THE
COUNTRY
FARMHOUSE
COOKBOOK

THE
COUNTRY
FARMHOUSE
COOKBOOK

400 RECIPES HANDED DOWN THE GENERATIONS, USING SEASONAL PRODUCE FROM THE
KITCHEN GARDEN AND RURAL SURROUNDINGS, ILLUSTRATED WITH 1400 PHOTOGRAPHS

SARAH BANBERY

HERMES
HOUSE

This edition is published by Hermes House, an imprint of Anness Publishing Ltd, Blaby Road, Wigston, Leicestershire LE18 4SE; info@anness.com

www.hermeshouse.com; www.annesspublishing.com

If you like the images in this book and would like to investigate using them for publishing, promotions or advertising, please visit our website www.practicalpictures.com for more information.

Publisher: Joanna Lorenz
Editorial Director: Helen Sudell
Executive Editor: Joanne Rippin
Designer: Adelle Morris
Recipes supplied by: Pepita Aris, Catherine Atkinson, Alex Barker, Michelle Berriedale-Johnson, Valerie Barrett, Ghillie Basan, Georgina Campbell, Carla Capalbo, Miguel de Castrol e Silva, Lesley Chamberlain, Maxine Clarke, Garole Clements, Frances Cleary, Matthew Drennan, Joanna Farrow, Jenni Fleetwood, Christine France, Brian Glover, Anja Hill, Christine Ingram, Silvena Johen Lauta, Bridget Jones, Lucy Knox, Janet Laurence, Sally Mansfield, Maggie Mayhew, Janny de Moor, Anna Mossesson, Claire Ptak, Keith Richmond, Rena Salaman, Jennie Shapter, Marlene Spieler, Liz Trigg, Christopher Trotter, Susanne Vandyck, Laura Washburn, Biddy White Lennon, Carol Wilson, Jeni Wright, Annette Yates.
Photography by: Martin Brigdale, Nicki Dowey, Ian Garlick, Amanda Heywood, Janine Hosegood, Dave Jordan, William Lingwood, Steve Moss, Craig Robertson, Jon Whitaker.
Production Controller: Christine Ni

ETHICAL TRADING POLICY

At Anness Publishing we believe that business should be conducted in an ethical and ecologically sustainable way, with respect for the environment and a proper regard to the replacement of the natural resources we employ. As a publisher, we use a lot of wood pulp in high-quality paper for printing, and that wood commonly comes from spruce trees. We are therefore currently growing more than 750,000 trees in three Scottish forest plantations: Berrymoss (130 hectares/320 acres), West Touxhill (125 hectares/305 acres) and Deveron Forest (75 hectares/185 acres). The forests we manage contain more than 3.5 times the number of trees employed each year in making paper for the books we manufacture.

Because of this ongoing ecological investment programme, you, as our customer, can have the pleasure and reassurance of knowing that a tree is being cultivated on your behalf to naturally replace the materials used to make the book you are holding.

Our forestry programme is run in accordance with the UK Woodland Assurance Scheme (UKWAS) and will be certified by the internationally recognized Forest Stewardship Council (FSC). The FSC is a non-government organization dedicated to promoting responsible management of the world's forests. Certification ensures forests are managed in an environmentally sustainable and socially responsible way. For further information about this scheme, go to www.annesspublishing.com/trees

Previously published in two separate volumes, *The Farmhouse Cookbook* and *The Illustrated Practical Book of Country Cooking*

NOTES

Bracketed terms are intended for American readers.
For all recipes, quantities are given in both metric and imperial measures and, where appropriate, in standard cups and spoons. Follow one set of measures, but not a mixture, because they are not interchangeable.
Standard spoon and cup measures are level. 1 tsp = 5ml, 1 tbsp = 15ml, 1 cup = 250ml/8fl oz.
Australian standard tablespoons are 20ml. Australian readers should use 3 tsp in place of 1 tbsp for measuring small quantities.
American pints are 16fl oz/2 cups. American readers should use 20fl oz/2.5 cups in place of 1 pint when measuring liquids.
Electric oven temperatures in this book are for conventional ovens. When using a fan oven, the temperature will probably need to be reduced by about 10–20°C/20–40°F. Since ovens vary, you should check with your manufacturer's instruction book for guidance.
The nutritional analysis given for each recipe is calculated per portion (i.e. serving or item), unless otherwise stated. If the recipe gives a range, such as Serves 4–6, then the nutritional analysis will be for the smaller portion size, i.e. 6 servings. The analysis does not include optional ingredients, such as salt added to taste.
Medium (US large) eggs are used unless otherwise stated.

PUBLISHER'S NOTE

Although the advice and information in this book are believed to be accurate and true at the time of going to press, neither the authors nor the publisher can accept any legal responsibility or liability for any errors or omissions that may have been made nor for any inaccuracies nor for any loss, harm or injury that comes about from following instructions or advice in this book.

CONTENTS

Introduction

Farmhouse cooking is essentially based on traditional peasant food that has evolved over the centuries. The authentic recipes of the countryside naturally rely on good ingredients and fresh seasonal produce, making use of all the fantastic richness of locally produced food throughout the year. Peasant and country dishes also include many more esoteric foods such as oysters and game which are today regarded as luxury items, but in the past would actually have been classified as poor man's food.

The hard-won knowledge and frugal habits of the country cook, developed with patience and skill over time, are reflected in our 21st-century concerns with the origin and provenance of ingredients. We are beginning to understand that local, fresh, seasonal produce has a better flavour and is far more nutritionally rich than food that is imported from far-flung countries out of season, and this is an area where country recipes shine.

The age-old custom of passing down tried-and-tested traditional family recipes from generation to generation, along with cherished cooking skills, equipment and utensils, means that country food has survived to be appreciated and enjoyed by each new generation of cooks.

The contemporary country kitchen

With a growing interest in cooking seasonally, in using organic produce and the simplest, freshest ingredients, the contemporary country kitchen retains much of what is best about traditional cooking, but with the added blessing of modern equipment, time-saving gadgets and appliances. Innovations such as pressure cookers and bread machines mean that the busy home cook can now recreate many of the more time-consuming recipes of the past in a fraction of the time, without losing any authentic taste. In modern kitchens, it is easier than ever to make the most of all the fresh, high-quality ingredients on which country cooking is based.

Homemade food

Farmhouse cooking is simply delicious home-made food using traditional raw materials, without any unnecessary waste. For example, many meat dishes involve long, slow cooking, making use of every possible part of an animal such as the trotters, the head and the offal. This thrifty custom has played a key role in developing some of the best-loved country meat recipes.

An integral part of this style of cooking was preserving food, which was an absolute necessity rather than an indulgence. Home baking and home smoking, along with pickling and salting, and making cheese and butter, were a natural part of living in the country and a matter of pride. Many a country larder contained neat rows of preserved fruit and vegetables in jars, with maybe a ham or some game hanging on a hook and a crock of salted fish ready to be eaten in the cold

Left Summer in the country means rich grazing for farm animals and an abundance of produce from the woods, fields and vegetable plot.

months of winter. Techniques such as making a rich stock from meat bones or vibrant crab apple jelly from windfall fruits illustrate the inventiveness that characterizes much country cooking.

The seasons

Culinary creativity was very important to the country cook, whose life revolved around the seasons. Traditional recipes tended to be structured around one central ingredient which was in season – spring vegetables tasting wonderful in a delicious soup, or pork as the main ingredient of a raised pie, for example. If there was an abundance of one crop, it was either used fresh in different ways or stored for the cold weather.

Spring could still be a time of year when the cook was largely reliant on preserved foods to support the few early vegetables, while the summer months provided plenty of fresh fruits, vegetables and salads from an overflowing kitchen garden. In the autumn, the country cook has traditionally relied heavily on wild foods to support the larder and pantry. Game from the fields and woods, as well as hedgerow fruits and nuts, complemented the last of the

summer crops. Winter recipes reflect the thriftiness of country cooking, with hearty stews making the most of the root vegetables, brassicas and dried beans and peas, and using bottled and pickled vegetables from the store cupboard to bulk up meagre winter crops.

Farmhouse traditions

The simple act of baking a certain loaf of bread or a special cake for a specific celebration or festival evolved over time to become an indelible part of country tradition. These rituals, treasured and passed down within families, connected people both to the rhythms of the countryside and to the traditions of their local community, marking the passing of the year. Harvest suppers, spiced Christmas drinks, festival sweetmeats and Easter cakes are all concocted from ancient recipes in the country kitchen.

Today, spending time in the kitchen baking a fruit cake, chopping home-grown vegetables to make soup or cooking wonderfully nutritious food

Left Country cooking techniques often rely on a few well-loved utensils, such as this traditional rolling pin, pastry cutters, mixing bowl and jug.

Above Home-grown local fruits such as these beautiful apples are used in many country recipes, such as a sweet pie or a savoury roast joint of meat.

from a few simple ingredients reconnects us to the countryside. Even growing a few herbs in pots on the window sill or making your own preserves can give a satisfying feeling of keeping up time-honoured culinary customs.

About the book

This book begins with a description of country cooking, its history, methods and ingredients, including some fascinating facts about the practical cooking techniques of our rural ancestors. There is also plenty of inspiration for growing your own produce, using it wisely when fresh, and preserving the inevitable glut to enjoy in the colder months.

There are eight chapters of recipes, ranging from simple, rustic soups and pot roasts to some best-loved regional specialities, puddings, breads and preserves. Many dishes can be prepared ahead of time or slow-cooked all day in traditional fashion, bringing the real taste of the country to your table.

Farmhouse Traditions

Throughout the centuries, cooks have prepared food for the family using whatever ingredients were available from the local area, fresh and in season. In the lean winter months, this would be supplemented by whatever had been preserved by bottling, pickling, salting or drying. Today we can be inspired by the thrifty methods of the past to make delicious meals that everyone will enjoy.

The history of country cooking

The development of our traditional cooking has its roots in pre-history. The earliest cooking would probably have been limited to roasting meat and game on a spit, toasting and grinding grain and using simple hollowed-out stones and bones to heat liquids over an open fire.

Early cooking techniques

Not until the development of settled agriculture and the introduction of pottery would cooking develop beyond the most basic methods. By the Middle Ages the resourceful country cook, restricted by the limitations of one-pot cooking on an open fire, relied on tasty dishes such as soups, stews and casseroles, spit-roasted meat and preserved fruit and vegetables for many months of the year. Bread dough was baked in a central public oven, since most of the rural populace would not have access to an oven at home.

Tools, equipment and utensils

From mankind's earliest days, much effort was put into developing tools for gathering, killing and cooking food. Clay, iron and bronze materials were

fashioned into pots used for cooking over the fire and also for preserving food. Utensils made of wood and metal, such as ladles and knives, became stronger and more reliable.

Well-tested techniques for preserving food were vital. As well as preserving fruit and vegetables in glass jars or earthenware crocks, many rural homes would smoke fish and meat in the chimney or in a home-built smokery.

The cook now had access to a broader range of cooking equipment, as well as specialist dairy tools for making butter and cheese. The Victorian era saw the introduction of a huge number of new cooking utensils and mass-produced kitchen gadgets such as fancy pastry cutters, cheese graters and potato peelers.

Fires and ovens

Cooking food over an open fire is the basis upon which all subsequent cooking has developed. The earliest pot ovens, domed iron pots placed over hot hearth stones, gave way to clay or brick-lined ovens similar to today's

Left Fruits such as cranberries, together with spices and herbs, were important ingredients for preserves.

Above Cherished kitchen utensils and equipment were often passed from one generation of cooks down to the next.

pizza ovens, but until the end of the 18th century, much cooking was still done over an open fire. Iron stoves began to appear in the late 18th century, but it was not until the 'cooking machines' or closed stoves appeared in Victorian kitchens that home cooking was really revolutionized.

By the 19th century the typical farmhouse kitchen had a fireplace with a chimney and a rudimentary range with its own ovens. The Aga stove or range cooker and other coal- or wood-fired ovens used today are still associated with a more traditional cooking style; they have certain limitations, but these stoves are often much loved by their owners, who have become experts in slow-cooking skills.

Larders and pantries

Keeping food fresh was a constant concern for the country cook. Storing vegetables and fruits in a cool place on stone floors with a good circulation of air meant they lasted longer. Eventually a larder cupboard or walk-in pantry was

Left *The American plantation kitchen had an open hearth for cooking, a hand-cranked meat mincer and copper pots.*

exchange an excess of produce. These markets became the focus of many rural communities, with people travelling long distances, often on foot, to buy and sell the essentials of life. Many towns and settlements grew up around the site of a regular market, and in some countries the right to hold a market was a highly valued privilege enshrined in writing. Although both regular markets and seasonal fairs were essentially trading institutions, they became a treasured part of the life of the country. In recent eras, when many countries have seen an increase in trade and movements of population, markets played an integral role both in the dissemination of new foods and cooking styles and in the preservation of ancient local customs.

constructed in every rural kitchen, as well as in many town basement kitchens. This was the ideal place to keep dairy products and meat in the best condition before the advent of refrigeration. It was also a good place for keeping dry stores of beans, peas and grains, and preserved foods and vegetables in glass or earthenware jars. Many farmhouses in dairy farming areas developed their own clean, cool dairies where the scrubbed stone floors and shelves gave the best conditions for making and storing butter and cheese.

Local markets

Markets were integral to country life and the rural economy. They developed from the basic need to barter or

Below *Fruit, vegetables and preserves are kept cool and dry in a pantry, along with dried herbs and garlic.*

Frugal food

For the earliest farmers, the earth needed to be coaxed into fertility, and their hard-won skills gradually developed over many years as a response to the challenges of living off the land. The popular image of the countryside as a bucolic and tranquil place belies the reality for rural communities all over the world; the poverty and hardship of country living has always demanded an inventive and frugal way of life. Almost all country cooking relies on good sense, forward planning, a talent for improvisation when times are hard and shared skills rooted in long experience.

Making the most of the countryside

Country economy is symbolized in the use of absolutely all parts of an animal. One or two pigs were often kept in country yards to be killed and eaten in the winter – an essential source of protein for the peasant farmer and his family. Virtually no part of the pig was thrown away: once the major cuts had been eaten as roasted joints and the lesser ones as stews, fat was rendered for lard, intestines were used for sausage cases, and hearts were stuffed and braised. In many countries of the world, pig's feet and ears are a delicacy.

Recipes using ingredients collected from the wild also bear witness to the country cook's frugal outlook. These delicious dishes include soups made from wild greens, herbs and even nettles. Game, fish, nuts and seeds were all hunted or collected to enrich and diversify the country diet. Foraging for food was considered not just a source of free ingredients, but also a positive pleasure when the day could be spent hunting or fishing, picking blackberries along a field edge or searching for mushrooms in the woods.

Economical food around the world

Around the world, peasant cooking has a great regard for frugal economy. Since peasant food traditionally uses whatever ingredients the local land has to offer, it is always both accessible and inexpensive, and often based around a limited number of staple, hearty ingredients cooked in a single pot.

Left To make the most of a pig, the meat was salted, smoked or preserved, and also made into sausages.
Right Home-grown tomatoes are perfect for cooking if you can resist eating them as soon as they are picked.

Above Good economy means taking advantage of what the fields, woods and hedgerows have to offer.

Scarcity of ingredients has led to great culinary invention in many countries, with the creation of new dishes and exciting ways to present familiar ingredients. In Turkey, for example, there are countless recipes based on the simple aubergine (eggplant), examples of which can be found in glistening deep purple piles in every market. These include the famous aubergine and tomato dish, Imam Bayildi.

In many countries, traditional meals vary only slightly across the borders, where the climate and ingredients are similar. The peasant dishes of Germany, such as Himmel und Erde, puréed potato and apple with blood sausage, and Sauerbrauten, a sweet and sour pot roast served with dumplings and cabbage, both remain distinctively German but share a common culinary heritage with other 'peasant' foods such as Irish Stew or French Cassoulet. The technique of marinating and slow cooking the less tender cuts of meat such as the shoulder, shanks and ribs resulted in mouth-watering casseroles, pot roasts and stews.

Waste not, want not

Leftovers feature prominently in country cooking. In Italy, rice left over from a risotto would be added to soups or made into Arancini – balls of cooked rice stuffed with cheese and deep-fried. Spanish Gazpacho, Italian Pappa al Pomodoro and English Queen of Puddings were all made to use up stale bread. Pizza is the ultimate peasant dish, a flour and olive oil dough base topped with tomato sauce and whichever vegetables and cheese are available.

Sourcing ingredients today

With the rise of the grass-roots movement that promotes traditionally raised food, today's resourceful cook can take advantage of the best their country has to offer. Financial imperatives paired with an increased desire to buy good, natural food means that many people are more educated about where their food comes from and what they should pay for it. Awareness of the amount of pesticides used in commercially grown crops and the less welcome effects of agro-chemicals and antibiotics used to rear livestock intensively means that many people are beginning to buy

organic and bio-dynamic foods instead. In particular, the furore over the advent of genetically modified crops has starkly illustrated the number of artificial processes associated with modern food production. In contrast, vegetable and fruit varieties grown organically may take longer to grow and have lower yields of uneven-sized crops, but they have time to develop more flavour and are nutritionally richer.

The reintroduction of traditional and rare-breed animals and an increased concern for animal welfare means that

Left A thick slice of home-baked bread, such as this cheese and onion loaf, is a delicious and filling country snack.

many more livestock and poultry are raised free-range and slaughtered in more humane conditions. Meat can often be sourced from farmers as many rural producers now sell direct to the consumer. Buying a whole or half animal from a farmer, butchered into convenient portions and ready for the freezer, means fantastic meat at a reasonable price.

Growing your own is the best way of ensuring freshness, but there are also increased opportunities for sourcing frugal ingredients. Farmers' markets, farm shops, co-operatives and box schemes offer locally grown and organic supplies which are, by definition, in season and fresh. Buying food from the person who grew or raised it has the added benefit of the exchange of knowledge, ideas and perhaps even recipes. In this way, the city-dwelling cook with an interest in traditional food can bridge the gap between urban and rural life.

Below Free-range meat from animals such as these sheep can be sourced direct from farmers and markets.

The kitchen garden

Growing fruits, vegetables and herbs has always been an integral part of the self-sufficiency of the country cook. A well-planned kitchen garden will provide an ongoing supply of fruit and vegetables throughout the year – just as one crop is coming to an end, a new one will take over – and as long as the cook has enough skill and imagination to make the most of a glut, to preserve everything that cannot be eaten immediately, and to plan ahead so that best use is made of the available space, the kitchen garden can be an inspiring place.

The renewed interest in 'growing your own' means that planting a kitchen garden is no longer solely the privilege of the rural population. Allotments, land shares, community gardens and urban plots, or even a pot or two in a small yard or on a windowsill, make home-grown fruits and vegetables available to all.

Nowadays, there are plenty of dwarf varieties available that crop well but take up limited space. Even vegetables such as runner (green) beans or aubergines (eggplants) – which would usually need a large area to grow in – can now be grown in containers on patios.

Grow your own

One of the major advantages of home-grown food is that it encourages the country cook to make recipes that are prepared from scratch. Having a handy selection of your favourite fruits, vegetables and herbs flourishing just outside the kitchen window is a huge help – and also an attractive addition to any back garden.

In order to avoid making expensive mistakes, it is a good idea to check the gardening catalogues for ideas and maybe borrow some books from the library before you start. There is plenty of practical advice to be had on the best varieties to grow, whatever the size and shape of your plot. The traditional varieties of many vegetables, including 'heirloom' varieties, often

Left Damsons are ideal for jam-making, and the trees look very pretty in spring with their snow-white blossom.

Above This neat kitchen garden has a recently harvested crop of onions drying on the ground before being stored.

taste fantastic, and you will have the additional pleasure of knowing that you are preserving our culinary heritage.

Containers and window boxes are a great way to start growing vegetables because they are manageable and can be very productive. Some climbing varieties of fruit and vegetables do not need deep soil and can be grown in grow bags or containers in a small space. A small herb garden or pots of herbs on a windowsill will offer an easy introduction to growing at home, with the attraction of fresh ingredients to hand for cooking. There is nothing quite like the aroma of a dish of new potatoes with home-grown mint or parsley sprinkled on top.

Another big incentive to start cultivating a small plot or vegetable garden is that it is an easy way to

While many crops can be harvested gradually over a long growing season, other fruits and vegetables will have a short but extravagantly abundant burst of activity, providing a big yield in just a few weeks.

For this reason, preserving has long been an integral part of getting the most from a home harvest, helping to avoid groans from the family as they face yet another courgette (zucchini) or tomato dish for supper. While many crops will freeze well, some fruits and vegetables do not respond favourably to this treatment, becoming soggy or tasteless, and so the old traditional methods of making jams, jellies, relishes and chutneys, and bottling, drying, salting and pickling come into their own.

The great value of home made preserves is in capturing the colours, textures, smells and tastes of summer at any time of the year. There is also the undeniably warm glow that comes from eating your own produce, preserved in your own kitchen, all year round.

Above A space for potting seeds is useful when growing fruits and vegetables at home or in an allotment.

introduce children to new fruits and vegetables which they might otherwise be reluctant to try. Windowsill gardening is ideal for children, as they can inspect the crop regularly.

Vegetable gardens can also be much more than a working part of the garden. Certain fruits and vegetables, such as potatoes, onions, lettuce and the dwarf varieties of beans, can be integrated into an ornamental garden, although this is not an easy option – both vegetables and flowers are going to need constant attention to keep them pest-free and avoid one variety swamping the others. Even if there is no room in the flower garden for vegetables, many fruit trees flourish against a sunny wall and also look extremely decorative, with their spring blossom and autumn fruits.

Plot to pantry

Growing fruit and vegetables can very easily result in over-production of certain varieties at particular times of the year.

Below Home-grown thyme, asparagus, onions, figs, radishes and carrots can go straight from the garden to the kitchen.

Seasonal food

Eating seasonally is as relevant today as it was centuries ago. Cooking and eating within the year's natural rhythm means that fruit and vegetable varieties are eaten when they are at their best in terms of flavour and ripeness, as well as nutritional qualities.

But it is not only the taste and goodness of traditional fresh food that should focus everyone's minds on buying seasonal produce. An increasing concern about the impact of fossil fuels used to transport foods from far-flung countries has added to the renewed interest in cooking and eating local produce. Awareness of food miles and reluctance to pay a premium price for tasteless out-of-season foods are now coupled with a desire to support local economies and reconnect with the seasons.

Seasonal recipes

In many regions of the world, shopping every day naturally means having the choice of produce restricted seasonally – but often this is no hardship as long as the cook is prepared to settle into a pattern of traditional cooking dictated by the harvests. This is where growing your own or buying local fresh produce

Above *Spring carrots are best when lightly cooked and simply served with butter and some chopped parsley.*

really pays dividends. Newly harvested fruits and vegetables that are cooked on the same day they are picked retain their natural goodness and will be eaten before their natural sugars turn to starch, thus making them sweeter and more flavoursome; they often have a better texture and cook more quickly.

Everyone can tell the difference between a bowl of fragrant, firm strawberries eaten at the height of the harvesting season in early summer, and the tired, soggy, tasteless examples bought in midwinter. But this also applies to other ingredients such as tomatoes, courgettes (zucchini), new potatoes, peaches, spring lamb and many more. Why not make good use of all these wonderful flavours when they are at their absolute peak?

Left *Succulent summer fruits such as strawberries are delicious in fruit fools, with ice cream or in a sweet pudding.*
Right *Orchard apples are perfect for autumn puddings such as crumbles, or baked with dried fruits and honey.*

Spring

As the first spring produce appears, it is time to move on from the casseroles and stews of the winter months and enjoy the vibrant new flavours of spring vegetables and early fruits. The best way to cook these fantastically fresh ingredients changes from long, slow cooking to quick stir-fries and grilling (broiling), or even serving raw in a salad.

Early spring is the ideal time to use up the last of the winter staple crops and pair them with new herbs and dressings, perhaps using the first wild greens in a casserole or simmering the new pink shoots of rhubarb and blending them with cream to make a tasty dessert. Later, spring shoots and tender young vegetables such as broad (fava) beans and new potatoes make interesting salads, and this is also the time of year when luxuries such as asparagus start to appear.

Summer

The sunshine brings the opportunity to make plain but exquisite dishes focusing on the best-quality ingredients. Early summer offers young, sweet vegetables

Left Many fruits and vegetables are at their best in the autumn, such as these pumpkins and squashes.

Winter

The colder months may be restricted in the variety of seasonal foods available, but winter is the time to bring out the preserved and stored foods hoarded in the summer and preserved in the autumn. There are still some fresh vegetables available, such as cabbages and Brussels sprouts, which do not reach their peak of flavour until the first frosts.

Late autumn cooking apples and berries can be stewed or baked in a pie. Beans and peas are a good store cupboard stand-by at this time of year and can be made into warming dinners for winter evenings; they taste great paired with root vegetables. Steamed puddings are essential winter warmers, and a home-baked fruit cake bursting with dried fruits is a tempting treat for the winter store cupboard.

Below Winter is the season for root vegetables, citrus fruits and dried fruit, which can be stored until needed.

such as new potatoes, lettuce, peas and beans; later, the focus moves to sun-ripened tomatoes and bell peppers, courgettes, marrows and main-crop potatoes. The soft fruits in the kitchen garden – raspberries, strawberries, peaches and apricots – are perfect for desserts such as fruit fools and tarts.

Cooking with warm weather in mind means making simple, light food – delicious fresh dishes such as chilled soups, salads, grilled (broiled) meat and fish, for example – to allow the flavour and texture of the produce to shine. Summer is also a good time to turn a glut of soft fruit and summer berries into cordials and cooling drinks, which are very welcome on a hot day.

Autumn

As summer draws to a close, the thrifty country cook begins to preserve the abundant harvest of fruits and vegetables and to make jams, pickles and other preserves. The autumn season is blessed with an overlap between the last of the summer produce and the first of the root vegetables and brassicas,

with the opportunity to start making hearty soups and roasting pumpkins, squashes, potatoes and parsnips.

Autumn is also the season for game, wild mushrooms and nuts, as well as being the perfect time to start making treats for Christmas such as fruit cake, pudding and presents of bottled fruit or spicy chutney.

Preserving and storing

Smoking, drying, bottling or making jams and chutneys are all major activities in the country kitchen. These techniques are really worth learning, even in an era when all kinds of foodstuffs are available the whole year round in the supermarket. Eating your own preserves, made with best-quality, tasty fruits and vegetables, is a reminder of summer in the depths of winter. There is no comparison between a cheap shop-bought strawberry jam with its high sugar content and red colouring, for example, and the darker colour and richer, purer flavour of home-made strawberry jam, bursting with fruit.

Jams, jellies and marmalades

Making delicious jams and jellies is the most common way to enjoy the summer's harvest all year round. Jams and jellies are particularly versatile preserves, with many uses in the country kitchen – they can be spread between the layers of a sponge cake, used as a dessert topping, or simply served with freshly made bread for tea.

Jam is made by simmering prepared fruits, either whole or chopped, with sugar. Fruits that are low in pectin, such as strawberries, make a soft-set jam, whereas those that are naturally full of

pectin, such as plums or gooseberries, make a firmer preserve. Compôtes are simply soft-set jams made with a little less sugar, served fresh, as they will not keep for long. Many traditional jellies are made from hedgerow crops such as crab apple, mint and elderflower, and these delicately flavoured preserves are usually served with meats or cheese.

Old-fashioned fruit butters and cheeses are preserves made with the fruit pulp left in a jelly bag after the juice has dripped. Making fruit butter requires less sugar than jam and the texture is softer – perfect for spreading.

Fruit cheeses have a firmer texture and are made from well-sieved (strained) thick fruit purées, often from fruits with lots of pips or stones such as damsons or quince. In contrast, fruit curds are made with the addition of butter and eggs, gently cooking the fruit to create a thick, sweet conserve which has a shorter shelf-life than other preserves because of the dairy content. Piquant lemon curd is the best known, but other fruits such as gooseberries, apricots and quince also lend themselves well to this treatment.

Marmalade is made in a similar way to jam, using citrus fruits. The fruit rind in marmalade needs longer cooking than the usual jam fruits, so water is

Above Home-made jams and jellies look very attractive when finished with pretty tops, to give as gifts.

added to the fruit and sugar while it is cooked. The marmalade can be flavoured with alcohol or fragrant spices such as ginger.

Pickles, chutneys and relishes

Both fruits and vegetables can be made into mouth-watering pickles and chutneys. Chutney is made with chopped fruit and/or vegetables simmered with varying amounts of spices, sugar and vinegar to a thick pulp and then stored in jars. As it improves with age, chutney stores very well and has a long shelf-life. It is particularly useful for using up end-of-season fruits such as windfall apples and green tomatoes, mixed with dried vine fruits such as sultanas (golden raisins) and currants.

In contrast, pickles are more often made with whole vegetables, such

Far left Stone fruits such as these ripe plums can be bottled, or made into jam, chutney or a rich fruit cheese.
Left Some autumn fruits, if carefully wrapped and properly stored, can last for many weeks or months into winter.

Far left Fruit or herb jellies are often served with roast meat, but are also delicious with cold pies or cheese.
Left Many herbs can be air-dried by tying them into bunches and hanging them in a cool, dry place.

bottling must be fresh and not too ripe. Stone (pit) fruits such as apricots and plums are particularly suitable for this method and look glorious with their beautiful colours shining through the glass jar.

Drying

Home-drying fruit and vegetables was long regarded as an important part of preserving. Dried vegetables are oven-, sun- or air-dried, and then often packed in oil, while dried fruits are kept in boxes. Fruit, vegetables and herbs will keep for many months when properly dried, and most characteristically have a particular intensity of flavour. Sun-drying crops such as tomatoes, aubergines (eggplants) and bell peppers is popular in the Mediterranean, India and the Middle East, where these vegetables grow easily and the sun is strong enough to preserve all the goodness quickly.

as baby onions, cauliflower florets or beetroot (beet). The vegetables are first salted or soaked to remove excess moisture, then packed into jars and covered in vinegar, with the addition of strong herbs and spices to add a really zingy taste to the mixture. Pickles do not require the long cooking of chutney, and benefit from being kept for a few weeks for the flavours to develop.

Both pickles and chutneys are usually served straight from the jar with cold meats, terrines, pies or cheese, but they can also be regarded as an instant ingredient to add zest to many winter dishes. Pickled onions can be rinsed and added to a robust casserole or stew, for example.

Relish is halfway between chutneys and pickles. It consists of coarsely chopped fruit or vegetables, spices and vinegar cooked together for a shorter time than chutney, so the vegetables tend to keep their shape. There are even traditional recipes for uncooked relishes that make the best of a summer glut – vegetables or fruits such as tomatoes, courgettes (zucchini), bell peppers or plums can be chopped and mixed

Right Pretty bottles can be re-used for pickling if they are sterilized and have new, air-tight tops.

with chillies, herbs and seasoning and served cold. These should be kept in the refrigerator and used within a few days.

Bottling

The technique of bottling is most often used for preserving best-quality whole fruits and vegetables. Fruit is usually bottled in syrup or alcohol to keep the colour and flavour of these pristine ingredients; vegetables are more often bottled in brine. Fruit and vegetables for

The Farmhouse Kitchen

Country recipes rely on traditional cooking techniques combined with the quality and freshness of the produce. This chapter gives an overview of all the basic ingredients used in farmhouse cooking, from the familiar fruits and vegetables of the kitchen garden to the autumn berries and nuts from the hedgerows, and from meat and dairy products to fish and shellfish.

Garden, field and orchard

In the past, most country gardens contained a few vegetables, a fruit tree or two and maybe a beehive or some chickens – all with one aim in mind, to put food on the table. Nowadays, many rural and city gardeners are turning at least part of their flower beds over to food production, and expressing an interest in traditional methods of harvesting, cooking and preserving. Even city-dwellers with no garden usually have access to the most wonderful fresh, seasonal produce in their local shops and markets.

Vegetables

The vegetable garden was always the basis of country cooking. Gardeners knew how to prepare the ground, rotate their crops to get the best from the nutrients in the soil and raise as many excellent vegetables as they could cram into their plot.

Bulb vegetables, including onions and shallots, garlic, leeks and salad onions, have always been a favourite in the country kitchen. They provide a quick and easy way of adding depth of flavour to many dishes.

Leafy greens and brassicas include broccoli, Brussels sprouts, cauliflower, cabbage, spinach, endive and salad leaves – all of which are best eaten very soon after picking.

Root vegetables such as potatoes, carrots, squash and parsnips are amazingly versatile winter vegetables. Often used as thickening agents in casseroles or stews, they can also be mashed, roasted, puréed or made into delicious velvety soups.

Peas, broad (fava) beans, French (green) beans, borlotti beans and corn grow prolifically but need lots of space, and should be harvested while young.

Asparagus is slow to establish in the garden and has a very short season, but should not be missed. Other summer vegetables that need the full warmth of the sun to ripen include tomatoes, bell peppers, avocados and aubergines (eggplants) – these grow well in hot countries or under glass in cooler areas.

Dried beans, peas and lentils

The number of varieties of the dried seeds of plant legumes runs into thousands. As they are inexpensive,

Above Courgettes are part of the squash family, which also includes pumpkins, marrows and gourds.

easy to grow and have a good storage life, dried beans, peas and lentils have long been an integral part of the country diet. They are high in protein and complex carbohydrates, low in fat and nutritionally rich.

Bean stews, salads, soups and casseroles, re-interpreted for each culture, appear in recipes from all over the world, such as Tuscan Ribollito or Southern Succotash Chicken Soup from the United States. Beans, peas and lentils can also be puréed and mashed into delicious dips and pâtés or included in curries and highly spiced meat dishes.

Fruits

An enormous number of fruit varieties are now available. Among the best-known are tree fruits such as apples, pears and quinces, which appear in the late summer and autumn, while stone (pit) fruits such as apricots, cherries,

Left A variety of healthy vegetables and fruits has always been part of the rural diet, especially in the summer.

Left Peaches and apricots are fragrant summer fruits – they are perfect in a sweet dessert or for making jam.

fragrant almond paste central to many seasonal celebration dishes and sweetmeats. Sweet chestnuts are also made into chestnut flour, which used to be a substitute for the more expensive wheat flour in peasant kitchens.

Seeds

Pumpkin seeds are delicious roasted and tossed with a little sea salt and eaten as a snack. Pine nuts, sesame seeds and sunflower seeds are all important, nutritionally rich elements in peasant cooking throughout Europe, North Africa and the Middle East, and form the basis of many traditional dishes.

Herbs

Easy to grow and versatile, herbs can be used fresh or dried, cooked or raw in both savoury and sweet dishes, and each has its own distinct flavour and texture. In slow-cooked recipes, a bouquet garni added at the beginning of cooking allows the flavour to permeate throughout the dish, while a sprinkling of chopped parsley or coriander (cilantro) on a bowl of cooked rice or vegetables adds freshness and colour.

damsons, greengages, nectarines, peaches and plums tend to ripen earlier in the year

Soft fruits and berries include bilberries, blackberries, black, white and red currants, blueberries, gooseberries, raspberries and strawberries, and are mainly summer and autumn crops, some of which can be found growing wild in the countryside.

Grapefruit, oranges, lemons, limes, mandarins and kumquats need consistent warmth and sunlight to flourish; in northern parts of the world they can only be grown indoors. Bananas, dates, figs, mangoes, pomegranates, melons and pineapples are some of the best-known 'exotic' fruits that can only be grown in hot, humid climates or in a heated greenhouse.

Central to the country larder is a good supply of preserved fruits, which keep well and can therefore be imported from warmer countries to the cooler parts of the world: dried vine fruits such as currants and sultanas (golden raisins) appear in numerous traditional European cakes and biscuits, and dried dates, figs and apricots are used extensively in Mediterranean and Middle Eastern savoury dishes.

Nuts

In country cooking, nut butters are often used to thicken soups and stews or added to stuffings and sauces, and nut oils are made into fragrant dressings. French cooks use walnuts and chestnuts extensively, and in Italy almonds are a staple ingredient, with

Left Each variety of nut has its own distinctive taste. Nuts can either be added to dishes or eaten as a snack.
***Right** Fresh herbs add essential flavour to country meals, and are very easy to grow on a sunny windowsill.*

Wild foods

In the past, foraging for wild roots and fruits was a vital part of country life, providing nutritious, succulent treats to supplement the kitchen garden and store cupboard. Wild food can also add variety and indeed a luxurious, unexpected flavour to some traditional dishes.

Rural cooks have always regarded the hedgerow and field as an extension to their larder, and this tradition survives today, with many families enjoying a day out with a picnic to pick the produce of the countryside. As long as care is taken to avoid poisonous varieties of fungi or polluted bushes near main roads, wild mushrooms and hedgerow fruits such as blackberries, elderberries and rosehips still present great possibilities for making delicious meals. They can occasionally be found in magnificent abundance, and the opportunity for preserving a glut of berries in the form of jam or jelly, for example, should not be missed.

Depending on your location, there is usually some sort of wild food available for gathering in every month of the year, including nuts and berries, wild greens, roots, herbs, seeds and flowers such as elderflowers and rosehips. In the early spring, there is a 'hungry gap', when the last winter vegetables are finishing, the spring vegetables have not yet appeared, and the store

cupboard is emptying fast. At such times, wild food such as watercress, nettles and mushrooms have been essential additions to the country diet.

Fruits and berries

In Europe, the autumn and early winter is a particularly rich time for foraging, with fruits such as blackberries, damsons, juniper berries, sloes, crab apples and rosehips all ready for picking.

The tradition of pickling, bottling and preserving these fruits and vegetables, storing nuts and drying fungi are all methods by which the country cook bolsters the store cupboard. In Spain, wild quince is customarily made into Membrillo, a sweet quince paste. Fruit wines, syrups and drinks made from windfall fruits feature in many cultures: cider made from apples, elderflower or damson wine and rosehip syrup are all traditional treats. Fiercely alcoholic vodka, gin and other spirits, made from

Above Hedgerows are a great source of wild berries, such as these blackberries which make lovely bramble jam.

bland grains or root vegetables, are often flavoured with herbs and berries such as juniper or sloes that were gathered in the autumn.

Green leaves

Since most cultivated vegetables are descended from native ancestors, there are many greens and leaves growing wild which make good additions to the cooking pot – spinach, nettles, rocket

Left These tiny, bright red crab apples can be harvested in the autumn to make tasty home-made apple jelly.
Right Full of healthy vitamin C, rosehips can be used for making delicious teas, syrups and jellies.

Left Many different kinds of wild mushrooms can be found in the woods and fields, especially in the autumn.

(arugula) and sorrel all grow abundantly and are delicious. Italian family recipes for Minestrone soup often include wild greens, such as dandelion leaves. English cooks often use horseradish root and mint made into piquant sauces to accompany a roast joint of meat.

Mushrooms and fungi

Wild mushrooms grow throughout the year, but autumn is often the most rewarding time for harvesting fungi because this season offers such an abundant and varied selection. They are delicious, but there are some varieties that are extremely poisonous. It is essential to take a good guidebook with you to identify edible varieties, or find an expert to check your collection. Bear in mind that many highly poisonous varieties look remarkably similar to edible ones.

Like many uncultivated foods, wild mushrooms tend to have a superior flavour to cultivated varieties, and they also have their own distinct texture and taste. Some fungi are found in large abundant groups, while others are less easy to spot. Many wild mushrooms dry very well, and highly prized varieties such as morels and ceps are an important winter ingredient in Italy and Spain.

Unlike most other foraging, mushroom collecting requires focus, knowledge and commitment, and especially so if it is truffles that are being hunted. In France and Italy, these are the most highly prized fungi, requiring great skill and commitment to find – preferably with the help of a truffle hound or pig to sniff out these delicacies.

Herbs and edible flowers

When collected from the wild, herbs generally have a stronger flavour than commercially cultivated varieties. They may grow in great profusion, and armfuls of some herbs can be gathered and dried for use in winter cooking. Native herbs tend to have an affinity with local foods. Hardy, woody-stemmed herbs such as rosemary, thyme and oregano grow prolifically in hot climates, and their pungent aroma works best when cooked with strong-tasting meat and fish, but they can also be used for infusing oils for cooking. More delicate herbs such as basil, sorrel or chervil are better used raw with vegetable, fish or chicken dishes.

Edible flowers such as nasturtiums and dandelions have been used for centuries, not just for their visual appeal but also for their delicate flavour in salads or preserves.

Folklore often credits these foods with beneficial properties – many herbs, flowers and wild foods are still used as remedies, such as feverfew for headaches and peppermint to aid digestion.

Below left Wild green plants from the countryside, such as these nettles, often feature in traditional recipes. Below Edible flowers, such as pansies, nasturtiums and rose petals, look pretty in salads and as cake decorations.

Fish and shellfish

Saltwater fish, freshwater fish and shellfish have long been recognized as a vital source of protein and minerals, supplementing the country diet of vegetables, cereals, dairy and meat. The earliest hunter-gatherers foraged the coastline for shellfish, and tidal zones of the seashore provided valuable sea vegetables, including seaweed.

Fish

There are countless classic fish recipes, and shellfish such as crab and prawns (shrimp) also appear in local dishes all over the world. Freshwater crayfish and eels, long considered peasant food, have been re-invented for the modern cook, and appear on menus alongside more glamorous companions such as scallops and oysters.

As many of our oceans are now over-fished, dishes once made to use up unwanted leftover fish from the catch – such as Bouillabaisse from southern France – are now regarded as rather a luxury. Smaller fish such as sardines, mackerel and herring, once the staple diet of Portuguese, Spanish and northern European fishermen,

are replacing fish such as cod, whose stocks are diminished through pollution and over-fishing.

Drying, salting, pickling and smoking were all traditional methods of preserving before canning and freezing procedures became available, and many countries have their own techniques depending on the variety of fish – for instance, tasty pickled or soused herring from Scandinavia, strong-flavoured smoked

Above left *Large whole fish such as sea bream or this sea bass are perfect for poaching or oven-roasting in foil.* ***Above*** *Wild salmon is delicious poached and served warm or cold with home-made herb mayonnaise.*

mackerel and salmon from Scotland and the acquired taste of salt cod from Spain and Portugal.

The seasons affect fish, just as they do the fruit and vegetable crop. It is worth investigating when native varieties are at their best, in terms of abundance and availability. Seasonality as the foundation of traditional cooking means that locally caught fish will give a really authentic flavour and texture.

When buying fresh fish, look out for unclouded, bright eyes, firm flesh and pink gills, and a pleasantly fresh aroma of the sea rather than a strong 'fishy' smell. Delicate white fish responds best to simple baking, steaming or grilling (broiling), perhaps with a few herbs and butter, while more substantial, meatier fish can take bolder handling and richer sauces.

Left *Fast-flowing inland rivers and streams are good sources of freshwater fish such as salmon and trout.*

Far left *There are many varieties of clam. They are quick to cook and taste great in pasta or risotto dishes.* ***Left*** *Oysters, once 'poor man's' food, are now a luxury, served fresh or deep-fried with tartare sauce.*

Each country has its own native species and plenty of traditional dishes to match; it is worth experimenting with whatever fish is available locally, as many recipes are transferable, but you should keep to the right kind of fish – white fish, flat fish or the nutritionally rich oily fish species.

Shellfish

The term 'shellfish' covers crustaceans such as prawns and shrimp, langoustines, lobster and crab, as well as molluscs and cephalopods such as clams, oysters, scallops, mussels, cockles, winkles, cuttlefish and squid.

Traditionally harvested from the sea shallows and caught in inland waters, shellfish proved a useful part of the diet of early mankind. Oyster and clam shells have been found in the archaeological remains of many of the earliest peoples, from the Aborigines of Australia to the Celts of the Scottish Outer Hebrides. Most shellfish recipes make the most of the delicate, salty flavour of these tasty morsels by cooking them when they are really fresh; some, such as oysters, are generally eaten raw.

Cured and preserved fish

Fish has been preserved in many different ways since ancient times. Drying, smoking, salting or preserving in vinegar or oil was once essential if the fish was to be enjoyed out of season. Freezing and canning have largely supplanted older methods of preservation, but smoking is still popular – less for its preservative qualities than for the texture and flavour it imparts.

In the pre-refrigeration days, salting fish was a necessity to preserve it on the long sea journey from the fishing grounds to port, but nowadays the salting process is more commonly used to create luxuries such as smoked salmon. The salting process draws moisture out of the fish, and as it dries, the flesh firms up, making it easier to carve and changing both its flavour and its texture.

Salt cod, or bacalao, as it is known in Spain, is still very popular in many European countries, and is used in dishes such as Brandade and Salt Cod

Right *Coastal communities have the advantage of choosing from the catch of the day as it lands on the quayside.*

Fritters. Salted and preserved anchovies were traded as long ago as Roman times, and salted, cured fish roe – Bottarga – remains a favourite food of the Portuguese.

Smoking preserves fish by a hot or cold smoking process. In cold smoking, the fish is first cured and then smoked at low temperatures for anything between 24 hours and 3 weeks. In contrast, hot smoking effectively 'cooks' the fish, as it is smoked at a higher temperature for between 6 and 12 hours.

Smoke houses have evolved slightly differently around the world, but generally the principle is the same: fish are salted, rinsed and then strung up to air dry, and finally smoked over smouldering woodchips or peat. The strength of the cure and length of smoking affects the colour and flavour of the fish, and adding sugar, juniper berries or other flavouring to the flesh will change its character. Oily fish such as eel respond particularly well to smoking.

Poultry and feathered game

Many a country garden, from the most prosperous farm to the tiniest cottage, once had a group of hens happily pecking in the dirt, jealously guarded by the resident cockerel, or a few ducks swimming on a tiny pond. These creatures were a fantastic source of eggs and meat and would be carefully protected from marauding foxes. Out in the woods and pastures, country people also had access to feathered game such as partridge, pheasant and grouse, which would be hunted and then cooked to make a tasty autumn or winter casserole, with their rich, dark flesh.

Chicken

The most popular and widely available poultry, chicken is a staple in most kitchens around the world, even though these days they are often bought in markets or shops. Traditional recipes use the whole bird; once the flesh of the chicken has been eaten, there is still the liver to make into pâté and the carcass to boil with a few vegetables for a rich jellied stock.

As with all country cooking, recipes have developed over the years to make the most of the kind of chicken available, whether it is a young spring chicken, at its best simply roasted with fresh herbs, or a laying hen past its

productive years, which is ideal for casseroles with plenty of vegetables and a full-flavoured gravy.

Traditional country chickens would have been raised in conditions now defined as 'free range' – they would have lived mainly in the open, foraging and feeding outside, eating a varied diet of grains and scraps from the kitchen, with plenty of space to establish their pecking order. The free-range and organic chickens now available in many shops and markets are likely to have a similar flavour and texture to those found in the traditional farmyard.

Above Organic free-range chickens are reared in the open air with plenty of space and opportunities to forage.

Turkey

Once only appearing at Thanksgiving or Christmas, the large, domesticated descendant of the North American wild turkey is now available all year round, as a whole bird, leg pieces or breast pieces. It makes a splendid roast dinner for a special occasion, accompanied by lots of vegetables and a light stuffing packed with fresh herbs.

Guinea fowl

Until recently regarded as game birds, guinea fowl are slightly smaller than chickens and have a more pronounced, stronger flavour; the hen birds are considered to be more tender. Sold as squabs, chicks or fowl, they can weigh

Far left A traditional roast turkey with all the trimmings is central to Christmas and Thanksgiving celebrations.
Left Guinea fowl are perfect for a casserole or a pot roast slow-cooked with fresh seasonal vegetables.

up to 2kg/4½lb, and are cooked in similar ways to chicken – they can be either roasted whole or sliced into pieces to make a delicious dish with a creamy sauce.

Duck and goose

These were traditionally wild game birds, but both duck and goose are now more widely available as they are bred and raised commercially. The rich flesh of duck and goose blends particularly well with orchard fruits such as apples, pears and quince, whose tartness cuts through the strong flavour of the meat. In France goose is often eaten with prunes. Goose was the proud centrepiece of many traditional English feasts and celebration meals, especially at Christmas.

Feathered game

Wild birds hunted for the table have long been a staple country food, being readily available in the woods and fields of many rural areas, mostly during the autumn and winter months. Wild birds tend to have a stronger flavour and denser texture than domestic poultry. Young game birds are usually roasted, and older birds are braised or stewed in much the same way as domestic chicken.

Above left *A male or 'cock' pheasant, with its colourful head feathers, is a common sight in the autumn woods.*
Above *Grouse are a wild game bird hunted only for a limited season, and much prized for their flavour.*

While the countryman would shoot his own, birds such as pheasant and quail are now reared commercially, and are widely available in shops and markets. Rarer birds such as grouse and woodcock are usually found only at specialist game dealers.

Perhaps the most widely available game bird is the pheasant, which originated in China and is related to the chicken. They are usually sold as a 'brace' – a hen and a cock bird – and the two birds are cooked together, roasted or braised in a large casserole dish with vegetables, herbs and spices such as juniper berries. As with most game birds, pheasant are low in fat and lean, with a strong, distinctive flavour, which develops according to how long they have been hung.

Grouse are truly wild game birds. They include the sage and red grouse, and the capercaillie, particularly prized for its distinctive flavour and lean flesh. The smaller birds are highly prized for their rich flavour; a single bird such as

partridge, pigeon or quail will serve only one person. Quail are pink-fleshed and succulent, quick to cook and often available part-boned. Their attractive speckled eggs are often used in canapés.

The rarest and most prized wild birds are woodcock and snipe. Both have dark, intensely flavoured meat, and are usually roasted whole (including their intestines and head) and served one per person.

Left *Goose has a rich, fatty meat that is delicious when served with berry sauces or fruit jellies.*
Right *The classic way to prepare partridge is to roast it whole with strips of bacon, and serve with cabbage.*

Meat and furred game

Central to the country diet, both domestically raised meat and wild game have always been a prime source of protein. While there are plenty of traditional recipes for roast meat as the centrepiece of a special meal, many country recipes call for the cheaper cuts of meat or offal, which work so well in rich, tasty stews and casseroles cooked gently and slowly in the oven.

Beef, lamb, pork and offal

The meat from domestic cattle is one of the most prized sources of protein, used in both everyday and celebration meals around the world. Generally 'prime' or 'rare' beef comes from a pedigree herd, while 'dairy cross' comes from a dairy cow, and veal is the paler, tender meat of a young calf up to the age of six months. Traditional methods of cooking beef vary hugely, depending on the cut, including everything from a standing rib roast of the best, most succulent meat to a homely shepherd's pie made of beef mince (ground meat).

Good-quality lamb should have light red, moist flesh with a good layer of firm, creamy fat. The leg and shoulder are usually roasted, but again there are plenty of lesser cuts that melt into tenderness when simmered slowly in stock with some vegetables and mint from the garden. In past centuries,

mutton was preferred to lamb because of its richer flavour; it has been unfashionable and difficult to obtain but is undergoing something of a comeback with the revival of interest in our culinary heritage.

Domesticated pork was regarded traditionally as a seasonal meat, much of which was processed, preserved and salted to provide ham, bacon and sausages throughout the winter. Good pork should be pale pink with creamy white fat and a pliable rind.

As 'rare breed' pork is now becoming fashionable again, many excellent and diverse traditional breeds have made a comeback.

Above There are many different kinds of beef cattle. Hand-fed animals will produce the most tender meat.

Offal was a natural part of the diet in the days when nothing was wasted from a precious carcass. It can be really delicious, and there are many traditional recipes from around the world for sausages, fricassees and casseroles made with these strong-tasting ingredients. Pig's blood is also used to make black pudding, known as Boudin Noir in France and blood sausage in Germany and the USA.

Preserved and processed meats

Age-old techniques of preserving meat include curing methods such as salting, pickling, air- or wind-drying and smoking. One of the best meats for preserving is pork, which makes delicious joints such as ham and bacon. These were once the mainstay of a farmhouse pantry.

Far left Young prime lamb chops are best simply cooked quickly on a griddle, barbecue or grill, with rosemary.
Left A stuffed tenderloin of pork wrapped in bacon to keep the meat moist makes an impressive lunch dish.

Far left Good sausages have a high meat content. Pan-fry them and serve with pickles and home-made bread.
Left Young rabbit and hare can be roasted, but are also good slowly casseroled with wine and vegetables.

Pâtés and terrines are a good way of using up leftover meat. The difference between the two is that a terrine usually contains layers of meat that are immediately visible once the dish is sliced up, whereas a pâté is a smoother, more blended mixture. Cold raised pies are simply a variation on the terrine, where pastry replaces the dish in which terrines are cooked. Traditional raised pies with lard-rich, hot-water pastry can last up to a month, and make perfect picnic fare.

Sausages are another important staple of country cooking, whether they are fresh, smoked or dried. Fresh sausages are made by blending chopped meat – usually pork – with fat, seasonings and spices, fresh or dried herbs, cereal or rusk stuffed into cleaned intestines. Sausages can be made from virtually any blend of meat, game or poultry, and some varieties contain no meat at all – the French country sausage andouillette, for instance, is made from tripe.

Dried sausages, such as salamis and chorizo, have been air-dried to extend the amount of time they will keep and, like North African merguez sausage, might have chilli and other dried herbs or spices added to them.

Furred game

Game animals, like game birds, are a vital part of the country kitchen. These days, venison is more likely to come from farmed deer than to be caught wild. The meat is dark and lean, and can be cooked in similar ways to beef, with the saddle, haunch and loin best suited to roasting and the fillet or boned loin providing a juicy, well-flavoured steak. Lesser cuts of venison can be slow-cooked or made into sausages or minced

(ground) meat. Venison is often marinated in red wine with tart juniper berries to tenderize the meat, and has a great affinity with other astringent fruits such as blackberries and redcurrants.

The smaller furred game such as rabbit and hare, which populate the countryside, naturally feature in many country recipes, and lend themselves to a wide variety of cooking methods, from casseroles to pies. Hare is larger and less common than rabbit, and is considered a delicacy, with its moist, rich flesh and distinctive flavour.

Wild boar meat is more widely available in recent years. Traditionally a game animal, this sturdy wild pig is hunted across Europe and prized for its rich, dark meat. It makes a wonderful stew with a full-bodied flavour.

Below Sheep which have grazed on particular ground, such as salt marshes, provide meat with a distinctive flavour.

Dairy produce and eggs

The country cook has always had access to the freshest milk, cream and eggs, and dairy produce is a very important part of rural cooking. Before the advent of the centralized dairy, many homes had their own cow for providing milk and a few chickens for fresh eggs. Making butter, cream and cheese was a regular ritual and a delicate skill often handed down among the women of the family. Any excess produce was useful for trading, and always found a market.

Milk, cream and yogurt

Domesticated cows, sheep and goats provide milk for the country kitchen, and this can be processed into wonderful thick cream and sour cream, butter, yogurt and cheeses of all kinds and flavours. Buffalo and camels also produce milk, providing a staple food for many cultures.

A rich source of calcium and vitamins, and infinitely versatile, milk can vary in fat content, with the richest full-fat (whole) milk being the best type for cooking.

Traditionally, buttermilk was the liquid left over after churning milk into butter, but today it is more likely to be formed by the addition of lactic acid bacteria to milk, creating a liquid with a thickish texture between milk and yogurt. With its piquant flavour,

buttermilk is used for pancakes, scones and bread, and for tenderizing meat or poultry before cooking.

Double (heavy) cream has a high butterfat content, and is therefore the most frequently used cream for cooking. Whipping cream and single or light cream have much less butterfat and are not so suitable for cooking, but they add richness to a sweet pudding or a white sauce.

Crème fraîche and sour cream are both manufactured products that can add creaminess and bite to a dish. Before the introduction of pasteurization, crème fraîche was created when the bacteria naturally present in cream fermented and thickened. Sour cream

Above Old-fashioned dairy containers like these were often made from pottery to keep the contents cool.

was made by letting fresh cream sour naturally, the acids and bacteria occurring in the cream producing a thick textured cream with a slightly acidic taste, ideal for stirring into savoury soups and casseroles or for adding a twist to a rich, sweet dessert.

Below left Dairy cows provide milk for a range of products, including butter, cream, yogurt and cheese.
Below Enamel bowls were used for separating curds from whey, and enamel pint pots for measuring milk.

Above Dairy butter, made into blocks or 'pats', was used fresh or salted down to preserve it for longer.

Above This farmhouse goat's cheese has a thick rind, showing it has been aged and has a well-developed flavour.

Yogurt is the bacterial fermentation of milk, to create curds. The most common is made from cow's milk, but sheep and goat's milk also makes good yogurt with a more tangy taste. Probably originating from India, Asia and southern Europe, yogurt may well have been introduced to the rest of the world by travelling nomads. As it has been made for thousands of years, there are many regional varieties. Greek (US strained plain) yogurt is strained to reduce the water content and produce a richer, thicker variety that can easily stand in for cream as a dessert topping. Middle Eastern yogurt – labneh – is thicker still, and used in many savoury dishes.

Butter and cheese

New butter was an everyday luxury in the country for those with access to fresh cream. It was churned from cream and then formed into butter 'pats' or 'rolls', and wrapped in linen or vine leaves to keep it cool and clean. Butter was used fresh and unsalted in the spring and summer, with any surplus salted down to help preserve it for autumn and winter. It is essential in

many cake and biscuit (cookie) recipes, lending flavour to a plain sponge cake or light pastry. It is also used in savoury sauces, or mixed with herbs and seasoning to melt over a simple fish dish or a grilled (broiled) steak. In India, ghee is made by heating butter and straining out the impurities, and this clarified butter is used widely in traditional country cooking.

Cheese, the most versatile and portable of all milk products, can be made from almost any type of milk. Some cheeses are produced with a mixture of two or three types of milk,

such as Greek halloumi and feta. The final flavour and texture of the cheese depends on many factors: the type of milk used, what other ingredients are added and how long the cheese is aged or matured.

Eggs

Fresh eggs are an integral part of country cooking, and are a hugely versatile ingredient. Hen's eggs are the most readily available, but duck, goose and quail eggs are also useful additions to the country kitchen – there are numerous traditional recipes which make the most of them in omelettes, cakes and savoury tarts.

Eggs should be kept cool in a pantry or refrigerator, but always brought up to room temperature before use. Always choose the freshest eggs available, especially for recipes such as mayonnaise or chocolate mousse, which use uncooked eggs. Vulnerable groups such as babies and the elderly should avoid eating raw egg.

Below left Free-range and organic chickens lay eggs that have a bright yolk colour and are nutritionally rich.
Below The freshest eggs should always be used for recipes that are made with raw egg, such as mayonnaise.

Baking ingredients

Some of the best-loved breads, cakes and biscuits (cookies) that we enjoy today are based on ancient traditional recipes. Early civilizations cooked flat, unleavened bread made simply from ground grains and water, and subsequently baking developed through the centuries with the addition of yeast to make leavened loaves. The first cakes were simply bread dough with added eggs or butter; many country cakes also contained fruit, nuts and seeds gathered wild from the hedgerows. Before commercially refined sugar was available, honey was used to sweeten baked goods. Many recipes for substantial country fruit cakes make the most of rather meagre ingredients, using very little flour, sugar and eggs with plenty of fruit and nuts, which gives a dark, moist cake that has a long storage life.

Unlike much country cooking, baking is based on careful attention to the amounts of each ingredient, and most recipes for cakes and bread rely on measuring by weight or by cup and spoon measures. Most baking also requires specific types of key basic ingredients such as flour. Strong bread flour, for instance, should only be used for baking bread, never cakes.

Like much that is best in country cooking, many rural baking recipes can be time-consuming to prepare, but the flavour and texture of a light home-made sponge cake or a tasty wholemeal (whole-wheat) loaf is well worth the effort.

Bread and cakes

Using only a few ingredients and with very simple equipment, bread-making was a skill which every traditional country cook needed to acquire. Although bread at its simplest is just flour, water, yeast and a little salt and sugar, many country breads are made with numerous other additions, including wholemeal flour, grains such as rye and barley, and oats or seeds added for extra texture and flavour.

Above There are many types of flour and they are not interchangeable – use the correct one to suit the recipe.

Through necessity, many peasant breads dispense with the need for yeast altogether. These include Irish soda bread, Turkish simit, American cornbread and unleaved breads such as Indian chapatis and Mexican tortillas. The need for bread which would keep well throughout the dark winter months led to the flat crisp breads of Scandinavia, while German and Polish peasants baked dark rye bread with added treacle or molasses to give a dense, sustaining texture.

Most of the best-loved, so-called 'fancy breads' were made from the dough left over from a weekly bread baking, with the addition of eggs, sugar, fruit or nuts to make sweetened loaves. Speciality breads with added spices and fruit were often made for celebrations or festivals: many had symbolic relevance, such as English hot cross buns to mark the Easter holiday.

Country cakes tend to be rather substantial, and based on simple but delicious ingredients rather than the elaborate cream-filled confections typical of pâtisserie. Many traditional cakes have their origins rooted in rituals and

Left Bread comes in a variety of shapes and colours, from dark fruity sweet loaves to the classic farmhouse plait.

Left Baking day was a regular country tradition, providing home-made cakes and muffins for the coming week.

make and transport, and make a good addition to a lunch box or picnic.

Tarts, pies and puddings are emblematic of the country kitchen, and sum up the sort of comfort food that traditional cooking does best. Pastry is a simple mixture of flour and fat, and is the basis of many of the best-known savoury country recipes, such as quiches, pasties, flans and pies. Its sweet form comes in many variations, such as doughnuts or fried churros from Spain. Sweet pastry made with almonds is widely used in Italian, Spanish and Middle Eastern cooking, and the almond-stuffed Gateau de Roi is still the traditional Christmas pastry of Provence.

Steamed puddings were popular in the country because they do not require an oven. A sponge or suet (US chilled, grated shortening) mixture is gently steamed in a covered bowl on the hob for an hour or two. These substantial puddings, often containing fruit inside the pastry crust, only need the addition of a jug (pitcher) of creamy custard to make a delicious sweet treat.

worship. The Chinese offered up round cakes at harvest time to honour a moon goddess, while the ancient Celts used cakes in rituals on the first day of spring.

All cultures developed their own versions of basic recipes, with home-made cakes in Eastern Europe tending to be darker, spicier and containing more fruit, while in the USA muffins are the ultimate portable breakfast. Plain, nutritious mixtures such as

oatcakes were peasant standbys eaten in place of bread during lean times when wheat was scarce or expensive.

Biscuits, pastry and puddings

From tray-baked flapjacks to crumbly shortbread, biscuits and cookies offered a variety of sweet treats to supplement a basic diet. Many traditional country cooks had a weekly baking day when they made enough cakes and biscuits (as well as bread) to last throughout the rest of the week.

From the simplest plain biscuits made from flour, sugar and a little fat, to rich, chocolate and nut-studded American cookies, the inventive cook has always made use of whatever was available in order to enliven plain dough mixtures. Tray bakes or bar cakes, such as brownies and flapjacks, are easy to

Left A home-made harvest loaf, shaped like a wheatsheaf to celebrate the end of the harvest, symbolizes the importance of our 'daily bread'.
Right Baked desserts and cakes make the most of the fruits and other ingredients available in each season.

Farmhouse Breakfasts

The old adage that breakfast is the most important meal of the day is perhaps most true in the farmhouse. Breakfast is often served well after the working day has begun, and dawn chores will have worked up a hearty appetite in those sitting down to a well-deserved break. This means that the first meal of the day needs to be rather more substantial than a cup of tea and a piece of toast.

Porridge

One of the world's oldest dishes, porridge remains a favourite way to start the day in many farmhouses, especially in the winter months. Brown sugar and milk, or honey and cream, are added, and perhaps for weekend breakfasts a tot of whiskey for a real Celtic touch.

Serves 4

1 litre/1¾ pints/4 cups water

115g/4oz/1 cup pinhead oatmeal

good pinch of salt

Variation Modern rolled oats can be used, in the proportion of 115g/4oz/ 1 cup rolled oats to 750ml/1¼ pints/ 3 cups water, plus a sprinkling of salt. This cooks more quickly than pinhead oatmeal. Simmer, stirring to prevent sticking, for about 5 minutes. Either type of oatmeal can be left to cook overnight in the slow oven of a range.

1 Put the water, pinhead oatmeal and salt into a heavy pan and bring to the boil over a medium heat, stirring with a wooden spatula. When the porridge is smooth and beginning to thicken, reduce the heat to a simmer.

2 Cook gently for about 25 minutes, stirring occasionally, until the oatmeal is cooked and the consistency smooth.

3 Serve hot with cold milk and extra salt, if required.

Energy 115Kcal/488kJ; Protein 3.6g; Carbohydrate 20.9g, of which sugars 0g; Fat 2.5g, of which saturates 0g; Cholesterol 0mg; Calcium 16mg; Fibre 2g; Sodium 304mg.

Wholesome muesli

Commercially made muesli really can't compete with this home-made version. This combination of seeds, grains, nuts and dried fruits works particularly well, but you can alter the balance of ingredients, or substitute others, if you like.

Serves 4

50g/2oz/½ cup sunflower seeds

25g/1oz/¼ cup pumpkin seeds

115g/4oz/1 cup porridge oats

115g/4oz/heaped 1 cup wheat flakes

115g/4oz/heaped 1 cup barley flakes

115g/4oz/1 cup raisins

115g/4oz/1 cup chopped hazelnuts, roasted

115g/4oz/½ cup unsulphured dried apricots, chopped

50g/2oz/2 cups dried apple, chopped

25g/1oz/⅓ cup desiccated (dry unsweetened shredded) coconut

1 Put the sunflower and pumpkin seeds in a dry frying pan, and cook over a medium heat for 3 minutes until golden, tossing the seeds regularly to prevent them burning.

2 When golden, transfer the seeds to a large plate, and spread them out to cool and crisp.

3 Mix the seeds with the remaining ingredients and when completely cool, store in an airtight container.

Variation Serve the muesli in a long glass layered with fresh raspberries and fromage frais or yogurt. Soak the muesli first in a little water or fruit juice in order to soften it slightly.

Energy 813kcal/3411kJ; Protein 20.8g; Carbohydrate 100.9g, of which sugars 33.4g; Fat 39g, of which saturates 5.5g; Cholesterol 0mg; Calcium 145mg; Fibre 12.4g; Sodium 55mg

Oat crunch cereal

Serve this tasty, crunchy granola-type cereal simply with milk or, for a summer breakfast when berries are in season, with yogurt and raspberries or blueberries.

Serves 6

200g/7oz/1¾ cups jumbo rolled oats

150g/5oz/1¼ cups pecan nuts, roughly chopped

90ml/6 tbsp maple syrup

75g/3oz/6 tbsp butter, melted

Farmhouse tip This crunchy oat cereal will keep in an airtight container for up to two weeks. Store in a cool, dry place.

1 Preheat oven to 1600C/3250F/Gas 3. Mix all the ingredients together and spread over a large baking tray.

2 Bake for 30–35 minutes, or until golden and crunchy. Leave to cool, then break up into clumps and serve.

Energy 443Kcal/1847kJ; Protein 6.5g; Carbohydrate 37.7g, of which sugars 13.1g; Fat 30.6g, of which saturates 4.6g; Cholesterol 1mg; Calcium 38mg; Fibre 3.4g; Sodium 152g.

Breakfast pancakes

A great way of using up eggs, pancakes are a lovely hearty way to start a working day.
Add a little more milk if you want thinner pancakes, and eat warm with butter and syrup.

Makes 25

400g/14oz/3¼ cups plain (all-purpose) flour

5 eggs

1 egg yolk

5ml/1 tsp salt

750ml/1¼ pints/3 cups milk

25g/1oz/2 tbsp butter

Variations Cook some thin rashers (strips) of bacon in a dry frying pan until crisp. Remove from the pan, pour in the batter and return the bacon. Serve with treacle (molasses) or a salad.
   Alternatively, add apple slices to the batter and serve with brown sugar and ground cinnamon.

1 Sift the flour into a bowl and make a well in the centre. Add the eggs, egg yolk and salt, mix the eggs and stir, gradually incorporating the flour.

2 Gradually add half the milk and beat with a hand-held electric mixer to make a smooth, thick batter. Gradually stir in the remaining milk. Cover and leave to rest in the refrigerator for 30 minutes.

3 Remove the batter from the fridge. Melt the butter in a small frying pan, and stir it into the batter.

4 Re-heat the frying pan, add a little oil and pour in some of the batter. When set, flip over and cook the other side until golden. Remove from the pan and keep warm. Repeat until all the batter is finished. Serve with butter and syrup.

Per pancake Energy 93kcal/392kJ; Protein 3.9g; Carbohydrate 13.8g, of which sugars 1.7g; Fat 2.9g, of which saturates 1.2g; Cholesterol 50mg; Calcium 65mg; Fibre 0.5g; Sodium 112mg.

Eggs Benedict

This is a great way to serve traditional English muffins, and is a favourite breakfast dish all over the world. It can also be enjoyed with smoked salmon instead of ham.

Serves 4

4 eggs

2 English muffins or 4 slices of bread

butter, for spreading

4 thick slices cooked ham, cut to fit the muffins

fresh chives, to garnish

For the sauce

3 egg yolks

30ml/2 tbsp fresh lemon juice

1.5ml/¼ tsp salt

115g/4oz/½ cup butter

30ml/2 tbsp single (light) cream

ground black pepper

1 To make the sauce, blend the egg yolks, lemon juice and salt in a food processor or blender for 15 seconds.

2 Melt the butter in a small pan until it bubbles; do not let it brown. With the motor running, slowly pour the hot butter into the food processor or blender through the feed tube in a slow stream. Turn off the machine as soon as all the butter has been added.

3 Pour the sauce into a bowl, placed over a pan of simmering water. Stir for 2–3 minutes, until thickened. If the sauce begins to curdle, whisk in 15ml/ 1 tbsp boiling water. Stir in the cream and season with pepper. Remove from the heat and keep warm over the pan.

4 Bring a shallow pan of lightly salted water to the boil. Break each egg into a cup, then slide it carefully into the water. Turn the white around the yolk with a spoon. Cook for about 4 minutes until the white is set. Remove the eggs from the pan with a slotted spoon, and drain on kitchen paper. Cut off any ragged edges.

5 While the eggs are poaching, split and toast the muffins or toast the slices of bread. Spread with butter while warm.

6 Place a piece of ham on each muffin half or slice of toast, then place an egg on top. Spoon the warm sauce over the eggs, garnish with chives and serve.

Energy 553kcal/2304kJ; Protein 19.8g; Carbohydrate 31.6g, of which sugars 2.2g; Fat 39.7g, of which saturates 18.9g; Cholesterol 427mg; Calcium 148mg; Fibre 1.3g; Sodium 635mg.

Traditional bacon and eggs

A hearty cooked breakfast is far more than the sum of its parts, and its enduring popularity shows how simple food, using the best ingredients, is a reliable recipe for success.

Serves 4

4 lamb's kidneys, halved and trimmed

wholegrain mustard, for spreading

8 rashers (strips) back or streaky (fatty) bacon, preferably dry-cured

275g/10oz black pudding (blood sausage), sliced

225g/8oz good quality sausages

butter or oil, for grilling or frying

4 tomatoes, halved

4–8 flat field (portabello) mushrooms

4 potato cakes or potato bread

4 eggs

sea salt and ground black pepper

chopped fresh chives or fresh parsley sprigs, to garnish

Variation This breakfast has several different variations, scramble the eggs, if you prefer, or grill the bacon and mushrooms, or add fried potatoes.

1 Spread the kidneys with a little mustard. Fry the bacon, black pudding, kidneys and sausages with butter or oil, as preferred, until crisp and browned. Remove from the pan and keep warm.

2 Meanwhile, fry or grill the halved tomatoes with knobs (pats) of butter, and fry or bake the flat field mushrooms, preferably in the juices from the bacon, kidneys and sausages, until they are just tender.

3 Fry the potato cakes or potato bread until warmed through and golden brown on both sides. Cook the eggs to your liking. Arrange everything on large, warm plates, and garnish with chopped chives or parsley sprigs. Serve at once.

Energy 894Kcal/3728kJ; Protein 50.6g; Carbohydrate 40.1g, of which sugars 5.5g; Fat 60.4g, of which saturates 20.1g; Cholesterol 618mg; Calcium 115mg; Fibre 3.5g; Sodium 2.25mg.

Smoked salmon and chive omelette

The addition of smoked salmon gives a really luxurious finish to this simple, classic dish.
You could try replacing the salmon and chives with chopped ham and parsley.

Serves 2

4 eggs

15ml/1 tbsp chopped fresh chives

50g/2oz smoked salmon, roughly chopped

a knob (pat) of butter

salt and ground black pepper

1 Beat the eggs until just combined, then stir in the chives and season with salt and pepper.

2 Heat the butter in a medium-sized frying pan until foamy. Pour in the eggs and cook over a medium heat for 3–4 minutes, drawing the cooked egg from around the edge into the centre of the pan from time to time.

3 At this stage, you can either leave the top of the omelette soft or finish it off under the grill (broiler), depending on how you like your omelette. Top with the smoked salmon, fold the omelette over and cut in half to serve.

Energy 221kcal/920kJ; Protein 19g; Carbohydrate 0.2g, of which sugars 0.2g; Fat 16.4g, of which saturates 5.9g; Cholesterol 400mg; Calcium 65mg; Fibre 0.1g; Sodium 641mg.

Grilled kippers with marmalade toast

The best English kippers are still cured in 19th century smokehouses. The bitter-sweet orange marmalade is an old-fashioned accompaniment that is well worth reviving.

Serves 2

melted butter, for greasing

2 kippers

2 slices of bread

soft butter, for spreading

orange marmalade, for spreading

1 Preheat the grill (broiler). Line the grill pan with foil – to help prevent fishy smells from lingering in the pan – and brush the foil with melted butter to stop the fish sticking.

2 Using kitchen scissors, or a knife, cut the heads and tails off the kippers.

3 Lay the fish, skin side up, on the buttered foil. Put under the hot grill and cook for 1 minute.

4 Turn the kippers over, brush the uppermost (fleshy) side with melted butter, put back under the grill and cook for 4–5 minutes.

5 Toast the bread and spread it first with butter and then with marmalade. Serve the sizzling hot kippers immediately with the marmalade toast.

Variation Cook the kippers sprinkled with cayenne pepper, and serve with a knob (pat) of butter and lemon wedges.

Energy 518kcal/2155kJ; Protein 33.9g; Carbohydrate 17.6g, of which sugars 5.9g; Fat 35.1g, of which saturates 7.6g; Cholesterol 121mg; Calcium 126mg; Fibre 0.4g; Sodium 1640mg

Bubble and squeak

Whether you have leftovers, or cook this old-fashioned farmhouse classic from fresh, be sure to give it a really good 'squeak' (fry) in the pan so it turns a rich golden brown.

Serves 4

60ml/4 tbsp vegetable oil

1 onion, finely chopped

450g/1lb floury potatoes, cooked and mashed

225g/8oz cooked cabbage or Brussels sprouts, finely chopped

salt and ground black pepper

1 Heat 30ml/2 tbsp oil in a heavy frying pan. Add the onion and cook, stirring frequently, until soft but not browned.

2 In a large bowl, mix together the potatoes and cooked cabbage or sprouts, and season with salt and plenty of pepper to taste.

Variation Use dripping or bacon fat, instead of the vegetable oil, if you can, for extra flavour.

3 Add the vegetables to the pan with the cooked onions, stir well, then press the vegetable mixture into a large, even cake.

4 Cook over a medium heat for about 15 minutes until the cake is browned underneath.

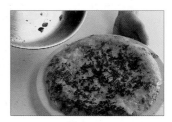

5 Invert a large plate over the pan, and, holding it tightly against the pan, turn them both over together. Lift off the frying pan, return it to the heat and add the remaining dripping, fat or oil. When hot, slide the cake back into the pan, browned side uppermost.

6 Cook over a medium heat for 10 minutes or until the underside is golden brown. Serve hot, in wedges.

Farmhouse tip If you don't have leftover cooked cabbage or Brussels sprouts, shred raw cabbage and cook both in boiling salted water until tender. Drain, then chop.

Energy 205kcal/857kj; Protein 3.5g; Carbohydrate 23.3g; of which sugars 4.2g; Fat 11.5g; of which saturates 1.2g; Cholesterol 0mg; Calcium 34mg; Fibre 3g; Sodium 15mg.

Bacon and potato floddies

This breakfast special from England's northeast is often served with eggs and sausages.
Floddies are said to have originally been cooked on shovels, over a fire, by canal workers.

Serves 4–6

250g/9oz potatoes, weighed after peeling

1 large onion

175g/6oz rindless streaky (fatty) bacon, finely chopped

50g/2oz/½ cup self-raising (self-rising) flour

2 eggs

oil or bacon dripping, for frying

salt and ground black pepper

Farmhouse tip Fry the floddies in oiled metal rings if you wish, for a neat circular shape.

1 Grate the potatoes onto a clean dish cloth, and then gather up the edges to make a pouch. Squeeze and twist the towel to remove the liquid.

2 Grate or finely chop the onion into a mixing bowl and add the potatoes, chopped bacon, flour and seasoning, mixing well.

3 Beat the eggs and stir into the potato mixture. Heat some oil in a large frying pan. Add generous tablespoonfuls of the potato mixture to the hot oil and flatten them to make thin cakes. Cook over a medium heat for 3–4 minutes on each side or until golden brown and cooked through. Lift out, drain on kitchen paper and serve.

Energy 214kcal/891kJ; Protein 8.8g; Carbohydrate 17.1g, of which sugars 3.5g; Fat 12.7g, of which saturates 3.4g; Cholesterol 82mg; Calcium 38mg; Fibre 1.4g; Sodium 397mg.

Country Soups

Nourishing and frugal, soups are a farmhouse speciality, using up seasonal gluts or making a limited amount of food feed a table full of hungry people. Whether you are making a hearty one-pot meal of beans and vegetables like Minestrone, or a simple appetizer such as Creamy Parsnip Soup, the bubbling pan on your stove will warm the kitchen and take very little effort to prepare.

Making stock

As every farmhouse cook will tell you, good home-made stock is the secret of successful soups and casseroles. Here are three stock recipes, which you can make in bulk and freeze.

Meat stock

Makes about 2 litres / 3½ pints/ 18 cups

1.75kg/4–4½lb beef bones, such as shin, leg, neck and clod, or veal or lamb bones, cut in 6cm/2½in pieces

2 onions, unpeeled, quartered

2 carrots, roughly chopped

2 celery sticks, with leaves if possible, roughly chopped

2 tomatoes, coarsely chopped

4 litres/6½ pints/16 cups water

a handful of parsley stalks

a few fresh thyme sprigs or 5ml/ 1 tsp dried thyme

2 bay leaves

10 black peppercorns, lightly crushed

1 Preheat the oven to 230°C/450°F/ Gas 8. Put the bones in a roasting pan or flameproof casserole and roast, turning occasionally, for 30 minutes or until they start to brown.

2 Add the vegetables and baste with the fat in the pan or casserole. Roast for a further 20–30 minutes or until the bones are well browned. Stir and baste occasionally.

3 Transfer the bones and vegetables to a stockpot. Spoon off the fat from the roasting pan or casserole, add a little water and bring to the boil, scraping in any residue from the bottom of the pan. Pour this liquid into the stockpot.

4 Add the remaining water to the stockpot. Bring just to the boil, skimming frequently to remove any foam. Add the herbs and peppercorns.

5 Partly cover the pot and simmer the stock for 4–6 hours, topping up the liquid as necessary.

6 Strain the stock. Skim as much fat as possible from the surface. If possible, cool the stock and then chill it; the fat will set in a layer on the surface and can be removed easily. You can then use the stock for meat-based soups, casseroles and stews, or freeze it for up to three months.

Chicken stock

Makes about 2.5 litres/4 pints/10 cups

1.2–1.4kg/2½–3lb chicken or turkey pieces; wings, backs and necks etc

2 onions, unpeeled, quartered

4 litres/6½ pints/16 cups water

2 carrots, roughly chopped

2 celery sticks, with leaves if possible, roughly chopped

a small handful of fresh parsley

a few fresh thyme sprigs or 5ml/1 tsp dried thyme

1 or 2 bay leaves

10–15 black peppercorns, lightly crushed

1 Put the chicken pieces and the onions in a stockpot. Cook over a medium heat, stirring occasionally, until lightly browned. Stir in the water. Bring to the boil. Skim the surface.

2 Add the remaining ingredients. Simmer for 3 hours. Strain, cool and chill. When cold, remove the fat from the surface. Use within 2 days for chicken soups or stews, or freeze.

Vegetable stock

Makes about 2.5 litres/4 pints/10 cups

2 large onions, peeled and coarsely chopped

2 leeks, sliced

3 garlic cloves, crushed

3 carrots, coarsely chopped

4 celery sticks, coarsely chopped

1 large strip of pared rind from an unwaxed lemon

a handful of parsley stalks

a few fresh thyme sprigs

2 bay leaves

2.5 litres/4 pints/10 cups water

1 Put the vegetables, lemon rind, herbs and water in a stockpot and bring to the boil. Skim the surface.

2 Reduce the heat and simmer, uncovered, for 30 minutes. Strain the stock and leave it to cool. Vegetable stock will keep for longer than meat or fish stock, but you should still use it within 3–4 days, or freeze it for up to 3 months.

Fish stock

Makes about 1.2 litres/2 pints/5 cups

1.5kg/3–3½lb white fish bones, including tails and heads, washed

2 large onions, peeled, roughly chopped

1 large leek, washed, roughly chopped

1 celery stick, roughly chopped

6 button mushrooms, sliced

6 black peppercorns

a few fresh parsley stalks

1.2 litres/2 pints/5 cups cold water

1 Cut the fish pieces into two or three pieces and place in a large pan.

2 Add the vegetables, peppercorns and parsley stalks to the pan. Pour in the water, bring to the boil, then skim. Reduce the heat and simmer for 20 minutes.

3 Strain the stock through a cloth-lined sieve (strainer) and leave until just cool. Chill for up to 2 days or freeze. Use for vegetable-based soups or casseroles.

Country vegetable soup

This satisfying soup captures all the flavours of the countryside and served, with bread is a meal in itself. The basil and garlic purée gives it extra colour and a wonderful aroma.

Serves 6–8

275g/10oz/1½ cups fresh shelled broad (fava) beans, or 175g/6oz/ ¾ cup dried haricot (navy) beans, soaked overnight in water to cover

2.5ml/½ tsp dried herbes de Provence

2 garlic cloves, finely chopped

15ml/1 tbsp olive oil

1 onion, finely chopped

2 small leeks, finely sliced

1 celery stick, finely sliced

2 carrots, finely diced

2 small potatoes, peeled and finely diced

115g/4oz French (green) beans

1.2 litres/2 pints/5 cups water

115g/4oz/1 cup peas, fresh or frozen

2 small courgettes (zucchini), finely chopped

3 tomatoes, skinned, seeded and finely chopped

a handful of spinach leaves, cut into thin ribbons

salt and freshly ground black pepper

fresh basil sprigs, to garnish

For the garlic purée

1 or 2 garlic cloves, finely chopped

15g/½oz/½ cup basil leaves

60ml/4 tbsp grated Parmesan cheese

60ml/4 tbsp extra virgin olive oil

1 To make the purée, process the garlic, basil and Parmesan until smooth. With the machine running, slowly add the olive oil. Set aside until ready to serve.

2 If using dried beans, boil vigorously for 10 minutes and drain. Place them or the fresh beans in a saucepan with the herbs and 1 garlic clove. Add water to cover by 2.5cm/1in. Bring to the boil and simmer for 10 minutes for fresh beans, or about 1 hour for dried beans.

3 Heat the oil in a large heavy pan. Fry the onion and leeks for 5 minutes, stirring occasionally.

4 Add the celery and carrots, with the remaining garlic clove. Stir together and cook for 10 minutes.

5 Add the potatoes, French beans and water. Bring to the boil, then cover and simmer for 10 minutes.

6 Add the peas, courgettes and tomatoes, with the reserved beans. Simmer for 25–30 minutes. Add the spinach, season to taste, and simmer for 5 minutes. To serve the soup, ladle into warmed bowls, swirl a spoonful of purée on the top of each one and garnish with basil.

Energy 197kcal/821kJ; Protein 8g; Carbohydrate 14g, of which sugars 5g; Fat 13g, of which saturates 3g; Cholesterol 7mg; Calcium 127mg; Fibre 3.7g; Sodium 122mg.

Rustic mushroom soup

Using a mixture of mushrooms gives real depth of flavour to this rustic soup – if you have some wild mushrooms include them for extra character. The cream gives a lovely finish.

Serves 4–6

20g/³⁄₄oz/1¹⁄₂ tbsp butter

15ml/1 tbsp oil

1 onion, roughly chopped

4 potatoes, about 250–350g/
9–12oz, roughly chopped

350g/12oz mixed mushrooms, such
as field (portabello) and button
(white)

1 or 2 garlic cloves, crushed

150ml/¹⁄₄ pint/²⁄₃ cup white wine or
dry (hard) cider

1.2 litres/2 pints/5 cups good chicken
stock

bunch of fresh parsley, chopped

salt and ground black pepper

whipped or sour cream, to garnish

◀ **1** Chop the mushrooms. Heat the butter and oil in a large pan, over medium heat. Stir in the onion and potatoes. Cover and sweat over a low heat for 5–10 minutes until softened.

2 Add the mushrooms, garlic and white wine or cider and stock to the pan. Season, bring to the boil and cook for 15 minutes, until tender.

3 Blend the soup with a hand blender or processor until smooth. Return to the rinsed pan, and add three-quarters of the parsley. Bring back to the boil, season, and garnish with cream and the remaining parsley.

Energy 155kcal/648kJ; Protein 3.3g; Carbohydrate 13.6g, of which sugars 3.4g; Fat 7.6g, of which saturates 3.1g; Cholesterol 11mg; Calcium 23mg; Fibre 2.1g; Sodium 117mg.

Garlic soup

An aromatic soup, best made with plenty of early-season garlic and good stock. This traditional recipe is not only delicious, but said to be a cure for colds and hangovers.

Serves 8

12 large garlic cloves, peeled

15ml/1 tbsp olive oil

15ml/1 tbsp melted butter

1 small onion, finely chopped

15g/¹⁄₂oz/2 tbsp plain (all-purpose)
flour

15ml/1 tbsp white wine vinegar

1 litre/1³⁄₄ pints/4 cups chicken stock

2 egg yolks, lightly beaten

bread croûtons, fried in butter,
to serve

1 Crush the garlic. Put the oil and butter into a pan, add the garlic and onion, and cook them gently for 20 minutes. Add the flour and stir to make a roux. Cook for a few minutes, then stir in the wine vinegar, stock and 1 litre/1³⁄₄ pints/4 cups water. Simmer for 30 minutes.

2 When ready to serve, whisk in the egg yolks. Do not allow the soup to boil again. Serve at once with the croûtons.

Farmhouse tip This garlic soup brings a great sense of well-being and is a real treat for garlic-lovers.

Energy 55kcal/229kJ; Protein 1.3g; Carbohydrate 3g, of which sugars 0.5g; Fat 4.4g, of which saturates 1.6g; Cholesterol 54mg; Calcium 12mg; Fibre 0.3g; Sodium 50mg.

Classic onion soup

Although onions keep well through the winter, the autumn onion harvest is a great opportunity to make this lovely soup. With delicious melting Gruyère croûtes floating in the bowl, it is a hearty meal in itself, perfect for a warming lunch as the seasons turn.

Serves 6

50g/2oz/¼ cup butter

15ml/1 tbsp olive or vegetable oil

2kg/4½lb yellow onions, peeled and sliced

5ml/1 tsp chopped fresh thyme

5ml/1 tsp caster (superfine) sugar

15ml/1 tbsp sherry vinegar

1.5 litres/2½ pints/6¼ cups good beef, chicken or duck stock

25ml/1½ tbsp plain (all-purpose) flour

150ml/¼ pint/⅔ cup dry white wine

45ml/3 tbsp brandy

salt and ground black pepper

For the croûtes

6–12 thick slices day-old French stick or baguette, about 2.5cm/1in thick

1 garlic clove, halved

15ml/1 tbsp French mustard

115g/4oz/1 cup coarsely grated Gruyère cheese

1 Melt the butter with the oil in a large pan. Add the onions and stir to coat them in the mixture.

2 Cook over a medium heat for 5–8 minutes, stirring once or twice, until the onions begin to soften. Stir in the thyme.

3 Reduce the heat to very low, cover the pan and cook the onions for about 20–30 minutes, stirring frequently, until they are very soft and golden yellow.

4 Uncover the pan and increase the heat slightly. Stir in the sugar and cook for 5–10 minutes, until the onions start to brown.

5 Add the sherry vinegar and increase the heat again, then continue cooking, stirring frequently, until the onions turn a deep, golden brown – this could take up to 20 minutes. Meanwhile, bring the stock to the boil in another pan.

6 Stir the flour into the onions and cook for about 2 minutes, then gradually pour in the hot stock. Add the wine and brandy, and season the soup to taste with salt and pepper. Simmer for 10–15 minutes.

7 For the croûtes, preheat the oven to 150°C/300°F/Gas 2. Place the slices of bread on a greased baking tray and bake for 15–20 minutes, until dry and lightly browned. Rub the bread with the cut surface of the garlic.

8 Spread the croûtes with the mustard, then sprinkle the grated Gruyère cheese over the slices.

9 Preheat the grill (broiler) on the hottest setting. Ladle the soup into a large flameproof pan or six flameproof bowls. Float the croûtes on the soup, then grill (broil) until the cheese melts, bubbles and browns. Serve the soup immediately.

Energy 484kcal/2030kJ; Protein 15.3g; Carbohydrate 67.2g, of which sugars 21.5g; Fat 15.1g, of which saturates 8.7g; Cholesterol 36mg; Calcium 314mg; Fibre 6.4g; Sodium 611mg.

Creamy parsnip soup

This is a spicy winter country soup. It can also be made with other root vegetables, such as carrots or celeriac. It is delicious garnished with parsnip crisps or fried garlic croûtons.

Serves 6

900g/2lb parsnips

50g/2oz/¼ cup butter

1 onion, chopped

2 garlic cloves, crushed

10ml/2 tsp ground cumin

5ml/1 tsp ground coriander

about 1.2 litres/2 pints/5 cups hot chicken stock

150ml/¼ pint/⅔ cup single (light) cream

salt and ground black pepper

chopped fresh chives or parsley and/or croûtons, to garnish

1 Peel and thinly slice the parsnips. Heat the butter in a large heavy pan then add the peeled parsnips and chopped onion with the crushed garlic. Cook until softened, stirring occasionally.

2 Add the cumin and coriander to the vegetable mixture and cook, stirring, for 1–2 minutes, then gradually blend in the hot chicken stock and mix well.

3 Cover and simmer for about 20 minutes, or until the parsnip is soft. Purée the soup, adjust the texture with extra stock or water if it seems too thick, and check the seasoning. Add the cream and reheat without boiling.

4 Serve immediately, sprinkled with chopped chives or parsley and/or croûtons, to garnish.

Energy 215kcal/899kJ; Protein 3.9g; Carbohydrate 21.3g, of which sugars 10.6g; Fat 13.3g, of which saturates 7.7g; Cholesterol 32mg; Calcium 92mg; Fibre 7.3g; Sodium 74mg.

Pear and watercress soup with Stilton croûtons

Pears and Stilton taste good when you eat them together after the main course – here, for a change, they are blended into a delicious soup that makes a lovely first course.

Serves 6

1 bunch watercress

4 medium pears, sliced

900ml/1½ pints chicken stock, preferably home-made

120ml/4fl oz double (heavy) cream

juice of 1 lime

salt and ground black pepper

For the croûtons

25g/1oz butter

30ml/1 tbsp olive oil

200g/7oz cubed stale bread

140g/5oz crumbled Stilton cheese

1 Keep back about a third of the watercress leaves. Place all the rest of the watercress leaves and stalks in a pan with the sliced pears, stock and a little seasoning. Bring to the boil, reduce the heat and simmer for about 15–20 minutes. Blend until smooth.

2 Reserving the best watercress leaves for garnishing, add the rest of the leaves and blend in a food processor to form a paste.

3 Add the cream and lime juice to the watercress paste, mix and season to taste. Pour the blended soup back into a pan, and add the watercress and cream mixture.

4 To make the croûtons, melt the butter and oil and fry the bread cubes until golden. Put the cheese on top and heat under a hot grill, until bubbling. Reheat the soup and pour into bowls. Divide the croûtons and remaining watercress leaves between the bowls to serve.

Energy 402kcal/1672kJ; Protein 10g; Carbohydrate 28g, of which sugars 12g; Fat 29g, of which saturates 15g; Cholesterol 58mg; Calcium 167mg; Fibre 1.8g; Sodium 844mg.

Leek and potato soup

A hearty classic, this soup is full of chunky vegetables. If you prefer a smooth version, press the soup through a sieve but don't process, as that will give the potatoes a gluey consistency.

2 Add the potatoes to the pan and cook for about 2–3 minutes, then add the stock and bring to the boil. Cover and simmer for 30–35 minutes.

3 Season to taste and remove the pan from the heat. Dice and stir in the remaining butter. Garnish with the chopped parsley and serve hot.

Serves 4

50g/2oz/¼ cup butter

2 leeks, washed and chopped

1 small onion, peeled and finely chopped

350g/12oz potatoes, peeled and chopped

900ml/1½ pints/3¾ cups chicken or vegetable stock

salt and ground black pepper

chopped fresh parsley, to garnish

1 Heat 25g/1oz/2 tbsp of the butter in a large pan over a medium heat. Add the leeks and onion and cook gently, stirring occasionally, for about 7 minutes, until they are softened but not browned.

Energy 179kcal/747kJ; Protein 3.2g; Carbohydrate 17.9g, of which sugars 4g; Fat 11g, of which saturates 6.7g; Cholesterol 27mg; Calcium 32mg; Fibre 3g; Sodium 88mg.

Bean and cabbage soup

This is a typical Italian farmhouse dish, designed to make the most of leftovers, including day-old bread and vegetables. Use dark-leaved curly kale or Savoy cabbage.

Serves 4

115g/4oz/generous ½ cup cannellini beans, soaked overnight and drained

8 garlic cloves, unpeeled

30ml/2 tbsp olive oil

6 celery sticks, chopped

3 carrots, chopped

2 onions, chopped

400g/14oz can plum tomatoes, drained

30ml/2 tbsp chopped fresh flat leaf parsley

grated rind and juice of 1 lemon

800g/1¾lb dark green cabbage leaves, sliced

1 day-old ciabatta loaf

salt and ground black pepper

olive oil, to serve

1 Put the beans in a pan and cover with fresh water. Bring to the boil and boil for 10 minutes. Drain again. Cover with fresh cold water and add six garlic cloves. Bring to the boil, cover and simmer for 45–60 minutes, until the beans are tender. (The cooking time depends on how old the beans are). Set the beans aside in their liquid.

2 Heat the oil in a pan. Peel and chop the remaining garlic and add it to the pan with the celery, carrots and onions.

3 Cook gently for 10 minutes, until beginning to soften. Stir in the tomatoes, parsley, lemon rind and juice. Cover and simmer for 25 minutes.

4 Add the sliced cabbage and half the cannellini beans with enough of their cooking liquid to cover all of the ingredients. Simmer for 30 minutes.

5 Meanwhile, process the remaining beans with a little of their cooking liquid in a food processor until just smooth. Add to the pan and pour in boiling water to thin the mixture to the consistency of a thick soup.

6 Remove the crust from the ciabatta loaf and tear the bread into rough pieces. Stir the torn chunks into the soup. Season well. This soup should be very thick, but add a little more boiling water to thin if you wish.

7 Ladle the soup into four serving bowls and drizzle a little olive oil over each. Serve immediately.

Energy 104kcal/436kJ; Protein 5.7g; Carbohydrate 14.5g, of which sugars 6.9g; Fat 3g, of which saturates 0.5g; Cholesterol 0mg; Calcium 78mg; Fibre 5.9g; Sodium 218mg.

Cream of celeriac and spinach soup

Celeriac has a wonderful flavour that is reminiscent of celery, but also adds a slightly nutty taste. Here it is combined with spinach to make a delicious soup.

Serves 6

1 leek

500g/1¼lb celeriac

1 litre/1¾ pints/4 cups water

250ml/8fl oz/1 cup dry white wine

200g/7oz fresh spinach leaves

milk (optional)

salt and ground black pepper

25g/1oz/⅓ cup pine nuts, dry roasted, and grated nutmeg, to serve

1 Trim and slit the leek. Rinse it under running water to remove any grit, then slice it thickly. Peel the celeriac and dice the flesh.

2 Mix the water and wine in a jug. Place the leek and celeriac, with the spinach, in a deep pan and pour over the liquid. Bring to the boil, lower the heat and simmer for 10–15 minutes, until the vegetables are soft.

3 Blend with a hand blender or in a processor. Return to a clean pan and season with salt, pepper and nutmeg. If the soup is too thick, thin with a little milk. Reheat, and serve with the roasted pine nuts and grated nutmeg.

Energy 77Kcal/319kJ; Protein 2.5g; Carbohydrate 24.8g, of which sugars 18.8g; Fat 19.5g, of which saturates 9.2g; Cholesterol 34mg; Calcium 102mg; Fibre 2.3g; Sodium 99mg.

Carrot and coriander soup

Root vegetables, such as carrots, are great for slow cooking. Their earthy flavour becomes rich and sweet when cooked over a gentle heat, and their texture becomes smooth when puréed.

Serves 4

450g/1lb carrots, preferably young and tender

15ml/1 tbsp sunflower oil

40g/1½oz/3 tbsp butter

1 onion, chopped

1 stick celery, plus 2–3 pale leafy tops

2 small potatoes, peeled

900ml/1½ pints/3¾ cups boiling vegetable stock

10ml/2 tsp ground coriander

15ml/1 tbsp chopped fresh coriander (cilantro)

150ml/¼ pint/⅔ cup milk

salt and ground black pepper

1 Trim and peel the carrots and cut into chunks. Heat the oil and 25g/1oz/2 tbsp of the butter in a large pan and fry the onion over a gentle heat for 3–4 minutes until softened but not brown.

2 Slice the celery and chop the potatoes, and add them to the onion in the pan. Cook for 2 minutes, then add the carrots and cook for a further 1 minute. Pour the boiling vegetable stock over the vegetables, then season with salt and ground black pepper.

3 Bring the liquid to the boil, then cover the pan with the lid and cook on a gentle for 45 minutes until the vegetables are tender.

4 Reserve 6–8 tiny celery leaves from the leafy tops for the garnish, then finely chop the remaining celery tops. Melt the remaining butter in a frying pan and add the ground coriander. Fry for about 1 minute, stirring constantly, until the aromas are released.

5 Reduce the heat under the pan and add the chopped celery tops and fresh coriander. Fry for about 30 seconds, then remove the pan from the heat.

6 Ladle the soup into a food processor or blender and process until smooth, then return to the cleaned pan. Add the celery tops and coriander, stir in the milk and reheat gently. Check the seasoning, then serve, garnished with the reserved celery leaves.

Energy 168Kcal/697kJ; Protein 3g; Carbohydrate 11.9g, of which sugars 9.2g; Fat 12.4g, of which saturates 6g; Cholesterol 24mg; Calcium 94mg; Fibre 3.1g; Sodium 758mg.

Beetroot soup

This rustic soup is a particular favourite in the rural communities of Russia and Eastern Europe. There are many variations and it is rare to find two recipes the same.

Serves 6

350g/12oz whole, uncooked beetroot

15ml/1 tbsp sunflower oil

115g/4oz rindless streaky bacon rashers, chopped

1 large onion, chopped

1 large carrot, cut into matchstick strips

3 celery sticks, thinly sliced

1.5 litres/2½ pints/6 cups chicken stock

about 225g/8oz tomatoes, skinned, seeded and sliced

about 30ml/2 tbsp lemon juice or wine vinegar

30ml/2 tbsp chopped fresh chives

115g/4oz white cabbage, thinly sliced

150ml/¼ pint/⅔ cup soured cream

salt and ground black pepper

1 Peel the beetroot, slice and then cut into very thin strips.

2 Heat the oil in a large, heavy pan and fry the bacon for 3–4 minutes. Add the onion to the pan, fry for 2–3 minutes.

3 Add the sliced carrot, celery and sliced beetroot. Cook for 4–5 minutes, stirring frequently, until most of the oil has been absorbed.

4 Add the stock, tomatoes, lemon juice or wine vinegar to the pan, together with half of the chopped chives.

5 Bring the soup to the boil, then lower the heat and simmer for about 30–40 minutes until the vegetables are completely tender.

6 Add the cabbage to the soup and simmer for 5 minutes until tender.

7 Season to taste and serve, swirled with a spoonful of sour cream and sprinkled with chopped chives.

Energy 137Kcal/574kJ; Protein 3.7g; Carbohydrate 18.2g, of which sugars 16.3g; Fat 6g, of which saturates 0.1g; Cholesterol 0mg; Calcium 22mg; Fibre 1.9g; Sodium 29mg.

Bean and pistou soup

This classic rustic soup from the countryside of the South of France makes the most of nourishing beans and vegetables with fresh pistou, the Provençal garlic and basil sauce.

Serves 4–6

150g/5oz/scant 1 cup dried haricot (navy) beans, soaked overnight

150g/5oz/scant 1 cup dried flageolet or cannellini beans, soaked overnight

1 onion, chopped

1.2 litres/2 pints/5 cups hot vegetable stock

2 carrots, roughly chopped

225g/8oz Savoy cabbage, shredded

1 large potato, about 225g/8oz, roughly chopped

225g/8oz French (green) beans, chopped

salt and ground black pepper

basil leaves, to garnish

For the pistou

4 garlic cloves

8 large sprigs basil leaves

90ml/6 tbsp olive oil

60ml/4 tbsp freshly grated Parmesan cheese

1 Drain the soaked haricot and flageolet or cannellini beans and place them in an ovenproof casserole or ceramic bean pot.

2 Add the chopped onion and pour over sufficient cold water to come 5cm/2in above the beans. Cover and place the casserole in an cold oven. Set the oven to 200°C/400°F/Gas 6 and cook for about 1½ hours, until tender.

3 Drain the beans and onions. Place half the beans and onions in a food processor or blender and process to a paste. Return the beans and paste to the casserole. Add the vegetable stock.

4 Add the chopped carrots, shredded cabbage, chopped potato and French beans to the pot. Season, cover and return the pot to the oven. Reduce the oven temperature to 180°C/350°F/Gas 4 and cook for 1 hour, or until all the vegetables are cooked.

5 Meanwhile, place the garlic and basil in a mortar and pound with a pestle, then gradually beat in the oil. Stir in the grated Parmesan.

6 Stir half of the pistou into the soup and then ladle into warmed bowls. Top each bowl of soup with a spoonful of the remaining pistou and serve, garnished with basil.

Energy 286kcal/1214kJ; Protein 19.8g; Carbohydrate 50.9g, of which sugars 11.1g; Fat 1.8g, of which saturates 0.3g; Cholesterol 0mg; Calcium 142mg; Fibre 16.1g; Sodium 36mg.

Country minestrone

An Italian country soup, made with pasta, beans and vegetables, which is a meal in itself.

Serves 4

45ml/3 tbsp olive oil

115g/4oz pancetta, any rinds removed, roughly chopped

2–3 celery sticks, finely chopped

3 medium carrots, finely chopped

1 medium onion, finely chopped

1–2 garlic cloves, crushed

2 x 400g/14oz cans chopped tomatoes

about 1 litre/1¾ pints/4 cups chicken stock

400g/14oz can cannellini beans, drained and rinsed

50g/2oz/½ cup short–cut macaroni

30–60ml/2–4 tbsp chopped flat leaf parsley, to taste

salt and ground black pepper

shaved Parmesan cheese, to serve

1 Heat the oil in a large pan. Add the pancetta, celery, carrots and onion and cook over a low heat for 5 minutes, stirring constantly, until the vegetables are softened.

2 Add the garlic and tomatoes, breaking them up with a wooden spoon. Pour in the stock. Season to taste and bring to the boil. Half cover the pan, lower the heat and simmer gently for 20 minutes, until the vegetables are soft.

3 Drain the beans and add to the pan with the macaroni. Bring to the boil again. Cover, lower the heat and continue to simmer for about 20 minutes more. Check the consistency and add more stock if necessary.

4 Stir in the parsley and taste for seasoning. Serve hot, sprinkled with plenty of Parmesan cheese.

Energy 198kcal/833kJ; Protein 15.6g; Carbohydrate 23.3g, of which sugars 3.9g; Fat 5.4g, of which saturates 1.4g; Cholesterol 30mg; Calcium 31mg; Fibre 3.2g; Sodium 224mg.

Summer minestrone

A light, colourful and delicious version of the country soup that is full of summer flavours.

Serves 4

45ml/3 tbsp olive oil

1 large onion, finely chopped

15ml/1 tbsp sun-dried tomato purée (paste)

450g/1lb ripe Italian plum tomatoes, peeled and finely chopped

450g/1lb green and yellow courgettes (zucchini), trimmed and chopped

3 waxy new potatoes, diced

2 garlic cloves, crushed

1.2 litres/2 pints/5 cups chicken stock

60ml/4 tbsp shredded fresh basil

50g/2oz/⅔ cup grated Parmesan cheese

salt and ground black pepper

1 Heat the oil in a large pan, then add the chopped onion and cook gently for about 5 minutes, stirring constantly.

2 Stir the sun-dried tomato purée in to the onion, and add the chopped tomatoes, chopped green and yellow courgettes, diced new potatoes and crushed garlic to the pan.

3 Mix together well and cook gently for 10 minutes, uncovered, shaking the pan frequently to stop the vegetables sticking to the base.

4 Carefully pour chicken stock in to the pan. Bring to the boil, lower the heat, half-cover the pan and simmer gently for 15 minutes or until the vegetables are just tender. Add more stock if necessary.

5 Remove the pan from the heat and stir in the basil and half the cheese. Taste for seasoning. Serve hot, sprinkled with the remaining cheese.

Energy 201kcal/839kJ; Protein 8.1g; Carbohydrate 18.1g, of which sugars 7.8g; Fat 11.2g, of which saturates 3.4g; Cholesterol 10mg; Calcium 170mg; Fibre 3g; Sodium 138mg.

Autumn pumpkin soup with yogurt

This smooth puréed soup is an absolute must during the pumpkin harvest, but at other times of the year you can replace it with butternut squash instead.

Serves 4

1kg/2¼lb prepared pumpkin flesh, cut into cubes

1 litre/1¾ pints/4 cups chicken or vegetable stock

10ml/2 tsp sugar

25g/1oz/2 tbsp butter

60–75ml/4–5 tbsp thick and creamy natural (plain) yogurt

salt and ground black pepper

1 Put the pumpkin cubes into a pan with the stock, and bring the liquid to the boil. Reduce the heat, cover the pan, and simmer for about 20 minutes, or until the pumpkin is tender.

2 Blend the soup or use a potato masher to mash the pumpkin flesh. Return the soup to the pan and bring back to the boil.

3 Add the sugar to the pan and season to taste with salt and pepper. Keep the pan over a low heat while you gently melt the butter in a small pan over a low heat.

4 Pour the soup into a tureen, or carefully ladle it into individual serving bowls. Swirl a little yogurt on to the surface of the soup and drizzle the melted butter over the top. Serve, with extra yogurt and black pepper.

Energy 97kcal/406kJ; Protein 2.6g; Carbohydrate 9.3g, of which sugars 8g; Fat 5.8g, of which saturates 3.6g; Cholesterol 14mg; Calcium 104mg; Fibre 2.5g; Sodium 51mg.

Garden pea and mint soup

New peas combined with freshly picked mint from the garden produce a velvety,
fresh-tasting soup with a wonderful taste of summer.

Serves 6

25g/1oz/2 tbsp butter

1 medium onion, finely chopped

675g/1½lb shelled fresh peas

1.5ml/¼ tsp sugar

1.2 litres/2 pints/5 cups chicken
or vegetable stock

handful of fresh mint leaves, plus
extra, to garnish

150ml/¼ pint/⅔ cup double
(heavy) cream

salt and ground black pepper

chopped fresh chives, to serve

1 Melt the butter in a large pan and
add the onion. Cook over a low
heat for about 10 minutes, stirring
occasionally, until soft and just brown.

2 Add the peas, sugar, stock and half
the mint. Cover and simmer gently for
10–15 minutes until the peas are tender.

3 Leave to cool slightly. Add the
remaining mint and process or blend
until smooth. Return the soup to the
pan and season to taste.

4 Stir in the cream and reheat gently
without boiling. Serve, garnished with
chopped chives.

Energy 121kcal/506kJ; Protein 6.1g; Carbohydrate 9.2g, of which sugars 5.2g; Fat 7g, of which saturates 4.2g; Cholesterol 18mg; Calcium 113mg; Fibre 3g; Sodium 123mg.

Country tomato soup

This creamy soup owes its great flavour to a generous mix of fresh and canned tomatoes, but in the summer it can be made with just ripe sweet and fragrant fresh tomatoes from the garden and garnished with a few fresh basil leaves from the herb plot.

Serves 4–6

25g/1oz/2 tbsp butter

1 medium onion, finely chopped

1 small carrot, finely chopped

1 celery stick, finely chopped

1 garlic clove, crushed

450g/1lb ripe tomatoes, roughly chopped

400g/14oz can chopped tomatoes

30ml/2 tbsp tomato purée (paste)

30ml/2 tbsp sugar

15ml/1 tbsp chopped fresh thyme or oregano leaves, plus extra for garnishing

600ml/1 pint/2½ cups chicken or vegetable stock

600ml/1 pint/2½ cups milk

salt and ground black pepper

1 Melt the butter in a large pan. Add the onion, carrot, celery and garlic.

2 Cook the vegetables over a medium heat for about 5 minutes, stirring occasionally, until soft and just beginning to brown. Stir in the tomatoes, purée, sugar, stock and chopped herbs.

3 Bring to the boil, then cover and simmer gently for about 20 minutes until all the vegetables are very soft. Process or blend the mixture until smooth, then press it through a sieve (strainer) to remove the skins and seeds, which can be discarded.

4 Return the sieved (strained) soup to the cleaned pan and stir in the milk. Reheat gently.

5 Stir, without allowing it to boil. Season with salt and pepper. Garnish with the remaining herbs and serve.

Energy 107kcal/447kJ; Protein 2.3g; Carbohydrate 11.4g, of which sugars 10.9g; Fat 6.1g, of which saturates 3.5g; Cholesterol 13mg; Calcium 50mg; Fibre 3.9g; Sodium 71mg.

Chunky country vegetable soup

Soup-making is an excellent way to make the most of freshly harvested seasonal vegetables. This substantial soup makes a hearty appetizer or a satisfying light meal, and goes well with chunks of crusty bread and wedges of cheese.

Serves 6

15ml/1 tbsp oil

25g/1oz/2 tbsp butter

2 medium onions, finely chopped

4 medium carrots, sliced

2 celery sticks, sliced

2 leeks, sliced

1 potato, cut into small cubes

1 small parsnip, peeled and cut into small cubes

1 garlic clove, crushed

900ml/1½ pints/3¾ cups vegetable stock

300ml/½ pint/1¼ cups milk

25g/1oz/4 tbsp cornflour (cornstarch)

handful of frozen peas

30ml/2 tbsp chopped fresh parsley

salt and ground black pepper

2 Add the stock to the pan and stir into the vegetables. Bring the mixture slowly to the boil, cover and simmer gently for 20–30 minutes until all the vegetables are tender but not too soft.

3 Whisk the milk into the cornflour, making a paste. Stir into the vegetables. Add the frozen peas. Bring to the boil and simmer for 5 minutes. Adjust the seasoning, stir in the parsley and serve.

1 Heat the oil and butter in a large pan and add the onions, carrots and celery. Cook over a medium heat for 5–10 minutes, stirring occasionally, until soft and just beginning to turn golden brown. Add the leeks, potato, parsnip and garlic and stir well together.

Energy 160kcal/665kJ; Protein 3.6g; Carbohydrate 11.5g, of which sugars 10g; Fat 11.4g, of which saturates 6.8g; Cholesterol 27mg; Calcium 72mg; Fibre 5.4g; Sodium 106mg.

Split pea and barley soup

This thick and warming soup is a winter standby for when fresh vegetables are in short supply. It makes a substantial starter, or a meal on its own with hot crusty bread.

Serves 6

225g/8oz/1¼ cups yellow split peas

25g/1oz/¼ cup pearl barley

1.75 litres/3 pints/7½ cups vegetable or ham stock

50g/2oz smoked streaky bacon, cubed

25g/1oz/2 tbsp butter

1 onion, finely chopped

2 garlic cloves, crushed

225g/8oz celeriac, cubed

15ml/1 tbsp chopped marjoram, plus extra to garnish

salt and ground black pepper

1 Rinse the peas and barley in a sieve under cold running water. Put in a bowl, cover with plenty of water and leave to soak overnight. The following day, drain the peas and barley, and rinse again in clean water.

2 Put the peas and barley in a large pan, pour in the stock and bring to the boil. Turn down the heat and simmer gently for 40 minutes.

3 Dry fry the bacon cubes in a frying pan for 5 minutes, or until well browned and crispy. Remove with a slotted spoon, leaving the fat behind, and set aside.

4 Add the butter to the frying pan, add the onion and garlic and cook gently for 5 minutes. Add the celeriac and cook for a further 5 minutes, or until the onion is just starting to colour.

5 Add the softened vegetables and bacon to the pan of stock, peas and barley. Season lightly with salt and pepper, then cover and simmer for 20 minutes, or until the soup is thick.

6 Stir in the marjoram, add extra black pepper to taste and serve garnished with marjoram.

Energy 209kcal/882kJ; Protein 11g; Carbohydrate 28g, of which sugars 2g; Fat 7g, of which saturates 3g; Cholesterol 14mg; Calcium 22mg; Fibre 4.6g; Sodium 635mg.

Lentil and bacon soup

Another good winter soup, this recipe makes the most of store-cupboard ingredients. Turnips, like potatoes, can be stored in a cool, dark place for weeks.

Serves 4

450g/1lb thick-sliced streaky (fatty) bacon, cubed

1 onion, roughly chopped

1 small turnip, roughly chopped

1 celery stick, chopped

1 carrot, sliced

1 potato, peeled and roughly chopped

75g/3oz/½ cup brown lentils

1 bouquet garni

ground black pepper

1 Heat a large pan and add the bacon. Cook for a few minutes, allowing the fat to run out.

2 Add all the vegetables to the pan, stir to mix and cook for 5 minutes, stirring occasionally. Rinse and drain the lentils, then stir into the pan.

3 Add the bouquet garni and seasoning to the pan and enough water to cover. Bring to the boil and simmer for 1 hour, or until the lentils are tender. Serve with crusty bread.

Energy 260Kcal/1091kJ; Protein 14.8g; Carbohydrate 24.6g, of which sugars 3.9g; Fat 12.1g, of which saturates 3.8g; Cholesterol 29mg; Calcium 42mg; Fibre 3.2g; Sodium 370mg.

Classic fish soup

Use whichever fish and shellfish you prefer for this tasty main-course dish, which is almost a stew rather than a soup. Serve with slices of home-made crusty brown or soda bread.

1 Melt the butter in a large heavy pan and cook the chopped onion and crushed garlic gently in it until softened but not browned. Add the chopped red pepper. Season with salt and pepper, the sugar and Tabasco sauce. Sprinkle the flour over and cook gently for 2 minutes, stirring. Gradually stir in the stock and add the tomatoes, with their juices and the mushrooms.

2 Bring to the boil over medium heat, stir well, then reduce the heat and simmer until the vegetables are soft. Add the milk and bring back to the boil.

3 Add the fish to the pan and simmer for 3 minutes, then add the mussels, if using, and cook for 3–4 minutes more, or until the fish is just tender but not breaking up. Discard any mussels that remain closed. Adjust the consistency with a little extra fish stock or milk, if necessary. Check the seasoning and serve immediately, garnished with parsley or chives.

Serves 6

25g/1oz/2 tbsp butter

1 onion, finely chopped

1 garlic clove, crushed or chopped

1 small red (bell) pepper, seeded and chopped

2.5ml/½ tsp sugar

a dash of Tabasco sauce

25g/1oz/¼ cup plain (all-purpose) flour

about 600ml/1 pint/2½ cups fish stock

450g/1lb ripe tomatoes, skinned and chopped, or 400g/14oz can chopped tomatoes

115g/4oz/1½ cups mushrooms, chopped

about 300ml/½ pint/1¼ cups milk

225g/8oz white fish, such as haddock or whiting, filleted and skinned, and cut into bitesize cubes

115g/4oz smoked haddock or cod, skinned, and cut into bitesize cubes

12–18 mussels, cleaned (optional)

salt and ground black pepper

chopped fresh parsley or chives, to garnish

Energy 142kcal/597kJ; Protein 13.9g; Carbohydrate 10.7g, of which sugars 7.1g; Fat 5.2g, of which saturates 2.9g; Cholesterol 36mg; Calcium 84mg; Fibre 1.7g; Sodium 91mg.

Clam, mushroom and potato chowder

This one-pot dish is hearty and substantial enough for supper. The chowder includes sweet, delicately flavoured clams and the earthy flavours of wild and cultivated mushrooms.

Serves 4

48 clams, scrubbed

50g/2oz/¼ cup unsalted butter

1 large onion, chopped

1 celery stick, sliced

1 carrot, sliced

225g/8oz assorted wild and cultivated mushrooms

225g/8oz floury potatoes, sliced

1.2 litres/2 pints/5 cups boiling light chicken or vegetable stock

1 thyme sprig

4 parsley stalks

salt and ground black pepper

thyme sprigs, to garnish

1 Place the clams in a large, heavy pan, discarding any that are open. Add 1cm/½in of water to the pan, then cover and bring to the boil.

2 Cook over a medium heat for 6–8 minutes, shaking the pan occasionally, until the clams are all opened (discard any clams that do not open). Drain the clams over a bowl and remove most of the shells, leaving some in the shells as a garnish.

3 Strain the cooking juices into the bowl, add all the cooked clams and set aside.

4 Add the butter, onion, celery and carrot to the pan and cook gently until softened but not coloured.

5 Add the assorted mushrooms to the pan, and cook for 3–4 minutes until their juices begin to appear. Add the potato slices, the clams and their juices, the chicken or vegetable stock, thyme sprig and parsley stalks.

6 Bring the chowder to the boil, then reduce the heat, cover and simmer for about 25 minutes.

7 Season to taste with salt and pepper, ladle into individual soup bowls, and serve, garnished with thyme sprigs.

Energy 203kcal/848kJ; Protein 10.8g; Carbohydrate 15.8g, of which sugars 5.2g; Fat 11.2g, of which saturates 6.8g; Cholesterol 60mg; Calcium 66mg; Fibre 2.4g; Sodium 696mg.

Southern succotash chicken soup

This traditional farm soup from the Deep South of America includes fresh corn kernels, beans and chicken for a satisfying lunch or supper. Serve with crackers or tortilla chips.

Serves 4

750ml/1¼ pints/3 cups chicken stock

4 skinless chicken breast fillets

50g/2oz/¼ cup butter

2 onions, chopped

115g/4oz piece rindless smoked streaky (fatty) bacon, chopped

25g/1oz/¼ cup plain (all-purpose) flour

4 cobs of corn

300ml/½ pint/1¼ cups milk

400g/14oz can butter (lima) beans, drained

45ml/3 tbsp chopped fresh parsley

salt and ground black pepper

1 Bring the chicken stock to the boil in a large pan. Add the chicken breasts and bring back to the boil. Reduce the heat and cook for 12–15 minutes, until cooked through and tender. Use a slotted spoon to remove the chicken from the pan and leave to cool. Reserve the stock.

2 Melt the butter in a pan over a low heat. Add the onions and cook for about 4–5 minutes, until softened but not brown.

3 Add the bacon to the pan and cook for 5–6 minutes, until beginning to brown. Sprinkle in the flour and cook for 1 minute, stirring constantly.

4 Gradually stir in the hot stock and bring to the boil, constantly stirring the mixture until the liquid is thickened. Remove from the heat.

5 Using a sharp knife, remove the kernels from the corn cobs. Stir the kernels into the pan with half the milk. Return the pan to the heat and cook, stirring occasionally, for about 12–15 minutes, until the corn is tender.

6 Cut the chicken into bitesize pieces and stir into the soup. Stir in the butter beans and the remaining milk. Bring to the boil and cook for 5 minutes, then season well and stir in the parsley.

Energy 539kcal/2267kJ; Protein 51.8g; Carbohydrate 37.4g, of which sugars 11.5g; Fat 21.4g, of which saturates 10.3g; Cholesterol 155mg; Calcium 155mg; Fibre 6.4g; Sodium 1120mg.

Sausage and pesto soup

This filling soup is a wonderful and satisfying one-pot winter warmer. It is equally good when made with classic green pesto or sun-dried tomato red pesto.

Serves 4

15ml/1 tbsp olive oil, plus extra for frying

1 red onion, chopped

450g/1lb smoked pork sausages

225g/8oz/1 cup red lentils

400g/14oz can chopped tomatoes

1 litre/1¾ pints/4 cups water

oil, for deep-frying

salt and ground black pepper

60ml/4 tbsp pesto and fresh basil sprigs, to garnish

1 Heat the oil in a large pan and cook the onion until softened. Coarsely chop all the sausages except one, and add them to the pan. Cook for 5 minutes, stirring, or until the sausages are cooked.

2 Stir in the lentils, tomatoes and water, and bring to the boil. Reduce the heat, cover and simmer for about 20 minutes.

3 Cool the soup slightly before pureéing it in a blender. Return the soup to the rinsed-out pan.

4 Cook the remaining sausage in a little oil in a small frying pan for 10 minutes, turning it often, or until lightly browned and firm.

5 Transfer to a chopping board or plate and leave to cool slightly, then slice thinly.

6 Heat the oil for deep-frying to 190°C/375°F or until a cube of bread browns in about 60 seconds. Deep-fry the sausage slices and basil until the sausages are brown and the basil leaves are crisp.

7 Lift the sausages and basil leaves out of the oil using a slotted spoon and allow to drain on kitchen paper.

8 Reheat the soup, add seasoning to taste, then ladle into warmed individual soup bowls.

9 Sprinkle each bowl of soup with the deep-fried sausage slices and basil, and swirl a little pesto through each portion. Serve with warm crusty bread.

Energy 656kcal/2741kJ; Protein 30.9g; Carbohydrate 46.7g, of which sugars 8.2g; Fat 39.7g, of which saturates 13.1g; Cholesterol 75mg; Calcium 250mg; Fibre 4.8g; Sodium 1109mg.

Bacon and barley broth

Use a good-sized bacon hock to flavour this soup, which is thick with barley and lentils.
This is a hearty peasant recipe, which makes a nutritious and comforting soup.

1 Soak the bacon in cold water overnight. Next morning, drain it and put it into a large pan with enough fresh cold water to cover it. Bring to the boil, skim off any scum that rises to the surface, and then add the barley and lentils. Bring back to the boil and simmer for about 15 minutes.

2 Add the vegetables to the pan with some pepper and the herbs. Bring back to the boil, reduce the heat and simmer for 1½ hours, until the meat is tender.

3 Lift the bacon hock from the pan with a slotted spoon. Remove the skin, then take the meat off the bones and break it into bitesize pieces. Return to the pan with the cabbage. Discard the herbs and cook for a little longer until the cabbage is cooked to your liking.

4 Adjust the seasoning and ladle into large serving bowls, garnish with parsley and serve with freshly baked brown bread.

Serves 6–8

1 bacon hock, about 900g/2lb

75g/3oz/⅓ cup pearl barley

75g/3oz/⅓ cup lentils

2 leeks, sliced, or onions, diced

4 carrots, diced

200g/7oz swede (rutabaga), diced

3 potatoes, diced

small bunch of herbs (thyme, parsley, bay leaf)

1 small cabbage, trimmed, quartered or sliced

salt and ground black pepper

chopped fresh parsley, to garnish

brown bread, to serve

Farmhouse tip Traditionally, the cabbage is simply trimmed and quartered, although it may be thinly sliced or shredded, if you prefer.

Energy 306kcal/1284kJ; Protein 17.7g; Carbohydrate 33.5g, of which sugars 8.3g; Fat 12.1g, of which saturates 4.3g; Cholesterol 35mg; Calcium 74mg; Fibre 4.6g; Sodium 1.05g.

Lamb and vegetable broth

A contemporary version of the classic farmhouse mutton soup, this meaty broth includes
lots of winter vegetables. It is very tasty served with chunks of soda bread.

Serves 6

675g/1½lb neck of lamb (US shoulder
or breast) on the bone

1 large onion

2 bay leaves

3 carrots, chopped

½ white turnip, diced

½ small white cabbage, shredded

2 large leeks, thinly sliced

15ml/1 tbsp tomato purée (paste)

30ml/2 tbsp chopped fresh parsley

salt and ground black pepper

1 Trim any excess fat from the meat. Chop the onion, and put the lamb and bay leaves in a large pan. Add 1.5 litres/ 2½ pints/6¼ cups water and bring to the boil. Skim the surface and then simmer for about 1½–2 hours. Remove the lamb on to a board and leave to cool until ready to handle.

2 Remove the meat from the bones and cut into small pieces. Discard the bones and return the meat to the broth. Add the vegetables, tomato purée and parsley, and season well. Simmer for another 30 minutes, until the vegetables are tender. Ladle into soup bowls and serve.

Energy 162kcal/675kJ; Protein 13.1g; Carbohydrate 8.5g, of which sugars 7g; Fat 8.6g, of which saturates 3.8g; Cholesterol 44mg; Calcium 42mg; Fibre 3g; Sodium 55mg.

Beef and split pea broth

A restorative and nutritious meaty broth that will taste even more delicious when reheated, this hearty country soup will warm and comfort on a dark winter evening.

Serves 6–8

450–675g/1–1½lb rib steak, or other stewing beef on the bone

2 large onions

50g/2oz/¼ cup pearl barley

50g/2oz/¼ cup green split peas

3 large carrots, chopped

2 white turnips, peeled and chopped into dice

3 celery stalks, chopped

1 large or 2 medium leeks, thinly sliced and washed in cold water

salt and ground black pepper

chopped fresh parsley, to serve

1 Bone the meat and put the bones and half an onion, roughly sliced, into a large pan. Cover with cold water, season with salt and pepper, and bring to the boil. Skim if necessary, then simmer until needed.

2 Meanwhile, trim any fat or gristle from the meat and cut into small pieces. Chop the remaining onions finely with a sharp knife.

3 Drain the stock from the bones, make it up with water to 2 litres/3½ pints/ 9 cups, and return to the rinsed pan with the meat, onions, barley and split peas.

4 Season, bring to the boil, and skim if necessary. Reduce the heat, cover and simmer for about 30 minutes.

5 Add the carrots, turnips, celery and leeks to the pan and simmer for a further 1 hour, or until the meat is tender. Check the seasoning and adjust if necessary.

6 Serve the soup immediately in large individual warmed bowls, generously sprinkled with the chopped parsley.

Energy 167kcal/705kJ; Protein 16g; Carbohydrate 21.4g, of which sugars 7.8g; Fat 2.6g, of which saturates 0.8g; Cholesterol 34mg; Calcium 54mg; Fibre 3.6g; Sodium 58mg.

Oxtail soup

Frugal country cooks utilize every part of an animal, and it is the most economical cuts that respond well to slow cooking – in this recipe oxtail becomes rich, dark and tender.

Serves 4–6

1 oxtail, cut into joints, total weight about 1.3kg/3lb

25g/1oz/2 tbsp butter

2 medium onions, chopped

2 medium carrots, chopped

2 celery sticks, sliced

1 bacon rasher (strip), chopped

2 litres/3½ pints/8 cups homemade beef stock

1 bouquet garni

2 bay leaves

30ml/2 tbsp plain (all purpose) flour

squeeze of fresh lemon juice

60ml/4 tbsp port, medium-sweet sherry or Madeira

salt and ground black pepper

5 When the oxtail has cooled sufficiently to handle, pick all the meat off the bones and cut it into small pieces.

6 Skim off any fat that has risen to the surface of the stock, then transfer the stock into a large pan. Add the pieces of meat and reheat.

1 Wash and dry the pieces of oxtail, trimming off any excess fat. Melt the butter in a large pan, and when foaming, add the oxtail a few pieces at a time and brown them quickly on all sides. Lift the meat out on to a plate.

2 To the same pan, add the onions, carrots, celery and bacon. Cook over a medium heat for 5–10 minutes, stirring, until the vegetables are softened.

3 Return the oxtail to the pan and add the stock, bouquet garni, bay leaves and seasoning. Bring just to the boil and skim off any foam. Cover and simmer gently for about 3 hours or until the meat is so tender that it is falling away from the bones.

4 Strain the mixture, discarding the vegetables, bouquet garni and bay leaves, and leave to stand.

7 With a whisk, blend the flour with a little cold water to make a smooth paste. Stir in a little of the hot stock, then stir the mixture into the pan. Bring to the boil, stirring, until the soup thickens slightly. Reduce the heat and simmer gently for about 5 minutes.

8 Season with salt, pepper and lemon juice to taste. Just before serving, stir in the port, sherry or Madeira.

Energy 459kcal/1914kJ; Protein 45.4g; Carbohydrate 6.5g, of which sugars 2.6g; Fat 26.8g, of which saturates 11.8g; Cholesterol 176mg; Calcium 36mg; Fibre 0.7g; Sodium 403mg.

Snacks and Appetizers

Farmhouse meals are not best known for dainty appetizers, but wholesome first courses to take the edge off a healthy hunger are a very good thing. Many of the recipes in this chapter also make great snacks or a stand by for when friends pop round unexpectedly, while the pâtés and terrines are great picnic and party dishes that can be prepared in advance.

Field mushrooms stuffed with hazelnuts

Large mushrooms filled with an aromatic mix of garlic and parsley and topped with crunchy chopped hazelnuts make a delicious appetizer. They can also served with grilled meats.

Serves 4

2 garlic cloves

grated rind of 1 lemon

90ml/6 tbsp olive oil

8 large field (portabello) mushrooms

50g/2oz/½ cup hazelnuts, coarsely chopped

30ml/2 tbsp chopped fresh parsley

salt and ground black pepper

1 Crush the garlic cloves with a little salt. Place in a bowl and stir in the grated lemon rind and the olive oil. If time allows, leave to infuse (steep).

2 Preheat the oven to 200°C/400°F/ Gas 6. Arrange the field mushrooms, stalk-side up, in a single layer in an ovenproof earthenware dish.

3 Drizzle over about 60ml/4 tbsp of the oil mixture and bake in the oven for about 10 minutes.

4 Remove the mushrooms from the oven and baste them with the remaining oil mixture, then sprinkle the chopped hazelnuts evenly over the top.

5 Bake for a further 10–15 minutes, or until the mushrooms are tender. Season with salt and pepper and sprinkle with chopped parsley. Serve immediately.

Farmhouse tip Almost any unsalted nuts can be used in place of the hazelnuts in this recipe – try pine nuts, cashew nuts, almonds or walnuts. Nuts can go rancid quickly so, for the freshest flavour, either buy nuts in small quantities or buy them in shells and remove the shells just before use.

Energy 255kcal/1052kJ; Protein 5.2g; Carbohydrate 1.7g, of which sugars 1g; Fat 25.4g, of which saturates 3.1g; Cholesterol 0mg; Calcium 43mg; Fibre 3.1g; Sodium 12mg.

Wild mushroom soufflés

Wild mushrooms would be ideal for this recipe. These delightful soufflés are remarkably easy to prepare, and are perfect either as an appetizer or light lunch.

Serves 4

25g/1oz/½ cup dried cep mushrooms

40g/1½oz/3 tbsp butter, plus extra for greasing

20ml/4 tsp grated Parmesan cheese

40g/1½oz/⅓ cup plain (all-purpose) flour

250ml/8fl oz/1 cup milk

50g/2oz/½ cup grated mature (sharp) Cheddar cheese

4 eggs, separated

2 sun-dried tomatoes in oil, drained and chopped

15ml/1 tbsp chopped fresh chives

salt and ground black pepper

Farmhouse tip A variety of different dried mushrooms are available – any can be used instead of the ceps.

1 Place the ceps in a bowl, pour over enough warm water to cover and leave to soak for 15 minutes. Grease four individual earthenware soufflé dishes with a little butter.

2 Sprinkle the grated Parmesan cheese into the soufflé dishes and rotate each dish to coat the sides with cheese. Preheat the oven to 190°C/375°F/Gas 5.

3 Melt the 40g/1½oz/3 tbsp of butter in a large pan, remove from the heat and stir in the flour. Cook over a low heat for 1 minute, stirring constantly. Remove the pan from the heat and gradually stir in the milk. Return to the heat and bring to the boil, stirring constantly, until the sauce has thickened.

4 Remove the sauce from the heat, then stir in the grated Cheddar cheese and plenty of seasoning. Beat in the egg yolks, one at a time, then stir in the chopped sun-dried tomatoes and the chives. Drain the soaked mushrooms, then coarsely chop them and add them to the cheese sauce.

5 Whisk the egg whites until they stand in soft peaks. Mix one spoonful into the sauce, then carefully fold in the remainder. Divide the mixture among the soufflé dishes and bake for 25 minutes, or until the soufflés are golden brown on top, well risen and just firm to the touch. Serve immediately – before they sink.

Energy 290kcal/1207kJ; Protein 14.7g; Carbohydrate 11.6g, of which sugars 3.9g; Fat 20.8g, of which saturates 11.2g; Cholesterol 232mg; Calcium 274mg; Fibre 0.6g; Sodium 305mg.

Pears with blue cheese and walnuts

The success of this dish depends on the quality of the pears, which must be very succulent, and, of course, the cheese. Use a soft blue cheese with a mild taste that won't overwhelm the walnuts and pears, such as Cashel Blue, Gorgonzola or Cambozola.

Serves 6

115g/4oz fresh cream cheese

75g/3oz mild, soft blue cheese

30–45ml/2–3 tbsp single (light) cream

115g/4oz/1 cup roughly chopped walnuts

6 ripe pears

15ml/1 tbsp lemon juice

mixed salad leaves, such as frisée, oakleaf lettuce and radicchio

6 cherry tomatoes

salt and ground black pepper

walnut halves and sprigs of fresh flat leaf parsley, to garnish

For the dressing

juice of 1 lemon

a little finely grated lemon rind

pinch of caster (superfine) sugar

60ml/4 tbsp olive oil

3 Arrange a bed of salad leaves on six plates – shallow soup plates are ideal – add a tomato to each and sprinkle over the remaining chopped walnuts.

4 Drain the pears well and pat dry with kitchen paper, then turn them in the prepared dressing and arrange, hollow side up, on the salad leaves.

1 Mash the cream cheese and blue cheese together in a bowl with a good grinding of black pepper. Blend in the cream until smooth. Add 25g/1oz/ ¼ cup chopped walnuts and stir in. Cover and chill until required.

2 Peel and halve the pears and scoop out the core. Place in a bowl of water with the lemon juice so they don't brown. Make the dressing: whisk the lemon juice, lemon rind, caster sugar and olive oil together and season.

5 Divide the cheese and walnut mixture between the six halved pears, and place on top of each. Spoon the dressing over the top. Garnish each pear with a walnut half and a sprig of flat leaf parsley before serving.

Energy 331Kcal/1373kJ; Protein 6.7g; Carbohydrate 16.3g, of which sugars 16.1g; Fat 27g, of which saturates 9.8g; Cholesterol 30mg; Calcium 120mg; Fibre 4.1g; Sodium 219mg

Potted cheese

The potting of cheese became popular in the 18th century, and it is still a great way to use up odd pieces left in the larder. Blend them with your chosen seasonings, adjusting the flavour before adding the alcohol. Serve with plain crackers, oatcakes or crisp toast.

Serves 4–6

250g/9oz hard cheese, such as mature Cheddar

75g/3oz/6 tbsp soft unsalted butter, plus extra for melting

1.5ml/¼ tsp ready-made English (hot) mustard

1.5ml/¼ tsp ground mace

30ml/2 tbsp sherry

ground black pepper

fresh parsley, to garnish

3 Spoon the mixture into a dish just large enough to leave about 1cm/½in to spare on top. Level the surface.

Variations Use some crumbled Stilton in place of the Cheddar and the same quantity of port in place of sherry.
  Some finely chopped chives could be added instead of mustard.

4 Melt some butter in a small pan, skimming off any foam that rises to the surface. Leaving the sediment in the pan, pour a layer of melted butter on top of the cheese mixture to cover the surface. Refrigerate until required.

5 Garnish with parsley and serve with thin slices of toast or crispbread.

1 Cut the cheese into rough pieces and put them into the bowl of a food processor. Use the pulse button to chop the cheese into small crumbs.

2 Add the butter, mustard, mace and a little black pepper and blend again until smooth. Taste and adjust the seasoning. Finally, blend in the sherry.

Energy 262kcal/1082kJ; Protein 10.7g; Carbohydrate 0.2g, of which sugars 0.2g; Fat 23.6g, of which saturates 15.2g; Cholesterol 70mg; Calcium 290mg; Fibre 0g; Sodium 363mg

Mushroom picker's pâté

One of the delights of country living is to rise early and go on a mushrooming expedition with an expert who knows precisely what to pick. This pâté is the perfect reward.

Serves 6

45ml/3 tbsp vegetable oil

1 onion, chopped

½ celery stick, chopped

350g/12oz mushrooms, sliced

150g/5oz/⅔ cup red lentils

475ml/16fl oz/2 cups water or vegetable stock

1 fresh thyme sprig

50g/2oz/4 tbsp almond nut butter

1 garlic clove, crushed

1 thick slice white bread, crusts removed

75ml/5 tbsp milk

15ml/1 tbsp lemon juice

4 egg yolks

celery salt and ground black pepper

Melba toast, to serve

1 Preheat the oven to 180°C/350°F/Gas 4.

2 In a large pan, fry the onion and celery in the oil, until lightly browned. Add the mushrooms to the pan and cook to soften for 3–4 minutes. Remove a spoonful of the mushroom pieces and set it aside.

3 Add the lentils, water or stock and thyme to the mushroom mixture. Bring to the boil, then lower the heat and simmer for 20 minutes or until the lentils are very soft.

4 Place the nut butter, garlic, bread and milk in a food processor and process until smooth.

5 Add the lemon juice and egg yolks and process briefly. Add in the lentil mixture, process until smooth, then season with the celery salt and pepper. Lastly, stir the reserved mushrooms into the mixture.

6 Spoon the mixture into a 1.2 litre/2 pint/5 cup pâté dish and cover with foil. Stand the dish in a roasting pan and pour in boiling water to come halfway up the sides of the dish. Cook the pâté for 50 minutes. Allow to cool completely before serving.

Farmhouse tip If you are using only cultivated mushrooms, an addition of 10g/⅓oz/3 tbsp of dried porcini will boost the flavour. Soak the dried mushrooms in warm water for 20 minutes before draining and adding to the pan with the fresh mushrooms.

Energy 285kcal/1189kJ; Protein 12g; Carbohydrate 21g, of which sugars 3g; Fat 17g, of which saturates 3g; Cholesterol 136mg; Calcium 84mg; Fibre5.7g; Sodium 261mg.

Baby aubergines with raisins and pine nuts

Make this simple appetizer a day in advance, to allow the flavours to develop. Ideal for an outdoor lunch in the garden, this dish goes well with warmed bread and a green salad.

Serves 4

250ml/8fl oz/1 cup extra virgin olive oil

juice of 1 lemon

30ml/2 tbsp balsamic vinegar

3 cloves

25g/1oz/⅓ cup pine nuts

25g/1oz/3 tbsp raisins

15ml/1 tbsp sugar

1 bay leaf

large pinch of dried chilli flakes

12 baby aubergines (eggplants), halved lengthways

salt and ground black pepper

1 Put 175ml/6fl oz/¾ cup of the olive oil in a jug. Add the lemon juice, vinegar, cloves, pine nuts, raisins, sugar and bay leaf. Stir in the chilli flakes and salt and pepper. Mix well and set aside.

Farmhouse tip Use sliced aubergines if baby ones are not obtainable, or try this recipe with grilled (bell) peppers.

2 Preheat the grill (broiler). Brush the aubergines with the remaining oil. Grill (broil) for 10 minutes, until slightly black, turning them halfway through.

3 Place the hot aubergines in a bowl, and pour over the marinade. Leave for 3–4 hours, preferably overnight, turning the aubergines once or twice. Serve at room temperature.

Energy 662kcal/2730kJ; Protein 3g; Carbohydrate 12g, of which sugars 12g; Fat 67g, of which saturates 9g; Cholesterol 0mg; Calcium 24mg; Fibre 3.8g; Sodium 109mg.

Roasted pepper salad

When roasted, red peppers acquire a marvellous smoky flavour that is wonderful with sun-dried tomatoes and artichoke hearts, for a true Italian farmhouse feel.

Serves 6

50g/2oz/½ cup drained sun-dried tomatoes in oil

3 red (bell) peppers

2 yellow or orange (bell) peppers

2 green (bell) peppers

30ml/2 tbsp balsamic vinegar

a few drops of chilli sauce

75ml/5 tbsp olive oil

4 canned artichoke hearts, sliced

1 garlic clove, thinly sliced

salt and ground black pepper

fresh basil leaves, to garnish

1 Preheat the oven to 200°C/400°F/ Gas 6. Slice the sun-dried tomatoes into thin strips. Set aside.

2 Put the whole peppers on an oiled baking sheet, and place in the hot oven for about 45 minutes until the skins are beginning to char. Remove from the oven, cover with a clean towel for 5 minutes, then peel and slice them.

3 Mix the vinegar and chilli sauce in a large bowl. Whisk in the oil, then season with a little salt and pepper. Add the peppers, artichokes, tomatoes and garlic to the bowl and toss. Serve, scattered with basil leaves.

Energy 216Kcal/890kJ; Protein 1.5g; Carbohydrate 8.1g, of which sugars 7.9g; Fat 19.9g, of which saturates 2.9g; Cholesterol 0mg; Calcium 22mg; Fibre 2.4g; Sodium 24mg.

Stuffed vine leaves with garlic yogurt

This is a classic Greek farmhouse dish, perfect to begin a long summer lunch, preferably in the garden.

Serves 6

225g/8oz packet preserved vine leaves, rinsed then soaked in boiling water for 10 minutes

1 onion, finely chopped

½ bunch spring onions (scallions), trimmed and finely chopped

60ml/4 tbsp chopped fresh parsley

10 large fresh mint sprigs, chopped

finely grated rind of 1 lemon

2.5ml/½ tsp crushed dried chillies

7.5ml/1½ tsp fennel seeds, crushed

175g/6oz/scant 1 cup long grain rice

120ml/4fl oz/½ cup olive oil

300ml/½ pint/1¼ cups boiling water

150ml/¼ pint/⅔ cup thick natural (plain) yogurt

2 garlic cloves, crushed

salt

lemon wedges, to serve

1 Mix the onion, spring onions, herbs, lemon rind, chillies, fennel seeds and rice with 25ml/1½ tbsp of the olive oil. Season with salt.

2 Drain and pat dry the vine leaves. Place one, veins uppermost, on a work surface and cut off any stalk. Place a heaped teaspoonful of the rice mixture near the stalk end. Fold the stalk end over the filling, then fold over the sides. Roll into a cigar shape. Repeat with the remaining leaves and filling.

3 Place any remaining leaves in the base of a heavy pan. Pack the stuffed leaves in a single layer in the pan. Spoon over the remaining oil, then add the measured boiling water.

4 Place a small plate over the leaves to keep them submerged. Cover and cook over a very low heat for 45 minutes, until tender and the liquid is absorbed.

5 Mix the yogurt and garlic in a small serving dish. Transfer the stuffed leaves to a plate and garnish with lemon wedges. Serve with the garlic yogurt.

Energy 339kcal/1407kJ; Protein 5.8g; Carbohydrate 32.2g, of which sugars 7.3g; Fat 20.9g, of which saturates 2.7g; Cholesterol 0mg; Calcium 95mg; Fibre 3.4g; Sodium 14mg.

Warm potato cakes with smoked salmon

Smoked wild salmon or trout are both delicious on these versatile little potato cakes.
They can also be served for breakfast with scrambled eggs and crispy bacon.

Serves 6

450g/1lb potatoes, cooked and mashed

75g/3oz/²⁄₃ cup plain (all-purpose) flour

2 eggs, beaten

2 spring onions (scallions), chopped

a little freshly grated nutmeg

50g/2oz/¼ cup butter, melted

150ml/¼ pint/²⁄₃ cup sour cream

12 slices of smoked salmon

salt and ground black pepper

chopped fresh chives, to garnish

1 Put the potatoes, flour, eggs and spring onions into a large bowl. Season with salt, pepper and a little nutmeg, and add half the butter. Mix thoroughly and shape into 12 small potato cakes.

Variation Top the potato cakes with smoked mackerel and a squeeze of lemon juice, if you like.

2 Heat the remaining butter in a non-stick pan and cook the potato cakes until browned on both sides.

3 To serve, mix the sour cream with some salt and pepper. Fold a piece of smoked salmon and place on top of each potato cake. Top with the cream and chives and serve immediately.

Energy 326kcal/1365kJ; Protein 21.9g; Carbohydrate 22.9g, of which sugars 2.3g; Fat 17g, of which saturates 8.6g; Cholesterol 119mg; Calcium 70mg; Fibre 1.2g; Sodium 1315mg.

Potted prawns

A favourite recipe in Victorian England, this was traditionally made with tiny brown shrimps that are fiddly to prepare; it is equally good with larger prawns. Serve with bread and butter.

Serves 4

225g/8oz/2 cups peeled prawns (shrimp)

225g/8oz/1 cup butter

pinch of ground mace

pinch of cayenne pepper

salt

dill sprigs, to garnish

lemon wedges and thin slices of brown bread and butter, to serve

1 Chop a quarter of the prawns. Melt 115g/4oz/¹⁄₂ cup of the butter slowly, carefully skimming off any foam that rises to the surface with a metal spoon.

2 Stir all the prawns, the mace, salt and cayenne into the pan and heat gently without boiling. Pour the prawn and butter mixture into four individual pots and leave to cool.

3 Heat the remaining butter in a clean small pan, then carefully spoon the clear butter over the prawns, leaving behind the sediment.

4 Leave until the butter is almost set, then place a dill sprig in the centre of each pot. Leave to set completely, then cover and chill until ready to serve.

5 Remove the prawns from the refrigerator 30 minutes before serving to bring up to room temperature. Serve with lemon wedges and thin slices of brown bread and butter.

Energy 461kcal/1901kJ; Protein 10.3g; Carbohydrate 0.4g, of which sugars 0.4g; Fat 46.6g, of which saturates 29.4g; Cholesterol 230mg; Calcium 55mg; Fibre 0g; Sodium 448mg.

Salt cod fritters with garlic aioli mayonnaise

A favourite dish of Portuguese and Spanish rural communities, salt cod fritters are delicious when served with an aromatic garlic mayonnaise. If you have any leftover aioli, it can be stirred into a bowl of cold potatoes to make a lovely potato salad.

Serves 6

450g/1lb salt cod

500g/1¼lb floury potatoes

300ml/½ pint/1¼ cups milk

6 spring onions (scallions), finely chopped

30ml/2 tbsp extra virgin olive oil

30ml/2 tbsp fresh chopped parsley

juice of ½ lemon, to taste

2 eggs, beaten

60ml/4 tbsp plain (all-purpose) flour

90g/3½oz/1⅓ cups dry white breadcrumbs

vegetable oil, for shallow frying

salt and ground black pepper

lemon wedges and salad, to serve

For the aioli

2 large garlic cloves

2 egg yolks

300ml/½ pint/1¼ cups olive oil

lemon juice, to taste

1 Soak the salt cod in cold water for 24 hours, changing the water about 5 times. The cod should swell as it rehydrates. Taste a tiny piece to ensure it is not too salty. Drain well.

2 Cook the potatoes, unpeeled, in a pan of boiling salted water for about 20 minutes, until tender. Drain, then peel and mash the potatoes.

3 Poach the cod very gently in the milk with half the spring onions for 10–15 minutes, or until it flakes easily. Remove the cod and flake it with a fork into a bowl, discarding bones and skin.

4 Add 60ml/4 tbsp mashed potato to the flaked cod and beat with a wooden spoon. Work in the olive oil, then gradually add the remaining potato. Beat in the remaining spring onions and parsley. Season with lemon juice and pepper to taste – it may need a little salt. Beat in 1 egg, then chill until firm.

5 Shape the mixture into 12 round cakes. Coat them in flour, then dip in the remaining egg and coat with the breadcrumbs. Chill until ready to fry.

6 Meanwhile, make the aioli. Place the garlic and a good pinch of salt in a mortar and pound to a paste with a pestle. Using a small whisk or a wooden spoon, gradually work in the egg yolks.

7 Add the olive oil, a drop at a time, until half is incorporated. When the sauce is as thick as soft butter, beat in 5–10ml/1–2 tsp lemon juice, then continue adding oil until the aioli is very thick. Adjust the seasoning, adding lemon juice to taste.

8 Heat 2cm/¾in depth of oil in a frying pan. Add the fritters and cook over a medium-high heat for 4 minutes. Turn over and cook for a further 4 minutes on the other side, until crisp and golden. Drain on kitchen paper, then serve with the aioli, lemon wedges and salad leaves.

Energy 653kcal/2721kJ; Protein 32.7g; Carbohydrate 28.1g, of which sugars 4.2g; Fat 46.4g, of which saturates 7.6g; Cholesterol 178mg; Calcium 123mg; Fibre 1.4g; Sodium 472mg.

Maryland crab cakes with tartare sauce

One of the most famous American country dishes, these crab cakes are a modern version of Baltimore crab cakes. The tasty white crab meat is coated in breadcrumbs and fried.

Serves 4

675g/1½lb fresh crab meat

1 egg, beaten

30ml/2 tbsp mayonnaise

15ml/1 tbsp Worcestershire sauce

15ml/1 tbsp sherry

30ml/2 tbsp chopped fresh parsley

15ml/1 tbsp finely chopped
fresh chives

45ml/3 tbsp olive oil

salt and ground black pepper

lemon wedges and salad leaves,
to serve

For the sauce

1 egg yolk

15ml/1 tbsp white wine vinegar

30ml/2 tbsp Dijon-style mustard

250ml/8fl oz/1 cup vegetable oil

30ml/2 tbsp fresh lemon juice

20g/¾oz/¼ cup finely chopped
spring onions (scallions)

30ml/2 tbsp chopped drained capers

few finely chopped sour dill pickles

60ml/4 tbsp chopped fresh parsley

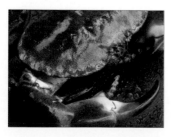

1 Pick over the crab meat, removing any shell or cartilage.

2 In a bowl, combine the beaten egg with the mayonnaise, Worcestershire sauce, sherry and herbs. Season, then gently fold in the crab meat. Divide the mixture into eight portions and gently form each one into an oval cake. Place on a baking sheet between layers of baking parchment and chill for 1 hour.

3 Make the sauce. In a bowl, beat the egg yolk. Add the vinegar, mustard and salt and pepper, and whisk for 10 seconds. Whisk in the oil in a slow, steady stream.

4 Add the lemon juice, spring onions, capers, pickles and parsley and mix well. Cover and chill for 30 minutes.

5 Preheat the grill (broiler). Brush the crab cakes with the olive oil. Place on an oiled baking sheet, in one layer.

6 Grill (broil) 15cm/6in from the heat until golden brown, about 5 minutes on each side. Serve the crab cakes hot with the tartare sauce, lemon wedges and salad leaves.

Variation You can use defrosted frozen or canned crab meat instead.

Energy 710kcal/2934kJ; Protein 33.8g; Carbohydrate 1.9g, of which sugars 1.7g; Fat 62.6g, of which saturates 8.1g; Cholesterol 225mg; Calcium 234mg; Fibre 0.2g; Sodium 1249mg.

Country-style pâté with leeks

A rough pâté is very much a feature of a farm kitchen.
Cooked slowly in advance, it makes a perfect lunch.

Serves 8

15g/½oz/1 tbsp butter

450g/1lb leeks (white and pale green parts), sliced

2 or 3 large garlic cloves, finely chopped

1kg/2¼lb lean pork leg or shoulder, trimmed and cubed

150g/5oz rindless smoked streaky bacon rashers (strips)

7.5ml/1½ tsp chopped fresh thyme

3 fresh sage leaves, finely chopped

¼ tsp quatre épices (mixed ground cloves, cinnamon, nutmeg and black pepper)

¼ tsp ground cumin

pinch of freshly grated nutmeg

½ tsp salt

5ml/1 tsp freshly ground black pepper

1 bay leaf

1 Melt the butter in a large, heavy frying pan, add the leeks, then cover and sweat over a low heat for 10 minutes, stirring occasionally. Add the garlic and continue cooking for about 10 minutes until the leeks are very soft, then set aside to cool.

2 Pulse the meat cubes in batches in a food processor to chop it coarsely. Alternatively, pass the meat through the coarse blade of a mincer (grinder). Transfer the meat to a large bowl and remove any white stringy bits. Reserve two bacon rashers for garnishing, then chop or mince (grind) the remainder, and mix with the pork in the bowl.

3 Preheat the oven to 180°C/350°F/ Gas 4. Line the base and sides of a 1.5 litre/2½ pint/6 cup terrine with baking parchment. Add the leek mixture, herbs and spices to the pork mixture, with the salt and pepper.

4 Spoon the mixture into the terrine, pressing it into the corners and compacting it. Tap firmly to settle the mixture and smooth the top. Arrange the bay leaf and bacon rashers on top, then cover tightly with foil.

5 Place the terrine in a roasting pan and pour in boiling water to come halfway up the side. Bake for 1¼ hours.

6 Drain off the water from the roasting pan, then return the terrine to the tin and place a baking sheet or plate on top. Weight this with two or three large cans or a foil-wrapped clean house brick while the pâté cools. Chill in the refrigerator overnight, before slicing and serving with toast or fresh bread.

Energy 211Kcal/884kJ; Protein 27.5g; Carbohydrate 1.3g, of which sugars 1g; Fat 10.7g, of which saturates 4.4g; Cholesterol 87mg; Calcium 20mg; Fibre 1.0g; Sodium 395g.

Country duck pâté with redcurrants

Depending on availability, chicken or duck livers can be used interchangeably to make this lovely country appetizer. The tart flavours and pretty colour and texture of the tiny red berries complement the rich pâté perfectly.

Serves 4–6

1 onion, finely chopped

1 large garlic clove, crushed

115g/4oz/½ cup butter

225g/8oz duck livers

10–15ml/2–3 tsp chopped fresh mixed herbs, such as parsley, thyme or rosemary

15–30ml/1–2 tbsp brandy

bay leaf (optional)

50–115g/2–4oz/¼ –½ cup clarified butter, or melted unsalted butter

salt and ground black pepper

a sprig of flat leaf parsley, to garnish

8 slices white bread, crusts removed

For the redcurrant sauce

30ml/2 tbsp redcurrant jelly

15–30ml/1–2 tbsp port

30ml/2 tbsp redcurrants

1 Cook the onion and garlic in 25g/1oz/2 tbsp of the butter in a pan over gentle heat, until just turning colour.

2 Trim the duck livers. Add to the pan with the herbs and cook together for about 3 minutes, or until the livers have browned on the outside but are still pink in the centre. Allow to cool.

3 Dice the remaining butter. Process the liver mixture in a food processor, gradually adding the cubes of butter by dropping them down the chute, to make a smooth purée.

4 Add the brandy, then check the seasoning and transfer the purée to a 450–600ml/½–1 pint/scant 2 cups dish, smoothing the top. Lay a bay leaf on top if you wish.

5 Seal the pâté by pouring clarified or unsalted butter over the top. Cool, and chill in the refrigerator until required.

6 To make the redcurrant sauce, put the redcurrant jelly, port and redcurrants into a small pan and bring gently to boiling point. Simmer for about 10 minutes to make a rich consistency. Leave to cool.

7 To make the Melba toast, toast the bread on both sides, then carefully slice each piece of toast vertically to make 16 very thin slices.

8 Place each piece of toast, with the untoasted side up, on a grill (broiler) rack and grill (broil) until golden. It can be stored in an airtight container for a few days, then warmed through to crisp up again just before serving.

9 Serve the chilled pâté, garnished with parsley and accompanied by Melba toast or toasted slices of brioche and the redcurrant sauce. Once the butter seal is broken, the pâté should be eaten within 2–3 days.

Energy 794kcal/3312kJ; Protein 101.3g; Carbohydrate 11.3g, of which sugars 9.9g; Fat 36.8g, of which saturates 19g; Cholesterol 2213mg; Calcium 73mg; Fibre 1.3g; Sodium 608mg.

Gamekeeper's terrine

Hare and other game are popular in country cooking, having been hunted as food for centuries. For tender meat and a good flavour, use young hare that has been properly hung. Rabbit would also be delicious in this terrine, or a mixture of minced pork and rabbit.

Serves 4–6

5 dried mushrooms, rinsed and soaked in warm water for 30 minutes

saddle, thighs, liver, heart and lungs of 1 hare

2 onions, cut into wedges

1 carrot, chopped

1 parsnip, chopped

4 bay leaves

10 allspice berries

300g/11oz calf's liver

165g/5½oz unsmoked streaky (fatty) bacon rashers (strips)

75g/3oz/1½ cups soft white breadcrumbs

4 eggs

105ml/7 tbsp 95 per cent proof Polish spirit or vodka

5ml/1 tsp freshly grated nutmeg

10ml/2 tsp dried marjoram

10g/¼oz juniper berries

4 garlic cloves, crushed

150g/5oz smoked streaky (fatty) bacon rashers (strips)

salt and ground black pepper, to taste

redcurrant jelly and green salad, to serve

Farmhouse tip To make sure the bacon doesn't shrink during cooking, stretch each rasher (strip) out thinly on a board with the back of a knife.

1 Drain the mushrooms and slice into strips. Put the pieces of hare in a large pan and pour in enough water to just cover. Add the onions, carrot, parsnip, mushrooms, bay leaves and allspice.

2 Bring to the boil, then cover and simmer gently for 1 hour. Add a pinch of salt and allow the meat to cool in the stock.

3 Slice the liver and 50g/2oz unsmoked bacon into small pieces and put in a medium pan. Add a ladleful of the stock and simmer for 15 minutes.

4 Preheat the oven to 180°C/350°F/Gas 4. Put two ladlefuls of the stock in a small bowl, add the breadcrumbs and leave to soak.

5 Remove the hare pieces, liver and bacon from the stock and chop finely with a large knife.

6 Transfer to a large bowl, then add the soaked breadcrumbs, eggs, Polish spirit or vodka, nutmeg, marjoram, juniper berries and crushed garlic. Season to taste and mix well to combine thoroughly.

7 Line a 1.2 litre/2 pint/5 cup ovenproof dish with the smoked and remaining unsmoked bacon rashers, making sure they overhang the edges. Spoon in the meat mixture and bring the overhanging bacon over the top. Cover with buttered baking parchment, then cover with a lid or foil.

8 Place the dish in a roasting pan containing boiling water, then put in the oven and bake for 1½ hours, or until a skewer pushed into the centre comes out clean and the juices run clear. Remove the baking parchment and lid or foil about 15 minutes before the end of cooking to allow the terrine to brown.

9 Remove from the oven, and take the dish out of the roasting pan. Cover the terrine with baking parchment and a board and weight down with a 900g/2lb weight (such as two cans).

10 Leave to cool, then turn out on to a serving dish. Serve in slices with redcurrant jelly and a green salad.

Energy 266kcal/1112kJ; Protein 27.1g; Carbohydrate 6.4g, of which sugars 1.4g; Fat 14g, of which saturates 5g; Cholesterol 182mg; Calcium 25mg; Fibre 0.3g; Sodium 432mg.

Egg and Cheese Dishes

There is usually a plentiful supply of freshly laid eggs and home-churned cheese in a farmhouse, and this chapter is full of recipes that combine the two. Ideal for a quick omelette when time is short, or a tasty bake for a weekday supper, eggs are the world's first fast food, while adding a tasty tangy cheese can transform a simple food into a complete meal.

Carrot and coriander soufflés

Use tender young carrots for this light-as-air dish. Souffles sink quickly so make sure you are ready to serve them the moment they are taken out of the oven.

Serves 4

450g/1lb young carrots

30ml/2 tbsp fresh chopped coriander (cilantro)

4 eggs, separated

salt and ground black pepper

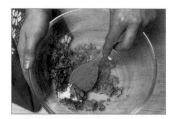 

1 Peel or scrub the carrots, then cook whole in boiling salted water for 20 minutes or until tender.

2 Drain the carrots, and blend to a smooth purée in a food processor or with a hand blender.

3 Preheat the oven to 200°C/400°F/ Gas 6. Transfer the puréed carrots to a bowl, season well, and stir in the chopped coriander.

4 Fold the separated egg yolks into the carrot mixture.

5 In a separate bowl, whisk the egg whites until stiff.

6 Fold the egg whites into the carrot mixture and pour into four greased ramekins. Bake for 20 minutes or until risen and golden. Serve immediately.

Energy 129kcal/539kJ; Protein 8g; Carbohydrate 9g, of which sugars 8g; Fat 7g, of which saturates 2g; Cholesterol 232mg; Calcium 67mg; Fibre 2.9g; Sodium 212mg.

Baked eggs with creamy leeks

This simple, homely appetizer can also be made with other vegetables such as spinach instead of the leeks. It is perfect for last-minute entertaining or quick dining.

Serves four

15g/½ oz/1 tbsp butter, plus extra for greasing

225g/8oz small, young leeks, very thinly sliced

75–90ml/5–6 tbsp whipping cream

freshly grated nutmeg

4 eggs

a few sage leaves

sunflower oil

salt and ground black pepper

Variation For a slightly different result, beat the eggs with the remaining cream and seasoning in step 4 then spoon over the leeks. Bake as normal.

1 Preheat the oven to 190°C/375°F/ Gas 5. Generously butter the base and sides of four ramekins.

2 Melt the butter in a frying pan and cook the leeks for 3–5 minutes over a medium heat, stirring, until softened.

3 Add 45ml/3 tbsp of the cream and cook over a gentle heat for 5 minutes until the leeks are very soft and the cream has thickened a little. Season with salt, pepper and nutmeg.

4 Place the ramekins in a small roasting pan and divide the leeks among them.

5 Break an egg into each, spoon over the remaining cream, and season. Pour boiling water into the pan to come about halfway up the sides of the dishes. Bake in the oven for 10 minutes, until just set.

6 Meanwhile, fry the sage leaves in a little oil until crisp and scatter over the top of the cooked eggs to serve.

Energy 149kcal/614kJ; Protein 4.4g; Carbohydrate 2.2g, of which sugars 1.8g; Fat 13.7g, of which saturates 7.5g; Cholesterol 123mg; Calcium 39mg; Fibre 1.3g; Sodium 64mg.

Cheese pudding

Old recipes for this classic dish involved cooking layers of toasted bread and cheese in the custard mixture. This version uses fresh breadcrumbs for a lighter result.

Serves 4

225g/8oz/2 cups grated mature (strong) Cheddar-style cheese

115g/4oz/2 cups fresh breadcrumbs

600ml/1 pint/2½ cups milk

40g/1½oz/3 tbsp butter

3 eggs, beaten

5ml/1 tsp wholegrain mustard

salt and ground black pepper

2 Place three-quarters of the grated cheese in a bowl together with the breadcrumbs and mix.

3 Put the remaining ingredients into a pan and stir well. Heat gently, stirring, until the butter has just melted (if the mixture gets too hot then the eggs will start to set).

4 Stir the warm liquid into the cheese mixture and pour into the prepared dish. Scatter the remaining cheese evenly over the top.

5 Put into the hot oven and cook for about 30 minutes or until golden brown and just set (a knife inserted in the centre should come out clean).

Variations Stir a small handful of chopped fresh parsley into the mixture before cooking, or put a layer of soft-cooked leeks in the bottom of the dish.

1 Preheat the oven to 200°C/400°F/ Gas 6. Butter the insides of a 1.2 litre/ 2 pint/5 cups ovenproof soufflé dish.

Energy 534kcal/2232kJ; Protein 27.5g; Carbohydrate 29.5g, of which sugars 7.9g; Fat 33.9g, of which saturates 20.2g; Cholesterol 227mg; Calcium 656mg; Fibre 0.6g; Sodium 803mg.

Spicy sausage and cheese tortilla

A colourful, Spanish-style omelette, which is delicious hot or cold. Cut into wedges and serve with a fresh tomato and basil salad, or wrap up for lunch boxes or a picnic.

Serves 4 to 6

75ml/5 tbsp olive oil

175g/6oz chorizo or spicy sausages, thinly sliced

675g/1½lb potatoes, peeled and thinly sliced

275g/10oz onions, halved and thinly sliced

4 eggs, beaten

30ml/2 tbsp chopped fresh parsley, plus extra to garnish

115g/4oz/1 cup Cheddar cheese, grated

salt and ground black pepper

1 Heat 15ml/1 tbsp of the oil in a non-stick frying pan, about 20cm/8in in diameter, and fry the chorizo until golden brown and cooked through. Lift out with a slotted spoon, drain on kitchen paper and set aside.

2 Add a further 30ml/2 tbsp oil to the pan and fry the potatoes and onions for 2–3 minutes, turning frequently (the pan will be very full).

3 Cover the pan tightly and cook over a gentle heat for about 30 minutes, turning the potatoes and onions occasionally, until all are softened and slightly golden in places.

4 In a bowl, mix the beaten eggs with the parsley, cheese, sausage, salt and pepper. Gently stir in the potatoes and onions until well coated.

5 Wipe out the pan with kitchen paper and heat the remaining 30ml/2 tbsp oil. Add the potato mixture and cook over a very low heat, until the egg begins to set. Use a metal spatula to prevent the tortilla from sticking to the sides.

6 Preheat the grill to hot. When the base of the tortilla has set, which should take about 5 minutes, protect the pan handle with foil and place under the grill until the tortilla is set and golden. Cut into wedges and serve, garnished with parsley.

Energy 409kcal/1703kJ; Protein 14.9g; Carbohydrate 28.3g, of which sugars 6.8g; Fat 26.7g, of which saturates 9.5g; Cholesterol 157mg; Calcium 212mg; Fibre 2.7g; Sodium 438mg.

Cheese and potato patties

Serve these delicious little potato cakes with a simple tomato salad for an imaginative appetizer or light lunch. Use a strong Cheddar instead of Roquefort if you wish.

Serves 4

500g/1¼lb potatoes, boiled in their skins until soft

115g/4oz Roquefort cheese

4 spring onions (scallions), finely chopped

45ml/3 tbsp chopped fresh dill

1 egg, beaten

15ml/1 tbsp lemon juice

plain (all-purpose) flour, for dredging

45ml/3 tbsp olive oil

salt and ground black pepper

1 Drain the potatoes, peel of the skins, and in a large bowl, mash while still warm. Crumble the Roquefort cheese into the potatoes and add the spring onions, dill, egg and lemon juice.

2 Season with a little salt (the cheese will be salty) and pepper. Stir well.

3 Cover the mixture and chill in the refrigerator until firm. Divide the mixture into walnut-sized balls, then flatten them slightly. Dredge with flour.

4 Heat the oil in a frying pan and fry the patties until golden on each side. Drain on kitchen paper and serve.

Energy 230Kcal/960kJ; Protein 8.4g; Carbohydrate 20.9g, of which sugars 2.3g; Fat 13.1g, of which saturates 2.3g; Cholesterol 68mg; Calcium 122mg; Fibre 1.4g; Sodium 446mg.

Hot cheese dip

Fontina is an Italian medium-fat cheese with a rich salty flavour, a little like Gruyère, which makes a good substitute. This wonderfully rich dip makes a good appetizer served with warm crusty bread.

Serves 4

250g/9oz Fontina or Gruyère cheese, diced

250ml/8fl oz/1 cup milk

15g/½oz/1 tbsp butter

2 eggs, lightly beaten

ground black pepper

Farmhouse tip Do not overheat the sauce, or the eggs may curdle. A very gentle heat will produce a lovely smooth sauce.

1 Put the cheese in a bowl with the milk and leave to soak for 2–3 hours. Transfer to a double boiler or a heatproof bowl set over a pan of simmering water.

2 Add the butter and eggs and stir gently until the cheese has melted to a smooth sauce. Remove from the heat, season with pepper and serve in a warmed serving dish.

Energy 250Kcal/1039kJ; Protein 15.6g; Carbohydrate 3g, of which sugars 3g; Fat 19.7g, of which saturates 12g; Cholesterol 145mg; Calcium 290mg; Fibre 0g; Sodium 320mg.

Summer quiche

The strong Mediterranean flavours of tomatoes, peppers and anchovies complement the cheesy pastry beautifully in this unusual quiche, which is perfect for a summer lunch.

Serves 6–8

For the pastry

225g/8oz/2 cups plain (all-purpose) flour

pinch of salt

pinch of dry mustard

115g/4oz/½ cup butter, chilled and cubed

50g/2oz Gruyère cheese, grated

For the filling

50g/2oz can of anchovies in oil, drained

50ml/2fl oz/¼ cup milk

30ml/2 tbsp French mustard

45ml/3 tbsp olive oil

2 large Spanish (Bermuda) onions, sliced

1 red (bell) pepper, seeded and very finely sliced

3 egg yolks

350ml/12fl oz/1½ cups double (heavy) cream

1 garlic clove, crushed

175g/6oz mature (sharp) Cheddar cheese, grated

2 large tomatoes, thickly sliced

salt and ground black pepper

30ml/2 tbsp chopped fresh basil, to garnish

1 First make the pastry. Place the flour, salt and mustard powder in a food processor, add the butter and process the mixture until it resembles breadcrumbs.

2 Add the cheese and process again briefly. Add enough iced water to make a stiff dough: it will be ready when the dough forms a ball. Wrap with plastic wrap and chill for 30 minutes.

3 Meanwhile, make the filling. Soak the anchovies in the milk for 20 minutes. Drain away the milk.

4 Roll out the chilled pastry and line a 23cm/9in loose-based flan tin. Spread over the mustard and chill for a further 15 minutes.

5 Preheat the oven to 200°C/400°F/ Gas 6. Heat the oil in a frying pan and cook the onions and red pepper until soft.

6 In a separate bowl, beat the egg yolks, cream, garlic and Cheddar cheese together; season well.

7 Arrange the tomatoes in a single layer in the pastry case. Top with the onion and pepper mixture and the anchovy fillets, the pour over the egg mixture.

8 Bake the tart in the oven for 30–35 minutes. When the top is firm and golden brown, remove from the oven.

9 Leave the tart to stand for 5–10 minutes, sprinkle over the basil and serve warm or at room temperature.

Energy 564kcal/2340kJ; Protein 9g; Carbohydrate 28g, of which sugars 6g; Fat 47g, of which saturates 25g; Cholesterol 177mg; Calcium 173mg; Fibre 2.3g; Sodium 605mg.

Feta and olive tartlets

Delicious for lunch or a snack, these crisp little tarts showcase the best Mediterranean farmhouse flavours. They freeze well and can be stuffed with a variety of fillings.

Serves 4

25g/1oz sun-dried aubergine (eggplant) slices

300ml/½ pint/1¼ cups boiling water

45ml/3 tbsp sunflower oil

1 onion, thinly sliced

150g/5oz/2 cups button (white) mushrooms, sliced

1 garlic clove, crushed

12–16 cherry tomatoes, halved

8 black or green olives, pitted and chopped

115g/4oz/1 cup feta cheese, crumbled

350g/12oz ready-made puff pastry

salt and ground black pepper

Farmhouse tip Choose cherry tomatoes on the vine for the very best flavour in these tartlets.

1 Preheat the oven to 200°C/400°F/ Gas 6. Place the aubergine slices in a shallow dish. Pour over the boiling water and leave to soak for 10 minutes. Rinse in cold water, drain and dry on kitchen paper. Cut the aubergine slices in half or quarters, depending on their size.

2 Heat 30ml/2 tbsp of the sunflower oil in a frying pan and fry the onion over a medium heat for 4–5 minutes. Add the mushrooms and cook for 3–4 minutes, or until the onions are light golden. Remove and set aside.

3 Heat the remaining oil in the frying pan, add the aubergine slices and garlic and lightly fry for 1–2 minutes. Lightly oil four individual clay pots.

4 Mix the halved tomatoes with the onions, mushrooms, aubergines, olives and feta cheese and divide among the clay pots. Season well.

5 Roll out the pastry thinly into a rectangle, then cut out four rounds, each slightly larger than the diameter of the clay pots.

6 Place the pastry rounds on top of the vegetable and cheese mixture, tucking any overlapping pastry down inside the dish.

7 Bake the tarts for about 20 minutes, or until the pastry is risen and golden. Allow to cool slightly, then carefully invert on to plates to serve.

Energy 506kcal/2105kJ; Protein 11.1g; Carbohydrate 35.9g, of which sugars 4.1g; Fat 37.2g, of which saturates 5.2g; Cholesterol 20mg; Calcium 175mg; Fibre 1.6g; Sodium 989mg.

Leek and onion tarts

Leeks are a great winter vegetable, and when combined with sliced onion and grated Gruyére cheese, these tarts make a good addition to a picnic, buffet or a vegetarian lunch.

Serves 6

25g/1oz/2 tbsp butter, plus extra for greasing

1 onion, thinly sliced

450g/1lb/4 cups leeks, thinly sliced

2.5ml/½ tsp dried thyme

50g/2oz/½ cup Gruyère cheese, grated

3 eggs

300ml/½ pint/1¼ cups single (light) cream

pinch of freshly grated nutmeg

salt and ground black pepper

mixed salad leaves, to serve

For the pastry

175g/6oz/1½ cups plain (all-purpose) flour

75g/3oz/6 tbsp cold butter

1 egg yolk

30–45ml/2–3 tbsp cold water

1 To make the pastry, sift the flour into a large bowl and add the cold butter. Using your hands, gently rub the butter into the flour until the mixture resembles fine breadcrumbs.

2 Add the egg yolk and enough water to form a stiff dough. Form into a ball, wrap and chill for 30 minutes.

3 Butter six 10cm/4in tartlet tins (muffin pans). On a floured surface, roll out the dough until 3mm/⅛in thick then cut rounds and line the tins, pressing the pastry into the sides. Prick the bases and chill for 30 minutes. Preheat the oven to 190°C/375°F/Gas 5.

4 Line the pastry cases with foil and fill with baking beans. Place on a baking sheet and bake for 6–8 minutes until golden at the edges. Remove the foil and beans, and bake for 2 minutes more. Transfer to a wire rack to cool. Reduce the oven temperature to 180°C/350°F/Gas 4.

5 In a large frying pan, melt the butter over a medium heat, then add the onion, leeks and thyme, and cook for 10–12 minutes until soft and tender.

6 In a medium bowl, beat the eggs, cream, nutmeg and salt and pepper together. Place the pastry cases on a baking sheet and pour in the egg mixture, then sprinkle each with cheese, dividing it evenly.

7 Bake the tartlets for 15–20 minutes until set and golden. Transfer the tartlets to a wire rack to cool slightly, then remove them from the tins and serve warm or at room temperature with a selection of fresh salad leaves.

Energy 422kcal/1755kJ; Protein 11.5g; Carbohydrate 26.8g, of which sugars 3.9g; Fat 30.4g, of which saturates 17.7g; Cholesterol 200mg; Calcium 189mg; Fibre 2.7g; Sodium 215mg.

Caramelized onion tart

This is a good recipe for when onions are harvested and have a milder flavour. The tart makes a delicious main course, served warm and accompanied by a green salad.

Serves 4–6

175g/6oz/1½ cups plain (all-purpose) flour

75g/3oz/6 tbsp butter, chilled

30–45ml/2–3 tbsp iced water

For the filling

50g/2oz/¼ cup butter

900g/2lb onions, thinly sliced

1 egg, plus 2 egg yolks

250ml/8fl oz/1 cup double (heavy) cream

1.5ml/¼ tsp freshly grated nutmeg

salt and ground black pepper

1 Process the flour, a pinch of salt and the chilled butter or butter and lard in a food processor until reduced to fine crumbs. Add the iced water and process briefly to form a dough. Wrap in plastic wrap and chill for 40 minutes.

2 Melt the butter in a large pan and add the onions and a pinch of salt. Turn them in the butter. Cover and cook the onions very gently, stirring frequently, for 30–40 minutes. Cool slightly.

Variations Try adding chopped fresh herbs such as thyme.
This tart is also delicious made with cheese pastry; add 50g/2oz/⅔ cup grated Parmesan to the flour.

3 Preheat the oven to 190°C/375°F/ Gas 5. Roll out the dough thinly and use to line a 23–25cm/9–10in loose-based flan tin (pan). Line with foil or baking parchment and baking beans, then bake blind for 10 minutes.

4 Remove the foil or parchment and baking beans, and bake for another 4–5 minutes, until the pastry is lightly cooked to a pale brown colour (blonde is a good description). Reduce the oven temperature to 180°C/350°F/Gas 4.

5 Beat the egg, egg yolks and cream together. Season with salt, lots of black pepper and the grated nutmeg. Place half the onions in the pastry shell and add half the egg mixture. Add the remaining onions, then pour in as much of the remaining custard as you can.

6 Place on a baking sheet and cook for 40–50 minutes, or until the custard is risen, browned and set in the centre. Serve warm rather than piping hot.

Energy 905kcal/3748kJ; Protein 15g; Carbohydrate 36.7g, of which sugars 3g; Fat 78.2g, of which saturates 47.1g; Cholesterol 384mg; Calcium 272mg; Fibre 1.6g; Sodium 383mg.

Smoked salmon quiche

The rich salmon and cream filling of this light but richly-flavoured quiche perfectly complements the melt-in-the-mouth potato pastry.

Serves 6

For the potato pastry

115g/4oz floury maincrop potatoes, diced

225g/8oz/2 cups plain (all-purpose) flour, sifted

115g/4oz/8 tbsp butter, diced

$\frac{1}{2}$ egg, beaten

10ml/2 tsp chilled water

For the filling

275g/10oz smoked salmon

6 eggs, beaten

150ml/$\frac{1}{4}$ pint/$\frac{2}{3}$ cup whole milk

300ml/$\frac{1}{2}$ pint/1$\frac{1}{4}$ cups double (heavy) cream

30–45ml/2–3 tbsp chopped fresh dill

30ml/2 tbsp capers, chopped

salt and ground black pepper

salad leaves and fresh dill, to serve

1 Boil the potatoes in a large pan of lightly salted water for 15 minutes or until tender. Drain well through a colander and return to the pan. Mash the potatoes until smooth and set aside to cool completely.

2 Place the flour in a bowl and rub in the butter to form fine crumbs. Beat in the potatoes and egg. Bring the mixture together, adding a little chilled water.

3 Roll the pastry out on a floured surface and use to line a deep 23cm/9in round, loose-based, fluted flan tin (pan). Chill for 1 hour.

4 Place a baking sheet in the oven to preheat it. Chop the salmon into bite-size pieces and set aside. Preheat the oven to 200°C/400°F/Gas 6.

5 For the filling, beat the eggs, milk and cream together. Then stir in the dill and capers and season with pepper. Add in the salmon and stir to combine.

6 Remove the pastry case from the refrigerator, prick the base and pour the mixture into it. Bake on a baking sheet for 35–45 minutes. Serve warm with mixed salad leaves and some more dill.

Farmhouse tip To ensure the base cooks through, it is important to preheat a baking sheet in the oven first.

Energy 679Kcal/2825kJ; Protein 23.3g; Carbohydrate 34.1g, of which sugars 2.7g; Fat 51.1g, of which saturates 28.9g; Cholesterol 317mg; Calcium 142mg; Fibre 1.4g; Sodium 1070mg.

Cheese and bacon flan

Flans are great country fare, ideal for al fresco meals. To pack for a picnic, double-wrap the tin in foil and wait until you arrive before cutting into slices.

2 Fry the chopped bacon on a medium heat until crisp and browned.

3 Drain the bacon. Pour off most of the fat from the pan, add the onion and cook gently for about 15 minutes.

4 Beat the eggs and cream in a bowl, and season with salt and pepper.

Serves 6–8

1 x quantity potato pastry (see page 118)

15ml/1 tbsp Dijon mustard

175g/6oz/6 rindless streaky (fatty) bacon rashers (strips), chopped

3 eggs

350ml/12fl oz/1½ cups single (light) cream

1 onion, chopped

150g/5oz Gruyère cheese, diced

salt and ground black pepper

1 Preheat the oven to 200°C/400°F/Gas 6. Roll out the pastry and line a 23 cm/9 in flan tin (pan). Prick the base of and bake for 15 minutes. Brush with mustard and bake for 5 minutes more. Stand on a wire rack to cool and reduce the oven to 180°C/350°F/Gas 4.

5 Sprinkle half the cheese over the pastry case, then the onion, followed by the bacon and remaining cheese. Pour on the egg mixture and bake for 35–45 minutes until set. Serve warm, garnished with parsley.

Energy 494kcal/2055kJ; Protein 18g; Carbohydrate 25g, of which sugars 3g; Fat 37g, of which saturates 21g; Cholesterol 183mg; Calcium 340mg; Fibre 1.3g; Sodium 730mg.

Chard omelette

This traditional flat omelette can also be made with fresh spinach, but the large leaves of Swiss chard – a variety of white beet – are more authentic.

Serves 6

675g/1½lb Swiss chard leaves, without stalks

60ml/4 tbsp olive oil

1 large onion, sliced

5 eggs

salt and ground black pepper

fresh parsley sprig, to garnish

1 Wash the chard well in several changes of water and pat dry. Stack four or five leaves at a time and slice across into thin ribbons. Steam the chard until wilted, then drain in a sieve (strainer) and press out any liquid with the back of a spoon.

2 Heat half the olive oil in a large frying pan. Add the onion and cook over a medium-low heat for about 10 minutes until soft, stirring occasionally. Add the chard and cook for a further 2–4 minutes until the leaves are tender.

3 Beat the eggs in a large bowl. Season with salt and pepper, then stir in the cooked vegetables.

4 Heat the remaining oil in a large frying pan, pour in the egg mixture and reduce the heat to medium low. Cook the omelette, covered, for 5–7 minutes until the egg mixture is set around the edges and almost set on top.

5 To turn the omelette over, loosen the edges and slide it on to a large plate. Place the frying pan upside down over the omelette and, holding both tightly, carefully invert pan and plate.

6 Cook the omelette for a further 2–3 minutes. Slide the omelette on to a serving plate and serve hot or at room temperature, garnished with parsley.

Energy 200kcal/832kJ; Protein 9g; Carbohydrate 6g, of which sugars 3g; Fat 16g, of which saturates 3g; Cholesterol 193mg; Calcium 98mg; Fibre 0.6g; Sodium 374mg.

Omelette with herbs

Sometimes the simplest dishes are the most satisfying. Fresh farm eggs, lightly soured cream and fresh herbs make a speedy but superb meal.

Serves 1

2 eggs

15g/¹⁄₂oz/1 tbsp butter

15ml/1 tbsp crème fraîche or sour cream

15ml/1 tbsp chopped fresh mixed herbs (such as tarragon, chives, parsley or marjoram)

salt and ground black pepper

Variations Other omelette fillings could include sautéed sliced mushrooms, diced ham or crumbled crisp bacon, creamed spinach or thick tomato sauce and grated cheese.

1 Beat the eggs and salt and pepper in a bowl. Melt the butter in an omelette pan until foamy, then pour in the eggs.

2 When the mixture starts to set on the base of the pan, lift up the sides with a spatula and tilt the pan to allow the uncooked egg to run underneath.

3 When the omelette is set, but still soft on top, spoon the crème fraîche or soured cream over the centre and sprinkle with the herbs. With a palette knife, lift one edge of the omelette and fold it over the middle. Tilt the pan so that the omelette folds in thirds and slide it out on to a plate.

Energy 95Kcal/393kJ; Protein 7g; Carbohydrate 0.2g, of which sugars 0.2g; Fat 7.7g, of which saturates 2.9g; Cholesterol 196mg; Calcium 44mg; Fibre 0.4g; Sodium 91g.

Egg-stuffed tomatoes

Effective, and surprisingly easy to prepare, this combination of eggs with tomatoes makes a quick, filling lunch. For the most enjoyable result, eat immediately.

Serves 4

175ml/6fl oz/³⁄₄ cup mayonnaise

30ml/2 tbsp snipped fresh chives

30ml/2 tbsp torn fresh basil leaves

30ml/2 tbsp chopped fresh parsley

4 ripe tomatoes

4 hard-boiled eggs, sliced

salt and white pepper

lettuce leaves and ground black pepper, to serve

1 Mix the mayonnaise and herbs in a small bowl and set aside. Place the tomatoes stalk-end down and make deep cuts to within 1cm/¹⁄₂in of the base. Make the same number of cuts as there are slices of egg.

2 Fan open the tomatoes and sprinkle with salt and white pepper, then insert an egg slice into each slit. Place each stuffed tomato on a plate with lettuce leaves, grind over some black pepper, and serve with the herb mayonnaise.

Energy 309Kcal/1276kJ; Protein 7.6g; Carbohydrate 3.6g, of which sugars 3.4g; Fat 29.6g, of which saturates 5.2g; Cholesterol 214mg; Calcium 62mg; Fibre 1.5g; Sodium 223mg.

Baked cheese polenta with tomato sauce

Polenta, or cornmeal, is a staple country food in Italy. Cooked, cut into squares when set, then baked with a tomato sauce, it makes a satisfying meal.

Serves 4

1 litre/1¾ pints/4 cups water

5ml/1 tsp salt

250g/9oz/2¼ cups quick-cook polenta

5ml/1 tsp paprika

2.5ml/½ tsp grated nutmeg

30ml/2 tbsp olive oil

1 large onion, finely chopped

2 garlic cloves, crushed

2 x 400g/14oz cans tomatoes

15ml/1 tbsp tomato purée (paste)

5ml/1 tsp sugar

75g/3oz Gruyère cheese, grated

salt and ground black pepper

1 Preheat the oven to 200°C/400°F/ Gas 6. Line a 28 x 18cm/11 x 7in baking tin (pan) with plastic wrap.

2 Bring the water to the boil with the salt, pour in the polenta in a steady stream and cook, stirring constantly for 5 minutes or until it forms a thick mass.

3 Beat in the paprika and nutmeg, then pour into the prepared tin and smooth the surface. Leave to cool and set.

4 Heat the oil in a large pan and cook the onion and garlic until soft. Add the tomatoes, tomato purée and sugar, and season to taste. Bring to the boil, lower the heat and simmer for 20 minutes.

5 Turn the polenta on to a board, and cut into squares. Place half the squares in a greased baking dish. Spoon over half the tomato sauce, and sprinkle with half the cheese. Repeat. Bake for 25 minutes, and serve warm.

Energy 415kcal/1734kJ; Protein 13.4g; Carbohydrate 57.5g, of which sugars 10g; Fat 14g, of which saturates 4.9g; Cholesterol 18mg; Calcium 180mg; Fibre 3.6g; Sodium 707mg.

Poached eggs with spinach

When the vegetable garden yields fresh spinach, serve this simple dish with farm-fresh poached eggs, and a delicious, creamy hollandaise sauce.

Serves 4

25g/1oz/2 tbsp butter

450g/1lb young spinach leaves

½ tsp vinegar

4 eggs

salt and ground black pepper

For the hollandaise sauce

2 egg yolks

15ml/1 tbsp lemon juice

15ml/1 tbsp water

175g/6oz/¾ cup butter

salt and white pepper

1 First make the hollandaise sauce. Blend the egg yolks, lemon juice and water in a processor to a smooth paste.

2 Melt the butter in a small pan until foaming. With the machine running, slowly pour the hot butter into the processor in a thin stream. Season the thickened sauce with more lemon juice if needed and salt and pepper. Transfer the sauce to a warmed bowl, cover and keep warm.

Farmhouse tip For a well-shaped poached egg, swirl the water whirlpool-fashion and slip the egg into the centre.

3 Melt the butter in a heavy frying pan over a medium heat. Add the spinach and cook until wilted, stirring occasionally. Season and keep warm.

4 Bring a pan of lightly salted water to the boil and add the vinegar. Break an egg into a saucer and slide the egg into the water. Reduce the heat and simmer for 2–3 minutes until the white is set but the yolk is still soft. Remove with a slotted spoon, drain and keep warm. Poach the remaining eggs one at a time in the same way.

5 To serve, spoon the spinach on to warmed plates and make a hollow in each mound. Place the eggs on top and pour over a little hollandaise sauce.

Energy 521kcal/2147kJ; Protein 13g; Carbohydrate 2g, of which sugars 2g; Fat 51g, of which saturates 29g; Cholesterol 439mg; Calcium 249mg; Fibre 4.4g; Sodium 649mg.

Eggs in pepper nests

Pepper strips look pretty and provide an interesting base for baked eggs topped with cream. Served with crusty bread, this makes a good first course.

Serves 4

2 red (bell) peppers and 1 green (bell) pepper, halved and seeded

30ml/2 tbsp olive oil

1 large onion, finely sliced

2 garlic cloves, crushed

5–6 tomatoes, skinned and chopped

a sprig of fresh rosemary

120ml/4fl oz/½ cup passata (bottled, strained tomatoes)

4 eggs

40ml/8 tsp single (light) cream

pinch of cayenne pepper

salt and ground black pepper

1 Preheat the oven to 180°C/350°F/ Gas 4. Thinly slice the peppers. Heat the oil in a large pan, and fry the onion and garlic for about 5 minutes.

2 Add the peppers to the onion and fry for 10 minutes. Stir in the tomatoes, rosemary and passata, and seasoning. Cook gently for 10 minutes more until the peppers are soft.

3 Transfer the mixture equally into four ovenproof dishes.

4 Make a hole in the centre of each and break in an egg. Spoon 10ml/2 tsp cream over the yolk of each egg and sprinkle with black pepper and cayenne.

5 Bake for 12–15 minutes until the white of the egg is lightly set. Serve at once with crusty bread.

Energy 248kcal/1032kJ; Protein 11g; Carbohydrate 15g, of which sugars 13g; Fat 16g, of which saturates 4g; Cholesterol 237mg; Calcium 78mg; Fibre 2.4g; Sodium 166mg.

Eggs baked in ham and potato hash

A traditional hash is a great way to serve leftover ham and potatoes, and is easy to prepare. You can replace the ham with corned beef if you wish.

Serves 6

50g/2oz/¼ cup butter

1 large onion, chopped

350g/12oz cooked ham, diced

450g/1lb cooked potatoes, diced

115g/4oz/1 cup grated Cheddar cheese

30ml/2 tbsp tomato ketchup

30ml/2 tbsp Worcestershire sauce

6 eggs

few drops of Tabasco sauce

salt and freshly ground black pepper

chopped fresh chives, to garnish

1 Preheat the oven to 160°C/325°F/ Gas 3. Melt half the butter in a pan, fry the onion until soft, tip into a bowl and stir in the ham, potato, cheese, ketchup, seasoning and Worcestershire sauce.

2 Spread the hash in a buttered ovenproof dish. Bake for 10 minutes.

3 Make six hollows in the hash. Break each egg in turn into a small bowl or saucer and slip into one of the hollows.

4 Melt the remaining butter. Season with Tabasco sauce, then dribble the seasoned butter over the eggs and hash. Bake for 15–20 minutes or until the eggs are set. Garnish with chopped chives and serve.

Energy 305kcal/1275kJ; Protein 19.7g; Carbohydrate 18.2g, of which sugars 5.9g; Fat 17.2g, of which saturates 9.9g; Cholesterol 135mg; Calcium 180mg; Fibre 1.5g; Sodium 1020mg.

Pasta with cheese and cream

This rich and filling dish can be rustled up really quickly, in the time it takes to cook the pasta. It is perfect for a family supper when time is short and appetites are large.

Serves 4

400g/14oz/3½ cups dried pasta

3 egg yolks

105ml/7 tbsp freshly grated Parmesan cheese

200g/7oz/scant 1 cup ricotta cheese

60ml/4 tbsp double (heavy) cream

whole nutmeg

40g/1½oz/3 tbsp butter

salt and ground black pepper

1 Cook the pasta according to the instructions on the packet. Meanwhile, mix the egg yolks, grated Parmesan and ricotta together in a bowl. Then mix in the cream.

2 Grate nutmeg into the egg, cheese and cream mixture, then season with plenty of black pepper and a little salt.

3 Drain the pasta thoroughly when cooked, retain a little of the cooking liquid. Return the pan to the heat. Add the butter to the pan and melt, then add the drained pasta and toss vigorously over a medium heat until the pasta is really hot.

4 Turn off the heat under the pan and add the ricotta mixture. Stir well with a large spoon for 10–15 seconds until all the pasta is coated; add a little cooking water if it needs thinning. Serve at once in warmed individual bowls.

Farmhouse tip The best pasta shape for this recipe is elicoidali. If you can't get them, use rigatoni or another pasta shape that has ridges.

Energy 670kcal/2816kJ; Protein 29.2g; Carbohydrate 75.7g, of which sugars 4.9g; Fat 30g, of which saturates 16.5g; Cholesterol 220mg; Calcium 359mg; Fibre 2.9g; Sodium 357mg.

Bread and cheese bake

This is a great way to use up the previous day's bread, and if you have some cheese that is looking past its best, use that too, in place of the Parmesan and Cheddar.

Serves 4

butter or olive oil, for greasing

1 pint/625ml/2½ cups milk

3 eggs, beaten

1½oz/45g Parmesan cheese, grated

a pinch of cayenne pepper

5 large, thick slices of white bread

8oz/225g Cheddar cheese, grated

salt and ground black pepper

1 Grease an oval baking dish with the butter or olive oil.

2 In a mixing bowl combine the milk, eggs, 3 tablespoons of the Parmesan cheese, the cayenne and salt and pepper to taste.

3 Cut the bread slices in half. Arrange 5 of the pieces in the bottom of the buttered dish, overlapping the slices if necessary.

4 Sprinkle the bread with two-thirds of the Cheddar cheese. Top with the remaining bread.

5 Pour the egg mixture evenly over the bread. Press the bread down gently so that it will absorb the egg mixture. Sprinkle the top evenly with the remaining Parmesan and Cheddar cheeses. Let it stand until the bread has absorbed most of the egg mixture; this will take at least 30 minutes.

6 Preheat the oven to 425°F/220°C/ Gas 7. Set the baking dish in a roasting pan. Add enough boiling water to the pan to come halfway up the sides of the baking dish.

7 Place in the oven and bake for 30 minutes, or until the pudding is lightly set and browned. If the pudding browns too quickly before setting, cover loosely with foil and reduce the temperature slightly. Serve hot.

Energy 664kcal27701kJ; Protein 34g; Carbohydrate 34g, of which sugars 9g; Fat 44g, of which saturates 26g; Cholesterol 285mg; Calcium 806mg; Fibre 2.1g; Sodium 1076mg.

Fish and Shellfish

Whether the fish you eat comes from a nearby river, seashore or fishmonger, the same farmhouse principles of good cooking remain the same: fresh, seasonal and local ingredients, simply cooked, make the best meals. Here you will find recipes using all types of fish to create hearty suppers and quick and easy family dinners, from delicious fish pies to frugal fishcakes.

Smoked mackerel with roasted blueberries

Fresh blueberries burst with flavour when roasted, and their sharpness complements the rich flesh of mackerel very well. This recipe is perfect for using the berries when in season.

Serves 4

15g/½oz/2 tsp plain (all-purpose) flour

4 smoked peppered mackerel fillets

50g/2oz/4 tbsp unsalted butter

juice of ½ lemon

salt and ground black pepper

For the roasted blueberries

450g/1lb blueberries

25g/1oz/2 tbsp sugar

15g/½oz/1 tbsp unsalted butter

salt and ground black pepper

1 Preheat the oven to 200°C/400°F/ Gas 6. Sprinkle each fish with the flour to coat it, it doesn't need seasoning as the fish will be salty and is already coated in pepper, if you buy plain mackerel fillets, however, season the flour with a little salt and pepper. Dot the butter on the fillets and bake in the hot oven for 20 minutes.

2 Place the blueberries, sugar, butter and seasoning in a separate small roasting pan and roast them in the oven at the same time as the mackerel, basting occasionally, for 15 minutes.

3 To serve, drizzle the lemon juice over the roasted mackerel, accompanied by the roasted blueberries.

Energy 656kcal/2729kJ; Protein 25g; Carbohydrate 23g, of which sugars 20g; Fat 52g, of which saturates 17g; Cholesterol 169mg; Calcium 51mg; Fibre 1.8g; Sodium 1138mg.

Fresh mackerel with gooseberry relish

Packed with beneficial oils, fresh mackerel is not only tasty but very nutritionally rich. The tart gooseberries in this recipe are a perfect accompaniment to any type of oily fish.

Serves 4

4 whole mackerel, cleaned

60ml/4 tbsp olive oil

For the sauce

250g/9oz gooseberries

25g/1oz/2 tbsp soft light brown sugar

5ml/1 tsp wholegrain or Dijon mustard

salt and ground black pepper

1 For the sauce, wash and trim the gooseberries and then roughly chop them, so there are some pieces larger than others.

2 Cook the gooseberries in a little water with the sugar in a small pan. A thick and chunky purée will form. Add the mustard, and season to taste with salt and ground black pepper.

Farmhouse tips Turn the grill (broiler) on well in advance as the fish need a fierce heat to cook quickly. If you love the fish but don't like the smell, try barbecuing them outside.

   The foil lining in the grill (broiling) pan is to catch the smelly drips. Simply roll it up and throw it away afterwards, leaving a nice clean pan.

3 Preheat the grill (broiler) to high and line the grill (broiling) pan with foil. Using a sharp knife, slash the fish two or three times down each side, then season and brush with the olive oil.

4 Place the fish in the grill pan and grill (broil) for about 4 minutes on each side until cooked. You may need to cook them for a few minutes longer if they are particularly large. The slashes will open up to speed cooking, and the skin should be lightly browned. To check that they are cooked properly, use a small sharp knife to pierce the skin and check for uncooked flesh.

5 Place the mackerel on warmed plates and spread generous dollops of the gooseberry relish over them. Pass the remaining sauce around at the table.

Energy 576Kcal/2390kJ; Protein 38.1g; Carbohydrate 8.4g, of which sugars 8.4g; Fat 43.5g, of which saturates 8.2g; Cholesterol 108mg; Calcium 43mg; Fibre 1.5g; Sodium 128mg.

Haddock in cider sauce

Both smoked and unsmoked, haddock is a popular fish that finds its way into many traditional dishes. Its firm, meaty flesh is beautifully complemented by the cider sauce.

2 Pour in most of the cider, reserving 30ml/2 tbsp for the sauce. Cover and bring to the boil, reduce the heat and simmer for 10 minutes, or until the fish is just cooked.

3 Strain 300ml/½ pint/1¼ cups of the fish liquor into a measuring jug (cup). In a small pan, mix the cornflour with the reserved cider, then gradually whisk in the fish liquor.

4 Bring to the boil, whisking, for about 2 minutes, until it is smooth and thickened. Add more cooking liquor, if necessary, to make a pouring sauce.

5 Remove the pan from the heat, stir in the single cream, and season to taste with salt and freshly ground black pepper.

6 To serve, remove any skin from the fish, arrange on individual hot serving plates with the onion over the vegetables, and pour the sauce over.

Serves 4

675g/1½lb haddock fillet

1 medium onion, thinly sliced

1 bay leaf

2 sprigs fresh parsley

10ml/2 tsp lemon juice

450ml/¾ pint/2 cups dry (hard) cider

25g/1oz/¼ cup cornflour (cornstarch)

30ml/2 tbsp single (light) cream

salt and ground black pepper

1 Cut the haddock fillet into four equal portions and place in a pan big enough to hold them neatly in a single layer. Add the onion, bay leaf, parsley and lemon juice, and season with salt.

Energy 227Kcal/964kJ; Protein 32.8g; Carbohydrate 11.8g, of which sugars 5.2g; Fat 2.6g, of which saturates 1.1g; Cholesterol 65mg; Calcium 50mg; Fibre 0.5g; Sodium 128mg.

Plaice with sorrel and lemon butter sauce

Sorrel is a delicate wild herb that grows in early spring and has a lovely lemony taste, which does not overwhelm the flavour of the fish. This sauce would also work with turbot or brill.

Serves 4

200g/7oz/scant 1 cup butter

500g/1¼lb plaice fillets, skinned and patted dry

30ml/2 tbsp chopped fresh sorrel

90ml/6 tbsp dry white wine

a little lemon juice

1 Heat half the butter in a large frying pan and place the fillets skin side down. Cook briefly, just to firm up, reduce the heat and turn the fish over. The fish will be cooked in less than 5 minutes.

2 Try not to let the butter brown or allow the fish to colour. Remove the fish fillets from the pan and keep warm between two plates. Cut the remaining butter into chunks. Add the chopped sorrel to the pan and stir.

3 Add the wine, then the butter, swirling it in and not allowing the sauce to boil. Stir in a little lemon juice. Serve the fish with the sorrel and lemon butter spooned over, with some crunchy green beans and new potatoes, if you like.

Energy 494kcal/2047kJ; Protein 25.7g; Carbohydrate 0.5g, of which sugars 0.5g; Fat 43.3g, of which saturates 26.4g; Cholesterol 170mg; Calcium 98mg; Fibre 0.3g; Sodium 501mg.

Grilled sea bass with fennel

Fennel has an unmistakable flavour, which goes particularly well with fish. If sea bass is not available, use a small salmon, or individual river trout for this recipe.

Serves 6–8

1 sea bass, about 1.75kg/4–4½lb in weight, cleaned

60–90ml/4–6 tbsp olive oil

10–15ml/2–3 tsp fennel seeds

2 large fennel bulbs, trimmed and quartered, with some of the fronds reserved

60ml/4 tbsp Pernod

salt and ground black pepper

1 With a sharp knife, make three or four deep cuts in both sides of the fish. Brush both sides with a little olive oil and season with salt and pepper. Preheat the grill (broiler).

2 Sprinkle the fennel seeds in the stomach cavity and the cuts. Set aside.

3 Remove the core from the fennel and slice thinly. Put the fennel slices on the grill rack and drizzle with oil. Grill for 4 minutes on each side until tender. Transfer the fennel to a large dish or platter and keep warm.

4 Place the fish on the grill rack and grill (broil) for 10–12 minutes on each side, brushing occasionally with oil. Transfer to the platter on top of the fennel. Garnish with the fronds. Heat the Pernod in a pan, light it and pour it, flaming, over the fish. Serve at once.

Energy 180Kcal/750kJ; Protein 19.9g; Carbohydrate 1.2g, of which sugars 1.1g; Fat 8.1g, of which saturates 1.2g; Cholesterol 80mg; Calcium 146mg; Fibre 1.6g; Sodium 76mg.

Barbecued stuffed sardines

Perfect for summer barbecues, this recipe can also be made with trout. Simply grill, griddle or barbecue the fish, and serve with sliced cucumber and lemon wedges.

Serves 4

15ml/1 tbsp currants

4 good-sized sardines

30ml/2 tbsp olive oil

6 spring onions (scallions), finely sliced

2–3 garlic cloves, crushed

5ml/1 tsp cumin seeds, crushed

5ml/1 tsp sumac

15ml/1 tbsp pine nuts

1 small bunch flat leaf parsley, leaves finely chopped

salt and ground black pepper

For basting

45ml/3 tbsp olive oil

juice of 1 lemon

5–10ml/1–2 tsp sumac

1 Prepare the barbecue, if using. Soak four wooden skewers in cold water for 30 minutes. Soak the currants in warm water for about 15 minutes, then drain them.

2 Slit the sardines from head to tail with a sharp knife and remove the backbone by gently massaging the area around it to loosen it. Using your fingers, carefully prise out the bone, snapping it off at each end, while keeping the fish intact. Rinse the fish and pat it dry.

3 Heat the oil in a large, heavy frying pan, stir in the spring onions and cook until soft. Add the garlic, cumin and sumac.

4 Add the pine nuts and currants to the onions and spices, stir them into the mixture and fry until the pine nuts begin to turn golden.

5 Toss in the parsley, and season to taste with salt and pepper. Leave to cool. Heat the grill (broiler), if using.

6 Place each sardine on a flat surface and spread the filling inside each one. Seal closed with the skewers.

7 Mix together the olive oil, lemon juice and sumac, and brush some of it over the sardines.

8 Place the fish on the rack over the hot coals, or under the grill (broiler) and cook them for 2–3 minutes on each side over a medium heat, basting them with the remainder of the olive oil mixture.

Farmhouse tip Sumac is a Middle-eastern spice, which is easily available. If you can't find it, however, use a little lemon zest instead.

Energy 265kcal/1098kJ; Protein 16.7g; Carbohydrate 4g, of which sugars 3.1g; Fat 20.3g, of which saturates 3.6g; Cholesterol 0mg; Calcium 90mg; Fibre 0.4g; Sodium 88mg.

Classic fish and chips

Nothing beats a piece of cod cooked to a crisp served with freshly made chips (French fries). The batter should be light and crisp and the fish should melt in the mouth.

Serves 4

450g/1lb potatoes

groundnut oil for deep-fat frying

4 x 175g/6oz cod fillets

For the batter

75g/3oz/²⁄₃ cup plain (all-purpose) flour

1 egg yolk

10ml/2 tsp oil

175ml/6fl oz/³⁄₄ cup water

pinch of salt

1 Cut the potatoes into 5mm/¼in thick slices. Cut each slice again to make 5mm/¼in chips.

2 Heat the oil in a deep fat fryer to 180°C/350°F. Add the chips to the fryer and cook for 3 minutes, then remove from the pan and shake off all fat. Set to one side.

Farmhouse tip Use fresh rather than frozen fish for the very best texture and flavour. If you have to use frozen fish, defrost it thoroughly and make sure it is dry before coating with batter.

3 To make the batter, sift the flour into a bowl and add the remaining ingredients. Beat well until smooth. Set aside until ready to use.

4 Cook the chips again in the fat for a further 5 minutes or so until they are really crisp. Drain on kitchen paper and season with salt. Keep hot in a low oven while you cook the pieces of fish.

5 Dip the fish into the batter, making sure they are evenly coated, and shake off any excess.

6 Carefully lower the fish into the fat and cook for 5 minutes. Drain on kitchen paper. Serve with lemon wedges and the chips.

Variation Although cod is the traditional choice for fish and chips, it is increasingly difficult to buy. You can also use haddock. Rock salmon, sometimes known as huss or dogfish, also has a good flavour.

Energy 399kcal/1668kJ; Protein 28.9g; Carbohydrate 38g, of which sugars 2.2g; Fat 14.6g, of which saturates 7.6g; Cholesterol 181mg; Calcium 62mg; Fibre 0.5g; Sodium 974mg.

Fried trout with citrus and basil

Here, fillets of freshwater trout or sea trout are pan-fried and served with a fresh, citrus sauce. This light, summer supper is very good served with new potatoes and a salad.

4 Season the fish and coat each in flour. Heat the remaining oil in a frying pan and add the fish. Fry for 2–3 minutes on each side until cooked, then transfer to a plate and keep hot in the oven.

5 Add the butter and the marinade to the frying pan and heat gently, stirring until the butter has melted. Season with salt and pepper, then stir in the sugar. Continue cooking the sauce gently for 4–5 minutes until it has slightly thickened.

6 Tear half the basil leaves and add them to the pan. Pour the sauce over the fish and garnish with the remaining basil and the orange and lemon slices.

Serves 4

4 trout fillets, each about 200g/7oz

2 lemons

3 oranges

105ml/7 tbsp olive oil

45ml/3 tbsp plain (all-purpose) flour

25g/1oz/2 tbsp butter

5ml/1 tsp soft light brown sugar

15g/¹/₂oz/¹/₂ cup fresh basil leaves

salt and ground black pepper

1 Arrange the trout fillets in the base of a non-metallic shallow dish. Grate in the zest from one lemon and two of the oranges, then squeeze these fruits and pour the combined juices into a jug (pitcher). Slice the remaining fruits and reserve to use as a garnish.

2 Add 75ml/5 tbsp of the oil to the citrus juices. Beat with a fork and pour over the fish. Cover and marinate in the refrigerator for at least 2 hours.

3 Preheat the oven to 150°C/300°F/ Gas 2. Using a fish slice or metal spatula, carefully remove the trout from the marinade.

Farmhouse tip Basil leaves bruise very easily, so they should always be torn, snipped with scissors or used whole rather than cut with a knife. Don't use any leaves that are shrivelled or have brown patches on them.

Energy 266Kcal/1119kJ; Protein 40.5g; Carbohydrate 7.9g, of which sugars 7.7g; Fat 8.3g, of which saturates 0.2g; Cholesterol 0mg; Calcium 140mg; Fibre 1.7g; Sodium 177mg.

Griddled trout with bacon

Salty, flavourful bacon makes a good foil to the sweet, mild taste of trout, and here it also
helps to keep the fish moist and tender by protecting it from the fierce heat.

Serves 4

25g/1oz/1 tbsp plain (all-purpose)
flour

4 medium-sized trout, cleaned and
gutted

75g/3oz streaky (fatty) bacon rashers
(strips)

50g/2oz/4 tbsp butter

15ml/1 tbsp olive oil

juice of ½ lemon

salt and ground black pepper

1 Pat the trout dry with kitchen paper
and mix the flour and seasoning
together. Use the seasoned flour to dust
each side of the fish thoroughly. Preheat
the grill (broiler).

2 Wrap each trout tightly in the streaky
bacon. Place directly under the hot grill
for 5–8 minutes on each side until the
bacon is crisp and browned. Serve the
trout immediately, with the lemon juice
drizzled on top.

Energy 289kcal/1211kJ; Protein 33g; Carbohydrate 5g, of which sugars 0g; Fat 15g, of which saturates 5g; Cholesterol 121mg; Calcium 39mg; Fibre 0.2g; Sodium 425mg.

Trout fillets with spinach and mushroom sauce

Field mushrooms form the basis of this rich sauce, served with trout that has been filleted
to make it easier to eat. Serve with new potatoes and braised baby corn and carrots.

Serves 4

4 medium-sized brown or rainbow
trout, filleted and skinned to make
8 fillets

For the spinach and mushroom sauce

75g/3oz/6 tbsp butter

¼ medium onion, chopped

225g/8oz mushrooms, chopped

300ml/½ pint/1¼ cups hot chicken
stock

225g/8oz frozen chopped spinach

10ml/2 tsp cornflour (cornstarch),
mixed to a paste with 15ml/1 tbsp
cold water

150ml/¼ pint/⅔ cup crème fraîche

grated nutmeg

salt and ground black pepper

new potatoes, and baby corn
braised with carrots, to serve

3 Stir the cornflour paste into the
mushroom mixture. Bring to the boil,
then simmer gently to thicken. Purée
the mixture. Add the crème fraîche and
season with salt, pepper and nutmeg.
Blend briefly, then scrape into a serving
jug (pitcher) and keep warm.

4 Melt the remaining butter in a large
non-stick frying pan. Season the trout
and cook for 6 minutes, turning once.
Serve with the sauce either poured over
or served separately, accompanied by
new potatoes and baby corn braised
with carrots

1 To make the sauce, melt two-thirds of
the butter in a frying pan and fry the
onion until soft. Add the mushrooms
and cook until the juices run.

2 Stir in the stock and the spinach and
cook, stirring, until the spinach has
thawed completely.

Energy 289kcal/1211kJ; Protein 33g; Carbohydrate 5g, of which sugars 0g; Fat 15g, of which saturates 5g; Cholesterol 121mg; Calcium 39mg; Fibre 0.2g; Sodium 425mg.

Trout with almonds

This quick and easy recipe for freshly caught trout combines the fish with almonds, a classic accompaniment handed down for generations in many different countries.

Serves 2

2 trout, about 350g/12oz each, cleaned

40g/1½oz/6 tbsp plain (all-purpose) flour

50g/2oz/¼ cup butter

25g/1oz/¼ cup flaked (sliced) almonds

30ml/2 tbsp dry white wine

salt and ground black pepper

1 Season the flour with salt and pepper and coat the trout. Melt half the butter in a large frying pan. When foaming, add the trout and cook for 6–7 minutes on each side, until the skin is golden and the flesh is opaque. Transfer to plates and keep hot.

2 Add the remaining butter to the pan and cook the almonds until just lightly browned. Add the wine to the pan and boil for 1 minute, stirring constantly, until slightly syrupy. Pour or spoon the sauce and almonds over the fish, and serve at once.

Energy 475kcal/1978kJ; Protein 39.2g; Carbohydrate 7.6g, of which sugars 0.8g; Fat 32.2g, of which saturates 12.4g; Cholesterol 187mg; Calcium 101mg; Fibre 1.2g; Sodium 249mg.

Tuna with garlic, tomatoes and herbs

Use fresh, rather than dried herbs if you wish. Serve with fried potatoes.

Serves 4

4 tuna steaks, about 2.5cm/1in thick (175–200g/6–7oz each)

30–45ml/2–3 tbsp olive oil

3–4 garlic cloves, finely chopped

60ml/4 tbsp dry white wine

3 ripe tomatoes, skinned, seeded and chopped

15–30ml/1–2 tbsp dried mixed herbs

salt and ground black pepper

fresh basil, to garnish

fried potaotes, to serve

1 Season the tuna steaks with salt and pepper. Set a heavy-based frying pan over a high heat. When very hot, add the oil and swirl to coat. Add the tuna steaks and press down gently, then reduce the heat to medium and cook for 6–8 minutes, turning once, until the steaks are tender but still slightly pink in the centre.

2 Transfer the tuna to a warmed serving plate and keep hot. Add the garlic to the pan and fry for a few seconds, then pour in the wine and boil rapidly until reduced by half. Add the tomatoes and herbs and cook for 2–3 minutes. Season with pepper and pour over the fish steaks. Garnish with fresh basil leaves and serve with fried potatoes..

Energy 322kcal/1352kJ; Protein 42g; Carbohydrate 3g, of which sugars 2g; Fat16g, of which saturates 3g; Cholesterol 49mg; Calcium 59mg; Fibre 0.8g; Sodium 188mg.

Whole baked salmon with watercress sauce

Served as an impressive centrepiece, this whole baked salmon would make a stunning focal point for a country dining table. Healthy and delicious, the dish is equally good served hot or cold. The peppery watercress sauce and fresh cucumber complement the salmon perfectly.

Serves 6–8

2–3kg/4½–6½lb salmon, cleaned, with head and tail left on

3–5 spring onions (scallions), thinly sliced

1 lemon, thinly sliced

1 cucumber, thinly sliced

salt and ground black pepper

sprigs of fresh dill, to garnish

lemon wedges, to serve

For the sauce

3 garlic cloves, chopped

200g/7oz watercress leaves, or rocket (arugula), finely chopped

40g/1½oz/¾ cup finely chopped fresh tarragon

300g/11oz/1¼ cups mayonnaise

15–30ml/1–2 tbsp lemon juice

200g/7oz/scant 1 cup unsalted butter

1 Preheat the oven to 180°C/350°F/ Gas 4. Rinse the salmon and lay it on a large piece of foil. Stuff the fish with the sliced spring onions and lemon. Season with salt and black pepper.

2 Loosely fold the foil around the fish and fold the edges over to seal. Bake in the preheated oven for about 1 hour.

3 Remove the fish from the oven and leave it to stand, still wrapped in the foil, for about 15 minutes. Then gently unwrap the foil parcel and set the salmon aside to cool.

4 When the fish has cooled, carefully lift it on to a large plate, still covered with lemon slices. Cover the fish tightly with clear film (plastic wrap) and chill for several hours in the refrigerator.

5 Remove the lemon slices from the top of the fish. Use a blunt knife to lift up the edge of the skin and carefully peel the skin away from the flesh, avoiding tearing the flesh. Pull out any fins at the same time. Carefully turn the salmon over and repeat on the other side. Leave the head on for serving, if you wish. Discard the skin.

Variation If you prefer to poach the fish rather than baking it, you will need to use a fish kettle. Place the salmon on the rack in the kettle. Cover the salmon completely with cold water, place the lid over to cover, and slowly bring to a simmer. Cook for 5–10 minutes per 450g/1lb until tender. The fish is cooked when pink and opaque.

6 To make the sauce, put the garlic, watercress, tarragon, mayonnaise and lemon juice in a food processor or bowl, and process or mix to combine.

7 Melt the butter, then add to the watercress mixture a little at a time, processing or stirring until the butter has been incorporated and the sauce is thick and smooth. Cover and chill.

8 Arrange the cucumber slices in overlapping rows along the length of the fish, so that they look like large fish scales. You can also slice the cucumber diagonally to produce longer slices for decoration. Trim the edges with scissors. Serve the fish, garnished with dill and lemon wedges, with the watercress sauce alongside.

Farmhouse tip Do not prepare the sauce too long before serving because it will discolour. Alternatively, add the watercress just before serving.

Energy 1044kcal/4323kJ; Protein 51.6g; Carbohydrate 1.4g, of which sugars 1.2g; Fat 92.4g, of which saturates 28.5g; Cholesterol 231mg; Calcium 135mg; Fibre 0.7g; Sodium 558mg.

Salmon in puff pastry

This is an elegant party dish, in which the rice and eggs makes the salmon go much further. With everything enclosed in crispy puff pastry it makes a meal in itself.

Serves 6

450g/1lb puff pastry, thawed if frozen

1 egg, beaten

3 hard-boiled eggs

90ml/6 tbsp single (light) cream

200g/7oz/1¾ cups cooked long grain rice

30ml/2 tbsp chopped fresh parsley

10ml/2 tsp chopped fresh tarragon

675g/1½lb fresh salmon fillets

40g/1½oz/3 tbsp butter

juice of ½ lemon

salt and ground black pepper

1 Preheat the oven to 190°C/375°F/Gas 5. Roll out two-thirds of the pastry into a large oval, measuring about 35cm/14in in length. Cut into a fish shape and place on a lightly greased baking sheet. Use the trimmings to make narrow strips. Brush one side of each strip with a little beaten egg and secure in place around the rim of the pastry to make a raised edge.

2 Prick the base all over with a fork, then bake for 8–10 minutes until the sides are well risen and the pastry is lightly golden. Leave to cool.

3 In a bowl, mash the hard-boiled eggs with the cream, then stir in the cooked rice. Add the parsley and tarragon and season. Spoon on to the pastry.

4 Cut the salmon into 2cm/¾in chunks. Melt the butter until it starts to sizzle, then add the salmon. Turn the pieces over in the butter so that they colour but do not cook through.

5 Remove from the heat and arrange the salmon pieces on top of the rice, piled in the centre. Stir the lemon juice into the butter in the pan, then spoon the mixture over the salmon pieces.

6 Roll out the remaining pastry, and cut out a semi-circle piece for head portion and a tail shape for the tail. Brush both pieces of pastry with a little beaten egg and place on top of the fish, pressing down firmly to secure. Score a criss-cross pattern on the tail.

7 Cut the remaining pastry into small circles and, starting from the tail end, arrange the circles in overlapping lines to represent scales. Add an extra one for an eye. Brush the whole fish shape with the remaining beaten egg.

8 Bake for 10 minutes, then reduce the temperature to 160°C/325°F/Gas 3 and cook for a further 15–20 minutes until the pastry is evenly golden. Slide the fish on to a serving plate and serve.

Farmhouse tip If the pastry is browning too quickly, cover it with foil during cooking. It is important to cook the pie for the recommended time, so the salmon is completely cooked.

Energy 668kcal/2782kJ; Protein 31g; Carbohydrate 36.6g, of which sugars 0.7g; Fat 45.3g, of which saturates 14g; Cholesterol 209mg; Calcium 98mg; Fibre 1.1g; Sodium 389mg.

Catch of the day fish stew

In coastal areas, fish suppers are based on what has been landed that morning. This recipe can be adapted to your favourite seafood, or to what you buy at the fishmongers.

Serves 4

30ml/2 tbsp olive oil

1 large onion, roughly chopped

1 leek, roughly chopped

2 garlic cloves, crushed

450g/1lb ripe tomatoes, roughly chopped

5ml/1 tsp tomato purée (paste)

1.3kg/3lb fish bones

a piece of pared orange peel

a few parsley stalks and fennel fronds

1 bay leaf

250ml/8fl oz/1 cup dry white wine

whisky or pastis, such as Pernod (optional)

1kg/2¼lb mixed fish fillets, such as salmon, sole and haddock, cut into chunks, and prepared shellfish

salt and ground black pepper

chopped fresh parsley, to garnish

2 Put in the fish bones, orange peel, herbs and wine, and add a little salt and ground black pepper. Then add enough water just to cover. Bring to a gentle boil, then reduce the heat and simmer for 30 minutes.

3 Strain the soup into a clean pan, pressing the juices out of the solid ingredients with the back of a spoon.

4 Bring the liquid back to the boil and check for seasoning and texture. If you like, add a splash of whisky or Pernod. The fish takes just minutes to cook so add the firmer, larger pieces first, such as monkfish or salmon and mussels in the shell, and end with delicate scallops or prawn (shrimp) tails. Do not allow the stew to boil once you add the fish.

5 Serve in warmed soup plates, garnished with chopped fresh parsley.

1 Heat the olive oil in a large pan on a medium heat, then sweat the onion and leek, stirring all the time, until soft. Add the garlic, tomatoes and tomato purée to the pan, and cook for 5 minutes, stirring occasionally.

Energy 341kcal/1432kJ; Protein 47.5g; Carbohydrate 6.5g, of which sugars 5.8g; Fat 7.8g, of which saturates 1.2g; Cholesterol 115mg; Calcium 53mg; Fibre 2.3g; Sodium 165mg.

Seafood and tomato casserole

There's no more pleasant way of spending an evening than sitting around the table and tucking into an excellent seafood stew, accompanied by freshly baked bread.

Serves 6

45ml/3 tbsp olive oil

2 large onions, chopped

1 green (bell) pepper, seeded and sliced

3 carrots, chopped

3 garlic cloves, crushed

30ml/2 tbsp tomato purée (paste)

2 x 400g/14oz cans chopped tomatoes

45ml/3 tbsp chopped fresh parsley

5ml/1 tsp chopped fresh thyme

15ml/1 tbsp shredded fresh basil leaves

120ml/4fl oz/½ cup dry white wine

450g/1lb raw, peeled and deveined, or cooked, peeled prawns (shrimp)

1.5kg/3–3½lb mussels or clams (in shells), or a mixture, thoroughly cleaned and scrubbed

900g/2lb halibut or other firm, white fish fillets, cut in 5cm/2in chunks

350ml/12fl oz/1½ cups fish stock

salt and ground black pepper

chopped fresh herbs, to garnish

1 Heat the oil in a flameproof casserole. Add the onions, green pepper, carrots and garlic and cook on a medium heat for about 5 minutes, until tender.

2 Stir in the tomato purée, canned tomatoes, herbs and wine. Bring to the boil, lower the heat and simmer for 20 minutes.

3 Add the prawns, mussels and/or clams, fish pieces and stock or water. Season with salt and pepper to taste, and bring back to the boil.

Farmhouse tip Serve the soup with some garlic mayonnaise spooned on top, if you like.

4 Simmer for 5–6 minutes, until the prawns turn pink, the fish flakes easily and the mussels and clams open, remove and discard any unopened shells. If using cooked prawns, add them for the last 2 minutes only. Serve the casserole in large soup plates, garnished with chopped herbs.

Energy 352Kcal/1483kJ; Protein 55g; Carbohydrate 9g, of which sugars 8.5g; Fat 9g, of which saturates 1.5g; Cholesterol 245g; Calcium 246mg; Fibre 2.6g; Sodium 412mg.

Cod and bean casserole with saffron

Another classic fish casserole this recipe has the unusual addition of butter beans, which add carbohydrates and bulk so that an entire meal is cooked in one pot. Serve with hunks of crusty bread and a crisp green side salad.

Serves 6–8

1 large red (bell) pepper

45ml/3 tbsp olive oil

4 rashers (strips) streaky (fatty) bacon, roughly chopped

4 garlic cloves, finely chopped

1 onion, sliced

10ml/2 tsp paprika

5ml/1 tsp smoked paprika (pimentón)

large pinch of saffron threads

400g/14oz can butter (lima) beans, drained and rinsed

600ml/1 pint/2½ cups fish stock

6 plum tomatoes, quartered

350g/12oz fresh skinned cod fillet, cut into large chunks

45ml/3 tbsp chopped fresh coriander (cilantro), plus a few sprigs to garnish

salt and ground black pepper

crusty bread, to serve

1 Preheat the grill (broiler) and line the pan with foil. Halve the red pepper and scoop out the seeds.

2 Place the red pepper, cut-side down, in the grill (broiler) pan and cook under a hot heat for about 10–15 minutes, until the skin is black and charred.

3 Put the pepper into a plastic bag, seal and leave for 10 minutes to steam, which will make the skin easier to remove.

4 Remove the pepper from the bag, peel and chop into large pieces.

5 Heat the olive oil in a pan, then add the chopped streaky bacon and the chopped garlic. Fry for about 2 minutes, then add the sliced onion.

6 Cover the pan and cook for about another 5 minutes until the onion is soft. Stir in the paprika and smoked paprika (pimentón), the saffron, and a generous amount of salt and pepper.

7 Stir the beans into the pan and add just enough of the stock to cover them. Bring to the boil and simmer, uncovered, for about 15 minutes, stirring occasionally to prevent it from sticking.

8 Stir in the chopped pepper and tomato quarters. Drop in the cubes of cod and bury them in the sauce.

9 Cover and simmer for 5 minutes until the fish is cooked. Stir in the chopped coriander.

10 Divide the stew equally between six to eight warmed soup plates or bowls, garnishing each one with the coriander sprigs. Serve with lots of crusty bread.

Farmhouse tip If you prefer to use dried beans, soak them in water overnight, rinse and then boil for 40–50 minutes, depending on the beans.

Energy 449kcal/1883kJ; Protein 44.5g; Carbohydrate 25.3g, of which sugars 3.9g; Fat 19.5g, of which saturates 3g; Cholesterol 84mg; Calcium 85mg; Fibre 9.8g; Sodium 403mg.

Cod, basil and tomato pie

A great dish to prepare in advance and then bake 30 minutes before you're ready to eat, this fish pie can be served with lots of fresh parsley and a mixed salad.

Serves 8

1kg/2lb smoked cod fillet

1kg/2lb cod fillet

600ml/1 pint milk

2 sprigs basil

1 sprig lemon thyme

75g/3oz butter

1 onion, peeled and chopped

75g/3oz plain (all-purpose) flour

30ml/2 tbsp tomato purée (paste)

2 tbsp chopped basil

12 medium-sized potatoes

50g/2oz butter

300ml/½ pint milk

salt and ground black pepper

1 tbsp chopped parsley

1 Place both kinds of fish in a roasting pan with the milk, 1.2 litres/2 pints water and herbs. Simmer for about 3–4 minutes. Leave to cool in the liquid for about 20 minutes.

2 Drain the fish, reserving the liquid for use in the sauce. Flake the fish, taking care to remove any skin and bone, which should be discarded.

3 Melt the butter in a pan, add the onion and cook for about 4 minutes until tender but not browned. Add the flour, tomato purée and half the basil.

4 Gradually add the reserved fish stock, adding a little more milk if necessary to make a fairly thin sauce. Bring to the boil, season, and add the remaining basil. Add the fish carefully and stir gently. Transfer to an ovenproof dish.

5 Boil the potatoes until tender. Add the butter and milk, and mash well. Add salt and pepper to taste.

6 Preheat the oven to 180°C/350°F/ Gas 4. Cover the fish mixture with the mashed potato, forking to create a pattern. Bake for 30 minutes. Serve with chopped parsley.

Energy 495kcal/3846kJ; Protein 71g; Carbohydrate 49g, of which sugars 3g; Fat 51g, of which saturates 5g; Cholesterol 269mg; Calcium 153mg; Fibre 3.3g; Sodium 1236mg.

Mixed fish gratin

Cheese sauce with fish is popular with everyone, from children to sophisticated adult diners; this gratin will please the whole family with its rich and creamy taste.

Serves 4

400g/14oz firm fish fillets, such as monkfish, salmon, turbot or cod

200g/7oz cooked shrimp and/or shelled cooked mussels, or peeled uncooked scampi (extra large shrimp)

1 litre/1¾ pints/4 cups fish stock

100g/3½oz/scant ½ cup butter

50g/2oz/½ cup plain (all-purpose) flour

100ml/3½fl oz/scant ½ cup dry white wine or dry vermouth

100ml/3½fl oz/scant ½ cup double (heavy) cream

115g/4oz/1 cup grated cheese (see Farmhouse tip)

45ml/3 tbsp chopped fresh parsley

salt and ground white pepper

crusty bread, to serve

Farmhouse tip Use any mixture of cheeses but a mixture of Gruyère and Parmesan cheese works well. Add a mixture of cheese and breadcrumbs for a crunchy topping if you wish.

1 Preheat the oven to 200°C/400°F/ Gas 6. Grease a 1.2 litre/2 pint/5 cup baking dish or four individual dishes.

2 Cut the fish fillets into even cubes, removing any stray bones.

3 Bring the fish stock to the boil in a large pan. Add the fish cubes, reduce the heat and poach for 2 minutes. If using scampi, poach them for 1 minute, until barely pink.

4 As soon as the fish pieces are cooked, lift them out with a slotted spoon and layer in the dish or dishes. Season and cover to keep warm. Reserve the fish stock.

5 Melt the butter in a pan. When the butter begins to foam, whisk in the flour and stir for 2 minutes.

6 Stirring all the time, add 500ml/ 17fl oz/generous 2 cups of the reserved fish stock, saving the rest to thin the sauce later if necessary. Add the white wine or vermouth and simmer for 3 minutes, stirring, then add the cream. Season and simmer for 1 minute more.

7 Remove from the heat and add the grated cheese, reserving 45ml/3 tbsp for the topping. Stir in the grey shrimp and/or mussels, with 15ml/1 tbsp of the parsley, and spoon evenly over the fish. Sprinkle with the reserved cheese.

8 Bake for 10–15 minutes, until the cheese melts and turns golden. Sprinkle with the remaining parsley and serve with crusty bread.

Energy 612Kcal/2541kJ; Protein 36g; Carbohydrate 10.5g, of which sugars 1g; Fat 45.3g, of which saturates 27.9g; Cholesterol 190mg; Calcium 358mg; Fibre 0.4g; Sodium 531mg.

Herbed halibut pastry layer

The mixed fresh herbs in this dish add their own special flavours to the creamy fish.

Serves 2

250g/9oz puff pastry

butter, for greasing

1 egg, beaten

1 small onion

1 tbsp fresh ginger, grated

7ml/½ tbsp oil

150ml/¼ pint/⅔ cup fish stock

15 ml/1 tbsp dry sherry

350g/12oz halibut fillet, cooked and flaked

225g/8oz crab meat

salt and white pepper

1 avocado, peeled and chopped, and tossed in the juice of 1 lime

1 mango, peeled

1 tbsp chopped mixed parsley, thyme and chives, to garnish

1 Roll the pastry out into a square 25 x 25 cm/10 x 10 in, trim the edges and place on a buttered baking sheet. Prick with a fork, then rest it in the refrigerator for 30 minutes. Preheat the oven to 230°C/450°F/Gas 8. Brush with beaten egg, and bake for 10 minutes.

2 Let the pastry cool for a few minutes, then cut it twice across in one direction and once in the other to make six pieces. Leave to cool completely.

3 Fry the onion and ginger in the oil until tender. Add the fish stock and sherry, and simmer for 5 minutes. Add the halibut and crab, and season. Chop the mango reserving a few slices for garnishing. Add the avocado and the mango to the fish.

4 Build up alternate layers of fish and pastry, starting and finishing with a piece of pastry. Serve with mango slices.

Energy 919kcal/1223kJ; Protein 10g; Carbohydrate 41g, of which sugars 2g; Fat 11g, of which saturates 11g; Cholesterol 2mg; Calcium 98mg; Fibre 3.9g; Sodium 289mg.

Salmon and ginger pie

You need to begin this delicious pie a day in advance to give the fish time to marinate.

Serves 4–6

800g/1¾lb middle cut of salmon

45ml/3 tbsp walnut oil

15ml/1 tbsp lime juice

2 tsp chopped fresh lemon thyme

30ml/2 tbsp white wine

400g/14oz puff pastry

50g/2oz/½ cup flaked (sliced) almonds

3–4 pieces preserved stem ginger in syrup, chopped

salt and ground black pepper

1 Split the salmon in half, remove all the bones and skin and divide into 4 fillets. Mix the oil, lime juice, thyme, wine and pepper, and pour over the fish. Cover and leave to marinate overnight in the refrigerator.

2 Divide the pastry into 2, one slightly larger than the other, and roll out – the smaller piece needs to take 2 of the salmon fillets, and the second piece needs to be about 5cm/2in larger all the way round.

3 Drain the fillets, and discard the marinade. Preheat the oven to 190°C/375°F/Gas 5.

4 Place 2 of the fillets on the smaller piece of pastry, and season. Add the almonds and ginger and cover with the other 2 fillets. Season again, cover with the second piece of pastry and seal. Brush with beaten egg and bake for 40 minutes. Serve warm.

Energy 623kcal/2493kJ; Protein 33g; Carbohydrate 29g, of which sugars 5g; Fat 43g, of which saturates 4g; Cholesterol 67mg; Calcium 92mg; Fibre 2.6g; Sodium 334mg.

Cod poached in onion sauce

Cod is often served with little preparation. Although it can be delicious in its simplest form, it sometimes deserves more sophisticated treatment, as in this recipe.

Serves 6

300ml/½ pint/1¼ cups olive oil	5ml/1 tsp chopped fresh celery leaves
2 onions, thinly sliced	15ml/1 tbsp chopped fresh parsley
3 garlic cloves, thinly sliced	300ml/½ pint/1¼ cups water
3 large well-flavoured tomatoes, roughly chopped	6 cod steaks
5ml/1 tsp sugar	juice of 1 lemon
5ml/1 tsp chopped fresh dill	salt and ground black pepper
5ml/1 tsp chopped fresh mint	extra dill, mint or parsley, to garnish

1 Heat the oil in a large pan and cook the onions until golden. Add the garlic, tomatoes, sugar, dill, mint, celery leaves and parsley. Pour in the water. Season, then simmer for 25 minutes, until the liquid has reduced by one-third.

2 Add the cod and simmer for 10–12 minutes, until just cooked. Remove from the heat and pour over the lemon juice. Cover and leave to stand for about 20 minutes, then arrange the cod in a dish and spoon the cooled sauce over the top. Serve at room temperature, or cold.

Energy 561kcal/2319kJ; Protein 19g; Carbohydrate 7g, of which sugars 5g; Fat 51g, of which saturates 7g; Cholesterol 46mg; Calcium 30mg; Fibre 1.4g; Sodium 132mg.

Leek and monkfish with thyme sauce

Monkfish is a well-known fish now, and widely available, thanks to its excellent flavour and firm texture. Radiccio leaves add a sharp flavour and some texture to this creamy dish.

Serves 4

1kg/2lb monkfish, cubed

75g/3oz/generous ⅓ cup butter

4 leeks, sliced

1 tbsp plain (all-purpose) flour

150ml/¼ pint/⅔ cup fish or vegetable stock

2 tsp finely chopped fresh thyme, plus extra to garnish

juice of 1 lemon

150ml/¼ pint/⅔ cup single (light) cream

salt and ground black pepper

radicchio, to garnish

1 Season the fish to taste. Melt a third of the butter in a frying pan, and fry the fish briefly. Set side.

2 In a small pan, melt another third of the butter, stir in the flour, and gradually add the stock, stirring all the time. As it thickens, add the thyme and lemon juice. Cover and keep warm.

3 Fry the leeks in the frying pan with the last of the butter until softened.

4 Return the monkfish to the pan with the leeks, and cook gently for a few minutes. Pour in the sauce, warm through, stirring to mix, and season to taste. Serve, garnished with thyme and serve with radicchio leaves.

Energy 369kcal/1554kJ; Protein 43g; Carbohydrate 9g, of which sugars 4g; Fat 18g, of which saturates 11g; Cholesterol 80mg; Calcium 105mg; Fibre 4.4g; Sodium 268mg.

Pan-fried garlic sardines

This rustic dish from rural Spain makes a perfect summer lunch, and could also be cooked on the barbeque. Use sprats or fresh anchovies instead if sardines are not available.

Serves 4

8 fresh sardines, cleaned and gutted

30ml/2 tbsp olive oil, plus extra for drizzling

4 garlic cloves

finely grated rind of 2 lemons

30ml/2 tbsp chopped fresh parsley

salt and ground black pepper

For the tomato bread

2 large ripe beefsteak tomatoes

8 slices crusty bread

1 Heat the oil in a frying pan and cook the garlic cloves until soft. Remove the garlic from the pan, and when cool, slice thinly and set aside.

2 Fry the sardines in the garlic-infused oil for 4–5 minutes. Sprinkle over the lemon rind, parsley and seasoning and keep warm.

3 Cut the tomatoes in half around the circumference. Toast the slices of bread on both sides.

4 Rub the cut side of the tomatoes on to the toast so that the juice and some of the flesh adheres. Discard the skins. Drizzle with olive oil and serve with a sardine and a few slices of garlic on top.

Energy 513Kcal/2149kJ; Protein 47.4g; Carbohydrate 27.9g, of which sugars 4.5g; Fat 24.1g, of which saturates 5.8g; Cholesterol 0mg; Calcium 279mg; Fibre 2g; Sodium 504mg.

Stuffed sardines

A sultana and pine nut stuffing takes simple sardines to a more sophisticated level. Add some fried potatoes and wilted greens for dinner, or serve as they are as an appetizer.

Serves 4

8 fresh sardines, cleaned and gutted

30ml/2 tbsp olive oil

75g/3oz/1½ cups breadcrumbs

50g/2oz/⅓ cup sultanas (golden raisins)

50g/2oz/⅔ cup pine nuts

50g/2oz can anchovy fillets, drained

60ml/4 tbsp chopped fresh parsley

1 onion, finely chopped

salt and ground black pepper

lemon wedges, to garnish

3 Stuff each sardine with the mixture. Close the fish firmly and closely pack them together in a single layer in an ovenproof dish.

4 Scatter any remaining filling over the sardines and drizzle with a little olive oil. Bake for 30 minutes and serve with lemon wedges.

1 Preheat the oven to 200°C/400°F/ Gas 6. Heat the oil in a frying pan and fry the breadcrumbs until golden.

2 Add the sultanas, pine nuts, anchovies, parsley, onion and seasoning to the breadcrumbs and stir fry for a further 2–3 minutes.

Energy 596kcal/2481kJ; Protein 36.1g; Carbohydrate 21.1g, of which sugars 9.8g; Fat 41.3g, of which saturates 6.8g; Cholesterol 0mg; Calcium 215mg; Fibre 1.3g; Sodium 467mg.

Seafood pie

A taste of the sea, a good fish pie includes both fresh and smoked fish – ideal farmhouse winter fare when the fishing fleets are hampered by gales and fresh fish is in short supply. Add shellfish such as mussels, and a few capers and dill, if you wish, for extra piquancy.

Serves 4–5

450g/1lb haddock or cod fillet

225g/8oz smoked haddock or cod

150ml/¼ pint/⅔ cup milk

150ml/¼ pint/⅔ cup water

1 slice of lemon

1 small bay leaf

a few fresh parsley stalks

For the sauce

25g/1oz/2 tbsp butter

25g/1oz/¼ cup plain (all-purpose) flour

5ml/1 tbsp lemon juice, or to taste

45ml/3 tbsp chopped fresh parsley

salt and ground black pepper

For the topping

450g/1lb potatoes, boiled in salted water and mashed

25g/1oz/2 tbsp butter

1 Preheat the oven to 190°C/375°F/ Gas 5. Rinse the fish, cut it into manageable pieces and put into a pan with the milk, water, lemon, bay leaf and parsley stalks.

2 Bring the fish slowly to the boil, then simmer gently for 15 minutes until tender. Strain and reserve 300ml/ ½ pint/1¼ cups of the cooking liquor. Leave the fish until cool, then flake the cooked flesh and discard the skin and bones. Set aside.

3 To make the sauce, melt the butter in a heavy pan, add the flour and cook for 1–2 minutes over low heat, stirring constantly.

4 Gradually add the reserved cooking liquor, stirring well to make a smooth sauce.

Variations Almost any mixture of prepared seafood can go into this pie, you can also use frozen. Cut the fish into roughly the same size, and large scallops or prawns (shrimp) in half.

Try adding other soft herbs such as chervil, dill or chives to the sauce, or a teaspoon of wholegrain mustard.

5 Simmer the sauce gently for about 1–2 minutes, then remove the pan from the heat and stir in the flaked fish, chopped parsley and lemon juice. Season to taste with salt and black pepper.

6 Turn into a buttered 1.75 litre/3 pint/ 7½ cup pie dish or shallow casserole, cover evenly with the mashed potato for the topping, smoothing with the back of a fork if necessary. Cut the butter into small pieces and dot the potato with the butter.

7 Cook the pie in the preheated oven for about 20 minutes, or until it is thoroughly heated through. The potato topping should be golden brown and crunchy.

8 Divide the pie among four or five warmed plates and serve immediately with a lightly cooked green vegetable, such as fresh broccoli florets.

Energy 336kcal/1413kJ; Protein 35.1g; Carbohydrate 24.3g, of which sugars 0.9g; Fat 11.6g, of which saturates 6.7g; Cholesterol 87mg; Calcium 45mg; Fibre 1.7g; Sodium 587mg.

Chunky salmon and potato fishcakes

The secret of a good fishcake is to make it with freshly prepared fish and potatoes, home-made breadcrumbs and plenty of interesting seasoning. This recipe makes a great mid-week supper, and you can serve the fishcakes with tartare sauce or garlic mayonnaise.

Serves 4

450g/1lb cooked salmon fillet

450g/1lb freshly cooked potatoes, mashed

25g/1oz/2 tbsp butter, melted

10ml/2 tsp wholegrain mustard

15ml/1 tbsp each chopped fresh dill and chopped fresh flat leaf parsley

grated rind and juice of ½ lemon

15g/½oz/1 tbsp plain (all-purpose) flour

1 egg, lightly beaten

150g/5oz/generous 1 cup dried breadcrumbs

60ml/4 tbsp sunflower oil

salt and ground white pepper

rocket (arugula) leaves and fresh chives, to garnish

lemon wedges, to serve

1 Flake the cooked salmon, watching carefully for and discarding any skin and bones. Place the flaked salmon in a bowl with the mashed potato, melted butter and wholegrain mustard. Mix well, then stir in the chopped fresh dill and parsley, lemon rind and juice. Season to taste.

2 Divide the mixture into eight portions and shape each into a ball, then flatten into a thick disc. Dip the fishcakes first in flour, then in egg and finally in breadcrumbs, coating evenly.

3 Heat the oil in a frying pan until very hot. Fry the fishcakes in batches until golden brown and crisp all over. As each batch is ready, drain on kitchen paper and keep hot.

4 Warm some plates and place two fishcakes on each one. Garnish with rocket leaves and chives, and serve with lemon wedges.

Variations Almost any fresh white or hot-smoked fish is suitable; smoked cod and haddock are particularly good.
  A mixture of smoked and unsmoked fish also works well, as does a mixture of salmon and chopped prawns (shrimp).

Energy 586kcal/2453kJ; Protein 29.8g; Carbohydrate 49.9g, of which sugars 3.2g; Fat 31g, of which saturates 7.2g; Cholesterol 117mg; Calcium 79mg; Fibre 1.3g; Sodium 266mg.

Grilled scallops with bacon

This simple recipe combines succulent scallops and crispy bacon with butter that has just begun to burn but not quite. This gives the dish a lovely nutty smell and a mouthwatering texture. It is delicious served with minted peas and sautéed potatoes.

Serves 4

12 rashers (strips) streaky (fatty) bacon

12 scallops

225g/8oz/1 cup unsalted butter

juice of 1 lemon

30ml/2 tbsp chopped fresh flat leaf parsley

ground black pepper

1 Preheat the grill (broiler) to high. Wrap a rasher of bacon around each scallop so it goes over the top and not round the side.

2 Cut the butter into chunks and put them into a small pan over a low heat.

3 Meanwhile grill (broil) the scallops with the bacon facing up so it protects the meat. The bacon fat will help to cook the scallops. This will take only a few minutes; once they are cooked, set aside and keep warm.

Farmhouse tip Put the scallops on to warmed plates just as the butter is coming to the right colour, then add the lemon juice, to keep the food at just the right temperature.

◄ **4** Allow the butter to turn a nutty brown colour, gently swirling it from time to time. Just as it is foaming and darkening, take off the heat and add the lemon juice so it bubbles and foams.

5 Place the scallops on warmed plates, garnish with plenty of chopped fresh parsley and pour the lemon butter over.

Energy 665kcal/2749kJ; Protein 24.4g; Carbohydrate 2.7g, of which sugars 0.6g; Fat 62g, of which saturates 34.7g; Cholesterol 189mg; Calcium 51mg; Fibre 0.5g; Sodium 1240mg.

Moules marinière

Serve this French country classic with a big bowl of chips (French fries) and chunks of bread to soak up the sauce. As an alternative, you could try cooking the mussels in light beer.

Serves 2

25g/1oz/2 tbsp butter

300ml/½ pint/1¼ cups dry white wine

1kg/2¼lb mussels, cleaned

45ml/3 tbsp chopped fresh parsley

salt and ground black pepper

Farmhouse tip Use line-grown mussels if possible. Tip them into the sink and rinse several times in cold water before draining well.

1 Heat the butter in a large pan until foaming, then pour in the wine. Bring to the boil.

2 Discard any open mussels that do not close when sharply tapped, and add the remaining ones to the pan.

3 Cover with a tight-fitting lid and cook over a medium heat for 4–5 minutes, shaking the pan every now and then. By this time, all the mussels should have opened. Discard any that are still closed.

4 Line a large sieve (strainer) with kitchen paper and strain the mussels and their liquid through it. Transfer the mussels to warmed serving bowls.

5 Pour the liquid into a small pan and bring to the boil. Season with salt and pepper and stir in the parsley. Pour over the mussels and serve immediately.

Energy 189kcal/799kJ; Protein 26.4g; Carbohydrate 2.4g, of which sugars 1.9g; Fat 3.1g, of which saturates 0.5g; Cholesterol 60mg; Calcium 308mg; Fibre 0.4g; Sodium 319mg.

Dressed crab with asparagus

Considerably cheaper than lobster, crab meat is just as juicy and flavourful, and at its best when asparagus comes into season. Try this crab dish with a splash of Tabasco sauce.

Serves 4

24 asparagus spears, washed

4 dressed crabs

30ml/2 tbsp mayonnaise

15ml/1 tbsp chopped fresh parsley

bread, dressed salad leaves and lemon wedges, to serve

1 Trim the bases off the asparagus. Boil in a pan of water for about 7 minutes, until tender. Plunge the spears into iced water to stop them from cooking further. Drain them when cold, and pat dry with kitchen paper.

2 Scoop out the white crab meat from the shells and claws and place it in a bowl. If you can't find fresh crabs, you can use the same amount of canned or frozen white crab meat. Ensure the meat is completely defrosted and place on to kitchen paper to dry.

3 Add the mayonnaise and chopped fresh parsley and combine with a fork.

4 Place the mixture into the crab shells and add six asparagus spears per serving. Serve with crusty bread and a handful of lightly dressed salad leaves.

Energy 207kcal/859kJ; Protein 19.5g; Carbohydrate 3g, of which sugars 2.8g; Fat 13g, of which saturates 1.9g; Cholesterol 72mg; Calcium 157mg; Fibre 2.6g; Sodium 540mg.

Prawn, chilli and potato stew

This quick and tasty shellfish stew makes the most of new potatoes that have plenty of flavour. You could add extra chilli if you prefer the dish really hot, then serve with a garden salad and crusty bread to mop up the sauce.

Serves 4

675g/1½lb small new potatoes

15g/½oz/½ cup coriander (cilantro)

350g/12oz jar tomato and chilli sauce

300g/11oz cooked peeled prawns (shrimp), thawed and drained if frozen

salt

1 Cook the potatoes in lightly salted, boiling water for 15 minutes, until tender. Drain and return to the pan.

2 Finely chop half the coriander and add to the pan with the tomato and chilli sauce and 90ml/6 tbsp water. Bring to the boil, reduce the heat, cover and allow to simmer gently for 5 minutes.

3 Stir in the prawns and heat until they are warmed through. Do not overheat the prawns or they will quickly shrivel, becoming tough and tasteless. Spoon into bowls and serve, sprinkled with the remaining coriander, torn into pieces.

Energy 218kcal/924kJ; Protein 16.9g; Carbohydrate 30.4g, of which sugars 5.4g; Fat 4.1g, of which saturates 0.7g; Cholesterol 146mg; Calcium 84mg; Fibre 2.9g; Sodium 171mg.

Seafood spaghetti

One of Italy's most famous country recipes, this tasty dish using carpet shell clams is an effortlessly easy supper or lunch dish that can be made with any small clams. It is lovely served with a green salad of peppery leaves.

Serves 4

1kg/2¼lb fresh clams

60ml/4 tbsp olive oil

45ml/3 tbsp chopped fresh flat leaf parsley

120ml/4fl oz/½ cup dry white wine

350g/12oz dried spaghetti

2 garlic cloves

salt and ground black pepper

1 Scrub the clams under cold running water, discarding any that are open or that do not close when sharply tapped against the work surface.

2 Heat half the oil in a large pan, add the clams and 15ml/1 tbsp of the parsley and cook over a high heat for a few seconds.

3 Pour in the wine, then cover tightly. Cook for 5 minutes, shaking the pan frequently, until the clams have opened. Meanwhile, cook the pasta in salted boiling water according to the instructions on the packet.

4 Using a slotted spoon, transfer the clams to a bowl, discarding any that have failed to open.

5 Strain the liquid and set it aside. Put eight clams in their shells to one side, then remove the rest from their shells.

6 Heat the remaining oil in the clean pan. Fry the garlic cloves until golden, crushing them with the back of a spoon. Remove the garlic with a slotted spoon and discard.

7 Add the shelled clams to the garlic-suffused oil in the pan, gradually add some of the strained liquid from the clams, then add plenty of pepper.

8 Cook for about 1–2 minutes, gradually adding a little more liquid as the sauce reduces. Add the remaining parsley and cook for 1–2 minutes more.

9 Drain the pasta, add it to the pan and toss well. Serve in individual dishes, carefully scooping the shelled clams from the bottom of the pan and placing some of them on top of each serving.

10 Garnish with the reserved clams in their shells, and serve immediately.

Energy 519kcal/2187kJ; Protein 30.9g; Carbohydrate 67.7g, of which sugars 3.4g; Fat 13.5g, of which saturates 2g; Cholesterol 84mg; Calcium 142mg; Fibre 3.2g; Sodium 1508mg.

Seafood risotto

Risotto is a rustic dish that can be adapted to take advantage of whatever is in season.

Serves 4

60ml/4 tbsp sunflower oil

1 onion, chopped

2 garlic cloves, crushed

225g/8oz/generous 1 cup arborio rice

105ml/7 tbsp white wine

1.5 litres/2½ pints/6 cups hot fish stock

350g/12oz raw seafood, such as prawns (shrimp), mussels, squid rings or clams, prepared according to type

grated rind of ½ lemon

30ml/2 tbsp tomato purée

15ml/1 tbsp chopped fresh parsley

salt and ground black pepper

1 Heat the oil in a heavy pan and fry the onion and garlic gently until soft. Add the rice and stir well to coat all the grains with oil. Pour in the wine and stir over a medium heat until it has been absorbed.

2 Ladle in 150 ml/¼ pint/⅔ cup of the hot stock and cook, stirring, until the liquid is absorbed. Continue stirring and adding stock, until half is left. This should take about 10 minutes.

3 Stir in the seafood and cook for 2–3 minutes. Add the remaining stock as before, until the rice is cooked. It should be quite creamy and the grains just tender. Stir in the lemon rind, tomato purée and parsley. Season with salt and pepper, and serve warm.

Energy 404Kcal/1693kJ; Protein 28.1g; Carbohydrate 56.3g, of which sugars 1.1g; Fat 3.9g, of which saturates 1.9g; Cholesterol 228mg; Calcium 200mg; Fibre 0.2g; Sodium 301mg.

Prawn skewers

These are delicious, whether grilled or cooked on the barbecue, ideal for a summer party.

Serves 4

900g/2 lb raw tiger prawns (jumbo shrimp), peeled

60ml/4 tbsp olive oil

45ml/3 tbsp vegetable oil

175g/6oz/1¼ cups very fine dry breadcrumbs

1 garlic clove, crushed

15ml/1 tbsp chopped fresh parsley

salt and ground black pepper

lemon wedges, to serve

1 Slit the prawns down their backs and remove the dark veins with the point of a knife. Rinse in cold water and pat dry. Mix the oils in a large bowl and add the prawns, turning them in the oil to coat evenly.

2 Add the breadcrumbs, garlic and parsley to the bowl, with salt and pepper to taste. Toss the oiled prawns in the mixture to coat them evenly.

3 Cover the bowl, and leave the prawns to marinate for 1 hour, during which time the breadcrumbs will adhere to them. Preheat the grill.

4 Thread the prawns on to four skewers, curling them up as you do so, so that the tail is skewered in the middle. Place the skewers in the grill pan and cook for about 2 minutes on each side, until golden. Serve with lemon wedges.

Energy 563kcal/2356kJ; Protein 45g; Carbohydrate 34g, of which sugars 1g; Fat 28g, of which saturates 4g; Cholesterol 439mg; Calcium 237mg; Fibre 2.5g; Sodium 859mg.

Poultry Dishes

There is probably nothing more closely identified with the farmyard than chicken,
and it is a universally favourite family food. Whether roasted, baked in a pie,
braised or casseroled, poultry dishes are always popular at the dinner table.
You will also find some delicious turkey recipes here, for everyday suppers or
special occasion and celebration meals.

Country chicken and mushroom pie

A family favourite, this classic farmhouse pie includes dried mushrooms, which give an intense mushroom flavour, topped with a melt-in-the-mouth pastry crust.

Serves 6

15g/½oz/¼ cup dried porcini mushrooms

50g/2oz/¼ cup butter

30ml/2 tbsp plain (all-purpose) flour

250ml/8fl oz/1 cup hot chicken stock

60ml/4 tbsp single (light) cream

1 onion, coarsely chopped

2 carrots, sliced

2 celery sticks, coarsely chopped

50g/2oz/¾ cup fresh mushrooms, quartered

450g/1lb cooked chicken meat, cubed

50g/2oz/½ cup fresh or frozen peas

salt and ground black pepper

beaten egg, to glaze

For the pastry

225g/8oz/2 cups plain (all-purpose) flour

1.5ml/¼ tsp salt

115g/4oz/½ cup cold butter, diced

65g/2½oz/⅓ cup white vegetable fat, diced

60–120ml/4–8 tbsp chilled water

1 To make the pastry, sift the flour and salt into a bowl. Cut or rub in the butter and white vegetable fat until the mixture resembles fine breadcrumbs. Sprinkle with 90ml/6 tbsp chilled water and mix until the dough holds together. If the dough is too crumbly, add a little more water, 15ml/1 tbsp at a time.

2 Gather the dough into a ball and flatten it into a round. Wrap and chill for at least 30 minutes.

3 To make the filling, put the mushrooms in a bowl. Cover with hot water and soak for 30 minutes. Drain in a muslin- (cheesecloth-) lined sieve (strainer), then dry on kitchen paper. Preheat the oven to 190°C/375°F/Gas 5.

4 Melt half of the butter in a heavy pan. Whisk in the flour and cook until bubbling, whisking constantly. Add the hot stock and whisk over a medium heat until the mixture boils. Cook for 2–3 minutes, then whisk in the cream. Season to taste, and set aside.

5 Heat the remaining butter in a non-stick frying pan and cook the onion and carrots over a low heat for 5 minutes. Add the celery and fresh mushrooms and cook for 5 minutes more. Stir in the cooked chicken, peas and drained porcini mushrooms.

6 Add the chicken mixture to the hot cream sauce and stir to mix. Adjust the seasoning if necessary. Spoon the mixture into a 2.5 litre/4 pint/2½ quart oval baking dish.

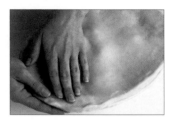

7 Roll out the pastry to a thickness of about 3mm/⅛in. Cut out an oval 2.5cm/1in larger all around than the dish. Lay the pastry over the filling. Gently press around the edge of the dish to seal, then trim off the excess pastry. Crimp the edge of the pastry by pushing the forefinger of one hand into the edge and, using the thumb and forefinger of the other hand, pinch the pastry. Continue all round the pastry edge.

8 Press together the pastry trimmings and roll out again. Cut out mushroom shapes with a knife and stick them on to the pastry lid with beaten egg. Glaze the lid with egg and cut several slits in the pastry to allow the steam to escape. Bake the pie for about 30 minutes, until the pastry has browned. Serve hot.

Energy 576kcal/2403kJ; Protein 23.8g; Carbohydrate 39.6g, of which sugars 4.7g; Fat 36.9g, of which saturates 20.3g; Cholesterol 127mg; Calcium 104mg; Fibre 3.1g; Sodium 334mg.

Traditional roast chicken with herb stuffing

A staple of traditional country cooking, a simply roasted free-range chicken with herbs and home-made stuffing is hard to beat. Serve with roast potatoes, sausages, rolled bacon and seasonal vegetables, along with a fruit jelly such as cranberry sauce or elderberry jelly.

Serves 6

1 large chicken, about 1.8kg/4lb, with giblets and neck if possible

1 small onion, sliced

1 small carrot, sliced

small bunch of parsley and thyme

15g/½oz/1 tbsp butter

30ml/2 tbsp chicken fat or oil

6 rashers (strips) of streaky (fatty) bacon

salt and ground black pepper

For the stuffing and gravy

1 onion, finely chopped

50g/2oz/¼ cup butter

150g/5oz/2½ cups fresh white breadcrumbs

15ml/1 tbsp fresh chopped parsley

15ml/1 tbsp fresh chopped mixed herbs, such as thyme, marjoram and chives

finely grated rind and juice of ½ lemon

1 small egg, lightly beaten (optional)

15ml/1 tbsp plain (all-purpose) flour

1 Remove the giblets from the chicken; also remove the piece of fat which is found just inside the vent and put this fat into a roasting pan – it can be rendered down and used when cooking the roast potatoes. Wipe out the inside of the bird thoroughly. Separate the liver from the rest of the giblets, chop it and set it aside to use in the gravy.

2 Put the giblets and the neck into a pan with the sliced onion and sliced carrot, the bunch of parsley and thyme and a good sprinkling of salt and pepper. Add enough cold water to cover generously, bring to the boil and leave to simmer gently for about 1 hour. Strain the chicken stock and discard the giblets. Preheat the oven to 200°C/400°F/Gas 6.

3 Meanwhile, make the herb stuffing: cook the chopped onion in the butter in a large pan over a low heat without colouring for a few minutes until it is just beginning to soften.

4 Remove from the heat, and add the breadcrumbs, fresh herbs and grated lemon rind. Mix thoroughly. Mix in the lemon juice, beaten egg, if using, and salt and pepper. (The egg will bind the stuffing and make it firmer when cooked, but it can be omitted if you prefer a lighter, more crumbly texture.)

5 Spoon the stuffing into the neck cavity of the chicken, without packing it in too tightly, and secure the opening with a small skewer. Spread the breast with the butter, then put the chicken fat or oil into a roasting pan and lay the bird in it. Season and lay the bacon rashers over the top of the bird to protect it in the oven.

6 Weigh the stuffed chicken and work out the cooking time at 20 minutes per 450g/1lb plus 20 minutes more, then put into the preheated oven. After 20 minutes, reduce the temperature to 180°C/350°F/Gas 4 for another 45–60 minutes, or until cooked. Test by inserting a sharp knife between the body and thigh: if the juices run clear with no hint of blood, it is cooked.

7 Transfer the cooked chicken to a serving dish and allow it to rest for 10 minutes while you make the gravy.

8 To make the gravy, pour off the excess fat from the roasting pan, then add the finely chopped liver and stir over a low heat for 1 minute, or until it has turned light brown. Sprinkle in just enough flour to absorb the remaining chicken fat and cook gently, stirring to blend, for 1 or 2 minutes. Gradually add some of the giblet stock, scraping the pan to dissolve the residues and stirring well to make a smooth gravy.

9 Bring to the boil, stirring, gradually adding more stock until the consistency is as you like it. Adjust the seasoning, and then pour into a heated sauceboat to hand round separately.

10 Carve the chicken. Serve on heated plates with the herb stuffing and gravy.

Energy 562kcal/2342kJ; Protein 40.9g; Carbohydrate 23.2g, of which sugars 2.7g; Fat 34.5g, of which saturates 11.9g; Cholesterol 216mg; Calcium 72mg; Fibre 1.5g; Sodium 381mg.

Lemon and garlic pot roast chicken

Pot-roasting is at the heart of rustic cooking. Easy to prepare and slow-cooked, this is a great family dish that can simmer away happily in the oven.

Serves 4

30ml/2 tbsp olive oil

25g/1oz/2 tbsp butter

175g/6oz/1 cup smoked lardons, or roughly chopped streaky (fatty) bacon

8 garlic cloves, peeled

4 onions, quartered

10ml/2 tsp plain (all-purpose) flour

600ml/1 pint/2½ cups chicken stock

2 lemons, thickly sliced

45ml/3 tbsp chopped fresh thyme

1 chicken, about 1.3–1.6kg/3–3½lb

2 x 400g/14oz cans flageolet, cannellini or haricot (navy) beans, drained and rinsed

salt and ground black pepper

1 Preheat the oven to 190°C/375°F/ Gas 5. Heat the oil and butter in a flameproof casserole that is large enough to hold the chicken with a little room around the sides. Add the lardons and cook until golden. Remove with a slotted spoon and drain on kitchen paper.

2 Add the garlic and onions and brown over a high heat. Stir in the flour, then the stock. Return the lardons to the pan with the lemon, thyme and seasoning.

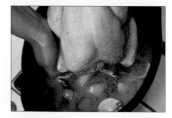

3 Bring to the boil, stirring constantly until thickened, then place the chicken on top. Season well. Transfer the casserole to the oven. Cook for 1 hour, basting the chicken once or twice during cooking to ensure it stays moist.

4 Baste the chicken again. Stir the beans into the casserole and return it to the oven for a further 30 minutes, or until the chicken is cooked through and tender. Carve the chicken into thick slices and serve with the beans.

Energy 887kcal/3696kJ; Protein 62.5g; Carbohydrate 45.5g, of which sugars 12.9g; Fat 51.7g, of which saturates 16g; Cholesterol 256mg; Calcium 187mg; Fibre 13.9g; Sodium 1519mg.

Chicken baked with forty cloves of garlic

Don't worry about the amount of garlic in this dish, it becomes soft, sweet and fragrant.
The dough seal is an old-fashioned way of making sure the chicken stays moist and tender.

Serves 4–5

5–6 whole heads of garlic

15g/½oz/1 tbsp butter

45ml/3 tbsp olive oil

1.8–2kg/4–4½lb chicken

150g/5oz/1¼ cups plain (all-purpose)
flour, plus 5ml/1 tsp

75ml/5 tbsp white port, or other
white, fortified wine

2–3 fresh tarragon or rosemary sprigs

30ml/2 tbsp crème fraîche

few drops of lemon juice

salt and ground black pepper

3 Pour the remaining oil over the
chicken and season to taste with salt
and pepper. Rub all over to coat.

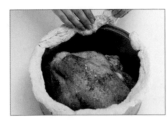

4 Mix the main batch of flour with
enough water to make a dough. Roll
into a sausage and press around the rim
of the pot, then press on the lid, folding
the dough up and over it to create a
tight seal. Cook for 1½ hours.

5 Lift off the lid and remove the chicken
and whole garlic to a serving platter.
Remove the herb sprigs, then place the
casserole on the stove and whisk the
garlic cloves in with the juices.

6 Add the crème fraîche to the sauce,
with a little lemon juice to taste. Carve
the chicken, and serve with the whole
garlic heads and the sauce.

1 Separate three of the heads of garlic
into cloves and peel. Remove the first
layer of papery skin from the remaining
heads of garlic and leave whole.
Preheat the oven to 180°C/350°F/Gas 4.

2 Heat the butter and 15ml/1 tbsp of the
olive oil in a flameproof casserole that is
just large enough to take the chicken
and garlic. Add the chicken and cook
over a medium heat, turning frequently,
for 10 minutes, until it is browned all
over. Sprinkle in 5ml/1 tsp flour and
cook for 1 minute. Add the port or wine.
Tuck in the whole heads of garlic and
the peeled cloves with the herb sprigs.

Energy 787kcal/3276kJ; Protein 51.3g; Carbohydrate 33.2g, of which sugars 1g; Fat 50.6g, of which saturates 14.5g; Cholesterol 248mg; Calcium 77mg; Fibre 2.2g; Sodium 212mg.

Chicken and corn casserole

The traditional way to serve this American farmhouse stew is with scones (biscuits); use the recipe for cobbler topping opposite, and bake in the oven if you wish to do the same.

Serves 6

1.75kg/4lb chicken, cut into pieces

paprika

30ml/2 tbsp olive oil

25g/1oz/2 tbsp butter

450g/1lb onions, chopped

1 green or yellow (bell) pepper, cored, seeded and chopped

400g/14oz can chopped tomatoes

250ml/8fl oz/1 cup white wine

475ml/16floz/2 cups chicken stock

45ml/3 tbsp chopped fresh parsley

2.5ml/$\frac{1}{2}$ tsp Tabasco sauce

15ml/1 tbsp Worcestershire sauce

275g/10oz/2 cups corn kernels (fresh, frozen, or drained canned)

150g/5oz/1 cup broad (fava) beans (fresh or frozen)

20g/$\frac{3}{4}$oz/3 tbsp plain (all-purpose) flour

salt and ground black pepper

flat leaf parsley sprigs, to garnish

1 Rinse the chicken pieces under cold water and pat dry with kitchen paper. Sprinkle lightly with salt and paprika.

2 Heat the oil and butter in a large, heavy-based saucepan. Add the chicken pieces and fry until golden brown on all sides. Remove with tongs and set aside.

3 Reduce the heat to low and cook the onions and pepper for 8–10 minutes, until softened. Stir in the tomatoes, wine, stock, parsley and sauces. Turn up the heat and bring to the boil.

4 Return the chicken to the pan, pushing it down in to the sauce. Cover, reduce the heat and simmer for 30 minutes, stirring occasionally.

5 Add the corn and beans. Partly cover and cook for 30 minutes more.

6 Mix the flour with a little water to make a paste. Gradually add 175ml/ 6fl oz/$\frac{3}{4}$ cup of the hot liquid from the pan. Stir this mixture into the stew and season with salt and pepper. Cook for 5–8 minutes more, stirring occasionally. Garnish and serve.

Energy 370kcal/1549kJ; Protein 32g; Carbohydrate 23g, of which sugars 9g; Fat 18g, of which saturates 5g; Cholesterol 115mg; Calcium 72mg; Fibre 4.3g; Sodium 412mg.

Chicken and mushroom cobbler

There's something very homely about a cobbler, with its scone topping and satisfying filling. Adding wild mushrooms enriches the flavour but button mushrooms are fine.

Serves 4

60ml/4 tbsp vegetable oil

1 onion, chopped

1 celery stick, sliced

1 small carrot, peeled and diced

3 skinless, chicken breast portions

450g/1lb/4 cups mixed field (portabello) mushrooms and wild mushrooms, sliced

40g/1½oz/6 tbsp plain (all-purpose) flour

500ml/18fl oz/2¼ cups hot chicken stock

10ml/2 tsp Dijon mustard

30ml/2 tbsp medium sherry

10ml/2 tsp wine vinegar

salt and ground black pepper

For the cobbler topping

275g/10oz/2½ cups self-rising flour

pinch of celery salt

pinch of cayenne pepper

115g/4oz/½ cup butter, diced

50g/2oz/½ cup grated Cheddar cheese

150ml/¼ pint/⅔ cup cold water

1 beaten egg, to glaze

1 Preheat the oven to 200°C/400°F/ Gas 6. Heat the oil in a large pan and fry the onion, celery and carrot gently for 8–10 minutes, to soften. Cube the chicken, then add to the pan and cook briefly. Add the mushrooms, fry until the juices run, then stir in the flour.

2 Remove the pan from the heat and gradually stir in the stock. Return to the heat, and simmer to thicken, stirring all the time. Stir in the mustard, sherry, vinegar and seasoning.

3 To make the topping, sift the flour, celery salt and cayenne into a bowl. Rub in the butter and half the cheese until the mixture resembles coarse breadcrumbs. Add the water and combine without over-mixing.

4 Turn the dough on to a floured board, form it into a round and flatten to a thickness of about 1cm/½in. Cut out as many 5cm/2in shapes as you can, using a cutter.

5 Transfer the chicken mixture to a 1.2 litre/2 pint/5 cup pie dish, then overlap the cobbler around the edge. Brush with beaten egg, scatter with the remaining cheese and bake for 25–30 minutes until the topping has risen well.

Energy 828kcal/3463kJ; Protein 38g; Carbohydrate 66g, of which sugars 5g; Fat 48g, of which saturates20g; Cholesterol 197mg; Calcium 395mg; Fibre 7.0g; Sodium 1064mg.

Chicken braised in red wine

A quintessential French country casserole, this dish is a fricassée made with a cock bird, cooked long and slow in red wine to tenderize the meat.

2 Use a slotted spoon to transfer the cooked ingredients to a plate. Halve the chicken breast portions, then brown on all sides, along with the thighs, in the pan. Return the shallots, garlic, mushrooms and bacon to the casserole and pour in the red wine.

3 Tie the ingredients for the bouquet garni in a bundle in a small piece of muslin (cheesecloth) and add to the casserole. Bring to the boil, reduce the heat and cover the casserole, then simmer for about 35 minutes.

4 To make the beurre manié, cream the butter and flour together in a small bowl, using your fingers or a spoon to make a smooth paste.

5 Add small lumps of this paste to the bubbling casserole, stirring well until each piece has melted into the liquid before adding the next. When all the paste has been added, bring back to the boil and simmer for 5 minutes.

6 Check the seasoning, remove the bouquet garni and serve, garnished with chopped fresh parsley and accompanied by boiled potatoes.

Farmhouse tip Tie the bouquet garni with string to the handle of the casserole, if you wish, to make it easier to find and discard before serving.

Serves 6

45ml/3 tbsp light olive oil

12 shallots

225g/8oz rindless streaky (fatty) bacon rashers (strips), chopped

3 garlic cloves, finely chopped

225g/8oz small mushrooms, halved

3 boneless chicken breast portions

6 boneless chicken thighs

1 bottle red wine

salt and ground black pepper

45ml/3 tbsp chopped fresh parsley, to garnish

For the bouquet garni

3 sprigs each of fresh parsley, thyme and sage

1 bay leaf

4 peppercorns

For the beurre manié

25g/1oz/2 tbsp butter, softened

25g/1oz/¼ cup plain (all-purpose) flour

1 Heat the oil in a large casserole, add the shallots and cook for 5 minutes. Increase the heat, add the bacon, garlic and halved mushrooms and cook for 10 minutes more, stirring frequently.

Energy 496kcal/2067kJ; Protein 39.2g; Carbohydrate 5g, of which sugars 1.8g; Fat 26.9g, of which saturates 8.5g; Cholesterol 153mg; Calcium 47mg; Fibre 1.1g; Sodium 600mg.

Country chicken casserole

Tender chunks of root vegetables are the ideal winter comfort food. When cooked slowly in a casserole with chicken, the natural sugars in the vegetables become mellow and intense.

Serves 4

350g/12oz onions

350g/12oz leeks

225g/8oz carrots

450g/1lb swede (rutabaga)

30ml/2 tbsp oil

4 chicken portions, about 900g/2lb total weight

115g/4oz/½ cup green lentils

475ml/16fl oz/2 cups chicken stock

300ml/½ pint/1¼ cups apple juice

10ml/2 tsp cornflour (cornstarch)

45ml/3 tbsp crème fraîche

10ml/2 tsp wholegrain mustard

30ml/2 tbsp chopped fresh tarragon

salt and ground black pepper

fresh tarragon sprigs, to garnish

3 Add the onions to the casserole and cook for 5 minutes, stirring, until they begin to soften. Add the leeks, carrots, swede and lentils to the casserole and stir over a medium heat for 2 minutes.

4 Return the chicken to the pan, then add the stock, apple juice, salt and pepper. Bring to the boil and cover. Reduce the heat and cook for 50–60 minutes, until tender.

5 Blend the cornflour with about 30ml/2 tbsp water to make a paste, then add to the casserole with the crème fraîche, mustard and tarragon.

6 Adjust the seasoning to taste, then simmer the casserole gently for about 2 minutes, stirring constantly, until thickened slightly. Garnish with the tarragon sprigs, and then serve in individual bowls.

1 Prepare the onions, leeks, carrots and swede, and roughly chop them into even pieces.

2 Heat the oil in a large flameproof casserole. Season the chicken portions with plenty of salt and pepper and brown them in the hot oil until golden, in batches if necessary. Remove from the pan and drain on kitchen paper.

Energy 477kcal/2010kJ; Protein 46.8g; Carbohydrate 45.7g, of which sugars 24.9g; Fat 13.2g, of which saturates 4.5g; Cholesterol 118mg; Calcium 151mg; Fibre 8.1g; Sodium 141mg.

Bacon, chicken and leek pudding

Old-fashioned suet puddings were once a favourite way to make food go further. Serve this with seasonal vegetables or a green salad tossed lightly in an oil and vinegar dressing.

Serves 4

200g/7oz unsmoked lean, rindless bacon, preferably in one piece

400g/14oz skinless boneless chicken pieces, preferably thigh meat

2 small or medium leeks, finely chopped

30ml/2 tbsp finely chopped fresh parsley

175g/6oz/1¼ cups self-raising (self-rising) flour

75g/3oz/½ cup shredded suet (US chilled, grated shortening)

120ml/4fl oz chicken or vegetable stock, or water

ground black pepper

butter for greasing

1 Cut the bacon and chicken into bitesize pieces into a large bowl. Mix them with the leeks and half the parsley. Season with black pepper.

2 Sift the flour into a separate large bowl and stir in the suet and the remaining parsley. With a round-bladed knife, stir in sufficient cold water to make a soft dough.

3 On a lightly floured surface, roll out the dough to a circle measuring about 33cm/13in across. Cut out one quarter of the circle (starting from the centre, like a wedge), roll up and reserve.

4 Lightly butter a 1.2 litre/2 pint pudding bowl. Use the rolled out dough to line the buttered bowl, pressing the cut edges together to seal them and allowing the pastry to overlap the top of the bowl slightly.

5 Spoon the bacon and chicken mixture into the lined bowl, packing it neatly and taking care not to split the pastry. Pour the chicken or vegetable stock over the bacon mixture, making sure it does not overfill the bowl.

6 Roll out the reserved pastry into a circle to form a lid and lay it over the filling, pinching the edges together to seal them well. Cover with baking parchment (pleated in the centre to allow the pudding to rise) and then a large sheet of foil (again pleated at the centre). Tuck the edges under and press them tightly to the sides of the bowl until well sealed.

7 Steam the pudding over boiling water for about 3½ hours. Check the water level occasionally. Uncover the pudding, slide a knife around the sides and turn out on to a warmed serving plate.

Energy 535kcal/2236kJ; Protein 28.2g; Carbohydrate 39.4g, of which sugars 2.9g; Fat 31.3g, of which saturates 14.8g; Cholesterol 86mg; Calcium 111mg; Fibre 4g; Sodium 999mg.

Hen in a pot with parsley sauce

Every country family used to keep hens, and the older ones were destined for the table. As they are harder to find nowadays, a boiling fowl can be replaced with a large roasting bird.

Serves 6

1.6–1.8kg/3½–4lb boiling fowl

½ lemon, sliced

small bunch of parsley and thyme

675g/1½lb carrots, cut into chunks

12 shallots, peeled

For the sauce

50g/2oz/¼ cup butter

50g/2oz/½ cup plain (all-purpose) flour

15ml/1 tbsp lemon juice

60ml/4 tbsp finely chopped fresh parsley

150ml/¼ pint/⅔ cup milk

salt and ground pepper

fresh parsley sprigs, to garnish

1 Put the chicken into a large pan with enough water to cover. Add the sliced lemon and parsley and thyme, and season well with salt and pepper. Cover the pan and bring to the boil, then reduce the heat and simmer over a gentle heat for 2½ hours, turning several times during cooking.

2 Add the carrots and whole shallots to the pot and cook for another 30–40 minutes, or until the chicken and the vegetables are tender.

3 Using a slotted spoon, lift the chicken on to a serving dish, arrange the vegetables around it and keep warm. Remove the herbs and lemon slices from the cooking liquor and discard.

4 Bring the liquor back to the boil and boil, uncovered, to reduce the liquid by about a third. Strain and leave to settle for 1–2 minutes, then skim the fat.

5 Melt the butter in a pan, add the flour and cook, stirring, for 1 minute.

6 Gradually stir the stock into the butter and flour mixture, and bring to the boil. Add the lemon juice, parsley and the milk. Adjust the seasoning and simmer the sauce for another 1–2 minutes.

7 To serve, pour a little of the sauce over the chicken and the carrots and shallots, then garnish with a few sprigs of parsley. Pour the rest of the sauce into a heated sauceboat and hand round separately.

Energy 509Kcal/2114kJ; Protein 36.2g; Carbohydrate 20.1g, of which sugars 12.2g; Fat 31.9g, of which saturates 11.4g; Cholesterol 195mg; Calcium 109mg; Fibre 4g; Sodium 214mg.

Devilled chicken

A 19th-century way to use up cooked meats, 'devilling' adds spicy seasoning to pep up leftovers. This recipe uses the technique to give freshly prepared chicken a pungent flavour.

2 In a large bowl, mix the oil, chutney, Worcestershire sauce, mustard, cayenne, ginger and seasoning. Add the chicken pieces and toss them in the mixture, until well coated. Cover and leave to stand for 1 hour.

3 Preheat the oven to 200°C/400°F/ Gas 6. Arrange the chicken pieces in a single layer on a non-stick baking sheet, brushing them with any extra sauce.

4 Put the chicken pieces into the hot oven and cook for about 35 minutes until they are a crisp, deep golden brown and cooked through (test them by inserting a small sharp knife or skewer – the juices should run clear). Turn them over once or twice during cooking to encourage even browning.

Serves 4–6

6 chicken drumsticks

6 chicken thighs

15ml/1 tbsp oil

45ml/3 tbsp chutney, finely chopped

15ml/1 tbsp Worcestershire sauce

10ml/2 tsp English (hot) mustard

1.5ml/¼ tsp cayenne pepper

1.5ml/¼ tsp ground ginger

salt and ground black pepper

1 With a sharp knife, make several deep slashes in the chicken pieces, cutting down to the bone.

Variation Instead of chutney, try using the same quantity of tomato ketchup or mushroom ketchup, or a teaspoon of finely chopped fresh chilli.

Energy 299kcal/1254kJ; Protein 47.4g; Carbohydrate 0.3g, of which sugars 0.3g; Fat 12g, of which saturates 2.6g; Cholesterol 236mg; Calcium 41mg; Fibre 0.6g; Sodium 207mg.

Chicken with sloe gin and juniper

Juniper is found in gin, and this dish is flavoured with both sloe gin and juniper. Sloe gin is easy to make and has a wonderful flavour; the recipe can be found on page 494.

Serves 8

2 tbsp butter

30ml/2 tbsp sunflower oil

8 chicken breast fillets, skinned

350g/12 oz carrots, cooked

1 clove garlic, peeled and crushed

1 tbsp finely chopped parsley

60ml/2fl oz/¼ cup chicken stock

60ml/2fl oz/¼ cup red wine

60ml/2fl oz/¼ cup sloe gin

1 tsp crushed juniper berries

salt and ground black pepper

a bunch of basil, to garnish

◀ **1** Melt the butter with the oil in a pan, and sauté the chicken fillets until they are browned on all sides.

2 In a food processor, combine all the remaining ingredients except the basil, and blend to a smooth purée. If the mixture seems too thick, add a little more red wine.

3 Put the chicken in a pan, pour the sauce over the top and cook until the chicken for 15 minutes, until it is cooked through. Adjust the seasoning and serve garnished with basil.

Energy 210kcal/82kJ; Protein 30g; Carbohydrate 4g, of which sugars 3g; Fat 8g, of which saturates 3g; Cholesterol 95mg; Calcium 19mg; Fibre 1.2g; Sodium 178mg.

Puff pastry chicken pies

These versatile little pies can be filled with different kinds of meat. Although chicken is the most popular, they are also good with a mixture of game and chicken, or with fish or shellfish. They make a tempting afternoon snack, or you could have two or three of them, either hot or cold, with a refreshing salad for a delicious light lunch.

Makes about 12

1 chicken, weighing 1.6–2kg/3½–4½lb

45ml/3 tbsp olive oil

1 sausage, weighing about 250g/9oz

150g/5oz bacon

1 garlic clove

10 black peppercorns

1 onion, stuck with 2 cloves

a bunch of parsley, chopped

4 thyme or marjoram sprigs

juice of 1 lemon or 60ml/4 tbsp white wine vinegar

butter, for greasing

500g/1¼lb puff pastry, thawed if frozen

plain (all-purpose) flour, for dusting

2 egg yolks, lightly beaten

salt

1 Cut the chicken into pieces. Heat the oil in a large, heavy pan. Add the chicken, in batches if necessary, and cook over a medium-low heat, turning occasionally, for about 10 minutes, until golden brown on all sides. Place all the pieces back in the pan.

2 Add the sausage, bacon, garlic, peppercorns, onion, parsley, thyme and lemon juice or vinegar. Pour in just enough water to cover and bring to the boil. Lower the heat, cover and simmer for 45–50 minutes, or until tender.

3 Remove all the meat from the stock with a slotted spoon. Then return the stock to the heat and cook, uncovered, until slightly reduced. Strain the stock into a bowl and season with salt to taste.

4 Remove and discard the chicken skin and bones and cut the meat into small pieces. Cut the sausage and bacon into small pieces. Mix all the meat together. Preheat the oven to 200°C/400°F/Gas 6. Grease a 12-cup muffin tin (pan) with butter.

5 Roll out the pastry thinly on a lightly floured surface and stamp out 12 rounds with a 7.5cm/3in cutter.

6 Gather the trimmings together and roll out thinly again, then stamp out 12 rounds with a 6cm/2½in cutter. Place the larger rounds in the cups of the prepared tin, pressing the pastry to the side with your thumb, and divide the meat among them.

7 Spoon in a little of the stock, then brush the edges with beaten egg yolk and cover with the smaller rounds, pinching the edges to seal.

8 Brush the remaining egg yolk over the top to glaze and make a small hole in the centre of each pie with a wooden cocktail stick (toothpick).

9 Bake for 15–25 minutes, until golden brown. Remove from the oven and leave to cool before serving.

Variation You can use the following dough as an alternative to puff pastry. Sift 500g/1¼lb/5 cups plain (all-purpose) flour into a bowl and make a well in the centre. Add 5 eggs and about 150g/5oz/⅔ cup of the leftover chicken fat to the well and mix together, adding some stock if necessary. Blend well, then shape the dough into a ball and leave to rest, wrapped in clear film (plastic wrap), for 30 minutes before rolling out.

Per pie Energy 368kcal/1534kJ; Protein 24.5g; Carbohydrate 18.3g, of which sugars 1.2g; Fat 22.8g, of which saturates 4.3g; Cholesterol 109mg; Calcium 44mg; Fibre 0.2g; Sodium 547mg.

Classic roast turkey with country stuffing

Traditionally served at Christmas or Thanksgiving, roast turkey is a splendid celebration dish. The rich herb stuffing in this recipe is made with calf's liver, but lamb's liver would be fine, too. Serve with cranberry jelly, which will taste even better if you make it yourself (see tip).

Serves 6

1 turkey, about 4.5–5.5kg/10–12lb, washed and patted dry with kitchen paper

25g/1oz/2 tbsp butter, melted

salt and ground black pepper

cranberry sauce, to serve

For the stuffing

200g/7oz/3½ cups fresh white breadcrumbs

175ml/6fl oz/¾ cup milk

25g/1oz/2 tbsp butter

1 egg, separated

1 calf's liver, about 600g/1lb 6oz, finely chopped

2 onions, finely chopped

90ml/6 tbsp chopped fresh dill

10ml/2 tsp clear honey

salt and ground black pepper,

Farmhouse tip Make your own cranberry sauce by placing 225g/8oz/ 2 cups cranberries, a finely chopped onion, 150ml/¼ pint/⅔ cup port and 115g/40oz/½ cup caster (superfine) sugar, in a pan. Cook for 10 minutes, or until tender. Mix the finely grated zest and juice of an orange with 2.5ml/½ tsp English mustard powder and 2.5ml/½ tsp cornflour (cornstarch) and stir into the pan. Heat gently, stirring, until the sauce thickens. Cool, cover and chill ready for serving. The sauce will keep in the refrigerator for up to a week.

1 To make the stuffing, put the breadcrumbs and milk in a large bowl and soak until swollen and soft.

2 Melt the butter in a frying pan and mix 5ml/1 tsp with the egg yolk.

3 Heat the remaining butter in a frying pan and add the finely chopped calf's liver and onions. Fry gently for 5 minutes, until the onions are golden brown. Remove from the heat and leave to cool.

4 Preheat the oven to 180°C/350°F/ Gas 4. Add the cooled liver mixture to the soaked breadcrumbs and milk, then add the butter and egg yolk mixture, with the chopped dill, clear honey and seasoning.

5 In a clean bowl, whisk the egg white to soft peaks, then fold into the stuffing mixture, stirring gently to combine thoroughly.

6 Season the turkey inside and out with salt and pepper. Stuff the cavity with the stuffing mixture, then weigh to calculate the cooking time. Allow 20 minutes per 500g/1¼lb, plus an additional 20 minutes. Tuck the legs of the turkey inside the cavity and tie the end shut with string. Brush the outside with melted butter and transfer to a roasting pan. Place in the oven and roast for the calculated time.

7 Baste the turkey regularly during cooking, and cover with foil for the final 30 minutes if the skin becomes too brown. To test whether the turkey is cooked, pierce the thickest part of the thigh with a knife; the juices should run clear.

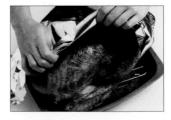

8 Remove the turkey from the oven, cover with foil and leave to rest for about 15 minutes. Carve into thin slices, then spoon over the juices and serve with the stuffing and cranberry jelly.

Energy 740kcal/3126kJ; Protein 112.3g; Carbohydrate 35.9g, of which sugars 7.3g; Fat 13.5g, of which saturates 6.6g; Cholesterol 507mg; Calcium 122mg; Fibre 1.7g; Sodium 517mg.

Turkey with apples and bay leaves

Apples from the orchard combine with bay leaves and Madeira to create a delicious turkey casserole with a handsome garnish. Serve with patty pan squash for an autumn feel.

Serves 4

75g/3oz/6 tbsp butter

675g/1½lb turkey breast fillets, cut into 2cm/¾in slices

4 cooking apples, peeled and sliced

3 bay leaves

90ml/6 tbsp Madeira

150ml/¼ pint/⅔ cup chicken stock

10ml/2 tsp cornflour (cornstarch)

150ml/¼ pint/⅔ cup double (heavy) cream

salt and ground black pepper

1 Preheat the oven to 180°C/350°F/ Gas 4. Melt a third of the butter in a large, shallow pan and fry the turkey breast fillets until sealed on all sides. Transfer to a casserole and add half the remaining butter and half the apple slices and cook gently for 1–2 minutes.

2 Tuck the bay leaves around the turkey breasts. Stir in 60ml/4 tbsp Madeira and all the stock. Simmer for 3–4 minutes, then cover and bake for 40 minutes.

3 Mix the cornflour to a paste with a little of the cream, then stir in the rest of the cream. Add this mixture to the casserole, season, stir well, then return to the oven for 10 minutes to thicken.

4 To make the apple garnish, melt the remaining butter in a frying pan and gently fry the remaining apple slices until just tender. Add the remaining Madeira and set it alight. Once the flames have died down, continue to cook the apple slices until they are lightly browned. Arrange them on top of the turkey casserole and serve.

Energy 552kcal/2295kJ; Protein 42g; Carbohydrate 13g, of which sugars 13g; Fat 37g, of which saturates 23g; Cholesterol 188mg; Calcium 36mg; Fibre 2.0g; Sodium 389mg.

Turkey escalopes

These crisp-coated, fried steaks can be made with turkey, chicken or veal. Serve with a selection of vegetables for a quick supper. Use any leftovers for a delicious sandwich.

Serves 4

4 boneless turkey or chicken breast fillets, each weighing about 175g/6oz

juice of 1 lemon

2 garlic cloves, chopped

plain (all-purpose) flour, for dusting

1–2 eggs

15ml/1 tbsp water

about 50g/2oz/½ cup breadcrumbs

2.5ml/½ tsp paprika

a mixture of vegetable and olive oil, for shallow frying

salt and ground black pepper

lemon wedges, to serve

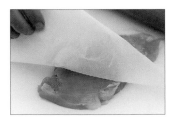

1 Lay each piece of meat between two sheets of baking parchment and pound with a mallet or the end of a rolling pin until it is about half its original thickness and fairly even.

2 In a bowl, combine the lemon juice, garlic, salt and pepper. Coat the meat in it, then leave to marinate.

3 Meanwhile, put three shallow dishes in a row. Fill one dish with flour, beat the egg and water together in another, and mix the breadcrumbs, salt, pepper and paprika together in the third.

4 Working quickly, dip each fillet into the flour, then the egg, then the breadcrumbs. Then arrange the fillets on a plate and chill for at least 30 minutes, and up to 2 hours.

Farmhouse tip Resting the breaded fillets will ensure the coating sticks, and doesn't fall off while frying.

5 In a large, heavy frying pan, heat the oil until it will turn a cube of bread dropped into the oil golden brown in 30–60 seconds. Carefully add the crumbed fillets (in batches if necessary) and fry until golden brown, turning once. Remove and drain on kitchen paper. Serve immediately with lemon wedges and a selection of vegetables.

Energy 368kcal/1546kJ; Protein 45.4g; Carbohydrate 14.7g, of which sugars 0.6g; Fat 14.6g, of which saturates 2.3g; Cholesterol 170mg; Calcium 27mg; Fibre 0.5g; Sodium 125mg.

Country raised pie

A classic raised pie takes quite a long time to make, but it is a perfect winter treat and makes a very impressive centrepiece for a Christmas party.

Serves 12

1 small duck

1 small chicken

350g/12oz pork belly, minced (ground)

1 egg, lightly beaten

2 shallots, finely chopped

2.5ml/¹⁄₂ tsp ground cinnamon

2.5ml/¹⁄₂ tsp grated nutmeg

5ml/1 tsp Worcestershire sauce

finely grated rind of 1 lemon

150ml/¹⁄₄ pint/²⁄₃ cup red wine

175g/6oz ham, cut into cubes

salt and ground black pepper

For the jelly

all the meat bones and trimmings

2 carrots

1 onion

2 celery sticks

15 ml/1 tbsp red wine

1 bay leaf

1 whole clove

1 sachet of gelatine (about 15g/1oz)

For the pastry

225g/8oz/1 cup white vegetable fat

300ml/¹⁄₂ pint/1¹⁄₄ cups boiling water

675g/1¹⁄₂lb/6 cups plain (all-purpose) flour

1 egg, beaten with a pinch of salt

1 Cut as much meat from the raw duck and chicken as possible, removing the skin and sinews. Cut the duck and chicken breasts into cubes and set aside.

2 Mix the rest of the duck and chicken meat with the minced pork, egg, shallots, spices, Worcestershire sauce, lemon rind and salt and pepper. Add the red wine and leave for about 15 minutes for the flavours to develop.

3 To make the jelly, place the meat bones and trimmings, carrots, onion, celery, wine, bay leaf and clove in a large pan, and cover with 2.75 litres/5 pints/12¹⁄₂ cups of water. Bring to the boil, skimming off any scum, and simmer gently for 2¹⁄₂ hours.

4 To make the pastry, place the fat and water in a pan and bring to the boil. Sift the flour and a pinch of salt into a bowl, and pour on the liquid. Mix with a wooden spoon, then leave to cool.

5 When the dough is cool enough to handle, knead it well and leave to stand in a warm place, covered with a cloth, for 20–30 minutes. Preheat the oven to 200°C/400°F/Gas Mark 6.

6 Grease a 25 cm/10 in loose-based deep cake tin (pan). Roll out about two-thirds of the pastry thinly enough to line the cake tin. Make sure there are no holes and allow enough pastry to leave a little hanging over the top.

7 Fill the pie with a layer of half the minced-pork mixture; then top this with a layer of the cubed duck and chicken breast-meat, and cubes of ham. Top with the remaining minced pork. Brush the overhanging edges of pastry with water and cover with the remaining rolled-out pastry. Seal the edges well. Make two large holes in the top and decorate with any pastry trimmings.

8 Bake the pie for 30 minutes. Brush the top with the egg and salt mixture. Turn down the oven to 180°C/350°F/Gas 4. After 30 minutes cooking, loosely cover the pie with foil to prevent the top getting too brown, and bake it for a further 1 hour.

9 Strain the stock after 2¹⁄₂ hours. Let it cool, then remove the fat from the top. Measure 600 ml/1 pint/2¹⁄₂ cups of stock. Heat it gently to just below boiling point and whisk the gelatine into it until no lumps are left. Add the remaining stock and leave to cool.

10 When the pie is cool, place a funnel through one of the holes and pour in as much of the stock as possible, letting it come up to the holes in the crust. Leave to set for at least 24 hours before slicing and serving.

Energy 518kcal/2164kJ; Protein 22g; Carbohydrate 44g, of which sugars 1g; Fat 29g, of which saturates 11g; Cholesterol 118mg; Calcium 97mg; Fibre 2.0g; Sodium 230mg.

Country Game

Quintessentially rural, game has supplemented the farmhouse diet for generations. Whether you are able to bag a brace of pheasants yourself, or have a good local game merchant on hand, the recipes in this chapter cover all the available types of game, from duck to rabbit, while many classic recipes use hedgerow and seasonal ingredients, reflecting how truly local fresh game is.

Duck with damson ginger sauce

Wild damsons or plums have a sharp taste that make a lovely fruity sauce to serve with these simple and quick-to-cook pan-fried duck breasts. This delicious sauce would also be good with other rich meats such as venison, pheasant or goose.

3 Meanwhile, with a sharp knife, score the fat on the duck breast portions in several places without cutting into the meat. Brush the oil over both sides of the duck. Sprinkle a little salt and pepper on the fat side only.

4 Preheat a griddle pan or heavy frying pan. When hot, add the duck breast portions, skin side down, and cook over medium heat for about 5 minutes or until the fat is evenly browned and crisp.

Serves 4

250g/9oz fresh damsons

5ml/1 tsp ground ginger

45ml/3 tbsp sugar

10ml/2 tsp wine vinegar or sherry vinegar

4 duck breast portions

15ml/1 tbsp oil

salt and ground black pepper

1 Put the damsons in a pan with the ginger and 45ml/3 tbsp water. Bring to the boil, cover and simmer gently for about 5 minutes, or until the fruit is soft. Stir frequently and add a little extra water if the fruit looks as if it is drying out or sticking to the bottom of the pan.

2 Stir in the sugar and vinegar. Press the mixture through a sieve (strainer) to remove stones (pits) and skin. Taste the sauce and add more sugar (if necessary) and seasoning to taste.

5 Turn over and cook the meat side for 4–5 minutes. Lift out and leave to rest for 5–10 minutes.

6 Slice the duck on the diagonal and serve with the sauce.

Farmhouse tip Both the duck and the sauce are good served cold too. Serve with simple steamed vegetables, crisp salads or in sandwiches.

Energy 275kcal/1157kJ; Protein 29.9g; Carbohydrate 17.5g, of which sugars 17.5g; Fat 12.5g, of which saturates 2.4g; Cholesterol 165mg; Calcium 39mg; Fibre 1.1g; Sodium 167mg.

Roast farmyard duck with apples and cider

The combination of the apples and cider in this recipe makes a fine sauce that
complements the rich meat of roast duck or goose perfectly. Serve with a selection
of vegetables, including roast potatoes and, perhaps, some red cabbage.

Serves 4

2kg/4½lb oven-ready duck

300ml/½ pint/1¼ cups dry (hard)
cider

60ml/4 tbsp double (heavy) cream

salt and ground black pepper

For the stuffing

75g/3oz/6 tbsp butter

115g/4oz/2 cups fresh white
breadcrumbs

450g/1lb cooking apples, peeled,
cored and diced

15ml/1 tbsp sugar, or to taste

freshly grated nutmeg

1 Preheat the oven to 200°C/400°F/
Gas 6. To make the stuffing, melt the
butter in a pan and fry the breadcrumbs
until golden brown. Add the apples to
the breadcrumbs with salt, pepper, the
sugar and a pinch of nutmeg. Mix well.

2 Wipe the duck out with a clean, damp
cloth, and remove any obvious excess
fat (including the flaps just inside the
vent). Rub the skin with salt. Stuff the
duck with the prepared mixture, then
secure the vent with a small skewer.

3 Weigh the stuffed duck and calculate
the cooking time, allowing 20 minutes
per 450g/1lb. Prick the skin all over
with a fork to allow the fat to run out
during the cooking time, then lay it on
top of a wire rack in a roasting pan,
sprinkle with freshly ground black
pepper and put it into the preheated
oven to roast.

4 About 20 minutes before the end of
the estimated cooking time, remove the
duck from the oven and pour off all
the fat that has accumulated under the
rack (reserve it for frying). Slide the duck
off the rack into the roasting pan, and
pour the cider over it. Return to the oven
and finish cooking, basting occasionally.

5 When the duck is cooked, remove it
from the pan and keep warm while you
make the sauce. Set the roasting pan
over a medium heat and boil the cider
to reduce it by half. Stir in the cream,
heat through and season. Meanwhile,
remove the stuffing from the duck.
Carve the duck into slices or quarter
it using poultry shears. Serve with a
portion of stuffing and the cider sauce.

Energy 572kcal/2397kJ; Protein 31.5g; Carbohydrate 34.6g, of which sugars 13.1g; Fat 33.1g, of which saturates 17.8g; Cholesterol 211mg; Calcium 74mg; Fibre 2.4g; Sodium 498mg.

Duck, pork and bean casserole

If ever there was a dish that exemplifies farmhouse cooking, it is this famous French casserole, or cassoulet. Use canned beans if you wish in place of the dried.

Serves 6–8

675g/1½lb/3½ cups dried cannellini or haricot (navy) beans

900g/2lb belly pork, preferably salted

4 large duck breasts

60ml/4 tbsp olive oil

2 onions, chopped

6 garlic cloves, crushed

2 bay leaves

1.5ml/¼ tsp ground cloves

60ml/4 tbsp tomato purée (paste)

8 good-quality sausages

4 tomatoes, skinned and quartered

75g/3oz/1½ cups white breadcrumbs

salt and freshly ground black pepper

Farmhouse tip Alter the proportions and types of meat and vegetables if you wish. Turnips, carrots and celeriac make suitable substitutes, while lamb and goose can replace the pork and duck.

1 Put the beans in a large bowl and cover with plenty of cold water. Leave to soak overnight. If using salted belly pork, soak it overnight in water, too.

2 Drain the beans and put them in a large pan with fresh water to cover. Cover and bring to the boil. Boil rapidly for 10 minutes. Drain and set the beans aside.

3 Drain the pork and cut it into large pieces, discarding the rind. Halve the duck breasts. Heat 30 ml/2 tbsp of the oil in a frying pan and fry the pork in batches, until it is browned.

4 Put the beans in a large, heavy pan with the onions, garlic, bay leaves, ground cloves and tomato purée. Stir in the browned pork and pour in just enough water to cover.

5 Bring the liquid to the boil, then reduce the heat to the lowest setting and simmer, covered, for 1½–2 hours until the beans are tender.

6 Preheat the oven to 180°C/350°F/ Gas 4. Heat the rest of the oil in a frying pan and fry the duck breasts and sausages until browned.

7 Cut the sausages into smaller pieces. Transfer the bean mixture to a large casserole. Stir in the fried sausages and duck breasts and quartered tomatoes, with salt and pepper to taste.

8 Remove the lid and sprinkle the casserole with a layer of breadcrumbs. Bake for 45 minutes more until the crust is golden. Serve hot.

Energy 776kcal/3254kJ; Protein 59g; Carbohydrate 52g, of which sugars 7g; Fat 39g, of which saturates 11g; Cholesterol 170mg; Calcium 230mg; Fibre 20.4g; Sodium 611mg.

Duck breasts with harvest plums

Duck breasts are often cooked separately to the legs, as they cook beautifully fast but stay moist and tender, whereas the legs respond better to longer, slower cooking.

Serves 4

4 duck breasts, skinned

2 tsp crushed stick cinnamon

50g/2oz butter

1 tbsp plum brandy (or Cognac)

250ml/8fl oz chicken stock

250ml/8fl oz double cream

6 red plums, stoned (pitted)

salt and ground black pepper

6 sprigs coriander (cilantro) leaves, plus some extra to garnish

1 Preheat the oven to 190°C/375°F/ Gas 5. Score the duck breasts, sprinkle with salt and press the cinnamon on to both sides. Melt half the butter in a pan and fry on both sides to seal, then place in an ovenproof dish with the butter and bake for 6–7 minutes.

2 Remove the dish from the oven and return the contents to the pan. Add the brandy and set it alight. When the flames have died down, remove from the pan and keep warm. Add the stock and cream to the pan, and simmer gently until reduced and thick. Adjust the seasoning.

3 Slice the plums. In a pan, melt the other half of the butter and fry the plums, reserving a few for garnishing, to just cook the fruit through. Add the coriander. Slice the duck breasts and pour some sauce around each one, then garnish with slices of plum, black pepper and chopped coriander.

Energy 606kcal/2512kJ; Protein 26g; Carbohydrate 8g, of which sugars 8g; Fat 52g, of which saturates 30g; Cholesterol 250mg; Calcium 63mg; Fibre 1.9g; Sodium 449mg.

Duck stew with shallots

In this traditional recipe the sweetness of the shallots balances the saltiness of the olives and complements the richness of the duck. Serve with buttered cabbage if you wish.

Serves 6–8

2 ducks, about 1.4kg/3¼lb each, quartered, or 8 duck leg quarters

225g/8oz/1½ cups shallots, peeled

30ml/2 tbsp plain (all-purpose) flour

350ml/12fl oz/1½ cups dry red wine

475ml/16fl oz/2 cups duck or chicken stock

1 bouquet garni

115g/4oz/1 cup stoned (pitted) green or black olives, or a combination

salt, if needed, and ground black pepper

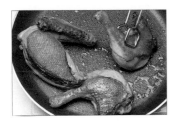

1 Put the duck portions, skin side down, in a large frying pan. Cook over a medium heat for 10–12 minutes until well browned, then turn to colour evenly. Cook in batches if necessary.

2 Pour 15ml/1 tbsp of the duck fat into a large, flameproof casserole. Place the casserole over a medium heat and cook the shallots until evenly browned, stirring frequently.

3 Sprinkle the flour into the shallots, and cook for 2 minutes more, stirring frequently. Gradually add the wine, stirring constantly.

4 Add the duck pieces to the casserole, together with the stock and bouquet garni. Bring to the boil, then reduce the heat, cover and simmer for about 40 minutes, stirring occasionally.

5 Rinse the olives in cold water. If they are very salty, put them in a pan, cover with water and bring to the boil, then drain and rinse. Add the olives to the casserole and continue cooking for a further 20 minutes, until tender.

6 Transfer the duck, shallots and olives to a plate. Strain the cooking liquid, skim off all the fat and return the liquid to the pan. Boil to reduce by about one-third, then adjust the seasoning and return the duck and vegetables to the casserole. Simmer gently for a few minutes to heat through, and serve.

Energy 317kcal/1332kJ; Protein 36g; Carbohydrate 10g, of which sugars 3g; Fat 15g, of which saturates 4g; Cholesterol 188mg; Calcium 63mg; Fibre 2.3g; Sodium 1128mg.

Duck and chestnut casserole

Serve this rustic casserole with a mixture of mashed potatoes and celeriac, for a real autumn supper and to help soak up the rich duck juices.

2 Add the onions to the pan and brown them well for 10 minutes.

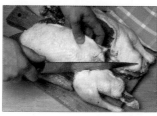

3 Add the mushrooms and cook for a few minutes more. Deglaze the pan with the red wine and boil to reduce the volume by half. Meanwhile, preheat the oven to 180°C/350°F/Gas Mark 4.

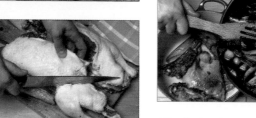

Serves 4–6

1.75kg/4½lb duck

45ml/3 tbsp olive oil

175g/6oz small onions

100g/4oz field (portabello) mushrooms

300ml/½ pint/1¼ cups red wine

300ml/½ pint/1¼ cups beef stock

225g/8oz canned chestnuts

salt and ground black pepper

1 Joint the duck into eight pieces. Heat the oil in a large frying pan and brown the duck pieces, in batches if necessary. Remove from the frying pan and place in a large casserole with a lid.

4 Transfer the wine, onions and mushrooms to the casserole, add the stock and stir in the chestnuts, season well, cover with the lid and and cook in the oven for 1½ hours, until the meat is tender. Serve with mashed potato and celeriac

Energy 405kcal/1689kJ; Protein 22.2g; Carbohydrate 16.2g, of which sugars 4.4g; Fat 24.7g, of which saturates 6.4g; Cholesterol 134mg; Calcium 41mg; Fibre 2.1g; Sodium 125mg.

Duck breast with field turnips

Duck is often served at festive occasions. In this recipe, duck breasts are combined with turnips, an ancient vegetable widely used since medieval times in stews and hotpots.

Serves 4

4 duck breasts, skin on

15ml/1 tbsp clear honey

1kg/2¼lb fresh young turnips

50g/2oz/¼ cup unsalted butter

15ml/1 tbsp sherry vinegar

salt and ground pepper

chopped fresh parsley, to garnish

Farmhouse tip Don't use duck breast fillets with the fat removed, as you need this to keep the meat tender and moist during cooking.

1 Rinse the duck breasts and pat them dry with kitchen paper. Trim off any sinew. Using a sharp knife, cross hatch the fatty skin on each breast and rub with honey on both sides. Take care to cut right through the fatty skin without piercing the meat.

2 Scrub, rinse and dry the turnips and slice them thinly. Melt the butter in a frying pan over medium-high heat. Add the turnips and fry for 10 minutes, stirring occasionally until they start to brown.

3 Meanwhile, put the duck breasts, skin-side down, in a large non-stick frying pan. Cook over medium heat for about 5 minutes or until the fat runs and the skin becomes crisp and golden.

4 Drain off any excess fat from the duck breasts, if necessary. Season to taste.

5 Using tongs, turn the duck breasts over and cook the other side for 5–6 minutes. Do not overcook. Season again. Remove from the heat, cover with foil or a lid and set aside for 4–5 minutes.

6 Add the sherry vinegar to the turnips and stir over the heat for 3 minutes until reduced. Season to taste and spoon on to warm plates.

7 Slice the duck breasts thinly and fan over the turnips, spooning a little of the juices from the pan on top. Garnish with the chopped herbs and serve.

Farmhouse tip Cook duck breast like you would a fine filet mignon – so that it is pink and tender in the middle.

Energy 591kcal/2446kJ; Protein 13.7g; Carbohydrate 14.7g, of which sugars 14.2g; Fat 53.7g, of which saturates 18.1g; Cholesterol 27mg; Calcium 134mg; Fibre 6g; Sodium 191mg.

Roast wild duck with mushroom sauce

Wild duck is more strongly flavoured than the domestic bird and contains much less fat; it therefore benefits from cooking in a liquid to keep it tender.

Serves 4

2 x 1.2kg/2½lb mallards, dressed and barded weight

50g/2oz/4 tbsp butter

1 onion, halved and sliced

½ celery stick, chopped

1 small carrot, chopped

75ml/5 tbsp Madeira or sherry

10 large dried morel mushrooms

225g/8oz wild mushrooms, sliced

600ml/1 pint/2½ cups hot chicken stock

1 fresh thyme sprig

10ml/2 tsp wine vinegar

salt and ground black pepper

parsley sprigs, steamed broccoli and carrot matchsticks, to serve

1 Preheat the oven to 190°C/375°F/ Gas 5. Season the ducks all over.

2 Heat half the butter in a pan and fry the onion, celery and carrot for about 5 minutes. Transfer the vegetables to a large casserole.

3 Add the remaining butter to the pan. When it is foaming, brown the ducks on all sides. Place them in the casserole.

4 Pour the Madeira or sherry into the pan used for frying, and bring to the boil. Pour this liquid over the birds. Bake in the oven for 40 minutes.

5 Tie all the mushrooms in a piece of muslin (cheesecloth). Add the stock and thyme to the casserole. Immerse the muslin bag in the liquid. Cover and return to the oven for 40 minutes more.

6 Transfer the birds to a serving platter and keep hot; set the mushrooms aside. Remove the thyme from the braising liquid, then purée the vegetables and liquid. Pour the purée back into the casserole and stir the mushrooms into the sauce. Add the vinegar and seasoning and heat through gently.

7 Garnish the ducks with parsley and carrot. Serve with mushroom sauce.

Energy 383kcal/1603kJ; Protein 39g; Carbohydrate 6g, of which sugars 4g; Fat 23g, of which saturates 10g; Cholesterol 214mg; Calcium 53mg; Fibre 5.9g; Sodium 672mg.

Guinea fowl with cabbage

Originally a game bird, but now domesticated and available all year round, guinea fowl has a flavour somewhere between chicken and pheasant.

Serves 4

15ml/1 tbsp vegetable oil

1.2–1.4kg/2½–3lb guinea fowl, trussed

15g/½oz/1 tbsp butter

1 large onion, halved and sliced

1 large carrot, halved and sliced

1 large leek, sliced

450g/1lb green cabbage, such as Savoy, sliced or chopped

120ml/4fl oz/½ cup dry white wine

120ml/4fl oz/½ cup chicken stock

1 or 2 garlic cloves, finely chopped

salt and ground black pepper

1 Preheat the oven to 180°C/350°F/ Gas 4. Heat half the oil in a large, flameproof casserole and cook the guinea fowl until golden brown on all sides. Transfer to a plate.

2 Add the remaining oil with the butter to the casserole. Cook the onion, carrot and leek over a low heat for 5 minutes, stirring occasionally.

3 Add the cabbage and cook for about 3–4 minutes until slightly wilted, stirring occasionally. Season the vegetables with salt and pepper.

4 Place the guinea fowl on its side on the vegetables. Add the wine, bring to the boil, then add the stock and garlic. Cover and cook in the oven for 25 minutes, then turn the bird on to the other side and cook for 20–25 minutes more, until the juices run clear when pierced with a knife.

5 Transfer the bird to a board and leave to rest for 5–10 minutes, then cut into four or eight pieces. With a slotted spoon, transfer the cabbage to a warmed serving dish and place the pieces of guinea fowl on top. Skim any fat from the casserole, then serve the cooking juices separately.

Energy 369kcal/15398kJ; Protein 33g; Carbohydrate 13g, of which sugars 11g; Fat 21g, of which saturates 7g; Cholesterol 244mg; Calcium 121mg; Fibre 5.8g; Sodium 293mg.

Guinea fowl and spring vegetable ragoût

Equally delicious if made with chicken or rabbit, this light stew makes the best of kitchen garden vegetables, including tender baby leeks. Finish with plenty of chopped parsley.

2 Season the flour with salt and pepper and toss the guinea fowl in it. Fry the portions in the oil remaining in the pan until browned on all sides. Transfer to a casserole. Preheat the oven to 180°C/ 350°F/Gas 4. Add the remaining oil to the pan and cook the onion until soft.

3 Add the garlic to the pan and fry for 4 minutes. Stir in the pancetta and wine.

4 Tie the herbs into a bundle and add to the pan. Bring to the boil, then simmer gently for 3–4 minutes. Pour into the casserole and season. Cover and cook in the oven for 40 minutes.

5 Add the carrots and turnips to the casserole and cook, covered, for another 30 minutes, until the vegetables are just tender. Add the leeks and cook for 20 minutes more.

6 Transfer the guinea fowl and vegetables to a warmed serving dish. Place the casserole on the stove and boil vigorously over a high heat until the juices are reduced by about half.

Serves 4

45ml/3 tbsp olive oil

115g/4oz pancetta, cut into lardons

30ml/2 tbsp plain (all-purpose) flour

2 × 1.2–1.6kg/2½–3½lb guinea fowl, each jointed in 4 portions

1 onion, chopped

1 head of garlic, separated into cloves and peeled

1 bottle dry white wine

fresh thyme sprig

1 fresh bay leaf

a few parsley stalks

250g/9oz baby carrots

250g/9oz baby turnips

6 slender leeks, cut into pieces

250g/9oz frozen peas, cooked for 2 minutes

15ml/1 tbsp French herb mustard

15g/½oz flat leaf parsley, chopped

15ml/1 tbsp chopped fresh mint

salt and ground black pepper

1 Heat 30ml/2 tbsp of the oil in a large frying pan and cook the pancetta over a medium heat until lightly browned. Remove from the pan and set aside.

7 Stir in the cooked peas and cook gently for 2–3 minutes, then stir in the mustard and adjust the seasoning. Stir in most of the parsley and the mint. Pour the sauce over the guinea fowl. Sprinkle the remaining parsley over the top and serve.

Energy 862kcal/3579kJ; Protein 52g; Carbohydrate 23.4g, of which sugars 11g; Fat 50.5g, of which saturates 13.6g; Cholesterol 227mg; Calcium 138mg; Fibre 8.3g; Sodium 558mg.

Farmhouse potted goose

Potting is a traditional way to preserve cooked meat. It is commonly made with goose or duck, but also with pork or rabbit. Using salted meat means it will last for weeks.

Makes 1 jar

4 goose legs

1 thyme sprig

1 bay leaf

10 black peppercorns

4 juniper berries, lightly crushed

1 small onion, quartered

1 medium carrot, roughly sliced

1 celery stick, quartered

2 garlic cloves in their skins

50g/2oz/4 tbsp goose fat

15ml/1 tbsp chopped parsley

sea salt and ground black pepper

1 Place the goose legs in a bowl and add the herbs, peppercorns and juniper berries. Rub plenty of salt into the flesh. Cover and refrigerate for 12–15 hours.

2 Preheat the oven 160°C/325°F/Gas 3. Rub the salt and herbs off the goose legs, rinse in cold water and pat dry.

3 Place the goose in a casserole with the vegetables and goose fat and just cover with water. Bring to a simmer. Cover the dish and transfer to the oven for 3–4 hours, until the flesh is falling off the bones. Top up the liquid if necessary during the cooking time.

4 Once the legs are cooked remove from the pan to cool. Strain the stock, together with all the fat, in to a bowl and set aside. Discard the vegetables.

5 Remove and discard the skin from the goose and pull the meat off the bones, shredding it with your fingers and transferring to a large bowl as you go.

6 When the fat has solidified, separate it from the stock. Warm the fat and the stock in separate pans, so the fat melts.

7 Add all but 30ml/2 tbsp of the melted fat to the shredded meat, add a little of the warmed stock and beat vigorously. Add a little more stock and beat again, taste for saltiness and continue to beat in as much stock as you can until the mixture is creamy and soft, and just salty enough. Then beat in the parsley.

8 Transfer to a jar or airtight container, smooth the top and pour over the reserved fat. Chill until needed. Serve with toast and gherkins or fruit chutney.

Energy 1727kcal/7161kJ; Protein 117.6g; Carbohydrate 0.4g, of which sugars 0.3g; Fat 139.3g, of which saturates 20.4g; Cholesterol 47mg; Calcium 70mg; Fibre 0.7g; Sodium 606mg.

Roast pheasant with port

Many farmers – and their fortunate friends – have a regular supply of pheasant in the shooting season. This is an excellent way of cooking them.

Serves 4

2 oven-ready hen pheasants, about 675g/1½lb each

50g/2oz/4 tbsp butter, softened

8 fresh thyme sprigs

2 bay leaves

6 rindless streaky (fatty) bacon rashers (strips)

15ml/1 tbsp plain (all-purpose) flour

175ml/6fl oz/¾ cup game or chicken stock, plus more if needed

15ml/1 tbsp redcurrant jelly

45–60ml/3–4 tbsp port

freshly ground black pepper

1 Preheat the oven to 230°C/450°F/Gas 8. Line a large roasting pan with a sheet of strong foil large enough to enclose the pheasants. Lightly brush the foil with oil.

2 Wipe the pheasants with damp kitchen paper and remove any extra fat or skin. Using your fingertips, carefully loosen the skin of the breasts.

3 Spread the butter between the skin and breast meat of each bird. Tie the legs securely with string, then lay thyme sprigs and a bay leaf over the breast of each bird.

4 Lay the bacon over the breasts, place the birds in the tin and season with pepper. Bring up the foil and enclose the birds. Roast for 20 minutes, then reduce the oven to 190°C/375°F/Gas 5 and cook for 40 minutes more.

5 Uncover the birds and roast 10–15 minutes more. Transfer the birds to a board and leave to stand for 10 minutes before carving.

6 Pour the juices into the roasting tin and skim off any fat. Sprinkle in the flour and stir over a medium heat until smooth. Whisk in the stock and redcurrant jelly and bring to the boil.

7 Simmer until the sauce thickens slightly, then stir in the port and adjust the seasoning. Strain the sauce and serve with the carved pheasants and rashers of crispy bacon.

Energy 526kcal/2195kJ; Protein 50.1g; Carbohydrate 6.4g, of which sugars 4.5g; Fat 29g, of which saturates 8.2g; Cholesterol 25mg; Calcium 104mg; Fibre 2g; Sodium 798mg.

Braised pheasant with chestnuts and bacon

Towards the end of their season pheasant can be a little tough, so are best braised. Try this delicious casserole enriched with wild mushrooms and chestnuts.

Serves 4

2 mature pheasants

50g/2oz/4 tbsp butter

75ml/5 tbsp brandy

12 button or pickling (pearl) onions, peeled

1 celery stick, chopped

50g/2oz rindless unsmoked streaky (fatty) bacon, cut into strips

25g/1oz/3 tbsp plain (all-purpose) flour

500ml/18fl oz/2¼ cups hot chicken stock

175g/6oz/1½ cups peeled chestnuts

15g/½oz/¼ cup dried ceps, soaked in warm water for 20 minutes

15ml/1 tbsp lemon juice

salt and freshly ground black pepper

watercress sprigs, to garnish

1 Preheat the oven to 170°C/325°F/ Gas 3. Season the pheasants. Melt half the butter in a casserole and brown the birds all over. Remove the birds and set aside and pour off the fat.

2 Return the casserole to the heat. Add the brandy, stir to incorporate the sediment, then pour over the pheasant.

3 Melt the remaining butter. Lightly brown the onions, celery and bacon. Stir in the flour, cook for 1 minute, then gradually stir in the stock. Add the chestnuts and mushrooms, then replace the pheasants and their juices. Bring to a gentle simmer, cover and cook in the oven for 1½ hours.

4 Transfer the pheasants and vegetables to a serving plate. Skim off any fat from the sauce, bring it back to the boil, add the lemon juice and season to taste.

5 Pour the sauce into a jug and garnish the birds with watercress sprigs. Serve, sliced, with gravy.

Energy 883Kcal/3699kJ; Protein 86.8g; Carbohydrate 32.3g, of which sugars 6.9g; Fat 41.6g, of which saturates 15.8g; Cholesterol 35mg; Calcium 205mg; Fibre 2.9g; Sodium 920mg.

Roast pheasant with sherry mustard sauce

It is best to use only young pheasants for roasting – older birds are tougher and suitable for casseroles. Serve this succulent dish with potatoes, bread sauce and winter vegetables.

Serves 4

2 young oven-ready pheasants

50g/2oz/¼ cup softened butter

200ml/7fl oz/scant 1 cup sherry

15ml/1 tbsp Dijon mustard

salt and ground black pepper

Farmhouse tip To help the pheasant stay tender, cover the pan with foil if you wish. Remove 10–15 minutes before the end of cooking, to brown the skin.

1 Preheat the oven to 200°C/400°F/ Gas 6. Put the pheasants in a roasting pan and spread the butter all over both birds. Season with salt and pepper.

2 Roast the pheasants for 50 minutes, basting often to stop the birds from drying out. When the pheasants are cooked, take them out of the pan and leave to rest on a board, covered with foil.

3 Meanwhile, place the roasting pan over a medium heat. Add the sherry and season with salt and pepper. Simmer for 5 minutes, until the sherry has slightly reduced, then stir in the mustard. Carve the pheasants and serve with the sherry and mustard sauce.

Energy 692kcal/2897kJ; Protein 81.7g; Carbohydrate 1.2g, of which sugars 1.1g; Fat 34.2g, of which saturates 14.5g; Cholesterol 27mg; Calcium 133mg; Fibre 0g; Sodium 456mg.

Pheasant and wild mushroom ragoût

This rich and delicious way to prepare pheasant uses shallots, garlic cloves, port and a mixture of wild mushrooms for a good variety of flavour and texture.

Serves 4

4 pheasant breasts, skinned

15ml/1 tbsp oil

12 shallots, halved

2 garlic cloves, crushed

75g/3oz wild mushrooms, sliced

75ml/2$\frac{1}{2}$fl oz/$\frac{1}{3}$ cup port

150ml/$\frac{1}{4}$ pint/$\frac{2}{3}$ cup chicken stock

sprigs of fresh parsley and thyme

1 bay leaf

grated rind of 1 lemon

200ml/7fl oz/scant 1 cup double (heavy) cream

salt and ground black pepper

1 Dice and season the pheasant breasts. Heat the oil in a heavy pan and colour the pheasant meat quickly. Remove from the pan and set aside.

2 Add the halved shallots to the pan, fry quickly to colour a little, then add the crushed garlic and sliced wild mushrooms. Reduce the heat and cook gently for 5 minutes.

3 Pour the port and stock into the pan and add the herbs and lemon rind. Reduce the liquid a little. When the shallots are nearly cooked, add the cream, reduce to thicken, then return the meat. Allow to cook for a few minutes before serving.

Farmhouse tip Serve with pilaff rice: fry a chopped onion, stir in 2.5cm/1in cinnamon stick, 2.5ml/$\frac{1}{2}$ tsp crushed cumin seeds, 2 crushed cardamom pods, a bay leaf and 5ml/1 tsp turmeric. Add 225g/8oz/generous 1 cup long grain rice. Stir until well coated. Pour in 600ml/1 pint/2$\frac{1}{2}$ cups boiling water, cover, then simmer gently for 15 minutes. Transfer to a serving dish, cover with a dish towel and leave for 5 minutes.

Energy 530kcal/2200kJ; Protein 34.1g; Carbohydrate 7.4g, of which sugars 5.9g; Fat 33g, of which saturates 20.2g; Cholesterol 69mg; Calcium 91mg; Fibre 1.1g; Sodium 114mg.

Roast young grouse with rowanberries

Young grouse can be identified by their pliable breastbone, legs and feet, and their claws will be sharp. They have very little fat, so bacon is used here to protect the breasts.

Serves 2

2 young grouse

6 rashers (strips) bacon

2 sprigs of rowanberries or 1 lemon, quartered, plus 30ml/2 tbsp extra rowanberries (optional)

50g/2oz/¼ cup butter

150ml/¼ pint/⅔ cup red wine

150ml/¼ pint/⅔ cup water

5ml/1 tsp rowan jelly

salt and ground black pepper

1 Wipe the grouse with kitchen paper. Preheat the oven to 200°C/400°F/Gas 6.

1 Lay the bacon over the breasts of the grouse, and place them side by side in a roasting pan.

2 If you have rowanberries, place one sprig in the cavity of each grouse as well as a little butter. Otherwise, put a lemon quarter in each cavity.

3 Roast the grouse in the preheated oven for 10 minutes, then remove the bacon and pour in the wine. Return to the oven for 10 minutes.

4 Baste the birds with the juices and cook for a further 5 minutes. Remove the birds from the pan and keep warm. Add the water and rowan jelly to the pan and simmer gently until the jelly melts. Strain into another pan, add the rowanberries, if using, and simmer until the sauce just begins to thicken. Season with salt and ground black pepper.

Variation If rowanberries are hard to find, you can replace them with dried cranberries or sour cherries, which will give a similar result.

Energy 423kcal/1763kJ; Protein 43.8g; Carbohydrate 1.5g, of which sugars 1.5g; Fat 24g, of which saturates 10.8g; Cholesterol 51mg; Calcium 43mg; Fibre 0g; Sodium 902mg.

Grouse with orchard fruit stuffing

In the late summer and autumn, when grouse are in season, orchard fruits such as apples, plums and pears make a perfect stuffing. Try serving with creamy mashed potatoes.

Serves 2

juice of ½ lemon

2 young grouse

50g/2oz/¼ cup butter

4 Swiss chard leaves

50ml/2fl oz/¼ cup Marsala

salt and ground black pepper

For the stuffing

2 shallots, finely chopped

1 tart cooking apple, peeled, cored and chopped

1 pear, peeled, cored and chopped

2 plums, halved, stoned (pitted) and chopped

large pinch of mixed (apple pie) spice

Farmhouse tip In this recipe, the birds are steamed, and it is important that the casserole has a tight-fitting lid, so the liquid does not evaporate.

1 Sprinkle the lemon juice over the grouse and season well with salt and pepper. Melt half the butter in a flameproof casserole, add the grouse and cook for 10 minutes, or until browned. Use tongs to remove the grouse from the casserole and set aside.

2 Add the shallots to the fat remaining in the casserole and cook until softened but not coloured. Add the apple, pear, plums and mixed spice, and cook for about 5 minutes, or until the fruits are just beginning to soften. Remove from the heat.

3 Spoon the hot fruit mixture into the body cavities of the birds, pushing it in to fill them well.

4 Truss the birds neatly with string. Smear the remaining butter over the birds, and wrap them in the chard leaves. Replace them in the casserole.

5 Pour in the Marsala and heat until simmering. Cover tightly and simmer for 20 minutes, or until the birds are tender, taking care not to overcook them. Leave to rest in a warm place for about 10 minutes before serving.

Energy 508kcal/2121kJ; Protein 46.9g; Carbohydrate 19.5g, of which sugars 18.7g; Fat 24.3g, of which saturates 13.8g; Cholesterol 53mg; Calcium 185mg; Fibre 4.2g; Sodium 406mg.

Pigeon pie

This rich pie is based upon a traditional dish, using a mixture of pigeon meat, eggs, spices and nuts.

Serves 6

3 pigeons

50g/2oz/4 tbsp butter

1 onion, chopped

1 cinnamon stick

2.5ml/½ tsp ground ginger

30ml/2 tbsp chopped coriander (cilantro)

45ml/3 tbsp chopped fresh parsley

pinch of ground turmeric

15ml/1 tbsp caster sugar

2.5ml/½ tsp ground cinnamon

115g/4oz/1 cup toasted almonds, finely chopped

6 eggs, beaten

175g/6oz/¾ cup butter, melted

16 sheets filo pastry

1 egg yolk

salt and ground black pepper

cinnamon and icing (confectioners') sugar, to garnish

1 Wash the pigeons and place them in a heavy pan with the butter, onion, cinnamon stick, ginger, coriander, parsley and turmeric. Season with salt and pepper. Add enough water to cover, bring to the boil, reduce the heat, cover and simmer gently for about 1 hour, until the pigeon is tender.

2 Strain off the stock and reserve. Skin and bone the pigeons, and use your fingers to shred the flesh into bitesize pieces. Preheat the oven to 180°C/ 350°F/Gas 4. Mix the sugar, cinnamon and almonds in a bowl.

3 Measure 150 ml/¼ pint/⅔ cup of the reserved stock into a small pan. Add the eggs and mix well. Stir over a low heat almost set. Season with salt and pepper.

4 Brush a 30cm/12in diameter ovenproof dish with some melted butter and lay a sheet of pastry in the dish. Brush with butter and repeat with five more sheets of pastry. Cover with the almond mixture, then half the egg mixture. Moisten with a little stock.

5 Layer four more sheets of filo, brushing with butter. Lay the meat on top, then add the remaining egg mixture and more stock. Cover with all the remaining pastry, brushing each sheet with butter. Tuck in any overlap.

6 Brush the pie with egg yolk and bake for 40 minutes. Raise the oven temperature to 200°C/400°F/Gas 6, and bake for 15 minutes more, until the pastry is crisp and golden. Garnish with cinnamon and icing sugar, and serve.

Energy 628kcal/2607kJ; Protein 27.1g; Carbohydrate 15.1g, of which sugars 1.6g; Fat 51.7g, of which saturates 6.6g; Cholesterol 224mg; Calcium 113mg; Fibre 2.1g; Sodium 130mg.

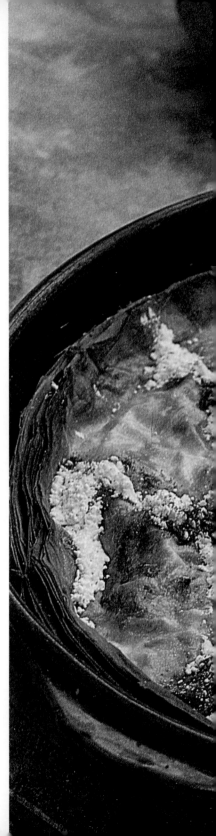

Pigeon with mushrooms

The breasts are the best part of the pigeon, and here the carcass is used to make a rich sauce. Use the strongest-flavoured mushrooms you can find for this dish to add flavour.

Serves 6

6 pigeon, cleaned

90ml/6 tbsp olive oil

1 large onion, chopped

2 garlic cloves, finely chopped

450g/1lb/6 cups brown cap (cremini) or small open-cap field (portabello) mushrooms (use wild mushrooms, if possible)

150g/5oz Serrano or other cured ham, diced

150ml/¼ pint/⅔ cup red wine

salt and ground black pepper

60ml/4 tbsp chopped fresh parsley, to garnish

fried potatoes, to serve

For the stock

1 large onion, unpeeled, roughly chopped

2 carrots, roughly chopped

1 celery stick, roughly chopped

6 tough parsley stalks, snapped or bruised

1 bay leaf

1 garlic clove, unpeeled but crushed

4 sprigs of fresh thyme

12 black peppercorns, crushed

1 First prepare the pigeons. Find the bird's wishbone by pushing your forefinger and thumb in the neck end. It runs up each side; snap it out. Once this is gone, it is easy to take off the breast portions.

2 Cut down on one side of the breastbone with a large knife, then scrape along the rib cage, to get the breast meat off whole. Repeat this, and season the meat.

3 Cut the pigeon carcasses across the ribs and flatten them in a large pan. Add all the stock ingredients and just cover with water. Simmer gently for about 1½ hours to make a rich dark stock. Allow to cool slightly, then strain into a large bowl.

4 Heat 30ml/2 tbsp of the olive oil in a large shallow casserole and fry the onion and garlic for a few minutes, until soft. Meanwhile, pull the stalks out of the mushroom caps, chop the stalks finely and add to the casserole.

Farmhouse tip Pigeons are available in abundance while they are in season, and many country recipes only use the breast, discarding the rest of the bird or using it to make stock.

5 Add the ham cubes to the casserole and fry briefly, stirring. Pour in the wine and 250ml/8fl oz/1 cup of the stock. Simmer gently to reduce a little.

6 Heat 30ml/2 tbsp oil in a large frying pan. Put the pigeon breasts in the pan, skin downward and fry for 2 minutes on each side. Remove them to the casserole and simmer for 2–3 minutes.

7 Fry the mushroom caps, in 30ml/ 2 tbsp oil. Arrange the pigeon breasts on a platter. Add the mushrooms, spoon the ham and sauce over the pigeon, and sprinkle with parsley.

Energy 495kcal/2057kJ; Protein 42g; Carbohydrate 9g, of which sugars 7g; Fat 33g, of which saturates 8g; Cholesterol 253mg; Calcium 77mg; Fibre 4.0g; Sodium 659 mg.

Game pie

This impressive country pie can be made with whatever game birds are available. Add in some freshly foraged mushrooms, and serve the pie with puréed Jerusalem artichokes and winter greens such as purple sprouting broccoli or Brussels sprouts.

Serves 8–10

2 game birds, such as skinless pheasant and/or pigeon

225g/8oz lean stewing steak, trimmed and cut in thin strips

115g/4oz streaky (fatty) bacon

butter, for frying

2 medium onions, finely chopped

1 large garlic clove, crushed

15ml/1 tbsp plain (all-purpose) flour

about 300ml/½ pint/¼ cup chicken stock

15ml/1 tbsp tomato purée (paste)

15ml/1 tbsp chopped fresh parsley

a little grated lemon rind

15ml/1 tbsp redcurrant jelly

50–115g/2–4oz button (white) mushrooms, halved if large

pinch of freshly grated nutmeg

milk or beaten egg, to glaze

salt and ground black pepper

For the rough-puff pastry

225g/8oz/2 cups plain (all-purpose) flour

2.5ml/½ tsp salt

5ml/1 tsp lemon juice

115g/4oz/½ cup butter, diced

1 To make the rough-puff pastry, sift the flour and salt into a large bowl. Add the lemon juice and the butter, and enough cold water to bind the ingredients together.

2 Turn the dough on to a floured board and roll into a long strip. Fold into three and press the edges together. Half-turn the pastry, rib it with the rolling pin to equalize the air in it then roll into a strip once again. Repeat three more times.

3 Slice the pheasant or pigeon breasts from the bone and cut the meat into thin strips.

4 Cut the bacon into strips, and cook it gently in a heavy frying pan until the fat runs. Add some butter and brown the pigeon or pheasant and sliced stewing steak, a little at a time.

5 Remove the meats from the pan and set aside. Cook the onions and garlic in the fat for 2–3 minutes over a medium heat. Remove and add to the meats. Stir the flour into the remaining fat in the pan and cook for 1–2 minutes, then gradually stir in enough stock to make a fairly thin gravy.

6 Add the tomato purée, parsley, lemon rind, redcurrant jelly, nutmeg and mushrooms to the gravy. Season to taste and add the nutmeg.

7 Return the browned meats, chopped onion and garlic to the pan containing the gravy, and mix well before turning into a deep 1.75 litre/3 pint/7½ cup pie dish. Leave to cool. Meanwhile, preheat the oven to 220°C/425°F/Gas 7.

8 Roll the prepared pastry out to make a circle 2.5cm/1in larger all round than the pie dish, and cut out to make a lid for the pie. Wet the rim of the pie dish and line with the remaining pastry strip. Dampen the strip and cover with the lid, pressing down well to seal.

9 Trim away any excess pastry and knock up the edges with a knife. Make a hole in the centre for the steam to escape and use any pastry trimmings to decorate the top. Glaze the top of the pie with milk or beaten egg.

10 Bake the pie in the oven for about 20 minutes, until the pastry is risen, then reduce the oven to 150°C/300°F/Gas 2 for 1½ hours, until cooked. Protect the pastry from over-browning if necessary, by covering it with a double layer of baking parchment. Serve the pie hot with seasonal vegetables.

Energy 448kcal/1871kJ; Protein 28.3g; Carbohydrate 29.5g, of which sugars 5.3g; Fat 24.9g, of which saturates 9.5g; Cholesterol 55mg; Calcium 67mg; Fibre 1.5g; Sodium 393mg.

Raised game pie

The perfect picnic food traditionally taken on country shoots, this stylish dish makes a spectacular centrepiece. The hot water crust pastry is surprisingly easy to make.

Serves 10

25g/1oz/2 tbsp butter

1 onion, finely chopped

2 garlic cloves, finely chopped

900g/2lb mixed boneless game meat, such as skinless pheasant and/or pigeon breast, venison and rabbit, diced

30ml/2 tbsp chopped fresh herbs such as parsley, thyme or marjoram

salt and ground black pepper

For the pâté

50g/2oz/¼ cup butter

2 garlic cloves, finely chopped

450g/1lb chicken livers, rinsed, trimmed and chopped

60ml/4 tbsp brandy

5ml/1 tsp ground mace

For the hot water crust pastry

675g/1½lb/6 cups strong white bread flour

5ml/1 tsp salt

115ml/3½fl oz/scant ½ cup milk

115ml/3½fl oz/scant ½ cup water

115g/4oz/½ cup lard, diced

115g/4oz/½ cup butter, diced

beaten egg, to glaze

For the jelly

300ml/½ pint/1¼ cups game or beef consommé

2.5ml/½ tsp powdered gelatine

1 Melt the butter in a small pan until foaming, then add the onion and garlic, and cook until softened but not coloured. Remove from the heat and mix with the diced game meat and the chopped mixed herbs. Season well, cover and chill.

2 To make the pâté, melt the butter in a pan until foaming. Add the garlic and chicken livers and cook until the livers are just browned. Remove the pan from the heat and stir in the brandy and mace. Purée the mixture in a blender or food processor until smooth, then set aside and leave to cool.

3 To make the pastry, sift the flour and salt into a bowl and make a well in the centre. Place the milk and water in a pan. Add the lard and butter and heat gently until melted, then bring to the boil and remove from the heat as soon as the mixture begins to bubble.

4 Pour the hot liquid into the well in the flour and beat until smooth. Cover and leave until cool enough to handle.

5 Preheat the oven to 200°C/400°F/ Gas 6. Roll out two-thirds of the pastry and line a springform 23cm/9in raised pie mould. Add half the game mixture and press it down. Add the pâté, then top with the remaining game.

6 Roll out the remaining pastry to form a lid. Brush the edge of the pastry lining the mould with water and cover the pie with the lid. Trim off any excess. Pinch the edges together to seal. Make two holes in the centre of the lid and glaze with egg. Use pastry trimmings to roll out leaves to garnish the pie. Brush with egg.

7 Bake the pie for 20 minutes, cover with foil and cook for a further 10 minutes. Reduce the oven temperature to 150°C/300°F/Gas 2. Glaze the pie again with beaten egg and cook for a further 1½ hours, keeping the top covered loosely with foil.

8 Remove the pie from the oven and leave to stand for 15 minutes. Increase the oven temperature to 200°C/400°F/ Gas 6. Stand the mould on a baking sheet and remove the sides. Now glaze the sides of the pie with beaten egg and cover the top with foil, then cook for a final 15 minutes to brown. Cool completely, then chill overnight.

9 For the jelly, heat the game or beef consommé in a small pan until just starting to bubble, whisk in the gelatine until dissolved and leave to cool until just setting. Using a small funnel, carefully pour the jellied consommé into the holes in the pie. Chill. This pie will keep in the refrigerator for up to 3 days. Serve sliced, with lettuce and pickles.

Energy 731kcal/3058kJ; Protein 44g; Carbohydrate 54.3g, of which sugars 2.5g; Fat 32g, of which saturates 17.9g; Cholesterol 223mg; Calcium 163mg; Fibre 2.3g; Sodium 444mg.

Country rabbit sauté

Rabbit has always been a farmhouse favourite. Town dwellers eager to try this recipe should look out for packs of rabbit portions, sold at the supermarket.

1 Put the rabbit in a bowl. Add the wine, vinegar, oregano and bay leaves and toss lightly. Cover and marinate for several hours or overnight.

2 Remove the seeds from the chilli and chop it finely. Set it aside. Drain the rabbit portions, reserving the marinade, and pat dry on kitchen paper. Heat the oil in a large frying pan and fry the rabbit on all sides until golden, then remove with a slotted spoon. Fry the onions until beginning to colour.

3 Remove the onions from the pan and add the chilli, garlic and paprika. Cook, stirring, for about 1 minute. Add the reserved marinade, with the stock. Season lightly.

Serves 4

675g/1½lb rabbit portions

300ml/½ pint/1¼ cups dry white wine

15ml/1 tbsp sherry vinegar

several fresh oregano sprigs

2 bay leaves

1 fresh red chilli

90ml/6 tbsp olive oil

175g/6oz baby (pearl) onions or shallots, peeled

4 garlic cloves, sliced

10ml/2 tsp paprika

150ml/¼ pint/⅔ cup chicken stock

salt and ground black pepper

flat leaf parsley sprigs, to garnish

4 Return the rabbit to the pan with the onions. Bring to the boil, then reduce the heat, cover and simmer for about 45 minutes until the rabbit is tender. Serve, garnished with a few sprigs of flat leaf parsley, if you like.

Energy 311Kcal/1294kJ; Protein 23.2g; Carbohydrate 9.5g, of which sugars 2.6g; Fat 20.4g, of which saturates 4.1g; Cholesterol 83mg; Calcium 65mg; Fibre 0.9g; Sodium 52mg.

Rabbit salad with garden chard

Chard is a delicious vegetable which can be used in place of spinach and prepared in the same way. This quick method for cooking rabbit is only good for the saddle.

Serves 4

15ml/1 tbsp groundnut (peanut) oil

2 saddles of rabbit, approx 250g/9oz each in weight

mixed salad leaves

salad dressing

50g/2oz/¼ cup butter

225g/8oz ruby chard leaves

salt and ground black pepper

1 Heat a frying pan and pour in the oil, allowing it to get quite hot. Dry and season the rabbit and place in the oil, skin side down. Brown lightly, reduce the heat and turn the saddles over on to the rib side. Cover and cook over a very low heat for about 7 minutes. Turn off the heat, and leave to rest.

2 Wash the chard thoroughly, and then remove and discard the central stalks. Chop roughly.

3 Remove the rabbit from the pan, and place on a chopping board. Heat the butter in the pan and, as soon as it is melted and sizzling, throw in the chard.

4 Season and toss to coat, and keep stirring as it cooks. When the chard is wilted, remove the pan from the heat.

5 Toss the salad leaves with dressing and place in the centre of four plates.

6 Slice the rabbit fillets from the back of the saddle and remove the small fillets from underneath as well. Cut thinly and strew the meat evenly over the salad. Place the warm chard on top and serve.

Energy 287kcal/1192kJ; Protein 29g; Carbohydrate 1g, of which sugars 0.9g; Fat 18.5g, of which saturates 9.1g; Cholesterol 115mg; Calcium 126mg; Fibre 1.2g; Sodium 238mg.

Slow-braised rabbit

Long, slow cooking is the secret to the tender rabbit in this dish. It is delicious served with potatoes boiled in their skins and lightly cooked green vegetables such as leeks.

Serves 4–6

1 rabbit, prepared and jointed by the butcher

30ml/2 tbsp seasoned flour

30ml/2 tbsp olive oil or vegetable oil

25g/1oz/2 tbsp butter

115g/4oz streaky (fatty) bacon

1 onion, roughly chopped

2 or 3 carrots, sliced

1 or 2 celery sticks, trimmed and sliced

300ml/½ pint/1¼ cups chicken stock

300ml/½ pint/1¼ cups dry (hard) cider or stout

a small bunch of parsley leaves, chopped

salt and ground black pepper

1 Soak the joints in cold salted water for at least 2 hours, then pat them dry with kitchen paper and toss them in seasoned flour. Preheat the oven to 200°C/400°F/Gas 6.

2 Heat the oil and butter together in a heavy flameproof casserole. Shake off (and reserve) any excess flour from the rabbit joints and brown them on all sides. Lift out and set aside.

3 Add the bacon to the casserole and cook for a few minutes, then remove and set aside with the rabbit.

4 Add the vegetables to the casserole and cook until just colouring. Add the remaining seasoned flour to absorb the fats in the casserole. Stir over a low heat, gradually adding the stock and cider or stout, to make a smooth sauce.

5 Return the rabbit and bacon to the casserole, and mix in half of the parsley. Season with salt and pepper.

6 Cover the casserole with a lid and cook in the oven for 15–20 minutes, then reduce the temperature to 150°C/300°F/Gas 2 for 1½ hours, or until the rabbit is tender. Add the remaining parsley and serve.

Energy 368kcal/1535kJ; Protein 32.9g; Carbohydrate 10.5g, of which sugars 5.8g; Fat 19.7g, of which saturates 8g; Cholesterol 133mg; Calcium 88mg; Fibre 1.4g; Sodium 567mg.

Spicy rabbit and onion stew

Slow-cooked rabbit was a crucial part of the rural diet in past generations; this dish includes pounded garlic, bread and vinegar, which gives it a Mediterranean character.

Serves 4

675g/1½lb rabbit, jointed

300ml/½ pint/1¼ cups dry white wine

15ml/1 tbsp sherry vinegar

several oregano sprigs

2 bay leaves

30ml/2 tbsp plain (all-purpose) flour

90ml/6 tbsp olive oil

175g/6oz baby (pearl) onions, peeled and left whole

4 garlic cloves, sliced

150ml/¼ pint/⅔ cup chicken stock

1 dried chilli, seeded and finely chopped

10ml/2 tsp paprika

salt and ground black pepper

crusty bread, to serve

1 Put the rabbit in a bowl. Add the wine, vinegar, oregano and bay leaves and toss together. Marinate for several hours or overnight in the refrigerator.

2 Drain the rabbit, reserving the marinade, and pat it dry with kitchen paper. Season the flour and use to dust the marinated rabbit.

3 Heat the oil in a large, wide flameproof casserole or frying pan. Fry the rabbit pieces until golden on all sides, then remove them and set aside.

4 Fry the onions until they are beginning to colour, then reserve on a separate plate.

5 Add the garlic to the pan and fry, then add the strained marinade, with the chicken stock, chilli and paprika.

6 Return the rabbit and the reserved onions to the pan. Bring to a simmer, then cover and simmer gently for about 45 minutes until the rabbit is tender. Check the seasoning, adding more vinegar and paprika if necessary. Serve the stew hot, in warmed serving bowls, with some crusty bread.

Farmhouse tip Rather than cooking on the stove, you can bake the stew in the oven at 180°C/350°F/Gas 4 for about 50 minutes.

Energy 311kcal/1294kJ; Protein 23.2g; Carbohydrate 9.5g, of which sugars 2.6g; Fat 20.4g, of which saturates 4.1g; Cholesterol 83mg; Calcium 65mg; Fibre 0.9g; Sodium 52mg.

Casseroled rabbit with thyme

This is the sort of home cooking found in farmhouse kitchens and cosy neighbourhood restaurants in France, where rabbit is treated much like chicken and enjoyed frequently.

3 Melt the butter and oil in a large flameproof casserole. Cook the rabbit pieces until golden.

4 Pour the wine into the casserole and boil for 1 minute, then add enough of the stock to just cover the meat. Add the herbs and garlic. Cover and simmer gently for 1 hour.

Serves 4

40g/1½oz/6 tbsp flour

1.2kg/2½lb rabbit

15g/½oz/1 tbsp butter

15ml/1 tbsp olive oil

250ml/8fl oz/1 cup red wine

350–475ml/12–16fl oz/1½–2 cups chicken stock

15ml/1 tbsp fresh thyme leaves

1 bay leaf

2 garlic cloves, finely chopped

10–15ml/2–3 tsp Dijon mustard

salt and ground black pepper

1 Joint the rabbit into 8 portions. Put the flour in a plastic bag and season with salt and pepper.

2 One at a time, drop the rabbit pieces into the bag and shake to coat them with the seasoned flour. Tap off the excess and set aside. Any excess flour can be discarded.

5 When cooked, stir the mustard into the casserole, then lift the rabbit pieces on to a warmed serving platter. Season the sauce, then pour over the rabbit. Serve immediately, accompanied by some mashed potato.

Energy 257kcal/1076kJ; Protein 29g; Carbohydrate 9g, of which sugars 1g; Fat 12g, of which saturates 5g; Cholesterol 72mg; Calcium 83mg; Fibre 0.4g; Sodium 653mg.

Farmhouse venison pie

This satisfying pie combines venison in a rich gravy with a potato and parsnip topping.
If you assemble in advance and cook later, increase the cooking time to 45–60 minutes.

Serves 4

45ml/3 tbsp sunflower oil

1 onion, chopped

1 garlic clove, crushed

3 rindless streaky (fatty) bacon
rashers (strips), chopped

675g/1½lb minced (ground) venison

115g/4oz/1 cup button (white)
mushrooms, chopped

30ml/2 tbsp flour

475ml/16fl oz/2 cups beef stock

150ml/¼ pint/⅔ cup ruby port

2 bay leaves

5ml/1 tsp chopped fresh thyme

5ml/1 tsp Dijon mustard

15ml/1 tbsp redcurrant jelly

675g/1½lb potatoes, peeled and cut
into large chunks

450g/1lb parsnips, peeled and cut
into large chunks

1 egg yolk

50g/2oz/4 tbsp butter

grated nutmeg

45ml/3 tbsp chopped fresh parsley

salt and ground black pepper

1 Heat the oil in a large frying pan and
fry the onion, garlic and bacon for
about 5 minutes. Add the venison and
mushrooms and cook, stirring, until
browned. Stir in the flour and cook for
1–2 minutes, then add the stock, port,
herbs, mustard, redcurrant jelly and
seasoning. Bring to the boil, cover and
simmer for 30–40 minutes, until tender.

2 Preheat the oven to 200°C/400°F/
Gas 6. Bring a pan of lightly salted
water to the boil and cook the potatoes
and parsnips for 20 minutes or until
tender. Drain and mash, then mix in the
egg yolk, butter, nutmeg and parsley.
Season to taste with salt and pepper.

3 Spoon the venison mixture into a
large pie dish. Shake to level the
surface. Spoon the potato and parsnip
mixture over the meat and smooth over
to cover. Bake in the oven for
30–40 minutes, until the top is golden
brown. Serve at once.

Energy 723Kcal/3033kJ; Protein 48.5g; Carbohydrate 59.6g, of which sugars 20.4g; Fat 30.3g, of which saturates 11.2g; Cholesterol 174mg; Calcium 128mg; Fibre 9g; Sodium 447mg.

Wild venison stew

This simple, yet deeply flavoured stew makes a wonderful supper dish, incorporating rich red wine and sweet redcurrant jelly with the salty bacon. This recipe also works beautifully with diced beef, and is even more delicious reheated the following day.

Serves 4

1.3kg/3lb stewing venison (shoulder or topside), trimmed and diced

50g/2oz/¼ cup butter

225g/8oz piece of streaky (fatty) bacon, cut into 2cm/¾in lardons

2 large onions, chopped

1 large carrot, peeled and diced

1 large garlic clove, crushed

30ml/2 tbsp plain (all-purpose) flour

1 bay leaf

200g/7oz button (white) mushrooms, sliced

30ml/2 tbsp redcurrant jelly

sprig of fresh thyme

½ bottle red wine

beef stock

salt and ground black pepper

1 Dry the diced venison thoroughly using kitchen paper. Set aside.

2 Melt the butter in a large, heavy pan then brown the bacon lardons over a medium-high heat, stirring occasionally. Reduce the heat slightly to medium and add the onions and carrot, stir in and brown lightly.

3 Add the venison to the pan along with the garlic and stir into the mixture. Sprinkle on the flour and mix well. Add the sliced mushrooms and redcurrant jelly and stir in.

▶ **4** Place the thyme in the pan and pour in the wine, together with enough beef stock to just cover.

5 Cover the pan and simmer over a very low heat until the meat is cooked and very tender, this will take approximately 1½–2 hours.

6 Serve hot, accompanied by rustic bread or creamy mashed potato, and green vegetables of your choice, or cool and chill for reheating the next day.

Energy 727kcal/3045kJ; Protein 83.8g; Carbohydrate 17.5g, of which sugars 14.4g; Fat 31.3g, of which saturates 13.8g; Cholesterol 226mg; Calcium 70mg; Fibre 2.9g; Sodium 985mg.

Venison pie with root vegetable mash

A variation on cottage pie, this tasty game pie has tender pieces of venison cooked in a rich gravy, and is topped with creamy root vegetables such as sweet potatoes, parsnips and swede. It makes an excellent winter supper dish, served with steamed green vegetables.

Serves 6

30ml/2 tbsp olive oil

2 leeks, trimmed and chopped

1kg/2¼lb minced (ground) venison

30ml/2 tbsp chopped fresh parsley

300ml/½ pint/1¼ cups game consommé or stock

salt and ground black pepper

For the topping

1.5kg/3¼lb mixed root vegetables, such as sweet potatoes, parsnips and swede (rutabaga), coarsely chopped

15ml/1 tbsp horseradish sauce

25g/1oz/2 tbsp butter

1 Heat the oil in a pan. Add the leeks and cook for about 8 minutes, or until softened and beginning to brown.

2 Add the minced venison to the pan and cook for about 10 minutes, stirring frequently, or until the meat is well browned. Stir in the chopped parsley, consommé and seasoning, then bring to the boil, cover and simmer for about 20 minutes, stirring occasionally.

3 Meanwhile, preheat the oven to 200°C/400°F/Gas 6 and prepare the topping. Cook the vegetables in boiling, salted water to cover for 15–20 minutes. Drain and mash with the horseradish sauce, butter and pepper.

4 Spoon the venison mixture into an ovenproof dish and top with the mashed vegetables. Bake for 20 minutes, or until piping hot and beginning to brown.

Energy 307kcal/1291kJ; Protein 39.8g; Carbohydrate 13.2g, of which sugars 12.5g; Fat 12g, of which saturates 4.1g; Cholesterol 93mg; Calcium 154mg; Fibre 5.8g; Sodium 176mg.

Rustic Meat Dishes

Freshly baked pies, slow-cooked pot roasts and flavoursome casseroles showcase all that is best in country cooking. From simple Sunday roasts to weekday dishes such as Shepherd's Pie and Rustic Meat Loaf, there is a meat recipe for every day in this chapter. Many of the recipes use economic cuts of meat and seasonal vegetables, so you can really make the most of the revival in home cooking.

Roast beef with Yorkshire puddings

A quintessential Sunday lunch classic, this is the well-loved 'roast beef of old England', traditionally served with crisp Yorkshire puddings, golden roast potatoes and a selection of seasonal vegetables, all covered in gravy and accompanied by a tangy horseradish cream. In Yorkshire the puddings are often served before the meat, with the gravy, as a first course.

Serves 6–8

rib of beef joint, weighing about 3kg/6½lb

oil, for brushing

salt and ground black pepper

For the Yorkshire puddings

115g/4oz/1 cup plain (all-purpose) flour

1.5ml/¼ tsp salt

1 egg

200ml/7fl oz/scant 1 cup milk

oil or beef dripping, for greasing

For the horseradish cream

60–75ml/4–5 tbsp finely grated fresh horseradish

300ml/½ pint/1¼ cups sour cream

30ml/2 tbsp cider vinegar or white wine vinegar

10ml/2 tsp caster (superfine) sugar

For the gravy

600ml/1 pint/2½ cups good beef stock

Farmhouse tip If fresh horseraddish is unavailable use a jar of preserved grated horseradish instead.

1 Preheat the oven to 220°C/425°F/Gas 7. Weigh the joint and calculate the cooking time required as follows: 10–15 minutes per 500g/1¼lb for rare beef, 15–20 minutes for medium and 20–25 minutes for well done.

2 Put the joint into a large roasting pan. Brush it all over with oil and season with salt and pepper. Put into the hot oven and cook for 30 minutes, until the beef is browned. Lower the oven temperature to 160°C/325°F/Gas 3 and cook for the calculated time, spooning the juices over the meat occasionally during cooking.

3 For the Yorkshire pudding, sift the flour and salt into a bowl and break the egg into it. Make the milk up to 300ml/½ pint/1¼ cups with water and gradually whisk into the flour to make a smooth batter. Leave to stand while the beef cooks. Generously grease with oil or dripping eight Yorkshire pudding tins (muffin pans) measuring about 10cm/4in, and set aside.

4 For the horseradish cream, put all the ingredients into a bowl and mix well. Cover and chill until required.

5 At the end of its cooking time, remove the beef from the oven, cover with foil and leave to stand for 30–40 minutes while you cook the Yorkshire puddings and make the gravy.

6 Increase the oven temperature to 220°C/425°F/Gas 7 and put the prepared tins on the top shelf for 5 minutes until very hot. Pour in the batter and cook for about 15 minutes until well risen, crisp and golden brown.

7 To make the gravy, transfer the beef to a warmed serving plate. Pour off the fat from the roasting pan, leaving the meat juices. Add the stock to the pan, bring to the boil, scraping up the meat deposits, and bubble until reduced by about half. Season to taste.

8 Carve the beef and serve with the gravy, Yorkshire puddings, roast potatoes and horseradish cream.

Energy 1037kcal/4338kJ; Protein 129g; Carbohydrate 15.1g, of which sugars 4.1g; Fat 51.5g, of which saturates 24.3g; Cholesterol 352mg; Calcium 123mg; Fibre 0.5g; Sodium 249mg.

Slow-cooked beef stew

In the South of France, this farmhouse stew is called a daube, taking its name from the daubière, the earthenware pot it was cooked in. It is improved by being cooked a day ahead.

Serves 6–8

30–60ml/2–4 tbsp olive oil

225g/8oz lean salt pork or thick-cut rindless streaky (fatty) bacon, diced

1.75kg/4–4½lb stewing beef, cut into 7.5cm/3in pieces

750ml/1¼ pints/3 cups red wine

4 carrots, thickly sliced

2 large onions, coarsely chopped

3 tomatoes, skinned, seeded and chopped

15ml/1 tbsp tomato purée (paste)

2–4 garlic cloves, very finely chopped

1 bouquet garni

5ml/1 tsp black peppercorns

1 small onion, studded with 4 cloves

grated rind and juice of 1 orange

30–45ml/2–3 tbsp chopped parsley

salt and ground black pepper

1 Heat 30ml/2 tbsp of the olive oil in a large, heavy frying pan and cook the salt pork or bacon, stirring frequently, until the fat runs. Raise the heat and cook for 4–5 minutes more, until browned. Transfer with a slotted spoon to a large, flameproof casserole.

2 Add enough beef to the frying pan to fit easily in one layer. Cook for 6–8 minutes until browned, turning to colour all sides, then transfer the meat to the casserole. Brown the rest of the meat in the same way, adding a little more oil if needed.

3 Pour the wine in to the casserole and, if needed, add enough water to cover the beef and bacon. Bring to the boil over a medium heat, skimming off any foam that rises to the surface.

4 Add the carrots, onions, tomatoes, tomato purée, garlic, bouquet garni and peppercorns to the casserole.

5 Add the clove-studded onion and stir all the ingredients into the meat. Cover tightly and simmer over a low heat for about 3 hours. Skim off any fat. Season, discard the bouquet garni and onion and stir in the orange rind and juice and the parsley.

Energy 463kcal/1934kJ; Protein 56g; Carbohydrate 9g, of which sugars 8g; Fat 23g, of which saturates 7g; Cholesterol 148mg; Calcium 50mg; Fibre 2.5g; Sodium 681mg.

Beef casserole with beans and eggs

This traditional Jewish stew, called 'cholent', is usually cooked throughout Friday night, ready to be eaten on the Sabbath. This Sephardi version contains eggs.

Serves 6–8

225g/8oz/1¼ cups haricot (navy) or butter (lima) beans, soaked overnight in water

30–60ml/2–4 tbsp oil

10 small onions, halved

2 carrots, diced

1.5kg/3–3½lb stewing steak, cubed

6 small hard-boiled eggs in their shells

5ml/1 tsp paprika

5ml/1 tsp tomato purée (paste)

600ml/1 pint/2½ cups boiling water or beef stock

salt and ground black pepper

3 Stir the paprika and tomato purée into the oil left in the pan. Add salt and pepper and cook for 1 minute. Stir in the boiling water or stock to incorporate the sediment, then pour the mixture over the meat and eggs.

4 Cover the casserole and cook for at least 8 hours or until the meat is very tender, adding more liquid if it is needed. Take out the eggs, remove the shells and return them to the casserole before serving.

1 Preheat the oven to 110°C/225°F/ Gas ¼. Drain the beans, place them in a pan and cover with fresh water. Bring to the boil. Cook rapidly for 10 minutes, skimming off the white froth and any bean skins that come to the surface. Drain.

2 Heat half the oil in a frying pan and sauté the onions for about 10 minutes, then transfer to a casserole, with the carrots and beans. Heat the remaining oil and brown the beef in batches. Place it on top of the vegetables. Tuck the eggs between the pieces of meat.

Energy 492/2060kJ; Protein 53g; Carbohydrate 10g, of which sugars 8g; Fat 23g, of which saturates 7g; Cholesterol 263mg; Calcium 102mg; Fibre 7.6g; Sodium 365mg.

Pot roast beef with stout

Use a boned and rolled joint such as brisket, silverside or topside for this slow-cooked dish, where the vegetables are cooked with the beef and the meat becomes meltingly tender.

Serves 6

30ml/2 tbsp vegetable oil

900g/2lb rolled brisket of beef

2 medium onions, roughly chopped

2 celery sticks, thickly sliced

450g/1lb carrots, cut into large chunks

675g/1½lb potatoes, peeled and cut into large chunks

30ml/2 tbsp plain (all-purpose) flour

450ml/¾ pint/2 cups beef stock

300ml/½ pint/1¼ cups stout

1 bay leaf

45ml/3 tbsp chopped fresh thyme

5ml/1 tsp soft light brown sugar

30ml/2 tbsp wholegrain mustard

15ml/1 tbsp tomato purée (paste)

salt and ground black pepper

1 Preheat the oven to 180°C/350°F/ Gas 4. Heat the oil in a large flameproof casserole and brown the beef until golden brown all over.

2 Lift the beef from the pan and drain on kitchen paper. Add the onions to the pan and cook for about 4 minutes, until just beginning to soften and brown.

3 Add the celery, carrots and potatoes to the casserole and cook over a medium heat for 2–3 minutes, or until they are just beginning to colour.

4 Add the flour and cook for a further 1 minute, stirring constantly. Gradually pour in the beef stock and the stout. Heat until the mixture comes to the boil, stirring frequently.

5 Stir in the bay leaf, thyme, sugar, mustard, tomato purée and seasoning. Place the meat on top, cover tightly and transfer the casserole to the hot oven.

6 Cook for about 2½ hours, or until tender. Adjust the seasoning, to taste. To serve, carve the beef into thick slices and serve with the vegetables and plenty of gravy.

Energy 415kcal/1743kJ; Protein 36g; Carbohydrate 35.6g, of which sugars 13.1g; Fat 14g, of which saturates 4.4g; Cholesterol 81mg; Calcium 66mg; Fibre 4.2g; Sodium 284mg.

Braised beef and country vegetables

In the past, this dish would have been left to gently cook all day, but it is just as tasty when slow cooked for just a few hours. It is delicious served with suet dumplings or crusty bread.

Serves 4–6

1kg/2¼lb lean stewing steak, cut into 5cm/2in cubes

45ml/3 tbsp plain (all-purpose) flour

45ml/3 tbsp oil

1 large onion, thinly sliced

1 large carrot, thickly sliced

2 celery sticks, finely chopped

300ml/½ pint/¼ cup beef stock

30ml/2 tbsp tomato purée (paste)

5ml/1 tsp dried mixed herbs

15ml/1 tbsp dark muscovado (molasses) sugar

225g/8oz baby potatoes, halved if necessary

2 leeks, thinly sliced

salt and ground black pepper

Variation Replace the potatoes with dumplings. Sift 175g/6oz/1½ cups self-raising (self-rising) flour and stir in 75g/3oz/½ cup shredded suet (US chilled, grated shortening), 30ml/2 tbsp chopped parsley and seasoning. Stir in water to make a soft dough and divide the mixture into 12 balls. In step 6, stir in the leeks and put the dumplings on top. Cover and cook for 15–20 minutes more.

1 Preheat the oven to 150°C/300°F/ Gas 2. Season the flour and use to coat the beef cubes.

2 Heat the oil in a large, flameproof casserole. Add a small batch of meat, cook quickly until browned on all sides and, with a slotted spoon, lift out on to a plate. Repeat with the remaining beef until it is all cooked.

3 Add the onion, carrot and celery to the casserole. Cook over medium heat for about 10 minutes, stirring frequently, until they begin to soften and brown slightly on the edges.

4 Return the meat to the casserole and add the stock, tomato purée, herbs and sugar, at the same time scraping up any sediment that has stuck to the casserole. Heat until the liquid nearly comes to the boil.

5 Cover with a tight-fitting lid and put into the hot oven. Cook for 2–2½ hours, or until the beef is tender.

6 Gently stir in the potatoes and leeks, cover and continue cooking for a further 30 minutes or until the potatoes are soft.

Energy 450kcal/1880kJ; Protein 41.3g; Carbohydrate 23.6g, of which sugars 10.3g; Fat 21.7g, of which saturates 7.3g; Cholesterol 97mg; Calcium 63mg; Fibre 3.5g; Sodium 137mg.

Beef and red wine stew

Beef cooked 'Burgundy style' in red wine with chopped bacon, baby onions and mushrooms and simmered for hours at a low temperature produces a rich, dark gravy and melt-in-the-mouth meat. Serve with creamy mashed potato.

Serves 6

175g/6oz rindless streaky (fatty) bacon rashers (strips), chopped

900g/2lb lean braising steak, such as top rump of beef or braising steak

30ml/2 tbsp plain (all-purpose) flour

45ml/3 tbsp sunflower oil

25g/1oz/2 tbsp butter

12 shallots

2 garlic cloves, crushed

175g/6oz/2½ cups mushrooms, sliced

450ml/¾ pint/scant 2 cups robust red wine

150ml/¼ pint/⅔ cup beef stock

1 bay leaf

2 sprigs each of fresh thyme, parsley and marjoram

salt and ground black pepper

mashed potato, to serve

Variation Instead of the rindless streaky (fatty) bacon rashers (strips), use lardons, which are available from supermarkets.

1 Preheat the oven to 160°C/325°F/ Gas 3. Heat a large flameproof casserole, then add the bacon and cook, stirring occasionally, until the pieces are crisp and golden brown.

2 Meanwhile, cut the meat into 2.5cm/ 1in cubes. Season the flour and use to coat the meat. Use a slotted spoon to remove the bacon from the casserole and set aside. Add and heat the oil, then brown the beef in batches and set aside with the bacon.

3 Add the butter to the fat remaining in the casserole. Cook the shallots and garlic until starting to colour, then add the mushrooms and cook for a further 5 minutes. Replace the bacon and meat, and stir in the wine and stock. Tie the bay leaf, thyme, parsley and marjoram together into a bouquet garni and add to the casserole.

4 Cover and cook in the oven for 1½ hours, or until the meat is tender, stirring once or twice. Add salt and pepper to taste and serve with creamy mashed potatoes.

Farmhouse tip This casserole freezes very well. Transfer the mixture to a dish so that it cools quickly, then pour it into a rigid plastic container. Push all the cubes of meat down into the sauce or they will dry out. Freeze for up to 2 months. Thaw overnight in the refrigerator, then transfer to a flameproof casserole and add 150ml/ ¼ pint/⅔ cup water. Stir well, bring to the boil, stirring occasionally, and simmer steadily for at least 15 minutes, or until the meat is piping hot.

Energy 749kcal/3117kJ; Protein 63.3g; Carbohydrate 15.2g, of which sugars 8.8g; Fat 40.3g, of which saturates 14g; Cholesterol 167mg; Calcium 69mg; Fibre 2.8g; Sodium 868mg.

Braised oxtail

While oxtail requires long, slow cooking to tenderize the meat, the resulting complex flavour and rich texture are well worth the effort. This dish is traditionally served with simple boiled potatoes to soak up the gravy, though mashed potatoes would be good too.

Serves 6

2 oxtails, trimmed, cut into pieces, total weight about 1.5kg/3lb 6oz

30ml/2 tbsp flour, seasoned with salt and pepper

45ml/3 tbsp oil

2 large onions, sliced

2 celery sticks, sliced

4 medium carrots, sliced

1 litre/1¾ pints/4 cups beef stock

15ml/1 tbsp tomato purée (paste)

finely grated rind of 1 small orange

2 bay leaves

few sprigs of fresh thyme

salt and ground black pepper

chopped fresh parsley, to garnish

1 Preheat the oven to 150°C/300°F/ Gas 2. Coat the pieces of oxtail in the seasoned flour, shaking off and reserving any excess.

2 Heat 30ml/2 tbsp oil in a large flameproof casserole and add the oxtail in batches, cooking quickly until browned all over. Lift out and set aside. Add the remaining oil to the pan, and stir in the onions, celery and carrots.

3 Cook the vegetables quickly, stirring occasionally, until beginning to brown. Tip in any reserved flour, then add the stock, tomato purée and orange rind.

Farmhouse tip This dish benefits from being made in advance. When cooled completely, any fat can be removed before reheating if you wish.

4 Heat until bubbles begin to rise to the surface, then add the herbs, cover and put into the hot oven. Cook for 3½–4 hours until the oxtail is very tender.

5 Remove from the oven and leave to stand, covered, for 10 minutes before skimming off the surface fat. Adjust the seasoning and garnish with parsley.

Energy 341kcal/1426kJ; Protein 30.9g; Carbohydrate 13.6g, of which sugars 7.7g; Fat 18.6g, of which saturates 0.7g; Cholesterol 0mg; Calcium 54mg; Fibre 2.3g; Sodium 203mg.

Beef rib with onion sauce

Beef with a peppercorn crust, seared in a pan and then briefly roasted in the oven is a great way to cook this prized cut of meat. The onion sauce makes a superb accompaniment.

2 Meanwhile, make the sauce. Melt 40g/1½oz/3 tbsp of the butter in a pan and cook the onion for 3–5 minutes until softened. Add the wine, stock, redcurrant jelly and thyme and bring to the boil.

3 Reduce the heat and simmer for 30–35 minutes, until the liquid has evaporated and the sauce has thickened. Season with salt and pepper and keep hot.

4 Preheat the oven to 220°C/425°F/ Gas 7. Melt the remaining butter with the oil in a heavy, ovenproof frying pan. Add the meat and sear over a high heat for 1–2 minutes on each side. Immediately place the pan in the oven and roast for 8–10 minutes.

5 Transfer the beef to a board, cover loosely and leave to stand for 10 minutes. With a knife, loosen the meat from the rib bone, then carve into thick slices. Serve with the onion sauce.

Serves 2–4

1 beef rib with bone, about 1kg/2¼lb and about 4cm/1½in thick, well trimmed of fat

5ml/1 tsp lightly crushed black peppercorns

15ml/1 tbsp coarse sea salt, crushed

50g/2oz/4 tbsp butter

1 large red onion, sliced

120ml/4fl oz/½ cup fruity red wine

120ml/4fl oz/½ cup beef stock

15–30ml/1–2 tbsp redcurrant jelly

2.5ml/½ tsp dried thyme

30–45ml/2–3 tbsp olive oil

salt and ground black pepper

1 Wipe the beef with damp kitchen paper. Mix the crushed peppercorns and salt together and press on to both sides of the meat. Leave to stand, loosely covered, for 30 minutes.

Energy 540kcal/2255kJ; Protein 66g; Carbohydrate 10g, of which sugars 8g; Fat 27g, of which saturates 9g; Cholesterol 148mg; Calcium 37mg; Fibre 0.9g; Sodium 451mg.

Rustic meat loaf

Made with a mixture of minced beef, pork and veal, this tasty meat loaf has plenty of fresh herbs and seasoning, and is lovely served with a home-made tomato sauce.

Serves 6

25g/1oz/2 tbsp butter
or margarine

1 onion, finely chopped

2 garlic cloves, finely chopped

50g/2oz/½ cup finely chopped celery

450g/1lb lean minced (ground) beef

225g/8oz minced (ground) veal

225g/8oz minced (ground) pork

2 eggs

50g/2oz/1 cup fine fresh breadcrumbs

25g/1oz/½ cup chopped fresh parsley

30ml/2 tbsp chopped fresh basil

2.5ml/½ tsp fresh or dried thyme leaves

2.5ml/½ tsp salt

2.5ml/½ tsp pepper

30ml/2 tbsp Worcestershire sauce

50ml/2fl oz/¼ cup chilli sauce or tomato ketchup

6 bacon rashers (strips)

1 Preheat oven to 180°C/350°F/Gas 4. Melt the butter or margarine in a small frying pan over a low heat. Add the onion, garlic and celery and cook until softened, 8–10 minutes. Set aside.

2 Combine the onion, garlic and celery with all the other ingredients except the bacon in a bowl. Mix lightly, using a fork or your fingers. Do not overwork or the meat loaf will be too compact.

3 Form the meat mixture into an oval loaf on a shallow baking tin (pan).

4 Lay the bacon across the meat loaf. Bake for 1¼ hours, basting occasionally with the juices and bacon fat in the pan.

5 Remove from the oven and drain off the fat. Leave the meat loaf to stand for 10 minutes to firm up, before serving in thick slices.

Energy 286kcal/1189kJ; Protein 18.6g; Carbohydrate 11.9g, of which sugars 5.1g; Fat 18.5g, of which saturates 8.3g; Cholesterol 119mg; Calcium 62mg; Fibre 1g; Sodium 572mg.

Sunday best beef wellington

For a special occasion, nothing surpasses the succulent flavour of beef Wellington. Traditionally, the beef is spread with goose liver pâté, but many country cooks prefer a pâté made from woodland mushrooms, especially when they have picked them themselves.

Serves 4

675g/1½lb fillet steak, tied

15ml/1 tbsp vegetable oil

350g/12oz puff pastry

1 egg, beaten, to glaze

salt and ground black pepper

For the parsley pancakes

50g/2oz/½ cup plain flour

150ml/¼ pint/⅔ cup milk

1 egg

30ml/2 tbsp chopped fresh parsley

For the mushroom pâté

25g/1oz/2 tbsp butter

2 shallots or 1 small onion, chopped

450g/1lb/4 cups assorted wild and cultivated mushrooms, chopped

50g/2oz/1 cup white breadcrumbs

75ml/5 tbsp double cream

2 egg yolks

1 Preheat the oven to 220°C/425°F/Gas 7. Season the steak with black pepper. Heat the oil in a roasting pan and quickly sear to brown all sides.

2 Transfer to the oven and roast for 15 minutes for rare, 20 minutes for medium-rare or 25 minutes for well-done. Set aside to cool. Reduce the oven to 190°C/375°F/Gas 5.

3 To make the pancakes, beat together the flour, a pinch of salt, half the milk, the egg and parsley until smooth, then stir in the remaining milk. Heat a greased pan and pour in enough batter to coat the base. When set, flip over and cook the other side until browned. Continue with the remaining batter.

4 To make the mushroom pâté, melt the butter in a frying pan and fry the shallots or onion for 7–10 minutes to soften without colouring. Add the mushrooms and cook until the juices run. Increase the heat so that the juices evaporate. Combine the breadcrumbs, cream and egg yolks. Add to the mushroom mixture and mix to a smooth paste. Allow to cool.

5 Roll out the pastry to a 36 x 30cm/ 14 x 12in rectangle. Place two pancakes on the pastry and spread with mushroom pâté.

6 Place the beef on top of the pâté. Spread over any remaining pâté, then the remaining pancakes. Cut out and reserve four squares from the corners of the pastry, then moisten the pastry with egg and wrap the meat. Decorate with the reserved pastry trimmings.

7 Put the beef Wellington on a baking sheet and brush evenly with beaten egg. Bake in the oven for 40 minutes until the top is golden brown. To ensure that the meat is heated through, test with a meat thermometer. It should read 52–54°C/125–130°F for rare, 57°C/135°F for medium-rare and 71°C/ 160°F for well-done meat.

8 Serve the Wellington hot, in slices, with watercress if you wish.

Energy 902Kcal/3765kJ; Protein 50.4g; Carbohydrate 55.5g, of which sugars 4.8g; Fat 55.6g, of which saturates 16.3g; Cholesterol 297mg; Calcium 177mg; Fibre 2.1g; Sodium 529mg.

Roast beef with mushrooms and red peppers

A substantial and warming dish for cold, dark evenings. If you can't find small red peppers, use two large red (bell) peppers, cut into large chunks, instead.

Serves 8

1.5kg/3–3½lb piece of sirloin	300ml/½ pint/¼ cups beef stock
15ml/1 tbsp olive oil	30ml/2 tbsp Marsala
450g/4lb small red peppers	10ml/2 tsp dried mixed herbs
115g/4oz mushrooms	salt and ground black pepper
175g/6oz thick-sliced pancetta or smoked bacon, cubed	
50g/2oz/2 tbsp plain flour	
150ml/¼ pint/⅔ cup red wine	

1 Preheat the oven to 190°C/375°F/ Gas 5. Season the meat well. Heat the olive oil in a large pan. When very hot, brown the meat on all sides. Place in a roasting pan and cook for 1¼ hours.

2 Put the red peppers in the oven to roast for 20 minutes.

3 Near the end of the meat's cooking time, prepare the gravy. Wipe the mushrooms, and roughly chop the caps and stems.

4 Heat the frying pan again and add the pancetta or bacon. Cook until the fat runs freely from the meat. Add the flour and cook for a few minutes until the meat is browned.

5 Gradually stir in the red wine and the stock. Bring to the boil, stirring. Lower the heat and add the Marsala, herbs and seasoning.

6 Add the mushrooms to the pan and heat through.

7 Remove the sirloin from the oven and leave to stand for 10 minutes before carving it. Serve with the roasted peppers and the hot gravy.

Energy 343kcal/1437kJ; Protein 50g; Carbohydrate 9g, of which sugars 4g; Fat 12g, of which saturates 5g; Cholesterol 102mg; Calcium 38mg; Fibre 1.6g; Sodium 534mg.

Traditional beef stew and dumplings

This dish can cook in the oven while you go for a wintery walk to work up an appetite, simply add the dumplings and steam some greens when you get home.

Serves 6

25g/1oz/1 tbsp plain flour

1.2kg/2½lb stewing steak, cubed

30ml/2 tbsp olive oil

2 large onions, sliced

450g/1lb carrots, sliced

300ml/½ pint/1¼ cups stout, such as Guinness, or dark beer

3 bay leaves

10ml/2 tsp light brown soft sugar

3 fresh thyme sprigs

5ml/1 tsp cider vinegar

salt and ground black pepper

For the dumplings

115g/4oz/½ cup suet (US chilled grated shortening)

225g/8oz/2 cups self-raising (self-rising) flour

30ml/2 tbsp chopped mixed fresh herbs

about 150ml/¼ pint/⅔ cup water

1 Preheat the oven to 160°C/325°F/ Gas 3. Season the flour and sprinkle over the meat, tossing to coat.

2 Heat the oil in a large casserole and lightly sauté the onions and carrots. Remove the vegetables with a slotted spoon and reserve them.

3 Brown the meat well in batches in the casserole, adding a little more oil if necessary. Return all the vegetables to the casserole.

4 Add any leftover seasoned flour to the pan, stirring so that it combines with the oil. Add the Guinness or beer, bay leaves, sugar and thyme.

5 Bring the liquid to the boil, cover, and transfer to the oven. Cook for at least 1 hour and 40 minutes, before making the dumplings.

6 Mix the suet, flour and herbs together. Add enough water to make a soft, sticky dough. Form into small balls.

7 Stir the cider vinegar in to the meat and then add the dumplings on top. Cook for a further 20 minutes, covered, until the dumplings have cooked through. Serve hot.

Energy 648Kcal/2714kJ; Protein 50.3g; Carbohydrate 42.9g, of which sugars 10.6g; Fat 30.5g, of which saturates 11.2g; Cholesterol 152mg; Calcium 184mg; Fibre 4g; Sodium 297mg.

Beef in red wine with a potato crust

This recipe makes the best of braising beef by marinating it in red wine and topping it with a cheesy grated potato crust that bakes to a golden, crunchy consistency. This one-pot dish makes a satistfying meal on its own.

Serves 4

675g/1½lb stewing beef, diced

300ml/½ pint/1¼ cups red wine

3 juniper berries, crushed

slice of orange peel

30ml/2 tbsp olive oil

2 onions, cut into chunks

2 carrots, cut into chunks

1 garlic clove, crushed

225g/8oz/3 cups button (white) mushrooms

150ml/¼ pint/⅔ cup beef stock

30ml/2 tbsp cornflour (cornstarch)

salt and ground black pepper

For the crust

450g/1lb potatoes, grated

15ml/1 tbsp olive oil

30ml/2 tbsp creamed horseradish

50g/2oz/½ cup mature (sharp) Cheddar cheese, grated

1 Place the beef in a non-metallic bowl. Add the wine, berries, and orange peel and season with pepper. Mix the ingredients, then cover and leave to marinate for at least 4 hours or overnight.

2 Preheat the oven to 160°C/325°F/Gas 3. Drain the beef, reserving the marinade.

3 Heat the oil in a large flameproof casserole and fry the meat in batches for 5 minutes to seal. Add the onions, carrots and garlic and cook for 5 minutes. Stir in the mushrooms, red wine marinade and beef stock. Simmer.

4 Mix the cornflour with water to make a smooth paste. Stir into the pan. Season, cover and cook for 1½ hours.

5 Make the crust 30 minutes before the end of the cooking time for the beef. Start by blanching the grated potatoes in boiling water for 5 minutes. Drain well and then squeeze out all the extra liquid.

6 Stir in the remaining ingredients and then sprinkle evenly over the surface of the beef. Increase the oven temperature to 200°C/400°F/Gas 6 and cook the dish for a further 30 minutes so that the top is crispy and slightly browned.

Farmhouse tip Use a large grater on the food processor for the potatoes, or alternatively, grate them by hand with a traditional grater. They will hold their shape better while being blanched than if you use a finer blade.

Energy 474kcal/1973kJ; Protein 43g; Carbohydrate 6.1g, of which sugars 5.6g; Fat 28.8g, of which saturates 8.7g; Cholesterol 106mg; Calcium 53mg; Fibre 2.6g; Sodium 564mg.

Steak, mushroom and ale pie

This dish is a firm favourite on menus at restaurants specializing in traditional country fare. Preparing the filling the day before and allowing the meat and vegetables to rest overnight ensures a particularly tasty filling. The pie can be ready relatively quickly by topping with the pastry and baking. Serve with seasonal vegetables or a side salad.

Serves 4

25g/1oz/2 tbsp butter

1 large onion, finely chopped

115g/4oz/1½ cups field (portabello) mushrooms, halved

900g/2lb lean beef in one piece, such as rump or braising steak

30ml/2 tbsp plain (all-purpose) flour

45ml/3 tbsp sunflower oil

300ml/½ pint/1¼ cups stout or brown ale

300ml/½ pint/1¼ cups beef stock or consommé

500g/1¼lb puff pastry, thawed if frozen

beaten egg, to glaze

salt and ground black pepper

1 Melt the butter in a large, flameproof casserole, add the onion and cook gently, stirring occasionally, for about 5 minutes, or until it is softened. Add the halved mushrooms and continue cooking for a further 5 minutes, stirring.

2 Meanwhile, trim the meat and cut it into 2.5cm/1in cubes. Season the flour and toss the meat in it.

3 Remove the onion mixture from the casserole and set aside. Add the oil, then brown the steak in batches.

4 Replace the vegetables, then stir in the stout or ale and stock or consommé. Bring to the boil, reduce the heat and simmer for 1 hour, stirring occasionally. Season to taste and transfer to a 1.5 litre/ 2½ pint/6½ cup pie dish. Cover and leave to cool. If possible, chill the meat filling overnight, as this allows the flavour to develop. Preheat the oven to 230°C/450°F/Gas 8.

5 Roll out the pastry in the shape of the dish and about 4cm/1½in larger all around. Cut a 2.5cm/1in strip from the edge of the pastry. Brush the rim of the dish with water and press the pastry strip on it. Brush the pastry rim with beaten egg and cover the pie with the pastry lid. Press the lid firmly in place, then trim off the excess.

6 Use the blunt edge of a knife to tap the outside edge of the pastry, pressing it down with your finger as you seal in the filling. (This technique is known as knocking up.)

7 Pinch the pastry between your fingers to flute the edge. Roll out any remaining pastry trimmings and cut out shapes to garnish the pie, brushing the shapes with a little beaten egg before pressing them lightly in place.

8 Make a hole in the middle of the pie to allow steam to escape, brush the top carefully with beaten egg and chill for 10 minutes to rest the pastry.

9 Bake the pie for 15 minutes, then reduce the oven temperature to 200°C/ 400°F/Gas 6 and bake for a further 15–20 minutes, or until the pastry is risen and golden. Let the pie rest for a minute or two before serving.

Energy 1061kcal/4423kJ; Protein 58.8g; Carbohydrate 59.3g, of which sugars 7.6g; Fat 65.3g, of which saturates 24g; Cholesterol 164mg; Calcium 129mg; Fibre 3.2g; Sodium 622mg.

Steak and kidney pudding

One of the best-known English country dishes, this tasty pudding is a 19th-century recipe that originally contained oysters, but mushrooms are more often used today. You will need a steamer pan to cook the pudding, and five hours to keep an eye on it as it cooks.

Serves 6

500g/1¼lb lean stewing steak, cut into cubes

225g/8oz beef kidney or lamb's kidneys, skin and core removed and cut into small cubes

1 medium onion, finely chopped

30ml/2 tbsp finely chopped fresh herbs, such as parsley and thyme

30ml/2 tbsp plain (all-purpose) flour

275g/10oz/2½ cups self-raising (self-rising) flour

150g/5oz/1 cup shredded suet (US chilled, grated shortening)

finely grated rind of 1 lemon

about 120ml/4fl oz/½ cup beef stock or water

salt and ground black pepper

1 Put the stewing steak into a large bowl and add the kidneys, onion and chopped herbs. Sprinkle the plain flour and seasoning over the top and mix well.

2 To make the pastry, sift the self-raising flour into another large bowl. Stir in the suet and lemon rind. Add sufficient cold water to bind the ingredients and gather into a soft dough.

3 On a lightly floured surface, knead the dough gently, and then roll out to make a circle measuring about 35cm/14in across. Cut out one-quarter of the circle, roll up and set aside.

4 Lightly butter a 1.75 litre/3 pint heatproof bowl. Line the bowl with the rolled out dough, pressing the cut edges together and allowing the pastry to overlap the top of the bowl slightly.

5 Spoon the steak mixture into the lined bowl, packing it in carefully, so as not to split the pastry.

6 Pour in sufficient stock to reach no more than three-quarters of the way up the filling.

7 Roll the reserved pastry into a circle to form a lid and lay it over the filling, pinching the edges together to seal.

8 Cover the pudding with baking parchment, pleated in the centre to allow the pudding to rise, then cover again with a large sheet of foil (again pleated at the centre). Tuck the edges of the foil under and press them tightly to the sides of the basin until securely sealed (alternatively, tie with string).

9 Fill the pan with water, bring to the boil, add the steamer and pudding and cook for 5 hours, checking the water level every now and then.

10 Remove the foil and paper, slide a knife around the sides of the pudding and turn out on to a serving plate.

Energy 436kcal/1835kJ; Protein 31.1g; Carbohydrate 49.5g, of which sugars 4.8g; Fat 13.9g, of which saturates 3.6g; Cholesterol 166mg; Calcium 201mg; Fibre 1.9g; Sodium 380mg.

Veal casserole with broad beans

This fresh-tasting country stew, flavoured with sherry and plenty of garlic, is a made with new season spring vegetables. For a delicious flavour, be sure to add plenty of parsley just before serving. Lamb would be equally good cooked in this way.

Serves 6

45ml/3 tbsp olive oil

1.3–1.6kg/3–3½lb veal, cut into 5cm/2in cubes

1 large onion, chopped

6 large garlic cloves, unpeeled

1 bay leaf

5ml/1 tsp paprika

250ml/8fl oz/1 cup fino sherry

100g/4oz/scant 1 cup shelled, skinned broad (fava) beans

small bunch fresh flat leaf parsley

salt and ground black pepper

1 Heat 30ml/2 tbsp oil in a large flameproof casserole. Add half the meat and brown well on all sides. Transfer to a plate. Brown the rest of the meat and remove from the pan.

2 Add the remaining oil to the pan and cook the onion until soft. Return the meat to the casserole and stir well to mix with the onion.

3 Add the garlic cloves, bay leaf, paprika and sherry. Season. Bring to simmering point, then cover and cook very gently for 30–40 minutes.

4 Add the broad beans to the casserole about 10 minutes before the end of the cooking time. Chop the flat leaf parsley. Check the seasoning and stir in the parsley just before serving.

Energy 352kcal/1473kJ; Protein 47.4g; Carbohydrate 3.6g, of which sugars 1.3g; Fat 11.6g, of which saturates 2.8g; Cholesterol 182mg; Calcium 34mg; Fibre 1.2g; Sodium 244mg.

Veal and ham pie

Historically, the English love meat pies. This splendid version contains a mixture of diced veal, gammon and hard-boiled eggs. The flavours of the two meats marry perfectly in the delicate filling. Serve with green cabbage leaves and buttery mashed potato.

Serves 4

450g/1lb boneless shoulder of veal, diced

225g/8oz lean gammon (smoked or cured ham), diced

15ml/1 tbsp plain (all-purpose) flour mixed with a large pinch each of dry mustard and ground black pepper

25g/1oz/2 tbsp butter

15ml/1 tbsp sunflower oil

1 onion, chopped

600ml/1 pint/2½ cups chicken or veal stock

2 eggs, hard-boiled and sliced

30ml/2 tbsp chopped fresh parsley

For the pastry

175g/6oz/1½ cups plain (all-purpose) flour

75g/3oz/6 tbsp butter

iced water, to mix

beaten egg, to glaze

1 Preheat the oven to 180°C/350°F/Gas 4. Mix the veal and gammon in a bowl. Add the seasoned flour to the meat and toss well. Heat the butter and oil in a casserole until sizzling, then cook the meat mixture in batches until golden on all sides. Remove the meat from the pan.

2 Cook the onion in the fat remaining in the casserole until softened, but not coloured. Gradually stir in the stock, then replace the meat mixture and stir. Cover and cook in the oven for 1½ hours, or until the veal is tender.

3 To make the pastry, sift the flour into a bowl and rub in the butter with your fingers. Mix in enough iced water to bind into a soft dough.

4 Spoon the veal and gammon into a 1.5 litre/2½ pint/6¼ cup pie dish. Lay the hard-boiled egg over the top and sprinkle with the chopped parsley.

5 Roll out the pastry on a lightly floured work surface to about 4cm/1½in larger than the top of the pie dish.

6 Cover the pie dish with the pastry lid. Press down the rim to seal and trim the edges. Use the blunt edge of a knife and your fingers to pinch the pastry to flute the edge. Roll out any remaining pastry and cut out shapes to garnish the top, if you wish.

7 Brush the pie with beaten egg and bake for 30–40 minutes, or until the pastry is well-risen and golden brown. Serve hot with steamed green cabbage and creamy mashed potato.

Energy 621kcal/2595kJ; Protein 42.4g; Carbohydrate 39.2g, of which sugars 2.6g; Fat 33.8g, of which saturates 17.2g; Cholesterol 281mg; Calcium 128mg; Fibre 2.3g; Sodium 1007mg.

Veal casserole

In France, this farmhouse stew is known as a blanquette because it is enriched with cream, giving it a white colour. It is traditionally made with veal, but can also be made with lamb.

Serves 6

1.5kg/3–3½lb boneless veal shoulder

1.5 litres/2½ pints/6 cups veal or chicken stock

1 large onion, studded with 2 cloves

4 carrots, sliced

2 leeks, sliced

1 garlic clove, halved

1 bouquet garni

15ml/1 tbsp black peppercorns

65g/2½oz/5 tbsp butter

225g/8oz/2 cups mushrooms

225g/8oz/1½ cups shallots or baby (pearl) onions

15ml/1 tbsp sugar

40g/1½oz/⅓ cup flour

120ml/4fl oz/½ cup crème fraîche or double (heavy) cream

pinch of grated nutmeg

60ml/4 tbsp chopped fresh parsley

salt and white pepper

fresh herb sprigs, to garnish

1 Cut the veal in cubes and place it with the stock in a large, flameproof casserole. Bring to the boil, skim the surface, then add the studded onion, one of the sliced carrots, the leeks, garlic, bouquet garni and peppercorns. Cover, lower the heat and simmer for 1 hour until the veal is just tender.

2 Meanwhile melt 15g/½oz/1 tbsp of the butter in a frying pan and sauté the mushrooms until lightly golden. Transfer to a large bowl, using a slotted spoon.

3 Melt another 15g/½oz/1 tbsp of the butter in the pan and add the shallots or onions. Cook for 3–4 minutes, stirring, then sprinkle with the sugar and add about 90ml/6 tbsp of the veal cooking liquid.

4 Cover and simmer for 10–12 minutes until the onions are tender and the liquid has evaporated. Add the onions to the mushrooms.

5 When the veal is tender, transfer the cubes to the bowl of vegetables using a slotted spoon. Strain the veal cooking liquid and retain, discard the cooked vegetables and bouquet garni, then wash the casserole and return it to the heat.

6 Melt the remaining butter in the casserole, add the flour and cook for 1–2 minutes. Gradually whisk in the reserved stock. Bring to the boil, then lower the heat and simmer the sauce until smooth and slightly thickened. Add the remaining carrots and cook for a further 10 minutes until tender.

7 Whisk the cream into the sauce and simmer until thickened. Add the meat, mushrooms and onions and simmer for 10–15 minutes until the veal is tender.

8 Season with salt, white pepper and a little nutmeg, then stir in the chopped dill or parsley. Garnish with fresh herb sprigs and serve.

Energy 695kcal/2906kJ; Protein 63g; Carbohydrate 46g, of which sugars 31g; Fat 30g, of which saturates 16g; Cholesterol 189mg; Calcium 174mg; Fibre 9.9g; Sodium 713mg.

Lamb with honey, rosemary and cider

Country lamb with honey and rosemary are traditional partners. Here, they are teamed with cider and cooked until the meat is meltingly soft and the sweet juices are deliciously caramelized and golden. Slow-cooking this economic cut of lamb ensures that the finished dish is beautifully tender, and the addition of cider gives a lovely tangy flavour. Serve with some golden roast potatoes and green vegetables, such as spring greens.

Serves 4–6

1.5kg/3lb 6oz shoulder of lamb

2 garlic cloves, halved

fresh rosemary sprigs

75ml/5 tbsp clear honey

300ml/½ pint/1¼ cups dry (hard) cider, plus extra if necessary

lemon juice (optional)

salt and ground black pepper

1 Preheat the oven to 220°C/425°F/Gas 7. Rub the lamb with the cut garlic. Put the meat and the garlic in a deep roasting pan. Season with salt and pepper.

2 Make small slashes in the meat with a knife and push in a few small sprigs of rosemary.

3 Stir the honey into the cider until it has fully dissolved and then pour it over the lamb.

4 Put the roasting pan into the hot oven and cook for 20–30 minutes until the lamb has browned and the juices have reduced, begun to caramelize and turn golden brown. Keep checking to make sure the liquid does not dry up and brown too much. If so, add a little water.

5 Stir 300ml/½ pint water into the pan juices and spoon them over the lamb. Cover with a large tent of foil, scrunching the edges around the rim of the pan to seal them.

6 Put the pan back into the oven, reduce the temperature to 180°C/350°F/Gas 4 and cook for about another hour.

7 Remove the foil and spoon the juices over the lamb again. Turn the oven temperature back up to 220°C/425°F/Gas 7 and continue cooking, uncovered, for a further 10–15 minutes, until the lamb is crisp and brown.

8 Lift the lamb on to a serving plate and leave in a warm place to rest for 15 minutes before carving.

9 While the lamb is resting, spoon any excess fat off the top of the juices in the pan. Then taste the juices and adjust the seasoning, if necessary, adding lemon juice to taste. Put the roasting pan on the hob and bring just to the boil.

10 Serve the carved lamb with the juices spooned over.

Farmhouse tip Though it looks attractive when the rosemary stands proud of the lamb, it is likely to burn. Make sure the slashes are deep and that you push the rosemary sprigs into the lamb.

Variation Medium dry white wine, apple juice, light vegetable stock or water could be used in place of cider.

Energy 524kcal/2180kJ; Protein 35.3g; Carbohydrate 10.9g, of which sugars 10.9g; Fat 36.5g, of which saturates 17g; Cholesterol 153mg; Calcium 17mg; Fibre 0g; Sodium 130mg.

Roast shoulder of lamb with garlic potatoes

The potatoes are basted in the lamb juices while cooking, and become wonderfully garlicky, fragrant and sticky. Return the potatoes to the oven to keep warm while you leave the lamb to rest before carving, then serve along with a selection of seasonal vegetables.

Serves 4–6

675g/1½lb waxy potatoes, peeled and cut into large dice

12 garlic cloves, unpeeled

1 whole shoulder of lamb

45ml/3 tbsp olive oil

salt and ground black pepper

Farmhouse tip Shoulder of lamb has its fat distributed within the meat, which helps keep it tender. Make sure it still has the bone, as this will add to the flavour when it is cooking.

1 Preheat the oven to 180°C/350°F/ Gas 4. Put the potatoes and garlic cloves into a large roasting pan and season with salt and pepper. Pour over 30ml/2 tbsp of the oil and toss the potatoes and garlic to coat.

2 Place a rack over the roasting pan, so that it is not touching the potatoes. Place the lamb on the rack and drizzle over the remaining oil. Season with salt and pepper.

3 Roast the lamb and potatoes for about 2–2½ hours, or until the lamb is cooked through.

4 Halfway through the cooking time, carefully take the lamb and the rack off the roasting pan and turn the potatoes to ensure even cooking. Transfer the lamb, potatoes and garlic to a warmed serving platter.

Energy 668kcal/2775kJ; Protein 29.2g; Carbohydrate 20.8g, of which sugars 1.7g; Fat 52.6g, of which saturates 24.1g; Cholesterol 113mg; Calcium 22mg; Fibre 1.8g; Sodium 123mg.

Lamb and pearl barley casserole

The combination of pearl barley and carrots add texture, bulk and flavour to this comforting stew, giving a thick, flavourful sauce for the meat. Comfort food is at its best when served with boiled or baked potatoes and a green vegetable, such as spring cabbage.

Serves 6

675g/1½lb stewing lamb

15ml/1 tbsp oil

2 onions, sliced

675g/1½lb carrots, thickly sliced

4–6 celery sticks, sliced

45ml/3 tbsp pearl barley, rinsed

stock or water

salt and ground black pepper

chopped fresh parsley, to garnish

1 Trim the lamb and cut it into bitesize pieces. Heat the oil in a flameproof casserole and brown the lamb. Preheat the oven to 150°C/300°F/Gas 2.

2 Add the vegetables to the casserole and fry them briefly with the meat. Add the barley and enough stock or water to cover, and season to taste.

3 Cover the casserole and simmer gently in the oven, for 1–1½ hours until the meat is tender. You can also cook this on a very low heat on the stove top if you wish. Add extra stock during cooking if necessary. Serve garnished with the chopped fresh parsley.

Farmhouse tip The best cut of lamb for stewing is neck or shoulder, with some fat on the meat to keep it moist during cooking.

Energy 304kcal/1263kJ; Protein 23.2g; Carbohydrate 13g, of which sugars 11.3g; Fat 18g, of which saturates 7.5g; Cholesterol 84mg; Calcium 53mg; Fibre 3.6g; Sodium 110mg.

Lamb stew with shallots and new potatoes

This Italian farmhouse casserole is given a flavour boost at the end of cooking, with a piquant garlic and parsley garnish. The stew is a great all in one supper dish.

Serves 6

1kg/2¼lb boneless shoulder of lamb, trimmed of fat and cut into 5cm/2in cubes

1 garlic clove, finely chopped

finely grated rind of ½ lemon and juice of 1 lemon

90ml/6 tbsp olive oil

45ml/3 tbsp plain (all-purpose) flour

1 large onion, sliced

5 anchovy fillets in olive oil, drained

2.5ml/½ tsp caster (superfine) sugar

300ml/½ pint/1¼ cups white wine

475ml/16fl oz/2 cups lamb stock or half stock and half water

1 fresh bay leaf

fresh thyme sprig

fresh parsley sprig

500g/1¼lb small new potatoes

250g/9oz shallots, peeled but left whole

45ml/3 tbsp double (heavy) cream (optional)

salt and ground black pepper

For the garlic and parsley garnish

1 garlic clove, finely chopped

finely shredded rind of ½ lemon

45ml/3 tbsp chopped fresh flat leaf parsley

1 Mix the lamb with the garlic and the rind and juice of ½ lemon. Season with pepper and mix in 15ml/1 tbsp olive oil, then leave to marinate for 12–24 hours.

2 Drain the lamb, reserving the marinade, and pat the lamb dry with kitchen paper. Preheat the oven to 180°C/350°F/Gas 4.

3 Heat 30ml/2 tbsp olive oil in a large, heavy frying pan. Season the flour with salt and pepper and toss the lamb in it to coat, shaking off any excess. Seal the lamb on all sides in the hot oil. Do this in batches, transferring each batch of lamb to an ovenproof pan or flameproof casserole as you brown it. You may need to add an extra 15ml/1 tbsp olive oil to the pan.

4 Reduce the heat, add another 15ml/1 tbsp oil to the pan and cook the onion gently over a very low heat, stirring frequently, for 10 minutes, until softened and golden but not browned.

5 Add the anchovies and caster sugar, and cook, mashing the anchovies into the soft onion with a wooden spoon until well combined.

6 Add the reserved marinade, increase the heat a little and cook for about 1–2 minutes, then pour in the wine and stock or stock and water and bring to the boil. Simmer gently for about 5 minutes, then pour over the lamb.

7 Tie the bay leaf, thyme and parsley together and add to the lamb. Season with salt and pepper, then cover tightly and cook in the oven. After 1 hour, stir the potatoes into the stew and cook for a further 20 minutes.

8 Meanwhile, to make the gremolata, mix all the ingredients together. Place in a dish, cover and set aside.

9 Heat the remaining oil in a frying pan and brown the shallots on all sides, then stir them into the lamb.

10 Cover and cook for 30 minutes more, until the lamb is tender. Transfer the lamb and vegetables to a dish and keep warm. Discard the herbs.

11 Boil the cooking juices to reduce and concentrate them, then add the cream, if using, and simmer for 2–3 minutes.

12 Adjust the seasoning, adding a little lemon juice to taste. Pour this sauce over the lamb, sprinkle the gremolata on top and serve immediately on warmed plates.

Energy 553kcal/2311kJ; Protein 37g; Carbohydrate 26.2g, of which sugars 5.3g; Fat 30.6g, of which saturates 10.4g; Cholesterol 128mg; Calcium 79mg; Fibre 2.7g; Sodium 261mg.

Lamb stew with vegetables

This farmhouse stew is made with lamb and a selection of young tender spring vegetables such as carrots, new potatoes, baby onions, peas, French beans and especially turnips.

Serves 6

60ml/4 tbsp vegetable oil

1.5kg/3–3½lb lamb shoulder, boned, trimmed and cut into 5cm/2in chunks

120ml/4fl oz/½ cup water

45–60ml/3–4 tbsp plain flour

1 litre/1¾ pints/4 cups lamb stock

1 large bouquet garni

3 garlic cloves, lightly crushed

3 ripe tomatoes, skinned, seeded and chopped

5ml/1 tsp tomato purée (paste)

675g/1½lb small potatoes, peeled or scrubbed

12 baby carrots, scrubbed

115g/4oz French (green) beans, cut into 5cm/2in pieces

25g/1oz/2 tbsp butter

12–18 baby (pearl) onions or shallots, peeled

6 medium turnips, quartered

30ml/2 tbsp sugar

2.5m/½ tsp dried thyme

175g/6oz/1¼ cups peas

50g/2oz/½ cup mangetouts (snowpeas)

salt and ground pepper

45ml/3 tbsp chopped fresh parsley or coriander (cilantro), to garnish

1 Heat half the oil in a large, heavy frying pan. Brown the lamb in batches, adding more oil if needed, and place it in a large, flameproof casserole.

2 Add 45ml/3 tbsp of the water to the pan and boil for about 1 minute, stirring and scraping the base of the pan to release any bits, then pour the liquid into the casserole.

3 Sprinkle the flour over the browned meat in the casserole and set it over a medium heat. Cook for 3–5 minutes until the flour is browned and the fat absorbed. Gradually stir in the stock, the bouquet garni, garlic, chopped tomatoes and tomato purée. Season with salt and pepper.

4 Bring to the boil over a high heat. Skim the surface, reduce the heat and simmer, stirring occasionally, for about 1 hour until the meat is tender. Cool the stew to room temperature, cover and chill overnight.

5 About 1½ hours before serving, take the casserole from the fridge and lift off the solid fat. Set the casserole over a medium heat and bring to a simmer.

6 Cook the potatoes in a pan of boiling, salted water for 15–20 minutes, then transfer to a bowl and add the carrots to the same water. Cook for 4–5 minutes and transfer to the same bowl. Add the French beans and boil for 2–3 minutes. Transfer to the bowl with the other vegetables.

7 Melt the butter in a heavy frying pan and add the onions and turnips with a further 45 ml/3 tbsp water. Cover and cook for 4–5 minutes.

8 Sprinkle the sugar on to the onions and turnips, together with the thyme. Stir in and cook until the vegetables are caramelized. Transfer them to the bowl of vegetables.

9 Add the remaining water to the pan. Boil for 1 minute, incorporating the sediment, then add to the lamb.

10 When the lamb and gravy are hot, add the cooked vegetables to the stew and stir gently to distribute. Stir in the peas and mangetouts and cook for 5 minutes until they turn a bright green, then stir in 30ml/2 tbsp of the parsley or coriander.

11 Pour the stew into a large, warmed serving dish. Scatter over the remaining parsley or coriander and serve.

Energy 560Kcal/2346kJ; Protein 39.2g; Carbohydrate 41.9g, of which sugars 14.4g; Fat 27.4g, of which saturates 9.9g; Cholesterol 127mg; Calcium 90mg; Fibre 6.2g; Sodium 181mg.

Lancashire hotpot

Authentically made with mutton and lamb's kidney, this farmhouse favourite is now more often made with neck of lamb and a selection of hearty vegetables.

Serves 4

40g/1½oz/3 tbsp dripping, or 45ml/ 3 tbsp oil

8 middle neck lamb chops, about 1kg/2¼lb total weight

175g/6oz lamb's kidneys, cut into large pieces

1kg/2¼lb potatoes, thinly sliced

3 carrots, thickly sliced

450g/1lb leeks, sliced

3 celery sticks, sliced

15ml/1 tbsp chopped fresh thyme

30ml/2 tbsp chopped fresh parsley

small sprig of rosemary

600ml/1 pint/2½ cups veal stock

salt and ground black pepper

Variations Pork chops can be used instead of lamb. Use thick loin chops or boneless sparerib chops, as preferred.
Try adding the shredded leaves from a couple of sprigs of sage instead of the rosemary.

1 Preheat the oven to 170°C/325°F/ Gas 3. Heat the dripping or oil in a frying pan and brown the lamb chops and lamb's kidneys in batches, then reserve the fat.

2 In a large casserole, make alternate layers of lamb chops, kidneys, three-quarters of the potatoes and the carrots, leeks and celery, sprinkling the herbs and seasoning over each layer as you go. Tuck the rosemary sprig down the side of the casserole.

3 Arrange the remaining potatoes on top. Pour over the stock, brush with the reserved fat, then cover and bake for 2½ hours. Increase the oven temperature to 220°C/425°F/Gas 7. Uncover and cook for 30 minutes until well browned on top.

Energy 724kcal/3035kJ; Protein 51.6g; Carbohydrate 50g, of which sugars 8.7g; Fat 36.7g, of which saturates 13.6g; Cholesterol 278mg; Calcium 75mg; Fibre 7.3g; Sodium 233mg.

Mustard thatch lamb pie

This is a shepherd's pie with a twist. Adding mustard to the potato topping gives extra bite and a crunchy, golden topping. Serve with minted new peas or steamed broccoli.

Serves 4

800g/1¾lb floury potatoes, diced

60ml/4 tbsp milk

15ml/1 tbsp wholegrain mustard

a little butter

450g/1lb lean minced (ground) lamb

1 onion, chopped

2 celery sticks, thinly sliced

2 carrots, diced

30ml/2 tbsp cornflour (cornstarch) blended into 150ml/¼ pint/⅔ cup lamb or chicken stock

15ml/1 tbsp Worcestershire sauce

30ml/2 tbsp chopped fresh rosemary,

salt and ground black pepper

3 Stir in the stock and cornflour mixture. Bring to the boil, stirring constantly, then remove from the heat. Stir in the Worcestershire sauce and rosemary, and season with salt and pepper to taste.

4 Turn the lamb mixture into a 1.75 litre/3 pint/7 cup ovenproof dish and spread over the potato topping evenly, swirling with the edge of a knife. Bake for 30–35 minutes until golden on the top. Serve hot, with a selection of fresh vegetables.

Variations The original shepherd's pie is made with lamb. It can be made with minced beef, in which case it is called a cottage pie.

To vary the potato topping, try adding horseradish – either creamed or, for an even stronger flavour, freshly grated.

1 Cook the potatoes in a large pan of boiling lightly salted water until tender. Drain well and mash until smooth, then stir in the milk, mustard, butter and seasoning to taste. Meanwhile, preheat the oven to 200°C/400°F/Gas 6.

2 Fry the lamb in a non-stick pan, breaking it up with a fork, until browned. Add the onion, celery and carrots and cook for 2–3 minutes, stirring, to stop the mixture sticking to the base.

Energy 371kcal/1561kJ; Protein 26.5g; Carbohydrate 37.9g, of which sugars 7.7g; Fat 13.7g, of which saturates 6.2g; Cholesterol 86mg; Calcium 68mg; Fibre 3.3g; Sodium 194mg.

Roast leg of lamb with wild mushroom stuffing

Removing the thigh bone in a leg of lamb creates a cavity that can be filled with a delicious stuffing, in this case one made from wild mushrooms – the perfect treat for Sunday lunch.

Serves 4

1.75kg/4–4¹⁄₂lb leg of lamb, boned

salt and freshly ground black pepper

watercress or rocket (arugula), to garnish

For the wild mushroom stuffing

25g/1oz/**2 tbsp** butter

1 shallot or small onion, chopped

225g/8oz/2 cups assorted wild and cultivated mushrooms

¹⁄₂ garlic clove, crushed

1 fresh thyme sprig, chopped

25g/1oz crustless white bread, diced

2 egg yolks

For the wild mushroom gravy

60ml/4 tbsp red wine

400ml/14fl oz/1²⁄₃ cups hot chicken stock

5g/2 tbsp dried ceps, soaked in boiling water for 20 minutes

20ml/4 tsp cornflour (cornstarch) and 5ml/1 tsp Dijon mustard blended together with 15ml/ 1 tbsp water

2.5ml/¹⁄₂ tsp wine vinegar

knob (pat) of butter

1 Preheat the oven to 200°C/400°F/ Gas 6. To make the stuffing, melt the butter in a large frying pan and gently fry the shallot or onion until softened but without colouring.

2 Add the mushrooms, garlic and thyme to the pan. Cook, stirring, until the mushroom juices begin to run, then increase the heat so that they evaporate completely.

3 Transfer the mushrooms to a mixing bowl and add the bread and egg yolks. Season with salt and pepper and mix well. Allow to cool slightly.

4 Season the inside of the lamb cavity with salt and pepper, then spoon in the stuffing. Tie up the end with fine string and then tie around the joint so that it does not lose its shape.

5 Place the lamb in a roasting pan. Roast for 15 minutes per 450g/1lb for rare or 20 minutes per 450g/1lb for medium-rare. A 1.8kg/4lb leg will take 1 hour 20 minutes for medium-rare.

6 Transfer the lamb to a warmed serving plate. Spoon off all excess fat from the roasting pan and brown the sediment over a medium heat. Add the wine then the chicken stock and the mushrooms, with their soaking liquid.

7 Mix the cornflour and mustard in a cup; blend in the water. Stir into the stock and thicken. Add the vinegar. Season and stir in the butter.

8 Garnish the lamb with watercress and serve, carved into thick slices, together with the wild mushroom gravy.

Farmhouse tip Chop up any leftover meat, mix with stuffing and gravy, top with mashed potato, and bake for 30 minutes for a quick, easy pie.

Energy 758kcal/3170kJ; Protein 96g; Carbohydrate 9g, of which sugars 1g; Fat 37g, of which saturates 14g; Cholesterol 444mg; Calcium 61mg; Fibre 2.1g; Sodium 630mg.

Lamb with mint and lemon

Lamb has been served with mint for many years – it is a great combination, and new season spring lamb coincides perfectly with the first crop of mint.

Serves 8

8 lamb steaks, 225g/8oz each

grated rind and juice of 1 lemon

2 cloves garlic, peeled and crushed

2 spring onions (scallions), finely chopped

2 tsp finely chopped fresh mint leaves, plus extra leaves for garnishing

4 tbsp extra virgin olive oil

salt and ground black pepper

1 Make a marinade for the lamb by mixing all the other ingredients and seasoning to taste. Place the lamb steaks in a shallow dish and cover with the marinade. Refrigerate overnight.

2 Grill (broil) the lamb under a high heat until just cooked, basting with the marinade occasionally during cooking. Turn once during cooking. Serve, garnished with fresh mint leaves.

Energy 367kcal/1530kJ; Protein 44g; Carbohydrate g, of which sugars 0g; Fat 21g, of which saturates 6g; Cholesterol 158mg; Calcium 36mg; Fibre 0.1g; Sodium 155mg.

Lamb pie with pear, ginger and mint sauce

Cooking lamb with fruit accentuates the meat's sweetness and also cuts the richness; the pastry in this recipe keeps the dish beautifully moist as it bakes.

Serves 6

1 boned mid-loin of lamb, 1kg/2lb after boning

8 large sheets filo pastry

25g/1oz/scant 2 tbsp butter

salt and ground black pepper

For the stuffing

1 tbsp butter

1 small onion, chopped

115g/4oz wholemeal (whole-wheat) breadcrumbs

grated rind of 1 lemon

170g/6oz drained canned pears from a 400g/14oz can (rest of can, and juice, used for sauce)

2.5ml/½ tsp ground ginger

1 small egg, beaten

skewers, string and a large needle to make a roll

For the sauce

rest of can of pears, including juice

10ml/2 tsp finely chopped fresh mint

1 First, prepare the stuffing. Melt the butter in a pan and add the onion, cooking until soft. Preheat the oven to 180°C/350°F/Gas 4.

2 Put the butter and onion into a mixing bowl and add the breadcrumbs, lemon rind, pears and ginger. Season lightly. Using your hands, or a fork, add enough beaten egg to bind. Don't let the stuffing become too wet.

3 Spread the loin out, fat down, and season. Place the stuffing along the middle and roll, holding with skewers while you sew it together with string.

4 Heat a large baking pan in the oven and brown the loin slowly on all sides. This will take 20–30 minutes. Leave to cool completely, then store in the refrigerator until needed. Preheat the oven to 200°C/400°F/Gas 6.

5 Take two sheets of filo pastry and brush with melted butter. Overlap by about 13cm/5in to make a square. Place the next two sheets on top and brush with butter. Continue until all the pastry has been used.

6 Place the roll of lamb diagonally across one corner of the pastry. Fold the corner over the lamb, fold in the sides, and brush the pastry well with melted butter. Roll to the far corner of the sheet. Place join side down on a buttered baking sheet and brush with butter. Bake for about 30 minutes or until golden brown.

7 Blend the remaining pears with their juice and the mint to a smooth purée. Slice the lamb and serve with the pear and mint sauce.

Energy 440kcal/1850kJ; Protein 57g; Carbohydrate 21g, of which sugars 10g; Fat 16g, of which saturates 6g; Cholesterol 179mg; Calcium 69mg; Fibre 3.2g; Sodium 358mg.

Lamb and leeks with mint and spring onions

This is a lightly-flavoured dish which uses the best of seasonal ingredients. If you do not have any home-made chicken stock, use good ready-made stock rather than a stock cube.

Serves 6

2 tbsp sunflower oil

2kg/4lb lamb (fillet or boned leg)

10 spring onions (scallions), thickly sliced

3 young leeks, thickly sliced

1 tbsp flour

150ml/¼ pint white wine

300ml/½ pint chicken stock

15ml/1 tbsp tomato purée (paste)

15ml/1 tbsp sugar

30ml/2 tbsp fresh mint leaves, finely chopped, plus a few more to garnish

115g/4oz dried pears

1kg/2lb potatoes, peeled and sliced

30g/1¼oz butter, melted

salt and ground black pepper

1 Heat the oil and fry the cubed lamb to seal it. Transfer to a casserole. Preheat the oven to 180°C/350°F/Gas 4.

2 Fry the onions and leeks for 1 minute, stir in the flour and cook for another minute. Add the wine and stock and bring to the boil. Add the tomato purée, sugar, salt and pepper with the mint and chopped pears and pour into the casserole. Stir the mixture. Arrange the sliced potatoes on top and brush with the melted butter.

3 Cover and bake for 1½ hours. Then increase the temperature to 200°C/400°F/Gas 6, cook for a further 30 minutes, uncovered, to brown the potatoes. Garnish with mint leaves.

Energy 846kcal/3542kJ; Protein 70.3g; Carbohydrate 37.3g, of which sugars 10.1g; Fat 45.5g, of which saturates 20.3g; Cholesterol 263mg; Calcium 75mg; Fibre 4.5g; Sodium 347mg.

Pork and black bean stew

This simple Spanish country stew uses a few robust and economical ingredients, which when combined create a deliciously intense flavour.

Serves 5–6

275g/10oz/1½ cups black beans, soaked overnight

675g/1½lb boneless belly pork rashers (strips)

60ml/4 tbsp olive oil

350g/12oz baby (pearl) onions or shallots

2 celery sticks, thickly sliced

10ml/2 tsp paprika

150g/5oz chorizo, chopped

600ml/1 pint/2½ cups light chicken or vegetable stock

2 green (bell) peppers, seeded and cut into large pieces

salt and ground pepper

1 Preheat the oven to 160°C/325°F/ Gas 3. Drain the beans, place them in a pan and cover with plenty of fresh water. Bring to the boil, boil rapidly for 10 minutes, then drain.

2 Cut away any rind from the pork and cut the meat into large chunks.

Farmhouse tip This stew works well with any winter vegetable. Try adding chunks of leek, turnip, celeriac and even tiny whole new potatoes.

3 Heat the oil in a large frying pan and fry the onions or shallots and celery for 3 minutes. Add the pork and fry for 5–10 minutes until browned. Stir in the paprika and chorizo and fry for another 2 minutes. Transfer to a casserole.

4 Add the stock to the frying pan and bring to the boil. Season lightly, then pour over the meat and beans in the casserole. Cover and bake for 1 hour, then stir in the green peppers. Bake for 15 minutes more, and serve hot.

Energy 760Kcal/3159kJ; Protein 32.1g; Carbohydrate 37.3g, of which sugars 9.2g; Fat 54.7g, of which saturates 18.6g; Cholesterol 91mg; Calcium 85mg; Fibre 5.9g; Sodium 303mg.

Roast loin of pork with apple and spinach

Pork and apple are a well-loved combination, and loin of pork is a prime roasting joint. In this recipe, the pork is stuffed with apples, but these could be replaced with apricots or prunes.

Serves 6–8

1.6–1.8kg/3½–4lb loin of pork, boned and skinned

1 onion, sliced

juice of 1 orange

15ml/1 tbsp wholegrain mustard

30ml/2 tbsp demerara (raw) sugar

salt and ground black pepper

For the stuffing

50g/2oz spinach

50g/2oz/¼ cup dried apricots, chopped

50g/2oz Cheddar cheese, grated

1 cooking apple, peeled and grated

grated rind of ½ orange

1 Blanch the spinach in boiling water, chop, and put in a bowl with the other stuffing ingredients. Mix well together. Preheat the oven to 180°C/350°F/Gas 4.

2 Place the loin of pork, fat side down, on a board and place the stuffing down the centre. Roll the meat up and tie with cotton string. Season and put it into a roasting pan with the onion and 60ml/4 tbsp water. Cook uncovered for about 35 minutes per 450g/1lb.

3 About 40 minutes before the end of the estimated cooking time, pour off the cooking liquid into a small pan and discard the onion. Add the orange juice to the cooking liquid.

4 Spread the joint with mustard and sprinkle with the sugar. Return it to the oven and increase to 200°C/400°F/Gas 6 for 15 minutes or until crisp. Meanwhile, boil up the juices and reduce to make a thin sauce. Serve with the sliced meat.

Energy 330kcal/1385kJ; Protein 49.4g; Carbohydrate 6.9g, of which sugars 6.3g; Fat 11.6g, of which saturates 4.9g; Cholesterol 145mg; Calcium 105mg; Fibre 1.2g; Sodium 227mg.

Roast pork belly with caramelized vegetables

Topped with crackling, this meltingly tender pork is served with root vegetables. The layer of fat keeps the meat moist. To ensure crisp crackling, make sure the skin is dry before roasting.

Serves 4–6

1 small swede (rutabaga), weighing about 500g/1lb 2oz

1 onion

1 parsnip

2 carrots

15ml/1 tbsp olive oil

1.5kg/3½lb belly of pork, with the skin well scored

15ml/1 tbsp fresh thyme leaves or 5ml/1 tsp dried thyme

salt and ground black pepper

Farmhouse tip Ask your butcher to score (slash) the pork skin really well, or use a strong sharp blade and (with care) do it yourself.

1 Preheat the oven to 220°C/425°F/ Gas 7. Cut the vegetables into small cubes (about 2cm/¾in) and stir them with the oil in a roasting pan, tossing them until evenly coated. Pour in 300ml/½ pint/1¼ cups water.

2 Sprinkle the pork rind with thyme, salt and pepper, rubbing them well into the scored slashes in the pork belly. Place the pork on top of the vegetables, pressing it down so that it sits level, with the skin side uppermost.

3 Put the pork and vegetables into the hot oven and cook for about 30 minutes, by which time the liquid will have almost evaporated to leave a nice golden crust in the bottom of the pan. Remove the pan from the oven.

4 Add 600ml/1 pint/2½ cups cold water to the vegetables in the pan. Reduce the oven temperature to 180°C/350°F/Gas 4.

5 Cook for 1½ hours, or until the pork is tender and the juices run clear when the centre of the meat is pierced with a sharp knife. Check the oven during the final 30 minutes to make sure the liquid does not dry up, adding a little water if necessary.

6 If the crackling is not yet crisp enough, increase the oven temperature to 220°C/425°F/Gas 7 and continue cooking for another 10–20 minutes, adding extra water if necessary – just enough to prevent the vegetables from burning on the bottom of the pan.

7 With a sharp knife, slice off the crackling. Serve it with thick slices of the pork, some vegetables and the golden juices spooned over.

Energy 1014kcal/4194kJ; Protein 39.5g; Carbohydrate 9.4g, of which sugars 7.3g; Fat 91.2g, of which saturates 33.1g; Cholesterol 180mg; Calcium 81mg; Fibre 3.3g; Sodium 202mg.

Loin of pork with cashew and orange stuffing

The oranges and cashew nuts add contrasting flavours and textures to this stuffing, and combine well with the brown rice. Don't worry if the stuffing doesn't bind – the good thing about brown rice is that it retains its own texture.

Serves 6

1.5kg/3–3½lb boned loin of pork

15ml/1 tbsp plain flour

300ml/½ pint/1¼ cups white wine

salt and ground black pepper

fresh rosemary sprigs and orange slices, to garnish

For the stuffing

25g/1oz/2 tbsp butter

1 small onion, finely chopped

75g/3oz/scant ½ cup brown basmati rice, soaked for 30 minutes and then drained

350ml/12fl oz/1½ cups chicken stock

50g/2oz/½ cup cashew nuts

1 orange

50g/2oz/⅓ cup sultanas (golden raisins)

1 First cook the rice for the stuffing. Melt the butter in a frying pan and fry the chopped onion for 2–3 minutes until softened but not browned. Add the rice and cook for 1 minute, stirring, then pour in the chicken stock and bring to the boil. Lower the heat, cover and simmer for 35 minutes until the rice is tender and the liquid absorbed. Preheat the oven to 220°C/425°F/Gas 7.

2 While the rice is cooking, open out the loin of pork and cut two lengthways slits through the meat, making sure not to cut right through. Turn the meat over. Remove any excess fat, but leave a good layer; this will keep the meat moist during cooking.

3 Spread out the cashew nuts for the stuffing in a roasting pan and roast in the oven for 2–4 minutes until golden, be careful they don't scorch. Allow to cool, then chop roughly in a food processor. Leave the oven on.

4 Grate 5ml/1 tsp of the orange rind into a bowl, then peel the orange. Working over a bowl to catch the juice, cut the orange into segments. Chop them roughly.

5 Add the chopped orange segments to the cooked rice with the orange rind, roast cashew nuts and sultanas. Season well, then stir in 15–30ml/1–2 tbsp of the reserved orange juice. Don't worry if the rice doesn't bind – it should have a fairly loose consistency.

6 Spread a generous layer of stuffing along the centre of the pork. If you have any stuffing left over, put it in a heatproof bowl and set aside.

7 Roll up the loin and tie securely with kitchen string. Rub a little salt and pepper into the surface of the meat and place it in a roasting pan. Roast for 15 minutes then lower the oven to 180°C/350°F/Gas 4.

8 Roast for 2–2¼ hours more or until the meat juices run clear and without any sign of pinkness. Heat any extra stuffing in the covered bowl alongside the meat for the final 15 minutes.

9 Transfer the meat to a warmed serving plate and keep warm. Stir the flour into the meat juices remaining in the roasting pan, cook for 1 minute, then stir in the white wine. Bring to the boil, stirring until thickened, then strain into a jug (pitcher).

10 Remove the string from the meat before carving. Stud the pork with the rosemary and garnish with the orange slices. Serve with the gravy and any extra stuffing.

Farmhouse tip Pork is usually roasted until well done, though cooking times depend on your oven and the size of the joint. As a rule, allow 35–40 minutes at 180°C/350°F/Gas 4 per 450g/1lb for stuffed pork, plus an extra 15–20 minutes. Make sure the skin is completely dry before cooking.

Energy 638kcal/2675kJ; Protein 81.9g; Carbohydrate 19.8g, of which sugars 8.5g; Fat 25.8g, of which saturates 8.8g; Cholesterol 224mg; Calcium 37mg; Fibre 0.9g; Sodium 201mg.

Pork sausage and puff pastry plait

Country butchers sell a wonderful variety of sausages, including venison, pork and apple, and herb. All taste delicious when wrapped around a wild mushroom filling and baked in pastry.

Serves 4

50g/2oz/4 tbsp butter

½ garlic clove, crushed

15ml/1 tbsp chopped fresh thyme

450g/1lb assorted wild and cultivated mushrooms, sliced

50g/2oz/1 cup fresh white breadcrumbs

75ml/5 tbsp chopped fresh parsley

350g/12oz puff pastry

675g/1½lb best pork sausages

1 egg, beaten with a pinch of salt

salt and ground black pepper

1 Melt the butter in a large frying pan and soften the garlic, thyme and mushrooms gently for 5–6 minutes. When the mushroom juices begin to run, increase the heat to drive off the liquid, then stir in the breadcrumbs, parsley and seasoning.

2 Roll out the pastry on a floured surface to a 36 x 25cm/14 x 10in rectangle. Place on a large baking sheet. Skin the sausages.

3 Place half of the sausagemeat in a strip along the centre of the pastry. Cover with the mushroom mixture, then with the rest of the sausagemeat.

◄ **4** Make a series of slanting cuts in the pastry on either side of the filling. Fold each end of the pastry over the filling, moisten the pastry with beaten egg and then cross the top with alternate strips from each side. Allow to rest for 40 minutes. Preheat the oven to 180°C/350°F/Gas 4. Brush with a little more egg and bake for 1 hour.

Energy 822kcal/3424kJ; Protein 26g; Carbohydrate 55g, of which sugars 4g; Fat 58g, of which saturates 17g; Cholesterol 1350mg; Calcium 189mg; Fibre 6.2g; Sodium 2076mg.

Stove-top pork and sausage casserole

This dish is based on a rural Spanish recipe. You should be able to find the butifarra
sausages in a delicatessen but, if not, spicy Italian sausages will do.

Serves 4

30ml/2 tbsp olive oil

4 boneless pork chops, about
175g/6oz total weight

4 butifarra or spicy Italian sausages

1 onion, chopped

2 garlic cloves, chopped

120ml/4fl oz/½ cup dry white wine

4 plum tomatoes, chopped

1 bay leaf

30ml/2 tbsp chopped fresh parsley

salt and ground black pepper

green salad and crusty bread, to
serve

◀ **3** Stir in the wine, tomatoes and bay
leaf, and season with salt and pepper.
Add the parsley. Cover the pan and
cook for 30 minutes.

4 Remove the sausages from the pan
and cut into thick slices. Return them to
the pan and heat through. Serve hot
with a green salad and bread.

1 Heat the oil in a large, deep frying
pan. Cook the pork chops over a high
heat until browned on both sides, then
transfer to a plate.

2 Add the sausages, onion and garlic to
the pan and cook over a moderate heat
until the sausages are browned and the
onion softened, turning the sausages
two or three times during cooking.
Return the chops to the pan.

Farmhouse tip Ordinary round, or
cherry, tomatoes can be used if plum
are not available.

Energy 431kcal/1803kJ; Protein 44.3g; Carbohydrate 12.5g, of which sugars 7g; Fat 20.8g, of which saturates 6.5g; Cholesterol 127mg; Calcium 78mg; Fibre 2.4g; Sodium 618mg.

Sausage and potato casserole

Be sure to use good butcher's sausages for this traditional Irish farmhouse recipe, cooking the ingredients slowly to give the best results. Serve with some fresh soda bread.

Serves 4

15ml/1 tbsp vegetable oil

4 bacon rashers (strips), cut into 2.5cm/1in pieces

2 large onions, chopped

2 garlic cloves, crushed

8 large pork sausages

4 large baking potatoes, thinly sliced

1.5ml/¼ tsp fresh sage

300ml/½ pint/1¼ cups vegetable stock

salt and ground black pepper

soda bread, to serve

1 Preheat the oven to 180°C/350°F/ Gas 4. Grease a large ovenproof dish and set aside. Heat the oil in a frying pan. Add the bacon and fry for 2 minutes. Add the onions and fry for 5 minutes until golden. Add the garlic and fry for 1 minute, then remove the mixture from the pan and set aside. Fry the sausages in the pan for 5 minutes until golden brown.

2 Arrange the potatoes in the base of the prepared dish. Spoon the bacon and onion mixture on top. Season with the salt and pepper and sprinkle with the fresh sage.

3 Pour on the stock and top with the sausages. Cover and bake for 1 hour. Serve hot with fresh soda bread.

Energy 553kcal/2305kJ; Protein 17.4g; Carbohydrate 48.7g, of which sugars 10g; Fat 33.4g, of which saturates 11.8g; Cholesterol 51mg; Calcium 74mg; Fibre 4g; Sodium 1019mg.

Toad-in-the-hole

Resembling toads peeping out of holes, this country favourite can be made with any variety of sausage. Try venison or wild boar, and replace the chives with shredded fresh sage leaves.

Serves 4–6

175g/6oz/1½ cups plain (all-purpose) flour

30ml/2 tbsp chopped fresh chives (optional)

2 eggs

300ml/½ pint/1¼ cups milk

50g/2oz/¼ cup white vegetable fat (shortening) or lard

450g/1lb good-quality pork sausages

salt and ground black pepper

Farmhouse tip To ensure really light and crisp batter, ensure that the pan is very hot before adding the batter.

1 Preheat the oven to 220°C/425°F/Gas 7. Sift the flour into a bowl with a pinch of salt and pepper. Make a well in the centre of the flour. Whisk the chives, if using, with the eggs and milk, then pour this into the well in the flour. Gradually whisk the flour into the liquid to make a smooth batter. Cover and leave to stand for at least 30 minutes.

2 Put the fat into a small roasting pan and place in the oven for 3–5 minutes. Add the sausages and cook for 15 minutes, turning twice during cooking.

3 Pour the batter over the sausages and return to the oven. Cook for about 20 minutes, or until the batter is risen and golden. Serve immediately.

Energy 497kcal/2070kJ; Protein 14.5g; Carbohydrate 32.1g, of which sugars 3.8g; Fat 35.4g, of which saturates 13.6g; Cholesterol 109mg; Calcium 141mg; Fibre 1.3g; Sodium 616mg.

Cider-glazed ham

Succulent, moist and with plenty of flavour, this old-fashioned English country recipe keeps the meat tender with a lovely sticky glaze, which is complemented by the fruit and port sauce. It is perfect to share with friends and family at Christmas or any time of the year.

Serves 8–10

2kg/4½lb middle gammon (cured ham) joint

1 large or 2 small onions

about 30 whole cloves

3 bay leaves

10 black peppercorns

1.3 litres/2½ pints/5⅔ cups medium-dry (hard) cider

45ml/3 tbsp soft light brown sugar

For the cranberry sauce

350g/12oz/3 cups cranberries

175g/6oz/¾ cup soft light brown sugar

grated rind and juice of 2 clementines or 1 small orange

30ml/2 tbsp port

1 Calculate the cooking time for the gammon at 20 minutes per 450g/1lb, then place it in a large casserole or pan. Stud the onion or onions with 5–10 of the cloves and add to the casserole or pan with the bay leaves and peppercorns. Add 1.2 litres/2 pints/5 cups of the cider and enough water to just cover the gammon.

2 Heat until simmering and then carefully skim off the scum that rises to the surface using a large spoon or ladle. Start timing the cooking from the moment the stock begins to simmer.

3 Cover the gammon with a lid or foil and simmer gently for the calculated time. Towards the end of the cooking time, preheat the oven to 220°C/425°F/Gas 7.

4 Heat the sugar and remaining cider in a pan; stir until the sugar has dissolved. Simmer for 5 minutes to make a dark, sticky glaze. Remove the pan from the heat and leave to cool for 5 minutes.

5 Lift the gammon out of the pan. Carefully and evenly, cut the rind from the meat, then score the fat into a diamond pattern. Place the gammon in a large roasting pan or ovenproof dish.

6 Press a clove into the centre of each diamond, then carefully spoon over the glaze. Bake for 20–25 minutes, or until the fat is brown, glistening and crisp.

7 To make the sauce, simmer all the ingredients in a pan for 20 minutes, stirring. Transfer to a jug (pitcher). Serve the gammon sliced, hot or cold, with the cranberry sauce.

Farmhouse tips Leave the gammon until it is just cool enough to handle before removing the rind. Snip off the string using a sharp knife or scissors, then carefully slice off the rind, leaving a thick, even layer of fat. Use a narrow-bladed, sharp knife for the best results.

A large stockpot is ideal for the first stages of cooking a big piece of meat like this gammon, but a deep roasting pan will do, using a double thickness of foil as a cover and turning the meat once for even cooking.

Energy 447kcal/1873kJ; Protein 44.1g; Carbohydrate 25.6g, of which sugars 25.6g; Fat 18.8g, of which saturates 6.3g; Cholesterol 58mg; Calcium 35mg; Fibre 1.3g; Sodium 2203mg.

Ham with summer vegetables and eggs

An easy and tasty family supper dish, this is very straightforward to prepare, and you can vary the vegetables as you like. Serve with plenty of crusty Italian bread, such as ciabatta.

Serves 4

30ml/2 tbsp olive oil

1 onion, roughly chopped

2 garlic cloves, crushed

175g/6oz cooked ham

225g/8oz courgettes (zucchini)

1 red (bell) pepper, seeded and thinly sliced

1 yellow (bell) pepper, seeded and thinly sliced

10ml/2 tsp paprika

400g/14oz can chopped tomatoes

15ml/1 tbsp sun-dried tomato purée (paste)

4 eggs

115g/4oz/1 cup coarsely grated Cheddar cheese

salt and ground black pepper

crusty bread, to serve

3 Add the courgettes and peppers to the onion and garlic and continue to cook over a medium heat for a further 3–4 minutes.

4 Stir in the paprika, tomatoes, tomato purée, ham and seasoning. Bring to the boil and simmer gently for about 15 minutes.

5 Reduce the heat to low. Make four wells in the tomato mixture, break an egg into each and season. Cook over a gentle heat until the white begins to set.

6 Preheat the grill (broiler). Sprinkle the cheese over the vegetables and grill (broil) for about 5 minutes until the eggs are set. Serve immediately with bread.

1 Heat the olive oil in a deep frying pan. Add the onion and garlic and cook for 4 minutes, stirring frequently, or until just beginning to soften.

2 While the onions and garlic are cooking, cut the ham and courgettes into 5cm/2in long batons. Set the ham aside.

Energy 350kcal/1457kJ; Protein 24.4g; Carbohydrate 11.4g, of which sugars 10.7g; Fat 22.8g, of which saturates 9.3g; Cholesterol 244mg; Calcium 276mg; Fibre 3.1g; Sodium 817mg.

Bacon, egg and leek pie

The mild onion flavour of leeks is lovely with the bacon and eggs. The creamy filling is topped with flaky puff pastry, but shortcrust pastry would also work well.

Serves 4–6

15ml/1 tbsp olive oil

200g/7oz lean back bacon rashers (strips), trimmed of rinds and cut into thin strips

250g/9oz/2 cups leeks, thinly sliced

40g/1½oz/⅓ cup plain (all-purpose) flour

1.5ml/¼ tsp freshly grated nutmeg

450ml/¾ pint/scant 2 cups milk, plus extra for brushing

4 eggs

1 sheet ready-rolled puff pastry

salt and ground black pepper

1 Preheat the oven to 200°C/400°F/ Gas 6. Put the oil and bacon in a pan and cook for 5 minutes, stirring occasionally, until the bacon is golden brown. Add the leeks. Stir, cover and cook over medium heat for 5 minutes until softened, stirring once or twice. Stir in the flour and nutmeg. Remove from the heat and gradually stir in the milk.

2 Return to the heat and cook, stirring, until it thickens and boils. Season, then pour into a shallow ovenproof pie dish, measuring 25cm/10in in diameter. Make four wells in the sauce and break an egg into each one.

3 Brush the edges of the dish with milk. Lay the pastry over the dish. Trim off the excess pastry and use it to make the trimmings. Brush the backs with milk and stick them on the top of the pie.

4 Brush the pastry with milk and make a small central slit to allow steam to escape. Put into the oven and cook for about 40 minutes until the pastry is puffed up and golden brown, and the eggs have set.

Energy 202kcal/842kJ; Protein 13.4g; Carbohydrate 9.7g, of which sugars 4.4g; Fat 12.5g, of which saturates 4.2g; Cholesterol 149mg; Calcium 125mg; Fibre 1.1g; Sodium 592mg.

Vegetable Dishes and Salads

Tasty and nutritious, vegetables are vital to good health and well-being. Served simply with a little unsalted butter or a drizzle of olive oil and a scatter of chopped herbs, they are hard to beat. Seasonal treats such as asparagus and new potatoes are best eaten as fresh as possible, so always seek out local suppliers or enrol in a vegetable box scheme that will give access to what's available.

Savoury lentil loaf

Ideal as an alternative to the traditional meat roast, this wholesome lentil and nut loaf is perfect for special occasions. It is good served with a spicy fresh tomato sauce.

Serves 4

30ml/2 tbsp olive oil, plus extra for greasing

1 onion, finely chopped

1 leek, finely chopped

2 celery sticks, finely chopped

225g/8oz/3 cups mushrooms, chopped

2 garlic cloves, crushed

425g/15oz can lentils, rinsed and drained

115g/4oz/1 cup mixed almonds, hazelnuts and cashews, chopped

50g/2oz/½ cup plain (all-purpose) flour

50g/2oz/½ cup grated mature (sharp) Cheddar cheese

1 egg, beaten

45–60ml/3–4 tbsp chopped fresh mixed herbs

salt and ground black pepper

chives and sprigs of fresh flat leaf parsley, to garnish

1 Lightly grease and line with baking parchment the base and sides of a 900g/2lb loaf tin (pan) or terrine.

2 Heat the oil in a large pan, add the onion, leek, celery, mushrooms and garlic, then cook for 10 minutes, until the vegetables have softened. Do not let them brown.

3 Remove from the heat. Stir in the lentils, mixed nuts and flour, cheese, egg and herbs. Season well and mix.

4 Spoon the mixture into the prepared loaf tin, or terrine, pressing it right into the corners. Level the surface with a fork, then cover the tin with a piece of foil. Place the loaf tin inside a large deep-sided baking tray and pour in enough near-boiling water to come just over halfway up the side of the tin.

5 Cover and cook slowly for 1–2 hours, or until the loaf is firm to the touch.

6 Leave to cool in the tin for about 15 minutes, then turn out on to a serving plate. Serve hot or cold, cut into thick slices and garnished with herbs.

Energy 484Kcal/2019kJ; Protein 23.7g; Carbohydrate 34.1g, of which sugars 5.1g; Fat 29g, of which saturates 5.4g; Cholesterol 69mg; Calcium 238mg; Fibre 8.7g; Sodium 128mg.

Parsnips and chickpeas

This lightly spiced vegetable stew makes a nourishing meal for vegetarians. The chickpeas add substance as well as protein. Complete the meal with warmed naan breads.

Serves 4

5 garlic cloves, finely chopped

1 small onion, chopped

5cm/2in piece fresh root ginger, chopped

2 green chillies, seeded and finely chopped

75ml/5 tbsp cold water

60ml/4 tbsp groundnut (peanut) oil

5ml/1 tsp cumin seeds

10ml/2 tsp coriander seeds

5ml/1 tsp ground turmeric

2.5ml/½ tsp chilli powder

50g/2oz/½ cup cashew nuts, toasted and ground

225g/8oz tomatoes, peeled and chopped

400g/14oz can chickpeas, drained and rinsed

900g/2lb parsnips, cut into 2cm/¾in chunks

350ml/12fl oz/1½ cups boiling vegetable stock

juice of 1 lime, to taste

salt and ground black pepper

chopped fresh coriander (cilantro), toasted cashew nuts and natural (plain) yogurt, to serve

1 Reserve 10ml/2 tsp of the garlic, then place the remainder in a food processor with the onion, ginger and half the chilli. Add the water and blend to a smooth paste. Preheat the oven to 180°C/250°F/Gas 4.

2 Heat the oil in a large frying pan, add the cumin seeds and cook for a few seconds. Stir in the coriander seeds, turmeric, chilli powder and ground cashews. Add the ginger and chilli paste and stir-fry for 2–3 minutes.

3 Add the tomatoes to the pan and cook for 1 minute.

4 Transfer the mixture to a casserole dish. Add the chickpeas and parsnips to the pot and stir to coat in the spicy tomato mixture, then stir in the stock and season with salt and pepper. Cover with the lid and cook in the oven for 1 hour, or until the parsnips are tender.

5 Stir half the lime juice, the reserved garlic and green chilli into the stew. Re-cover and cook for 30 minutes more, then taste and add more lime juice if needed.

6 Spoon on to plates and sprinkle with fresh coriander leaves and toasted cashew nuts. Serve immediately with a generous spoonful of natural yogurt.

Energy 453Kcal/1899kJ; Protein 14.8g; Carbohydrate 50.1g, of which sugars 16.6g; Fat 23g, of which saturates 4.3g; Cholesterol 0mg; Calcium 148mg; Fibre 15.8g; Sodium 394mg.

Baked potatoes and three fillings

Potatoes baked in their skins until they are crisp on the outside and fluffy in the middle make an excellent and nourishing meal on their own, served with a crisp, green salad. For an even tastier supper, add one of these delicious and easy toppings.

Serves 4

4 medium baking potatoes

olive oil

sea salt

filling of your choice (see below)

1 Preheat the oven to 200°C/400°F/ Gas 6. Score the potatoes with a cross and rub all over with the olive oil.

2 Place on a baking sheet and cook for 45 minutes to 1 hour until a knife inserted into the centres indicates they are cooked.

Farmhouse tip Choose potatoes that are evenly sized and have undamaged skins, and scrub them thoroughly. If they are done before you are ready to serve them, take them out of the oven and wrap them up in a warmed cloth until they are needed.

3 Cut the potatoes open along the score lines and push up the flesh. Season and fill with your chosen filling.

Stir-fry vegetables

45ml/3 tbsp vegetable oil

2 leeks, thinly sliced

2 carrots, cut into sticks

1 courgette (zucchini), thinly sliced

115g/4oz baby corn, halved

115g/4oz/1½ cup button (white) mushrooms, sliced

45ml/3 tbsp soy sauce

30ml/2 tbsp dry sherry or vermouth

15ml/1 tbsp sesame oil

sesame seeds, to garnish

1 Heat the vegetable oil in a large frying pan until really hot. Add the leeks, carrots, courgette and baby corn and stir-fry together for about 2 minutes, then add the mushrooms and stir-fry for a further minute.

2 Mix the soy sauce, sherry or vermouth and sesame oil together in a small bowl, and pour over the vegetables. Heat through until just bubbling and sprinkle the sesame seeds over.

Red bean chilli

425g/15oz can red kidney beans, drained

200g/7oz/scant 1 cup low-fat cottage or cream cheese

30ml/2 tbsp mild chilli sauce

5ml/1 tsp ground cumin

1 Heat the beans in a pan or microwave and stir in the cottage or cream cheese, chilli sauce and cumin.

2 Serve topped with more chilli sauce.

Cheese and creamy corn

425g/15oz can creamed corn

115g/4oz/1 cup strong cheese, grated

5ml/1 tsp mixed dried herbs

fresh parsley sprigs, to garnish

1 Heat the corn gently with the cheese and mixed herbs until well blended.

2 Use to fill the potatoes and garnish with fresh parsley sprigs.

Variation For an even simpler supper, just top the baked potato with a knob (pat) of butter and some grated cheese, and serve with coleslaw.

Energy 223kcal/941kJ; Protein 7.3g; Carbohydrate 38.6g, of which sugars 8.3g; Fat 4.5g, of which saturates 0.8g; Cholesterol 0mg; Calcium 55mg; Fibre 5.4g; Sodium 1150mg.

Spicy-hot mixed bean chilli

Inspired by traditional Texan home cooking, this chilli is served with cornbread. The delicious topping makes it a filling one-pot meal with no need for accompaniments.

Serves 4

115g/4oz/generous ½ cup dried red kidney beans, soaked overnight

600ml/1 pint/2½ cups of water

115g/4oz/generous ½ cup dried black-eyed beans (peas)

1 bay leaf

15ml/1 tbsp vegetable oil

1 large onion, finely chopped

1 garlic clove, crushed

5ml/1 tsp ground cumin

5ml/1 tsp chilli powder

5ml/1 tsp mild paprika

2.5ml/½ tsp dried marjoram

450g/1lb mixed vegetables, such as potatoes, carrots, parsnips or celery

1 vegetable stock cube

400g/14oz can chopped tomatoes

15ml/1 tbsp tomato purée (paste)

salt and ground black pepper

For the cornbread topping

250g/9oz/2¼ cups fine cornmeal

30ml/2 tbsp wholemeal (whole-wheat) flour

7.5ml/1½ tsp baking powder

1 egg, plus 1 egg yolk, lightly beaten

300ml/½ pint/1¼ cups milk

1 Preheat the oven to 150°C/300°F/Gas 2. Drain the beans and rinse well, then place in a pan with the water and the bay leaf. Bring to the boil and boil rapidly for 10 minutes.

2 Remove the beans from the heat, then pour into a large ovenproof dish and put in the oven.

3 Heat the oil in a pan, add the onion and cook for 7–8 minutes. Add the garlic, cumin, chilli powder, paprika and marjoram and cook for 1 minute. Tip into the casserole dish and stir.

4 Prepare the vegetables, peeling or trimming as necessary, then cut into 2cm/¾in chunks. Add to the bean mixture. Cover with the lid and bake for 3 hours, or until the beans are tender.

5 Add the stock cube and tomatoes to the cooking pot, then stir in the tomato purée and season with salt and pepper.

6 Replace the lid and bake for a further 30 minutes until at boiling point.

7 For the topping, in a bowl, combine the cornmeal, flour, baking powder and a pinch of salt. Make a well in the centre and add the beaten egg and milk. Mix, then spoon over the bean mixture. Cover and cook for 1 hour, or until the topping is firm and cooked.

Energy 613Kcal/2595kJ; Protein 29.6g; Carbohydrate 97.4g, of which sugars 15.8g; Fat 14.5g, of which saturates 3.4g; Cholesterol 112mg; Calcium 257mg; Fibre 13.4g; Sodium 413mg.

Sweet-and-sour mixed bean hotpot

This dish, topped with sliced potatoes, is incredibly easy, making the most of dried and canned ingredients from the kitchen cupboard and combining them with a rich and tangy sauce.

Serves 6

40g/1½oz/3 tbsp butter

4 shallots, peeled and finely chopped

40g/1½oz/⅓ cup plain (all-purpose) or wholemeal (whole-wheat) flour

300ml/½ pint/1¼ cups passata (bottled strained tomatoes)

120ml/4fl oz/½ cup unsweetened apple juice

60ml/4 tbsp soft light brown sugar

60ml/4 tbsp tomato ketchup

60ml/4 tbsp dry sherry

60ml/4 tbsp cider vinegar

60ml/4 tbsp light soy sauce

400g/14oz can butter (lima) beans

400g/14oz can flageolet (small cannellini) beans

400g/14oz can chickpeas

175g/6oz green beans, cut into 2.5cm/1in lengths

225g/8oz/3 cups mushrooms, sliced

15ml/1 tbsp chopped fresh thyme

15ml/1 tbsp fresh marjoram

450g/1lb unpeeled potatoes

15ml/1 tbsp olive oil

salt and ground black pepper

fresh herbs, to garnish

1 Melt the butter in a pan, add the shallots and fry gently for 5–6 minutes, until softened. Add the flour and cook for 1 minute, stirring all the time, then gradually stir in the passata.

2 Rinse and drain the beans and chickpeas. Place in an ovenproof dish with the green beans and mushrooms and pour over the sauce. Stir in the thyme and marjoram, apple juice, sugar, tomato ketchup, sherry, vinegar and light soy sauce.

3 Bring the mixture to the boil, stirring constantly until it thickens. Season.

4 Preheat the oven to 180°C/350°F/ Gas 4. Thinly slice the potatoes and par-boil them for 5 minutes. Drain well.

5 Arrange the potato slices on top of the beans, overlapping them slightly. Brush with half the olive oil. Cover and cook for 1 hour, or until the potatoes are just tender.

6 Uncover and brush the remaining oil over the potatoes. Cook for a further 30 minutes, to brown the potato topping. Serve garnished with herbs.

Energy 483Kcal/2042kJ; Protein 18.5g; Carbohydrate 73.3g, of which sugars 24.8g; Fat 13.8g, of which saturates 4.5g; Cholesterol 14mg; Calcium 134mg; Fibre 10.9g; Sodium 826mg.

Butter bean stew

A hearty dish, which is substantial enough to be served on its own, this butter bean stew can also be served with a leafy salad and fresh, crusty bread.

Serves 4

115g/4oz/²⁄₃ cup butter (lima) beans, soaked overnight

30–45ml/2–3 tbsp olive oil

1 onion, chopped

2–3 garlic cloves, crushed

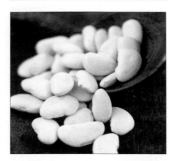

25g/1oz fresh root ginger, peeled and chopped

pinch of saffron threads

16 cherry tomatoes

generous pinch of sugar

handful of fleshy black olives, pitted

5ml/1 tsp ground cinnamon

5ml/1 tsp paprika

small bunch of flat leaf parsley

salt and ground black pepper

1 Place the beans in a large pan with plenty of water. Bring to the boil, boil for about 10 minutes, reduce the heat and simmer for 1–1¹⁄₂ hours until soft.

2 Drain the beans and refresh under cold water. Heat the olive oil in a heavy pan. Add the onion, garlic and ginger, and cook for about 10 minutes, or until softened but not browned. Stir in the saffron threads, followed by the cherry tomatoes and a sprinkling of sugar.

3 As the tomatoes begin to soften, stir in the butter beans. When the tomatoes have heated through, stir in the olives, ground cinnamon and paprika. Season to taste and sprinkle over the parsley. Serve immediately.

Farmhouse tip If you are in a hurry, you could use 2 x 400g/14oz cans of butter beans for this stew. Make sure you rinse the beans well before adding to the recipe as canned beans can tend to be salty.

Energy 117kcal/487kJ; Protein 3.5g; Carbohydrate 8.5g, of which sugars 2.2g; Fat 7.9g, of which saturates 1.2g; Cholesterol 0mg; Calcium 25mg; Fibre 3.3g; Sodium 635mg.

Chickpea rissoles

These chickpea rissoles are cheap to make, very appetizing and can be served with drinks, or as a starter, accompanied by radishes, rocket and olives.

Serves 4

300g/11oz/scant 1½ cups chickpeas, soaked overnight in water to cover

105ml/7 tbsp extra virgin olive oil

2 large onions, chopped

15ml/1 tbsp ground cumin

2 garlic cloves, crushed

3–4 fresh sage leaves, chopped

45ml/3 tbsp chopped flat leaf parsley

1 large (US extra large) egg, lightly beaten

45ml/3 tbsp self-raising (self-rising) flour

50g/2oz/½ cup plain (all-purpose) flour

salt and ground black pepper

radishes, rocket (arugula) and olives, to serve

1 Drain the chickpeas, rinse and drain again. Tip them into a large pan, cover with plenty of fresh cold water and bring them to the boil. Skim the froth from the surface of the water with a slotted spoon until the liquid is clear.

2 Cover the pan and cook for 1¼–1½ hours, or until the chickpeas are very soft. Alternatively, cook them in a pressure cooker under full pressure for 20–25 minutes.

3 Once the chickpeas are soft, set aside 30–45ml/2–3 tbsp of the liquid from the chickpeas, then strain them, discarding the rest of the liquid. Tip into a food processor, and process, adding enough of the reserved liquid to make a velvety mash.

4 Heat 45ml/3 tbsp of the olive oil in a large frying pan, add the onions and sauté until they are light golden. Add the cumin and the garlic and stir for a few seconds until their aroma rises. Stir in the chopped sage leaves and the parsley, and set aside.

5 Scrape the chickpea mash into a large bowl and add the egg, the self-raising flour and the fried onion and herb mixture. Add plenty of salt and pepper, and mix well.

Farmhouse tip Dampen your hands slightly when shaping the mixture, as this helps to prevent the mixture from sticking to them.

6 Take walnut-size pieces of the mixture and flatten them so that they look like thick, round mini-burgers. Coat the rissoles lightly in the plain flour. Heat the remaining olive oil in a frying pan and fry the rissoles in batches until they are crisp and golden on both sides. Drain on kitchen paper and serve hot with the radishes, rocket and olives.

Energy 552kcal/2312kJ; Protein 21.3g; Carbohydrate 63.7g, of which sugars 8.2g; Fat 25.3g, of which saturates 3.6g; Cholesterol 48mg; Calcium 234mg; Fibre 10.8g; Sodium 95mg.

Potatoes roasted with goose fat and garlic

Goose or duck fat gives the best flavour for roasting potatoes. In addition to the garlic,
try adding a couple of bay leaves and a sprig of rosemary or thyme to the roasting pan.
For a vegetarian version, use a generous piece of butter with a splash of olive oil.

Serves 4

675g/1½lb floury potatoes, such as
Maris Piper, peeled

30ml/2 tbsp goose fat

12 garlic cloves, unpeeled

salt and ground black pepper

1 Preheat the oven to 190°C/375°F/
Gas 5. Cut the potatoes into large
chunks and cook in a pan of salted,
boiling water for 5 minutes. Drain well
and give the colander a good shake
to fluff up the edges of the potatoes.
Return the potatoes to the pan and
place it over a low heat for 1 minute
to steam off any excess water.

2 Meanwhile, spoon the goose fat into
a roasting pan and place in the oven
until hot, about 5 minutes. Add the
potatoes to the pan with the garlic
and turn to coat in the fat. Season
well with salt and ground black pepper
and roast for 40–50 minutes, turning
occasionally, until the potatoes are
golden and tender.

Energy 185kcal/778kJ; Protein 2.9g; Carbohydrate 27.2g, of which sugars 2.2g; Fat 7.9g, of which saturates 3.2g; Cholesterol 7mg; Calcium 10mg; Fibre 1.7g; Sodium 19mg.

Colcannon

This traditional Irish dish is often served at Hallowe'en with a ring hidden inside it to predict the wedding of the person who finds it. You can use curly kale, cabbage or cavolo nero for a variation. Serve topped with a fried or poached egg, or with a stew or roast.

Serves 6–8

450g/1lb potatoes, peeled cut into chunks

450g/1lb curly kale or cabbage, lightly cooked

milk, if necessary

50g/2oz/2 tbsp butter, plus extra for serving

1 large onion, finely chopped

salt and ground black pepper

1 Cook the potatoes in lightly salted boiling water, until tender. Drain, return to the pan and mash until smooth.

2 Chop the cooked kale or cabbage, add it to the mashed potatoes and mix. Stir in a little milk if the mash is too stiff.

3 Melt a little butter in a large frying pan and add the onion. Cook until softened. Add to the potato and kale or cabbage and mix well.

4 Add the remainder of the butter to the hot frying pan. When very hot, turn the potato mixture in to the pan and spread it out. Fry until brown, then cut it roughly into pieces and continue frying until they are crisp on both sides. Serve in bowls or as a side dish, with plenty of butter.

Energy 306kcal/1281kJ; Protein 5.4g; Carbohydrate 40.6g, of which sugars 13.6g; Fat 14.6g, of which saturates 8.8g; Cholesterol 36mg; Calcium 104mg; Fibre 5.9g; Sodium 127mg.

Creamy layered potatoes

In this delicious and comforting winter dish, the slow-cooked potatoes soak up the cream and give a meltingly tender result. Serve with any kind of roasted meat.

Serves 6

1.5kg/3–3¹/₂lb large potatoes, peeled and sliced

2 large onions, sliced

75g/3oz/6 tbsp unsalted butter

300ml/¹/₂ pint/1¹/₄ cups double (US heavy) cream

salt and ground black pepper

Variation Add a couple of cloves of garlic, sliced, to the mixture in step 1, if you wish.

1 Preheat the oven to 200°C/400°F/Gas 6. Place the potatoes, onions, butter and cream in a large pan, stir gently to mix, bring to a simmer, and cook for about 15 minutes.

2 Transfer the potatoes and cream to an ovenproof dish, season and bake for 1 hour, until the potatoes are soft and tender, and all the liquid has been absorbed. Serve at once.

Energy 557kcal/2318kJ; Protein 7g; Carbohydrate 50g, of which sugars 7g; Fat 38g, of which saturates 23g; Cholesterol 95mg; Calcium 60mg; Fibre 5.2g; Sodium 172mg.

Spicy fried potatoes

This is a simple dish of fried potatoes given a hint of heat by tossing them with spiced vinegar. Sliced peppers add a splash of colour.

Serves 4

2 garlic cloves, sliced

2.5ml/½ tsp crushed chillies

2.5ml/½ tsp ground cumin

10ml/2 tsp paprika

30ml/2 tbsp red or white wine vinegar

675g/1½lb small new potatoes

75ml/5 tbsp olive oil

1 red or green (bell) pepper, seeded and sliced

olive oil and coarse sea salt, to serve

1 Crush the garlic, chillies and cumin in a mortar, then stir in the paprika and wine vinegar.

2 Bring a large pan of salted water to the boil and cook the potatoes, in their skins, for about 15 minutes until tender. Drain and cut into small chunks.

◀ **3** Transfer the potatoes to a large frying pan and sauté in the oil until they start to crisp at the edges. Add the spiced garlic mixture to the potatoes with the sliced pepper and continue to cook, stirring, for 2 minutes. Serve the potatoes warm, or leave until cold. Sprinkle with coarse sea salt, and a drizzle of olive oil, to serve.

Energy 300kcal/1253kJ; Protein 4g; Carbohydrate 29g, of which sugars 3g; Fat 20g, of which saturates 3g; Cholesterol 0mg; Calcium 20mg; Fibre 3.0g; Sodium 24mg.

Pepper and potato omelette

This substantial omelette is best eaten at room temperature in chunky wedges. It makes ideal picnicking food. Use a hard cheese, like Parmesan, or mature Cheddar.

Serves 4

2 medium-sized potatoes

45ml/3 tbsp olive oil, plus more if necessary

1 large onion, thinly sliced

2 garlic cloves, crushed

2 (bell) peppers, one green and one red, seeded and thinly sliced

6 eggs, beaten

115g/4oz/1 cup mature (sharp) Cheddar cheese, grated

salt and ground black pepper

Variation You can add any sliced and lightly cooked vegetable, such as courgette (zucchini) or broccoli, to this tortilla instead of the peppers.

1 Par-boil the potatoes in boiling water for about 10 minutes. Drain and cool slightly then slice thickly.

2 In a large non-stick or well-seasoned frying pan, heat the oil over a medium heat. Add the onion, garlic and peppers and cook for 5 minutes until softened.

3 Add the potatoes and continue frying, stirring occasionally, until the potatoes are tender.

4 Pour in half the beaten eggs, sprinkle half the cheese over this and then the remainder of the egg. Season. Finish with a layer of cheese. Reduce the heat to low and continue to cook without stirring, half-covering the pan with a lid to help set the eggs.

5 When the tortilla is firm, place the pan under a hot grill (broiler) to seal the top lightly. Leave in the pan to cool. Serve in wedges at room temperature.

Energy 321Kcal/1333kJ; Protein 13.1g; Carbohydrate 19.6g, of which sugars 10.2g; Fat 21.1g, of which saturates 8.3g; Cholesterol 123mg; Calcium 256mg; Fibre 3g; Sodium 254mg.

Baked potatoes with feta cheese and olives

These thinly sliced potatoes are cooked with Greek feta cheese and black and green olives in olive oil. This dish is a good one to serve with toasted pitta bread.

Serves 4

900g/2lb maincrop potatoes

150ml/¼ pint/⅔ cup olive oil

1 sprig rosemary

275g/10oz/2½ cups feta cheese, crumbled

115g/4oz/1 cup pitted black and green olives

300ml/½ pint/1¼ cups hot vegetable stock

ground black pepper

Farmhouse tip Make sure you choose Greek feta cheese, which has a completely different texture from Danish feta-style cheese.

1 Preheat the oven to 200°C/400°F/ Gas 6. Cook the potatoes in plenty of boiling water for 15 minutes. Drain and cool slightly. Peel the potatoes and cut into thin slices.

2 Brush the base and sides of a 1.5 litre/2½ pint/6¼ cup rectangular ovenproof dish with some of the olive oil.

3 Layer the potatoes in the dish with the rosemary, cheese and olives. Drizzle with the remaining olive oil and pour over the stock. Season with plenty of ground black pepper.

4 Cook for 35 minutes, covering with foil to prevent the potatoes from getting too brown. Serve hot, straight from the dish.

Energy 584Kcal/2429kJ; Protein 14.8g; Carbohydrate 37.3g, of which sugars 4g; Fat 42.7g, of which saturates 13.7g; Cholesterol 48mg; Calcium 279mg; Fibre 3.1g; Sodium 1662mg.

Rosemary roasties

These unusual roast potatoes require far less fat than conventional roast potatoes, and because they still have their skins they have more flavour, too.

Serves 4

1kg/2lb red potatoes

30ml/2 tsp sunflower oil

30ml/2 tbsp fresh rosemary leaves

salt and paprika

Farmhouse tip This recipe is also delicious with tiny salad potatoes, especially if you roast them with chunks of red onion.

Variation Replace the sunflower oil with walnut oil for a nutty flavour.

1 Preheat the oven to 240°C/475°F/ Gas 9. Scrub the potatoes. If they are large, cut them in half. Place in a pan of cold water and bring to the boil. Drain and allow the steam to evaporate for a few minutes to dry.

2 Drizzle the oil over the potatoes and shake the pan to coat them evenly.

3 Put the potatoes into a shallow roasting tin (pan). Sprinkle with the rosemary, salt and paprika. Roast for 30–45 minutes. Serve hot.

Energy 189Kcal/801kJ; Protein 4.3g; Carbohydrate 40.3g, of which sugars 3.3g; Fat 2.3g, of which saturates 0.4g; Cholesterol 0mg; Calcium 15mg; Fibre 2.5g; Sodium 28mg.

Baked courgettes in tomato sauce

This recipe is a good way to use the early summer glut of courgettes. Use homegrown, fresh tomatoes, cooked and puréed, instead of passata, if possible.

Serves 4

5ml/1 tsp olive oil

3 large courgettes (zucchini), thinly sliced

1/2 small red onion, finely chopped

300ml/1/2 pint/1 1/4 cups passata (bottled, strained tomatoes)

30ml/2 tbsp chopped fresh thyme

garlic salt and ground black pepper

fresh thyme sprigs, to garnish

1 Preheat the oven to 190°C/375°F/ Gas 5. Brush a baking dish with olive oil. Arrange half the courgettes and onion in the dish.

2 Spoon half the passata over the vegetables. Sprinkle with some of the fresh thyme, then season to taste with garlic salt and pepper. Repeat with the remaining ingredients. Cover the dish and bake for 40–45 minutes. Garnish with thyme sprigs and serve hot.

Energy 89Kcal/370kJ; Protein 4.3g; Carbohydrate 9.2g, of which sugars 8.6g; Fat 4.1g, of which saturates 0.7g; Cholesterol 0mg; Calcium 54mg; Fibre 3.2g; Sodium 235mg.

Farmhouse cheese-baked courgettes

This is an easy dish that makes a great accompaniment to a wide range of meat and fish dishes or a good vegetarian lunch. Use piquant farmhouse cheddar or mature goat's cheese.

Serves 4

4 courgettes (zucchini)

30ml/2 tbsp grated hard farmhouse cheese, such as Cheddar

about 25g/1oz/2 tbsp butter

salt and ground black pepper

1 Preheat the oven to 180°C/350°F/ Gas 4. Slice the courgettes in half, lengthways. Trim the ends and discard.

2 Butter a shallow baking dish and arrange the courgettes, cut side up, inside the dish.

3 Sprinkle the cheese over the courgettes, and sprinkle over a few knobs (pats) of butter.

4 Bake in the preheated oven for about 20 minutes, or until the courgettes are tender and the cheese is bubbling and golden brown. Serve immediately.

Energy 96kcal/395kJ; Protein 3.8g; Carbohydrate 1.9g, of which sugars 1.8g; Fat 8g, of which saturates 5g; Cholesterol 21mg; Calcium 82mg; Fibre 0.9g; Sodium 93mg.

Summer courgette and potato bake

This is a great dish for when courgettes and early crop potatoes are in season. Serve the oven-baked courgettes with a green salad for a satisfying vegetarian meal.

Serves 6

675g/1½lb courgettes (zucchini)

450g/1lb potatoes, peeled and cut into chunks

1 onion, finely sliced

3 garlic cloves, chopped

1 large red (bell) pepper, seeded and cubed

400g/14oz can chopped tomatoes

150ml/¼ pint/⅔ cup extra virgin olive oil

150ml/¼ pint/⅔ cup hot water

5ml/1 tsp dried oregano

45ml/3 tbsp chopped fresh flat leaf parsley, plus a few extra sprigs, to garnish

salt and ground black pepper

1 Preheat the oven to 190°C/375°F/ Gas 5. Scrape the courgettes lightly under running water to dislodge any grit and then slice them into thin rounds. Put them in a large baking dish and add the chopped potatoes, onion, garlic, red pepper and tomatoes.

2 Mix well, then stir in the olive oil, hot water and dried oregano.

3 Spread the mixture evenly, then season with salt and pepper. Bake for 30 minutes, then stir in the parsley and a little more water.

4 Return to the oven and cook for 1 hour, increasing the temperature to 200°C/400°F/Gas 6 for the final 10–15 minutes, so that the potatoes brown.

Energy 374kcal/1,554kJ; Protein 6.6g; Carbohydrate 28.6g, of which sugars 11.2g; Fat 26.7g, of which saturates 4g; Cholesterol 0mg; Calcium 86mg; Fibre 5.1g; Sodium 29mg.

Butter-braised lettuce, peas and spring onions

A well-loved French country recipe, this dish is traditionally served with pan-fried fish or
meat. Try adding fresh mint, or substituting mangetouts or sugar snaps for the peas.

Serves 4

50g/2oz/¼ cup butter

4 Little Gem (Bibb) lettuces, halved
lengthways

2 bunches spring onions (scallions),
trimmed

400g/14oz shelled peas (about
1kg/2¼lb in pods)

salt and ground black pepper

Variations Braise about 250g/9oz baby
carrots with the lettuce.
  Cook 115g/4oz chopped smoked bacon
in the butter. Use 1 bunch spring onions
(scallions) and some chopped parsley.

1 Melt half the butter in a wide, heavy
pan over a low heat. Add the lettuces
and spring onions.

2 Turn the vegetables in the butter,
then sprinkle in salt and plenty of
ground black pepper. Cover, and
cook the vegetables very gently for
5 minutes, stirring once.

3 Add the peas and turn them in the
buttery juices. Pour in 120ml/4fl oz/
½ cup water, then cover and cook over
a gentle heat for a further 5 minutes.
Uncover and increase the heat to
reduce the liquid to a few tablespoons.

4 Stir in the remaining butter. Transfer
to a warmed serving dish and serve.

Energy 161kcal/670kJ; Protein 9.1g; Carbohydrate 15.9g, of which sugars 6.8g; Fat 7.4g, of which saturates 3.7g; Cholesterol 13mg; Calcium 73mg; Fibre 6.5g; Sodium 47mg.

Fresh green beans and tomato sauce

This country summer dish can be made with whichever beans are in season, it makes a pretty accompaniment and can also be served with feta cheese, olives and flat bread.

Serves 4

800g/1¾lb green beans, trimmed

150ml/¼ pint/⅔ cup extra virgin olive oil

1 large onion, thinly sliced

2 garlic cloves, chopped

2 small potatoes, peeled and chopped into cubes

675g/1½lb tomatoes or a 400g/14oz can plum tomatoes, chopped

150ml/¼ pint/⅔ cup hot water

45–60ml/3–4 tbsp chopped fresh parsley

salt and ground black pepper

1 If the green beans are very long, cut them in half. Drop them into a bowl of cold water so that they are completely submerged. Leave them to absorb the water for a few minutes. To test if the beans are fresh, snap one in half. If it breaks crisply it is fresh; if it bends rather than breaking, the beans are not fresh.

2 Heat the olive oil in a large pan, add the onion and sauté until translucent. Add the garlic, then, when it becomes aromatic, stir in the potatoes and sauté the mixture for a few minutes. Add the tomatoes and the hot water and cook for 10 minutes.

3 Drain the beans, rinse them and drain again, then add them to the pan with a little salt and pepper to season. Cover and simmer for 10-15 minutes.

4 Stir in the chopped parsley, with a little more hot water if the mixture is dry. Cook for 5–10 minutes more, until the beans are very tender. Serve hot with slices of feta cheese, if you like.

Energy 350kcal/1,448kJ; Protein 6.6g; Carbohydrate 21.9g, of which sugars 13.4g; Fat 26.9g, of which saturates 4g; Cholesterol 0mg; Calcium 121mg; Fibre 7.7g; Sodium 25mg.

Sautéed broad beans with bacon

Broad beans have a natural affinity with bacon, especially when the beans are fresh and young, as their sweetness complements the saltiness of the meat. Use young tender broad beans or, if using larger beans, remove the skins to reveal the bright green inner bean.

Serves 4

30ml/2 tbsp olive oil

1 small onion, finely chopped

1 garlic clove, finely chopped

50g/2oz rindless smoked streaky (fatty) bacon, roughly chopped

225g/8oz broad (fava) beans, thawed if frozen

5ml/1 tsp paprika

15ml/1 tbsp sweet sherry

salt and ground black pepper

1 Heat the olive oil in a large frying pan or sauté pan. Add the chopped onion, garlic and bacon and fry over a high heat for about 5 minutes, stirring frequently, until the onion is softened and the bacon browned.

2 Add the beans and paprika to the pan and stir-fry for 1 minute. Add the sherry, lower the heat, cover and cook for 5–10 minutes until the beans are tender. Season with salt and pepper to taste, and serve hot or warm.

Energy 139kcal/577kJ; Protein 6.8g; Carbohydrate 8.2g, of which sugars 1.6g; Fat 9g, of which saturates 1.9g; Cholesterol 8mg; Calcium 38mg; Fibre 3.9g; Sodium 163mg.

Creamed leeks

Versatile leeks are a great winter vegetable, adding a subtle onion flavour to many dishes, including soups, casseroles, stews and stir-fries. Serve these creamed leeks on their own, or as a tasty accompaniment to grilled meats, such as chops, chicken or gammon.

Serves 4–6

4 large or 6 medium leeks

300ml/½ pint/1¼ cups milk

8 streaky (fatty) rashers (strips) of bacon, chopped (optional)

1 egg, lightly beaten

150ml/¼ pint/⅔ cup single (light) cream

15ml/1 tbsp wholegrain mustard

75g/3oz/¾ cup strong-flavoured cheese, grated

salt and ground black pepper

1 Slice the leeks into fairly large chunks. Put them into a pan with the milk. Season and bring to the boil. Reduce the heat and simmer for 15–20 minutes, or until tender. Drain well and turn the leeks into a buttered shallow baking dish, reserving the cooking liquor.

2 Meanwhile, if using the bacon, put it into a frying pan and cook gently to allow the fat to run, then turn up the heat a little and cook for a few minutes until it crisps up.

3 Remove from the pan with a slotted spoon and sprinkle the bacon over the leeks. Rinse out the pan that was used for the leeks.

4 Blend the beaten egg, single cream and mustard together and mix it with the reserved cooking liquor. Return to the pan and heat gently without boiling, allowing the sauce to thicken a little. Adjust the seasoning with salt and black pepper, then pour over the leeks and bacon.

5 Sprinkle the baking dish with grated cheese, and brown for a few minutes under a hot grill (broiler). Alternatively, the leeks may be served immediately without browning the top. Serve with plain grilled (broiled) meat or poultry, if you like.

Variations The bacon may be served separately, if you prefer.
  Omit the cheese topping and use the leeks and bacon to dress hot tagliatelle or spaghetti, or use in a risotto.
  The leeks could also be spread on to toast topped with cheese, and grilled for a light lunch.

Energy 238kcal/993kJ; Protein 18.6g; Carbohydrate 9g, of which sugars 7.9g; Fat 14.4g, of which saturates 7.3g; Cholesterol 90mg; Calcium 172mg; Fibre 3.5g; Sodium 830mg.

Stuffed onions

Although they could be eaten as a vegetarian dish, these stuffed onions make a wonderful accompaniment to meat dishes, or an appetizing supper dish with crusty bread and a salad.

Serves 3–4

6 medium or 4 large onions

4 tbsp cooked rice

4 tsp finely chopped fresh parsley, plus extra to garnish

4 tbsp mature (sharp) Cheddar cheese, plus extra for topping

2 tbsp olive oil

1 tbsp white wine, to moisten

salt and ground black pepper

1 Peel the onions leaving the tops and root bases intact. Place in a pan, cover with water, bring to the boil and cook for 15 minutes. Drain and set aside.

2 When the onions are cool enough to handle, cut off the tip of each onion, and remove the centre, leaving a shell 2–3 layers thick.

3 Grate the cheese, then combine with the remaining ingredients, moistening with enough wine to mix well. Preheat the oven to 180°C/ 350°F/Gas 4.

4 Fill the onions with the stuffing, sprinkling a little more cheese on top, and bake in the oven for 45 minutes. Serve garnished with parsley.

Energy 608kcal/2541kJ; Protein 16g; Carbohydrate 85g, of which sugars 27g; Fat 25g, of which saturates 8g; Cholesterol 24mg; Calcium 309mg; Fibre 8.5g; Sodium 395mg.

Stuffed tomatoes, with wild rice and corn

These tomatoes could be served as a light meal or as an accompaniment for meat or fish.
The wild rice gives extra flavour and texture to the dish.

Serves 4

8 medium tomatoes

50g/2oz corn kernels

2 tbsp white wine

50g/2oz cooked wild rice

1 clove garlic

50g/2oz grated Cheddar cheese

1 tbsp chopped fresh parsley

1 tbsp olive oil

salt and ground black pepper

1 Cut the tops off the tomatoes and remove the seeds with a small teaspoon. Scoop out all the flesh and chop finely – remember to chop the tops as well.

2 Preheat the oven to 180°C/350°F/Gas 4. Put the chopped tomato in a pan. Add the corn and the white wine. Cover with a close-fitting lid and simmer until tender. Drain the excess liquid.

3 Mix together all the remaining ingredients except the olive oil, seasoning to taste. Carefully spoon the mixture into the tomatoes, piling it higher in the centre. Drizzle the oil over the top, place in an ovenproof dish and bake at 180°C/350°F/Gas 4 for 15–20 minutes until cooked through.

Energy 145kcal/606kJ; Protein 5g; Carbohydrate 12g, of which sugars 6g; Fat 9g, of which saturates 3g; Cholesterol 12mg; Calcium 107mg; Fibre 2.8g; Sodium 205mg.

Baked tomatoes with mint

This is a high summer recipe that makes the most of falling-off-the-vine ripe tomatoes and fresh mint. Serve this attractive dish with grilled lamb or fish. It is ideal for a barbecue.

Serves 4

6 large ripe tomatoes

300ml/½ pint/1¼ cups double (heavy) cream

2 sprigs of fresh mint

olive oil, for brushing

a few pinches of caster (superfine) sugar

30ml/2 tbsp grated Bonnet cheese

salt and ground black pepper

Farmhouse tip Bonnet is a hard variety of goat's cheese but any other hard, well-flavoured cheese will do.

1 Preheat the oven to 220°C/425°F/ Gas 7. Bring a pan of water to the boil and have a bowl of iced water ready.

2 Cut the cores out of the tomatoes and make a cross at the base. Plunge the tomatoes into the boiling water for 10 seconds and then drop into the iced water. Leave to cool completely.

3 Put the cream and mint in a pan and bring to the boil. Reduce the heat and allow to simmer until it has reduced by about half.

4 Peel the cooled tomatoes and slice them thinly. Pat dry on kitchen paper.

5 Brush a shallow gratin dish lightly with a little olive oil. Layer the sliced tomatoes in the dish, overlapping slightly, and season with salt and ground black pepper. Sprinkle a little sugar over the top.

6 Strain the reduced cream evenly over the top of the tomatoes. Sprinkle on the cheese and bake in the preheated oven for 15 minutes, or until the top is browned and bubbling. Serve immediately from the gratin dish.

Energy 443kcal/1831kJ; Protein 5g; Carbohydrate 6.7g, of which sugars 6.7g; Fat 44.1g, of which saturates 27.4g; Cholesterol 113mg; Calcium 123mg; Fibre 1.8g; Sodium 105mg.

Oven-roast red onions

Serve these sticky, sweet and fragrant onions hot with roast chicken, or cold with a meat and platter. Alternatively, crumble over some fresh herb cheese and serve with crusty bread.

Serves 4

4 large or 8 small red onions

45ml/3 tbsp olive oil

6 juniper berries, crushed

8 small rosemary sprigs

30ml/2 tbsp balsamic vinegar

salt and ground black pepper

Farmhouse tips To help hold back the tears, chill the onions first for about 30 minutes, then remove the root end last. The root contains the largest concentration of the sulphuric compounds that make the eyes water.

If you don't have an onion baker, use a ceramic baking dish and cover with several layers of foil.

1 Soak a clay onion baker in cold water for 15 minutes, then drain. If the base of the baker is glazed, only the lid will need to be soaked.

2 Cut the onions from the tip to the root, cutting the large onions into quarters and the small onions in half. Trim the roots from the onions and remove the skins, if you like.

3 Rub the onions with olive oil, salt and pepper and the juniper berries. Place the onions in the baker, inserting the rosemary in among the onions. Pour the remaining olive oil and vinegar over.

4 Cover and place in an unheated oven. Set the oven to 200°C/400°F/Gas 6 and cook for 40 minutes. Remove the lid and cook for a further 10 minutes.

Energy 128kcal/530kJ; Protein 1.8g; Carbohydrate 11.9g, of which sugars 8.4g; Fat 8.6g, of which saturates 1.2g; Cholesterol 0mg; Calcium 38mg; Fibre 2.1g; Sodium 5mg.

Brussels sprouts with chestnuts

A traditional Christmas speciality, this combination of crisp, tender Brussels sprouts and chestnuts is perennially popular and a seasonal treat.

2 Return the chestnuts to the clean pan. Add the milk and enough water to cover the chestnuts. Simmer for 12–15 minutes. Drain and set aside.

3 Remove any wilted or yellow leaves from the Brussels sprouts. Trim the root end but leave intact or the leaves will separate. Using a small knife, cut a cross in the base of each sprout.

4 Melt the butter in a large, heavy frying pan, and cook the shallot for 1–2 minutes until just softened.

5 Add the sprouts and wine or water to the frying pan. Cover and cook over a medium heat for 6–8 minutes, shaking the pan occasionally and adding a little more water if necessary.

Serves 4–6

225g/8oz chestnuts

120ml/4fl oz/½ cup milk

500g/1¼lb/4 cups small tender Brussels sprouts

25g/1oz/2 tbsp butter

1 shallot, finely chopped

30–45ml/2–3 tbsp dry white wine or water

1 Cut a cross in the base of each chestnut. Bring a pan of water to the boil, drop in the chestnuts and boil for 6–8 minutes. Peel while still warm.

6 Add the poached chestnuts to the sprouts and toss gently, then cover and cook for a further 3–5 minutes. Serve at once as an accompaniment to roast meat or casseroles.

Energy 147kcal/614kJ; Protein 4g; Carbohydrate 19g, of which sugars 7g; Fat 6g, of which saturates 3g; Cholesterol 12mg; Calcium 66mg; Fibre 5.6g; Sodium 43mg.

Leeks in egg and lemon sauce

Tender young leeks, picked fresh from the vegetable plot, cooked and cooled in a tart creamy sauce, taste absolutely superb in this recipe.

Serves 4

675g/1½lb baby leeks, trimmed, slit and washed

15ml/1 tbsp cornflour

10ml/2 tsp sugar

2 egg yolks

juice of 1½ lemons

salt and ground black pepper

1 Lay the leeks in a single layer in a large pan, cover with water and add a little salt. Bring to the boil, lower the heat, cover and simmer for 4–5 minutes until just tender.

2 Transfer the leeks to a shallow serving dish. Mix 200ml/7fl oz/scant 1 cup of the cooking liquid with the cornflour in a small pan. Bring to the boil, stirring all the time, then cook for 1–2 minutes until the sauce thickens slightly. Stir in the sugar. Cool slightly.

3 Whisk the egg yolks with the lemon juice and stir gradually into the cooled sauce. Cook over a very low heat, stirring all the time, until the sauce is fairly thick. Immediately remove from the heat and continue stirring for 1 minute. Taste and add salt or sugar as necessary. Cool slightly.

4 Pour the sauce over the leeks. Cover and chill in the refrigerator for at least 2 hours. Serve sprinkled with freshly ground black pepper.

Farmhouse tip Do not let the sauce overheat after adding the egg yolks or it may curdle.

Energy 92kcal/389kJ; Protein 4g; Carbohydrate 11g, of which sugars 7g; Fat 4g, of which saturates 1g; Cholesterol 17mg; Calcium 27mg; Fibre 4.7g; Sodium 108mg.

Peas with lettuce and onion

Podding freshly picked peas is a traditional pastime in the farmhouse kitchen. Sweet young peas taste delicious when cooked with strips of lettuce.

Serves 4–6

15g/½oz/1 tbsp butter

1 small onion, finely chopped

1 small round lettuce, halved and sliced into thin strips

450g/1lb/3½ cups shelled fresh peas (from about 1.5kg/3½lb pods), or thawed frozen peas

45ml/3 tbsp water

salt and ground black pepper

1 Melt the butter in a heavy-based pan. Add the onion and cook over a medium-low heat for about 3 minutes until just softened. Place the lettuce strips on top of the onion and add the peas and water. Season lightly with salt and pepper.

2 Cover the pan tightly and cook the lettuce and peas over a low heat until the peas are tender – fresh peas will take 10–20 minutes, frozen peas about 5 minutes. Toss lightly, adjust the seasoning if necessary, and serve at once.

Energy 88kcal/364kJ; Protein 6g; Carbohydrate 10g, of which sugars 3g; Fat 3g, of which saturates 2g; Cholesterol 5mg; Calcium 26mg; Fibre 4.0g; Sodium 83mg.

Broad beans with cream

Skinned broad beans are a beautiful bright green, it may seem like a labour-intensive way to serve them, but the soft, sweet taste makes the time spent worthwhile.

Serves 4–6

450g/1lb shelled broad beans (from about 2kg/4½ lb pods)

90ml/6 tbsp crème fraîche or whipping cream

salt and ground black pepper

finely snipped chives, to garnish

1 Bring a large pan of lightly salted water to the boil and add the beans. Reduce the heat slightly and cook the beans for about 8 minutes until just tender. Drain, refresh under cold running water, then drain again.

2 Remove the skins by slitting each bean and gently squeezing out the kernel. Discard the skins.

Farmhouse tip Fresh butter (lima) beans can be served in the same way, and they don't need skinning.

3 Put the skinned beans in a saucepan with the cream and seasoning, cover and heat through gently. Sprinkle with the snipped chives and serve at once.

Energy 93kcal/387kJ; Protein 4g; Carbohydrate 5g, of which sugars 1g; Fat 7g, of which saturates 4g; Cholesterol 17mg; Calcium 23mg; Fibre 2.9g; Sodium 84mg.

Baked beans with sage

Sage thrives in the herb garden and is a somewhat neglected flavouring, mostly used for stuffings but little else. Here, it gives baked beans an incomparable taste.

Serves 6–8

600g/1lb 6oz/3¼ cups dried beans, such as cannellini

60ml/4 tbsp olive oil

2 garlic cloves, crushed

3 fresh sage leaves

1 leek, finely sliced

400g/14oz can chopped tomatoes

salt and ground black pepper

1 Place the beans in a bowl and cover with water. Soak for at least 6 hours, or overnight. Drain.

2 Preheat the oven to 180°C/350°F/ Gas 4. Heat the oil in a pan and sauté the garlic and sage for 3–4 minutes.

3 Put the beans in a casserole and add the leek, tomatoes and the oil, garlic and sage. Add enough water to cover. Cover the dish and bake for 1¾ hours.

4 Remove the dish from the oven, stir, and season with salt and pepper. Return the dish to the oven, uncovered, and cook for 15 minutes more. Remove from the oven, stir, and then allow to stand for around 5–10 minutes before serving as an accompaniment.

Energy 294kcal/1243kJ; Protein 17g; Carbohydrate 39g, of which sugars 4g; Fat 9g, of which saturates 1g; Cholesterol 0mg; Calcium 146mg; Fibre 18.0g; Sodium 101mg.

Glazed patty-pan squash

A traditional French-style dish that is usually made with mushrooms. Make sure that you cook the baby squash until they are tender, so they can fully absorb the delicious flavours.

Serves 4

175g/6oz patty-pan squash

250ml/8fl oz/1 cup white wine

juice of 2 lemons

fresh thyme sprig

bay leaf

bunch of fresh chervil, chopped

1.5ml/¼ tsp coriander seeds, crushed

1.5ml/¼ tsp black peppercorns, crushed

75ml/5 tbsp olive oil

1 Blanch the patty-pan squash in boiling water for 3 minutes, and then refresh them in cold water.

2 Place all the remaining ingredients in a large pan, add 150ml/¼ pint/⅔ cup of water and simmer for 10 minutes, covered.

3 Add the blanched patty-pans to the pan and cook for 10 minutes. Remove with a slotted spoon when they are cooked and tender.

4 Return the pan to the heat and reduce the liquid by boiling hard for 10 minutes. Strain it and pour it over the squashes. Leave until cool for the flavours to be absorbed. Serve cold.

Farmhouse tip You may not be able to get patty-pan squash, but this recipe can also be made with courgettes (zucchini), cut into thick chunks.

Energy 171Kcal/704kJ; Protein 0.4g; Carbohydrate 1.4g, of which sugars 1.1g; Fat 13.8g, of which saturates 2g; Cholesterol 0mg; Calcium 18mg; Fibre 0.5g; Sodium 3mg.

Aubergines with garlic and tomato

This is an unusual way of cooking aubergines (eggplant), which tend to absorb large amounts of oil when fried. Roasting the slices in the oven makes them slightly crisp.

Serves 2–4

2 aubergines (eggplant), about 225g/8oz each, sliced

2 garlic cloves, crushed

45ml/3 tbsp tomato purée (paste)

90–120ml/6–8 tbsp olive oil

2.5ml/½ tsp sugar

salt and ground black pepper

chopped flat leaf parsley, to garnish

1 Mix the garlic and tomato purée with 15ml/1 tbsp of the oil in a bowl. Add the sugar, salt and pepper.

2 Spread out the aubergines on kitchen paper. Sprinkle them with salt and leave for about 30 minutes, then rinse, drain and dry with kitchen paper. Preheat the oven to 190°C/375°F/Gas 5.

3 Pour about 60ml/4 tbsp of the oil into a baking tray and arrange the aubergine slices in a single layer. Spoon a little of the garlic tomato mixture over each one. Drizzle over the remaining oil, then bake for about 30 minutes. Arrange on a flat dish, garnish with chopped parsley and serve.

Energy 265kcal/1095kJ; Protein 2g; Carbohydrate 5g, of which sugars 5g; Fat 27g, of which saturates 4g; Cholesterol 0mg; Calcium 17mg; Fibre 2.6g; Sodium 128mg.

Beetroot with soured cream

Freshly lifted from the farmhouse garden, small beetroot make a delicious snack or side dish when simply boiled and served with sour cream.

Serves 4

450g/1lb small uncooked beetroot (beet)

300ml/½ pint/1¼ cups chilled soured cream

salt and ground black pepper

fresh dill sprigs, to garnish

Farmhouse tip To prepare the beetroot, cut off the leaves about 2.5cm/1in from the tops and remove the roots. Wash the beetroot, removing any dirt. Take care not to cut the beetroot or the colour will leach out.

1 Put the beetroot in a pan with water to cover generously. Season well, bring to the boil and simmer for 30–40 minutes. Drain the beetroot, and while they are still warm, use a knife to peel off the skin.

2 Spoon the chilled sour cream on to individual plates. Cut the beetroot into wedges and use one to make a pretty pink swirl. Arrange the wedges around the plates and garnish with sprigs of dill.

Energy 194kcal/807kJ; Protein 4g; Carbohydrate 11g, of which sugars 11g; Fat 15g, of which saturates 9g; Cholesterol 45mg; Calcium 93mg; Fibre 13.2g; Sodium 203mg.

Turnip tops with Parmesan and garlic

Farmhouse cooks know how to turn everyday ingredients into treats. Here, the tender leaves of young turnip tops are flavoured with onions, garlic and Parmesan cheese.

Serves 4

45ml/3 tbsp olive oil

2 garlic cloves, crushed

4 spring onions (scallions), sliced

350g/12oz turnip tops, thinly sliced, tough stalks removed

60ml/4 tbsp water

50g/2oz/²⁄₃ cup grated Parmesan cheese

salt and ground black pepper

shavings of Parmesan cheese, to garnish

1 Heat the olive oil in a large pan and stir-fry the garlic and sliced spring onions for 2 minutes. Add the turnip tops and stir-fry for 2–3 minutes so that the greens are coated in oil. Add the water.

2 Cook on a low heat, stirring frequently, until the greens are tender. Bring the liquid to the boil, allow the excess to evaporate, then stir in the Parmesan and seasoning. Serve with extra shavings of cheese.

Energy 169kcal/700kJ; Protein 6g; Carbohydrate 2g, of which sugars 2g; Fat 15g, of which saturates 4g; Cholesterol 12mg; Calcium 158mg; Fibre 1.1g; Sodium 196mg.

Spiced turnips with spinach and tomatoes

Sweet baby turnips, tender spinach and ripe tomatoes make tempting partners
in this simple vegetable stew, which makes the most of kitchen garden ingredients.

Serves 6

450g/1lb well-flavoured tomatoes,
skinned and chopped

60ml/4 tbsp olive oil

2 onions, chopped or sliced

450g/1lb baby turnips, peeled but
left whole

5ml/1 tsp paprika

60ml/4 tbsp water

2.5ml/$\frac{1}{2}$ tsp sugar

60ml/4 tbsp chopped parsley

450g/1lb young spinach

salt and ground black pepper

1 Heat the oil in a frying pan and fry
the onion for 5 minutes until golden.

2 Add the baby turnips, chopped
tomatoes, paprika and water to the pan
and cook until the tomatoes are pulpy.
Cover and continue cooking until the
baby turnips are soft.

3 Add the sugar and chopped parsley
to the pan, then add the spinach.

4 Stir carefully to mix and add a little
salt and pepper. Cook for a further
2–3 minutes until the spinach has
wilted. Serve the stew warm with
fresh bread. The dish can also be served
at room temperature.

Energy 77Kcal/320kJ; Protein 3.4g; Carbohydrate 8.3g, of which sugars 7.8g; Fat 3.6g, of which saturates 0.5g; Cholesterol 0mg; Calcium 172mg; Fibre 4.3g; Sodium 123mg.

Asparagus with hollandaise sauce

The asparagus season is short, and this country dish makes the most of its delicate and distinctive flavour. Asparagus can be served simply with melted butter drizzled over the top, but this delicious whisked hollandaise sauce makes it really special.

Serves 4

2 bunches of asparagus

30ml/2 tbsp white wine vinegar

2 egg yolks

115g/4oz butter, melted

juice of ½ lemon

salt and ground black pepper

Farmhouse tips Asparagus should be cooked and eaten as soon as possible, preferably on the day it is picked.
  Make stock with the woody ends of the asparagus rather than throwing them away, and add it to vegetable soups or sauces, or use for risotto.

1 Snap off the tough ends of the asparagus. Drop the spears into rapidly boiling water, cooking for 1–2 minutes until just tender. Test the thickest part of the stalk with a small sharp knife; take care not to overcook.

2 In a pan, bring the vinegar to the boil and bubble until it has reduced to just 15ml/1 tbsp. Remove from the heat and add 15ml/1 tbsp cold water.

3 Whisk the egg yolks into the vinegar and water mixture, then put the pan over a very low heat and continue whisking until the mixture is frothy and thickened.

4 Remove from the heat again and slowly whisk in the melted butter. Add the lemon juice and seasoning to taste. Serve the sauce immediately with the drained asparagus.

Energy 276kcal/1135kJ; Protein 5.3g; Carbohydrate 2.7g, of which sugars 2.6g; Fat 27.1g, of which saturates 15.9g; Cholesterol 162mg; Calcium 51mg; Fibre 2.1g; Sodium 180mg.

Jerusalem artichoke gratin

An under-appreciated vegetable, the Jerusalem artichoke – no relation to the globe artichoke – is sometimes known as the 'sun choke'. It has a distinctive nutty flavour and an appealing crunch. This creamy gratin side dish is the perfect accompaniment to roast meat or fried fish.

Serves 4

250ml/8fl oz/1 cup sour cream

50ml/2fl oz/¼ cup single (light) cream

675g/1½lb Jerusalem artichokes, scrubbed and coarsely chopped

40g/1½oz/½ cup mellow but flavoursome cheese, such as a mature Gouda

60ml/4 tbsp fresh breadcrumbs

salt

Variation Use a good mature English Cheddar instead of Gouda, if you wish.

1 Preheat the oven to 190°C/375°F/ Gas 5. Lightly grease an ovenproof dish. Stir together the sour cream and single cream in a mixing bowl, season with salt and stir to mix.

2 Add the Jerusalem artichokes to the cream and toss to coat evenly with the mixture. Spread the artichokes over the bottom of the prepared dish.

3 Sprinkle evenly with the cheese, then the breadcrumbs. Bake for about 30 minutes, until the cheese melts and the top is brown and bubbling.

Energy 296kcal/1230kJ; Protein 6.9g; Carbohydrate 27.6g, of which sugars 15.5g; Fat 18.1g, of which saturates 11.1g; Cholesterol 52mg; Calcium 186mg; Fibre 4.4g; Sodium 240mg.

Salsify and spinach bake

A less common winter root vegetable, salsify is also known as the oyster plant because of its colour and flavour. It is similar in shape to a long, thin carrot.

1 Preheat the oven to 160°C/325°F/ Gas 3. Add a quarter of the lemon juice to a large bowl of water. Top, tail and peel the salsify. Place each peeled root immediately in the lemon water, to prevent discoloration.

2 Bring a pan of water to the boil. Add the remaining lemon juice. Cut the salsify into 5cm/2in lengths, and simmer for 10 minutes, until just tender.

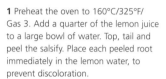

3 Meanwhile, cook the spinach in a large pan over a medium heat for 2–3 minutes until the leaves have wilted, shaking the pan occasionally. Place the stock, cream and seasoning in a small pan and heat through very gently, stirring.

4 Grease a baking dish generously with butter. Drain the salsify and spinach and arrange in layers in the prepared dish. Pour over the stock and cream mixture and bake for about 1 hour until the top is golden brown and bubbling.

Serves 4

juice of 2 lemons

450g/1lb salsify

450g/1lb fresh spinach leaves

150ml/¼ pint/⅔ cup vegetable stock

300ml/½ pint/1¼ cups single (light) cream

salt and ground black pepper

Energy 206kcal/853kJ; Protein 7g; Carbohydrate 15g, of which sugars 6g; Fat 16g, of which saturates 9g; Cholesterol 41mg; Calcium 309mg; Fibre 4.4g; Sodium 324mg.

Garden salad

You can use any fresh, edible flowers from your garden to add to this beautiful salad, but nasturtiums are the most often used in this way.

Serves 4

1 cos lettuce

175g/6oz rocket (arugula)

1 small frisée lettuce

fresh chervil and tarragon sprigs

15ml/1 tbsp snipped fresh chives

handful of mixed edible flower heads, such as nasturtiums or marigolds

For the dressing

45ml/3 tbsp olive oil

15ml/1 tbsp white wine vinegar

1/2 tsp French mustard

1 garlic clove, crushed

pinch of sugar

1 Wash the cos, rocket and frisée leaves and herbs, pat dry and mix together in a large bowl.

2 Whisk the dressing ingredients together. Toss into the salad, add the flower heads and serve.

Energy 122kcal/502kJ; Protein 1g; Carbohydrate 2g, of which sugars 2g; Fat 12g, of which saturates 2g; Cholesterol 0mg; Calcium 28mg; Fibre 1.5g; Sodium 2mg.

New potato salad

Potatoes freshly dug up from the garden are the best. Leave the skins on: just wash the dirt away. If you add the dressing when the potatoes are hot, the flavours will develop better.

Serves 6

900g/2lb baby new potatoes

2 green apples, cored and chopped

4 spring onions (scallions), chopped

3 celery sticks, finely chopped

150ml/¼ pint/⅔ cup mayonnaise

salt and ground black pepper

Variation The apple skin adds colour to the dish, but peel them if you wish.

1 Cook the potatoes in salted, boiling water for about 20 minutes, or until they are very tender.

2 Drain the potatoes well, and immediately add the remaining ingredients; stir until well mixed. Leave to cool and serve cold.

Energy 295kcal/1232kJ; Protein 3g; Carbohydrate 29g, of which sugars 6g; Fat 19g, of which saturates 3g; Cholesterol 19mg; Calcium 21mg; Fibre 2.9g; Sodium 205mg.

French bean salad

The secret of this recipe is to dress the beans while still hot, and serve at room temperature, to help the beans absorb the flavours of the dressing.

Serves 6

175g/6oz cherry tomatoes, halved

5ml/1 tsp sugar

450g/1lb French (green) beans, topped and tailed

175g/6oz feta cheese, cubed

salt and ground black pepper

For the dressing

90ml/6 tbsp olive oil

45ml/3 tbsp white wine vinegar

¼ tsp Dijon mustard

2 garlic cloves, crushed

salt and ground black pepper

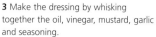

◀ **1** Preheat the oven to 230°C/450°F/Gas 8. Put the cherry tomatoes on a baking sheet and sprinkle over the sugar, salt and pepper.

2 Roast for 10 minutes, then leave to cool. Meanwhile, cook the beans in boiling, salted water for 10 minutes.

3 Make the dressing by whisking together the oil, vinegar, mustard, garlic and seasoning.

4 Drain the beans, and immediately pour the vinaigrette over them, mixing well. When the beans have cooled, stir in the roasted tomatoes and the feta cheese. Serve chilled.

Energy 237kcal/976kJ; Protein 6g; Carbohydrate 5g, of which sugars 4g; Fat 21g, of which saturates 6g; Cholesterol 20mg; Calcium 137mg; Fibre 2.6g; Sodium 60mg.

Marinated bean and courgette salad

This bright green, fresh and healthy salad makes the most of a summer glut of courgettes. Add some chopped soft herbs, such as chervil, dill or tarragon, and crumble over fresh ricotta or cubed mozzarella cheese. Serve as an accompaniment to meat and chicken dishes.

Serves 4

2 courgettes (zucchini), halved lengthways

400g/14oz can flageolet or cannellini beans, drained and rinsed

grated rind and juice of 1 unwaxed lemon

45ml/3 tbsp garlic-infused olive oil

salt and ground black pepper

1 Slice the halved courgettes and drop into boiling salted water for 2–3 minutes, or until just tender. Drain well and refresh under cold running water.

2 Transfer the courgettes to a bowl with the beans and stir in the oil, lemon rind and juice, and some salt and pepper. Chill for 30 minutes before serving.

Energy 106kcal/444kJ; Protein 5.5g; Carbohydrate 11.9g, of which sugars 3.5g; Fat 4.4g, of which saturates 0.7g; Cholesterol 0mg; Calcium 62mg; Fibre 4.4g; Sodium 228mg.

Garden tomato salad with peppers and oregano

Home-grown tomatoes fresh from the vine would be ideal here, but any ripe, juicy fruits combined with the marinated peppers would make a lovely appetizer or side dish for a summer buffet. Sprinkle over a few fresh basil leaves instead of the oregano, if you prefer.

Serves 4–6

2 marinated (bell) peppers, drained

6 ripe tomatoes, sliced

15ml/1 tbsp chopped fresh oregano

75ml/5 tbsp olive oil

30ml/2 tbsp white wine vinegar

coarse sea salt

1 If the marinated peppers are in large pieces, cut them into strips. Arrange the tomato slices and pepper strips on a serving dish, sprinkle with the oregano and season to taste with sea salt.

2 Whisk together the olive oil and vinegar in a jug (pitcher), decant into a bottle and pour the dressing over the salad. Serve immediately or cover and chill in the refrigerator until required.

Farmhouse tip For marinated (bell) peppers, wrap in foil and place on a baking sheet. Cook in a preheated oven at 180°C/350°F/Gas 4, or under a preheated grill (broiler), turning occasionally, for 20–30 minutes, until tender. Unwrap and when cool, peel, then halve and seed. Cut the flesh into strips and pack into a screw-top jar. Add olive oil to cover, close and store in the refrigerator for up to 6 days.

Energy 119kcal/494kJ; Protein 1.4g; Carbohydrate 6.9g, of which sugars 6.7g; Fat 9.7g, of which saturates 1.5g; Cholesterol 0mg; Calcium 17mg; Fibre 2.1g; Sodium 12mg.

Hot Puddings and Pies

Home baking is an essential element of farmhouse cooking, and no family supper would be complete without a proper pudding at the end of it. In the summer months this might be a light, cold confection, but in the autumn and winter one of the hot puddings and steaming pies you will find in this chapter, covered with custard or a thick dollop of fresh cream, is irresistible.

Steamed ginger and cinnamon syrup pudding

A traditional and comforting steamed pudding, which combines the warming flavours of
ginger and cinnamon. This pudding is lovely served with custard.

1 Set a full steamer or pan of water on
to boil. Lightly grease a 600ml/
1 pint/2½ cup pudding basin with
15g/½oz/1 tbsp butter. Place the
golden syrup in the basin.

2 Cream the remaining butter and
sugar together until light and fluffy.
Gradually add the eggs until the
mixture is glossy.

3 Sift the flour, baking powder and
cinnamon together and fold into the
mixture, with the stem ginger. Add the
milk to make a dropping consistency.

4 Spoon the batter into the basin and
smooth the top. Cover with a pleated
piece of baking parchment, to allow for
expansion during cooking. Tie securely
with string and steam for 1½–2 hours,
making sure that the water level is kept
topped up, to ensure a good flow of
steam to cook the pudding. Turn the
pudding out to serve it.

Serves 4

120g/4½oz/9 tbsp butter, softened

45ml/3 tbsp golden (light corn) syrup

115g/4oz/½ cup caster (superfine)
sugar

2 eggs, lightly beaten

115g/4oz/1 cup plain (all-purpose)
flour

5ml/1 tsp baking powder

5ml/1 tsp ground cinnamon

25g/1oz stem ginger,

finely chopped

30ml/2 tbsp milk

Energy 584kcal/2448kJ; Protein 7g; Carbohydrate 79g, of which sugars 57g; Fat 29g, of which saturates 17g; Cholesterol 181mg; Calcium 102mg; Fibre 1.0g; Sodium 430mg.

Christmas pudding

This pudding is the classic climax to a traditional Christmas dinner, but is made several months before and stored, wrapped in muslin, so the flavours can develop.

Serves 8

115g/4oz/1 cup plain (all-purpose) flour

pinch of salt

5ml/1 tsp ground mixed (apple pie) spice

2.5ml/$\frac{1}{2}$ tsp ground cinnamon

2.5ml/$\frac{1}{2}$ tsp freshly grated nutmeg

225g/8oz/1 cup suet (US chilled, grated shortening)

1 dessert apple, grated

225g/8oz/2 cups fresh white breadcrumbs

350g/12oz/2 cups soft (dark) brown sugar

50g/2oz flaked (sliced) almonds

225g/8oz/1$\frac{1}{2}$ cups seedless raisins

225g/8oz/1$\frac{1}{2}$ cups currants

225g/8oz/1$\frac{1}{2}$ cups sultanas (golden raisins)

115g/4oz ready-to-eat dried apricots

115g/4oz/$\frac{3}{4}$ cup chopped mixed peel

finely grated rind and juice of 1 lemon

30ml/2 tbsp black treacle (molasses)

3 eggs

300ml/$\frac{1}{2}$ pint/1$\frac{1}{4}$ cups milk

30ml/2 tbsp rum

clotted cream, to serve

1 Sift the flour, salt and spices into a large bowl. Add the grated fat, grated apple and other dry ingredients, including the grated lemon rind, to the bowl, and mix together.

2 Heat the treacle until warm and runny and pour into the dry ingredients.

3 Mix together the eggs, milk, rum and lemon juice in a bowl, and then stir into the dry mixture.

4 Spoon the mixture into two 1.2 litre/2 pint/5 cup basins. Overwrap the puddings with pieces of baking parchment, pleated to allow for expansion, and tie with string.

5 Steam the puddings in a steamer or over a pan of boiling water. Each pudding needs 10 hours' cooking and 3 hours' reheating. Remember to keep the water level topped up to keep the pans from boiling dry.

6 Serve the pudding warm, decorated with holly and accompanied by clotted cream or brandy butter.

Energy 448kcal/1902kJ; Protein 2.4g; Carbohydrate 99.8g, of which sugars 92.5g; Fat 7.1g, of which saturates 3.6g; Cholesterol 20mg; Calcium 67mg; Fibre 0.9g; Sodium 123mg.

Maple and pecan steamed pudding

Imagine a hot sponge cake, straight out of the oven but with less golden crust, a deeper sponge and more crumbliness – that's a steamed pudding. It can be flavoured with anything; maple syrup and pecan nuts are wonderful. Serve with home-made custard.

Serves 6

60ml/4 tbsp pure maple syrup

30ml/2 tbsp fresh brown breadcrumbs

115g/4oz/1 cup shelled pecan nuts, roughly chopped

115g/4oz/½ cup butter, softened

finely grated rind of 1 orange

115g/4oz/heaped ½ cup golden caster (superfine) sugar

2 eggs, beaten

175g/6oz/1½ cups self-raising (self-rising) flour, sifted

pinch of salt

about 75ml/5 tbsp milk

extra maple syrup and home-made custard, to serve

1 Butter a 900ml/1½ pint/3¾ cup heatproof pudding bowl generously. Stir the maple syrup, breadcrumbs and pecans together and spoon into the bowl.

2 Cream the butter with the orange rind and sugar until light and fluffy. Gradually beat in the eggs, then fold in the flour and salt. Stir in enough milk to make a loose mixture that will drop off the spoon if lightly shaken.

3 Carefully spoon the mixture into the bowl on top of the syrup and nuts. Cover with pleated, buttered baking parchment, then with pleated foil (the pleats allow for expansion). Tie string under the lip of the basin to hold the paper in place, then take it over the top to form a handle.

4 Place the bowl in a pan of simmering water, cover and steam for 2 hours, topping up with water as necessary.

5 Remove the string, foil and paper, then turn out the pudding and serve with extra maple syrup and a spoonful of home-made custard.

Energy 523kcal/2187kJ; Protein 7.7g; Carbohydrate 55.6g, of which sugars 29.9g; Fat 31.6g, of which saturates 12.7g; Cholesterol 108mg; Calcium 160mg; Fibre 1.9g; Sodium 345mg.

Winter fruit crumble

This recipe uses pears and dried fruits under the crumble topping, making it a deliciously warming winter pudding. At other times of the year, try gooseberries or rhubarb, flavoured with orange rind. The almond topping adds a specially rich texture.

Serves 6

175g/6oz/1½ cups plain (all-purpose) flour

50g/2oz/½ cup ground almonds

175g/6oz/¾ cup butter, diced

115g/4oz/½ cup soft light brown sugar

40g/1½oz flaked (sliced) almonds

1 orange

about 16 ready-to-eat dried apricots

4 firm ripe pears

1 Preheat the oven to 190°C/375°F/ Gas 5. To make the topping, sift the flour into a bowl and stir in the ground almonds. Add the butter and rub it into the flour until the mixture resembles rough breadcrumbs. Stir in 75g/3oz/ ⅓ cup sugar and the flaked almonds.

2 Finely grate 5ml/1 tsp rind from the orange and squeeze out its juice. Halve the apricots and put them into a shallow ovenproof dish. Peel the pears, remove their cores and cut the fruit into small pieces. Sprinkle the pears over the apricots. Stir the orange rind into the orange juice and sprinkle over the fruit. Sprinkle the remaining brown sugar over the top.

3 Cover the fruit completely with the crumble mixture and smooth over. Put into the hot oven and cook for about 40 minutes until the topping is golden brown and the fruit is soft (test with the point of a sharp knife).

Energy 615kcal/2569kJ; Protein 9.4g; Carbohydrate 65.7g, of which sugars 42.9g; Fat 36.7g, of which saturates 16.2g; Cholesterol 62mg; Calcium 150mg; Fibre 6.6g; Sodium 190mg.

Rhubarb and orange crumble

The almonds give this crumble topping a nutty taste and crunchy texture, while the tang of the orange juice and rind complements the tartness of the rhubarb.

Serves 6

900g/2lb rhubarb, cut in 5cm/2in lengths

75g/3oz/6 tbsp caster (superfine) sugar

finely grated rind and juice of 2 oranges

115g/4oz/1 cup plain (all-purpose) flour

115g/4oz/½ cup unsalted butter, chilled and cubed

75g/3oz/6 tbsp demerara (raw) sugar

115g/4oz/1¼ cups ground almonds

1 Preheat the oven to 180°C/350°F/ Gas 4. Place the rhubarb in a shallow ovenproof dish.

2 Sprinkle the caster sugar over the rhubarb, together with the orange rind and juice.

3 Sift the flour into a mixing bowl and add the butter. Rub the butter into the flour until the mixture resembles breadcrumbs. Add the demerara sugar and ground almonds and mix well.

4 Spoon the crumble mixture over the fruit to cover it completely. Bake for 40 minutes, until the top is browned and the fruit is cooked. Serve warm.

Energy 441kcal/1846kJ; Protein 7g; Carbohydrate 45g, of which sugars 30g; Fat 27g, of which saturates11g; Cholesterol 41mg; Calcium 222mg; Fibre 6.6g; Sodium 127mg.

Blackberry charlotte

A classic pudding, perfect for using late blackberries that have been picked from the hedgerow. Serve with lightly whipped cream or home-made custard.

Serves 4

65g/2½oz/5 tbsp unsalted butter

175g/6oz/3 cups fresh white breadcrumbs

50g/2oz/4 tbsp soft (light) brown sugar

60ml/4 tbsp golden (light corn) syrup

finely grated rind and juice of 2 lemons

50g/2oz walnut halves

450g/1lb blackberries

450g/1lb cooking apples, peeled, cored and finely sliced

1 Preheat the oven to 180°C/350°F/ Gas 4. Grease a 450ml/¾ pint/2 cup dish with 15g/½oz/1 tbsp of the butter.

2 Melt the remaining butter and add the breadcrumbs. Sauté them for 5–7 minutes, until the crumbs are a little crisp and golden. Leave to cool slightly.

3 Place the sugar, syrup, lemon rind and juice in a small pan and gently warm them. Mix in the crumbs.

4 Process the walnuts until finely ground and stir into the crumb mixture.

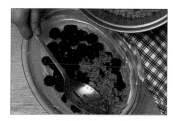

5 Arrange a thin layer of blackberries in the base of the dish. Top with a thin layer of crumbs.

6 Add a thin layer of apple, topping it with another thin layer of crumbs. Repeat the process with another layer of blackberries, followed by a layer of crumbs. Continue until you have used up all the ingredients, finishing with a layer of crumbs. The mixture can be piled well above the top edge of the dish, because it shrinks during cooking.

7 Bake for 30 minutes, until the topping is golden and the fruit is soft. Serve warm with custard or cream.

Energy 546Kcal/2294kJ; Protein 8.5g; Carbohydrate 81g, of which sugars 48.2g; Fat 23.1g, of which saturates 9.2g; Cholesterol 35mg; Calcium 133mg; Fibre 6.7g; Sodium 498mg.

Rice pudding with nutmeg

Originally a medieval treat, at a time when rice and sugar were expensive imports, rice pudding went on to become a farmhouse favourite. This simple pudding can be enlivened by adding a spoonful of preserves, or some brandy-soaked dried vine fruits or figs.

Serves 4

50g/2oz/4 tbsp butter, diced, plus extra for greasing

50g/2oz/¼ cup short grain or pudding rice

30ml/2 tbsp soft light brown sugar

900ml/1½ pints/3¾ cups milk

small strip of lemon rind

freshly grated nutmeg

Variation Add some sultanas (golden raisins), raisins or ready-to-eat dried apricots and cinnamon to the pudding. Try serving with fresh fruit such as raspberries or strawberries.

1 Preheat the oven to 150°C/300°F/ Gas 2. Butter a 1.2 litre/2 pint/5 cup shallow ovenproof dish.

2 Put the rice, sugar and butter into the dish and stir in the milk. Add the strip of lemon rind and sprinkle a little nutmeg over the surface. Put the pudding into the hot oven.

3 Cook the pudding for about 2 hours, stirring after 30 minutes and another couple of times during the next 1½ hours, until the rice is tender and the pudding is thick and creamy.

4 If you prefer skin on top, leave the pudding undisturbed for the final 30 minutes, or stir again. Serve with jam.

Energy 298kcal/1252kJ; Protein 8.8g; Carbohydrate 54.3g, of which sugars 21.5g; Fat 5.2g, of which saturates 1.4g; Cholesterol 143mg; Calcium 71mg; Fibre 0g; Sodium 185mg.

Bread and butter pudding with whiskey sauce

The ultimate comfort food and invented to use up stale bread, this dish becomes rather sophisticated with the addition of a boozy whiskey sauce. It is best served with vanilla ice cream or chilled cream – for an enjoyable contrast between the hot and cold.

Serves 6

8 slices of white bread, buttered

115–150g/4–5oz/²⁄₃–³⁄₄ cup sultanas (golden raisins), or mixed dried fruit

½ a whole nutmeg

150g/5oz/³⁄₄ cup caster (superfine) sugar

2 large eggs

300ml/½ pint/1¼ cups single (light) cream

450ml/¾ pint/scant 2 cups milk

5ml/1 tsp of vanilla extract

light muscovado (brown) sugar, for sprinkling (optional)

For the whiskey sauce

150g/5oz/10 tbsp butter

115g/4oz/generous ½ cup caster (superfine) sugar

1 egg

45ml/3 tbsp whiskey

1 Preheat the oven to 180°C/350°F/ Gas 4. Remove the crusts from the bread and put four slices, buttered side down, in the base of an ovenproof dish. Sprinkle with the fruit, grate over the nutmeg and 15ml/1 tbsp sugar.

2 Place the remaining four slices of bread on top, buttered side down, and sprinkle again with nutmeg and 15ml/1 tbsp sugar.

3 Beat the eggs lightly, add the cream, milk, vanilla extract and the remaining sugar, and mix well to make a custard. Pour this mixture over the bread, and sprinkle light muscovado sugar over the top, if you like to have a crispy crust.

4 Bake in the preheated oven for 1 hour, or until all the liquid has been absorbed and the pudding is risen and brown.

5 Meanwhile, make the whiskey sauce: melt the butter in a heavy pan, add the caster sugar and dissolve over gentle heat. Remove from the heat and add the egg, whisking vigorously, and then add the whiskey. Serve the pudding on hot serving plates, with the whiskey sauce poured over the top.

Energy 757kcal/3168kJ; Protein 11.7g; Carbohydrate 82g, of which sugars 65.2g; Fat 40.8g, of which saturates 24.3g; Cholesterol 207mg; Calcium 232mg; Fibre 0.9g; Sodium 472mg.

Honey and ginger baked apples

Baked apples are a country-cooking staple, and there are myriad different versions – they can be made with any type of eating apple and stuffed with vine fruits, spices and citrus fruits. This version uses honey and fresh ginger, and is accompanied by either vanilla sauce, sour cream or double cream. A final touch of luxury would be to fold a little whipped cream into the vanilla sauce before serving, then spooning ginger ice cream on top.

Serves 4

4 eating apples, such as Cox's Orange Pippin or Golden Delicious

30ml/2 tbsp finely chopped fresh root ginger

60ml/4 tbsp honey

25g/1oz/2 tbsp unsalted butter

60ml/4 tbsp medium white wine

vanilla sauce, sour cream or double (heavy) cream, to serve

For the vanilla sauce

300ml/½ pint/1¼ cups single (light) cream

1 vanilla pod (bean), split lengthways

2 egg yolks

30ml/2 tbsp caster (superfine) sugar

1 To make the vanilla sauce, put the cream and vanilla pod in a pan and heat to just below boiling point. Remove from the heat and leave to infuse for 10 minutes. Remove the vanilla pod.

2 Put the egg yolks and sugar in a bowl and whisk them together until pale and thick, then slowly pour in the cream, whisking all the time.

3 Return the pan to the heat and heat very gently until the cream is thick enough to coat the back of a wooden spoon. (If you draw a finger horizontally across the back of the spoon, the sauce should be thick enough not to run down through the channel.)

4 Remove from the heat and leave to cool. Either stir from time to time, or cover to prevent a skin forming.

5 Preheat the oven to 160°C/325°F/ Gas 3. Remove the cores from the apples leaving the stalk end intact, but remove the actual stalk. Fill each cavity with 2.5ml/½ tbsp chopped ginger and 15ml/1 tbsp honey.

6 Place the apples in an ovenproof dish, with the open end uppermost, and top each one with a little butter.

7 Pour in the wine and bake in the oven, basting frequently with the cooking juices, for about 45 minutes, until the apples are tender. Serve the apples with the vanilla sauce, sour cream or double cream.

Farmhouse tip If the sauce looks as though it may overheat, place the base of the pan into a bowl of cold water to cool and prevent it curdling.

Energy 331kcal/1381kJ; Protein 4.3g; Carbohydrate 27.8g, of which sugars 27.8g; Fat 22.3g, of which saturates 13.2g; Cholesterol 155mg; Calcium 89mg; Fibre 1.2g; Sodium 68mg.

Hot bramble and apple soufflés

Hedgerow brambles, blackberries, loganberries or blackcurrants would all work equally well
in this deliciously light pudding. Serve with lashings of thick cream or custard.

4 Put a spoonful of the fruit purée
into each prepared dish and smooth
the surface. Set the dishes aside.

5 Whisk the egg whites in a large
grease-free bowl until they form stiff
peaks. Very gradually whisk in the
remaining caster sugar to make a
stiff, glossy meringue mixture.

6 Fold in the remaining fruit purée and
spoon the flavoured meringue into the
prepared dishes. Level the tops with
a spatula, and run a table knife around
the edge of each dish.

Serves 6

butter, for greasing

150g/5oz/¾ cup caster (superfine)
sugar, plus extra for dusting

350g/12oz/3 cups blackberries

1 large cooking apple, peeled
and finely diced

grated rind and juice of 1 orange

3 egg whites

icing (confectioners') sugar, for dusting

1 Preheat the oven to 200°C/400°F/
Gas 6. Generously grease six 150ml/
¼ pint/⅔ cup individual soufflé dishes
with butter and dust with caster sugar,
shaking out the excess sugar.

2 Put a baking sheet in the oven to
heat. Cook the blackberries, diced apple
and orange rind and juice in a pan
for 10 minutes or until the apple has
pulped down well.

3 Press through a sieve (strainer) into
a bowl. Stir in 50g/2oz/¼ cup of the
caster sugar. Set aside to cool for
about 20–30 minutes.

7 Place the dishes on the hot baking
sheet and bake for 10–15 minutes until
the soufflés have risen well and are
lightly browned. Dust the tops with
icing sugar and serve immediately.

Farmhouse tip Running a table knife
around the inside edge of the dishes
before baking helps the soufflés to
rise evenly without sticking to the rim.

Energy 123kcal/522kJ; Protein 2.1g; Carbohydrate 30.1g, of which sugars 30.1g; Fat 0.1g, of which saturates 0g; Cholesterol 0mg; Calcium 38mg; Fibre 2g; Sodium 33mg.

Rhubarb spiral cobbler

A frugal yet delicious dish, this pudding makes the most of a seasonal glut, with a hearty topping made from storecupboard ingredients that children love helping to roll.

Serves 4

675g/1½lb rhubarb, sliced

45ml/3 tbsp orange juice

75g/3oz/6 tbsp caster (superfine) sugar

200g/7oz/1¾ cups self-raising (self-rising) flour

250ml/8fl oz/1 cup natural (plain) yogurt

grated rind of 1 medium orange

30ml/2 tbsp demerara (raw) sugar

5ml/1 tsp ground ginger

custard or double (heavy) cream, to serve

1 Preheat the oven to 200°C/400°F/Gas 6. Cook the rhubarb with the orange juice and two-thirds of the sugar until tender. Transfer to an ovenproof dish.

2 To make the topping, mix the flour with the remaining caster sugar, then gradually stir in enough of the yogurt to bind to a soft dough.

3 Roll out the dough on a floured surface to a 25cm/10in square. Mix together the orange rind, demerara sugar and ginger, then sprinkle this over the dough.

4 Roll up the dough quite tightly, then cut into about 10 slices. Arrange the dough slices over the rhubarb.

5 Bake the cobbler for 15–20 minutes, or until the spirals are well risen and golden brown. Serve warm with custard or a spoonful of cream.

Variation You can make this pudding with just about any fruit; try a mixture of apple and blackberry, or apricots with strawberries.

Energy 317Kcal/1355kJ; Protein 8.7g; Carbohydrate 72.6g, of which sugars 35.5g; Fat 1.3g, of which saturates 0.4g; Cholesterol 1mg; Calcium 443mg; Fibre 3.9g; Sodium 229mg.

Black cherry pudding

Also known as clafoutis, this is a batter pudding that originated in the Limousin area of central France. It is often made with cream and traditionally uses slightly tart black cherries, although other soft fruits such as apricots, peaches or plums will also give delicious results.

Serves 6

butter, for greasing

450g/1lb/2 cups black cherries, pitted

25g/1oz/¼ cup plain (all-purpose) flour

50g/2oz/½ cup icing (confectioners') sugar, plus extra for dusting

4 eggs, beaten

250ml/8fl oz/1 cup full-cream (whole) milk

30ml/2 tbsp cherry liqueur, such as Kirsch or Maraschino

1 Preheat the oven to 180°C/350°F/ Gas 4. Generously grease a 1.2 litre/ 2 pint/5 cup dish and spread the pitted black cherries in the bottom.

2 Sift the flour and icing sugar into a large mixing bowl, then gradually whisk in the beaten eggs until the mixture is smooth. Whisk in the milk until well blended, then stir in the liqueur.

3 Pour the batter into the baking dish. Transfer to the oven and bake for about 40 minutes, or until just set and golden brown. Insert a knife into the centre of the pudding to test if it is cooked in the middle; the blade should come out clean.

4 Allow the pudding to cool for at least 15 minutes. Dust liberally with icing sugar just before serving, either warm or at room temperature.

Variations Try using other liqueurs – almond-flavoured liqueur is delicious teamed with cherries, while hazelnut, raspberry or orange liqueurs also work well. You can also try other fruits, such as plums, apricots, blackberries or blueberries.

Energy 201Kcal/843kJ; Protein 6.7g; Carbohydrate 23.8g, of which sugars 20.7g; Fat 8.9g, of which saturates 4.3g; Cholesterol 142g; Calcium 89mg; Fibre 0.8g; Sodium 91mg.

Old-fashioned deep-dish apple pie

It is impossible to resist a really good home-baked apple pie. If you make your own shortcrust pastry and use eating apples bursting with flavour, and lots of butter and sugar, you can't go wrong. Serve this old-fashioned dish with thick cream or nutmeg ice cream.

Serves 6

900g/2lb eating apples

75g/3oz/6 tbsp unsalted butter

45–60ml/3–4 tbsp demerara (raw) sugar

3 cloves

2.5ml/½ tsp mixed (apple pie) spice

For the pastry

250g/9oz/2¼ cups plain (all-purpose) flour

pinch of salt

50g/2oz/¼ cup lard or white cooking fat, chilled and diced

75g/3oz/6 tbsp unsalted butter, chilled and diced

30–45ml/2–3 tbsp chilled water

a little milk, for brushing

caster (superfine) sugar, for dredging

clotted cream or ice cream, to serve

1 Preheat the oven to 200°C/400°F/Gas 6. Make the pastry first. Sift the flour and salt into a bowl. Rub in the lard or fat and butter. Stir in enough chilled water to bring the pastry together. Knead lightly, then wrap in clear film (plastic wrap) and chill for 30 minutes.

2 To make the filling, peel, core and thickly slice the apples. Melt the butter in a frying pan, add the sugar and cook for 3–4 minutes, allowing it to melt and caramelize. Add the apples and stir. Cook over a brisk heat until the apples take on a little colour, add the spices and tip out into a bowl to cool slightly.

3 Divide the pastry in two and, on a lightly floured surface, roll out into two rounds that will easily fit a deep 23cm/9in pie plate. Line the plate with one round of pastry. Spoon in the cooled filling and mound up in the centre.

4 Cover the apples with the remaining pastry, sealing and crimping the edges.

5 Make a 5cm/2in long slit through the top of the pastry to allow the steam to escape. Brush the pie with milk and dredge with caster sugar.

6 Place the pie on a baking sheet and bake in the oven for 25–35 minutes until golden and firm. Serve with dollops of thick cream or ice cream.

Energy 610kcal/2566kJ; Protein 8.1g; Carbohydrate 86.1g, of which sugars 40.2g; Fat 28.5g, of which saturates 8.8g; Cholesterol 14mg; Calcium 168mg; Fibre 8.1g; Sodium 413mg.

Peach and blueberry pie

With its attractive lattice pastry top, this colourful pie is bursting with plump blueberries and juicy peaches. It is good hot, or can be wrapped in its dish and transported to a picnic.

Serves 8

225g/8oz/2 cups plain (all-purpose) flour

2.5ml/½ tsp salt

150g/5oz/10 tbsp cold butter, diced

1 egg yolk, mixed with 30–45ml/ 2–3 tbsp iced water

For the filling

6 ripe peaches, peeled, pitted and sliced

225g/8oz/2 cups fresh blueberries, washed

150g/5oz/¾ cup sugar

30ml/2 tbsp lemon juice

40g/1½oz/⅓ cup plain (all-purpose) flour

25g/1oz/2 tbsp butter, chopped

1 For the pastry, place the flour, salt, and butter into a bowl. Rub in until the mixture resembles breadcrumbs. Mix in the egg and water and combine with a fork until the pastry holds together. Preheat the oven to 200°C/400°F/Gas 6.

2 Roll out two-thirds of the pastry to line a 23cm/9in fluted tin (pan). Use the rolling pin to trim the edges.

3 Gather the remaining pastry and roll out to 6mm/¼in thickness. Cut strips 1cm/½in wide. Chill the pastry case and the strips for 20 minutes.

4 Line the pastry case with baking parchment and fill with dried beans. Bake until the pastry case is just set, 12–15 minutes. Remove from the oven and carefully lift out the paper with the beans. Prick the bottom of the pastry case all over with a fork, then return to the oven and bake for 5 minutes more. Let the pastry case cool slightly before filling. Leave the oven on.

5 In a mixing bowl, combine the peach slices with the blueberries, sugar, lemon juice and flour. Spoon the fruit mixture evenly into the pastry case. Dot with the pieces of butter.

6 Weave a lattice top with the chilled pastry strips, pressing the ends to the baked pastry-case edge. Brush the strips with the milk.

7 Bake the pie for 15 minutes. Reduce the heat to 180°C/350°F/Gas 4, and continue baking until the filling is tender and bubbling and the pastry lattice is golden, about 30 minutes more. If the pastry gets too brown, cover loosely with a piece of foil. Serve the pie warm or at room temperature.

Farmhouse tip To skin fruits, place them in a large heat-proof bowl and cover with boiling water. Leave for 2–3 minutes then drain. The skin should slide off easily.

Energy 391kcal/1640kJ; Protein 4.7g; Carbohydrate 53g, of which sugars 27.7g; Fat 19.3g, of which saturates 11.7g; Cholesterol 72mg; Calcium 86mg; Fibre 2.9g; Sodium 139mg.

Apple tart

This is a lovely apple tart with a rich sweet pastry that goes perfectly with the sharp fruit.
For added flavour, scatter some toasted, flaked almonds over the top before serving.

Serves 8

For the pastry

115g/4oz/½ cup butter, softened

50g/2oz/4 tbsp caster (confectioner's) sugar

1 egg yolk

225g/8oz/2 cups plain (all-purpose) flour

For the filling

50g/2oz/4 tbsp unsalted butter

5 large tart green apples, peeled, cored and sliced

juice of ½ lemon

300ml/½ pint/1¼ cups double (heavy) cream

2 egg yolks

25g/1oz/2 tbsp caster (confectioners') sugar

50g/2oz/⅔ cup ground almonds

2.5ml/½ tsp vanilla extract

25g/1oz/2 tbsp flaked almonds, toasted, to garnish

1 Place the butter and sugar in a food processor and process until pale and fluffy. Mix the egg yolk in well.

2 Add the flour and process until you have a soft dough. Wrap the dough in plastic wrap and chill it for 30 minutes.

3 Roll the pastry out on a lightly floured surface to 22–25cm/9–10in diameter.

4 Line a tart tin (pan) with the pastry and chill again for 30 minutes. Preheat the oven to 220°C/425°F/Gas 7 and place a baking sheet in the oven to heat up. Line the pastry case with baking parchment and baking beans and bake on the baking sheet for 10 minutes. Then remove the beans and paper and cook for a further 5 minutes.

5 Turn the oven down to 190°C/375°F/Gas 5. To make the filling, melt the butter in a frying pan and lightly sauté the apples for 5–7 minutes. Sprinkle the apples with lemon juice.

6 Beat the cream and egg yolks with the sugar. Stir in the toasted ground almonds and vanilla extract. Arrange the apple slices on top of the warm pastry and pour over the cream mixture.

7 Bake for 25 minutes, until the cream is just about set – it tastes better if the tart is still slightly soft in the centre. Serve scattered with flaked almonds.

Energy 638kcal/2666kJ; Protein 7g; Carbohydrate 38g, of which sugars 16g; Fat 52g, of which saturates 29g; Cholesterol 197mg; Calcium 100mg; Fibre 4.3g; Sodium 29mg.

Classic treacle tart

A way of using up stale breadcrumbs, this tart is actually based on golden syrup rather than treacle or molasses. There are many variations on the basic recipe, but the hint of lemon in this one makes it particularly good. Serve it warm or cold, with custard or cream.

Serves 6

175g/6oz/1½ cups plain (all-purpose) flour

pinch of salt

40g/1½oz/3 tbsp white cooking fat

40g/1½oz/3 tbsp butter, diced

75g/3oz/1½ cups fresh breadcrumbs

2.5ml/½ tsp ground ginger (optional)

225g/8oz/1 cup golden (light corn) syrup

grated rind and juice of 1 lemon

1 Sift the flour and salt into a bowl and add the lard and butter. With the fingertips, rub the fats into the flour until the mixture resembles fine breadcrumbs. Stir in about 45ml/3 tbsp cold water until the mixture can be gathered together into a smooth ball of dough. Wrap the pastry and refrigerate for 30 minutes. Meanwhile, preheat the oven to 190°C/375°F/Gas 5.

2 Roll out the pastry on a lightly floured surface, and use to line a 20cm/8in flan tin (pan) or pie plate, reserving the trimmings.

3 Mix the breadcrumbs with the ginger, if using, and spread the mixture over the bottom of the pastry. Gently warm the syrup with the lemon rind and juice (on the stove or in the microwave) until quite runny, and pour evenly over the breadcrumbs.

4 Gather the reserved pastry trimmings into a ball, roll out on a lightly floured surface and cut into long, narrow strips. Twist these into spirals and arrange them in a lattice pattern on top of the tart, pressing them on to the edge to secure. Trim the ends.

5 Put into the hot oven and cook for about 25 minutes until the pastry is golden brown and cooked through and the filling has set.

Variations You could omit the lemon rind and juice for a sweeter version.
Sometimes finely crushed cornflakes are used in place of the breadcrumbs.

Energy 420kcal/1764kJ; Protein 4.1g; Carbohydrate 63.5g, of which sugars 35.1g; Fat 18.4g, of which saturates 11.3g; Cholesterol 46mg; Calcium 62mg; Fibre 1.1g; Sodium 344mg.

Bakewell tart

This is a modern version of the Bakewell pudding, which is made with puff pastry and has a custard-like almond filling. It is said to be the result of a 19th-century kitchen accident and is still baked in the original shop in the town of Bakewell, England.

Serves 4

For the pastry

115g/4oz/1 cup plain (all-purpose) flour

pinch of salt

50g/2oz/4 tbsp butter, diced

For the filling

30ml/2 tbsp raspberry or apricot jam

2 whole eggs and 2 extra yolks

115g/4oz/generous ½ cup caster (superfine) sugar

115g/4oz/½ cup butter, melted

55g/2oz/⅔ cup ground almonds

few drops of almond extract

icing (confectioners') sugar, to dust

1 Sift the flour and salt and rub in the butter until the mixture resembles fine crumbs. Stir in about 30ml/2 tbsp cold water and gather into a smooth ball of dough. Wrap and chill for 30 minutes. Preheat the oven to 200°C/400°F/Gas 6.

2 Roll out the pastry and use to line an 18cm/7in loose-based flan tin (pan). Spread the jam over the pastry.

3 Whisk the eggs, egg yolks and sugar together in a large bowl until the mixture is thick and pale. Gently stir the melted butter, ground almonds and almond extract in to the bowl. Mix together well to combine.

4 Pour the mixture over the jam in the pastry case (pie shell). Put the tart into the hot oven and cook for 30 minutes until just set and browned. Sift a little icing sugar over the top before serving warm or at room temperature.

Energy 700kcal/2919kJ; Protein 10.8g; Carbohydrate 57.1g, of which sugars 36.7g; Fat 49.9g, of which saturates 17.1g; Cholesterol 257mg; Calcium 110mg; Fibre 0.9g; Sodium 394mg.

Pecan pie

Almost an American institution, this classic country pie has a golden crust with a dense maple syrup filling, topped with pecans halves. Serve warm with whipped cream.

Serves 8

3 eggs

pinch of salt

200g/7oz/scant 1 cup soft dark brown sugar

120ml/4fl oz/½ cup golden (light corn) syrup

30ml/2 tbsp fresh lemon juice

75g/3oz/6 tbsp butter, melted

150g/5oz/1¼ cups chopped pecan nuts

50g/2oz/½ cup pecan halves

For the pastry

175g/6oz/1½ cups plain (all-purpose) flour

15ml/1 tbsp caster (superfine) sugar

5ml/1 tsp baking powder

2.5ml/½ tsp salt

75g/3oz/6 tbsp cold unsalted butter, cut into pieces

1 egg yolk

45–60ml/3–4 tbsp whipping cream

1 For the pastry, sift the flour, sugar, baking powder and salt into a bowl. Add the butter and rub in until the mixture resembles coarse breadcrumbs.

2 In a bowl, beat together the egg yolk and cream until blended. Pour the mixture into the flour mixture and stir with a fork.

3 Gather the pastry into a ball. On a lightly floured surface, roll it out to a thickness of 3mm/⅛in and use it to line a 23cm/9in fluted tin (pan).

4 Trim the overhang and flute the edge with your fingers. Chill for at least 20 minutes.

5 Preheat a baking sheet in the middle of a 200°C/400°F/Gas 6 oven. In a bowl, lightly whisk the eggs and salt. Add the sugar, syrup, lemon juice and butter. Mix well and stir in the chopped nuts.

6 Pour into the pastry case (pie shell) and arrange the pecan halves in concentric circles on top. Bake for 10 minutes. Reduce the heat to 170°C/325°F/Gas 3 and continue baking for 25 minutes.

Energy 587kcal/2449kJ; Protein 7.5g; Carbohydrate 56.7g, of which sugars 39.6g; Fat 38.3g, of which saturates 13.4g; Cholesterol 142mg; Calcium 82mg; Fibre 1.9g; Sodium 185mg.

Pumpkin pie

A version of this dish was baked by the earliest American settlers, and Thanksgiving would not be complete without it. Using canned pumpkin makes it a very easy pie to make.

Serves 8

450g/1lb cooked or canned pumpkin

250ml/8fl oz/1 cup whipping cream

2 eggs

115g/4oz/½ cup soft dark brown sugar

60ml/4 tbsp golden (light corn) syrup

7.5ml/1½ tsp ground cinnamon

5ml/1 tsp ground ginger

1.5ml/¼ tsp ground cloves

2.5ml/½ tsp salt

For the pastry

175g/6oz/1½ cups plain (all-purpose) flour

2.5ml/½ tsp salt

75g/3oz/6 tbsp cold butter, cut into pieces

40g/1½oz/3 tbsp cold white vegetable fat (shortening), cut into pieces

45–60ml/3–4 tbsp iced water

1 egg, beaten

1 For the pastry, sift the flour and salt into a bowl. Rub the butter and fat into the flour with your fingertips until it resembles coarse crumbs. Bind with iced water. Wrap in clear film (plastic wrap) and chill for 20 minutes.

2 Roll out the dough and line a 23cm/9in fluted pie tin (pan). Trim off the overhang. Roll out the trimmings and cut out leaf shapes.

3 Chill for about 20 minutes. Preheat the oven to 200°C/400°F/Gas 6.

4 Line the pastry case with baking parchment. Fill with baking beans and bake for 12 minutes. Remove paper and beans and bake until golden, 6–8 minutes more. Reduce the heat to 190°C/375°F/Gas 5.

5 Beat together the pumpkin, cream, eggs, sugar, golden syrup, spices and salt. Pour into the pastry case and bake for 25 minutes. Brush the pastry leaves with egg and place around the top of the pie. Bake for 10–15 minutes more.

Energy 434kcal/1809kJ; Protein 6.2g; Carbohydrate 35.3g, of which sugars 19.4g; Fat 30.8g, of which saturates 13.8g; Cholesterol 94mg; Calcium 108mg; Fibre 1.2g; Sodium 60mg.

Yellow plum tart

In this tart, glazed yellow plums sit atop a delectable almond filling in a crisp pastry shell.
When they are in season, greengages make an excellent alternative to the plums.

Serves 8

175g/6oz/1½ cups plain (all-purpose)
flour

pinch of salt

75g/3oz/scant ½ cup butter, chilled

30ml/2 tbsp sugar

a few drops of vanilla extract

45ml/3 tbsp iced water

cream or custard, to serve

For the filling

75g/3oz/⅓ cup sugar

75g/3oz/scant ½ cup butter,
softened

75g/3oz/¾ cup ground almonds

1 egg, beaten

30ml/2 tbsp plain (all-purpose) flour

450g/1lb plums or greengages,
halved and stoned (pitted)

For the glaze

45ml/3 tbsp apricot jam, strained

15ml/1 tbsp water

1 Sift the flour and salt into a bowl,
then rub in the chilled butter until the
mixture resembles fine breadcrumbs.
Stir in the caster sugar, vanilla extract
and enough of the iced water to make
a soft dough.

2 Knead the dough gently on a lightly
floured surface until smooth, then wrap
in plastic wrap and chill for 10 minutes.

3 Preheat the oven to 200°C/400°F/
Gas 6. Roll out the pastry and line a
23cm/9in fluted flan tin (pan), allowing
excess pastry to overhang the top. Prick
the base with a fork and line with non-
stick baking paper and baking beans.

4 Bake blind for 10 minutes, remove
the paper and beans, then return the
pastry case to the oven for 10 minutes.
Remove and allow to cool. Trim off any
excess pastry with a sharp knife.

5 To make the filling, beat together all
the ingredients except the fruit. Spread
on the base of the pastry case. Arrange
the plums or greengages on top,
placing them cut side down. Make a
glaze by heating the jam with the
water. Stir well, then brush a little of
the jam glaze over the top of the fruit.

6 Bake the tart for 50–60 minutes, until
the almond filling is cooked and the
plums or greengages are tender. Warm
any remaining jam glaze and brush it
over the top. Cut into slices and serve
with cream or custard.

Farmhouse tip Ceramic baking beans
are ideal for baking blind, but any dried
beans will do. You can use them over
and over again, but keep them in a
special jar, separate from the rest of
your dried beans, as you cannot use
them for conventional cooking.

Energy 361kcal/1510kJ; Protein 6g; Carbohydrate 38g, of which sugars 18g; Fat 22g, of which saturates 10g; Cholesterol 69mg; Calcium 72mg; Fibre 2.1g; Sodium 177mg.

Apple cake

If available, you should choose heritage apple varieties when making this lovely pudding. It has a crunchy top and is delicious served warm with cream, or cold for afternoon tea.

Serves 8–10

225g/8oz/2 cups self-raising (self-rising) flour

good pinch of salt

pinch of ground cloves

115g/4oz/½ cup butter, at room temperature

3 or 4 cooking apples

115g/4oz/generous ½ cup caster (superfine) sugar

2 eggs, beaten

a little milk, to mix

granulated (white) sugar, to sprinkle over

1 Preheat the oven to 190°C/375°F/Gas 5 and butter a 20cm/8in cake tin (pan).

2 Sift the flour, salt and ground cloves into a bowl. Cut in the butter and rub in until the mixture is like fine breadcrumbs. Peel and core the apples. Slice them thinly and add to the rubbed-in mixture with the sugar.

3 Mix in the eggs and enough milk to make a fairly stiff dough, then turn the mixture into the prepared tin and sprinkle with granulated sugar.

4 Bake in the preheated oven for 30–40 minutes, or until springy to the touch. When cool enough to handle, remove from the tin, and serve warm.

Per cake : Energy 2315kcal/9717kJ; Protein 37g; Carbohydrate 312.5g, of which sugars 145.3g; Fat 110.9g, of which saturates 64.1g; Cholesterol 702mg; Calcium 948mg; Fibre 10.7g; Sodium 1.68g.

Lemon meringue pie

This popular dessert is a 20th-century development of older English cheesecakes – open tarts with a filling of curds. It was particularly relished in the 1950s after the years of wartime rationing, when sugar, lemons and eggs became plentiful once more. The pie is best served at room temperature, with or without cream.

Serves 6

For the pastry

115g/4oz/1 cup plain (all-purpose) flour

pinch of salt

25g/1oz/2 tbsp white vegetable fat, diced

25g/1oz/2 tbsp butter, diced

For the filling

50g/2oz/¼ cup cornflour (cornstarch)

175g/6oz/¾ cup caster (superfine) sugar

grated rind and juice of 2 lemons

2 egg yolks

15g/½oz/1 tbsp butter, diced

For the meringue topping

2 egg whites

75g/3oz/½ cup caster (superfine) sugar

1 To make the pastry, sift the flour and salt into a bowl and add the lard and butter. With the fingertips, lightly rub the fats into the flour until the mixture resembles fine crumbs.

2 Stir in about 20ml/2 tbsp cold water until the mixture can be gathered together into a smooth ball of dough. (Alternatively, make the pastry using a food processor.) Wrap the pastry and refrigerate for at least 30 minutes. Meanwhile, preheat the oven to 200°C/400°F/Gas 6.

3 Roll out the pastry on a lightly floured surface and use to line a 20cm/8in flan tin (pan). Prick the base with a fork, line with baking parchment or foil, and add a layer of baking beans to prevent the pastry rising.

4 Put the pastry case (pie shell) into the hot oven and cook for 15 minutes. Remove the beans and parchment or foil, return the pastry to the oven and cook for a further 5 minutes until crisp and golden brown. Reduce the oven temperature to 150°C/300°F/Gas 2.

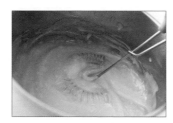

5 To make the lemon filling, put the cornflour into a pan and add the sugar, lemon rind and 300ml/½ pint/1¼ cups water. Heat the mixture, stirring constantly, until it comes to the boil and thickens. Reduce the heat and simmer very gently for 1 minute. Remove the pan from the heat and stir in the lemon juice.

6 Add the the egg yolks to the lemon mixture, one at a time and beating after each addition, and then stir in the butter. Tip the mixture into the baked pastry case and level the surface.

7 To make the meringue topping, whisk the egg whites until stiff peaks form then whisk in half the sugar. Fold in the rest of the sugar using a metal spoon.

8 Spread the meringue over the lemon filling, covering it completely. Cook for about 20 minutes until lightly browned.

Energy 357kcal/1497kJ; Protein 6.8g; Carbohydrate 42.8g, of which sugars 25.1g; Fat 18.9g, of which saturates 9g; Cholesterol 129mg; Calcium 108mg; Fibre 0.7g; Sodium 137mg

Chilled Desserts
and Ice Creams

In high summer, when berries are in season and the days are warm and long, there is nothing nicer than home-made ice cream or a cool, creamy dessert to finish a meal. In this chapter are tempting and impressive tarts, sorbets, ices and fools, which look beautiful but are easy to make in advance and chill until ready to serve.

Lemon meringue bombe with mint chocolate

This easy ice cream dessert will cause a sensation when you serve it – it is unusual, but is quite the most delicious combination of tastes that you can imagine.

Serves 6–8

2 large lemons

150g/5oz/¾ cup sugar

3 small sprigs fresh mint

150ml/¼ pint/¾ cup whipping cream

600ml/1 pint/3 cups natural (plain) yogurt

2 large meringues

225g/8oz good-quality mint chocolate, grated

1 Slice the rind off the lemons with a vegetable peeler, then squeeze them for juice. Place the lemon rind and sugar in a food processor and blend until the rind is finely shredded. Add the cream, yogurt and lemon juice and process thoroughly. Pour the mixture into a mixing bowl and add the meringues, roughly crushed.

2 Reserve one of the mint sprigs and chop the rest finely. Add to the mixture. Pour into a 1.2 litre/2 pint glass bowl and freeze for 4 hours.

3 When the ice cream has frozen, scoop out the middle and pour in the grated mint chocolate. Replace enough of the scooped-out ice cream to cover the chocolate, and refreeze.

4 When you are ready to serve the dessert, dip the basin in very hot water for a few seconds to loosen the ice cream, then turn the basin upside down over the serving plate. Decorate with grated chocolate and a sprig of mint. Serve in slices to show the chocolate centre.

Energy 349kcal/1465kJ; Protein 6g; Carbohydrate 44g, of which sugars 44g; Fat 18g, of which saturates 11g; Cholesterol 30mg; Calcium 173mg; Fibre 0.0g; Sodium 67mg.

Apple mint and pink grapefruit fool

Apple mint can easily run riot in the herb garden; this tangy dessert is an excellent way of using up an abundant crop. Use orange segments in place of the grapefruit if you wish.

Serves 4–6

500g/1lb tart apples, peeled, cored and sliced

225g/8oz pink grapefruit segments

45ml/3 tbsp clear honey

30ml/2 tbsp water

6 large sprigs apple mint, plus more to garnish

150ml/¼ pint/¾ cup double (heavy) cream

300ml/½ pint/1½ cups custard

1 Place the apples, grapefruit, honey, water and apple mint in a pan, cover and simmer for 10 minutes until soft. Leave in the pan to cool, then discard the apple mint. Purée the mixture in a food processor.

2 Whip the cream until it forms soft peaks, and fold into the custard, keeping 30ml/2 tbsp to decorate. Carefully fold the cream into the fruit mixture. Serve chilled and decorated with swirls of cream and sprigs of mint.

Energy 245kcal/1022kJ; Protein 3g; Carbohydrate 24g, of which sugars 22g; Fat 16g, of which saturates 10g; Cholesterol 42mg; Calcium 94mg; Fibre 2.4g; Sodium 43mg.

Rhubarb fool

This is a quick and simple dessert that makes the most of rhubarb when it is in season. You can use early or 'forced' rhubarb, which is a ravishing pink and needs very little cooking. Try adding a few drops of rosewater to the fruit as it cooks, and serve with shortbread.

1 Cut the rhubarb into pieces and wash thoroughly. Stew over a low heat with just the water clinging to it and the sugar. This takes about 10 minutes. Set aside to cool.

2 Pass the rhubarb through a fine sieve (strainer) so you have a thick purée.

3 Use equal parts of the purée, the whipped double cream and ready-made thick custard. Combine the purée and custard first, then fold in the cream. Chill in the refrigerator before serving. Serve with heather honey.

Serves 4

450g/1lb rhubarb, trimmed

75g/3oz/scant ½ cup soft light brown sugar

whipped double (heavy) cream and ready-made thick custard (for quantities, see step 3)

Variations You can use another fruit if you like for this dessert – try bramble fruits or apples. Other stewed fruits also work well, such as prunes or peaches. For something a little more exotic, you could try mangoes.
For a low-fat option, substitute natural (plain) yogurt for the cream.

Energy 439kcal/1828kJ; Protein 4.6g; Carbohydrate 34.1g, of which sugars 31.8g; Fat 31.7g, of which saturates 18.9g; Cholesterol 80mg; Calcium 233mg; Fibre 1.6g; Sodium 74mg.

Gooseberry and elderflower fool

The combination of gooseberry and elderflower is heavenly, especially in fruit fool,
a traditional dessert that dates back to the mid-17th century. Serve in pretty glasses,
with crisp little biscuits to add a contrast of texture.

Serves 4

500g/1¼lb gooseberries

300ml/½ pint/1¼ cups double
(heavy) cream

about 115g/4oz/1 cup icing
(confectioners') sugar, to taste

30ml/2 tbsp elderflower cordial

mint sprigs, to decorate

crisp biscuits (cookies), to serve

1 Place the gooseberries in a heavy
pan, then cover and cook over a low
heat, shaking the pan occasionally, until
tender. Transfer the gooseberries into a
bowl, crush them with a fork or potato
masher, then leave to cool completely.

2 Whip the cream until soft peaks
form, then fold in half the crushed fruit.
Add sugar and elderflower cordial to
taste. Sweeten the remaining fruit
to taste.

3 Layer the cream mixture and the
crushed gooseberries in four dessert
dishes or tall glasses, then cover and
chill until ready to serve. Decorate the
fool with mint sprigs and serve with
crisp sweet biscuits.

Variation When elderberries are in
season, cook 2–3 elderflower heads
with the gooseberries and omit the
elderflower cordial.

Energy 366kcal/1521kJ; Protein 3.5g; Carbohydrate 24.2g, of which sugars 21.8g; Fat 28.4g, of which saturates 16.7g; Cholesterol 70mg; Calcium 111mg; Fibre 1.9g; Sodium 41mg.

Country strawberry fool

This recipe uses a custard base rather than whipped cream. Fools don't keep well, and you need to make them on the day of eating, but leave enough time to chill them properly too.

Serves 4

300ml/½ pint/1¼ cups milk

2 egg yolks

90g/3½oz/scant ½ cup caster (superfine) sugar

few drops of vanilla essence

900g/2lb/8 cups ripe strawberries

juice of ½ lemon

300ml/½ pint/1¼ cups double (heavy) cream

To decorate

12 small strawberries

4 fresh mint sprigs

1 Whisk 30ml/2 tbsp milk with the egg yolks, 15ml/1 tbsp caster sugar and the vanilla essence.

2 Heat the remaining milk until it is just below boiling point. Stir the milk into the egg mixture. Rinse the pan out and return the mixture to it.

3 Gently heat and whisk until the custard thickens (it should be thick enough to coat the back of a spoon). Lay a wet piece of baking parchment on top of the custard, to prevent skin forming, and leave it to cool.

4 Purée the strawberries in a food processor or blender with the lemon juice and the remaining sugar.

5 Lightly whisk the cream until soft peaks form, then fold in the fruit purée and custard. Pour into glass dishes and decorate with the whole strawberries and sprigs of mint.

Energy 612kcal/2538kJ; Protein 7g; Carbohydrate 44g, of which sugars 44g; Fat 46g, of which saturates 28g; Cholesterol 214mg; Calcium 182mg; Fibre 5.2g; Sodium 70mg.

Autumn orchard pudding

This autumn version of a summer pudding makes the most of seasonal orchard fruits.
Serve with cream, lightly whipped with apple brandy or plain crème fraîche.

Serves 6–8

1 loaf white bread, 2 or 3 days old

675g/1½lb/6 cups mixed soft
fruit, such as blackberries,
autumn raspberries, late
strawberries, and peeled and
chopped eating apples

115g/4oz/generous ½ cup caster
(superfine) sugar or 75ml/
5 tbsp honey

1 Remove the crusts from the loaf
and slice the bread thinly. Use several
slices to line the base and sides of a
900ml–1.2 litre/1½–2 pint/3¾–5 cup
pudding bowl or soufflé dish, cutting
them carefully so that the pieces fit
closely together.

2 Put all the fruit into a wide, heavy
pan, sprinkle the sugar or honey over
and bring very gently to the boil. Cook
for 2–3 minutes, or until the sugar has
dissolved and the juices run.

3 Remove the pan from the heat and
set aside 30–45ml/2–3 tbsp of the
juices. Spoon the fruit and the
remaining juices into the prepared
bread-lined dish and cover the top
closely with the rest of the bread.

4 Put a plate that fits neatly inside the
top of the dish on top of the pudding
and weigh it down with a heavy can or
jar. Leave in the refrigerator for at least
8 hours, or overnight.

5 Before serving the pudding, remove
the weight and plate, cover the bowl
with a serving plate and turn upside
down to unmould. Use the reserved
fruit juice to pour over any patches
of the bread that have not been
completely soaked and coloured by the
fruit juices.

6 Serve the pudding cold, cut into
wedges, with lightly whipped chilled
cream or crème fraîche.

Energy 261kcal/1112kJ; Protein 7.7g; Carbohydrate 57.5g, of which sugars 27.1g; Fat 1.7g, of which saturates 0.4g; Cholesterol 0mg; Calcium 153mg; Fibre 4.2g; Sodium 398mg.

Poached spiced pears

The fragrant aroma of pears is greatly enhanced by gently poaching them in either spiced liquor or wine. Serve this dish warm or cold, with some cream whipped with icing sugar and pear liqueur, and perhaps some crisp, sweet biscuits to give a contrasting texture.

Serves 4

115g/4oz/½ cup caster (superfine) sugar

grated rind and juice of 1 lemon

2.5ml/½ tsp ground ginger

1 small cinnamon stick

2 whole cloves

4 firm ripe pears

Variations Omit the spices and instead flavour the water with ginger or elderflower cordial if you wish, or use white wine in place of water.

1 Put the sugar in a pan with 300ml/½ pint/1½ cups water, the lemon rind and juice, ginger and spices. Heat, stirring, until the sugar has dissolved.

2 Peel the pears, cut them in half lengthways and remove their cores.

3 Add the pear halves to the pan and bring just to the boil. Cover and simmer gently for about 5 minutes or until the pears are tender, turning them over in the syrup occasionally during cooking. Remove from the heat and leave to cool in the syrup before serving.

Energy 93kcal/392kJ; Protein 0.5g; Carbohydrate 23.6g, of which sugars 23.6g; Fat 0.2g, of which saturates 0g; Cholesterol 0mg; Calcium 17mg; Fibre 3.3g; Sodium 6mg.

Chilled berry pudding

A cross between a summer pudding and a trifle, this fragrant, light pudding makes the most of seasonal soft fruits and is a perfect summer dessert. Be sure to use a good loaf of farmhouse rather than processed sliced bread, to get the best texture and flavour.

Serves 4–6

550g/1lb 4oz/scant 1¼ cups mixed raspberries, blackberries, blackcurrants, redcurrants

50g/2oz/4 tbsp sugar

large thick slice of bread with crusts removed, about 125g/4½oz/2 cups without crusts

300ml/½ pint/1¼ cups double (heavy) cream

45ml/3 tbsp elderflower cordial

150ml/¼ pint/⅔ cup thick natural (plain) yogurt

Farmhouse tip During the seasons when fresh summer fruits are not as readily available, a bag of mixed frozen fruit works just as well in this recipe.

3 Spoon the fruit mixture over the bread and leave to cool.

Variation Instead of mixing yogurt into the topping, try using the same quantity of ready-made custard – it gives a richer, sweeter result to the finished dish.

4 Whip the cream with the cordial until stiff peaks begin to form. Gently stir in the yogurt and spoon the mixture over the top of the fruit.

5 Chill until required. Just before serving, decorate the top with the reserved fruit.

1 Reserve a few raspberries, blackberries, blackcurrants or redcurrants for decoration, then put the remainder into a pan with the sugar and 30ml/2 tbsp water. Bring just to the boil, cover and simmer gently for 4–5 minutes, until the fruit is soft and plenty of juice has formed.

2 Cut the bread into cubes, measuring about 2.5cm/1in, and put them into one large dish or individual serving bowls or glasses.

Energy 382kcal/1592kJ; Protein 5.2g, Carbohydrate 29.9g, of which sugars 20.2g; Fat 27.8g, of which saturates 16.9g; Cholesterol 69mg; Calcium 124mg; Fibre 2.6g; Sodium 144mg.

Eton mess

This 'mess' consists of whipped cream, crushed meringue and sliced or mashed strawberries, all mixed together. Don't make this in advance, as the meringue will go soggy.

Serves 4

450g/1lb ripe strawberries

45ml/3 tbsp elderflower cordial or orange liqueur

300ml/½ pint/1¼ cups double (heavy) cream

4 meringues or meringue baskets

Farmhouse tips Serve Eton mess just as it is or accompanied by crisp sweet biscuits (cookies).

Make the dish with other soft fruit, such as lightly crushed raspberries or blackcurrants.

This is a useful recipe for when you are trying to make a large meringue and it cracks, as you can just break it up completely and serve it this way.

1 Remove the green hulls from the strawberries and slice the fruit into a bowl, reserving a few for decoration.

2 Sprinkle with the elderflower cordial or fruit liqueur. Cover the bowl and chill for about 2 hours.

3 Whip the cream until soft peaks form. Crush the meringue into small pieces. Add the fruit and most of the meringue to the cream and fold in lightly.

4 Spoon into dishes and decorate with the reserved strawberries and meringue before serving.

Energy 526kcal/2182kJ; Protein 3.5g; Carbohydrate 32.8g, of which sugars 32.8g; Fat 40.4g, of which saturates 25.1g; Cholesterol 103mg; Calcium 60mg; Fibre 1.4g; Sodium 53mg

Mint and lemon balm sorbet

This is a light and refreshing sorbet to serve in summer after a generous meal. The individual iced bowls are a beautiful way to serve it, but you can make the sorbet on its own if you wish.

Serves 6–8

500g/1lb/2⅛ cups sugar

500ml/17fl oz/2⅛ cups water

6 sprigs mint, plus more to decorate

6 lemon balm leaves

250ml/8fl oz/1 cup white wine

30ml/2 tbsp lemon juice

herb sprigs, to decorate

1 Boil the sugar and water in a pan with the herbs. Remove from the heat and add the wine. Transfer to a freezer-proof container, and cool, then add the lemon juice. Place in the freezer, and when the mixture begins to freeze, stir briskly and replace. Repeat every 15 minutes for 3 hours.

2 To make the small ice bowls, pour about 1cm/½in cooled boiled water into small freezer-proof bowls and arrange some herbs in the water.

3 Freeze the herb water in the small bowls, then add a little water to cover the herbs and freeze again.

4 Place a small freezer-proof bowl inside each herb-water bowl so that it sits on the frozen water. Put a heavy weight inside. Fill the space between the bowls with more cooled boiled water. Float more herbs in this and freeze.

5 To release the ice bowls, warm the inner bowl with a small amount of very hot water and twist it out. Warm the outer bowl by standing it in very hot water for a few seconds, then turn out the ice bowl.

6 Spoon the frozen sorbet into the ice bowls and decorate with sprigs of your favourite herbs.

Energy 267kcal/1137kJ; Protein 0g; Carbohydrate 66g, of which sugars 66g; Fat 0g, of which saturates 0g; Cholesterol 0mg; Calcium 10mg; Fibre 0.0g; Sodium 4mg.

Summer fruit gâteau with heartsease

No one can resist the dainty appeal of little pansies. This cake would be lovely for a sentimental summer occasion in the garden.

Serves 6–8

16 pansy flowers

the white of 1 egg, for crystallizing

caster (superfine) sugar, as required, for crystallizing

100g/3¹⁄₂oz/scant ¹⁄₂ cup butter, softened, plus extra for greasing

100g/3³⁄₄ oz/scant ¹⁄₂ cup sugar

10ml/2 tsp clear honey

150g/5oz/1¹⁄₄ cups self-raising (self-rising) flour

3ml/¹⁄₂ tsp baking powder

30ml/2 tbsp milk

2 eggs

15ml/1 tbsp rosewater

15ml/1 tbsp Cointreau

icing (confectioner's) sugar, to decorate

450g/1lb/4 cups strawberries

strawberry leaves, to decorate

1 Crystallize the pansies by painting them with lightly beaten egg white and sprinkling with caster sugar. Leave to dry.

2 Preheat the oven to 190°C/ 375°F/ Gas 5. Grease and flour a ring mould.

◄ **3** In a large mixing bowl, place the butter, sugar, honey, flour, baking powder, milk and eggs. Beat well, with a wooden spoon until light and creamy.

4 Add the rosewater and the Cointreau to the bowl and mix well.

5 Pour the mixture into the ring mould and bake for 40 minutes. Allow to stand for a few minutes and then turn out on to a wire rack to go cold.

6 Put on a serving plate and sift icing sugar over the cake. Fill the cake centre with strawberries. Decorate with crystallized flowers and strawberry leaves.

Energy 198kcal/829kJ; Protein 3.1g; Carbohydrate 22.5g, of which sugars 17.7g; Fat 10.7g, of which saturates 0.4g; Cholesterol 47.7mg; Calcium 59mg; Fibre 0.8g; Sodium 121mg.

Mixed berry tart

The orange-flavoured pastry in the recipe is delicious with the fresh fruits of summer. Serve the tart with some extra shreds of orange rind scattered on top.

Serves 8

225g/8oz/2 cups plain (all-purpose) flour

115g/4oz/½ cup unsalted butter, diced

finely grated rind of 1 orange, plus extra to decorate

For the filling

300ml/½ pint/1¼ cups crème fraîche

finely grated rind of 1 lemon

10ml/2 tsp icing (confectioner's) sugar

675g/1½lb mixed summer berries, such as strawberries, blueberries and raspberries

1 To make the pastry, put the flour and diced butter in a large bowl. Rub in the butter until the mixture resembles fine breadcrumbs.

2 Add the orange rind and enough cold water to make a soft dough.

3 Roll the dough into a ball, then cover and chill in the refrigerator for at least 30 minutes.

4 Roll out the pastry on a floured surface, and use to line a 23cm/9in loose-based flan tin (pan). Chill for 30 minutes. Preheat the oven to 200°C/400°F/Gas 6.

5 Place a baking sheet in the oven to heat up. Line the raw pastry case with baking parchment and baking beans and bake blind on the baking sheet for 15 minutes. Remove the paper and beans and bake for 10 minutes more, until the pastry is golden. Allow to cool on a wire rack.

6 To make the filling, whisk the crème fraîche, lemon rind and icing sugar together and pour into the pastry case. Top with fruit, sprinkle with orange rind and serve in slices.

Energy 432kcal/1807kJ; Protein 6.7g; Carbohydrate 47.6g, of which sugars 21.8g; Fat 25.7g, of which saturates 14.6g; Cholesterol 160mg; Calcium 130mg; Fibre 2g; Sodium 150mg.

Lemon and lime cheesecake

Tangy cheesecakes, with their contrast between creamy filling and crisp buttery base, are always a hit. The lime syrup makes this version a citrus sensation.

Serves 8

150g/5oz/1½ cups digestive biscuits (graham crackers)

40g/1½oz/3 tbsp butter

For the topping

grated rind and juice of 2 lemons

10ml/2 tsp powdered gelatine

250g/9oz/generous 1 cup ricotta cheese

75g/3oz/⅓ cup caster (superfine) sugar

150ml/¼ pint/⅔ cup double (heavy) cream

2 eggs, separated

For the lime syrup

finely pared rind and juice of 3 limes

75g/3oz/⅓ cup caster (superfine) sugar

5ml/1 tsp arrowroot, mixed with 30ml/2 tbsp water

1 Lightly grease a 20cm/8in round springform cake tin. Place the biscuits in a food processor or blender and process until they form fine crumbs.

2 Melt the butter in a large pan, then stir in the crumbs until well coated. Spoon into the prepared cake tin (pan), press the crumbs down well in an even layer, then chill.

3 Place the lemon rind and juice in a small pan and sprinkle over the gelatine. Leave to stand for 5 minutes, then heat gently until the gelatine has melted. Set aside to cool slightly.

4 Beat the ricotta cheese and sugar in a bowl. Stir in the cream and egg yolks, then whisk in the gelatine mixture.

5 Whisk the egg whites in a grease-free bowl until they form soft peaks. Fold into the cheese mixture, then pour on to the biscuit base. Chill for 2–3 hours.

6 For the lime syrup, place the lime rind, juice and caster sugar in a pan. Bring to the boil, stirring, then boil for 5 minutes. Stir in the arrowroot mixture and continue to stir until the syrup boils again and thickens slightly. Chill.

7 When the cheesecake is completely set and chilled, spoon the lime syrup over the top. Remove from the tin and cut into slices to serve.

Energy 366kcal/1526kJ; Protein 6g; Carbohydrate 33.8g, of which sugars 23.5g; Fat 23.9g, of which saturates 13.8g; Cholesterol 105mg; Calcium 44mg; Fibre 0.4g; Sodium 166mg.

Curd cheese tart

The distinguishing characteristic of this tart is allspice, or 'clove pepper', made up of equal quantities of nutmeg, cloves and ground cinnamon. It tastes superb and is not too sweet.

Serves 8

90g/3½oz/scant ½ cup soft light brown sugar

large pinch of ground allspice

3 eggs, beaten

grated rind and juice of 1 lemon

40g/1½oz/3 tbsp butter, melted

450g/1lb/2 cups curd (farmer's) cheese

75g/3oz/scant ½ cup raisins

For the pastry

225g/8oz/2 cups plain (all-purpose) flour

115g/4oz/½ cup butter, diced

1 egg yolk

15–30ml/1–2 tbsp chilled water

1 To make the pastry, place the flour in a large mixing bowl and rub or cut in the butter until the mixture resembles fine breadcrumbs. Stir the egg yolk into the flour and add just enough of the water to bind the mixture together to form a dough.

Farmhouse tip Although it is not traditional, mixed spice (apple pie spice) would make a good substitute for the ground allspice.

2 Put the dough on a floured surface, knead lightly and briefly, then form into a ball. Roll out the pastry thinly and use to line a 20cm/8in fluted loose-based flan tin (pan). Cover with clear film (plastic wrap) and chill for about 15 minutes.

3 Preheat the oven to 190°C/375°F/ Gas 5. Mix the sugar with the ground allspice in a bowl, then stir in the eggs, lemon rind and juice, butter, curd cheese and raisins. Mix well.

4 Pour the filling into the pastry case, then bake for 40 minutes, or until the pastry is cooked and the filling is lightly set and golden brown. Cut the tart into wedges while it is still slightly warm, and serve with cream, if you like.

Energy 419Kcal/1753kJ; Protein 14.1g; Carbohydrate 42.2g, of which sugars 20.8g; Fat 23.6g, of which saturates 13.9g; Cholesterol 151mg; Calcium 132mg; Fibre 1.1g; Sodium 398mg.

Classic lemon tart

This is one dish where the colour of the yolks makes a real difference to the colour of the tart; the yellower the better. This tart can be served warm or chilled.

Serves 8

150g/5oz/1¼ cups plain (all-purpose) flour, sifted

50g/2oz/½ cup hazelnuts, toasted and finely ground

175g/6oz/scant 1 cup caster (superfine) sugar

115g/4oz/½ cup butter, softened

4 eggs

grated rind of 2 lemons and at least 175ml/6fl oz/¾ cup lemon juice

150ml/¼ pint/⅔ cup double (heavy) cream

Farmhouse tip Try rolling the pastry out over the base of the tin, so it is easier to lift it into the tin surround.

1 Mix together the flour, nuts and 25g/1oz/2 tbsp sugar, then gently work in the butter and, if necessary, 15–30ml/1–2 tbsp cold water, to make a soft dough. Chill for 10 minutes.

2 Roll out the dough and use to line a 20.5cm/8in loose-based flan tin (pan). If you find it too difficult to roll out, push the pastry into the flan tin. Chill for about 20 minutes.

3 Preheat the oven to 200°C/400°F/Gas 6. Line the pastry case with baking parchment, fill with baking beans, and bake for 15 minutes. Remove the paper and beans, and cook for a further 5–10 minutes.

4 Beat the eggs, lemon rind and juice, the remaining sugar and cream until blended. Pour into the pastry case. Bake for about 30 minutes, until just set.

Energy 268kcal/1122kJ; Protein 5.6g; Carbohydrate 27g, of which sugars 10.9g; Fat 16.1g, of which saturates 5.8g; Cholesterol 148mg; Calcium 57mg; Fibre 0.7g; Sodium 173mg.

Iced raspberry and almond trifle

This delicious combination of almondy sponge, sherried fruit, ice cream and mascarpone topping is sheer indulgence. The sponge and topping can be made a day in advance.

Serves 8–10

115g/4oz/½ cup unsalted butter, softened

115g/4oz/½ cup light muscovado (brown) sugar

2 eggs

75g/3oz/¾ cup self-raising (self-rising) flour

2.5ml/½ tsp baking powder

115g/4oz/1 cup ground almonds

5ml/1 tsp almond extract

15ml/1 tbsp milk

To assemble the trifle

500g/1¼lb/2½ cups mascarpone cheese

150g/5oz/⅔ cup Greek (US strained plain) yogurt

30ml/2 tbsp icing (confectioners') sugar

200ml/7fl oz/scant 1 cup medium sherry

300g/11oz/scant 3 cups raspberries

50g/2oz/½ cup flaked (sliced) almonds, toasted

90ml/6 tbsp fresh orange juice

250ml/8fl oz/1 cup vanilla ice cream

250ml/8fl oz/1 cup raspberry ice cream or sorbet

1 Preheat the oven to 180°C/350°F/ Gas 4. Grease and line a 20cm/8in round cake tin (pan). In a large bowl, beat the mascarpone in a bowl with the yogurt, icing sugar and 100ml/6 tbsp of the sherry. Place in the refrigerator.

2 Put the butter, sugar, eggs, flour, baking powder, almonds and almond extract in a large bowl and beat with an electric whisk for 2 minutes until creamy. Stir in the milk.

3 Spoon the mixture into the prepared tin, level the surface and bake for about 30 minutes or until just firm in the centre. Transfer to a wire rack to cool.

4 Cut the sponge into chunky pieces and place in a 1.75 litre/3 pint/7½ cup glass serving bowl. Scatter with half the raspberries and almonds.

5 Mix the orange juice with the remaining sherry, and pour over the cake and fruit in the serving bowl. Place the bowl in the refrigerator until you are ready to assemble the trifle.

6 To assemble, scoop the ice cream and sorbet into the serving bowl. Reserve a few of the raspberries and almonds for the decoration, then scatter the rest over the ice cream. Spoon over the mascarpone mixture and scatter with the reserved raspberries and almonds. If you wish, you can assemble the trifle in individual glass dishes instead.

Energy 330kcal/1382kJ; Protein 5g; Carbohydrate 35.9g, of which sugars 29.1g; Fat 17.7g, of which saturates 9.9g; Cholesterol 90mg; Calcium 102mg; Fibre 1.1g; Sodium 59mg.

Rich vanilla ice cream

This classic vanilla ice cream is quite superb and a great way of using up a farmhouse glut of cream and eggs. Serve it on its own, or use as the base for other ices and desserts.

Serves 6–8

300ml/½ pint/1¼ cups single (light) cream

1 vanilla pod (bean)

3 egg yolks

45ml/3 tbsp caster (superfine) sugar

10ml/2 tsp cornflour (cornstarch)

300ml/½ pint/1¼ cups double (heavy) cream, whipped

1 Put the cream in a small pan. Split the vanilla pod and scrape out the tiny seeds. Add them to the cream with the pod. Bring the cream just to the boil, then turn off the heat.

2 Whisk together the eggs, sugar and cornflour until pale and creamy. Remove the vanilla pod from the cream and whisk into the egg mixture. Return the mixture to the pan and bring to a simmer, stirring all the time. Cook gently until the custard coats the back of a wooden spoon, then leave to cool.

3 When cool whisk the custard and fold in the whipped cream. Spoon it into a freezer container and freeze, whisking once every hour for 2–3 hours, or churn in an ice-cream maker until almost frozen, then transfer to the freezer.

Energy 546kcal/2264kJ; Protein 6.8g; Carbohydrate 25.6g, of which sugars 24.4g; Fat 47.1g, of which saturates 27.4g; Cholesterol 309mg; Calcium 160mg; Fibre 0g; Sodium 60mg.

Brown bread ice cream

The secret of a good brown bread ice cream is not to have too many breadcrumbs and, for the best texture and deep, nutty flavour, to toast them until really crisp and well browned.

Serves 6–8

115g/4oz/2 cups wholemeal (whole-wheat) breadcrumbs

115g/4oz/½ cup soft (light) brown sugar

2 large (US extra large) eggs, separated

30–45ml/2–3 tbsp Irish Cream liqueur

450ml/¾ pint/scant 2 cups double (heavy) cream, whipped until stiff

1 Preheat the oven to 190°C/375°F/ Gas 5. Spread the breadcrumbs out on a baking sheet and toast them in the oven for about 15 minutes, or until crisp and well browned. Leave to cool.

2 Whisk the sugar and egg yolks together until light and creamy, then beat in the Irish Cream.

3 Stir the breadcrumbs and the whipped cream into the mixture with a spoon.

4 In a separate bowl, whisk the egg whites until stiff peaks form. Fold the whisked egg whites into the ice cream mixture, until completely combined.

5 Turn the mixture into a freezerproof container, cover and freeze for around 3 hours, whisking every hour, or churn in an ice-cream maker, until it is completely frozen, then transfer to the freezer. Allow to soften before serving.

Energy 561Kcal/2332kJ; Protein 6g; Carbohydrate 37.3g, of which sugars 23g; Fat 43.6g, of which saturates 25.7g; Cholesterol 179mg; Calcium 84mg; Fibre 0.4g; Sodium 196mg

Fresh strawberry ice cream

You can make the ice cream by hand if you freeze it over a period of several hours, whisking it every hour or so, but it is easier if you have an ice-cream maker.

2 Return the mixture to the clean pan and heat, stirring, until the custard just coats the back of the spoon. Pour the custard into a bowl, cover the surface with plastic wrap and set aside to cool.

3 Meanwhile, purée the strawberries with the lemon juice in a food processor or blender. Use a wooden spoon to press the strawberry purée through a sieve (strainer) into a bowl. Stir in the icing sugar and set aside.

4 Whip the cream to soft peaks, then gently but thoroughly fold it into the custard with the strawberry purée.

5 Pour the mixture into an ice cream maker. Churn for 20–30 minutes or until the mixture holds its shape.

6 Transfer the ice cream to a freezerproof container, cover and freeze until firm. Soften briefly before serving with the strawberries.

Serves 6

300ml/½ pint/1¼ cups creamy milk

1 vanilla pod (bean)

3 large (US extra large) egg yolks

225g/8oz/1½–2 cups strawberries

juice of ½ lemon

75g/3oz/¾ cup icing (confectioners') sugar

300ml/½ pint/1¼ cups double (heavy) cream

sliced strawberries, to serve

1 Pour the milk into a pan, add the vanilla pod and bring to the boil over a low heat. Remove from the heat. Leave for 20 minutes, then remove the vanilla pod. Strain the warm milk into a bowl containing the egg yolks; whisk well.

Energy 244kcal/1012kJ; Protein 2.4g; Carbohydrate 12.2g, of which sugars 10.4g; Fat 20.4g, of which saturates 12.1g; Cholesterol 51mg; Calcium 73mg; Fibre 0.7g; Sodium 32mg.

Mint ice cream

When mint is taking over the herb garden, this is a good recipe to make use of it. Ice cream is best eaten slightly softened, so take it out of the freezer 20 minutes before serving.

Serves 8

8 egg yolks

75g/3oz/6 tbsp caster (superfine) sugar

600ml/1 pint/2½ cups single (light) cream

1 vanilla pod (bean)

60ml/4 tbsp chopped fresh mint

1 Beat the egg yolks and sugar until they are pale and light using a hand-held electric beater or a balloon whisk. Transfer to a small pan.

2 In a separate pan, bring the cream to the boil with the vanilla pod.

3 Remove the vanilla pod and pour the hot cream on to the egg mixture, whisking briskly. Keep whisking to ensure the eggs are thoroughly mixed into the cream.

4 Gently heat the mixture until the custard thickens enough to coat the back of a wooden spoon. Leave to cool.

Farmhouse tip Don't throw away the vanilla pod once you have used it; dry it completely, then store in a jar of sugar to make vanilla sugar.

5 Stir in the mint and place in an ice-cream maker to churn for 3–4 hours. If you don't have an ice-cream maker, freeze until mushy and then whisk it to break down the ice crystals. Freeze for another 3 hours until it is softly frozen and whisk again. Finally freeze until hard: at least 6 hours.

Energy 206kcal/851kJ; Protein 5g; Carbohydrate 2g, of which sugars 2g; Fat 20g, of which saturates 11g; Cholesterol 243mg; Calcium 90mg; Fibre 0.0g; Sodium 31mg.

Country Kitchen Cakes

It is true that baking is an art, and probably the one most associated with a farmhouse kitchen, but it isn't hard to learn how to make perfect cakes. This chapter shows you how to create all the classics, from tea loaves to sponges, iced cakes and plain, so that you can fill your own kitchen with the enticing aromas of home-baked cakes.

Victoria sponge

This cake was named in honour of England's Queen Victoria, and is a favourite at village baking competitions. Fill with jam or preserves of your choice, or soft summer fruits.

Serves 6–8

3 large (US extra large) eggs

few drops of vanilla extract

175g/6oz/¾ cup butter, softened

175g/6oz/¾ cup caster (superfine) sugar

175g/6oz/1½ cups self-raising (self-rising) flour

about 60ml/4 tbsp jam

icing (confectioners') sugar, to dust

1 Preheat the oven to 180°C/350°F/ Gas 4. Butter two 20cm/8in sandwich tins (layer pans) and line the bases of each with baking parchment.

2 Lightly beat the eggs with the vanilla extract. In a large mixing bowl, whisk the butter with the sugar until the mixture is pale, light and fluffy.

3 Gradually add the eggs, beating well after each addition. Sift the flour over the top and, using a metal spoon, fold in lightly until the mixture is smooth.

4 Divide the mixture between the prepared tins and smooth the surface level. Bake for 20 minutes until golden and firm to the touch.

5 Leave the cakes to cool in the tins for a few minutes, then carefully turn out on to a wire rack. Remove the paper and leave to cool completely.

6 When the cakes are cold, sandwich the two halves together with plenty of jam. Finally, sift a little icing sugar over the top to cover the surface of the cake.

Variations Instead of vanilla extract, beat a little finely grated lemon rind into the butter and sugar mixture in step 2. Sandwich the cakes together with lemon curd.
   For a cream cake, sandwich with a thin layer of strawberry jam and a thick layer of whipped cream, topped with sliced fresh strawberries. Decorate the top of the cake with whipped cream and extra strawberries.

Energy 368kcal/1543kJ; Protein 4.6g; Carbohydrate 44.7g, of which sugars 28.5g; Fat 20.3g, of which saturates 12g; Cholesterol 118mg; Calcium 104mg; Fibre 0.7g; Sodium 241mg.

Iced chocolate cake

Chocolate cake is a staple of every self-respecting country tea table. A luxurious afternoon treat, this impressive cake with chocolate buttercream couldn't be more tempting.

Serves 10–12

225g/8oz/2 cups plain (all-purpose) flour

5ml/1 tsp bicarbonate of soda (baking soda)

50g/2oz/½ cup (unsweetened) cocoa powder

125g/4½oz/9 tbsp soft butter

250g/9oz/1¼ cups caster (superfine) sugar

3 eggs, beaten

250ml/8fl oz/1 cup buttermilk

For the chocolate buttercream

175g/6oz/1½ cups icing (confectioners') sugar

115g/4oz/½ cup butter, softened

few drops of vanilla extract

50g/2oz dark (bittersweet) chocolate

5 Beat in half the sifted icing sugar until smooth and light. Gradually beat in the remaining sugar and the vanilla extract. Break the chocolate into squares. Melt in a bowl over a pan of hot water or in a microwave oven on low.

1 Butter two 20cm/8in sandwich tins (layer pans) and line the bases with baking parchment. Preheat the oven to 180°C/350°F/Gas 4. Sift the flour with the bicarbonate of soda and cocoa and stir together.

2 Beat the butter and sugar until light and fluffy. Gradually beat in the eggs. Add the flour and buttermilk; mix well.

3 Spoon into the prepared tins. Place into the hot oven and bake for 30–35 minutes until firm to the touch. Turn out of the tins, peel off the paper and leave on a wire rack to cool completely.

4 To make the chocolate buttercream, sift the icing sugar into a bowl. In a separate bowl, beat the butter until very soft and creamy.

6 Mix the melted chocolate into the buttercream. Use half to sandwich the cakes together, and the rest on the top.

Energy 430kcal/1790kJ; Protein 7.8g; Carbohydrate 29.5g, of which sugars 28.8g; Fat 32.1g, of which saturates 13.6g; Cholesterol 96mg; Calcium 92mg; Fibre 1.9g; Sodium 125mg.

Boston cream pie

Actually a sponge cake filled with custard rather than cream and topped with a dark chocolate glaze, this cake is a reworking of the early American pudding cake pie.

Serves 8–10

225g/8oz/2 cups self-raising (self-rising) flour

15ml/1 tbsp baking powder

2.5ml/½ tsp salt

115g/4oz/½ cup butter, softened

200g/7oz/1 cup granulated (white) sugar

2 eggs

5ml/1 tsp vanilla extract

175ml/6fl oz/¾ cup milk

For the filling

250ml/8fl oz/1 cup milk

3 egg yolks

90g/3½oz/½ cup granulated (white) sugar

25g/1oz/¼ cup plain (all-purpose) flour

15g/½oz/1 tbsp butter

15ml/1 tbsp brandy or 5ml/1 tsp vanilla extract

For the chocolate glaze

25g/1oz cooking (unsweetened) chocolate

25g/1oz/2 tbsp butter

90g/3½oz/½ cup icing (confectioners') sugar, plus extra for dusting

2.5ml/½ tsp vanilla extract

about 15ml/1 tbsp hot water

1 Preheat the oven to 190°F/375°F/Gas 5. Butter two 20cm/8in shallow round cake tins (pans), and line the bases with baking parchment.

2 Sift the flour with the baking powder and salt.

3 Beat the butter and granulated sugar together until light and fluffy. Add the eggs one at a time, beating well after each addition. Stir in the vanilla. Add the milk and flour mixture alternately, mixing only enough to blend thoroughly. Do not over-beat the batter.

4 Divide the mixture between the prepared tins and spread it out evenly. Bake until a skewer inserted in the centre comes out clean, about 25 minutes.

5 Meanwhile, make the filling. Heat the milk in a small pan to boiling point. Remove from the heat.

6 In a heatproof mixing bowl, beat the egg yolks. Gradually add the granulated sugar and continue beating until pale yellow. Beat in the flour.

7 Pour the hot milk into the egg yolk mixture in a steady stream, beating constantly. When all the milk has been added, place the bowl over a pan of simmering water, or pour the mixture into the top of a double boiler. Heat for 30 minutes, stirring constantly, until thickened. Remove from the heat. Stir in the butter and brandy or vanilla. Chill for 2–3 hours or until set.

8 When the cake layers have cooled, use a large sharp knife to slice off the domed top to make a flat surface, if necessary. Place one layer on a serving plate and spread the filling on in a thick layer. Set the other layer on top, cut side down. Smooth the edge of the filling layer so it is flush with the sides of the cake layers.

9 For the glaze, melt the chocolate with the butter in a heatproof bowl set over a pan of hot water. When smooth, remove from the heat and beat in the icing sugar to make a thick paste. Add the vanilla. Beat in a little of the hot water. If the glaze does not have a spreadable consistency, add more water, 5ml/1 tsp at a time.

10 Spread the glaze evenly over the top of the cake, using a metal spatula. Dust the top with icing sugar. Because of the custard filling, any leftover cake must be chilled in the refrigerator, and can be stored for up to 3 days.

Energy 499kcal/2099kJ; Protein 6g; Carbohydrate 77g, of which sugars 53.1g; Fat 20.3g, of which saturates 12.1g; Cholesterol 146mg; Calcium 112mg; Fibre 1g; Sodium 296mg.

Swedish farmhouse plum and almond cake

Seasonal country cooking is an obvious necessity in cold areas that have fierce extremes of climate. Orchards have always been especially prized, and apple, pear and plum trees thrive in many cold countries. These fruits add sweetness, texture and variety to cakes. This sponge is best served warm and is equally good made with apricots or nectarines. The cardamom gives a hint of spice, which complements the fruit perfectly.

Serves 10–12

450g/1lb stone (pitted) fresh plums, coarsely chopped, plus 9 extra plums, stoned (pitted) and halved, to decorate

300ml/½ pint/1¼ cups water

115g/4oz/½ cup unsalted butter, softened

200g/7oz/1 cup caster (superfine) sugar

3 eggs

90g/3½oz/¾ cup toasted almonds, finely chopped

5ml/1 tsp bicarbonate of soda (baking soda)

7.5ml/1½ tsp baking powder

5ml/1 tsp ground cardamom

1.5ml/¼ tsp salt

250g/9oz/2¼ cups plain (all-purpose) flour

15ml/1 tbsp pearl sugar, or crushed sugar cubes, to decorate

250ml/8fl oz/1 cup double (heavy) cream

10ml/2 tsp vanilla sugar

10ml/2 tsp icing (confectioners') sugar

1 Place the chopped plums in a pan and add the water. Bring to the boil over a medium heat and cook for 10–15 minutes, until soft. Set aside to cool. You will need 350ml/12fl oz/ 1½ cups stewed plums for the cake.

2 Preheat the oven to 180°C/350°F/ Gas 4. Grease and flour a 24cm/9½in springform cake tin (pan).

3 Cream the butter with the sugar in a mixing bowl until light and fluffy. Beat in the eggs, one at a time.

4 Stir in the stewed plums and the almonds. Mix in the bicarbonate, baking powder, cardamom and salt.

5 Gradually stir in the flour, a few spoons at a time, and mix until blended.

6 Pour the mixture into the prepared tin. Place 15 plum halves around the circumference of the cake and the remaining three halves in the centre, cut sides down. Sprinkle the pearl sugar over the cake.

7 Bake for 1 hour, or until the top springs back when lightly touched. Cool in the tin for 15 minutes before unfastening the ring.

8 Beat the double cream until soft peaks form. Stir in the vanilla sugar and the icing sugar and beat until thick.

9 Serve the cake, still slightly warm, or at room temperature, in slices topped with a dollop of whipped cream.

Energy 311kcal/1308kJ; Protein 6.4g; Carbohydrate 44.5g, of which sugars 15.9g; Fat 13.2g, of which saturates 7.4g; Cholesterol 89mg; Calcium 86mg; Fibre 2.4g; Sodium 102mg.

Moist orange and almond cake

The key to this recipe is to cook the orange slowly first, so it is fully tender before being blended. Don't use a microwave to speed things up – this makes orange skin tough.

Serves 8–10

1 large orange, washed and pierced

3 eggs

225g/8oz/generous 1 cup caster (superfine) sugar

5ml/1 tsp baking powder

225g/8oz/2 cups ground almonds

25g/1oz/¼ cup plain (all-purpose) flour

icing (confectioner's) sugar, for dusting

whipped cream and orange slices (optional), to serve

1 Put the orange in a pan. Add water to cover. Bring to the boil, lower the heat, cover and simmer for 1 hour. Cool.

2 Preheat the oven to 180°C/350°F/ Gas 4. Grease a 20cm/8in round cake tin (pan) and line it with baking parchment. Cut the orange in half and discard the pips. Place the orange, skin and all, in a blender or food processor and purée until smooth and pulpy.

3 In a bowl, whisk the eggs and sugar until thick. Fold in the baking powder, almonds and flour. Fold in the purée.

4 Pour into the prepared tin and bake for 1 hour or until a skewer inserted into the middle comes out clean. Cool in the tin for 10 minutes, then turn out on to a wire rack, peel off the lining paper and cool completely.

5 Dust with icing sugar and serve in slices, with cream if you wish. For added colour, tuck thick orange slices under the cake just before serving.

Energy 187kcal/783kJ; Protein 5.1g; Carbohydrate 20g, of which sugars 18.2g; Fat 10.2g, of which saturates 1.1g; Cholesterol 41mg; Calcium 60mg; Fibre 1.4g; Sodium 19mg.

Courgette and double-ginger cake

Both fresh and preserved ginger are used to flavour this unusual tea bread. It is delicious served warm, cut into thick slices and spread with butter.

Serves 8–10

3 eggs

225g/8oz/generous 1 cup caster (superfine) sugar

250ml/8fl oz/1 cup sunflower oil

5ml/1 tsp vanilla extract

15ml/1 tbsp syrup from a jar of preserved stem ginger

225g/8oz courgettes (zucchini), grated

2.5cm/1in piece fresh root ginger, grated

350g/12oz/3 cups plain (all-purpose) flour

5ml/1 tsp baking powder

pinch of salt

5ml/1 tsp ground cinnamon

2 pieces preserved stem ginger, chopped

15ml/1 tbsp demerara (raw) sugar

1 Beat together the eggs and sugar until light and fluffy. Slowly beat in the oil until the mixture forms a batter.

2 Mix the vanilla extract and ginger syrup into the batter, then stir in the courgettes and fresh ginger. Preheat the oven to 190°C/ 325°F/Gas 5.

3 Lightly grease a 900g/2lb loaf tin. Sift the flour, baking powder, salt and cinnamon into the eggs, sugar and courgette mixture in batches. Beat well to combine after each addition.

Variation Grated carrots – and even parsnips – can be used in place of courgettes in this tea bread.

4 Pour the cake mixture in to the loaf tin (pan). Smooth and level the top, then sprinkle the chopped ginger and demerara sugar over the surface.

5 Bake for 1 hour until a skewer inserted into the centre comes out clean. Leave to cool for 20 minutes, then turn out on to a wire rack.

Energy 252Kcal/1060kJ; Protein 5.6g; Carbohydrate 35.6g, of which sugars 8.8g; Fat 10.7g, of which saturates 1.6g; Cholesterol 57mg; Calcium 73mg; Fibre 1.3g; Sodium 82mg.

Lemon-frosted whiskey cake

This light, moist cake has the subtle flavours of lemon and cloves. Thickly frosted with a zesty lemon icing, it makes a great winter cake using mostly store-cupboard ingredients.

4 Beat the yolks into the butter and sugar one at a time, adding a little of the flour with each egg and beating well after each addition. Gradually blend in the sultana and whiskey mixture, alternating with the remaining flour. Do not overbeat at this stage.

5 Whisk the egg whites until stiff, then fold them into the mixture with a metal spoon. Turn into the prepared tin and bake in the preheated oven for 1½ hours, or until well risen and springy to the touch. Turn out and cool on a rack.

Serves 8–10

225g/8oz/1⅓ cups sultanas (golden raisins)

grated rind of 1 lemon

150ml/¼ pint/⅔ cup Irish whiskey

175g/6oz/¾ cup butter, softened

175g/6oz/¾ cup soft light brown sugar

175g/6oz/1½ cups plain (all-purpose) flour

pinch of salt

1.5ml/¼ tsp ground cloves

5ml/1 tsp baking powder

3 large (US extra large) eggs, separated

For the icing

juice of 1 lemon

225g/8oz/2 cups icing (confectioners') sugar, sifted

crystallized lemon slices, to decorate (optional)

1 Put the sultanas and grated lemon rind into a bowl with the whiskey and leave overnight to soak.

2 Preheat the oven to 180°C/350°F/ Gas 4. Grease and line a loose-based 18cm/7in round deep cake tin (pan).

3 Cream the butter and sugar until light and fluffy. Sift the flour, salt, cloves and baking powder together into a bowl.

6 Make the icing: mix the lemon juice with the icing sugar and enough warm water to make a pouring consistency.

7 Lay a plate under the rack and pour the icing over the cake, letting it dribble down the sides. Any icing dripping on to the plate may be scooped up and put on top again. When the icing has set, decorate the cake with lemon slices, if you like.

Energy 469kcal/1973kJ; Protein 4.8g; Carbohydrate 71.1g, of which sugars 57.7g; Fat 16.7g, of which saturates 9.7g; Cholesterol 0.1g; Calcium 73.5mg; Fibre 0.9g; Sodium 0.13g.

Apple and cinnamon cake

Moist and spicy, this cake is perfect for packed lunches or afternoon tea. Spread thickly
with butter to make it extra special.

Serves 12–14

115g/4oz/½ cup butter, softened,
plus extra for greasing

200g/7oz/1¼ cups dried, stoned
(pitted) dates

1–2 tart eating apples or 1 cooking
apple, about 225g/8oz

7.5ml/1½ tsp mixed (apple pie) spice

5ml/1 tsp ground cinnamon

pinch of salt

75g/3oz/½ cup raisins

2 eggs, beaten

150g/5oz/1¼ cups wholemeal
(whole-wheat) flour, sifted

115g/4oz/generous 1 cup gram flour,
sifted with 10ml/2 tsp baking
powder

175ml/6fl oz/¾ cup unsweetened
coconut milk

3 Scrape the apple and date mixture
into a bowl and fold in the raisins and
beaten eggs alternately with the flours,
baking powder and coconut milk.
Transfer to the prepared tin and smooth
the surface level.

4 Bake for 30–40 minutes until dark
golden and firm to the touch. A skewer
inserted in the centre should come out
clean. Cool the cake in the tin for
15 minutes before turning out on to a
wire rack to cool completely.

1 Preheat the oven to 180°C/350°F/
Gas 4. Grease and line a deep 20cm/8in
square baking tin (pan). Combine the
butter and the dates in a processor.

2 Peel, core and grate the apple or
apples and add to the butter and date
mixture together with the mixed spice,
cinnamon and salt. Process until
thoroughly blended.

Energy 146.5kcals/613kJ; Protein 0g; Carbohydrate 21.4g of which sugars 10.7g; Fat, total 5.1g of which saturates 0.3g; Cholesterol 0g; Calcium 0mg; Fibre 2.45g; Sodium 172mg.

Carrot and parsnip cake

The grated carrots and parsnips in this deliciously light and moist cake add sweetness, while the unusual cooked meringue topping makes a wonderful contrast to the cake's crumb.

Serves 10–12

oil, for greasing

1 lemon

1 orange

15ml/1 tbsp caster (superfine) sugar

225g/8oz/1 cup butter, softened

225g/8oz/1 cup soft light brown sugar

4 eggs

225g/8oz/1²⁄3 cups carrot and parsnip, grated

115g/4oz/1¼ cups sultanas (golden raisins)

225g/8oz/2 cups self-raising (self-rising) wholemeal (whole-wheat) flour

5ml/1 tsp baking powder

For the meringue topping

50g/2oz/¼ cup caster (superfine) sugar

1 egg white

pinch of salt

1 Preheat the oven to 180°C/350°F/ Gas 4. Lightly grease a 20cm/8in loose-based cake tin (pan) and line the base with a circle of baking parchment.

2 Finely grate the lemon and orange rind. Put about half of it in a bowl, and mix with the caster sugar. Spread this on a sheet of baking parchment and leave in a warm place, to dry.

3 Cream the butter and sugar until pale and fluffy. Add the eggs gradually, then beat well. Stir in the unsugared rinds, the grated carrots and parsnips, 30ml/ 2 tbsp orange juice and the sultanas.

4 Gradually fold in the flour and baking powder, and spoon into the prepared tin. Bake for 1½ hours until risen, golden and just firm.

5 Leave the cake to cool slightly in the tin, then turn out on to a serving plate.

6 For the meringue topping, place the caster sugar in a bowl over a pan of simmering water with 30ml/2 tbsp of the remaining orange juice. Stir over the heat until the sugar begins to dissolve. Remove from the heat, add the egg white and salt, and whisk for 1 minute.

7 Return to the heat and whisk for a further 6 minutes until the mixture becomes stiff and glossy, holding a good shape. Allow to cool slightly, whisking frequently.

8 Swirl the cooled topping over the cake and leave to firm up for about 1 hour. To serve, sprinkle with the sugared lemon and orange rind, which should now be dry and crumbly.

Variation If you do not have any parsnips, just use carrots. Add a pinch of cinnamon if you wish.

Energy 414kcal/1734kJ; Protein 6.2g; Carbohydrate 52.8g, of which sugars 38.9g; Fat 21.3g, of which saturates 12.4g; Cholesterol 124mg; Calcium 47mg; Fibre 2.3g; Sodium 175mg.

Old-fashioned treacle cake

Quick to make and very moreish, this fruit-studded, crumbly cake would have originally been baked on a stove in a tin plate. The black treacle gives the cake a deep flavour.

Serves 8–10

250g/9oz/2¼ cups self-raising (self-rising) flour

2.5ml/½ tsp mixed (apple pie) spice

75g/3oz/6 tbsp butter, diced

35g/1oz/2 tbsp caster (superfine) sugar

150g/5oz/1 cup mixed dried fruit

1 egg

15ml/1 tbsp black treacle (molasses)

100ml/3½fl oz/scant ½ cup milk

3 Beat the egg and, with a small whisk or a fork, stir in the treacle and then the milk. Stir the liquid into the flour to make a fairly stiff but moist consistency, adding a little extra milk if necessary.

4 Transfer the cake mixture to the prepared dish or tin and level out the surface with a spoon.

5 Bake the cake in the hot oven for about 1 hour until it has risen, is firm to the touch and fully cooked through. To check if the cake is cooked, insert a small skewer in the centre – it should come out free of sticky mixture.

6 Leave the cake to cool completely for several hours. Serve it straight from the dish, cut into wedges.

1 Preheat the oven to 180°C/350°F/ Gas 5. Grease a shallow 20–23cm/ 8–9in ovenproof flan dish or baking tin (pan).

2 Sift the flour and spice into a large mixing bowl. Add the butter and, with your fingertips, rub it into the flour until the mixture resembles fine crumbs. Alternatively, you could do this in a food processor. Stir in the sugar and mixed dried fruit.

Variation Try varying the fruit in this recipe. Experiment with chopped ready-to-eat dried apricots and preserved stem ginger, or a packet of luxury dried fruit. Chopped dates or figs work well too, and make the cake more substantial.

Energy 209kcal/880kJ; Protein 3.7g; Carbohydrate 34g, of which sugars 15.2g; Fat 7.3g, of which saturates 4.2g; Cholesterol 36mg; Calcium 72mg; Fibre 1.1g; Sodium 67mg.

Lemon drizzle cake

This is a classic recipe, which is very easy to make. You can also make the cake with a large orange instead of the lemons; either way, it makes a zesty treat for afternoon tea.

Serves 6–8

175g/6oz/³⁄₄ cup caster (superfine) sugar, plus extra to decorate

finely grated rind of 2 lemons

225g/8oz/1 cup butter, softened

4 eggs

225g/8oz/2 cups self-raising (self-rising) flour

5ml/1 tsp baking powder

shredded rind of 1 lemon, to decorate

For the syrup

juice of 1 lemon

150g/5oz/³⁄₄ cup sugar

1 Preheat the oven to 160°C/325°F/ Gas 3. Grease a 1kg/2lb loaf tin or 18–20cm/7–8in round cake tin and line it with baking parchment.

2 Place the sugar in a small bowl and add the grated lemon rind. Mix together with a fork. In a large bowl cream the butter, add the lemon and sugar mixture and beat until fluffy.

3 Add the eggs and mix until smooth. Sift the flour and baking powder into a bowl and fold a third at a time into the mixture.

4 Turn the batter into the tin, smooth the top and bake for 1¹⁄₂ hours or until golden brown and springy to the touch.

5 To make the syrup, in a small pan slowly heat the juice with the sugar until dissolved.

6 Remove the cake from the oven but leave in the tin. Make several slashes in the top of the cake with a sharp knife, and pour over the syrup. Sprinkle the shredded lemon rind and sugar on top and leave to cool completely, before removing from the tin.

Energy 659kcal/2765kJ; Protein 8g; Carbohydrate 84.1g, of which sugars 56.2g; Fat 34.8g, of which saturates 21.4g; Cholesterol 213mg; Calcium 184mg; Fibre 1.2g; Sodium 466mg.

Pear and sultana teabread

This is an ideal teabread to make when pears are plentiful – an excellent use for windfalls.
It will freeze well, and makes a good lunchbox cake.

3 Core and grate the pear. Mix into the oat mixture with the flour, sultanas, baking powder, mixed spice and egg.

4 Spoon the mixture into the loaf tin and level the top. Bake for 50–60 minutes, or until a skewer inserted into the centre comes out clean.

Serves 6–8

25g/1oz/scant ⅓ cup rolled oats

50g/2oz/⅓ cup light brown sugar

30ml/2 tbsp pear or apple juice

30ml/2 tbsp sunflower oil

1 large or 2 small pears, quartered

115g/4oz/1 cup self-raising (self-rising) flour

115g/4oz/⅔ cup sultanas (golden raisins)

2.5ml/½ tsp baking powder

10ml/2 tsp mixed (apple pie) spice

1 egg

1 Preheat the oven to 180°C/350°F/Gas 4. Grease and line a 450g/1lb loaf tin (pan) with baking parchment.

2 Put the oats in a bowl with the sugar, pour over the pear or apple juice and oil, mix and set aside for 15 minutes.

5 Transfer the teabread on to a wire rack and peel off the lining paper. Leave to cool completely.

Farmhouse tip Health food shops sell concentrated pear and apple juice, ready for diluting as required.

Energy 184kcal/780kJ; Protein 3.1g; Carbohydrate 36.3g, of which sugars 23.1g; Fat 4g, of which saturates 0.6g; Cholesterol 24mg; Calcium 43mg; Fibre 1.8g; Sodium 16mg.

Bara brith fruited teabread

The name for this traditional Welsh loaf means 'speckled bread'. For a hint of citrus, add grated lemon or orange rind to the batter before baking. Spread with butter and honey.

Serves 10–12

225g/8oz/1⅓ cups mixed dried fruit and chopped mixed (candied) peel

225ml/8fl oz/1 cup hot, strong tea, strained

225g/8oz/2 cups self-raising (self-rising) flour

5ml/1 tsp mixed (apple pie) spice

25g/1oz/2 tbsp butter

100g/3½oz/½ cup soft dark brown sugar

egg, lightly beaten

Farmhouse tip The flavour of the loaf can be varied slightly by using different flavoured teas – try the distinctive perfume of Earl Grey.

1 Put the fruit into a heatproof bowl and pour the hot tea over it. Cover and leave to stand at room temperature for several hours or overnight.

2 Preheat the oven to 180°C/350°F/ Gas 4. Grease a 900g/2lb loaf tin (pan) and line it with baking parchment.

3 Sift the flour and the mixed spice into a large mixing bowl. Add the butter and, with your fingertips, rub it into the flour until the mixture starts to resemble fine breadcrumbs.

4 Stir the soft brown sugar into the flour and spice mixture, then add the dried fruit and its liquid along with the beaten egg. Stir well with a wooden spoon to make a mixture with a soft, dropping consistency.

5 Transfer the mixture to the prepared loaf tin and level the surface. Bake for about 1 hour or until a skewer inserted in the centre comes out clean. Turn out on a wire rack, remove the paper lining and leave to cool completely.

Energy 168kcal/715kJ; Protein 2.7g; Carbohydrate 36g, of which sugars 21.7g; Fat 2.5g, of which saturates 1.2g; Cholesterol 20mg; Calcium 47mg; Fibre 0.9g; Sodium 28.5mg.

Banana bread

Any very ripe bananas that have been abandoned in the fruit bowl are perfect for this recipe. This cake is always a favourite with children.

Serves 6–8

115g/4oz/½ cup butter, softened, plus extra for greasing

5ml/1 tsp bicarbonate of soda (baking soda)

225g/8oz/2 cups wholemeal (whole-wheat) flour

2 eggs, beaten

3 very ripe bananas

30–45ml/2–3 tbsp sweetened condensed milk

1 Preheat the oven to 180°C/350°F/Gas 4. Grease and base line a 23 x 13cm/9 x 5in loaf tin.

2 Cream the butter in a large bowl until it is fluffy. Sift the bicarbonate of soda with the flour, then add to the creamed butter, alternately with the beaten eggs.

Variation Sunflower seeds make a good addition to banana cake. Add about 50g/2oz/½ cup to the mixture just before baking.

3 Peel the bananas and slice them into a bowl. Mash them well, then stir them into the cake mixture. Mix in the condensed milk.

4 Spoon the mixture into the loaf tin and level the surface with a spoon. Bake for about 1¼ hours or until a fine skewer inserted in the centre comes out clean. Cool on a wire rack.

Energy 2265kcal/9548kJ; Protein 51.9g; Carbohydrate 372.4g, of which sugars 195.9g; Fat 73.6g, of which saturates 38.4g; Cholesterol 519mg; Calcium 461mg; Fibre 18.9g; Sodium 553mg.

Yorkshire parkin

This moist treacle cake is traditionally served cut into squares. In former days, when a quantity of parkin was being baked, one batch was sometimes eaten hot with apple sauce.

Makes 16–20 squares

300ml/½ pint/1¼ cups milk

225g/8oz/generous ½ cup golden (light corn) syrup

225g/8oz/generous ½ cup black treacle (molasses)

115g/4oz/½ cup butter

50g/2oz/¼ cup soft dark brown sugar

450g/1lb/4 cups plain (all-purpose) flour

2.5ml/½ tsp bicarbonate of soda (baking soda)

7.5ml/1½ tsp ground ginger

350g/12oz/3 cups medium oatmeal

1 egg, beaten

icing (confectioner's) sugar, to dust

1 Preheat the oven to 180°C/350°F/ Gas 4. Gently heat together the milk, syrup, treacle, butter and sugar, stirring until smooth; do not boil. Grease a 20cm/8in square cake tin (pan) and line the base and sides with baking parchment.

Farmhouse tip The flavour and texture of the cake improves if it is wrapped in foil and stored in an airtight container for several days.

2 Sift the flour into a bowl and add the bicarbonate of soda, ginger and oatmeal. Make a well in the centre and add the egg, then the warmed mixture, stirring to make a smooth batter.

3 Pour the batter into the tin and bake for about 45 minutes, until firm to the touch. Cool slightly in the tin, then turn out on to a wire rack to cool completely. Cut into squares and dust with icing sugar.

Energy 273kcal/1152kJ; Protein 5.3g; Carbohydrate 50g, of which sugars 20.1g; Fat 7.1g, of which saturates 3.3g; Cholesterol 23mg; Calcium 127mg; Fibre 1.9g; Sodium 102mg

Honey cake

The type of honey you choose affects the flavour of this cake. Use a darker honey in the recipe, then drizzle over a flower honey such as orange blossom while the cake is still warm.

2 In a pan, gently heat the butter, honey and sugar, stirring frequently until the sugar has dissolved. Set aside and leave to cool slightly.

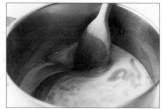

3 Beat the eggs and milk into the cooled mixture. Sift the flour over the top, stir in and beat well until smooth.

4 Place the mixture into the prepared tin, levelling the surface. Put into the hot oven and cook for about 30 minutes until well risen, golden brown and firm to the touch.

5 Leave the cake to cool in the tin for 20 minutes, then turn out, leaving the lining paper in place, on to a wire rack and leave to cool completely.

6 Peel off the paper and cut the cake into squares.

Serves 10–12

175g/6oz/¾ cup butter

175g/6oz/¾ cup clear honey

115g/4oz/½ cup soft (light) brown sugar

2 eggs, lightly beaten

15–30ml/1–2 tbsp milk

225g/8oz/2 cups self-raising (self-rising) flour

1 Grease and line a 23cm/9in square cake tin (pan) with baking parchment. Preheat the oven to 180°C/350°F/Gas 4.

Variation Add 5ml/1 tsp ground cinnamon or grated nutmeg to the flour in step 3.

Energy 152kcal/639kJ; Protein 1.9g; Carbohydrate 23.5g, of which sugars 13g; Fat 6.3g, of which saturates 3.8g; Cholesterol 26mg; Calcium 30mg; Fibre 0.4g; Sodium 49mg.

Dark and sticky gingerbread

This is a really special gingerbread. The secret of its dark richness lies in the amount of treacle used. Make it a couple of days in advance so it can develop its stickiness.

Serves 10–12

225g/8oz/2 cups plain (all-purpose) flour

10ml/2 tsp ground ginger

5ml/1 tsp mixed (apple pie) spice

a pinch of salt

2 pieces (preserved) stem ginger, drained and chopped

115g/4oz/½ cup butter, softened

115g/4oz/¾ cup dark muscovado (molasses) sugar, sifted

275g/10oz/scant 1 cup black treacle (molasses), at room temperature

2 eggs, beaten

2.5ml/½ tsp bicarbonate of soda (baking soda)

30ml/2 tbsp milk, warmed

butter or cream cheese, to serve

1 Preheat the oven to 160°C/325°F/Gas 3. Grease and line the base of an 18cm/7in square cake tin (pan).

2 Sift the flour, ground ginger, mixed spice and salt into a bowl. Add the chopped preserved stem ginger and toss it in the flour to coat.

3 In a large bowl, cream the butter and sugar together until fluffy.

4 Stir the treacle in to the butter and sugar mixture, gradually beat in the eggs, then fold in the flour mixture.

5 Dissolve the bicarbonate of soda in the milk and gradually beat this into the mixture. Pour the mixture into the prepared tin. Bake for 45 minutes.

6 Reduce the oven temperature to 150°C/300°F/Gas 2 and bake for a further 30 minutes. Remove from the oven when dark and slightly risen, and check the cake is cooked by inserting a metal skewer into the middle. If it comes out clean, the cake is cooked through. Don't worry if the gingerbread sinks slightly in the middle.

7 Cool the gingerbread for 5 minutes in the tin, then turn out and cool on a wire rack. At this stage, the gingerbread will be dark, but not sticky. Keep it for 2–3 days in an airtight container so the outside becomes sticky and moist. Slice when ready, then spread with butter or cream cheese.

Energy 189kcal/7994kJ; Protein 3g; Carbohydrate 33g, of which sugars 21g; Fat 27.5g, of which saturates 2.3g; Cholesterol 4.3mg; Calcium 49mg; Fibre 8.3g; Sodium 77mg.

Pound cake

The name for this traditional plain cake dates back to the 1700s in England, when the
ingredients were 1lb each of butter, sugar, eggs and flour.

Serves 6–8

450g/1lb/3 cups fresh raspberries,
strawberries or stoned (pitted)
cherries, or any combination

175g/6oz/³⁄₄ cup caster (superfine)
sugar, plus extra for sprinkling

15ml/1 tbsp lemon juice

175g/6oz/³⁄₄ cup butter, softened

3 eggs

grated rind of 1 orange

15ml/1 tbsp orange juice

175g/6oz/1½ cups plain (all-purpose)
flour, sifted

pinch of salt

10ml/2 tsp baking powder

1 Reserve a few whole, perfect berries
for decorating. In a food processor
fitted with the metal blade, process the
remaining fruit until smooth.

2 Add 30ml/2 tbsp of the sugar and the
lemon juice, then process again to
combine until the sugar dissolves. Strain
the sauce and chill. Preheat the oven to
180°C/ 350°F/Gas 4.

3 Line and grease a 20 x 10cm/8 x 4in
loaf tin (pan). Sprinkle the base and
sides of the tin lightly with sugar and
tip out any excess.

4 In a medium bowl, beat the butter
until creamy. Add the remaining sugar
and beat for 4–5 minutes until light and
fluffy, then add the eggs, one at a time,
beating well after each addition. Beat in
the orange rind and juice.

5 Sift over the flour, salt and baking
powder in batches, beating well after
each addition. Spoon the mixture into
the prepared tin and tap gently to
release any air bubbles. Bake for
35–40 minutes until the top of the
cake is golden and springs back
when touched.

6 Cool in the tin for 10 minutes, then
transfer the cake to a wire rack.
Remove the lining paper and serve
warm, in slices, with a little of the
sauce. Decorate with the reserved fruit.

Energy 366kcal/1533kJ; Protein 5.4g; Carbohydrate 42.7g, of which sugars 26.1g; Fat 20.5g, of which saturates 12.1g; Cholesterol 118mg; Calcium 71mg; Fibre 2.1g; Sodium 163mg.

Boiled fruit cake

The texture of this classic cake is quite distinctive – moist and plump as a result of boiling the dried fruit with the butter, sugar and milk.

2 Put the dried fruit in a large pan and add the butter, sugar and milk. Heat gently until the butter melts and the sugar dissolves, stirring occasionally.

3 Bring the mixture to the boil, then allow to bubble gently for about 2 minutes. Remove from the heat and cool slightly.

4 Sift the flour with the baking powder and mixed spice into a bowl. Add this and the eggs to the fruit mixture in batches and mix together well.

5 Pour the mixture into the prepared tin and smooth the surface.

6 Bake for about 1½ hours or until firm to the touch and the cake is cooked through – a skewer inserted in the centre should come out free of sticky mixture.

7 Leave in the tin to cool for 20–30 minutes, then turn out and cool completely on a wire rack.

Serves 8–10

350g/12oz/2 cups mixed dried fruit

225g/8oz/1 cup butter

225g/8oz/1 cup soft dark brown sugar

400ml/14fl oz/1⅔ cup milk

450g/1lb/4 cups self-raising (self-rising) flour

5ml/1 tsp baking powder

5ml/1 tsp mixed (apple pie) spice

2 eggs, beaten

1 Preheat the oven to 160°C/ 325°F/ Gas 3. Lightly grease a 20cm/8in round cake tin (pan) and line the base and sides with baking parchment.

Energy 515kcal/2168kJ; Protein 7.2g; Carbohydrate 79g, of which sugars 49.8g; Fat 20g, of which saturates 12.4g; Cholesterol 88mg; Calcium 235mg; Fibre 2.1g; Sodium 329mg.

Biscuits, Cookies
and Tray Bakes

Recreate the farmhouse kitchen by filling your home with the smell of baking,
and your cake tins with these delicious cookies and bakes. The ingredients used in
these recipes are wholesome and delicious. Oaty biscuits, nutty flapjacks and
fruity bars eaten in moderation are far healthier than similar shop-bought items,
and are perfect for children's lunchboxes and afternoon snacks.

Shortbread rounds

Shortbread should always be in the biscuit tin or cookie jar – it is so moreish. Serve these melting buttery biscuits with a cup of tea, or with fruit fools or junket. A traditional Scottish favourite, they can also be half-dipped into melted chocolate and left to set.

Makes about 24

450g/1lb/2 cups unsalted butter

225g/8oz/1 heaped cup caster (superfine) sugar

450g/1lb/4 cups plain (all-purpose) flour

225g/8oz/scant 1½ cups ground rice or rice flour

5ml/1 tsp salt

demerara (raw) sugar, to decorate

golden caster (superfine) sugar, for dusting

Farmhouse tips Ground rice adds a grittiness to the dough, distinguishing home-made shortbread from store bought varieties. Make sure all the ingredients are at room temperature. Salted butter has more flavour than unsalted, but if you only have salted, then use it – and omit the salt in step 3.

1 Preheat the oven to 190°C/375°F/ Gas 5.

2 In a food processor or bowl, cream the butter and sugar together until light, pale and fluffy. If you used a food processor, scrape the mixture out into a mixing bowl.

3 Sift together the flour, ground rice or rice flour and salt and stir into the butter and sugar with a wooden spoon, until the mixture resembles fine breadcrumbs.

4 Working quickly, gather the dough together with your hand, then put it on a clean work surface. Knead lightly together until it forms a ball but take care not to over-knead, or the shortbread will be tough and greasy. Lightly roll into a sausage shape, about 7.5cm/3in thick. Wrap in clear film (plastic wrap) and chill until firm.

5 Pour the demerara sugar on to a sheet of baking parchment. Unwrap the dough and roll in the sugar until evenly coated. Slice the roll into discs about 1cm/½in thick.

6 Place the discs on to two baking sheets lined with baking parchment, spacing well apart. Bake for 20–25 minutes until very pale gold (but not dark).

7 Remove from the oven and sprinkle with golden caster sugar. Allow to cool for 10 minutes before transferring to a wire rack to cool completely.

Energy 275kcal/1147kJ; Protein 2.5g; Carbohydrate 32g, of which sugars 10.2g; Fat 15.7g, of which saturates 9.8g; Cholesterol 40mg; Calcium 37mg; Fibre 0.8g; Sodium 197mg.

Cherry melting moments

As the name suggests, these crisp biscuits really do melt in the mouth. They have a texture like shortbread but are covered in rolled oats to give a crunchy surface and extra flavour. They are traditionally topped with a toothsome nugget of red glacé cherry.

Makes about 16–20

40g/1½oz/3 tbsp soft butter

65g/2½oz/5 tbsp white cooking fat

75g/3oz/6 tbsp caster (superfine) sugar

1 egg yolk, beaten

few drops of vanilla extract

150g/5oz/1¼ cups self-raising (self-rising) flour

rolled oats, for coating

4–5 glacé (candied) cherries

1 Preheat the oven to 180°C/350°F/ Gas 4. Beat together the butter, white cooking fat and sugar, then gradually beat in the egg yolk and vanilla extract.

2 Sift the flour over the butter and egg mixture, and stir to make a soft dough. Roll into 16–20 small balls.

3 Spread rolled oats on a sheet of baking parchment and toss the balls in them until evenly coated.

4 Place the balls, spaced slightly apart, on two baking (cookie) sheets. Flatten each ball a little with your thumb. Cut the cherries into quarters and place a piece of cherry on top of each biscuit (cookie). Put into the hot oven and cook for 15–20 minutes, until they are lightly browned.

5 Allow the biscuits to cool for a few minutes on the baking sheets, before transferring them to a wire rack to cool completely.

Energy 88kcal/370kJ; Protein 0.7g; Carbohydrate 10.9g, of which sugars 5.4g; Fat 5g, of which saturates 2.4g; Cholesterol 7mg; Calcium 30mg; Fibre 0.3g; Sodium 40mg.

Porridge biscuits

Nutritious, delicious and chewy, oats are a major ingredient in these traditional country biscuits. They are store-cupboard standbys, and you can embellish the recipe by adding whichever varieties of chopped nuts, dried fruits or seeds you have to hand.

3 Sift the flour and stir into the mixture in the pan, together with the oats, to make a soft dough.

4 Roll the dough into small balls and arrange them on the prepared baking sheets, leaving plenty of room for them to spread. Flatten each ball slightly with a palette knife or a metal spatula.

5 Put one tray into the hot oven and cook for 12–15 minutes until golden brown and cooked through.

6 Leave to cool on the baking sheet for 1–2 minutes, then carefully transfer to a wire rack to crisp up and cool completely, while you cook the remaining batches.

Makes about 18

115g/4oz/½ cup butter

115g/4oz/½ cup soft brown sugar

115g/4oz/½ cup golden (light corn) syrup

150g/5oz/1¼ cups self-raising (self-rising) flour

150g/5oz/1¼ cups rolled oats

1 Preheat the oven to 180°C/350°F/Gas 4. Line two baking (cookie) sheets with baking parchment, or grease with butter.

2 Gently heat the butter, sugar and golden syrup until the butter has melted and the sugar has dissolved. Remove from the heat and leave to cool slightly.

Variation Add 25g/1oz/¼ cup chopped toasted almonds or walnuts, or a small handful of dried fruit, such as raisins, sultanas (golden raisins), chopped dried figs, dates or apricots, in step 3.

Energy 151kcal/637kJ; Protein 1.8g; Carbohydrate 23.9g, of which sugars 11.9g; Fat 6g, of which saturates 3.3g; Cholesterol 14mg; Calcium 22mg; Fibre 0.8g; Sodium 59mg.

Ginger biscuits

These crisp little spiced biscuits are very versatile and completely delicious. You can cut them into any shape – but flowers, stars and hearts are the traditional forms. Make the dough the day before, to give it time to rest overnight. Serve on their own or with ice cream.

Makes about 50

250g/9oz/generous 1 cup butter

300g/9oz/1½ cups sugar

15ml/1 tbsp golden (light corn) syrup

15ml/1 tbsp treacle (molasses)

15ml/1 tbsp ground ginger

10ml/2 tsp ground cinnamon

10ml/2 tsp ground cloves

5ml/1 tsp ground cardamom

10ml/2 tsp bicarbonate of soda (baking soda)

450g/1lb/4 cups plain (all-purpose) flour

1 Put the butter, sugar, syrup, treacle, ginger, cinnamon, cloves and cardamom in a heavy pan and heat gently until the butter has melted.

2 Sift the flour and the bicarbonate of soda into a large heatproof bowl. Pour in the warm spice mixture and mix together until well blended.

3 Wrap the dough in clear film (plastic wrap) and put in the refrigerator overnight to rest.

4 Preheat the oven to 220°C/425°F/ Gas 7. Line several baking sheets with baking parchment. Knead the dough, then roll out on a lightly floured surface as thinly as possible. Cut the dough into shapes of your choice and place on the baking sheets.

5 Bake the biscuits (cookies) in the oven for about 5 minutes until golden brown, adding them in batches until all the biscuits are cooked. Leave to cool on the baking sheet. As you bake more cookies, they may take less time to cook through, so watch carefully.

Energy 31kcal/130kJ; Protein 0.2g; Carbohydrate 5.8g, of which sugars 4.2g; Fat 0.8g, of which saturates 0.5g; Cholesterol 2mg; Calcium 5mg; Fibre 0.1g; Sodium 13mg.

Butter biscuits

These crisp little biscuits are the French version of shortbread, but the higher proportion of butter makes them even richer. Handle them with care, as they break easily.

Makes about 20

200g/7oz/¾ cup butter, diced

6 egg yolks, lightly beaten

15ml/1 tbsp milk

225g/8oz/2 cups plain
(all-purpose) flour

175g/6oz/¾ cup caster
(superfine) sugar

1 Preheat the oven to 180°C/350°F/
Gas 4. Grease a large baking sheet.

2 Mix 15ml/1 tbsp of the beaten egg yolks with the milk, to make a glaze, and set aside.

3 Sift the flour into a large bowl and make a well in the centre. Add the remaining egg yolks, sugar and butter and, using your fingertips, work them together until smooth and creamy. Gradually incorporate the flour to make a smooth, slightly sticky dough.

4 Using floured hands, pat out the dough to a thickness of 8mm/⅜in and cut out rounds using a 7.5cm/3in cutter. Transfer to a baking sheet, brush each with a little egg glaze, then, using a knife, score to create a lattice pattern.

5 Bake for 12–15 minutes until golden. Cool on the sheet on a wire rack for 15 minutes, then remove the biscuits and leave to cool completely.

Energy 170kcal/711kJ; Protein 2.2g; Carbohydrate 19g, of which sugars 9.4g; Fat 10g, of which saturates 5.7g; Cholesterol 82mg; Calcium 32mg; Fibre 0.4g; Sodium 65mg.

Orange shortbread fingers

These are a perfect tea-time treat, and are so quick and easy to make that you can whip up a batch while you're making a soup or casserole. They will keep in an airtight tin for two weeks.

Makes about 18

115g/4oz/½ cup unsalted butter, softened

50g/2oz/4 tbsp caster (superfine) sugar, plus a little extra

finely grated rind of 2 oranges

175g/6oz/1½ cups plain (all-purpose) flour

1 Preheat the oven to 190°C/375°F/ Gas 5. Beat the butter and sugar together until they are soft and creamy. Beat in the orange rind.

2 Gradually add the flour and gently pull the dough together to form a soft ball. Roll the dough out on a lightly floured surface until about 1cm/½in thick.

3 Cut into fingers, sprinkle over a little extra caster sugar, prick with a fork and bake for about 20 minutes. Transfer to a wire rack to cool.

Energy 92kcal/383kJ; Protein 1g; Carbohydrate 10.5g, of which sugars 3.1g; Fat 5.4g, of which saturates 3.4g; Cholesterol 14mg; Calcium 16mg; Fibre 0.3g; Sodium 39mg.

Oaty chocolate-chip cookies

These crunchy cookies don't need rolling and cutting out, and are easy enough for children to make by themselves. They are sure to disappear as soon as they are put on the table.

Makes about 20

115g/4oz/½ cup butter

115g/4oz/½ cup soft dark brown sugar

2 eggs, lightly beaten

45–60ml/3–4 tbsp milk

5ml/1 tsp vanilla extract

150g/5oz/1¼ cups plain (all-purpose) flour

5ml/1 tsp baking powder

pinch of salt

115g/4oz/generous 1 cup rolled oats

175g/6oz plain (semisweet) chocolate chips

115g/4oz/1 cup pecan nuts, chopped

1 Cream the butter and sugar in a large bowl until pale and fluffy. Beat in the beaten eggs, a small amount at a time, then add the milk and vanilla extract, and beat thoroughly.

2 Sift in the flour, baking powder and salt, and stir in until well mixed. Fold in the rolled oats, chocolate chips and chopped pecan nuts.

3 Chill the mixture for at least 1 hour. Preheat the oven to 180°C/350°F/Gas 4. Grease two large baking trays.

4 Using two teaspoons, place mounds well apart on the trays and flatten with a spoon or fork.

5 Bake for 10–12 minutes until the edges are colouring. Leave on the trays for 5 minutes, then cool on wire racks.

Energy 139kcal/582kJ; Protein 1.7g; Carbohydrate 16.7g, of which sugars 11.1g; Fat 7.7g, of which saturates 3.9g; Cholesterol 19mg; Calcium 20mg; Fibre 0.5g; Sodium 33mg.

Creamed coconut macaroons

Finely grated creamed coconut gives these soft-centred cookies a rich creaminess. Cooking
the gooey mixture on baking parchment makes sure that the cookies are easily removed.

Makes about 18

50g/2oz creamed coconut, chilled

2 large (US extra large) egg whites

90g/3½ oz/½ cup caster (superfine)
sugar

75g/3oz/1 cup desiccated (dry
unsweetened shredded) coconut

1 Preheat the oven to 180°C/350°F/
Gas 4. Line a large baking sheet with
baking parchment.

2 Finely grate the creamed coconut.
Whisk the egg whites in a large bowl
until stiff. Whisk in the sugar, a little at
a time, until stiff and glossy. Fold in the
grated and desiccated coconut, using a
large, metal spoon.

3 Place dessertspoonfuls of the mixture,
spaced slightly apart, on the baking
sheet. Bake for 15–20 minutes, until
slightly risen and golden brown. Leave
to cool on the parchment, then transfer
to an airtight container.

Energy 65kcal/270kJ; Protein 0.7g; Carbohydrate 5.7g, of which sugars 5.7g; Fat 4.5g, of which saturates 3.9g; Cholesterol 0mg; Calcium 4mg; Fibre 0.6g; Sodium 9mg.

Peanut butter and jelly cookies

These cookies are a real hit with kids and adults alike. Give them a try – you'll love the crunchy nutty biscuits and sweet raspberry centres.

Makes 20–22

227g/8oz jar crunchy peanut butter (with no added sugar)

75g/3oz/6 tbsp unsalted butter, at room temperature, diced

90g/3½oz/½ cup golden caster (superfine) sugar

50g/2oz/¼ cup light muscovado (brown) sugar

1 large (US extra large) egg, beaten

150g/5oz/1¼ cups self-raising (self-rising) flour

250g/9oz/scant 1 cup seedless raspberry jam

1 Preheat the oven to 180°C/350°F/ Gas 4. Grease or line three or four baking sheets with baking parchment.

2 Put the peanut butter and unsalted butter in a large bowl and beat together with a wooden spoon until well combined and creamy.

3 Add the caster and muscovado sugars and mix. Add the beaten egg and blend well. Sift in the flour and mix in to make a stiff dough.

4 Roll the dough into walnut-size balls between the palms of your hands. Place the balls on the prepared baking sheets.

5 Gently flatten each dough ball with a fork to make a rough-textured cookie with a ridged surface. (Don't worry if the dough cracks slightly.)

6 Bake for 10–12 minutes, or until cooked but not browned. Using a palette knife or metal spatula, transfer to a wire rack to cool.

7 When the cookies are completely cool, spoon jam on to one cookie and top with a second. Continue to sandwich the cookies in this way. If you have made the cookies in advance, keep in an airtight container, and sandwich together just before serving.

Energy 169Kcal/709kJ; Protein 3.4g; Carbohydrate 21g, of which sugars 15.3g; Fat 8.5g, of which saturates 3.2g; Cholesterol 18mg; Calcium 35mg; Fibre 0.8g; Sodium 89mg.

Caraway and honey cookies

Lemon and caraway are a lovely combination of warm and tangy flavours, and honey complements them both. These biscuits are delicious served with cheese at the end of a meal.

Make 45–50

115g/4oz/½ cup butter, softened

225g/8oz/generous 1 cup caster (superfine) sugar

5ml/1 tsp honey

1 egg, beaten

15g/½oz caraway seeds

grated rind and juice of 1 lemon

350g/10½oz/2½ cups plain (all-purpose) flour, plus extra for dusting

2.5ml/½ tsp baking powder

1 Put the butter and sugar in a large bowl and cream together, using an electric mixer if you like, until the mixture is smooth and pale. Add the honey and mix again.

2 Add the egg, caraway, lemon juice and rind. Mix well, then sift in the flour and baking powder and gently fold in.

3 Transfer the mixture on to a floured surface and work to a firm dough. Form into a sausage shape, about 30cm/12in long, and wrap in baking parchment. Chill until firm.

Variation Prepare a thick chocolate sauce and drizzle over the cookies before serving.

◀ **4** Preheat the oven to 180°C/350°F/ Gas 4 and line a baking sheet with baking parchment. Unwrap the dough, and cut off slices about 5mm/¼in thick. Put them on the prepared baking sheet, spaced apart. Bake for 10 minutes, or until golden. Cool briefly on the baking sheet, then transfer to a wire rack to cool completely.

Energy 61kcal/255kJ; Protein 0.8g; Carbohydrate 10.2g, of which sugars 4.9g; Fat 2.1g, of which saturates 1.3g; Cholesterol 10mg; Calcium 13mg; Fibre 0.2g; Sodium 19mg.

Easter biscuits

These sweet, lightly spiced cookies have been part of English Easter festivities for generations, traditionally given tied in bundles of three to represent the Holy Trinity.

3 Sift the flour and spices over the mixture, then fold in the currants and peel, adding sufficient milk to make a fairly soft dough.

4 Knead the dough lightly on a floured surface then roll out to 5mm/¼in thick. Cut out circles using a 5cm/2in fluted biscuit (cookie) cutter. Arrange on the sheets and cook for 10 minutes.

Makes 16–18

115g/4oz/½ cup soft butter

85g/3oz/6 tbsp caster (superfine) sugar, plus extra for sprinkling

1 egg

200g/7oz/1¾ cups plain (all-purpose) flour

2.5ml/½ tsp mixed (apple pie) spice

2.5ml/½ tsp ground cinnamon

55g/2oz/scant ½ cup currants

15ml/1 tbsp chopped mixed (candied) peel

15–30ml/1–2 tbsp milk

1 Preheat the oven to 200°C/400°F/ Gas 6. Lightly grease two baking sheets or line with baking parchment.

2 Beat together the butter and sugar until light and fluffy. Separate the egg, reserving the white, and beat the yolk into the mixture.

5 Beat the egg white and brush gently over the biscuits (cookies). Sprinkle with caster sugar and return to the oven for 10 minutes until golden. Transfer to a wire rack to cool.

Energy 116kcal/485kJ; Protein 1.5g; Carbohydrate 15.4g, of which sugars 7g; Fat 5.7g, of which saturates 3.4g; Cholesterol 24mg; Calcium 25mg; Fibre 0.4g; Sodium 46mg.

Shrewsbury cakes

Despite being called 'cakes', these are crisp, lemony shortbread biscuits with fluted edges, which have been made and sold in the English town of Shrewsbury since the 17th century.

Makes about 20

115g/4oz/½ cup soft butter

140g/5oz/¾ cup caster (superfine) sugar

2 egg yolks

225g/8oz/2 cups plain (all-purpose) flour

finely grated rind of 1 lemon

1 Preheat the oven to 180°C/350°F/ Gas 4. Line two baking sheets with baking parchment.

4 Knead the dough lightly on a floured surface then roll it out to 5mm/¼in thick. Using a 7.5cm/3in fluted biscuit (cookie) cutter, cut out circles and arrange on the baking sheets.

5 Gather up the offcuts and roll out again to make more biscuits. Put into the hot oven and cook for about 15 minutes, until firm to the touch and lightly browned.

6 Transfer to a wire rack and leave to crisp up and cool completely.

Variations Omit the lemon rind and sift 5ml/1 tsp ground mixed (apple pie) spice with the flour in step 3.
  Add 25g/1oz/2 tbsp currants or raisins to the mixture in step 3.

2 In a mixing bowl, beat the softened butter with the sugar until pale, light and fluffy. Beat in each of the egg yolks one at a time, beating thoroughly after each addition.

3 Sift the flour over the top of the butter and sugar mixture, and add the lemon rind. Mix in and then gather up the mixture to make a stiff dough.

Energy 115kcal/482kJ; Protein 1.4g; Carbohydrate 16.1g, of which sugars 7.5g; Fat 5.4g, of which saturates 3.2g; Cholesterol 32mg; Calcium 23mg; Fibre 0.4g; Sodium 37mg.

Raspberry jam biscuits

These simple biscuits are given an extra dimension by the addition of sour cream. Make plenty, as they will be popular with all the family.

Makes about 25

100g/3¾oz/generous ½ cup caster (superfine) sugar

100g/3¾oz/scant ½ cup unsalted butter

1 egg

100ml/3½fl oz/scant ½ cup sour cream

350g/12oz/3 cups plain (all-purpose) flour

5ml/1 tsp baking powder (baking soda)

90ml/6 tbsp raspberry jam

1 Preheat the oven to 180°C/350°F/ Gas 4. Lightly grease and line two baking sheets.

2 Put the sugar and butter in a large bowl and beat together until light and fluffy. Beat in the egg, then mix in the sour cream.

3 Sift the flour and baking powder together, then add to the egg mixture and gather together to form a soft ball of dough.

4 On a lightly floured surface, roll out the dough to 5mm/¼in thickness then, using a floured 5cm/2in round cutter, cut out rounds and place, well-spaced, on the prepared baking trays.

5 Gather up the remnants, re-roll the dough, and cut out more rounds until it is all used up. Leave the rounds to rest for 15 minutes.

6 Press the centre of each round with your thumb or the back of a teaspoon, then spoon a little raspberry jam into the indentation. Bake for 12–15 minutes, until slightly risen and golden. Leave to cool on a wire rack.

Energy 28.5kcal/119kJ; Protein 0.04g; Carbohydrate 4.43g, of which sugars 1.7g; Fat 1.1g, of which saturates 0.6g; Cholesterol 4.6mg; Calcium 6.9mg; Fibre 0.1g; Sodium 7.6mg.

Oaty crisps

These biscuits are very crisp and crunchy – ideal to serve with coffee. Malt extract is often used in breadmaking, and can be found in stores that specialize in baking products.

Makes about 18

175g/6oz/1¾ cups rolled oats

75g/3oz/½ cup light muscovado (brown) sugar

1 egg

60ml/4 tbsp sunflower oil

30ml/2 tbsp malt extract

1 Preheat the oven to 190°C/375°F/Gas 5. Lightly grease two baking sheets. Mix the rolled oats and brown sugar in a bowl, breaking up any lumps in the sugar. Add the egg, sunflower oil and malt extract, mix well, then leave to soak for 15 minutes.

Variation To give these cookies a coarser texture, substitute jumbo oats for some or all of the rolled oats.

2 Using a teaspoon, place small heaps of the mixture well apart on the prepared baking sheets. Press the heaps into 7.5cm/3in rounds with the back of a dampened fork.

3 Bake the cookies for 10–15 minutes until golden brown. Leave them to cool on the baking sheet for 1 minute, then remove with a palette knife and cool completely on a wire rack.

Energy 86kcal/364kJ; Protein 1.6g; Carbohydrate 12.8g, of which sugars 5.7g; Fat 3.6g, of which saturates 0.4g; Cholesterol 11mg; Calcium 9mg; Fibre 0.7g; Sodium 12mg.

Tea finger cookies

The unusual ingredient in these cookies is Lady Grey tea – similar to Earl Grey but with the addition of Seville orange and lemon peel, which imparts a subtle flavour.

1 Beat the butter and sugar until light and creamy. Stir in the tea leaves. Beat in the egg, then fold in the flour.

2 Roll the dough on a lightly floured surface into a 23cm/9in long cylinder. Press down on the top of the dough cylinder with your hand to flatten slightly. Wrap the dough in clear film (plastic wrap) and chill for about 1 hour until the dough is firm enough to slice.

3 Preheat the oven to 190°C/375°F/ Gas 5. Line two or three baking sheets with baking parchment.

4 Using a sharp knife, cut the dough cylinder widthways into 5mm/¼in slices and place, slightly apart, on the prepared baking sheets.

5 Sprinkle the cookies with a little demerara sugar, then bake for 10–15 minutes until lightly browned. Transfer the cookies to a wire rack and leave to cool completely.

Makes about 36

150g/5oz/generous ½ cup unsalted butter, at room temperature, diced

115g/4oz/generous ½ cup light muscovado (brown) sugar

15–30ml/1–2 tbsp Lady Grey tea leaves

1 egg, beaten

200g/7oz/1¾ cups plain (all-purpose) flour

demerara (raw) sugar, for sprinkling

Energy 65kcal/270kJ; Protein 0.7g; Carbohydrate 7.7g, of which sugars 3.4g; Fat 3.7g, of which saturates 2.2g; Cholesterol 14mg; Calcium 11mg; Fibre 0.2g; Sodium 28mg.

Almond, orange and carrot bars

An out-of-this-world cookie version of the ever-popular carrot cake, these flavoursome, moist bars are best eaten fresh or stored in the refrigerator after making.

Makes 16

75g/3oz/6 tbsp unsalted butter, softened

50g/2oz/¼ cup caster (superfine) sugar

150g/5oz/1¼ cups plain (all-purpose) flour

finely grated rind of 1 orange

For the filling

90g/3½oz/scant ½ cup unsalted butter, diced

75g/3oz/scant ½ cup caster (superfine) sugar

2 eggs

2.5ml/½ tsp almond extract

175g/6oz/1½ cups ground almonds

1 parboiled carrot, coarsely grated

For the topping

175g/6oz/¾ cup cream cheese

30–45ml/2–3 tbsp chopped walnuts

1 Preheat the oven to 190°C/375°F/ Gas 5. Lightly grease a 28 x 18cm/11 x 7in shallow baking tin (pan). Put the butter, caster sugar, flour and orange rind into a bowl and rub together until it resembles coarse breadcrumbs. Add water, a teaspoon at a time, to mix to a firm but not sticky dough.

2 Roll the dough out on a floured surface and line the base of the tin.

3 To make the filling, cream the butter and sugar together. Beat in the eggs and almond extract. Stir in the ground almonds and the grated carrot. Spread over the base and bake for 25 minutes until firm in the centre. Leave to cool.

4 To make the topping, beat the cream cheese until smooth and spread it over the cooled filling. Sprinkle with chopped walnuts and cut into bars.

Energy 85kcal/355kJ; Protein 1.4g; Carbohydrate 5.3g, of which sugars 2.9g; Fat 6.6g, of which saturates 3g; Cholesterol 18mg; Calcium 20mg; Fibre 0.4g; Sodium 34mg.

Apricot and pecan flapjack

A tried-and-tested favourite made even more delicious by the addition of maple syrup, fruit and nuts. This is a real energy booster at any time of day – great for kids and adults alike.

Makes 10

150g/5oz/⅔ cup unsalted butter, diced

150g/5oz/⅔ cup light muscovado (brown) sugar

30ml/2 tbsp maple syrup

200g/7oz/2 cups rolled oats

50g/2oz/½ cup pecan nuts, chopped

50g/2oz/¼ cup ready-to-eat dried apricots, chopped

Variations You can substitute walnuts for the pecan nuts if you like, although the nutty flavour will not be quite so intense.

1 Preheat the oven to 160°C/325°F/ Gas 3. Lightly grease an 18cm/7in square shallow baking tin (pan).

2 Put the butter, sugar and maple syrup in a large heavy pan and heat gently until the butter has melted. Remove from the heat and stir in the oats, nuts and apricots until well combined.

3 Spread evenly in the prepared tin and, using a knife, score the mixture into ten bars. Bake for about 25–30 minutes, or until golden.

4 Remove the flapjack from the oven and cut through the scored lines. Leave until completely cold before removing from the tin.

Energy 240kcal/1000kJ; Protein 3.2g; Carbohydrate 18.3g, of which sugars 3.7g; Fat 17.6g, of which saturates 8.1g; Cholesterol 32mg; Calcium 21mg; Fibre 1.9g; Sodium 98mg.

Nut and chocolate chip brownies

Moist, dark and deeply satisfying – this is the ultimate chocolate brownie. Serve warm as a
dessert if you wish, with vanilla ice cream to contrast with the warm chocolatey brownie.

Makes 16

150g/5oz plain (semisweet)
chocolate, broken into squares

120ml/4fl oz/½ cup sunflower oil

215g/7½oz/1¼ cups light muscovado
sugar

2 eggs

5ml/1 tsp vanilla essence

65g/2½oz/⅔ cup self-raising (self-
rising) flour

60ml/4 tbsp cocoa powder

75g/3oz/¾ cup chopped
walnuts or pecan nuts

60ml/4 tbsp milk chocolate chips

1 Preheat the oven to 180°C/350°F/Gas
4. Lightly grease a shallow 19cm/7½in
square cake tin (pan).

2 Melt the plain chocolate in a
heatproof bowl over boiling water.
Allow to cool slightly.

3 Beat the oil, sugar, eggs and vanilla
extract together in a large bowl.

4 Stir in the melted chocolate, then
beat well until evenly mixed.

▶ **5** Sift the flour and cocoa powder
into the bowl and fold in thoroughly.

6 Stir in the chopped nuts and
chocolate chips, tip into the prepared
tin and spread evenly to the edges.

7 Bake the brownies in the oven for
30–35 minutes, or until the top is firm
and crusty. Cool in the tin before
cutting into squares and removing
from the tin.

Energy 235kcal/983kJ; Protein 3.4g; Carbohydrate 25.9g, of which sugars 22.2g; Fat 13.9g, of which saturates 3.8g; Cholesterol 25mg; Calcium 37mg; Fibre 1g; Sodium 49mg.

Luscious lemon bars

These bars are made from a crisp cookie base, covered with a tangy lemon topping. They make a delightful addition to the tea table on a warm summer's day in the garden.

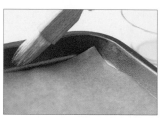

1 Preheat the oven to 180°C/350°F/ Gas 4. Line the base of a 20cm/8in square shallow cake tin (pan) with baking parchment and lightly grease the sides of the tin.

2 Process the flour, butter and icing sugar until the mixture comes together as a firm dough. Press evenly into the base of the tin using the back of a spoon.

3 Bake for 12–15 minutes until lightly golden. Cool in the tin.

4 To make the topping, whisk the eggs in a bowl until frothy. Add the caster sugar, a little at a time, whisking well between each addition. Whisk in the lemon rind and juice, flour and soda. Pour over the cookie base. Bake for 20–25 minutes, until set and golden.

5 Leave to cool slightly. Cut into twelve bars and dust lightly with icing sugar. Leave to cool completely.

Makes 12

150g/5oz/1¼ cups plain (all-purpose) flour

90g/3½oz/7 tbsp unsalted butter, chilled and diced

50g/2oz/½ cup icing (confectioners') sugar, sifted

For the topping

2 eggs

175g/6oz/scant 1 cup caster (superfine) sugar

finely grated rind and juice of 1 large lemon

15ml/1 tbsp plain (all-purpose) flour

2.5ml/½ tsp bicarbonate of soda (baking soda)

icing (confectioners') sugar, for dusting

Energy 189kcal/795kJ; Protein 2.5g; Carbohydrate 30.3g, of which sugars 19.8g; Fat 7.3g, of which saturates 4.2g; Cholesterol 48mg; Calcium 35mg; Fibre 0.4g; Sodium 59mg.

Walnut and honey bars

A sweet, custard-like filling brimming with nuts sits on a crisp pastry base. These scrumptious bars are pure heaven to bite into, especially if eaten while still slightly warm.

Makes 12–14

175g/6oz/1½ cups plain (all-purpose) flour

30ml/2 tbsp icing (confectioners') sugar, sifted

115g/4oz/½ cup unsalted butter, diced

For the filling

300g/11oz/scant 3 cups walnut halves

2 eggs, beaten

50g/2oz/¼ cup unsalted butter, melted

50g/2oz/¼ cup light muscovado (brown) sugar

90ml/6 tbsp dark clear honey

30ml/2 tbsp single (light) cream

1 Preheat the oven to 190°C/375°F/ Gas 5. Lightly grease a 28 x 18cm/ 11 x 7in shallow tin (pan).

2 Put the flour, icing sugar and butter in a food processor and process until the mixture forms crumbs. Using the pulse button, add 15–30ml/1–2 tbsp water – enough to make a firm dough.

3 Roll the dough out on baking parchment and line the base and sides of the tin. Trim the edges.

4 Prick the base, line with foil and baking beans and bake blind for 10 minutes. Remove the foil and beans. Return the base to the oven for about 5 minutes, to crisp. Remove from the oven and set on a wire tray to cool.

5 For the filling, sprinkle the walnuts over the base. Whisk the eggs, butter, sugar, honey and cream together in a large bowl, then pour into the base. Bake for 25 minutes, cut into bars, leave to cool, then remove from the tin.

Energy 333kcal/1386kJ; Protein 5.4g; Carbohydrate 21.4g, of which sugars 11.7g; Fat 25.7g, of which saturates 7.8g; Cholesterol 53mg; Calcium 49mg; Fibre 1.1g; Sodium 85mg.

Cranberry muffins

Light and fluffy, muffins are best eaten fresh for breakfast or brunch. These are very easy to make, and give a lovely contrast between sweet cake mixture and sharp berries.

Makes 12

350g/12oz/3 cups plain
(all-purpose) flour

15ml/1 tsp baking powder

pinch of salt

115g/4oz/½ cup caster
(superfine) sugar

2 eggs

150ml/5fl oz/⅔ cup milk

50ml/2fl oz/4 tbsp corn oil

finely grated rind of 1 orange

150g/5oz/1¼ cups cranberries

1 Preheat the oven to 190°C/375°F/ Gas 5. Line 12 deep muffin tins (pans) with paper cases. Mix the flour, baking powder, salt and caster sugar together in a large bowl.

2 In a separate bowl, lightly beat the eggs with the milk and oil.

3 Add the beaten egg mixture to the dry ingredients and blend to a smooth batter. Stir in the orange rind and cranberries. Divide the mixture between the paper cases and bake for 25 minutes until risen and golden. Leave to cool in the tins for a few minutes, and serve warm or cold.

Energy 184Kcal/780kJ; Protein 4.3g; Carbohydrate 34.4g, of which sugars 12.2g; Fat 4.3g, of which saturates 0.9g; Cholesterol 32mg; Calcium 66mg; Fibre 1.1g; Sodium 19mg.

Blueberry muffins

This is perhaps the classic American farmhouse muffin. Add some chopped pecans or walnuts for extra crunch, or replace the blueberries with raspberries if you wish.

Makes 12

180g/6¼oz/generous 1½ cups plain (all-purpose) flour

60g/2¼oz/generous ¼ cup sugar

10ml/2 tsp baking powder

pinch of salt

2 eggs

50g/2oz/¼ cup butter, melted

175ml/6fl oz/¾ cup milk

5ml/1 tsp vanilla extract

5ml/1 tsp grated lemon rind

175g/6oz/1½ cups fresh blueberries

1 Preheat the oven to 200°C/400°F/ Gas 6. Grease a 12-cup muffin tin (pan) or arrange 12 paper muffin cases on a baking tray.

2 Sift the flour, sugar, baking powder and salt into a large mixing bowl. In another bowl, whisk the eggs until blended. Add the melted butter, milk, vanilla and lemon rind to the eggs, and stir thoroughly to combine.

5 Spoon the batter into the muffin tin or paper cases, leaving enough room for the muffins to rise.

6 Bake for 20–25 minutes, until the tops spring back when touched lightly. Leave the muffins in the tin, if using, for 5 minutes before turning out on to a wire rack to cool a little before serving.

3 Make a well in the dry ingredients and pour in the egg mixture. With a large metal spoon, stir until the flour is just moistened, but not smooth.

4 Add the blueberries to the muffin mixture and gently fold in; being careful not to crush any of the berries while you stir them.

Farmhouse tip If you want to serve these muffins for breakfast, prepare the dry ingredients the night before to save time.

Energy 236kcal/992kJ; Protein 4.9g; Carbohydrate 34.7g, of which sugars 12.4g; Fat 9.6g, of which saturates 5.6g; Cholesterol 54mg; Calcium 88mg; Fibre 1.4g; Sodium 82mg.

Home-baked Breads and Scones

Making your own bread is a time-honoured farmhouse tradition, and when the aroma of newly baked bread and cakes is in the air, everyone makes a beeline for the kitchen. The anticipation of feasting on these delights is almost as enjoyable as the eating, and the baking itself can be almost therapeutic. The following recipes provide a selection of recipes that will be enjoyed by all the family.

Basic yeast bread

Make this dough into any shape you like, such as braids, bloomers, or rolls. Bread must be made with strong bread flour as it has a high gluten content, which rises better.

Makes 4 loaves

25g/1oz fresh yeast

10ml/2 tsp caster (superfine) sugar

900ml/1½ pints/3¾ cups tepid water, or milk and water mixed

15ml/1 tbsp salt

1.3kg/3lb/12 cups strong white bread flour, preferably unbleached

50g/2oz/scant ¼ cup white vegetable fat (shortening) or 50ml/2fl oz/¼ cup vegetable oil

1 Cream the yeast and caster sugar together in a measuring jug (cup), add about 150ml/¼ pint/⅔ cup of the measured liquid and leave in a warm place for about 10 minutes to froth up.

2 Meanwhile, mix the salt into the flour and rub in the fat (if using oil, add it to the remaining liquid).

3 Using an electric mixer with a dough hook attachment, or working by hand in a mixing bowl, add the yeast mixture and remaining liquid to the flour, and work it in to make a firm dough which leaves the bowl clean.

4 Knead well on a floured surface, or in the mixer, until the dough has become firm and elastic. Return to the bowl, cover lightly with a dish towel and leave in a warm place to rise for an hour, or until it has doubled in size. The dough will be springy and full of air. Meanwhile, oil four 450g/1lb loaf tins (pans).

5 Turn the dough out on to a floured work surface and knock back (punch down), flattening it out with your knuckles to knock the air out. Knead lightly into shape again, divide into four pieces and form into loaf shapes.

6 Place the dough in the loaf tins, pushing down well to fit into the corners, then leave to rise again for another 20–30 minutes. Meanwhile, preheat the oven to 230°C/450°F/Gas 8.

7 When the dough has risen just above the rims of the tins, bake the loaves in the centre of the oven for 30 minutes, or until browned and shrinking a little from the sides of the tins; when turned out and rapped underneath they should sound hollow. Cool on wire racks.

Variation For brown bread, replace the white flour with wholemeal (wholewheat) flour, or half and half white and wholemeal bread flour.

Per loaf Energy 1223kcal/5185kJ; Protein 30.7g; Carbohydrate 256.4g, of which sugars 7.5g; Fat 15.2g, of which saturates 6.3g; Cholesterol 0mg; Calcium 457mg; Fibre 10.1g; Sodium 1.48g.

Cottage loaf

Snipping both sections of the dough at intervals looks attractive and also helps
this classic country loaf to rise and expand in the oven while it cooks.

4 Turn out on to a lightly floured surface
and knock back (punch down). Knead
for 2–3 minutes, then divide into two-
thirds and one-third and shape into balls.

5 Place the balls of dough on the baking
sheets. Cover with inverted bowls and
leave to rise, in a warm place, for about
30 minutes. Gently flatten the top of the
larger round of dough and, with a sharp
knife, cut a cross in the centre, about 4cm/
1½in across. Brush with a little water
and place the smaller round on top.

Makes 1 large round loaf

675g/1½ lb/6 cups unbleached
strong white bread flour

10ml/2 tsp salt

20g/¾ oz fresh yeast

400ml/14fl oz/1⅔ cups lukewarm water

Farmhouse tips To ensure a well-
shaped cottage loaf, the dough needs
to be dry and firm enough to support
the weight of the top ball.
   Alternatively, make smaller, individual
rolls – bake them for 25 minutes.

1 Lightly grease two baking sheets. Sift
the flour and salt together into a large
bowl and make a well in the centre.

2 Mix the yeast in 150ml/¼ pint/⅔ cup
of the water until dissolved. Pour
into the centre of the flour with
the remaining water and mix to
a firm dough.

3 Knead on a lightly floured surface
for 10 minutes until smooth and elastic.
Place in a lightly oiled bowl, cover with
lightly oiled plastic wrap and leave to
rise, in a warm place, for about 1 hour,
or until doubled in bulk.

6 Press a hole through the middle of
the top ball with your thumb and first
two fingers. Snip both balls round the
sides at 5cm/2in intervals. Cover with
lightly oiled clear film (plastic wrap) and
rest for about 10 minutes.

7 Set the oven to 220°C/425°F/Gas 7
and place the bread on the lower shelf.
It will finish expanding as the oven heats
up. Bake for 35–40 minutes, or until
golden brown. Cool on a wire rack.

Per loaf Energy 2302kcal/9788kJ; Protein 63.5g; Carbohydrate 524.5g, of which sugars 10.1g; Fat 8.8g, of which saturates 1.4g; Cholesterol 0mg; Calcium 946mg; Fibre 20.9g; Sodium 3950mg.

Poppy seed bloomer

This satisfying white poppy seed bread, which is a version of the chunky baton loaf found throughout Europe, is made using a slower rising method and with less yeast than usual. It produces a longer-keeping loaf with a fuller flavour. The dough takes about 8 hours to rise, so you'll need to start making the bread early in the morning.

Makes 1 large loaf

675g/1½ lb/6 cups unbleached strong white bread flour

10ml/2 tsp salt

15g/½ oz fresh yeast

430ml/15fl oz/1⅞ cups water

For the topping

2.5ml/½ tsp salt

30ml/2 tbsp water

poppy seeds, for sprinkling

Farmhouse tip You can get the cracked appearance of this loaf by spraying the oven with water before baking. If the underside is not crusty at the end of baking time, turn the loaf over, switch off the heat and leave in the oven for 5–10 minutes.

1 Lightly grease a baking sheet. Sift the flour and salt together into a large bowl and make a well in the centre.

2 Mix the yeast and 150ml/¼ pint/ ⅔ cup of the water in a bowl. Mix in the remaining water. Add to the centre of the flour. Mix, gradually incorporating the surrounding flour, until the mixture forms a firm dough.

3 Turn out on to a lightly floured surface and knead the dough for at least 10 minutes, until smooth and elastic. Place the dough in a lightly oiled bowl, cover with lightly oiled clear film (plastic wrap) and leave to rise, at cool room temperature, about 15–18°C/60–65°F, for 5–6 hours, or until doubled in bulk.

4 Knock back (punch down) the dough, turn out on to a lightly floured surface and knead it thoroughly and quite hard for about 5 minutes. Return the dough to the bowl, and re-cover. Leave to rise, at cool room temperature, for 2 hours.

5 Knock back again and repeat the thorough kneading. Leave the dough to rest for 5 minutes, then roll out on a lightly floured surface into a rectangle 2.5cm/1in thick. Roll the dough up from one long side and shape it into a square-ended thick baton shape about 33 × 13cm/13 × 5in.

6 Place it seam side up on a lightly floured baking sheet, cover and leave to rest for 15 minutes. Turn the loaf over and place on the greased baking sheet. Plump up by tucking the dough under the sides and ends. Using a sharp knife, cut six diagonal slashes on the top.

7 Leave to rest, covered, in a warm place, for 10 minutes. Meanwhile preheat the oven to 230°C/450°F/Gas 8.

8 Mix the salt and water together and brush this glaze over the bread. Sprinkle with poppy seeds. Spray the oven with water, bake the bread immediately for 20 minutes, then reduce the oven temperature to 200°C/400°F/Gas 6. Bake for 25 minutes more, or until golden. Transfer to a wire rack to cool.

Variation You could also use sesame, or nigella seeds instead of poppy seeds, or a mixture of seeds, if you wish.

Per loaf Energy 2302kcal/9787kJ; Protein 63.5g; Carbohydrate 524.5g, of which sugars 10.1g; Fat 8.8g, of which saturates 1.3g; Cholesterol 0mg; Calcium 946mg; Fibre 20.9g; Sodium 3950mg.

Seeded wholemeal loaf

Home-made bread creates one of the most evocative smells in country cooking.
Eat this on the day of making, to enjoy the superb fresh taste.

1 Dissolve the yeast with a little of the milk and the sugar to make a paste. Place both flours plus any bran from the sieve (strainer) and the salt in a large warmed bowl. Rub in the butter until the mixture resembles breadcrumbs.

2 Add the yeast mixture, remaining milk and egg, and mix into a soft dough. Knead on a floured board for 15 minutes. Lightly grease the mixing bowl and put the dough back in the bowl, covering it with a piece of oiled cling film (plastic wrap). Leave to double in size in a warm place for at least an hour.

3 Knock (punch) the dough down and knead it for a further 10 minutes. Preheat the oven to 200°C/400°F/Gas Mark 6. To make round loaves, divide the dough into four pieces and shape them into flattish rounds. Place them on a floured baking sheet and leave to rise for a further 15 minutes. Sprinkle the loaves with the mixed seeds. Bake for about 20 minutes until golden and firm.

Makes 4 rounds

20g/¾oz fresh yeast

300ml/½ pint/1¼ cups warm milk

5ml/1 tsp caster (superfine) sugar

225g/8oz/1½ cups strong wholemeal (whole-wheat) bread flour, sifted

225g/8oz/2 cups strong white bread flour, sifted

5ml/1 tsp salt

50g/2oz/4 tbsp butter, diced

1 egg, lightly beaten

30ml/2 tbsp mixed seeds

Note The recipe will make 4 round loaves or 2 standard loaves. For standard loaves, put the knocked-back dough into two greased loaf tins. Leave to rise for 45 minutes and then bake for 45 minutes, until the loaf sounds hollow when turned out of the tin and knocked on the base.

Per loaf Energy 576kcal/2423kJ; Protein 20g; Carbohydrate 83g, of which sugars 7g; Fat 20g, of which saturates 10g; Cholesterol 95mg; Calcium 242mg; Fibre 7.2g; Sodium 626mg.

Granary cob

A loaf made with granary flour, which is a brand of flour that contains added malted wheat grains, has a particularly rustic look and a lovely nutty flavour.

Makes 1 loaf

450g/1lb/4 cups granary (whole-wheat) or malthouse flour

12.5ml/2½ tsp salt

15g/½oz fresh yeast

wheat flakes, cracked wheat, or rolled oats for sprinkling

1 Lightly flour a baking sheet. Mix the flour and 10ml/2 tsp of the salt together in a large bowl and make a well in the centre. Place in a very low oven for 5 minutes to warm.

2 Measure 300ml/½ pint/1¼ cups lukewarm water. Mix the yeast with a little of the water, then blend in the rest. Pour the yeast mixture into the centre of the flour and mix to a dough.

3 Turn out on to a lightly floured surface and knead for about 10 minutes, until smooth and elastic. Place in a lightly oiled bowl, cover with lightly oiled clear film (plastic wrap) and leave to rise in a warm place for 1¼ hours, or until doubled in bulk.

4 Turn the dough out on to a floured surface. Knead for 2–3 minutes, then roll into a ball. Place on the baking sheet. Cover with a bowl and leave to rise in a warm place for 30–45 minutes.

5 Preheat the oven to 230°C/450°F/ Gas 8 towards the end of the rising time. Mix 30ml/2 tbsp water with the remaining salt and brush evenly over the bread. Sprinkle the loaf with wheat flakes, cracked wheat or a handful of rolled oats.

6 Bake the bread for 15 minutes, then reduce the oven temperature to 200°C/400°F/Gas 6 and bake for a further 20 minutes, or until the loaf is firm to the touch and sounds hollow when tapped on the base. Cool on a wire rack.

Per loaf Energy 1395kcal/5931kJ; Protein 57.1g; Carbohydrate 287.6g, of which sugars 9.4g; Fat 9.9g, of which saturates 1.4g; Cholesterol 0mg; Calcium 172mg; Fibre 40.5g; Sodium 4926mg.

Onion, olive and Parmesan bread

Versatile and delicious, this tasty bread is made with olive oil and cornmeal. Try it cut into chunks and dipped into olive oil. It is also wonderful as a base for bruschetta or filled with mozzarella and prosciutto, and makes lovely crispy croûtons for tossing into a salad.

Makes 1 large loaf

350g/12oz/3 cups unbleached strong white bread flour, plus a little extra

115g/4oz/1 cup yellow cornmeal, plus a little extra

rounded 5ml/1 tsp salt

15g/½oz fresh yeast or 10ml/2 tsp active dried yeast

5ml/1 tsp muscovado (molasses) sugar

270ml/9fl oz/generous 1 cup warm water

5ml/1 tsp chopped fresh thyme

30ml/2 tbsp olive oil, plus a little extra for greasing

1 onion, finely chopped

75g/3oz/1 cup freshly grated Parmesan cheese

90g/3½oz/scant 1 cup pitted black olives, halved

1 Mix the flour, cornmeal and salt in a warmed bowl. If using fresh yeast, cream it with the sugar and gradually stir in 120ml/4fl oz/½ cup of the warm water. If using dried yeast, stir the sugar into the water and then sprinkle the dried yeast over the surface. Leave in a warm place for 10 minutes, until frothy.

2 Make a well in the centre of the dry ingredients and pour in the yeast liquid and a further 150ml/¼ pint/⅔ cup of the remaining warm water.

3 Add the chopped fresh thyme and 15ml/1 tbsp of the olive oil and mix thoroughly with a wooden spoon, gradually drawing in the dry ingredients until they are fully incorporated. Add a dash more warm water, if necessary, to make a soft, but not sticky, dough.

4 Knead the dough on a lightly floured work surface for 5 minutes, until smooth and elastic. Place in a clean, lightly oiled bowl and place in a polythene bag or cover with oiled clear film (plastic wrap). Set aside to rise in a warm, not hot, place for 1–2 hours or until well risen.

5 Meanwhile, heat the remaining olive oil in a heavy frying pan. Add the onion and cook gently for 8 minutes, until softened. Set aside to cool.

6 Brush a baking sheet with olive oil. Turn out the dough on to a floured work surface. Knead in the onions, followed by the Parmesan and olives.

7 Shape the dough into a rough oval loaf. Sprinkle a little cornmeal on the work surface and roll the bread in it, then place on the prepared baking sheet. Make several slits across the top.

8 Slip the baking sheet into the polythene bag or cover with oiled clear film, and leave to rise in a warm place for about 1 hour, or until well risen.

9 Preheat the oven to 200°C/400°F/ Gas 6. Bake for 30–35 minutes, or until the bread sounds hollow when tapped on the base. Cool on a wire rack.

Variation Alternatively, shape the dough into a loaf, roll in cornmeal and place in an oiled loaf tin (pan). Leave to rise in the tin, then bake as in step 8.

Per loaf Energy 1142kcal/4803kJ; Protein 37.4g; Carbohydrate 182.5g, of which sugars 6.4g; Fat 32.5g, of which saturates 10.4g; Cholesterol 38mg; Calcium 733mg; Fibre 8.4g; Sodium 1428mg.

Brown soda bread

Perhaps the easiest to make of all loaves, soda bread is yeast-free and so doesn't need time to rise. It is baked straightaway and is best eaten on the day it is made. It tastes delicious spread with unsalted butter and topped with a fruity jam or a slice of farmhouse cheese.

Makes 1 loaf

450g/1lb/4 cups wholemeal (whole-wheat) flour

175g/6oz/1½ cups plain (all-purpose) flour

7.5ml/1½ tsp bicarbonate of soda (baking soda)

5ml/1 tsp salt

about 450ml/¾ pint/scant 2 cups buttermilk

Variation Cream of tartar can be added to the dry ingredients to provide the acid reaction instead of buttermilk.

1 Preheat the oven to 200°C/400°F/Gas 6, and grease a baking sheet. Combine the dry ingredients in a mixing bowl and stir in enough buttermilk to make a fairly soft dough. Turn on to a work surface dusted with wholemeal flour, and knead lightly until smooth.

2 Form the dough into a circle, about 4cm/1½in thick. Place it on the baking sheet and mark a deep cross in the top with the blunt side of a knife.

3 Bake for about 45 minutes, or until the bread is browned and sounds hollow when tapped on the base. Cool on a wire rack. If a soft crust is preferred, wrap the loaf in a clean dish towel while cooling.

Farmhouse tip Buttermilk can be cultured easily, using a 'buttermilk plant'. Heat 450ml/¾ pint/scant 2 cups skimmed milk to lukewarm by adding 150ml/¼ pint/⅔ cup boiling water, then add 25g/1oz yeast and 10ml/2 tsp sugar.

Pour into a sterilized screw-top or preserving jar, allowing enough space for the contents to be shaken. Place on its side in a warm, dark place and shake several times a day for 4–6 days, while the buttermilk plant is forming, then remove the jar and open it carefully.

Strain the soured milk into a jug (pitcher); the lumpy pieces of yeast left in the strainer become the buttermilk plant and can be washed and used again.

Leftover milk can be added to the jar daily if there is room – it will thicken and sour, taking as little as 2 days in summer, 4–5 in winter.

Remember to always wash all the old milk from the yeast and sterilize the jar.

Per loaf Energy 2262kcal/9643kJ; Protein 88.5g; Carbohydrate 465.4g, of which sugars 31.4g; Fat 18.9g, of which saturates 6.5g; Cholesterol 27mg; Calcium 1.37g; Fibre 34.2g; Sodium 2.18g.

Cheese and onion cornbread

Full of flavour, and very easy to make, this American wheat-free cornbread is delicious served freshly baked, warm or cold in slices, either on its own or spread with butter. It makes an ideal accompaniment to soups, stews and chillies instead of potatoes or rice.

Makes 1 loaf

15ml/1 tbsp sunflower oil

1 onion, thinly sliced

175g/6oz/1½ cups gluten-free cornmeal

75g/3oz/¾ cup rice flour

25g/1oz/¼ cup soya flour

15ml/1 tbsp gluten-free baking powder

5ml/1 tsp sugar

5ml/1 tsp salt

115g/4oz/1 cup coarsely grated mature Cheddar cheese, plus extra for the topping

200ml/7fl oz/scant 1 cup tepid milk

2 eggs

40g/1½oz/3 tbsp butter, melted

1 Preheat the oven to 190°C/375°F/ Gas 5. Grease a 900g/2lb loaf tin (pan). Heat the oil in a frying pan, add the onion and cook gently for 10–15 minutes until softened, stirring occasionally. Set aside to cool.

2 Place the cornmeal, rice flour, soya flour, baking powder, sugar and salt in a bowl and combine thoroughly.

3 Stir the cheese into the cornmeal mixture. Beat together the milk, eggs and melted butter. Add to the flour mixture and mix well.

4 Stir in most of the cooled, cooked onions, reserving some, and mix again.

5 Spoon the onion mixture into the prepared tin and level the surface, Scatter the reserved onions, and some grated cheese on top and bake for about 30 minutes until the bread has risen and is golden brown.

6 Turn out on to a wire rack to cool slightly and serve warm. Alternatively, leave it on the rack until completely cold, and store wrapped in foil. Warm again before serving.

Farmhouse tip If you have any leftover cornbread, which has gone a little stale, use it cubed as one of the ingredients in a stuffing for turkey or chicken.

Per loaf Energy 2314kcals/9631kJ; Protein 83g; Carbohydrate 220g, of which sugars 21.2g; Fat 121g, of which saturates 42g; Fibre – NSP 9g; Sodium 3100mg

Drop scones

Centuries ago, drop, scones were cooked on a flat metal griddle set on an open fire, long before ovens were common. These little scones are delicious spread with jam.

2 Add the egg and half the milk, then gradually incorporate the surrounding flour to make a smooth batter. Beat in the remaining milk.

3 Lightly grease the griddle or pan. Drop tablespoons of the batter on to the surface, leaving them until they bubble and the bubbles begin to burst.

Makes 18

225g/8oz/2 cups self-raising (self-rising) flour

2.5ml/½ tsp salt

15ml/1 tbsp caster (superfine) sugar

1 egg, beaten

300ml/½ pint/1¼ cups skimmed milk

Variation For savoury scones, omit the sugar and add 2 chopped spring onions (scallions) and 15ml/1 tbsp freshly grated Parmesan cheese to the batter.

1 Preheat a griddle, or a heavy frying pan. Sift the flour and salt into a mixing bowl. Stir in the sugar and then make a well in the centre of the dry ingredients.

4 Turn the drop scones over with a palette knife or spatula and cook until the underside is golden. Keep the cooked drop scones warm and moist by wrapping them in a clean dish towel while cooking successive batches.

Energy 55kcal/235kJ; Protein 2.1g; Carbohydrate 11.3g, of which sugars 1.8g; Fat 0.5g, of which saturates 0.1g; Cholesterol 11mg; Calcium 40mg; Fibre 0.4g; Sodium 12mg.

Scones with jam and cream

For many people, English afternoon tea without a plate of scones would be unthinkable.
Quick and easy to make, these are best served fresh and warm from the oven.

Makes about 12

450g/1lb/4 cups self-raising (self-rising) flour, or 450g/1lb/4 cups plain (all-purpose) flour and 10ml/2 tsp baking powder

5ml/1 tsp salt

55g/2oz/¼ cup butter, chilled and cut into small cubes

15ml/1 tbsp lemon juice

about 400ml/14fl oz/1⅔ cups milk, plus extra to glaze

butter, jam and cream, to serve

1 Preheat the oven to 230°C/450°F/ Gas 8. Sift the flour, baking powder (if using) and salt into a mixing bowl, and stir to mix through. Add the butter and rub it lightly into the flour with your fingertips until the mixture resembles fine, even-textured breadcrumbs.

2 Whisk the lemon juice into the milk and leave for about 1 minute to thicken slightly, then pour into the flour mixture and mix quickly to make a soft but pliable dough. The softer the mixture, the lighter the resulting scones will be, but if it is too sticky they will spread during baking and lose their shape.

3 Knead the dough briefly, then roll it out on a lightly floured surface to a thickness of at least 2.5cm/1in. Using a 5cm/2in biscuit (cookie) cutter, and dipping it into flour each time, stamp out 12 rounds. Place the dough rounds on a well-floured baking sheet. Re-roll the trimmings and cut out more scones.

4 Brush the tops with a little milk, then put into the hot oven and cook for about 20 minutes, or until risen.

5 Remove from the oven and wrap the scones in a clean dish towel to keep them warm and soft until ready to eat. Eat the scones with butter, plenty of jam and a generous dollop of clotted or whipped double (heavy) cream.

Variation To make fruit scones, add a handful of sultanas (golden raisins) to the dry mixture at the end of step 1. Serve warm, spread generously with plenty of butter.

Energy 177kcal/749kJ; Protein 4.7g; Carbohydrate 30.7g, of which sugars 2.2g; Fat 4.8g, of which saturates 2.8g; Cholesterol 12mg; Calcium 93mg; Fibre 1.2g; Sodium 43mg.

Cheese scones

These delicious scones make a good tea-time treat. They are best served fresh and still warm, spread with butter or cream cheese. They also go well with soup.

Makes 12

225g/8oz/2 cups plain (all-purpose) flour

12.5ml/2½ tsp baking powder

2.5ml/½ tsp dry mustard powder

pinch of salt

50g/2oz/4 tbsp butter, chilled

75g/3oz Cheddar cheese, grated

150ml/¼ pint/⅔ cup milk

1 egg, beaten

1 Preheat the oven to 230°C/450°F/ Gas 8. Sift the flour, baking powder, mustard powder and salt into a mixing bowl. Add the butter and rub it into the flour mixture until the mixture resembles breadcrumbs. Stir in 50g/ 2oz of the cheese.

2 Make a well in the centre and add the milk and egg. Mix gently to a soft dough, then turn out on to a lightly floured surface. Roll and cut it into triangles or squares. Brush lightly with milk and sprinkle with the remaining cheese. Bake for 15 minutes, or until well risen, and serve warm.

Energy 133Kcal/557kJ; Protein 4.3g; Carbohydrate 15.2g, of which sugars 0.9g; Fat 6.4g, of which saturates 3.8g; Cholesterol 32mg; Calcium 91mg; Fibre 0.6g; Sodium 82mg.

Oatcakes

These are very simple to make and are an excellent addition to a cheese board. The oatcakes will keep in an airtight tin for up to 2 weeks.

Makes 24

225g/8oz/1⅔ cups medium oatmeal

75g/3oz/¾ cup plain (all-purpose) flour

1.5ml/¼ tsp bicarbonate of soda

5ml/1 tsp salt

25g/1oz/2 tbsp white vegetable fat

25g/1oz/2 tbsp butter

Farmhouse tip Add the water a little at a time; if the dough is too wet, the oatcakes won't crisp up so well.

1 Preheat the oven to 220°C/425°F/ Gas Mark 7. Place the oatmeal, flour, soda and salt in a large bowl.

2 Gently melt the two fats together in a small pan.

3 Add the melted fats and enough boiling water to make a dry dough. Turn out on to a surface sprinkled with a little oatmeal, roll out and cut into circles. Bake on ungreased baking trays for 15 minutes, then cool on wire racks.

Energy 102Kcal/429kJ; Protein 2.7g; Carbohydrate 16g, of which sugars 0g; Fat 3.4g, of which saturates 1g; Cholesterol 4mg; Calcium 12mg; Fibre 1.5g; Sodium 142mg.

Walnut and caramelized onion scones

These savoury scones are delicious served warm with butter, artisan cheese and fruit chutney. They can be made as bite-sized scones for a party, topped with cheese or ham.

Makes 10–12

90g/3½oz/7 tbsp butter

15ml/1 tbsp olive oil

1 Spanish (Bermuda) onion, chopped

5ml/1 tsp cumin seeds, lightly crushed

200g/7oz/1¾ cups self-raising (self-rising) flour

5ml/1 tsp baking powder

25g/1oz/¼ cup fine oatmeal

5ml/1 tsp light unrefined muscovado (brown) sugar

90g/3½oz/scant 1 cup chopped walnuts

5ml/1 tsp chopped fresh thyme

120–150ml/4–5fl oz/½–⅔ cup buttermilk

a little milk or soya milk

sea salt and ground black pepper

1 Melt 15g/½oz/1 tbsp of the butter with the oil in a small pan and cook the onion gently, covered, for 10–12 minutes. Uncover, then continue to cook gently until it begins to brown.

2 Add half the cumin seeds and increase the heat slightly. Continue to cook, stirring occasionally, until the onion begins to caramelize. Cool. Preheat the oven to 200°C/400°F/Gas 6.

3 Sift the flour and baking powder into a large bowl and add the oatmeal, sugar, 2.5ml/½ tsp salt and black pepper. Add the remaining butter and rub in until the mixture resembles fine breadcrumbs.

4 Add the cooked onion and cumin mixture, chopped walnuts and fresh thyme, then bind to make a soft, but not sticky, dough with the buttermilk.

5 Roll or pat out the mixture to an even thickness of just over 1cm/½in. Stamp out 10–12 scones using a 5–6cm/2–2½in plain round cutter.

6 Place the scones on a floured baking tray, glaze with the milk or soya milk and sprinkle with a little salt and the remaining cumin seeds.

7 Bake the scones for 12–15 minutes until risen and golden brown. Cool for a few minutes on a wire rack and serve warm, spread with butter.

Energy 131kcal/543kJ; Protein 1.8g; Carbohydrate 3g, of which sugars 1.3g; Fat 12.6g, of which saturates 4.6g; Cholesterol 17mg; Calcium 23mg; Fibre 0.5g; Sodium 51mg.

Three-herb potato scones

These flavoursome scones are perfect served warm, split in two, spread with butter and stuffed with hand-carved ham and Parmesan shavings as a filling.

Makes 12

225g/8oz/2 cups self-raising (self-rising) flour

5ml/1 tsp baking powder

pinch of salt

50g/2oz/4 tbsp butter, diced

25g/1oz potato flakes

15ml/1 tbsp chopped fresh parsley

15ml/1 tbsp chopped fresh basil

15ml/1 tbsp chopped fresh oregano

150ml/¼ pint/⅔ cup milk

1 Preheat the oven to 180°C/350°F/Gas 4. Sift the flour into a bowl with the baking powder and salt. Rub in the butter with your fingertips to form crumbs. Place the potato flakes in bowl and pour over 200ml/7fl oz/scant 1 cup boiling water. Beat well and cool.

2 Stir the potatoes into the dry ingredients with the herbs and milk.

3 Bring the mixture together to form a soft dough. Turn out on to a floured surface and knead gently for a few minutes, until soft and pliable.

Farmhouse tip Don't be tempted to overseason the mixture, as once cooked the baking powder can also increase the salty flavour of the finished scone and this can overpower the taste of the herbs.

4 Roll the dough out on a floured surface to about 4cm/1½in thickness, and stamp out rounds using a 7.5cm/3in cutter.

5 Reshape any remaining dough and re-roll for more scones. Place the scones on to a greased baking dish and brush the surfaces with a little more milk.

6 Cook for 15–20 minutes and serve warm. They can be eaten plain, or with a filling, such as cheese and pickle, or slices of ham.

Energy 46kcal/193kJ; Protein 1g; Carbohydrate 8.1g, of which sugars 0.4g; Fat 1.3g, of which saturates 0.2g; Cholesterol 0mg; Calcium 12mg; Fibre 0.5g; Sodium 3mg.

Teatime crumpets

These traditional crumpets are made with a yeast batter and cooked in metal rings on a griddle. Once cooked, they then need to be toasted, and are equally tasty with either savoury or sweet toppings – try golden syrup, honey or preserves, or sliced ham or cheese.

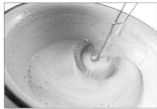

2 Whisk vigorously to make a thick smooth batter. Cover and leave in a warm place for about 1 hour until the mixture has a spongy texture. Re-whisk the batter before cooking.

3 Lightly oil and heat a griddle or heavy frying pan. Brush the inside of three or four 8cm/3½in diameter metal rings, place on the hot surface and leave for 1–2 minutes until hot.

4 Spoon the batter into the rings to a depth of about 1cm/½in. Cook over a medium heat for about 6 minutes until the top surface is set and bubbles have burst open to make holes.

5 Lift off the rings and flip the crumpets over, cooking the second side for just 1 minute until lightly browned, then transfer to a wire rack to cool. Repeat with the remaining crumpet mixture. To serve, toast the crumpets on both sides and butter generously.

Makes about 10

225g/8oz/2 cups plain (all-purpose) flour

2.5ml/½ tsp salt

2.5ml/½ tsp bicarbonate of soda (baking soda)

5ml/1 tsp easy-blend (rapid-rise) yeast

150ml/¼ pint/⅔ cup milk

oil, for greasing

1 Sift the flour, salt and bicarbonate of soda into a bowl and stir in the yeast. Make a well in the centre. Heat the milk with 200ml/7fl oz/scant 1 cup water until lukewarm and tip into the well.

Per crumpet Energy 93kcal/393kJ; Protein 3g; Carbohydrate 16.5g, of which sugars 1g; Fat 2.1g, of which saturates 1g; Cholesterol 21mg; Calcium 48mg; Fibre 0.6g; Sodium 21mg.

English muffins

In the past muffins got their distinctive floury crust from being baked directly on the brick or stone oven floor. They are perfect served warm, split open and buttered for afternoon tea; or try them toasted, split and topped with ham and eggs for brunch.

Makes 9

450g/1lb/4 cups unbleached strong white bread flour

7.5ml/1½ tsp salt

350–375ml/12–13fl oz/1½–1⅔ cups lukewarm milk

2.5ml/½ tsp caster (superfine) sugar

15g/½oz fresh yeast

15ml/1 tbsp melted butter or olive oil

rice flour or semolina, for dusting

Farmhouse tip Muffins should be cut around the outer edge only using a sharp knife and then torn apart. If toasting, toast the whole muffins first and then split them in half.

1 Generously flour a non-stick baking sheet. Very lightly grease a griddle. Sift the flour and salt together into a large bowl and make a well in the centre. Blend 150ml/¼ pint/⅔ cup of the milk, sugar and yeast together. Stir in the remaining milk and butter or oil.

2 Add the yeast mixture to the centre of the flour and beat for 4–5 minutes until smooth and elastic. The dough will be soft but just hold its shape. Cover with lightly oiled clear film (plastic wrap) and leave to rise, in a warm place, for 45–60 minutes, or until doubled in bulk.

3 Turn out on a floured surface and knock back (punch down). Roll out to 1cm/½in thick. Using a 7.5cm/3in plain cutter, cut out nine rounds.

4 Dust with rice flour or semolina and place on the prepared baking sheet. Cover and leave to rise in a warm place for about 20–30 minutes.

5 Warm the griddle over a medium heat. Carefully transfer the muffins in batches to the griddle. Cook slowly for about 7 minutes on each side or until golden brown. Transfer to a wire rack to cool.

Energy 200kcal/851kJ; Protein 6g; Carbohydrate 41.1g, of which sugars 3g; Fat 2.5g, of which saturates 0.7g; Cholesterol 2mg; Calcium 117mg; Fibre 1.5g; Sodium 350mg.

The Farmhouse Pantry

As well as preserving the taste of summer fruits and vegetables, it is immensely satisfying to make your own jams, jellies and relishes. Country-style home-made ones always taste better than store-bought varieties, and make lovely gifts. Spicy and fruity relishes enliven the simplest of rustic dishes, and stirring a bubbling pot of preserves is a highly pleasurable rural pastime.

Tomato chutney

A great recipe for using up a glut of greenhouse tomatoes, this spicy chutney is delicious with a selection of cheeses and crackers, or with cold meats.

Makes about 1.5kg/3lb

900g/2lb tomatoes

225g/8oz/1⅓ cups raisins

225g/8oz onions, chopped

225g/8oz/generous 1 cup caster (superfine) sugar

600ml/1 pint/2½ cups malt vinegar

1 Skin the tomatoes and roughly chop. Put them in a preserving pan.

2 Add the raisins, onions and caster sugar to the pan.

3 Pour over the vinegar. Bring to the boil and let it simmer for 2 hours, uncovered. Pot into sterilized jars. Seal with a waxed disc and cover with a tightly fitting cellophane top. Store in a cool, dark place. The chutney will keep unopened for up to a year. Once opened, store in the refrigerator and consume within a week.

Per batch Energy 1733kcal/7384kJ; Protein 14.9g; Carbohydrate 436.7g, of which sugars 431.6g; Fat 4g, of which saturates 0.9g; Cholesterol 0mg; Calcium 342mg; Fibre 16.6g; Sodium 236mg.

Windfall pear chutney

The bullet-hard pears that litter the ground underneath old pear trees after
high winds are ideal for this tasty chutney.

Makes about 2kg/4½lb

675g/1½lb pears, peeled
and cored

3 onions, chopped

175g/6oz/1 cup raisins

1 cooking apple, peeled, cored and
chopped

50g/2oz/⅓ cup preserved stem
ginger

115g/4oz/1 cup walnuts, chopped

1 garlic clove, chopped

grated rind and juice of 1 lemon

600ml/1 pint/2½ cups cider vinegar

175g/6oz/1 cup soft brown sugar

2 cloves

5ml/1 tsp salt

1 Peel the pears then chop roughly and
put them in a bowl. Add the onions,
raisins, apple, ginger, walnuts and
garlic, with the lemon juice and rind.

2 Put the vinegar, sugar, cloves and salt
into a pan. Gently heat, stirring until
the sugar has dissolved, then bring to
the boil briefly and pour over the fruit.
Cover and leave overnight. The
following day, transfer the mixture to a
preserving pan and boil gently for
1½ hours until soft.

3 ◄ Spoon into warm, sterilized jars.
Seal with a waxed disc and cover with a
cellophane top. Store in a dark cool
place for up to a year. Once opened,
store in the refrigerator. Serve with cold
meats or bread and cheese.

Per batch Energy 2496kcal/10480kJ; Protein 32g; Carbohydrate 415g, of which sugars 400g; Fat 82g, of which saturates 7g; Cholesterol 0mg; Calcium 512mg; Fibre 24.3g; Sodium 2205mg.

Green tomato chutney

This is a classic chutney for using the last tomatoes of summer that just never seem to ripen. Apples and onions contribute essential flavour, which is enhanced by the addition of spice. This zesty chutney is good in sandwiches, for barbecues and with burgers.

Makes about 2.5kg/5$\frac{1}{2}$lb

1.8kg/4lb green tomatoes, chopped

450g/1lb cooking apples, peeled, cored and chopped

450g/1lb onions, chopped

2 large garlic cloves, crushed

15ml/1 tbsp salt

45ml/3 tbsp pickling spice

600ml/1 pint/2$\frac{1}{2}$ cups cider vinegar

450g/1lb/2$\frac{1}{4}$ cups granulated (white) sugar

1 Place the tomatoes, apples, onions and garlic in a pan and add the salt.

2 Tie the pickling spice in a piece of muslin (cheesecloth) and add to the ingredients in the pan.

3 Add half the vinegar to the pan and bring to the boil. Reduce the heat, then simmer for 1 hour, or until the chutney is reduced and thick, stirring frequently.

4 Put the sugar and remaining vinegar in a pan and heat gently until the sugar has dissolved, then add to the chutney. Simmer for 1$\frac{1}{2}$ hours until thick, stirring the mixture occasionally.

5 Remove the muslin bag from the chutney, then spoon the hot chutney into warmed sterilized jars. Cover and seal immediately. Allow the chutney to mature for at least 1 month before using.

Per batch Energy 2398kcal/10,233kJ; Protein 21.6g; Carbohydrate 601.7g, of which sugars 591.3g; Fat 6.8g, of which saturates 1.8g; Cholesterol 0mg; Calcium 495mg; Fibre 31.5g; Sodium 2177mg.

Plum and cherry relish

This simple sweet-and-sour fruit relish complements rich poultry, game or meat, such as roast duck or grilled duck breasts. You can strain a few spoonfuls into a sauce or gravy to give fruity zest and flavour, as well as adding an appetizing splash of bright red colour.

Makes about 350g/12oz

350g/12oz dark-skinned red plums

350g/12oz/2 cups cherries

2 shallots, finely chopped

15ml/1 tbsp olive oil

30ml/2 tbsp dry sherry

60ml/4 tbsp red wine vinegar

15ml/1 tbsp balsamic vinegar

1 bay leaf

90g/3½oz/scant ½ cup demerara (raw) sugar

1 Halve and pit the plums, then roughly chop the flesh. Pit all the cherries and cut them in half.

2 Cook the shallots gently in the oil for 5 minutes, or until soft. Add the fruit, sherry, vinegars, bay leaf and sugar.

3 Slowly bring the mixture to the boil, stirring until the sugar has dissolved completely. Increase the heat and cook briskly for about 15 minutes, or until the relish is very thick and the fruit tender.

4 Remove the bay leaf and spoon the relish into warmed sterilized jars. Cover and seal. Store the relish in the refrigerator and use within 3 months.

Farmhouse tip Use a large preserving pan in which the mixture comes only half-way up the side. Always use just-ripe or slightly under-ripe fruits, as the pectin levels reduce when the fruit ripens.

Per batch Energy 804kcal/3407kJ; Protein 6.5g; Carbohydrate 170.3g, of which sugars 168.9g; Fat 11.8g, of which saturates 1.6g; Cholesterol 0mg; Calcium 156mg; Fibre 9.6g; Sodium 21mg.

Mint sauce

In England, mint sauce is the traditional and inseparable accompaniment to roast lamb.
Its fresh, tart and astringent flavour is the perfect foil to the rich, strongly flavoured meat.
As well as being extremely simple to make, it is infinitely superior to the store-bought varieties.

Makes about 250ml/8fl oz/1 cup

1 large bunch mint

105ml/7 tbsp boiling water

150ml/¼ pint/⅔ cup wine vinegar

30ml/2 tbsp granulated (white) sugar

Farmhouse tip To make a quick and speedy Indian raita for serving with crispy poppadums, simply stir a little mint sauce into a small bowl of natural (plain) yogurt. Serve the raita alongside a bowl of tangy mango chutney.

1 Using a sharp knife, chop the mint very finely and place it in a 600ml/ 1 pint/2½ cup jug (pitcher). Pour the boiling water over the mint and leave to infuse for about 10 minutes.

2 When the mint infusion has cooled and is lukewarm, stir in the wine vinegar and sugar. Continue stirring (but do not mash up the mint leaves) until the sugar has dissolved completely.

3 Pour the mint sauce into a warmed sterilized bottle or jar. Seal the jar, label it with the date and store in the refrigerator or a cool, dark place.

Farmhouse tip This mint sauce keeps for up to 6 months when stored in the refrigerator, but is best when used within 3 weeks.

Energy 161kcal/685kJ; Protein 3.9g; Carbohydrate 36.6g, of which sugars 31.3g; Fat 0.7g, of which saturates 0g; Cholesterol 0mg; Calcium 226mg; Fibre 0g; Sodium 17mg.

Real horseradish sauce

Fiery, peppery horseradish sauce is the essential accompaniment to roast beef, and is also delicious with smoked salmon. Take care when handling it, and wash your hands afterwards.

Makes about 200ml/7fl oz/scant 1 cup

45ml/3 tbsp freshly grated horseradish root

15ml/1 tbsp white wine vinegar

5ml/1 tsp granulated (white) sugar

pinch of salt

150ml/¼ pint/⅔ cup thick double (heavy) cream, for serving

Farmhouse tip To counteract the potent fumes of the horseradish, keep the root submerged in water while you chop and peel it. Use a food processor to do the fine chopping or grating, and avert your head when removing the lid.

1 Place the grated horseradish in a bowl, then add the white wine vinegar, granulated sugar and just a pinch of salt.

2 Stir the ingredients together, mixing them well until they are thoroughly combined and smooth.

3 Pour the mixture into a sterilized jar. It will keep in the refrigerator for up to 6 months.

4 A few hours before you intend to serve the sauce, stir the cream into the horseradish and leave to infuse. Stir once again before serving.

Per batch Energy 774kcal/3190kJ; Protein 2.8g; Carbohydrate 9.9g, of which sugars 9.8g; Fat 80.7g, of which saturates 50.1g; Cholesterol 206mg; Calcium 98mg; Fibre 1.1g; Sodium 40mg.

Herb mustard

This fragrant, hot mustard may be used either as a delicious condiment or for coating meats such as chicken and pork, or oily fish such as mackerel, before cooking. It is also fabulous when smeared thinly on cheese on toast, for an added bite.

Makes about 300ml/½ pint/1¼ cups

75g/3oz/scant ½ cup white mustard seeds

50g/2oz/¼ cup soft light brown sugar

5ml/1 tsp salt

5ml/1 tsp whole peppercorns

2.5ml/½ tsp ground turmeric

200ml/7fl oz/scant 1 cup distilled malt vinegar

60ml/4 tbsp chopped fresh mixed herbs, such as parsley, sage, thyme and rosemary

1 Put the mustard seeds, sugar, salt, whole peppercorns and ground turmeric into a food processor or blender and process for about 1 minute, or until the peppercorns are coarsely chopped.

2 Gradually add the vinegar to the mustard mixture, 15ml/1 tbsp at a time, processing well between each addition, then continue processing until a coarse paste forms.

3 Add the chopped fresh herbs to the mustard and mix well, then leave to stand for 10–15 minutes until the mustard thickens slightly.

4 Spoon the mustard into a 300ml/ ½ pint/1¼ cup sterilized jar. Cover the surface of the mustard with a baking parchment disc, then seal with a screw-top lid or a cork, and label. Store the unopened jars in a cool, dark place for up to 3 months.

Per batch Energy 553kcal/2324kJ; Protein 23.4g; Carbohydrate 69.1g, of which sugars 53.4g; Fat 34.5g, of which saturates 1.1g; Cholesterol 3mg; Calcium 374mg; Fibre 2.5g; Sodium 23mg.

Honey mustard

Delicious home-made mustards mature to make the most aromatic of condiments. This honey mustard is richly flavoured and is wonderful served with meats and cheeses, or stirred into sauces and salad dressings to give an extra peppery bite.

Makes about 500g/1¼lb

225g/8oz/1 cup mustard seeds

15ml/1 tbsp ground cinnamon

2.5ml/½ tsp ground ginger

300ml/½ pint/1½ cups white wine vinegar

90ml/6 tbsp dark clear honey

Farmhouse tip Use well-flavoured clear honey for this recipe. Set (crystallized) honey does not have the right consistency and will not work well.

1 Put the mustard seeds in a bowl with the cinnamon and ginger, and pour over the white wine vinegar. Stir well to mix, then cover and leave to soak overnight in a cool place.

2 The next day, put the mustard mixture in a mortar and pound with a pestle, adding the honey very gradually.

3 Continue pounding and mixing until the mustard resembles a stiff paste. If the mixture becomes too stiff, add a little extra vinegar to achieve the desired consistency.

4 Spoon the mustard into four warmed sterilized jars. Seal and label the jars, then store in a cool, dark place or in the refrigerator. Keep refrigerated after opening, and use within 4 weeks.

Per batch Energy 1276kcal/5345kJ; Protein 65.4g; Carbohydrate 115.3g, of which sugars 68.8g; Fat 101.5g, of which saturates 3.4g; Cholesterol 9mg; Calcium 747mg; Fibre 0g; Sodium 21mg.

Pickled spiced red cabbage

This delicately spiced and vibrant-coloured pickle is an old-fashioned favourite to serve with bread and cheese for an informal lunch, or to accompany pies, terrines or cold cuts.

Makes about 1–1.6kg/2¼–3½lb

675g/1½lb/6 cups red cabbage, shredded

1 large Spanish (Bermuda) onion, sliced

30ml/2 tbsp sea salt

600ml/1 pint/2½ cups red wine vinegar

75g/3oz/6 tbsp light muscovado (brown) sugar

15ml/1 tbsp coriander seeds

3 cloves

2.5cm/1in piece fresh root ginger

1 whole star anise

2 bay leaves

4 eating apples

1 Put the cabbage and onion in a bowl, add the salt and mix well until thoroughly combined.

2 Transfer the mixture into a colander over a bowl and leave to drain overnight.

3 The next day, rinse the salted vegetables, drain well and pat dry using kitchen paper. Transfer back to the colander.

4 Pour the vinegar into a pan, add the sugar, spices and bay leaves and boil. Remove from the heat and leave to cool.

5 Core and chop the apples, then layer with the cabbage and onions in sterilized preserving jars. Pour over the cooled spiced vinegar. Seal the jars and store for 1 week before eating. Eat within 2 months. Once opened, store in the refrigerator.

Per batch Energy 674kcal/2868kJ; Protein 12g; Carbohydrate 161.4g, of which sugars 159.3g; Fat 2g, of which saturates 0g; Cholesterol 0mg; Calcium 405mg; Fibre 23g; Sodium 64mg.

Traditional pickled onions

Essential for a ploughman's lunch, pickled onions should be crunchy and pungent, and stored for at least 6 weeks so the flavours develop. Try making some for Christmas.

Makes about 4 jars

1kg/2¼lb pickling (pearl) onions

115g/4oz/½ cup salt

750ml/1¼ pints/3 cups malt vinegar

15ml/1 tbsp sugar

2–3 dried red chillies

5ml/1 tsp brown mustard seeds

15ml/1 tbsp coriander seeds

5ml/1 tsp allspice berries

5ml/1 tsp black peppercorns

5cm/2in piece fresh root ginger, sliced

2–3 blades mace

2–3 fresh bay leaves

1 To peel the onions, trim off the root ends, but leave the onion layers attached. Cut a thin slice off the top (neck) end of the onion. Place the onions in a bowl, then cover with boiling water. Leave to stand for about 4 minutes, then drain. The skin should then be easy to peel using a small, sharp knife.

2 Place the peeled onions in a bowl and cover with cold water, then drain the water into a large pan. Add the salt and heat to dissolve, then cool before pouring the brine over the onions.

3 Place a plate inside the top of the bowl and weigh it down slightly so that it keeps all the onions submerged in the brine. Leave to stand for 24 hours.

4 Meanwhile, place the vinegar in a large pan. Wrap all the remaining ingredients, except the bay leaves, in a piece of muslin (cheesecloth). Bring to the boil, simmer for about 5 minutes, then remove the pan from the heat. Set aside, cover and leave in a cool place overnight to infuse.

5 The next day, drain the onions, rinse and pat dry. Pack them into sterilized 450g/1lb jars. Add some or all of the spice from the vinegar, except the ginger slices. The pickle will become hotter if you add the chillies. Pour the vinegar over to cover and add the bay leaves. (Store leftover vinegar in a bottle for another batch of pickles.)

6 Seal the jars with non-metallic lids and store in a cool, dark place for at least 6 weeks before eating.

Per batch Energy 109kcal/454kJ; Protein 3.1g; Carbohydrate 24.5g, of which sugars 18.6g; Fat 0.5g, of which saturates 0g; Cholesterol 0mg; Calcium 67mg; Fibre 3.6g; Sodium 8mg.

Sweet piccalilli

Undoubtedly one of the most popular relishes, piccalilli can be eaten with grilled sausages, ham, chops or cold meats, or a strong, well-flavoured cheese such as Cheddar. It should contain a good selection of fresh, crunchy vegetables in a smooth mustard sauce.

Makes about 1.8kg/4lb

1 large cauliflower

450g/1lb pickling (pearl) onions

900g/2lb mixed vegetables, such as marrow (large zucchini), cucumber, French (green) beans

225g/8oz/1 cup salt

2.4 litres/4 pints/10 cups cold water

200g/7oz/1 cup granulated (white) sugar

2 garlic cloves, peeled and crushed

10ml/2 tsp mustard powder

5ml/1 tsp ground ginger

1 litre/1¾ pints/4 cups distilled (white) vinegar

25g/1oz/¼ cup plain (all-purpose) flour

15ml/1 tbsp turmeric

1 Prepare the vegetables. Divide the cauliflower into small florets; peel and quarter the pickling onions; seed and finely dice the marrow and cucumber; trim the French beans, then cut them into 2.5cm/1in lengths.

2 Layer the vegetables in a large glass or stainless steel bowl, generously sprinkling each layer with salt. Pour over the water, cover the bowl with clear film (plastic wrap) and leave to soak for about 24 hours.

3 Drain the soaked vegetables and discard the brine. Rinse well in several changes of cold water to remove as much salt as possible, then drain them thoroughly.

4 Put the sugar, garlic, mustard, ginger and 900ml/1½ pints/3¾ cups of the vinegar in a preserving pan. Heat gently, stirring occasionally, until the sugar has dissolved.

5 Add the vegetables to the pan, bring to the boil, reduce the heat and simmer for 10–15 minutes, or until they are almost tender.

6 Mix the flour and turmeric with the remaining vinegar and stir into the vegetables. Bring to the boil, stirring, and simmer for 5 minutes, until the piccalilli is thick.

7 Spoon the piccalilli into warmed sterilized jars, cover and seal. Store in a cool, dark place for at least 2 weeks. Use within 1 year. Once opened, store in the refrigerator for up to two weeks.

Farmhouse tip Traditional preserving pans are copper, but if you don't have a preserving pan, any stainless steel, shallow and wide-topped pan will be suitable – the large surface area will help evaporation during cooking, which gives a good result.

Per batch Energy 1358kcal/5757kJ; Protein 34.1g; Carbohydrate 300.8g, of which sugars 266g; Fat 12g, of which saturates 1.2g; Cholesterol 0mg; Calcium 555mg; Fibre 20.6g; Sodium 4011mg.

Bottled cherry tomatoes

Cherry tomatoes, bottled in their own juices, are the perfect accompaniment to country ham, and make a welcome appearance through the winter months.

Makes 1kg/2¼lb

1kg/2¼lb cherry tomatoes

salt (see method)

granulated sugar (see method)

fresh basil leaves

5 garlic cloves per jar

1 Preheat the oven to 120°C/250°F/ Gas ½. Prick each tomato at least once with a toothpick or sharp knife.

2 Pack the tomatoes into clean, dry 1 litre/1¾ pint/4 cup preserving jars, adding 5ml/1 tsp each of salt and sugar to each jar.

3 Fill the jars to within 2cm/¾in of the top, tucking the basil leaves and garlic among the tomatoes. Rest the lids on the jars, but do not seal.

4 Stand on a baking sheet lined with a layer of cardboard or newspaper and place in the oven.

5 After about 45 minutes, when the juice is simmering, remove from the oven and seal. Store in a cool place and use within 6 months.

Pickled beetroot

This rich coloured preserve is a perennial favourite.

Makes 450g/1lb

450g/1lb beetroot (beets), cooked and peeled

1 large onion, sliced

300ml/½ pint/1¼ cups cider vinegar

150ml/¼ pint/⅔ cup water

50g/2oz/¼ cup sugar

1 Slice the beetroot and pack it into a jar, layering it with the sliced onion. Pour the vinegar and water into a saucepan. Add the sugar and bring to the boil.

2 Pour the liquid over the beetroot and seal the jar. Store in a cool place and use within 1 month, or longer if kept in the fridge.

Per batch Energy 249kcal/1053kJ; Protein 10g; Carbohydrate 45g, of which sugars 41g; Fat 4g, of which saturates 1g; Cholesterol 0mg; Calcium 120mg; Fibre 13.0g; Sodium 4062mg.
Per batch Energy 511kcal/2160kJ; Protein 12g; Carbohydrate 107g, of which sugars 99g; Fat 1g, of which saturates 0g; Cholesterol 0mg; Calcium 164mg; Fibre 16.2g; Sodium 322mg.

Yogurt cheese in olive oil

Simple cheesemaking has always been a farmhouse tradition, and this recipe from Greece is an easy one to start with. The mild-tasting, fresh cheese balls are delicious on toast.

Makes about 900g/2lb

800g/1³⁄₄lb/3¹⁄₂ cups Greek (US strained, plain) yogurt

2.5ml/¹⁄₂ tsp salt

10ml/2 tsp dried chillies, crushed

15ml/1 tbsp fresh rosemary, chopped

15ml/1 tbsp fresh thyme, chopped

about 300ml/¹⁄₂ pint/1¹⁄₄ cups olive oil, preferably garlic-flavoured

1 Sterilize a large square of muslin (cheesecloth) in boiling water. Squeeze and lay over a large plate. Mix the yogurt with the salt and pour on to the centre of the muslin. Draw up the sides and tie with string.

2 Suspend the bag from a cupboard handle or similar suitable hook, with a bowl placed underneath to catch the whey. Leave for 2–3 days until the yogurt stops dripping.

3 Mix the chillies and herbs together. Take teaspoonfuls of the cheese and roll into balls with your hands. Carefully lower into two sterilized 450g/1lb glass preserving jars, sprinkling each layer with some of the herb mixture.

4 Pour the oil over the cheese until completely covered. Store in the refrigerator for up to 3 weeks. To serve the cheese, spoon out of the jars with a little of the flavoured olive oil and spread on slices of lightly toasted bread.

Per batch Energy 1331kcal/5488kJ; Protein 24g; Carbohydrate 7.5g, of which sugars 7.5g; Fat 138.2g, of which saturates 33.8g; Cholesterol 0mg; Calcium 563mg; Fibre 0g; Sodium 758mg.

Rosemary oil

This pungent oil is ideal drizzled over meat or vegetables before grilling, and is also good with fish.

Makes 600ml/1 pint/2¹⁄₂ cups

600ml/1 pint/2¹⁄₂ cups olive oil

5 fresh rosemary sprigs

1 Transfer the oil to a pan and heat until warm but not too hot.

2 Add four rosemary sprigs and simmer gently to infuse. Put the reserved rosemary sprig in a clean bottle.

3 Strain the oil, pour in the bottle and seal tightly. Allow to cool and store in a cool, dark place. Use within a week.

Thyme vinegar

This vinegar is delicious sprinkled over salmon before poaching.

Makes 600ml/1 pint/2¹⁄₂ cups

600ml/1 pint/2¹⁄₂ cups white-wine vinegar

5 fresh thyme sprigs, washed and patted dry with kitchen paper

3 garlic cloves, peeled

1 ▶ Place the vinegar in a large pan on a low heat. Add four thyme sprigs and the garlic and heat gently.

2 Put the reserved thyme sprig in a sterilized bottle, strain the vinegar, and pour into the bottle.

3 Seal the bottle tightly, allow to cool and store in a cool, dark place. The vinegar may be kept unopened for up to 3 months; once opened use within 2–3 weeks.

Per batch Energy 5404kcal/22218kJ; Protein 0g; Carbohydrate 1g, of which sugars 0g; Fat 600g, of which saturates 8 6g; Cholesterol 0mg; Calcium 37mg; Fibre 05.6g; Sodium 558mg.
Per batch Energy 151kcal/616kJ; Protein 4g; Carbohydrate 36g, of which sugars 15g; Fat 12g, of which saturates 2g; Cholesterol 0mg; Calcium 78mg; Fibre 0.0g; Sodium 2mg.

Spiced apple cider jelly

This wonderfully spicy jelly goes well with cheese and crackers, or spread on to toast.

Makes about 1.3kg/3lb

900g/2lb tart cooking apples, washed and coarsely chopped, with skins and cores intact

900ml/1¼ pints/3¾ cups sweet cider

juice and pips (seeds) of 2 oranges

1 cinnamon stick

6 whole cloves

150ml/½ pint/⅔ cup water

about 900g/2lb/4½ cups preserving or granulated (white) sugar, warmed

3 Measure the strained juice into a preserving pan. Add 450g/1lb/ 2¼ cups warmed sugar for every 600ml/1 pint/2½ cups juice.

4 Heat, stirring, over a low heat until the sugar has dissolved. Increase the heat and boil, without stirring, for 10 minutes, or until the jelly reaches setting point (105°C/220°F).

5 Remove from the heat and skim off any scum. Ladle into warmed sterilized jars. Leave to cool, then cover, seal and label the jars. Store in a dark cupboard for up to 6 months.

1 Put the apples, cider, orange juice and pips, cinnamon, cloves and water in a large pan. Bring to the boil, cover and simmer for about 1 hour.

2 Leave to cool slightly, then pour the fruit into a scalded jelly bag suspended over a non-metallic bowl, and leave to drain overnight.

Per batch Energy 3975kcal/16,950kJ; Protein 5.4g; Carbohydrate 990.6g, of which sugars 990.6g; Fat 0.3g, of which saturates 0g; Cholesterol 0mg; Calcium 561mg; Fibre 4.8g; Sodium 123mg.

Dill pickle

Easy to grow in any kitchen herb garden, dill goes well with fish; these spiced cucumbers make the ideal accompaniment to cold poached salmon, or any smoked fish.

Makes about 2.5 litres/4 pints/10 cups

6 small cucumbers

475ml/16fl oz/2 cups water

1 litre/1¾ pints/4 cups white wine vinegar

115g/4oz/½ cup salt

3 bay leaves

45ml/3 tbsp dill seed

2 garlic cloves, slivered

1 Slice the cucumbers into medium-thick slices. Put the water, vinegar and salt in a pan. Bring to the boil, then immediately remove from the heat.

2 Layer the herbs and garlic between slices of cucumber in sterilized preserving jars until full, then cover with the warm salt and vinegar mixture.

3 When the liquid is cold, close the jars. Leave on a sunny windowsill for at least 1 week before using.

Per batch Energy 291kcal/1174kJ; Protein 10g; Carbohydrate 17g, of which sugars 14g; Fat 2g, of which saturates 0g; Cholesterol 0mg; Calcium 262mg; Fibre 4.2g; Sodium 45265mg.

Poached spiced plums in brandy

Bottling spiced fruit is a great way to preserve summer flavours for eating in winter. Serve these with whipped cream as a dessert, or on top of muesli and yogurt for breakfast.

Makes 900g/2lb

600ml/1 pint/2½ cups brandy

rind of 1 lemon, peeled in a long strip

350g/12oz/1⅔ cups caster (superfine) sugar

1 cinnamon stick

900g/2lb plums

1 Put the brandy, lemon rind, sugar and cinnamon in a pan and heat gently to dissolve the sugar. Add the plums and poach for 15 minutes, or until soft.

2 Remove the plums with a slotted spoon and set aside. Reduce the syrup by a third by rapid boiling. Strain it over the plums, then bottle them in sterilized jars. Seal tightly. Store for up to 6 months.

Per batch Energy 3035kcal/12,792kJ; Protein 7.1g; Carbohydrate 444.9g, of which sugars 444.9g; Fat 0.9g, of which saturates 0g; Cholesterol 0mg; Calcium 302mg; Fibre 14.4g; Sodium 39mg.

Spiced pickled pears

These delicious pears not only make a delicious dessert, but are also the perfect accompaniment for cooked ham. They will keep for up to a year unopened.

Makes 900g/2lb

900g/2lb pears

600ml/1 pint/2½ cups white-wine vinegar

225g/8oz/1⅛ cups sugar

1 cinnamon stick

5 star anise

10 whole cloves

1 Peel the pears, keeping them whole and leaving on the stalks. Heat the vinegar and sugar together in a large pan until the sugar has dissolved. Add the pears and poach for 15 minutes, covered, turning occasionally.

2 Add the cinnamon, star anise and cloves, and simmer for 10 minutes. Remove the pears and pack tightly into sterilized jars. Simmer the syrup for 15 minutes more and pour over the pears.

3 Seal the jars tightly and store in a cool, dark place. Once opened, store in the refrigerator for up to a week.

Per batch Energy 1379kcal/5835kJ; Protein 6g; Carbohydrate 330g, of which sugars 330g; Fat 2g, of which saturates 0g; Cholesterol 0mg; Calcium 187mg; Fibre 0.0 g; Sodium 76mg.

Apple and mint jelly

This jelly is delicious stirred into just-cooked, buttered garden peas, as well as an accompaniment to the more traditional rich roasted meat such as lamb.

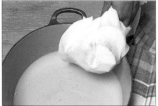

2 Pour through a jelly bag, allowing it to drip overnight. Do not squeeze the bag or the jelly will become cloudy.

3 Measure the amount of juice. To every 600ml/1 pint/2½ cups of juice, add 500g/1¼lb/2¾ cups granulated sugar.

4 Place the juice and sugar in a large pan and heat gently. Dissolve the sugar and then bring to the boil. Test for setting, by pouring about 15ml/1 tbsp into a saucer and leaving to cool slightly. If a wrinkle forms on the surface when pushed with a fingertip, the jelly will set. When a set is reached, leave to cool.

Makes about 1.5kg/3lb

900g/2lb cooking apples

granulated (white) sugar

45ml/3 tbsp chopped fresh mint

1 ▶ Chop the apples roughly and put them in a preserving pan. Add enough water to cover, bring to the boil, then simmer until the fruit is soft.

5 Stir in the mint and pour into sterilized jars. Seal each with a waxed disc and a tightly fitting cellophane top. Store in a cool, dark place. The jelly will keep unopened for up to a year. Once opened, keep in the refrigerator and consume within a week.

Per batch Energy 3865kcal/16495kJ; Protein 3g; Carbohydrate 1026g, of which sugars 1026g; Fat 1g, of which saturates 0g; Cholesterol 0mg; Calcium 145mg; Fibre 19.8g; Sodium 64mg.

Lemon and lime curd

Serve this soft, smooth, intensely-flavoured spread with toast or muffins, as an alternative to jam. It can also be used to make jam tarts or as a tangy filling for a sponge cake.

Makes 2 3 450g/1 lb jars

115g/4oz/½ cup unsalted butter

3 eggs

grated rind and juice of 2 lemons

grated rind and juice of 2 limes

225g/8oz/1⅛ cups caster (superfine) sugar

1 Set a large heatproof mixing bowl over a pan of simmering water. Lightly beat the eggs in a bowl.

2 Add the butter to the bowl above the pan, and then pour in the beaten eggs.

3 Add the lemon and lime rinds and juices to the beaten egg and butter in the pan, then add the sugar.

Farmhouse tip Buy unwaxed lemons and limes, if possible. If not, wash the fruit in warm water to remove the wax, before grating the zest.

◄ **4** Stir the mixture with a wooden spoon constantly until it thickens, then pour into sterilized jars. Seal each jar with a waxed disc and a tightly fitting cellophane top. Store in a cool, dark place. The curd will keep unopened for up to a month. Once opened, keep in the refrigerator and consume within a week.

Per batch Energy 1143kcal/4780kJ; Protein 25g; Carbohydrate 3g, of which sugars 3g; Fat 115g, of which saturates 68g; Cholesterol 960mg; Calcium 154mg; Fibre 0.1g; Sodium 271mg.

Hedgerow jelly

In the autumn, foraged hedgerow fruits such as damsons, blackberries and elderberries are wonderful for this delightful country jelly. Serve with cold meats or cheese.

Makes about 1.3kg/3lb

450g/1lb damsons, washed

450g/1lb/4 cups blackberries, washed

225g/8oz/2 cups raspberries

225g/8oz/2 cups elderberries, washed

juice and pips (seeds) of 2 large lemons

about 1.3kg/3lb/6½ cups preserving or granulated (white) sugar, warmed

1 Put the fruit, lemon juice and pips in a large pan. Add water to just below the level of the fruit. Cover and simmer for 1 hour. Mash the fruit, then leave to cool slightly.

2 Pour the fruit mash into a scalded jelly bag, which has been suspended over a non-metallic bowl. Leave to drain overnight. Don't squeeze the bag as this will cloud the jelly.

3 Measure the strained juice into a preserving pan. Add 450g/1lb/ 2¼ cups sugar for every 600ml/ 1 pint/2½ cups strained fruit juice.

4 Heat the mixture, stirring, over a low heat until the sugar has dissolved.

5 Increase the heat and boil rapidly without stirring for 10–15 minutes, or until the jelly reaches setting point (105°C/220°F).

6 Remove the pan from the heat and skim off any scum using a slotted spoon.

7 Ladle into warmed, sterilized jars and seal. Leave to cool, then label and store for up to 6 months.

Per batch Energy 5229kcal/22,306kJ; Protein 9.3g; Carbohydrate 1382.8g, of which sugars 1382.8g; Fat 0.4g, of which saturates 0g; Cholesterol 0mg; Calcium 799mg; Fibre 8.6g; Sodium 86mg.

Three-fruit marmalade

Home-made marmalade may be time-consuming to make, but the results are incomparably better than store-bought varieties.

Makes about 1.5kg/3lb

350g/12oz oranges

350g/12oz lemons

700g/1½lb grapefruit

2.5 litres/4½ pints/10¼ cups water

2.75kg/6lb granulated (white) sugar

1 Rinse and dry the oranges, lemons and grapefruit.

2 Put the whole fruit in a preserving pan. Add the water and let it simmer for about 2 hours.

3 Remove the fruit from the pan, retaining all the cooking liquid inside the pan. When cool enough to handle, quarter each fruit. Scrape the pulp away from the skin, and add it to the cooking liquid in the pan.

4 Cut all the orange, lemon and grapefruit rinds into thin slivers.

5 Add the slivers to the pan. Add the sugar. Gently heat until the sugar has dissolved. Increase the heat and boil rapidly until setting point is reached.

6 Leave to stand for 1 hour to allow the peel to settle. Pour into sterilized jars. Seal each jar with a waxed disc and a tightly fitting cellophane top. Store in a cool, dark place for up to a year.

Per batch Energy 6106kcal/26,049kJ; Protein 13.2g; Carbohydrate 1612.4g, of which sugars 1612.4g; Fat 0.6g, of which saturates 0g; Cholesterol 0mg; Calcium 1020mg; Fibre 8.9g; Sodium 115mg.

Blackcurrant jam

Dark, jewelled blackcurrants look and taste fabulous in this classic fruity jam. Serve on hot buttered toast, crumpets or croissants, or use as a filling for cakes.

Makes about 1.3kg/3lb

1.3kg/3lb/12 cups blackcurrants

grated rind and juice of 1 orange

475ml/16fl oz/2 cups water

1.3kg/3lb/6½ cups granulated (white) sugar, warmed

30ml/2 tbsp cassis (optional)

1 Place the blackcurrants, orange rind and juice and water in a large heavy pan. Bring to the boil, reduce the heat and simmer for 30 minutes.

2 Add the warmed sugar to the pan and stir over a low heat until the sugar has dissolved.

3 Bring the mixture to the boil and cook for about 8 minutes, or until the jam reaches setting point (105°C/220°F).

4 Remove the pan from the heat and skim off any scum from the surface using a slotted spoon.

5 Leave to cool for 5 minutes, then stir in the cassis, if using.

6 Pour the jam into warmed sterilized jars and seal. Leave the jars to cool completely, then label and store in a cool, dark place. The jam will keep for up to 6 months.

Per batch Energy 5504kcal/23,503kJ; Protein 18.4g; Carbohydrate 1448.7g, of which sugars 1448.7g; Fat 0.1g, of which saturates 0g; Cholesterol 0mg; Calcium 1474mg; Fibre 46.9g; Sodium 122mg.

Cherry berry conserve

Tart cranberries add an extra dimension to this delicious berry conserve. It is perfect for adding to sweet sauces, serving with roast duck, or for spreading on hot crumpets.

Makes about 1.3kg/3lb

350g/12oz/3 cups fresh cranberries

1kg/2¼lb/5½ cups cherries, pitted

120ml/4fl oz/½ cup blackcurrant or raspberry syrup

juice of 2 lemons

250ml/8fl oz/1 cup water

1.3kg/3lb/6½ cups preserving or granulated (white) sugar, warmed

4 Bring the fruit to the boil, then cook for 10 minutes, or to setting point (105°C/220°F).

5 Remove the pan from the heat, and skim off and discard any scum using a slotted spoon. Leave to cool for 10 minutes, then stir gently and pour into warmed sterilized jars. Seal and store in a cool, dark place for 6 months.

Farmhouse tip The cranberries must be cooked before the sugar is added, otherwise they will become tough.

1 Put the cranberries in a food processor and process until coarsely chopped. Scrape into a pan and add the cherries, fruit syrup and lemon juice.

2 Add the water to the pan. Cover and bring to the boil, then simmer for 20–30 minutes, or until the cranberries are very tender.

3 Add the sugar to the pan and heat gently, stirring, until the sugar has completely dissolved.

Per batch Energy 5859kcal/24,986kJ; Protein 16.7g; Carbohydrate 1540.4g, of which sugars 1540.4g; Fat 1.4g, of which saturates 0g; Cholesterol 0mg; Calcium 844mg; Fibre 14.6g; Sodium 105mg.

Strawberry jam

This classic jam is always popular, and a great way to use surplus strawberries. Make sure the jam is allowed to cool before pouring into jars, otherwise the fruit will float to the top.

Makes about 2.25kg/5lb

1kg/2¼lb strawberries

juice of 2 lemons

900g/2lb/4 cups sugar

1 Hull the strawberries by squeezing slightly and pulling out the stalk.

2 Put the strawberries in a pan with the lemon juice. Mash a few of the strawberries. Let the fruit simmer for 20 minutes or until softened.

3 Add the sugar and let it dissolve slowly over a gentle heat. Then let the jam boil rapidly until a setting point is reached.

4 Leave to stand until the strawberries are well distributed through the jam. Pour into warmed, sterilized jars, cover and seal.

5 Store in a cool dark place. The jam may be kept unopened for up to a year. Once opened, keep in the refrigerator and consume within 2 weeks.

Per batch Energy 3816Kcal/16259kJ; Protein 12.5g; Carbohydrate 1000g, of which sugars 1000g; Fat 1g, of which saturates 0g; Cholesterol 0g; Calcium 637mg; Fibre 11g; Sodium 114mg

Crab apple jelly

Crab apple trees are so pretty with abundant flowers and glowing red fruit, and though in the garden they are mainly decorative, this jelly is a delicious way to make use of the fruit.

Makes about 1kg/2¹/₄lb from each 600ml/1 pint/2¹/₂ cups liquid

preserving sugar (see method)

1kg/2¹/₄lb crab apples

3 cloves

1 Preheat the oven to 120°C/250°F/Gas Mark ¹/₂. Put the preserving sugar in a heatproof bowl and warm in the oven for 15 minutes. Wash the apples and cut them in half but do not peel or core. Place the apples and cloves in a large pan.

2 Pour in water to cover. Bring to the boil, reduce the heat and simmer until soft. Strain the mixture into a bowl. Measure the juice and add 450g/1lb/ 2 cups sugar for each 600ml/1 pint/ 2¹/₂ cups of juice. Pour into a pan and heat gently. Stir until the sugar dissolves, then boil rapidly until the setting point is reached. Pour into warm, sterilized jars and seal.

Rosehip and apple jelly

This frugal recipe makes the most of windfall apples, and rosehips gathered from the hedgerows.

Makes about 1kg/2¹/₄lb from each 600ml/1 pint/2¹/₂ cups liquid

1kg/2¹/₄lb windfall apples, peeled, trimmed and quartered

450g/1lb firm, ripe rosehips, roughly chopped in a processor

300ml/¹/₂ pint/1¹/₄ cups boiling water

preserving sugar

1 Place the apples in a preserving pan, just cover with water, and bring to the boil. Cook until the apples are pulpy.

2 Add the chopped rosehips to the cooked apples and boiling water, reduce the heat and leave to simmer for 10 minutes, then remove from the heat and allow to stand for 10 minutes more. Pour the mixture into a thick jelly bag suspended over a bowl and leave to strain overnight.

3 The following day, preheat the oven to 120°C/250°F/Gas¹/₂. Measure the juice and allow 400g/14oz/1³/₄ cups preserving sugar for each 600ml/1 pint/ 2¹/₂ cups of liquid. Warm the sugar.

4 Pour the juice into a pan, bring to the boil, stir in the warmed sugar until dissolved, then boil until a setting point is reached. Finally, pour the jelly into warm, sterilized jars and seal securely. Store for up to 6 months.

Per batch Energy 3218kcal/13733kJ; Protein 2g; Carbohydrate 854g, of which sugars 854g; Fat 1g, of which saturates 0g; Cholesterol 0mg; Calcium 127mg; Fibre 16.5g; Sodium 60mg.
Per batch Energy 5684kcal/24,259kJ; Protein 8.4g; Carbohydrate 1505.7g, of which sugars 1505.7g; Fat 0.5g, of which saturates 0g; Cholesterol 0mg; Calcium 761mg; Fibre 7.7g; Sodium 94mg.

Homemade Drinks and Sweets

Before sweet shops started to appear on the high street, soft drinks and sweetmeats would all have been made in the home. Here is a collection of favourite recipes, from lemonade to coconut ice, and from hot toddies to toffee apples, which will enable you to spend happy hours in the kitchen with results that will delight your family and friends.

Traditional lemonade

Fresh lemonade has been a country drink for many generations, since lemons first became available in Northern Europe in the 15th century. Now, although still popular in rural areas, this homemade version is just as likely to be on the menu in a contemporary café.

Serves 4–6

3 lemons

115g/4oz/generous ½ cup sugar

1 Pare the skin from the lemons with a vegetable peeler and squeeze the juice from the lemons.

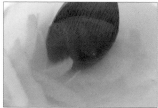

2 Put the lemon rind and sugar into a bowl, add 900ml/1½ pints/3¾ cups boiling water and stir well until the sugar has dissolved. Cover and leave until cold.

3 Add the lemon juice, mix well and strain into a jug (pitcher). Chill. Serve with plenty of ice.

Variation Old-fashioned lemonade made with freshly squeezed lemons is a far cry from the carbonated commercial varieties. This version can be topped up with soda water or sparkling water if you want some fizz.

Per glass Energy 115Kcal/489kJ; Protein 0.2g; Carbohydrate 30.4g, of which sugars 30.4g; Fat 0g, of which saturates 0g; Cholesterol 0mg; Calcium 17mg; Fibre 0g; Sodium 2mg.

Apple and ginger beer

Several small fruit producers make delicious natural pressed apple juice – use it if possible when making this cocktail. If you have your own apple tree, it is well worth investing in an apple press of your own so that you can be sure of using the whole of your crop.

Serves 8–10

1.2 litres/2 pints/5 cups unsweetened apple juice

juice of 1 lemon

4 small red-skinned eating apples

1.2 litres/2 pints/5 cups ginger beer

ice cubes, to serve

lemon slices or mint, to decorate

1 Mix the apple juice and lemon juice in a large glass jug (pitcher)

2 Wash and core the apples, but do not peel them. Slice thinly and add the slices to the jug.

3 Stir well and, to prevent browning, check that all the slices are immersed. Cover and set aside in the refrigerator to chill until required.

▶ **4** Shortly before serving, add some ice cubes and the ginger beer to the jug, and decorate with lemon slices, or sprigs of mint. Serve in tall glasses.

Per glass Energy 82Kcal/352kJ; Protein 0.2g; Carbohydrate 21.4g, of which sugars 21.4g; Fat 0.2g, of which saturates 0g; Cholesterol 0mg; Calcium 15mg; Fibre 0.4g; Sodium 11mg

Summer punch

Summertime means a long, cool drink and a lazy afternoon picnic in the garden. The beautiful borage flowers add the final essential ingredient. Here, the tastes of cucumber and mint are complemented by the flavour of the borage flower.

Serves 4–6

several sprigs of borage

¼ cucumber, halved and thinly sliced

1 small orange

¼ bottle Pimm's, chilled

several sprigs of mint and/or lemon balm

ice cubes

1 bottle lemonade (lemon soda) or ginger beer

1 To prepare the flowers, remove each flower-head from the green calyx by gently teasing it out. It should come away easily.

2 Chop the orange into small chunks, leaving the skin on. Put in a large jug (pitcher) with the sliced cucumber.

3 Pour the Pimm's into the jug, and add the mint and/or lemon balm, followed by the borage and ice cubes.

4 Slowly pour in the lemonade or ginger beer, making sure it doesn't fizz up too much. Stir to mix through, check if it is cold enough and add more ice if needed.

5 Serve the Pimm's in tall glasses, with flowers on top of each glass.

Per glass Energy 90kcal/380kJ; Protein 0g; Carbohydrate 17g, of which sugars 17g; Fat 0g, of which saturates 0g; Cholesterol 0mg; Calcium 26mg; Fibre 0.6g; Sodium 21mg.

Simply strawberry smoothie

Nothing evokes a sense of summer wellbeing more than the scent and flavour of sweet, juicy strawberries. This smoothie uses an abundance of these fragrant fruits so, if possible, make it when the season is right and local ones are at their most plentiful.

Serves 2

400g/14oz/3½ cups strawberries, plus extra to decorate

30–45ml/2–3 tbsp icing (confectioners') sugar

200g/7oz/scant 1 cup Greek (US strained plain) yogurt

60ml/4 tbsp single (light) cream

1 Hull the strawberries and place them in a blender or food processor with 30ml/2 tbsp of the icing sugar. Blend to a smooth purée, scraping the mixture down from the side of the bowl with a rubber spatula, if necessary.

Farmhouse tip You can replace the strawberries with other fruits if they are not in season. Try using fresh bananas instead to make another very popular milkshake.

◀ **2** Add the yogurt and cream and blend again until smooth and frothy.

3 Check the sweetness, adding a little more sugar if you find the flavour too sharp, and a little milk to thin if necessary. Pour into glasses and serve decorated with extra strawberries.

Per glass Energy 286Kcal/1195kJ; Protein 9.1g; Carbohydrate 30.4g, of which sugars 30.4g; Fat 16.2g, of which saturates 8.9g; Cholesterol 17mg; Calcium 217mg; Fibre 2.2g; Sodium 93g.

Garden mint milkshake

If you have mint growing in your garden, pick some for this recipe, as the fresher the mint, the better the flavour will be. The mint is infused in a sugar syrup, then left to cool before being blended to an aromatic, frothy shake with yogurt and creamy milk.

Serves 2

25g/1oz/1 cup fresh mint

50g/2oz/¼ cup caster (superfine) sugar

200g/7oz/scant 1 cup natural (plain) yogurt

200ml/7fl oz/scant 1 cup full cream (whole) milk

15ml/1 tbsp lemon juice

crushed ice cubes

icing (confectioners') sugar, to decorate

1 Pull out four small mint sprigs and set aside. Roughly snip the remaining leaves into a small pan. Add the sugar and pour over 105ml/7 tbsp water.

2 Heat the mixture, stirring occasionally, until the sugar dissolves, then boil for 2 minutes. Remove the pan from the heat and set aside until the syrup is completely cool.

3 Pour the cooled syrup through a sieve (strainer) into a jug (pitcher), pressing the mint against the side of the sieve with the back of a spoon. Pour into a blender or food processor.

4 Add the yogurt and milk to the syrup and blend until smooth and frothy. Add two of the reserved mint sprigs and the lemon juice and blend until specked with pretty green flecks.

5 Put the crushed ice in tall glasses or tumblers and pour over the milkshake. Dust the mint sprigs with icing sugar and use to decorate the glasses. Serve.

Per glass Energy 230kcal/950kJ; Protein 8g; Carbohydrate 1g, of which sugars 1g; Fat 22g, of which saturates 4g; Cholesterol 232mg; Calcium 52mg; Fibre 0.3g; Sodium 186mg.

Honey and banana milkshake

This delicious drink demonstrates just how smooth and creamy and filling a milkshake can be. Bananas make a healthy, energy-boosting addition to drinks – this one is almost a meal in itself, but you need to serve it straight away.

Serves 2

2 bananas

30ml/2 tbsp clear honey

15ml/1 tbsp lemon juice

300ml/½ pint/1¼ cups milk

4 scoops vanilla ice cream

▶ **3** Add milk and two scoops of ice cream to the blender or food processor, then blend until smooth.

4 Divide the milkshake between 2 tall glasses and top each one with another scoop of ice cream. Serve immediately with a little drizzle of honey on top if you wish.

1 Break the bananas into pieces and put in a blender or food processor with the honey and lemon juice.

2 Blend the mixture until very smooth, stopping and scraping it down from the side of the bowl with a rubber spatula, if necessary.

Per glass Energy 416Kcal/1749kJ; Protein 6.1g; Carbohydrate 68.4g, of which sugars 65.6g; Fat 15g, of which saturates 8.9g; Cholesterol 10g; Calcium 117mg; Fibre 2.3g; Sodium 81g.

Sloe gin

The small, purple fruit of the blackthorn shrub grow widely in the hedgerows. The tart, astringent berries are not much used except for infusing in alcohol to make sloe gin.

Makes 2–3 bottles

450g/1lb/4 cups ripe sloes (black plums)

225g/8oz/generous 1 cup caster (superfine) sugar

1 litre/1¾ pint/4 cups gin

1 Check through the sloes and discard any damaged or unsound fruit. Rinse the sloes and remove the stalks. Prick each sloe at least once with a silver or stainless steel fork or use a wooden cocktail stick (toothpick).

2 Select several wide-necked screw-top or easy-to-seal sterilized jars and arrange alternate layers of fruit and sugar in them. Top up the jars with gin, and close them tightly. Store for at least 3 months in a cool, dark place.

3 Shake the jars gently every now and then to help extract and distribute the flavour evenly. When ready, strain into a jug (pitcher) and then pour into sterilized bottles and store for another 3 months if possible.

Per bottle Energy 1554Kcal/6486kJ; Protein 0.6g; Carbohydrate 117.6g, of which sugars 117.6g; Fat 0g, of which saturates 0g; Cholesterol 0mg; Calcium 60mg; Fibre 0g; Sodium 7mg.

Gaelic coffee

A good Gaelic coffee, also called Irish coffee, is an exercise in contrasts and a rare treat indeed – and often taken as an alternative to dessert.

Serves 1

25ml/1½ tbsp Irish whiskey

about 150ml/¼ pint/⅔ cup hot strong black coffee

demerara (raw) sugar, to taste

about 50ml/2fl oz/¼ cup lightly whipped double (heavy) cream

1 Measure the whiskey into a stemmed glass, or one with a handle. Pour in enough freshly made strong black coffee to come to about 1cm/½in from the top.

2 Sweeten to taste and stir vigorously to dissolve the sugar and create a small whirlpool in the glass.

3 Top the coffee with the lightly whipped cream, poured over the back of the teaspoon. It will settle on the top to make a distinct layer in creamy contrast to the dark coffee underneath. (It is important that the coffee should be very hot to contrast with the chilled cream.) Serve immediately and do not stir in the cream.

Rum tea toddy

Rum isn't just good with coffee. It also goes well with tea.

Serves 1

30ml/2 tbsp light rum

2.5ml/½ tsp clear honey

2.5ml/½ tsp ground cinnamon

slice of lemon

1 teacup hot black tea, such as Darjeeling or Assam

piece of crystallized (candied) ginger

1 Place the rum, honey, cinnamon, slice of lemon and tea in a pan and gently warm until just about to boil.

2 Pour into a mug and add the ginger. Sip while hot.

Per cup Energy 262Kcal/1081kJ; Protein 1g; Carbohydrate 5.5g, of which sugars 5.5g; Fat 20.1g, of which saturates 12.6g; Cholesterol 53mg; Calcium 31mg; Fibre 0g; Sodium 13mg.
Per cup Energy 78kcal/325kJ; Protein 0g; Carbohydrate 3g, of which sugars 3g; Fat 0g, of which saturates 0g; Cholesterol 0mg; Calcium 5mg; Fibre 0.0g; Sodium 0mg.

Hot whiskey toddy

Hot toddies are sheer luxury, especially if you are feeling a little down or under the weather; this one is warming, soothing and has a lovely, almost fresh taste.

Serves 2

2 strips of pared lemon rind

4 slices of fresh root ginger

5ml/1 tsp honey

175ml/6fl oz/¾ cup water

175ml/6fl oz/¾ cup Scotch whisky, Irish whiskey or American bourbon

1 Put the lemon rind, ginger, honey and water in a small pan and bring to the boil. Remove from the heat and leave to infuse for 5 minutes.

2 Stir the alcohol into the pan, and allow time for it to warm through. Rest a silver spoon in warmed glasses and strain in the warm toddy. Sip slowly.

Buttered rum

Hot buttered rum is luxurious and pampering; save it for when you need some serious comfort.

Serves 2

475ml/16fl oz/2 cups milk

15ml/1 tbsp caster (superfine) sugar

1 cinnamon stick

175ml/6fl oz/¾ cup dark navy rum

25g/1oz/2 tbsp salted butter, chopped into small pieces

freshly grated nutmeg

1 Heat the milk in a pan with the sugar and cinnamon stick. Pour in the rum and heat gently for 1–2 minutes.

2 Pour the mixture into warmed mugs and dot the surface with the butter. Grate nutmeg over the top.

3 The top of each drink will soon be covered with a very thin layer of golden yellow melted butter, and sipping the hot, milky rum and nutmeg through this mixes the saltiness of the butter into the drink.

Per cup Energy 207kcal/856kJ; Protein 0g; Carbohydrate 3g, of which sugars 13g; Fat 0g, of which saturates 0g; Cholesterol 20mg; Calcium 0mg; Fibre 0.0g; Sodium 11mg.
Per cup Energy 4741kcal/1963kJ; Protein 8g; Carbohydrate 19g, of which sugars 19g; Fat 20g, of which saturates 13g; Cholesterol 60mg; Calcium 284mg; Fibre 0.0g; Sodium 178mg.

Spiced hot chocolate

Hot chocolate is a wonderful treat – for breakfast, as a teatime treat on a winter afternoon or before bed to help you sleep. Adding cardamom gives an extra fragrant aroma.

Serves 6

900ml/1½ pints/3¾ cups milk

2 cardamom pods, bruised

200g/7oz plain (semisweet) chocolate, broken into pieces, or half plain (semisweet) and half milk chocolate

◄ **1** Put the milk in a pan with the cardamom pods and bring to the boil. Add the pieces of chocolate and whisk until melted.

2 Using a slotted spoon, remove the cardamom pods and discard. Pour the hot chocolate into heatproof glasses, mugs or cups and sip slowly.

Per cup Energy 359Kcal/1567kJ; Protein 10g; Carbohydrate 42g, of which sugars 42g; Fat 18g, of which saturates 11g; Cholesterol 6g; Calcium 127mg; Fibre 0g; Sodium 100g.

Vanilla fudge

This classic sweet was first devised in Scotland in the early 1700s, and was then called 'tablet'; the softer variation 'fudge' was devised in America, and quickly spread to Europe. The beating of the mixture gives it the grainy texture that is typical of many fudges.

Makes about 1kg/2¼lb

300ml/½ pint/1¼ cups full-fat (whole) milk

½ vanilla pod (bean), seeds scraped

900g/2lb/4½ cups caster (superfine) sugar

125g/4¼ oz unsalted butter, cut into 1cm/½in cubes, plus extra for greasing

10ml/2 tsp vanilla extract

tiny pinch of salt

1 Grease a 20cm/8in square baking tin (pan) and line with baking parchment. Prepare an ice-water bath.

2 Put the milk, scraped vanilla seeds and pod, sugar and butter in a large, heavy pan and cook over a moderate heat, stirring constantly, until the sugar has completely dissolved and the butter has melted.

3 Increase the heat and bring the mixture to the boil. Cover with a tight-fitting lid and cook for 2 minutes, then remove the lid.

4 Without stirring, let the mixture cook at a slow rolling boil for about 10 minutes, or until it reaches the soft-ball stage (114°C/238°F).

5 Immediately place the pan over the ice-water bath for a few seconds. Remove the vanilla pod with a fork or slotted spoon and discard. Stir in the vanilla extract and salt.

6 Place the pan in a cool part of the kitchen until it is lukewarm or about 43°C/110°F. Do not stir.

7 Once it reaches this temperature, beat with a wooden spoon until it is thick, smooth and creamy.

8 Pour into the prepared tin and leave it to cool completely.

9 Cut it into squares in the tin, then lift it out by the sides of the parchment and serve. Store in an airtight container.

Per total amount Energy 4665Kcal/19743kJ; Protein 14.7g; Carbohydrate 954.9g, of which sugars 954.9g; Fat 113.8g, of which saturates 74.7g; Cholesterol 330g; Calcium 841mg; Fibre 0g; Sodium 1157g.

Old-fashioned chocolate fudge

This timeless classic is a smooth fudge that is not worked, but instead is simply melted to the perfect temperature and poured into a tin to set. This version uses dark, intense chocolate, which cuts through the sweetness, but you could use milk chocolate if you prefer.

Makes about 1.2kg/2½lb

800g/1¾lb/4 cups caster (superfine) sugar

250ml/8fl oz/1 cup full-fat (whole) milk

75g/3oz/6 tbsp unsalted butter, cut into 1cm/½in cubes, plus extra for greasing

350g/12oz dark (bittersweet) chocolate (70% cocoa solids), chopped into small pieces

5ml/1 tsp vanilla extract

1 Grease a 20 x 30cm/8 x 12in rectangular baking tin (pan) and line with baking parchment. Prepare an ice-water bath.

2 Put the sugar, milk and butter in a large heavy pan and cook over a moderate heat, stirring constantly, until the sugar dissolves.

3 When the sugar is dissolved and the butter is melted, stop stirring. Bring the mixture to the boil.

▶ **4** Without stirring, let the mixture cook at a slow rolling boil for about 10 minutes, or until it reaches the soft-ball stage (114°C/238°F). Stir in the chopped chocolate.

5 Immediately place the pan over the ice water bath for a few seconds. Stir in the vanilla extract. Pour into the tin. Leave to cool.

6 Lift out of the tin by the sides of the parchment paper and place on a chopping board. Cut into squares and serve. Store in an airtight container.

Per total amount Energy 5707Kcal/24098kJ; Protein 28.8g; Carbohydrate 1074.8g, of which sugars 1056.3g; Fat 173.2g, of which saturates 105.6g; Cholesterol 239mg; Calcium 856mg; Fibre 0g; Sodium 787mg.

Peanut butter fudge

This fudge has a fabulous texture. The combination of smooth, creamy peanut butter and melted milk chocolate result in a silkiness that cannot be attained in any other way.

3 When the sugar has dissolved and the butter has melted, bring the mixture to the boil.

4 Without stirring, let the mixture cook at a slow rolling boil for about 10 minutes, or until it reaches the soft-ball stage (114°C/238°F).

5 Remove the pan from the heat and stir in the peanut butter.

Makes about 1.3kg/3lb

750g/1lb 13oz/3¾ cups caster (superfine) sugar

250ml/8fl oz/generous 1 cup golden (light corn) syrup

300ml/½ pint/1¼ cups double (heavy) cream

75g/3oz/6 tbsp unsalted butter, cut into 1cm/½ in cubes

200g/7oz smooth, natural (unsweetened) peanut butter

150g/5oz roasted and salted peanuts, chopped

100g/3¾oz milk chocolate (35% cocoa solids), chopped

1 Grease a 20cm/8in square baking tin (pan) and line with baking parchment or waxed paper.

2 Put the sugar, golden syrup, cream and butter in a large, heavy pan and cook over a moderate heat, stirring constantly, until the sugar dissolves.

6 Gently fold in the nuts and chopped chocolate. Pour into the prepared baking tin and leave it to cool completely. This can take up to 8 hours.

7 Carefully lift the fudge out of the tin, using the sides of the parchment paper, and place on a cutting surface. Cut into small squares and serve, or store in an airtight container.

Variation You could also use crunchy peanut butter if you prefer, but it will change the consistency of the fudge.

Per total amount Energy 8274Kcal/34696kJ; Protein 96.6g; Carbohydrate 1091g, of which sugars 1068g; Fat 434.7g, of which saturates 185.1g; Cholesterol 572mg; Calcium 791mg; Fibre 19.8g; Sodium 2705mg.

Coconut ice

Thought to have been invented by the Victorians, this classic sweet is very easy to make at home. The use of coconut milk instead of milk in this version enhances the taste.

Makes about 1.3kg/3lb

butter, for greasing

750g/1lb 13oz/3¾ cups caster (superfine) sugar

300ml/½ pint/1¼ cups coconut milk

2.5ml/½ tsp salt

275g/10oz/generous 3½ cups desiccated (dry unsweetened) coconut

2–3 drops pink food colouring (optional), or any other colour

1 Grease a 20cm/8in square tin (pan) and line with baking parchment or waxed paper.

2 Combine the sugar, coconut milk and salt in a heavy pan and stir over a medium heat until the sugar has dissolved.

3 Bring the mixture to the boil, add the desiccated coconut and stir to combine.

4 Pour two-thirds of the mixture into the prepared tin, and spread evenly.

5 Combine the remaining one-third of the mixture with a few drops of pink food colouring in the pan, then quickly pour it over the first layer in the tin. Spread evenly, making sure you don't disturb the first layer.

6 Smooth the top with a metal spatula, pressing down slightly.

7 Allow the coconut ice to cool completely. This may take a few hours.

8 Lift out of the tin by the sides of the parchment or waxed paper and place on a cutting surface. Cut into squares and serve. Store in an airtight container.

Variations You could replace the coconut milk with an equal quantity of full-fat (whole) milk. Or try adding a splash of rum at step 3.

Per total amount Energy 4682Kcal/19746kJ; Protein 20.1g; Carbohydrate 816.1g, of which sugars 816.1g; Fat 171.4g, of which saturates 147.4g; Cholesterol 0mg; Calcium 548mg; Fibre 37.7g; Sodium 452g.

Chocolate macaroons

These lovely sweets combine moist coconut with dark chocolate; eat them before the chocolate has set completely to experience them at their best.

Makes about 18

2 egg whites

125g/4¼oz caster/generous ½ cup (superfine) sugar

pinch of salt

10ml/2 tsp honey

100g/3¾oz/generous 1 cup desiccated (dry unsweetened) coconut

2.5ml/½ tsp vanilla extract

100g/3¾oz dark (bittersweet) chocolate, broken into pieces

1 Preheat the oven to 160°C/325°F/ Gas 3. Line a baking sheet with baking parchment.

2 Combine the egg whites, sugar, salt, honey dessicated coconut and vanilla extract in a heavy pan and cook over a medium heat for about 7 minutes, stirring constantly, until the mixture is opaque and sticky. The coconut should just begin to scorch on the bottom of the pan.

3 Transfer the coconut mixture to a bowl and allow it to cool completely.

4 Drop tablespoonfuls of the mixture on to the baking sheet.

5 Using the end of a wooden spoon, make small depressions in the centre of each macaroon.

6 Place in the oven and bake for about 12 minutes, until the macaroons are just golden around the edges.

7 Place the chocolate in a heatproof bowl and position over a pan of barely simmering water, making sure the water does not touch the bowl. Leave until the chocolate is melted.

8 Transfer the melted chocolate to a piping (pastry) bag with a fine nozzle and fill the indented centre of each macaroon with chocolate.

9 Leave to cool, until the chocolate is almost set, then serve immediately. These macaroons are best eaten on the day they are made, but they can be stored in an airtight container for up to 1 week.

Farmhouse tip Instead of using a piping (pastry) bag, put the melted chocolate in a sealable food storage bag. Tilt the bag so the chocolate is in one corner, then snip off the corner of the bag to make a small hole through which the chocolate can be piped.

Energy 93Kcal/390kJ; Protein 0.9g; Carbohydrate 11.6g, of which sugars 11.3g; Fat 5.1g, of which saturates 3.9g; Cholesterol 1mg; Calcium 7mg; Fibre 0.8g; Sodium 9mg.

Cinder toffee

This toffee is an old favourite in many parts of the world, and must be the simplest to make. It is known by lots of names, including yellow man, hokey pokey and sponge candy.

Makes about 300g/11oz

butter, for greasing

60ml/4 tbsp water

225g/8oz/generous 1 cup caster (superfine) sugar

15ml/1 tbsp golden (light corn) syrup

1.5ml/¼ tsp bicarbonate of soda (baking soda), sifted

5ml/1 tsp warm water

1 Prepare an ice-water bath. Grease a shallow baking tray and set aside.

2 Put the water in heavy pan and cover with the sugar and golden syrup. Heat gently until the sugar dissolves. Increase the heat and bring to the boil without stirring until the syrup reaches just over the hard-crack stage (154°C/310°F) and begins to colour.

3 Remove the syrup from the heat and arrest the cooking by placing it over the ice-water bath for a moment.

4 Dissolve the bicarbonate of soda in the warm water.

5 Carefully pour the bicarbonate of soda and water into the sugar syrup. At this point, the mixture should bubble and froth up quite fiercely, so stand back and take great care.

6 Stir the mixture to disperse the bubbles throughout, working quickly, before pouring into the prepared baking tray.

7 When cooled, break into pieces. Wrap the shards in cellophane, baking parchment or waxed paper. Store in an airtight container.

Per total amount Energy 931Kcal/3973kJ; Protein 1.2g; Carbohydrate 247g, of which sugars 247g; Fat 0g; Cholesterol 0g; Calcium 123mg; Fibre 0g; Sodium 54g.

Bonfire toffee

Dark, intensely flavoured and satisfyingly hard and brittle to crunch on, this traditional British toffee is the perfect accompaniment to fireworks and fun on 5 November.

Makes about 600g/1lb 6oz

125g/4¼oz/generous ½ cup unsalted butter, plus extra for greasing

225ml/7.5fl oz/scant 1 cup black treacle (molasses)

200g/7oz/scant 1 cup demerara (raw) sugar

tiny pinch of salt

1 Grease a shallow baking tray. Melt the butter in a large, heavy pan over a low heat.

2 Add the black treacle, the demerara sugar and salt to the pan, and let them gently dissolve into the butter.

3 Once they have completely dissolved, turn the heat up to medium and bring to the boil. Boil until the mixture is just below the hard-crack stage (154°C/310°F). Pour the syrup into the baking sheet.

◄ **4** Leave the toffee to cool; this should only take about 20 minutes. When it is cold, break into shards.

► **5** As this is very sticky toffee, wrap the shards individually in pieces of baking parchment, if you wish, before storing in an airtight container.

Per total amount Energy 2386Kcal/10037kJ; Protein 4.5g; Carbohydrate 386.3g, of which sugars 386.3g; Fat 102.1g, of which saturates 67.5g; Cholesterol 288mg; Calcium 1263mg; Fibre 0g; Sodium 1167g.

Toffee apples

These delicious treats are a favourite with children at country fairs and village fêtes, especially around harvest time. The sweet caramel contrasts wonderfully with the crisp apple.

Makes 8

8 small or medium eating apples

115g/4oz/½ cup unsalted butter

200g/7oz/1 cup granulated (white) sugar

150ml/¼ pint/⅔ cup double (heavy) cream

15ml/1 tbsp soft light brown sugar

125g/4¼oz golden (light corn) syrup

2.5ml/½ tsp vanilla extract

1.5ml/¼ tsp salt

1 Wash and dry the apples. Push lollipop sticks or wooden dowels into the stem-end of the apples.

2 Prepare an ice-water bath and line a shallow baking tray with baking parchment.

3 Place all of the remaining ingredients in a large, heavy pan and heat gently over a medium heat. Stir, until everything is dissolved together into an emulsified mass.

4 Once the sugar has completely dissolved, increase the heat and bring the mixture to the boil. Cook until it reaches the soft-ball stage (114°C/238°F).

5 Remove the toffee from the heat and arrest the cooking by placing the pan over the ice-water bath.

6 Leave the mixture to cool to 82°C/180°F before dipping the apples into the toffee, holding them by their sticks and rolling them to coat in toffee all the way round.

Farmhouse tip Buy wooden dowels at a hardware or paint store. Use pruning shears to trim the dowels to the desired length. Dowels come in a few different widths. Choose ones that will be sturdy enough to hold on to while eating your apple, but not so thick that it splits the apple when you insert it.

7 Place the apples on the prepared baking sheet, stick-end up, until the toffee hardens. If it slips off, leave it to cool slightly and dip again into the pan.

8 Eat the toffee apples immediately or store in an airtight container at room temperature for up to 3 days.

Per toffee apple Energy 366Kcal/1534kJ; Protein 0.8g; Carbohydrate 46.9g, of which sugars 46.9g; Fat 21.9g, of which saturates 13.4g; Cholesterol 57mg; Calcium 33mg; Fibre 1.1g; Sodium 160mg.

Peanut brittle

The addition of bicarbonate of soda is what gives peanut brittle its texture. The raising action introduces thousands of tiny air bubbles into the sugar syrup, making it crunchy and giving the brittle its characteristic, almost opalescent, quality.

Makes 600g/1lb 6oz

grapeseed or groundnut (peanut) oil, for greasing

175g/6oz/¾ cup caster (superfine) sugar

115g/4oz golden (light corn) syrup

5ml/1 tsp salt

250g/9oz raw peanuts

25g/1oz/2 tbsp unsalted butter, cubed

2.5ml/½ tsp vanilla extract

2.5ml/½ tsp bicarbonate of soda (baking soda), dissolved in 5ml/1 tsp water

1 Combine the sugar, golden syrup, salt and 60ml/4 tbsp water in a large, heavy pan. Heat gently over a low heat until the sugar dissolves. Turn the heat up to medium and boil until the syrup reaches the hard-ball stage (130°C/266°F).

2 Add the peanuts and stir until the syrup reaches the hard-crack stage (154°C/310°F).

3 Remove the pan from the heat and stir in the butter and vanilla. Line a baking sheet with baking parchment and grease it lightly with oil.

4 Fold the bicarbonate of soda and water into the peanut mixture, then pour on to the baking sheet.

5 When cool enough to touch, use oiled hands to pull the brittle from the sides, stretching it to make holes.

6 Allow the brittle to cool completely, and then use the back of a spoon to break it up completely.

7 Serve the peanut brittle immediately or store in an airtight container for a few days.

Per total amount Energy 2626Kcal/11011kJ; Protein 65.3g; Carbohydrate 305g, of which sugars 289.2g; Fat 135.4g, of which saturates 34g; Cholesterol 58mg; Calcium 276mg; Fibre 15.5g; Sodium 514mg.

Caramel-buttered popcorn

Gooey, buttery caramel-coated popcorn is a fabulous treat. This recipe is very simple and great to make with kids. They love the popping of the popcorn and will be especially delighted that they can eat the delicious results immediately.

Makes 300g/11oz

30ml/2 tbsp vegetable oil

100g/3¾oz dried popcorn kernels

100g/3¾oz salted butter

100g/3¾oz golden (light corn) syrup

1 Warm the oil in a heavy pan that has a tight fitting lid, over a medium-high heat. Add the popcorn kernels and cover with the lid.

2 Cook, shaking occasionally as the corn pops against the lid. When the popping stops (after a few minutes), remove the pan from the heat and open the lid to release a little steam. Set the pan aside.

3 Melt the butter and golden syrup together in a separate large pan, stirring constantly to combine.

◀ **4** Transfer the popcorn to a large mixing bowl and pour over the syrup. Mix well. Serve immediately or keep for a few days in an airtight container or sealed bags.

Variation If you prefer salty popcorn to sweet, omit the syrup and add 2.5ml/ ½ tsp salt to the butter in step 3.

Per total amount Energy 1440Kcal/6054kJ; Protein 6.3g; Carbohydrate 232.8g, of which sugars 186.3g; Fat 60g, of which saturates 6g; Cholesterol 54mg; Calcium 18mg; Fibre 0g; Sodium 168g.

Index

Picture
acknowledgements

t=top, b=bottom, l=left, r=right
iStockphoto: 11t, 27b, 28t,
29tl, 29tr, 32bl.

Moments of
Unreason

The Practice of
Canadian Psychiatry
and the Homewood
Retreat, 1883–1923

CHERYL KRASNICK
WARSH

McGill-Queen's University Press
Montreal and Kingston • London • Buffalo

© McGill-Queen's University Press 1989
ISBN 0-7735-0701-9

Legal deposit fourth quarter 1989
Bibliothèque nationale du Québec

Printed in Canada on acid-free paper

This book has been published with the help of a
grant from the Canadian Federation for the
Humanities, using funds provided by the Social
Sciences and Humanities Research Council of
Canada. Publication has also been assisted by a grant
from the Hannah Institute for the History of
Medicine.

Canadian Cataloguing in Publication Data

Warsh, Cheryl Lynn Krasnick, 1957–
      Moments of unreason: the practice of Canadian
      psychiatry and the Homewood Retreat, 1833–1923
      Includes index.
      Bibliography: p.
      ISBN 0-7735-0701-9
      1. Homewood Retreat – History.   2. Psychiatric
      hospitals – Ontario – Guelph – History –
      19th century.   3. Psychiatry – Canada – History –
      19th century. I. Title.
      RC447.W37 1989   362.2'1'0971343   C89-090213-5

The illustrations are from the Homewood Sanitarium
Collection and are used by permission of the
Homewood Sanitarium. Patients in the photographs
are portrayed by staff members, except for those in
the jacket illustration whose faces are turned away
from the camera.

To the cherished memory of my father

Eternity is less familiar and not more
astounding to me than the complexity, the
boundless products, of our moral and mental
mechanisms. There are times when I seem to
hang awed over the abyss of my own mind,
with wonder near akin to terror. That out of
this world of thought, feelings, and memories
should come, to the most healthy nature, at
times inexplicable desires, moments of
unreason, impulses which defy analytic
research, even brief insanities, is not strange to
me ... If Hamlet wondered, we have even
greater cause to wonder.

S. Weir Mitchell,
*Dr. North and
His Friends*, 1915

Contents

Tables and Figures

FIGURES

Acknowledgments

Many individuals have contributed their knowledge and expertise towards the completion of this book. Dr Samuel Shortt, the supervisor of the thesis from which it was derived, challenged me, with patient encouragement and understated criticisms, to respond with my best efforts. Dr Klaus Hansen of Queen's University provided genial support and a formidable knowledge of American historiography, while Dr Roger Hall of The University of Western Ontario is a constant ally and a good friend. The aid of the reference, interlibrary loan, and archival staffs of the libraries of Queen's University, University of Guelph, University of Toronto, McGill University, University of New Brunswick, University of Western Ontario, and the Academy of Medicine is acknowledged with thanks. Special thanks as well go to Barbara Craig of the Archives of Ontario. William Hamilton, Dr M.O. Vincent, Dr John A. Watt, and the staff of the Homewood Sanitarium are thanked for opening their files to a stranger; I hope they will be pleased with the result.

Drs Ramsay Cook, James McSherry, George Rawlyk, Andrew Scull, and the anonymous SSHRC readers offered useful comments on parts or all of this book. McGill-Queen's University Press has been a pleasure to work with, and I would particularly like to thank Philip Cercone and Mary Norton. The financial support of the Hannah Institute for the History of Medicine and Associated Medical Services, Canadian Psychiatric Association, Queen's University, and the Social Sciences and Humanities Research Council is gratefully acknowledged. This study is about families, and in that, I have been blessed. Jeffrey Krasnick took time out of his own studies to assist his sister in data entry and cross-tabulations. My parents, Ruth and Jerry Krasnick, supported four children through most of the long years of post-graduate studies and provided us with opportunities they had never known. Finally, my husband, Michael Warsh, kept me company by undertaking legal studies, which made for a stimulating domestic environment; his insights helped to shape this text.

Nurses and patients on the extensive grounds surrounding the institution, c. 1915. While in other photographs staff members represented patients to ensure anonymity, the women with their faces away from the camera in this picture are probably actual patients.

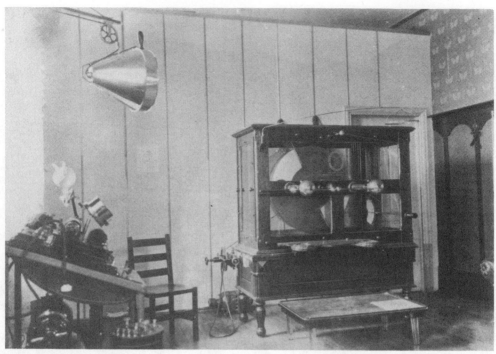

The electrotherapy room. The use of galvanic, faradic, and static electricity was a popular fin-de-siècle therapy. Recommended in the medical literature for a wide variety of complaints, including gynaecological disorders, at the Homewood Retreat electrotherapy was used only for muscular problems, digestive disorders, and its sedative effect.

Above, Dr Alfred Hobbs (centre) and his staff, c. 1910. Hobbs instituted uniforms for his nurses and attendants shortly after his appointment. References for the numbers on the picture have been lost.

Right, Dr Stephen Lett, medical superintendent, 1883–1901. Lett was an early Canadian specialist in the treatment of alcoholism and drug addiction.

Left, the acute division, c. 1910. Violent, destructive, and other "refractory" patients would be confined in these shuttered rooms for as long as their excitement phase lasted.

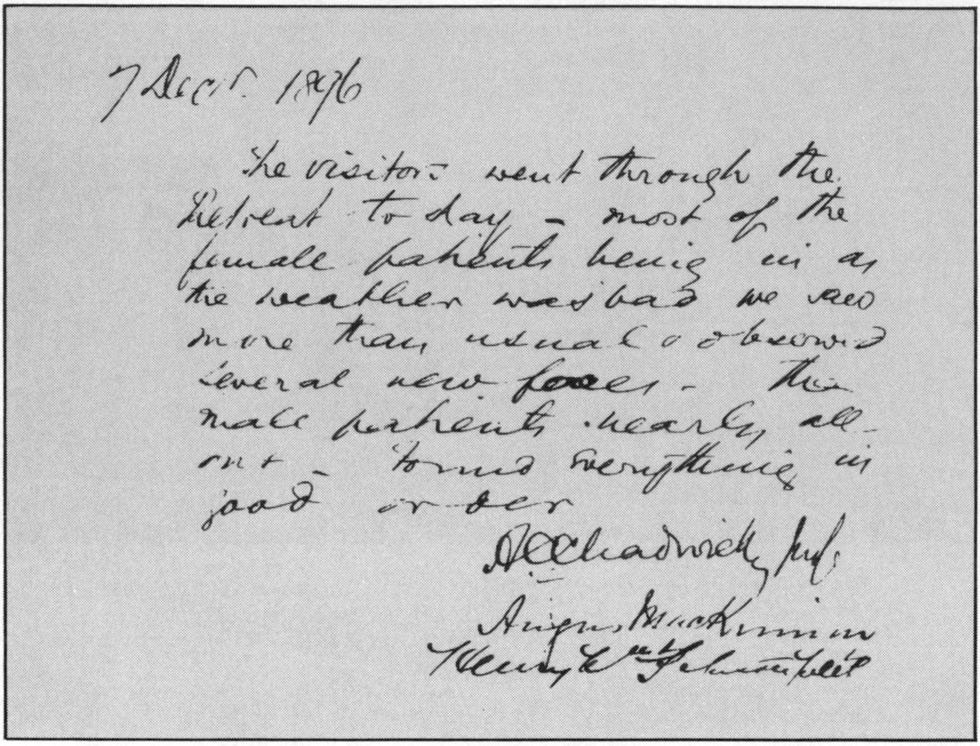

7 Dec. 1896

The visitors went through the Retreat to day — most of the female patients being in as the weather was bad we saw more than usual & observed several new faces — the male patients nearly all out — found everything in good order

A.C. Chadwick J.P.

[signatures]

A page from the Board of Visitors Minute Book, 1896. The Board of Visitors, an independent body of local magistrates, civil servants, and physicians, made unannounced visits throughout the year.

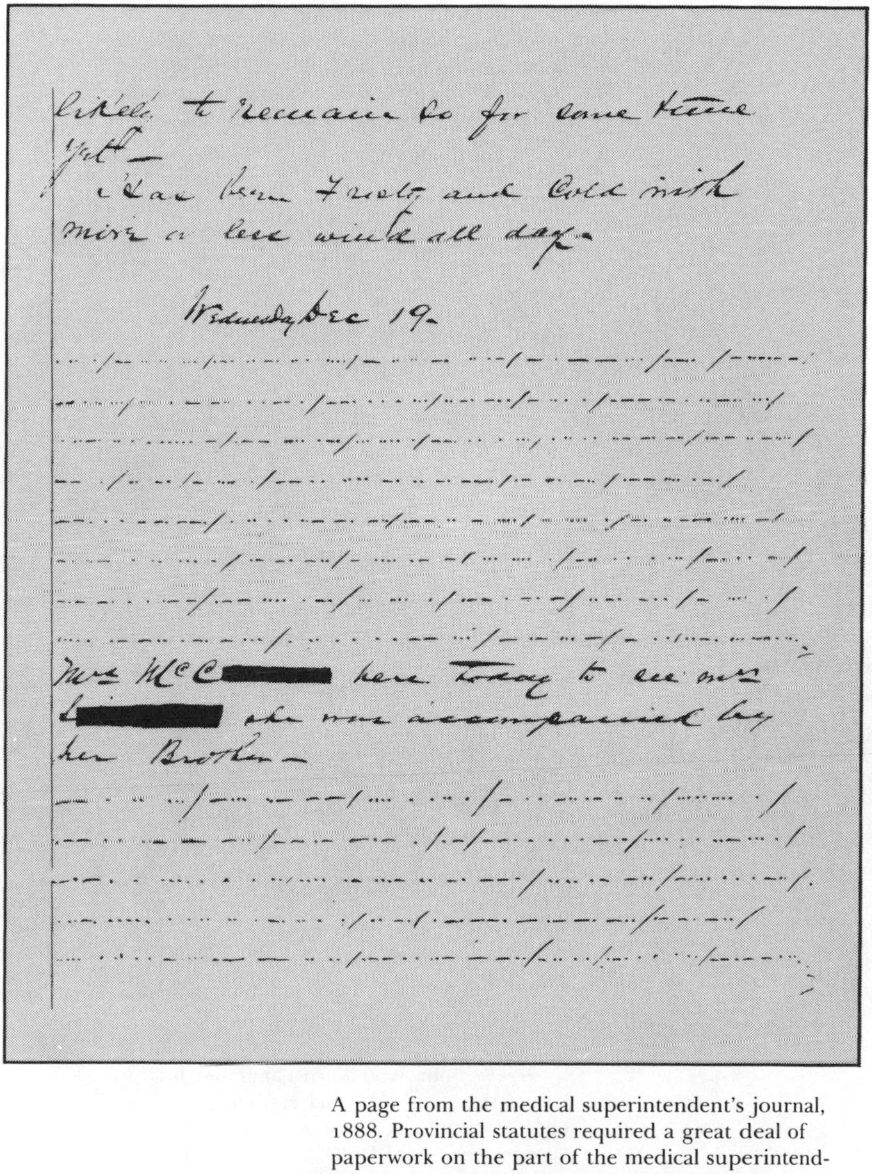

likely to remain so for some time yet —

It has been Frosty and Cold with more or less wind all day.

Wednesday Dec 19 —

[Morse code]

Mrs. McC▓▓▓▓ here today to see Mrs ▓▓▓▓▓ she was accompanied by her Brother —

[Morse code]

A page from the medical superintendent's journal, 1888. Provincial statutes required a great deal of paperwork on the part of the medical superintendent. Dr Lett's daily journal recorded weather conditions, patients' behaviour, and problems with staff. During late 1888 and 1889, Lett resorted to morse code to record his suspicions that his matron, Alice Finch, was supplying patients and staff members with alcohol and drugs.

The continuous bath. Hydrotherapy was Dr Hobb's innovation in the control and sedation of excited or insomniac patients. Although the continuous bath was alleged to avoid the baneful effects of mechanical restraints or excessive medication, overuse or negligent supervision could have tragic consequences.

Above right, John Woodburn Langmuir, first president of the Homewood Retreat. Langmuir, a driving, forthright bureaucrat, was the guiding force in the development of Ontario's social welfare network.

Right, Dr Alfred Hobbs, second medical superintendent, 1910–23. Under Hobbs, an excellent administrator and publicist, the Homewood Retreat began a period of expansion and growth.

Moments of Unreason

Introduction

The Homewood Retreat of Guelph, Ontario, established in 1883, was an early Canadian venture in corporate health care. The founders of the first large private asylum for nervous and mental disorders in the Dominion intended to address a growing need in late Victorian society – the mental health care of the middle class. The 1880s were a period of pervasive mistrust of public mental institutions. Private asylums, that is, institutions that appeared to profit from madness, also came under public suspicion because they were popularly associated with an older European tradition of madhouses and keepers. However, by the late nineteenth century in North America, the proprietary asylum was a far different creature. It depended upon its clientele, patrons and patients, for economic survival, and this dependence gave rise to both subtle and overt direction on the part of these rate payers.

Although the historiography of individual asylums, particularly of private institutions, is limited, it has gradually been expanding since William Parry-Jones's examination of English private madhouses of the eighteenth and nineteenth centuries was published in 1972.[1] In his study of the Lancaster (England) Asylum for pauper lunatics, John Walton engaged in intensive investigation of a single institution and its case records to determine the daily experiences of the patients as well as the motivations of the founders and administrators. Walton concluded that "even the most carefully nurtured and firmly established of 'moral treatment' regimes was vulnerable, in the long run, to the combined pressures of increased scale, cheeseparing economies, overworked medical superintendence, aging patient populations, and untrained, undersupervised nursing staff."[2] Anne Digby reached similar conclusions in her examination of the York Retreat, the model for nineteenth-century asylums in the western world.

Digby's computer-assisted study of York's case histories demonstrated that, even in the cloistered atmosphere of the Quaker experiment, asylum care evolved from moral treatment into a "more repressive moral management."[3]

On this side of the Atlantic, Nancy Tomes's study of the Pennsylvania Hospital for the Insane, also a private Quaker asylum and modelled after the York Retreat, is the major contribution to the historiography of the private asylum. Tomes's work addressed two historical problems: "Whom did the asylum serve and how did it function simultaneously as a medical and social institution?" She concluded that the needs of the families were foremost in the decision to commit members of the middle class to an institution.[4] In the United States, nineteenth-century institutional mental health care was of three types: the massive state-run public asylums, such as the Worcester (Massachussetts) State Hospital, which Gerald Grob has examined, and the Utica and Willard Asylums (New York), which Ellen Dwyer has more recently investigated,[5] the private charitable asylums such as the Pennsylvania Hospital, and the private, profit-making institutions of which no major study has yet been undertaken.

In Canada, the situation was somewhat different, and this is reflected in the historiography. Probably due to a limited population base and a tradition of government intervention in social welfare, Canadian asylums were primarily provincial institutions and the model public asylum network was in the province of Ontario. Thomas Brown's examination of the Provincial Lunatic Asylum at Toronto demonstrated that a Canadian institution was characterized by the best and worst features of asylums elsewhere: a succession of increasingly sophisticated and adept medical superintendents and a decline in the use of mechanical restraints, but also overcrowding, deteriorating facilities, and a growing chronic population.[6] Catharine Sims's study of the smaller provincial asylum at Kingston found similar features.[7] S.E.D. Shortt's examination of the London, Ontario Asylum for the Insane, similar in scope to Tomes's work, addressed both the institution and its medical superintendent, Richard M. Bucke, placing each within the context of nineteenth-century psychiatry.[8]

Apart from the provincial public asylums and the convent-run asylums in the province of Quebec, Canadian institutional mental health care was limited to small and ephemeral establishments and to the Homewood Retreat, a unique, privately owned, profit-oriented institution. The blurring of public and private that is characteristic of Canadian life also helped make this asylum unusual. Its founder,

John W. Langmuir, was the guiding force behind the public institutional network in Ontario; the Homewood Retreat therefore was never far from the psychiatric or social welfare mainstream. In this study of Homewood, by using a computer-assisted analysis of the case histories and institutional records of the Homewood Retreat, I document the social and therapeutic functions of the asylum from the perspective of its various human components. Such documentation should, among other things, provide instructive reference points for comparing public, private, and charitable institutions. What social needs, for example, were met by a private and for-profit institution, and what does this subsequently augur for corporate health care in contemporary society?

The following statistical framework was employed in this study. Using a random start, every fifth male and every third female admission between 1883 and 1920 were selected, the ratio of men to women reflecting the predominance of female admissions after 1900. Cases with extremely sparse data, such as no date of discharge or personal information, were discarded and replaced by a more complete matching case (that is, same sex, diagnosis, and year of admission). Cases noting only date of discharge and diagnosis were retained. The sample comprised 567 male and 567 female patients. All tables and graphs, unless otherwise noted, were derived from this sample. Significant narrative data has been culled from patient files that were not part of the sample. Such cases will be cited by date of admission. To ensure anonymity, all sample cases, commencing with female patients, have been alphabetized and then renumbered so that they do not correspond with the patient numbers listed in either the register or the casebook. The patient sample with the new numbers has been deposited with the Archives of Ontario, where the Homewood Sanitarium Collection is now housed, and with the Homewood Sanitarium. The sample population will be identified by given name, first initial of surname, the number assigned for the purposes of this study, and the year of first admission. In rare instances where anonymity might be compromised, the generic 'X' will replace the surname initial.

CHAPTER TWO

Retreat From the Madhouse: Ontario's First Experiment in Corporate Health Care

Watch for some season of vexation, and then, by proper insinuations and a pitying tone of voice, work up the patient to a due pitch of passion; then lay on blisters; and before his agitation of spirits has time to subside, hurry him away violently to a madhouse, so denominated, that is to say, one of the graves of mind, body and estate, much more dreadful than the Bastille and Inquisition [1796].[1]

The keeping of madhouses has long been a gainful trade ... and many have realized very large fortunes by the confinement of their fellow-creatures [1829].[2]

It would be impossible to secure a more complete privacy, or a more pleasant seclusion than is enjoyed amongst the grassy slopes, shaded walks and the lovely lawns of the Homewood Sanitarium. Here you feel the perfect charm of refined seclusion; here you feel that while the world is near, you are sheltered from its grosser side. It is perfect peace, perfect rest. It is the Homewood [1915].[3]

The madhouse, the retreat, or the proprietary asylum did not enjoy a favourable reputation in the eighteenth century, nor did it fare much better for most of the nineteenth. Yet in 1883, a group of prominent, affluent Canadian gentlemen, some of whom had long years of experience in public service, formed the Homewood Retreat Association, a commercial, social and medical venture which in the year of its centenary was praised as one of the country's "super hospitals."[4] Homewood is notable from a historical perspective not simply for its success and longevity but for the similarities in purpose and experiences it shared with the madhouses of an earlier period. The Homewood Retreat was certainly no Bastille, but it was similarly removed from that "perfect peace, perfect rest" so fulsomely described in its promotional literature. (See appendices 1 and 2.)

William L. Parry-Jones has defined the private madhouse as a "privately owned establishment for the reception and care of insane persons, conducted as a business proposition for the personal profit of the proprietor or proprietors."[5] He traces its roots in Great Britain to the early seventeenth century when destitute lunatics were boarded out at parish expense in private homes. The insane from wealthier families were usually personally attended by physicians or clergymen. By the mid-eighteenth century, madhouses had proliferated and acquired such a reputation for cruelty and mismanagement that in 1774 Parliament executed the Act for Regulating Madhouses, which provided rudimentary guidelines for inspection and for medical certification of patients.[6] At the century's end, the successful work of William Tuke in York, England, and Philippe Pinel in Paris in the use of non-restraining techniques and treatment by psychological rather than physical discipline brought into even sharper relief the alleged abuses of the private houses.

The English Madhouse Act of 1828 required certification of insanity by two physicians or magistrates to assuage fears, promulgated in the penny press, that sane persons were being committed by rapacious relatives who, abetted by the keepers of the private houses, coveted their estates. More comprehensive legislation appeared with the Lunatic Asylums Act of 1842, which established a board of commissioners to inspect all the asylums throughout England and Wales. The commissioners' report, completed in 1844, was the first complete survey of private licensed houses in the country, and many of its recommendations were embodied in the Lunatics Act of 1845. All counties in England and Wales were compelled to provide for their insane poor, and the majority of county asylums were built in the twenty years subsequent to this Act.[7] With the channelling of the pauper lunatics into the public system, the private houses were forced to look elsewhere for their clientele. By improving their premises and their images, the private asylums (as they were known by the 1850s) began to cater to the middle and upper classes.

The evolution of asylum care in British North America was somewhat different. In Upper Canada, the first legislation providing relief for the destitute insane was passed in 1832; it endorsed the old boarding-out system.[8] In 1839, in accord with British events, the legislative assembly authorized the construction of a model asylum in Toronto, although it was not until 1850 that a permanent institution was built. Within a short time, due primarily to a rapid influx of chronic cases, expansion became necessary, and a network of public asylums was built within a thirty-year period. Asylums were opened at Fort Malden (Amherstburg) in 1859 and at Orillia in 1861; then both were replaced by the London Asylum in 1870. The Rockwood Asylum for the Criminally Insane was opened in 1856, while in 1876 the Hamilton Asylum was completed and the Orillia Asylum was re-opened.[9]

In an instance where legislation preceded the event, the Private Lunatic Asylums Act was passed in Upper Canada in 1853, some thirty years before a private house was established. It has been suggested that the statute was passed under pressure from the British government following the passage of the Lunatic Act there in 1845, and indeed the 1853 legislation shared many of the same goals and concerns.[10] The comprehensive nature of the 1853 act ensured that any future private asylum in the province would avoid the most serious abuses prevalent in the worst of the British madhouses. The Canadian asylum would be subject to periodic visits by a board of "three or more Justices and one physician at least," none of whom was allowed to have any pecuniary interest in the asylum. The proprietor was required to submit a "true and full" description of his and other financial interests in the institution, a blueprint of the buildings, and a record and description of every patient. All construction and alterations had to be approved by a clerk of the peace. Complete notations of patient histories had to be kept in "the book of admissions," "the medical visitation book," and "the case book," all of which were to be presented to the board of visitors for inspection. The commitment of any patient to the asylum required the written certification of two medical practitioners after separate examinations. Bowing to the reality of asylum care in 1853, the act also allowed the admission of a patient to a private home, but only after the premises had been inspected by the visitors, and a "private return" submitted to a clerk of the peace.[11] Clearly the weighty bureaucratic requirements under which the private asylum would labour rendered its establishment in the province unfeasible for any but the most serious entrepreneurs. It is scarcely surprising therefore that the Homewood Retreat, Ontario's first private asylum, was founded by the men most intimately involved in asylum management: the administrators and physicians of the province's public asylums.

Homewood's founder and first president was John Woodburn Langmuir. Born in Ayrshire, Scotland in 1835 and immigrating to Canada in 1849, Langmuir was a successful businessman in Picton, Ontario, where he was elected mayor in 1858. A loyal Liberal, Langmuir was appointed first inspector of prisons and public charities in

1868, and in that capacity he created a modern, centralized system of institutions which included insane asylums, prisons, orphanages, and reformatories. In 1882 Langmuir resigned his government office to take part in the creation of the Toronto General Trust Corporation, the first Canadian trust company (Canada Permanent today), becoming general manager and vice-president of the corporation.[12] The establishment of the trust company was partly the result of his experiences in the collection of maintenance costs from the estates of the insane and the management of estates seized by the government after their owners had been certified as insane. In like fashion, while serving as inspector he had come in contact with many affluent families who required asylum care for a relation, but who were reluctant to use the facilities of the public asylums. In 1873, he recommended, unsuccessfully at the time, that beds at the Provincial Lunatic Asylum at Toronto be converted into more luxurious accommodations for paying patients. "The well-to-do," he argued, "were compelled to send their insane relatives to private asylums in the neighbouring States."[13] This created great hardship for the patient and family, and clearly indicated a need for some kind of appropriate accommodation in Canada. Langmuir's successor as inspector, W.T. O'Reilly, agreed that "as regards the insane persons of the wealthy class, it is manifest that our public Asylums, admirable as they are, cannot afford such persons the partial seclusion and special personal attention which they desire and are prepared to pay for ... Over and above this, it is not desirable that insane persons who can afford to pay well for comforts and luxuries should be admitted into our crowded public Asylums, to the exclusion of those who can barely afford to pay ... and for whose benefit [they] are more especially intended."[14]

General hospital care for the middle class was a phenomenon of the late Victorian and Edwardian periods. Until the 1880s, such hospitals were perceived as charity institutions for the destitute where the sick were expected to adhere to a strict moral code in order to heal their souls as well as their bodies.[15] Believed to be cursed with infectious diseases and a high mortality rate, hospitals were generally avoided by those able to pay a visiting physician. With increased geographical mobility, however, greater numbers of working- and middle-class people found themselves in need of health care far from their homes and so were forced to enter the hospitals. At the same time, advances in antisepsis and asepsis, anaesthesia and surgery made the hospitals safer and more complicated operations possible – though only in a hospital setting. Advanced medical technology also enhanced the influence of the physicians in the hospitals, thereby emphasizing a scientific rather than a moralistic view of the patient.[16]

In contrast to the slow acceptance by the middle class of hospitalization for medical or surgical reasons, mental illness, by its very nature, was not seen as curable in the home. At the point that an individual's behaviour became intolerably disruptive to the family, or dangerous to the community, or where there was a lack of resources, both human and financial, to care for the individual in the home, families were willing to identify a member as insane, neurotic, or addicted and seek outside accommodation for them.[17] This willingness dovetailed nicely with a basic premise of nineteenth-century psychiatry or moral treatment, namely that the patient's environment was partially responsible for the mental disorder and that removal to a new, controlled environment was the first step towards recovery. Belief in the value of serene rural surroundings and a strict regimen of food, rest, and hygiene meant that for the middle class mental care was institutional care.

Langmuir, deciding to act on his conviction, set about providing private asylum care for those who could afford to pay for it. He convinced Stephen Lett, the assistant medical officer of the Toronto Asylum, to join him in the venture. The two had become friends when they both served in the army during the Fenian raids of 1866. Langmuir and Lett, who was also to become the Homewood Retreat's first medical superintendent, each purchased one-third of the original stock issue. For the attending physician to be a major investor in a private asylum was not without precedent, particularly in Britain, but Lett's anomalous position as both physician and director would later provide difficulties for himself and the board.[18]

The other founding members were men such as William B. Jarvis, the sheriff of York county, who shared with Langmuir both commercial and political interests. Following his death in 1887, Jarvis was replaced on the board of directors by his son Frederick C. Jarvis, a lawyer, leading Toronto Anglican, and director of the prestigious Wycliff and Havergal colleges. Jarvis would succeed Langmuir as chairman of the board in 1915. Another director, Robert Jaffray, like Langmuir, was involved in a number of commercial interests, including insurance, railroads, electricity, sugar, banking, and publishing. He also served on the board of the Toronto General Trust Corporation and the Niagara Falls Commission, and he was appointed a senator in 1905.[19]

Edmund Allen Meredith, a notable figure in Victorian politics and education, was the son-in-law of Sheriff Jarvis, the vice-president of Toronto General Trust Corporation, and Homewood's fifth director. Born in Ireland in 1817, he graduated from Trinity College in 1837. After studying law, he immigrated to Canada in 1842 and articled with his brother, Sir William Meredith, who was to become chief justice of Quebec. He received a master's degree from Bishop's College and was subsequently called to the bars of Ireland and both Canadas. McGill College appointed Meredith principal and mathematics lecturer in 1846. Although he resigned the following year to become assistant provincial secretary of Upper Canada, he remained an active governor of McGill and was instrumental in the acquisition of the university's charter in 1852. After Confederation, Meredith was appointed under-secretary of state for the province of Ontario. He gained an international reputation in the fields of prison reform and juvenile delinquency in his capacity as inspector and later chairman of the Canadian Prison Board. Meredith retired from public office in 1878.[20]

Homewood's remaining original board members were Edward Galley, a Toronto contractor, and James A. Hedley, editor of the *Monetary Times*. The founding members were connected by family,[21] politics (most were active Liberals), philanthropy, and commercial pursuits. Virtually all were associated with the Toronto General Trust Corporation, where Homewood's board meetings were held; in some ways, the asylum may be seen as an outgrowth of the financial corporation. Unlike other philanthropic endeavours in which its founders were engaged, however, the retreat was created for the benefit of the very class to which they belonged.

When Homewood's board of directors held their first meeting on 19 May 1883, two important topics were discussed, property and legislation. The city of Guelph was chosen for its "healthful" high altitude and fresh spring water and for its central location. Sixty miles northwest of Toronto, Guelph was linked through the Grand Trunk Railway line to the metropolitan Toronto area, to a rich agricultural hinterland, and to the neighbouring states of New York, Michigan, and Pennsylvania. With a population in 1881 of under ten thousand, the town was also sufficiently small and isolated to assure anonymity for the asylum's middle-class charges.[22] The site chosen by the board was the nineteen-acre estate that a prominent Guelph attorney and member of parliament, Donald Guthrie, had put on the market. The Guthrie property was adjacent to the city, but it was flanked on one side by a large homestead and on the other by the Speed River (which was to claim a steady toll in suicidal and accidental deaths).

With respect to legislation, certain amendments were necessary to the 1853 act to make the venture viable, although Langmuir was not able to secure their passage until 1885, a year after the retreat had begun operation. The act had only allowed for admission of Ontario residents; by amendment, non-residents with two certificates from other than Ontario physicians were accepted provided that a provincial practitioner also certified the patient within three days of admission. (This clause, as it turned out, would provide a steady source of revenue for Guelph's physicians.) Since the amended act also allowed patients to be discharged on a probationary basis, the paperwork on re-admissions was reduced. The retreat was also made subject to the inspection of the provincial inspector, as well as the board of visitors, by the consent of both the government and the institution. Although the Homewood Retreat had been subject to de facto inspection since its opening, the formal enactment of this requirement was used to bolster community confidence in the asylum.[23]

Of greatest significance for the future of the retreat was section 5 of the amended act, which allowed for the admission of non-insane individuals for the treatment of "epilepsy, hysteria, chorea-amentia, or any nervine or physical ailment" by voluntary application with the signature of one physician. The percentage of voluntary nervous patients would determine whether the institution would most resemble a madhouse or a rest home, and there apparently was a wide pool of such patients from which the retreat could draw an income. Indeed the late nineteenth century was called "the nervous age." The diagnosis of nervousness was an innocuous one and far more acceptable to the paying patient than that of insanity.[24] As table 1 indicates, nervous cases comprised a very substantial segment of the patient population at the Homewood Retreat. "Neurasthenia," or nervous exhaustion, was in fact the primary diagnosis; among men, only alcoholics were admitted in greater numbers between 1883 and 1920. Fortunately, from Homewood's point of view, the provisions of the act of 1873 for the reclamation of habitual drunkards had made it possible for private asylums to admit inebriates (as physicians then termed alcoholics) who were considered to be "reasonably hopeful subject(s) for treatment," as voluntary patients.[25] Those who were dangerous or who squandered their property could be sent to a private asylum by court order.

With such a wide market to serve, it was not surprising that the directors were optimistic about the venture. In 1883 there were 538 paying patients in Ontario's public asylums, or thirteen percent of total admissions, generating an annual revenue of sixty thousand dollars. Daniel Hack Tuke, grandson of the founder of the York Retreat in England, commented that this "certainly point(ed) to the

Table 1
Diagnoses upon Admission

Diagnosis	Female	Male	Total
Neurasthenia	192	144	336
Alcoholism	23	168	191
Depression	85	45	130
Addiction	51	51	102
Dementia Praecox	55	27	82
Agitation	49	21	70
Delusion	31	12	43
Syphilitic disorders	0	33	33
Multiple addictions	12	19	31
Senility	16	13	29
Manic-depression	13	8	21
Epilepsy	7	8	15
Puerperal psychosis	12	n/a	12
Involutional melancholia	4	1	5
Psychosthenia	2	3	5
Imbecility	3	0	3
Other physical disorders	11	11	22
Not given	1	3	4
Total	567	567	1134

probable success of a private asylum which ha(d) recently been established in Guelph." Inspector O'Reilly concurred that the institution was "destined to form an important supplement to the public Asylums of this Province, as well as to the Dominion at Large."[26]

The retreat was opened on 1 January 1884. With a capacity for twenty-five male and twenty-five female patients, it consisted of the estate mansion, or Manor, with offices, reception rooms, and music hall on the ground floor and quarters for the medical superintendent on the first floor. A two-storied wing with female wards on the ground floor and male wards above had been added to the mansion. The rooms and corridors were wide and spacious, and each ward had a sitting room furnished with sofas, easy chairs, mirrors, carpets, and fireplaces. When it became apparent that male applicants were far outnumbering females, a spiral staircase was built from the lower to upper ward and half of the female quarters was used for male patients. Each ward was connected by a corridor to the dining rooms, which were segregated by sex, and to the conservatory and the billiard room. A bowling alley, gymnasium, bowling green, tennis court, and toboggan run were added later.[27]

By 1889, Lett was advertising the asylum widely, mailing thousands of copies of the retreat's prospectus to physicians in Canada and the United States. (See appendix 1.) Since Homewood's locale was its greatest asset, the pamphlets emphasized the arcadian splendours of the grounds: "A growth of natural woodland, extending down the hill and across the lower level, sweeps along the banks of the river ... And the tall trees rise with towering energy to struggle for the revivifying sunlight and air." The retreat also placed advertisements in Canadian and American medical journals and in a few daily newspapers, and it became common practice to invite visiting physicians to tour the retreat whenever the Canadian Medical Association or other professional group met in Toronto. Occasionally, members of the board were able to use "a little personal influence" to have portions of the annual report to the provincial legislature published in the Toronto Globe.[28]

However, it was soon evident that the number of admissions was not meeting expectations in spite of the active publicity program, the optimism, the market possibilities, and the luxurious accommodations at Homewood. As it turned out, the greatest threat to survival was competition. Rival institutions were established in Flint, Michigan (1892), Verdun, Quebec, where the Protestant Asylum for the Insane maintained a private ward (1892), and Allandale, near Barrie, Ontario (1912). The most crippling move, however, was the creation of a "Superior Ward" at the Provincial Asylum in Toronto simultaneously with Homewood's establishment. The public asylum administrators had finally heeded Langmuir's recommendation of a decade before and opened a paying wing in direct competition with his own investment. This decision was particularly harmful to Homewood because Torontonians and residents of surrounding communities were a significant proportion of its admissions. (See table 4.) Compounding the problem was Homewood's location: both physicians and family often preferred to keep patients closer to their homes in Toronto.

Homewood was also unable to match Toronto's lower rates – rates made possible because the government was partially subsidising those "much superior" accommodations for paying patients. Although Homewood's charges were less than those in American asylums, they were usually about double those the Toronto Asylum charged for a private room and at least three times as much as for standard public asylum accommodation. In 1885, for example, the basic rate at Homewood was $10 per week compared to $2.50 or less per week for standard accommodations at public asylums and $4 to $5 per week for a private room at the Toronto Asylum. Homewood did use a sliding scale of charges with the cost to the patient dependent upon the amount of medical attention required, on whether private nursing was necessary, and on the type of accommodation chosen. In the early years the best suite, which consisted of bedroom, bath, and sitting room cost $20 per week. Drug cases, which required constant nursing and physician care, at least for the first week, were charged a higher rate.[29]

Certainly Homewood's patients were, for the most part, from middle class backgrounds, as tables 2 and 3 illustrate. As would be expected at a private asylum, there was a striking difference between occupations of patients at the Homewood Retreat and those of patients in public asylums. According to S.E.D. Shortt's recent study of the public asylum at London, Ontario, farmers and labourers comprised fully sixty-two percent of the male population there in 1900.[30] Among Homewood's male patients, however, farmers, artisans, and unskilled labourers totalled only 23.5 percent. Merchants, professionals, and other white collar workers comprised forty-five percent of the male population. Since classes of women cannot be derived from standard occupational tables, further calculation was made of parental or spousal occupations. While such data remains sketchy, the figures do suggest the higher status of Homewood's patients in general.

However, the economic status of most of the patients could not alone ensure the success of the institution. Despite the superintendents' preference for nervous cases, in its formative years Homewood found its fortunes tied to the admission of inebriates. Regrettably, from a financial perspective, alcoholic cases were unsatisfactory because of a very high rate of turnover. So dependent was the retreat on the short-term alcoholic admissions, however, that when Inspector O'Reilly attempted to enforce compliancy with the Inebriate Act, under which patients were required to remain a minimum of one year in treatment, Langmuir argued that he might as well "close the institution" since applicants would go to American asylums.[31]

In 1887, Homewood's financial situation was so bleak that the board of directors considered selling the property to the government. Instead they reduced expenses to the lowest level upon which the asylum could be run "reasonably efficient(ly)" and the following year cut Lett's salary from $1700 to $1350. In 1889 the financial picture improved although two-thirds of the admissions were the capricious male alcoholics, and the board considered excluding female patients altogether.[32] During these years, Lett was regarded as employee rather than as professional by both the board of directors and the patrons. He was swamped with work. Homewood was severely understaffed, and his salary remained tied to the amount of dividends the shareholders received. The institution's unstable

Table 2
Occupations of Patients

	Female		Male	
Occupation	No.	%	No.	%
Merchant/manufacturer[a]	4	1	88	16
Professional[b]	70	12	92	16
Other white collar[c]	35	6	75	13
Artisan/skilled labour[d]	12	2	26	5
Farming[e]	4	1	76	13.5
Semi/unskilled labour[f]			13	2
Housekeeping[g]	330	58		
Other[h]			14	2.5
No occupation	21	4	10	2
Not given	91	16	173	30
Total	567	100	567	100

Occupational structure used here and in table 3 was devised by Gordon Darroch in "Occupational Structure, Assessed Wealth and Homeowning during Toronto's Early Industrialization, 1861–1899," *Histoire Sociale/Social History* 16, no. 32 (November 1983): 381–410.

[a]Merchant/manufacturer includes businessperson, storekeeper, insurance agent, lumberman, restaurant/hotelkeeper, real estate agent, railroad executive, brewer, distiller, banker, contractor, music dealer, stockbroker, liverykeeper, food buyer, mine operator, bookseller.

[b]Professional includes principal, professor, physician, artist, dentist, veterinarian, engineer, senator, barrister, editor, clergy, architect, judge, military, bishop, gentleman, nurse, schoolteacher, nun, music teacher, lady, librarian, writer, designer, accountant, publisher, mayor, school founder, "well off."

[c]Other white collar includes clerk, sales, officework, student, civil servant, bookkeeper, medical student, telegrapher, druggist, manager, advertiser, fire brigade, companion, student, bank teller, photographer, governess, telephone operator, law student, police, railroad conductor, secretary.

[d]Artisan/skilled labour includes mail carrier, tailor, clothier, bricklayer, machinist, molder, painter, shoemaker, watchmaker, jeweller, shirtcutter, electrician, tinsmith, butcher, smelterer, telephone technician, milliner, seamstress, dressmaker, linotype operator, stone mason, carpenter, cabinet maker, auto assembly.

[e]Farming includes beekeeper, miller, farmwork.

[f]Semi/unskilled labour includes barber, apprentice, chef, delivery, caretaker, jailor, junk dealer, laundry, janitor, waiter, driver, newspaper collector, labourer, mariner.

[g]Housekeeping includes housewife, "at home," "living alone," housework.

[h]Other includes entertainer, retired, various, bankrupt.

Table 3
Occupations of Parents or Spouses of Patients

	Female		Male	
Occupation	No.	%	No.	%
Merchant/manufacturer	77	13.5	57	10
Farming	61	11	69	12
Professional	76	13.5	49	9
Other white collar	29	5	13	2
Artisan/skilled labour	11	2	9	1.5
Semi/unskilled labour	8	1.5	2	.5
Other	4	.5	75	13
Not given	301	53	293	52
Total	567	100	567	100

Note: See table 2 for an explanation of occupational categories.

position affected therapeutics as well. Lett's preferred therapy for alcoholics and addicts was a lengthy course of gradual withdrawal, but few patients could be induced to remain for a full session. The situation improved slightly in 1896 when, due to Lett's growing reputation in the treatment of addiction, the number of addicts admitted increased. The institution attempted to reap the greatest benefits by fixing the price of habit cases at fifteen dollars per week despite the extra attention addicts required. The higher admission rate, however, was not to be maintained.[33]

At the March, 1900 board meeting, Langmuir submitted Lett's letter which read in part: "I do not see how we can continue. You will observe ... that we have only nineteen patients at present; of these four will be going out in a few days and none are coming to take their place. [This will leave us with a revenue] totally too small to run the institution, and even this we are not sure of." The board was forced to conclude that a private asylum "was not renumerative in the province" and opened negotiations with the government and private investors to sell the property.[34]

Neither group showed much interest. Unexpectedly, however, by the end of the year, the financial crisis had passed. Lett noted that "as our female population has increased beyond its normal figure, I have restored to the use of the female department that portion of their corridor which some years ago was set apart for male patients. This not only gives me more room for females but a better classification." This sudden increase in female patients was due to the growing acceptance of the institution by the medical community and meant a reversal in Homewood's fortunes. (See figure 1.) However, Lett, suffering from a fatal neurological disorder, was growing too ill to reap the benefits. By 1901, he had become "very seriously ill," and the daily running of the asylum was left to his wife Annie and a visiting physician while the board searched for a new superintendent.[35]

The board of directors selected Alfred Thomas Hobbs, formerly the assistant physician at the London Asylum. From the outset, Hobb's relations with the board were on a much more professional footing, despite (or perhaps because of) the fact that he did not personally invest in the corporation until 1906. Hobbs was hired on a three-year renewable contract. He demanded and received $1500 per annum plus maintenance, a free hand in management, the services of a fifth-year medical student, and, significantly, twenty-five percent of profits on patients over the first twenty-eight.[36]

Hobb's administration (he retired in 1923) was a period of growth for Homewood. He immediately changed the name from retreat to sanitarium to heighten the emphasis upon nervous cases. By 1903, he was able to report "a very substantial increase in the number of patients" and to recommend expansion to stave off competition and avoid turning away applicants. In that year, although a nurses' home, lodge house, and superintendent's residence were constructed to increase capacity, patients were still being kept "on stretchers and couches" six months later. A full-time assistant physician was added to the staff in 1904, and Hobbs was able to declare the sanitarium "equal to any institution on the Continent."[37]

The best indicator of the change in Homewood's fortunes was its policy towards the inebriate patients who had been so critical to the survival of the institution in its early years. By 1905, eighty percent of the patients were either nervous or "mental" cases, and Hobbs had the luxury to propose what Lett could not: "the less (Homewood) is known as an inebriate institution, the better its moral atmosphere in the eyes of the profession and the more attractive (it is) to the general public." In 1907, when two new buildings were opened, the long-desired separation of patients with different mental problems became possible. The original asylum, or Manor, was used to house addicts, inebriates, and incurable cases. The Colonial was a modern wing used for acute nervous and mental cases while the Vista was a small wing for those requiring "temporary isolation."[38]

There was expansion in the area of therapeutics as well, with the construction of facilities for hydrotherapy, electrotherapy, and massage; a fully-equipped operating room was built in 1907, and an arts and crafts department in 1908. Hobbs started Homewood's own

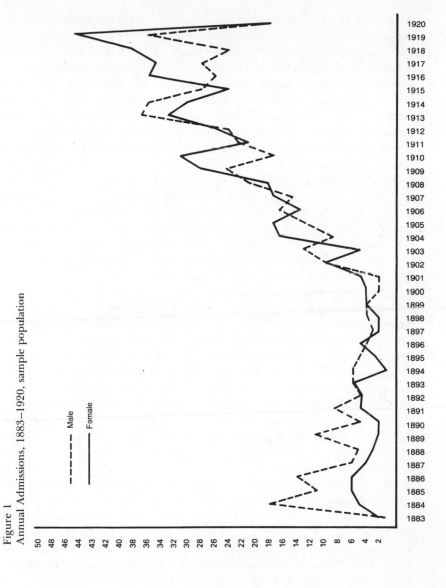

Figure 1
Annual Admissions, 1883–1920, sample population

nursing school in 1906, and the hospital staff was expanded to include a professionally trained occupational therapist and dietitian. In 1911 the original Manor was destroyed by fire. There were no injuries since it housed ambulatory habit cases, and Hobbs was able to use the accident as an opportunity to fully modernize the institution. A bungalow was built as a cottage for "disturbed and maniacal" patients in which a "battery of continous baths" for their treatment (and control) was situated. A new Vista was built for permanent patients, as well as a dining hall and kitchen block with a series of "seven handsome dining rooms," with quarters for male nurses and kitchen staff above. Beneath the dining hall was an amusement hall and arts and crafts department which was "fitted up in a workmanlike manner, with a series of benches, tools (and) looms for weaving." The new Manor contained fifty bedrooms, some with bathrooms ensuite, and all with hot and cold running water. It also included "large and cozy sitting rooms, and handsome drawing rooms, solariums, verandahs and billard rooms."[39]

The Great War, and accompanying economic constraints, produced a minor shortage of patients as Homewood's rates became more a luxury. There was also a shortage of staff since male attendants were in short supply due to enlistment, and prospective female employees were finding a wide variety of other attractive callings and professions. To help business, Hobbs offered to embark upon a North American tour to visit physicians, but the board remained unconvinced by either his motives or the likely results.[40] Fortunately, by 1922 admissions were again at a high level, so that upon his retirement in 1923, Hobbs left two legacies: expansion and solvency.

The Homewood Retreat in practice was neither madhouse nor clone of the public asylums. It operated under legal constraints which made procedures and treatments as visible as in the public asylums, yet it lacked the stability and funding enjoyed by the government institutions. The private nature of Homewood also left it prey to the vagaries of the public. Far from being an instrument of social control, the institution was forced to adapt to the desires and needs of its clientele. It was clear from Lett's experiences that as long as asylum care was a buyer's market, professional autonomy would be superseded by the need to make a profit. Hobbs, in contrast, was able to assert his authority over the patients and, to a lesser degree, the board. This was partly due to personality but primarily because the retreat had become a financial success.

CHAPTER THREE

Asylum Superintendents and the Medical Community, 1883–1923

The success of the proprietary asylum was largely dependent upon the ability and reputation of the medical superintendent. While he had the opportunity to try increasingly varied therapeutic alternatives, he also faced competition from other institutions and practitioners taking advantage of the same opportunity. In the 1880s many young physicians were no longer satisfied with relying on the traditions of moral management that had dominated psychiatric thinking in the 1860s and 1870s. They emphasized physical causation, although there were still traditionalists who remained convinced that neurological investigation alone did not provide the answers for mental disease.

The shifting contours of psychiatric care from 1883 to 1923 are reflected in the careers of Homewood's first two medical superintendents, Stephen Lett and Alfred Hobbs. Their different approachs to psychiatric care mirrored the changes in therapeutic rationale. Lett, apprenticed in traditional moral treatment and influenced by late Victorian hereditarianism, had little expectation of being able to cure insanity. He maintained, rather, that controlled surroundings, good diet, and moderate exercise would alleviate symptoms. Alfred Hobbs's professional career, on the other hand, coincided with the rising expectation that insanity could be cured through interventionist methods such as radical surgery. By endeavouring to incorporate American and European therapeutic innovations into his therapy, Hobbs attempted to bring Homewood into step with the most modern of North American asylums. The careers of both men also demonstrate that if the era in which an individual trained partly determined his approach to therapy, the era in which he worked determined the appeal to his patients of the therapy he offered. But choice of treatment was also based on attracting the attention of family physicians. The proprietary asylum required a steady stream of paying patients, directed to it by referring physicians whose selection of a particular institution might be greatly influenced by the professional stature of the medical superintendent. Should his specialty target a need in the community, the benefits for the institution could be immediate. Possibly more than at any time in its history, Homewood's fortunes would be tied to the reputations of the two individuals who steered it into the twentieth century.

Stephen Lett, the son of an Anglican minister, was born into a respectable if undistinguished family in Kilkenny, Ireland in 1847. After his family immigrated to Canada, Lett was educated at Upper Canada College and joined the militia in 1862, serving at Port Colborne, Welland and at Fort Erie during the Fenian raids of 1866. Lett left the military service in 1870 to become a member of the College of Physicians and Surgeons of Ontario. He was then appointed assistant medical officer at the Malden Lunatic Asylum in Amherstburg, Ontario, most likely at the behest of his friend, John Langmuir, the inspector of prisons and public charities. Since Malden was absorbed by the large regional London Lunatic Asylum after the latter's construction, Lett's sojourn in Amherstburg was only months in duration, but apparently he had sufficient opportunity to meet and court Annie MacLeod, daughter of a former member of parliament, John MacLeod. When the couple were wed in 1874, Lett enhanced his social standing considerably and solidified his relationship with the "right" (Liberal) political party of his superiors.[1] In the long run, Lett's swift securement of a desirable, steady asylum position probably hurt his career, since the deficiencies in his training would later hinder him. Like other gentlemen-professionals of his generation, he would find himself eclipsed by a new educated elite in the rising professional class.[2] Becoming assistant medical superintendent of the newest and largest Ontario asylum, however, within a year of entering the medical profession, Lett must have considered his position and prospects to be fortunate indeed.

At the London Asylum, Lett spent seven years working with and learning from the experienced Henry Landor, a dedicated alienist whose prior appointments had been in the British asylum system. It was a successful working relationship; Lett was able to absorb the temperate common-sensical approach to psychiatry of a traditional moral manager, who believed that healthful diet, rest, occupation, and amusement, with the judicious use of mechanical restraints and of alcohol as a sedative, could best alleviate the grosser symptoms of insanity. Landor was not optimistic about curing mental illness, based as it was, he believed, upon an hereditary taint. Although the discharge rate during his administration (1870–77) was only twenty-eight percent, he was not discouraged. "No reliable conclusion," he wrote, "can ever be drawn, as to the success of asylum treatment in any institution, without a careful and rational valuation of the facts represented by its statistics. A bad workman may spoil good materials, but a good one can hardly make a good article out of bad material ... Just so it is with the human mind. We cannot make it over again, and turn it out better than God has made it."[3]

Landor's justification of low discharge rates as the inevitable consequence of genetic transmission was a position common to alienists. As S.E.D. Shortt suggests, heredity became the "single most significant etiological factor in accounting for madness" after 1880; it provided "material and increasingly reductionist answers to problems of human individuality and pathology."[4] Nineteenth-century concepts of heredity were painted in broad strokes, including the assumptions that acquired characteristics were inherited, that heredity was a process that carried through to weaning, and that "character, disease, and temperament were inherited in the forms of tendencies and predispositions, not as discrete and unitary qualities."[5]

The Darwinian model of evolution through natural selection provided a logical premise for the explanation of a seemingly exponential increase in insanity, crime, and poverty. Benedict Morel, Cesare Lombroso, and Richard Krafft-Ebbing, among others, speculated that insanity, alcoholism, idiocy, and nervousness were different manifestations of a particular hereditary flaw which would produce successively more serious personality, mental, and physical disorders through the generations until the family line would ultimately become extinct. The prevalence of certain families or ethnic groups in asylums, prisons, and workhouses was thus explained. The compilation of patient histories and the discovery of insane or nervous relatives served to confirm, among alienists, the veracity of hereditarianism.[6]

Hereditarianism also crystallized the basic psychiatric belief in the somatic origins of mental disease into a dogma that had, if not a therapeutic solution, at least an etiological explanation that was scientifically satisfactory, as well as professionally comforting. The best efforts of psychiatry had not cured insanity; in fact, late nineteenth-century institutions produced far fewer positive results than the early asylums apparently had. Hereditarian somaticism, therefore, provided justification for the continued public and private support of mental institutions, if only to contain and control the degenerate; it

shifted blame for the failure of mental therapeutics from the alienists
to the patients; and it also allowed the physicians to turn their attention to more professionally satisfying concerns, such as preventive
psychiatry. The mental hygiene movement, organized by, among
others, Clifford Beers and Adolf Meyer in the United States and
Clarence Hincks in Canada in the early twentieth century, pushed
for the prevention of insanity and poverty through restrictions on
immigration, reproduction, and alcohol consumption, but also wid-
ened the field of professional psychiatric endeavour to the community outside the asylum.[7]

Besides dependence on moral management, the use of restraints,
and a belief in the influence of heredity upon insanity, Landor endowed Lett with a temperate view concerning the use of alcohol in
therapeutics. Like Joseph Workman and Daniel Clark of the Toronto
Asylum, Landor believed that alcohol was particularly efficacious in
restoring the "vital powers" of feeble patients.[8] In any case, he did
not see alcohol from the emotion-laden perspective of the advocates
of prohibition, but as one element, properly used, of the alienist's
materia medica. This temperate attitude certainly served Lett well
in his years at the Homewood Retreat when alcoholics became a
significant proportion of the patient population. At the same time,
many alcoholics probably returned to Homewood because of the
sympathetic response and benign treatment they received from Lett.
Lett generally, therefore, was fortunate in having had Landor as a
medical instructor.

Landor was more than that, of course, to Lett. Their relationship
as mentor and protegé was one in which Lett would empathize with
his superior's growing disillusionment with the Ontario asylum system. "I cannot live in comfort," Landor complained to Langmuir,
"with a perpetual blister on me arising from the conviction that I
am occupying a position without proper authority." When Landor
had trained and was first installed as head of a psychiatric institution
in the 1850s, superintendency involved control of virtually every
aspect of asylum management and treatment. By the 1870s, however,
government moves to centralize and rationalize public institutions
had resulted in a substantial loss of that power. The incident which
precipitated Landor's complaint was the peremptory demand, by
the superintendent of the Hamilton Asylum, that a certain patient
be released into his custody. That superintendent was Richard Maurice Bucke, who had said, Lett reported to Landor, "these are your
orders" and "threw" them at him. Landor was outraged: "it is the
first time in my life that I have known a physician ... (to) take without
notice a patient away. The transaction ... want(s) of common courtesy

to me." This inauspicious episode marked the beginning of a lifetime's antagonism between Stephen Lett and Richard Bucke.[9]

Upon Landor's death, Lett applied for the position of medical superintendent at London, a post for which he had been groomed for seven years. To his extreme dismay, Lett learned that not only was he passed over for the promotion, but he was to work under the command of Bucke. "The fates," as Langmuir consoled, did indeed seem to be against him.[10] No two men were less likely to work harmoniously than Lett and Bucke. Stephen Lett, whose handsome figure, military career, and marriage prepared him for the role of Canadian gentleman, considered his lack of education to be more than compensated for by his practical experience. Richard Bucke, although of distinguished lineage, had been crippled during youthful adventures in prospecting; to compensate for his disability, he had devoted himself to academic achievement. He subsequently complained of the necessity of being in "the position of a hanger-on waiting to have a bone thrown him." That "bone" was the superintendency of the Hamilton Asylum in 1876, and of London's in the following year; Bucke's patron, his poker-playing crony W.T. Pardee, was Ontario's provincial secretary and Langmuir's superior.[11]

Given Lett's protracted hostility and Bucke's sanctimonious eccentricities, it was not surprising that within two months of the new administration, Bucke informed Langmuir that "all pretensions of friendship must cease between (Lett's) family and mine," obstensibly because Lett would not help entertain Bucke's friends. Langmuir subsequently decided in 1877 that, for the sake of the institution, Lett should be transferred to Toronto.[12] With this decision, Toronto's Daniel Clark felt the cold wind of Langmuir's peremptory bureaucratic style. When W.G. Metcalfe, for whom Lett was to be exchanged, was curtly informed that "in the interests of the public service" he was to be uprooted to London, he regretted that he had unsuccessfully performed his duties, "as that is the only construction I can put upon your ... totally unexpected notice of transfer" and to an "inferior position" at that. He promptly resigned, supported by Clark, who hoped that "no such change is intended without my consent." When the physicians realized that Langmuir did indeed intend it, Metcalfe, who had no better prospects, meekly withdrew his resignation and offered his services as telegraph operator.[13]

The lack of autonomy suffered by the physicians in the Ontario public mental health care system was symptomatic of the psychiatric profession in the 1880s – the specialty continued to exist on the fringes of medicine even though asylum appointments were usually more secure than private practice, particularly during periods of economic depression. In the 1890s, for instance, there was a surplus of physicians in Ontario. Yet these institutional appointments were purchased at the cost of professional autonomy.[14] The medical superintendents of corporate, proprietary, and public asylums alike were answerable to boards of directors or government departments for their managerial and therapeutic decisions.[15] While the 1880s and 1890s would see the expansion of psychiatry into private practice, it would be decades before asylum work would not be the experience of the majority of psychiatrists in Canada. Few Ontario Victorian alienists, in fact, would not have been affected by the dynamic, creative, and authoritarian leadership of J.W. Langmuir.

At Toronto, Lett directed his energies towards the improvement of his deficient academic record. In 1878, he took his bachelor of medicine from Toronto University and in the following year his doctor of medicine. During his six years at Toronto, Lett would work under Daniel Clark, one of the most interesting figures in psychiatry in Victorian Canada. A Scottish-born, Ontario-trained physician who had served as a military surgeon during the American civil war, Clark attained a number of important professional positions; he became president of the Ontario College of Physicians and Surgeons, vice-president of the prestigious New York Medico-Legal Society, and president of the Association of Medical Superintendents of American Institutions for the Insane (AMSAII). He acquired an international reputation for his prolific contributions to medical literature, including monographs on alcoholism, self-abuse, mental diseases, and the legal ramifications of insanity.[16] In articles such as "Reflexes in Psychiatry," Clark outlined his opposition to the theory of brain localization of insanity that gained acceptance among neurologists in the late nineteenth century.[17]

Neurology in North America originated with the work of George M. Beard, William A. Hammond, and S. Weir Mitchell who, like Clark, had been military surgeons. The American physicians discovered that localized nerve damage resulting from head wounds could affect speech, behaviour, and sensations – producing symptoms previously associated solely with the mind.[18] Following the work of the German clinician Wilhelm Griesinger, who claimed that "all mental disease was brain disease," the North American neurologists developed a localized somatic view of mental illness.[19] Insanity was considered to be the consequence of a morbid condition localized in a specific area of the brain, and, it was believed, with advances in surgical and diagnostic techniques, all mental disease could ultimately be understood and treated. This perspective was given a great boost with the discovery, first in 1852, that general paresis of the insane (GPI), a degenerative neural disorder, was caused by syphilis. The GPI syndrome, which was characterized by extensive lesions in the brain resulting in personality disorders, became the model for all mental illness, as researchers searched for the lesions that must produce, they reasoned, other forms of insanity.[20]

Daniel Clark, however, was not convinced that all insanity and nervous disorders could ultimately be traced to localized nerve damage.[21] His views on the importance of heredity in the creation of insanity, and the importance of a holistic, rather than localized, approach to mental therapeutics, were in fact consistent with those of Henry Landor and most other asylum physicians of their generation. These views would be absorbed by Stephen Lett, although Clark's international reputation and varied commitments may have actually meant that his influence within his asylum and subsequently upon his assistant physicians was diminished.[22]

Lett made the best of his time in Toronto. His minor squabble with Langmuir over the retention of his personal horse and carriage demonstrated his attempt to preserve some vestige of a gentlemanly lifestyle although, at the salary of assistant physician, he was finally forced to sell the conveyance. When he was transferred in June 1883 to Hamilton, however, his prospects must have looked bleak indeed.[23] Three years earlier, Charles Kirk Clarke had written of his experiences at the Hamilton Asylum: "it was like a horrible dream ... The staff were an impossible, and in many instances, an immoral and uncontrollable rabble."[24] At this stage in their professional lives, Clarke and Lett were sharing the difficulties common to assistant physicians. As asylums grew in population, the numbers of assistant physicians to whom the daily management of the wards was left grew as well. For many of these assistants, further advancement was stalled by lack of superintendencies, so that opportunities lay in the growth of small proprietary asylums. As heads of proprietary hospitals, these physicians were eligible for membership in the AMSAII and "could more easily establish themselves as experts in psychological medicine."[25]

Thus it was fortunate indeed for Lett that his desire for an escape from Hamilton concurred with Langmuir's interest in forming a proprietary asylum for the middle-class insane of Ontario. With the formation of the Homewood Retreat Association, Lett finally reaped the benefits of his longstanding friendship (and that of his in-laws) with Langmuir. Lett's personal ties, his desire to leave the public system in which he was not likely to soon advance, his residence in Toronto, which made it easy for him to participate in the meetings and plans, Langmuir's retirement from public service, and Annie Lett's financial contribution – all of these factors made Lett the obvious choice for the position of superintendent. Langmuir's relationship with Lett also rendered the latter personally and professionally loyal to him; previous examples of Langmuir's imperious style of leadership demonstrated the necessity for a malleable, subservient medical superintendent. It was ironic, and inevitable, that the same qualities of malleability and subservience would backfire; they were to render Lett a relatively inefficient administrator and an ineffective publicist for the institution.

At the Homewood Retreat, Lett had frequent difficulties in asserting authority over his employees. Hampered by a disorderly staff, rowdy patients, and poor working conditions (his office was so cold he wore an overcoat in winter), Lett found himself on a treadmill; without a luxurious, smooth-running facility, he could not attract new patients.[26] Yet without the patients, no improvement or additional staffing could take place. As noted in chapter 1, a brief respite in low admission rates did take place in the late 1880s and 1890s with the admission of alcoholic and drug-addicted patients, even though they were regarded by the board, the public, and other patients alike as an unsatisfactory population. Nonetheless, it was to this same troublesome patient population that Lett looked to carve out a professional niche. He believed his area of expertise, the treatment of such patients, could not fail to attract patients "as both Canada and the United States are swarming with opium habituates." He therefore published a number of lengthy articles on "The Treatment of Drunkards" in newspapers in Toronto, Guelph and Ottawa,[27] and submitted scholarly articles to professional journals such as the *Quarterly Journal of Inebriety*. One of the highlights of Lett's career must have been the speech he gave before the British Society for the Study and Cure of Inebriety, a society which included Norman Kerr, T.D. Crothers, and other British and North American experts in the field, and which elected him a member. The retreat subsequently printed four thousand copies of Lett's paper and distributed them to general practitioners in Canada and the United States.[28]

Lett's therapeutic philosophy, as delineated in his articles, was that substance dependency was a disease and not a vice and should be treated as such. The superintendent further absolved prospective patients from most of the guilt arising from their condition by stating that inebriety was a disease to which there was a marked hereditary predisposition, a claim in keeping with his basic belief in the importance of heredity in all neurotic and psychotic disorders.[29] In

1900, just as Homewood was becoming an established institution, and Lett a respected authority on the addictions, he grew too ill to continue practising medicine and died in 1905. Alfred Thomas Hobbs was chosen as his successor.

Hobbs's background was solidly upper-middle class and his educational record impeccable. Hobbs was born in 1866 in Cumavor, Wales and educated at King's College, London and Oxford. He immigrated to Canada with his parents and received medical degrees from Toronto University (M.B. 1890) and Western University (M.D. 1890). In 1890 he also became a member of the College of Physicians and Surgeons and began a practice in Waterford, Ontario.[30] Richard Bucke's personal and political relationship with his brother, Thomas Saunders Hobbs, likely smoothed the way for his appointment to the London Asylum in 1891. Thomas Hobbs, a leading member of London's mercantile establishment was president of Hobbs Hardware, Hobbs Manufacturing, and the Indian Cordage Company, and an active member of the London Liberal party.[31] That Thomas Hobbs took an interest in his brother's career was demonstrated by the fact that he became a shareholder of the Homewood Sanitarium.

Bucke and Hobbs became a famous team in London. Shortly after his appointment, Hobbs took a two-month course in gynaecological surgery in New York at public expense.[32] His skills were put to use at London where, assisted by Bucke, he began operating on female patients to repair damaged or diseased internal organs. Encouraged by the alleged psychological improvements these patients experienced, the two physicians began systematic experimentation in the surgical treatment of insanity.[33] More important in terms of career, particularly for Hobbs, than whether or not the experiment was controversial, or whether or not the operations were successful, was that controversy of this type was not necessarily negative. Both Bucke and Hobbs excelled in public relations; whether presenting their findings, jointly or separately, or gathering support from physicians or special interest groups, both men used the surgical experiments to establish themselves as well-known figures in the nascent field of Canadian gynaecology. It was therefore with very sincere regret that Bucke learned of Hobbs's decision to resign from the asylum in order to take up private practice. "I feel (it) very much both personally and from the point of view of the institution," he admitted, "I may say ... that Dr. Hobbs has been the most efficient assistant I have ever had."[34] The purported cause for Hobbs's resignation was a "serious (affliction)" of the heart caused by the "overstrain" of climbing four long flights of stairs to the surgery. Without minimizing Hobbs's physical ill-health, that his serious affliction at the age of thirty-four would not prevent him from living an additional thirty-one years – twenty of which would be in the extremely stressful role of medical superintendent – probably indicated other motivations were also present. With his reputation established, Hobbs was in an excellent position to join many other neurologists and surgeons in private practice.

Neurologists such as Hobbs concurred with William Hammond that "whether in health or disease, the mind is to be studied from a purely material standpoint, and not as a mysterious principle to be looked upon with awe as something entirely beyond our reach." The premise that insanity could be treated like any other physical disease implied that insanity did not require institutionalization, but could be treated at the physician's office. Hammond had further stated in 1876 that "it is not a matter of doubt that many insane persons are sent to lunatic asylums who could ... be better attended to in their own homes under the care of the family physician."[35] By the 1880s, among those able to pay higher fees, many prospective patients chose to seek the advice of the neurologists, instead of the general practitioner, in cases of mental disorder – in effect, accepting and spurring on the movement towards specialization in medicine. Alfred Hobbs's qualifications placed him in an excellent position for a successful career as a specialist in neuropsychiatry.

The provincial secretary certainly thought Hobbs was making a personally advantageous career move. When the physician applied for a retiring allowance, he was told "plain gratuity (is) not necessarily justified in cases where an officer finds the work does not agree with him ... I was given to understand that you were ... preparing yourself ... for active practice. I clearly recollect that I expressed my disapproval of (your) trip (to improve) your gynaecological knowledge." The secretary was of the opinion that Hobbs's practice was "much more lucrative than your former position was," and he added, Hobbs had "the distinct advantage of a considerable experience in gynaecology work gained in your (asylum) service ... and with a large reputation as a specialist in gynaecological research and practice."[36] However lucrative the potential for Hobbs's private practice was, he did not long remain in it. One year after his resignation, he was hired to succeed Stephen Lett at the Homewood Retreat.

Alfred Hobbs was an inspired choice; not only was he nationally recognized as a psychiatrist but also as a specialist in gynaecology. He had what, despite his best efforts, Lett had lacked, particularly in the early years of the Homewood Retreat: a reputation of sufficient standing to attract the attention of the referring physicians, that crucial link between the family and the institution. By the 1880s, physicians had established themselves as family advisors. More than any other individual, the physician was able to enter the family circle "on terms of intimacy and become a party to family secrets in the natural course of his duties." The historians John and Robin Haller suggest that "like the priest's confessional, the minister's study, or the lawyer's office, the doctor's consultation and examination rooms became a sacred setting in which confidential conversation might take place, and the Victorians could give vent to feelings, emotions, fears, and anxieties that afflicted them."[37] Few family secrets could have been more personal or agonizing than mental illness.

When these practitioners were confronted with cases of neuroses or psychoses, they were often at a loss with respect to procedure. As Dr Judson Andrews noted in 1893, general physicians had obtained little or no instruction in psychiatry in medical schools and later offered poor perscriptive advice, such as travel, to patients in the early stages of mental illness, when, instead active treatment was desirable. Campbell Meyers affirmed that knowledge of psychiatry was crucial for the general practitioner since it was to his care "such cases must inevitably first come."[38] By explaining the warning symptoms and proper actions to be taken by general practitioners, neurologists and alienists were establishing the scope of their expertise and situating their own specialties in superior rank to the general physicians. Extra-institutional neurology, in the long run, facilitated the upgrading of the status of asylum physicians by taking psychiatry out of the realm of the esoteric, separating it from conventional medicine, and recommending institutionalization in certain instances. The didactic neurological literature established the asylum as one arm or avenue of the total psychiatric community available to the middle class.

The family physicians might first attempt their own version of S. Weir Mitchell's rest cure: extended bed rest, overfeeding, and perhaps sedatives. Mitchell himself had affirmed that one of the benefits of his cure was that any physician could employ it.[39] When this failed, or the patient's condition made such care unfeasible, the physician had to consider institutionalization. This was a very serious decision to make, particularly for a physician with a longstanding professional relationship with a family. To suggest that a family place kindred in an asylum far from their home required great confidence in the institution. In this regard, an institution run by a superintendent of known reputation would seem a safe choice. Alfred Hobbs enjoyed such a reputation and appreciated the importance of courting family physicians. In 1905, in justifying expansion of the facilities, he argued that if cases requiring immediate care were refused for lack

Table 4
Place of Residence of Patients prior to Commitment to Homewood

LARGE CANADIAN URBAN CENTRES		SMALLER CANADIAN URBAN CENTRES	
Toronto	179 (15%)[a]	Berlin/Waterloo	16
Montreal	66	Brantford	14
Ottawa	54	Guelph	14
Hamilton	51	St Thomas	13
London	18	Owen Sound	12
Windsor	15	Peterborough	11
Total	383 (34%)[a]	Total	80 (7%)

OUTSIDE ONTARIO		NON-URBAN CENTRES IN ONTARIO	
Manitoba	28	(by counties)[b]	
Saskatchewan	16	Waterloo	23
Nova Scotia	14	Perth	22
Alberta	14	Bruce	20
Quebec	12	Welland	19
(excluding Montreal)		Halton, Wellington	18
New Brunswick	3	Oxford, Simcoe, Huron	17
Prince Edward Island	3	Middlesex	16
British Columbia	3	Grey, Lincoln	15
Newfoundland	1	Peel	14
Total	94 (8%)	Lambton	11
OUTSIDE CANADA		Haldimand, Elgin, Durham	10
New York	32	Total	272
Michigan	13		
Other US States	18	Other Counties	127
Bermuda	1		
Total	64 (6%)	Total Ontario Counties	399 (35%)

[a]Percentage of sample population (n = 1134) for whom place of residence was noted. The records of 114 patients, or ten percent of the sample population, did not note place of residence prior to commitment.
[b]Patients from Ontario counties are considered to be living in rural areas.

of space, they "will go elsewhere ... To maintain the goodwill of (an) ever increasing and influential clientele of physicians, (we) must be able to cater to their wants." Hobbs visited various centres in Ottawa, Montreal, and Edmonton with some success to drum up business for the sanitarium.[40]

The role of the referring physician was particularly important as a consequence of the chronic problem of competition faced by the proprietary asylum. Table 4 illustrates the importance of Toronto and southwestern Ontario to the institution. That particular pockets of population such as Peterborough and Owen Sound were sources of frequent admissions probably indicated the crucial importance of links with particular local physicians. As demonstrated in table 5, a sampling of physicians who referred two or more patients to Home-

Table 5
Physicians Referring Patients to Homewood

No. of Referrals	Name	City	Yr. Referrals Made	Specialty
2	James Austin	Windsor	1916	general practitioner
7	William Barber	Toronto	1912–13	physician, Tor. Asylum
3	Irving Cameron	Toronto	1904–19	general practitioner
11	Wm, John & Jas Caven	Toronto	1901–13	consulting physicians
4	John Chabot	Ottawa	1899–1917	general practitioner
13	C.K. Clarke	Toronto	1907–25	super., Tor. Asylum
6	Peter Dewar	Windsor	1916–17	general practitioner
5	R.B. Echlin	Ottawa	1916	general practitioner
2	Ewart Ferguson	Toronto	1912	bacteriologist
5	J.T. Fotheringham	Toronto	1914–25	neurologist
5	James Gow	Windsor	1913–15	general practitioner
6	James Halliday	Peterborough	1887	general practitioner
3	Edward Hodge	Toronto	1908–12	general practitioner
10	Goldwin Howland	Toronto	1913–19	neurologist
4	Charles Husband	Hamilton	1913	general practitioner
8	Arthur Johnson	Toronto	1885–1920	neurologist
4	Warren Lyman	Ottawa	1915–16	general practitioner internist
3	Donald McGillivray	Toronto	1913	general practitioner
6	Campbell Meyers	Toronto	1914	neurologist
3	Alfred Nixon	Georgetown	1897–1919	general practitioner
5	Gerald O'Reilley	Hamilton	1909	general practitioner
4	William Parry	Toronto	1890	general practitioner
3	Thomas Roddick	Montreal	1895	surgeon
9	Colin Russel	Montreal	1908	neurologist
3	Arthur Smith	Perth	1914	general practitioner
3	Grant Stewart	Montreal	1914–18	general practitioner
3	Charles Toole	Brussels	1902–4	general practitioner
6	Joseph Workman	Toronto	1885–90	super., Tor. Asylum

wood, James T. Halliday of Peterborough, for instance, particularly patronised the institution in 1887. Certainly, the referrals of individual country or town physicians helped to compensate for the dearth of admissions from the metropolitan centre. Also to be noted is the growing degree of specialization among the profession. In the 1880s, referring physicians were general practitioners; after about 1910, however, referrals were made in greater frequency by specialists in neurology or psychiatry – a specialization centred in large cities. (James Halliday, John Leo Chabot, and Charles A. Toole, for example, were general practitioners. William Barber, Charles K.

Clarke, Joseph Workman and Campbell Meyers were institutional psychiatrists although Meyers also maintained a private practice in neurology.)

Although general practitioners and institutional alienists were the usual referring physicians in the nineteenth century, in the twentieth century, they would be joined by physicians who specialized in neurology outside the institutions. While the figures in table 5 are by no means conclusive, they do suggest that specialization in Canadian medicine became significant after the turn of the century. In Homewood's case histories, occasional mention was made by referring physicians of other patients they had sent. In Mary I.'s (#232, 1910) letter of introduction, for instance, Dr J.W. McLean of Cape Breton inquired about the prospects of another woman he had admitted. Thomas Roddick of Montreal's Royal Victoria Hospital and Frank Beemer of the Hamilton Asylum both sent personal friends to the "special care" of Lett and Hobbs respectively.[41]

Along with his professional reputation, crucial for the attraction of patients to the Homewood Retreat, Alfred Hobbs added the advantage of a specialty in the field of gynaecology. As has been demonstrated by a number of historians in recent years, the treatment of nervous and mental diseases in women was a lucrative specialty in late Victorian psychiatry. Elaine Showalter has labelled madness "the female malady." Statistically, women tended to be over-represented as patients in lunatic asylums and in non-institutional forms of psychiatry, a pattern which became apparent at the Homewood Retreat at the turn of the century. Contemporaries attempted to blame the growing rate of female admissions on the feminine condition itself. Defects in the female reproductive system were linked in medical literature and in the popular press to mental and physical instability. Many women and their families subsequently sought advice and treatment from physicians for a variety of real and imagined ailments.[42]

As will be discussed in chapter 4, increased admissions might have resulted from a society with limited opportunities for socially redundant women. The vogue in psycho-gynaecology might have legitimated the institutionalization of such women and incidentally ensured the success of the asylum. For the individual practitioner dealing with a disturbed woman and her distressed family, where better to turn than to the institution run by Alfred Hobbs, known expert in gynaecological disorders? While sexual surgery had been discontinued for ethical and political reasons in Ontario's public asylums (C.K. Clarke of the Kingston Asylum charged the London physicians with engaging in "meddlesome gynaecology" and "mutilating helpless lunatics"), this did not detract greatly from the generally-held belief among practitioners of the influence of the reproductive organs upon mental health.[43]

Hobbs's professional specialty therefore fulfilled a community need with lasting benefits for the Homewood Sanitarium. By 1906, the institution was sufficiently solvent to permanently employ an assistant superintendent, Edward C. Barnes, to oversee the daily medical care of the patients. Barnes received his M.D. from London's Western University and was in private practice for three years before taking up the position at Homewood at the age of twenty-seven. He was expected to succeed Hobbs as superintendent, but in 1920 he accepted the superintendency of the Selkirk, Manitoba Mental Hospital, which he administered for twenty-three years.[44] Barnes's departure from Homewood left a void that Hobbs, in anticipation of retirement, attempted to fill with the appointment of Harvey Clare. Clare was a logical choice for the position. A gold medal graduate of Trinity University, he had served in all of Ontario's mental hospitals. In 1914, he was appointed to the position of medical director of the Reception Hospital in Toronto and in 1919 became medical director of the Ontario mental health system. In this capacity, he was a member of the board of visitors to the Homewood Sanitarium. It is probable that he declined the position offered in 1920 since it would have meant demotion in status to the assistant superintendent level. The board of directors would not find a replacement for Hobbs until his actual retirement in 1923. At that point, Clare was medical superintendent of the Toronto Asylum.[45]

The board was finally able to attract Clarence B. Farrar, one of the leading figures in early twentieth-century Canadian psychiatry, to the position. Farrar was a graduate of Harvard and Johns Hopkins medical school and had studied under Kraepelin and Alzheimer. After a series of joint hospital and university appointments, he was named chief psychiatrist of the Department of Soldier Civil Reestablishment (Veteran's Affairs). The appointment of a psychiatrist with Farrar's outstanding qualifications was a coup for the board of directors – one which they badly needed. In soliciting opinions, the board was told by other physicians that while they expressed "their warm support" for Hobbs, an institution caring for involuntary patients "may expect at times to receive unjust, untrue and uncalled for criticism."[46] A prestigious appointment was therefore all the more necessary. However, having made such an appointment, the Homewood Sanitarium was not able to keep Clarence Farrar long. By 1925, probably feeling isolated in Guelph from political, medical, and educational events, he accepted the superintendency of the newly-built Toronto Psychiatric Hospital and the positions of professor and head of the department of psychiatry at the University of Toronto. He would be replaced by Dr Harvey Clare, whose administration lasted for seventeen years.

The modern psychiatric hospital Clare was to develop was built upon the legacies of Alfred Hobbs and Stephen Lett. Their efforts and varied fortunes reflected the transformations in their profession at the end of the century. Lett's social and political connections, so crucial to institutional appointment in the nineteenth century, would fail to compensate in the new educational meritocracy for his academic deficiencies. So too would his failure – probably due to illness – to keep abreast of medical innovation limit the appeal of his asylum to potential patrons and their physicians. As the options for mental health care to middle-class patients increased, particularly with the rise of the office-based neuropsychiatrist, it was inevitable that moral managers, like Stephen Lett, would be left behind.

Alfred Hobbs may be viewed as a transitional figure in Canadian institutional psychiatry. He, like Lett, was a product of the public asylum system, yet his surgical studies and experiments placed him in the realm of neuropsychiatry. The expansion of both physical plant and human resources during his tenure at the Homewood Sanitarium was in accordance with the requisites of the modern, specialized institution.[47] However, the internal disarray in the institution during his illness prior to retirement demonstrated that little real advancement had been made upon the Victorian tradition of one man, one asylum.

Homewood's experiences with referring physicians reflected transformations in the medical profession in general, as referrals increasingly were the province of mental health specialists. Psychiatry prior to the 1880s was asylum medicine; its practitioners tended to be isolated from the medical mainstream. With advances in neurology and the development of neuropsychiatry, the scope of mental health care was expanded to the wider community, and asylums like Homewood found themselves competing for fees with office-based physicians. The expansion of psychiatry outside the asylum, however, upgraded the profession as a whole and established psychiatrists as experts on the mind.

CHAPTER FOUR

The Medical World of the Asylum: Diagnostics and Therapeutics

When Stephen Lett and Alfred Hobbs advanced to the position of medical superintendent of the Homewood Retreat, no doubt they hoped to leave their mark upon Canadian psychiatry. Indeed, in both diagnostics and therapeutics, the men would be able to exploit advances in the medical community and, through the use of increasingly sophisticated techniques, steer their institution into the scientific, research-oriented medical mainstream. But, as will be demonstrated in this and succeeding chapters, their contribution to psychiatry would be continually compromised by patients' intrusive families, by independently minded and unskilled employees, and by the recalcitrant patients themselves, as well as by the economic necessities that required they use treatments they did not believe in.

In this chapter the diagnostic and therapeutic techniques Lett and Hobbs used for treating mental illness are described. The actual practices at Homewood are considered in their historical context, and the development of the two physicians' techniques and by association, the progress of Homewood as a mental institution, viewed accordingly.

DIAGNOSTICS

The initial diagnosis of the patient in the asylum was a crucial step in his or her psychiatric career. Diagnosis determined, in the short term, the ward in which the patient would be placed and the kind of treatment, although, as will be demonstrated, treatment did not necessarily derive from diagnosis. In the long term, diagnosis might result in a lifetime classification that could colour attitudes towards the patient both inside the asylum and after the patient's discharge.

During the period that Lett and Hobbs were superintendents at Homewood, innovations in diagnostics led many physicians to refine the classifications of insanity and alter the criteria upon which these classifications were based. Ideally, detailed analyses resulted from lengthy interviews that also determined the physical health of the patients; such analyses supplanted vague judgments based upon third-hand information. Lett's diagnostic classifications were the traditional divisions of insanity: mania, dementia, and melancholia, derived primarily from the certificates of the referring physicians. His diagnostic innovation was in the field of addictions, where he perfected urinalysis testing for traces of opiates, cocaine, and other drugs in the patient. Lett was particularly interested in hereditary influence, a factor that from the mid-century had been considered the most significant cause of insanity. Thus the physician's certificate usually included the family's history as well as his own observations. Most physicians' comments, however, were derived from a cursory single examination and limited to a description of superficial characteristics and behaviour during the admitting interview. A certificate in 1887 recorded these observations, for example: "During my visit (Susan A., #13, 1887) became restless and walked about in an exalted way uttering distressed sounds as if from fear. When questioned she did not answer but became more excited and tried to get out of the room. The facial expression, condition of tongue, eyes, etc. were those indicative of (an) unsound mind."

In 1901, Lett, foremost a moral manager, was succeeded by Hobbs, a committed somaticist. Hobbs was considerably more systematic in the use of diagnostic techniques such as physical examinations. He adopted more sophisticated blood and urine testing techniques, and detailed patient histories were taken to determine the physiological bases for the mental disturbance. Since his personal interest was in the field of gynaecology and the influence of the reproductive organs upon mental health, he recommended that case histories of female mental patients include information on the condition of the reproductive organs, and such was faithfully recorded during his regime.[1]

A number of international innovations during Hobbs's administration also influenced the nature of his diagnostics. Among them was the system of classification devised by the German doctor, Emil Kraepelin (1856–1926), one of the greatest clinicians in nineteenth-century psychiatry. In his *Kompendium der Psychiatrie*, published in its final form in 1899, Kraepelin stressed the importance of arriving at an accurate diagnosis, based upon a complete detailed case history and upon clinical observation.[2] Kraepelin's achievement was to focus attention on the "fundamental course of mental illness – its form –

rather than the superficial content of the psychotics' thought processes [e.g. 'religious mania']."[3]

Because Kraepelin was pessimistic about the prognosis of most psychoses, he was a fervent advocate of prevention and prophylaxis. He differentiated between the external causes of insanity, such as alcoholism and exhaustion, and the internal causes, including age, sex, occupation, and most importantly, heredity. His most immediate contribution was the re-classification, through extensive clinical observation, of insanity into three basic forms of functional psychoses: dementia praecox, paranoia, and manic-depressive psychosis. The shortcoming in Kraepelin's work was that the innovation ended at classification. At too many asylums, classification substituted for treatment, particularly among the mass of patients formerly labelled neurasthenic, and now diagnosed with dementia praecox, for whom Kraepelin considered the prognosis to be gloomy. When in 1909, Hobbs took a three-month leave of absence from Homewood "to visit the medical centres of Europe," it was his intention "to spend at least a month at the Psychiatric Clinic of Munich to observe the methods of Kraepelin, who is recognized as the leader of the German school of medical science of which we are followers."[4] Upon his return, the old classifications of dementia, melancholia, and mania were replaced by Kraepelian typology.

The diagnoses of referring physicians also became more sophisticated, as general practitioners were replaced by specialists in neuropsychiatry. Compare the 1887 certificate, cited above, with the letter admitting Mary Louise L. (#284, 1905), written by Charles Burr, superintendent of Oak Grove Hospital of Flint, Michigan. Burr's observations, which echoed the sentiments Richard Bucke had expressed some thirty years earlier (see p. 109) demonstrated some of the special stresses faced by institutional psychiatrists.

Dear Dr Hobbs,
I could say that Miss L. was 'neurasthenic' in the sense that all patients whose nervous systems are reduced are neurasthenic, but ... [this] case is manic-depressive insanity of the recurrent type.
I apprehend that you will have little or no trouble with Miss L. for several months. The acme of excitement was long ago reached and passed ... In depression she will be found a delightful member of the household. I will leave you to discover for yourself her relations to the establishment during the excited period, and do not wish to prejudice the case in advance ... If you should have her under observation during [the first attack of excitement], you will still have doors, windows, and furniture for the use of other people ... Not to hold up a picture too darkly shaded, I might add

that the damage to furniture will not be the worst of it. Damage to feelings, while not estimable in dollars and cents is still a factor not altogether negligible in the case of a patient's care ...

The patient is gifted and has had an unusually fine education, [so that] you will readily understand that her capabilities for mischief making in excitement are enhanced and are considerably above average. I think, on the other hand, her appreciation during periods of comfort and quiescence of kindness or of attentions is ample ... While at one time I felt that I had considerable influence with her, I am satisfied that it is worn out, and that another medical guide and counsellor and friend is necessary. Miss L. is an accomplished musician, has what is practically a perfect acquaintance with French, a liberal smattering of German and Italian, is clever in versification, sees through things quickly, and is an excellent whist player ...

Yours truly,
Charles W. Burr

The other great clinician whose work had immediate impact on Homewood's diagnostics was Adolf Meyer (1866–1950), the most influential American psychiatrist of the progressive period. A neuropathologist by training, Meyer campaigned against the dogmatism of the neurological establishment and emphasized the importance of environmental, as well as physical, influences on mental illness. Meyer was a great admirer of Kraepelin but was opposed to the pessimism and subsequent abandonment of active treatment arising from his negative prognostications.[5]

Meyer was a strong advocate of the use of clinical history and observation to overcome the "doctrine of psycho-physical parallelism which has governed science during the last fifty years or more," that is, the doctrine "that psychology deals with the mind as physiology deals with the body." The difficulty in accepting psychology as an objective science, he argued, lay in the "hesitancy to accept a frankly biologic view of the reactions and behaviour of man. As soon as mental attitudes and mental activities are accepted as definite functions of a living organism ... psychology ceases to be a puzzle supposedly resisting the objective methods of science." Thus Meyer attempted to unify the somaticist orientation with new advances in psychological therapy. According to Meyer, the first step in the proper diagnosis and treatment of mental illness was to "trace the plain life history of a person" and record it on a life chart, to include all the physical and emotional events of the individual's life.[6]

Meyer developed his life chart after his depressing sojourns at the custodial state hospitals of Kankakee, Illinois and Worcester, Massachusetts. He argued that neurotic and psychotic patients should be actively treated following the compilation of proper case histories and diagnosis. At the asylums, he introduced thorough interviews and physical examinations, as well as staff conferences where diagnoses were collectively made after a short period of clinical observation on the wards.[7] The impact of Meyer's work on Homewood was apparent, though limited, during the Hobbs administration. Hobbs initiated, in 1908, semi-weekly conferences and collective diagnoses, while the patient histories became more detailed and included significant life events.[8] Although the actual life chart was not included in the case files, appendix 3 is a sample of a life chart as derived from a patient history.

Unfortunately, as happened all too often in other institutions, innovations in treatment did not keep pace with innovation in diagnostic techniques. In 1916, for example, ward classification was still based not on forms and frequency of treatment, as Meyer had recommended, but on manageability. At Homewood, voluntary and committed patients remained sub-divided into "those who are suffering in a serious manner and who may be dangerous to themselves or others, and into an indeterminate class: also into a class consisting of those who are under observation for discharge: each class being separated by being allotted to a separate building." Ward therapy was practiced insofar as the patients were "moved from one class to another and from one building to another according to the degree of progress or change made in the several classes."[9]

The psychotherapeutic revolution at the turn of the century had little impact upon Homewood during the Hobbs administration. Conflict, repression, and complex were not part of his medical vocabulary although the concepts could not have been unknown. During the Great War, Homewood sheltered a number of officers suffering from shell-shock who had been sent to the institution by Colin K. Russel, head of the Canadian Special Hospital for Nervous Diseases at Ramsgate, England and a leading Montreal neurologist. While Russell developed a psychotherapeutic view of the causes of shell-shock, which he termed the consequence of conflict between "self-preservation" and "moral sense," his treatment of infantry cases reflected the exigencies of the war effort, in that it consisted of punitive measures, including the use of electric shocks, to render the treatment less desirable than combat duty. Significantly, it was only officers who received the benevolent Homewood rest cure.[10]

The view of many somaticists that shell-shock victims in the infantry were primarily malingerers was challenged by the psychotherapists, including Sigmund Freud, who considered the disorder to be a manifestation of psychic trauma.[11] However Freudian ideas did not gain wide acceptance in institutions in North America until the 1920s, and Hobbs did not differ from other members of the conservative medical establishment in Canada for whom Freudian precepts were too controversial to be accepted.[12] C.K. Clarke at the Toronto Asylum, for example, branded Freudianism "sex problems ad nauseum," and sanction for "free love" and "savagery." Freud's outspoken disciple, Ernest Jones, was the first director of the Psychiatric Out-patient Clinic in Toronto between the years 1908 and 1913, but he found the Canadian medical profession to be even more smitten with somaticism and hereditarianism than their American brethren. More importantly, the conservative Canadians believed in the innocence of childhood, purity of mind, and the relative asexuality of women that comprised the 'civilized' sexual morality Freudianism apparently challenged.[13]

Professional considerations along with practical ones also impeded acceptance of Freudian concepts. Psychoanalysis lent itself to patients who were "intelligent, educated (and) of sound moral character."[14] The system, ideally suited for those in professions or business, might well supersede the sanitarium for its convenience, personalized attention, and lack of stigma. It is not surprising therefore that Hobbs had little enthusiasm for Freudian teachings. He did however make some attempts at psychotherapy in its earlier American form as popularized by the work of Morton Prince and Adolf Meyer; in this incarnation, psychotherapy was called moral suasion.[15] Like the contemporary and popular faith-healing cults, psychotherapists in conversation with patients used encouragement, persuasion, and positive thinking to "cheer" patients out of their neuroses.

In Canadian psychotherapy before Freud, the commonly held approach to the interview was expressed in 1897 by J.V. Anglin of Montreal who instructed, "When your patient has delusions and talks about them, simply say, if you say anything, that you cannot see as he does, and then change the subject. Be frank with him, but don't antagonize. Patients should not only be discouraged in talking about their delusions, but about all their symptoms." Anglin endorsed a solidly somatic view which was also practiced at Homewood. He argued that "there is little dread of insanity in any one who sleeps well and holds his own in weight."[16]

Although after 1900, Hobbs's interviews with patients became increasingly detailed, they were primarily concerned with a description of patient behaviour and his or her physical state. Along with a particular interest in the gynaecological and obstetrical histories of his female patients, he subjected the patients to tests to determine orientation for place and person, memory, attention, and insight into their own conditions. The word association test, however, was not used. Following the initial diagnostic interview, the patient would be sent to the wards for the prescribed traditional treatments: hydrotherapy, electrotherapy, and massage. Through brief conversations during the ward physician's weekly visits, the mental state would be determined as, for example, "cheerful," "depressed," or "maintaining delusions." No further psychological treatment was remarked upon.

The most detailed transcripts of patient conversations were those that recorded interviews with paranoid or clearly delusional patients whose mental illness was self-evident. The instances where any sexual details were recorded were primarily from conversations initiated by the patient. Consider, for instance, the case of Clara B. (#27, 1916). Her condition appeared to be the result of sexual dysfunction; she had had a hysterectomy but later became "excited" and had a "secondary operation – which was said to be circumcision." She subsequently sent love letters to her surgeon. Clara was not questioned on sexual matters by Dr Barnes, but approached the subject herself, requesting that the stenographer and nurse leave the room. Once she was left alone with the physician, she immediately began describing her occasional "sexual uneasiness" and subsequent "self-abuse." Her confessions were not discussed further by Barnes, and her treatment was limited to over-feeding and participation in arts and crafts. (See appendix 4.)

THERAPEUTICS

The view of mental health commonly held by asylum physicians in the 1880s was that every part of the body was related and could affect every other part including the mind. Illness, exhaustion, deformity, or organic dysfunction were cited as causative factors in the disturbance of mental health, as were hereditary predisposition and environment. Treatment, therefore, could not be localized to the brain, but would be holistic, to restore a balance to the organism, a balance that since the time of Galen was the perceived sign of health. This would be accomplished by strengthening the body through the prescription of a balanced diet, healthful environment, exercise, fresh air, tonics, and purges. The asylum provided the optimum physical conditions to allow the natural recuperative powers of the body to mend itself.[17] However, interventionist measures were professional requisites. Such measures reassured "the patient or his

Table 6
Prescribed Treatments

	Male	Female	Total
Drugs (excluding salvarsan)	35	39	74
Hydrotherapy	19	22	41
Salvarsan	15	2	17
Surgery	8	5	13
Tonics	4	6	10
Special diet (e.g. diabetic)	1	4	5
Obstetrical/gynecological surgery	n/a	5	5
Massage	0	3	3
Gynecological examination	n/a	3	3
Electricity	1	1	2
Treatments of an unspecified nature	5	4	9
No active treatment	127	181	308
Unknown	116	170	286

Note: The files of 308 patients indicated no active treatment, while the files of 286 patients lacked data recorded after admission. This table does not include addiction withdrawal therapy.

friends that something is being done for him in accordance with the idea that still lies deep-rooted in most human minds that for every disease there is some curative drug."[18]

At a private institution, the necessity to demonstrate that something was "being done" was all the more urgent; competition from other avenues of treatment required that in the public mind, at the very least, the institution should be perceived as progressive and active. Neither Lett nor Hobbs had a clear-cut program of treatment; both used an amalgam of the traditional (occupations, amusements, and tonics); personal preferences (withdrawal therapy and gynaecological surgery); the fashionable (electrotherapy, hydrotherapy, the rest cure, and the gold cure, an alcoholism treatment); and the innovative (chemotherapy). Table 6 illustrates the variety and frequency of active treatments received by patients in the sample population. What is immediately apparent is that many, if not the majority of patients, received no active treatment at all.

Given the Homewood Retreat's proprietary status, it was appropriate that one of the few places where the methods of treatment were described was in its advertising literature. One typical circular described treatments as ranging from diet, physical exercise, the rest cure, electricity, and baths to "salt rubs, irrigations, or massage." The mental condition of the patient was to be improved "by means of normal sleep, freedom from worry, cheerful surroundings, quiet and intelligent nursing attention, and some occupation that will interest but not irritate." This circular, printed in 1934 (see appendix 5), might just as well have been written in 1894 when almost every therapeutic measure cited was in common practice.[19]

THE REST CURE

The fundamental feature of sanitarium treatment at Homewood as well as elsewhere was the rest cure. S. Weir Mitchell developed his hugely successful program to treat neurasthenia (acute nervous exhaustion) in 1875. The components of the rest cure included isolation to separate the patient from over-indulgent but well-meaning relatives; bed rest and limited mental diversion to rebuild limited and spent nervous energy; over-feeding on a milk-based diet to replace the needed "red corpuscles" and counteract the loss of weight commonly accompanying neurasthenia; and massage or electrotherapy to benefit muscles and bones wasted by the extended period of inactivity. The rest cure was a popular form of therapy for neurologists, psychotherapists, and asylum physicians alike.[20] In 1904, Toronto neurologist Campbell Meyers was recommending the rest cure to general practitioners at the earliest signs of neurasthenia and cerebrasthenia to avoid the possibility of insanity developing. Cerebrasthenia, or "brain exhaustion," was caused by "mental overwork" accompanied by excitement, worry, grief, trauma, pregnancy, or lactation. Its symptoms included lack of concentration and self-confidence and diminished will-power. The patient became morbidly introspective, and discussed his or her symptoms with "non-medical men in a distinctly thoughtless manner." The most important element of the treatment of cerebrasthenia, Meyers stressed, was isolation, which removed "irritation" (both to the patient and the family) and permitted the "useful action of drugs."[21]

Large public asylums also felt the influence of the popular treatment. The massage department at the London Asylum was established, according to Hobbs, as the favoured method "devoted to the increase of body weight and the generation of force known to us as vital energy," both important components of Mitchell's treatment.[22] A true indication of the lasting impact of the rest cure was its persistence in the face of the great psychiatric model for the twentieth century – psychotherapy. In 1908, looking back over thirty-three years of the rest cure treatment, Mitchell revealed the inter-generational conflicts in the use of mental therapeutics. Just as he had in his youth criticized the old guard of moral managers, in his maturity he criticized the renewed attack of the psychological approach upon somaticism. "Now we are to deal with what you say to the patient," he complained, "as well as what you do," and he linked psychoanalysis with "Eddyism [Christian Science], mind cure [and] soul cure," popular but medically disreputable faith-healing movements which relied on psychotherapeutic techniques. Mitchell denied the truth of the "gathering belief" that neurasthenia was purely a psychogenic malady. "I know that it often has a background ... of hysteria or hypochondria, but I also know that there is a goodly proportion of neurasthenia which has no more psychic origin or symptoms than has a colic."[23] "Put off advice until bodily vigor (is restored)," Mitchell advised, then "reason, implore, counsel, appeal to duty, affection, taste, desire for health ... be a sternly judging moralist or the humorous comrade of the minute." Despite "the elaborate and novel studies in psychologic diagnosis, the laboratory aids, the association tests, the mind-probing examinations" which characterized the new psychoanalysis, Mitchell maintained that "you cure the body and somehow find that the mind also is cured."[24]

Despite Mitchell's protestations, the lasting value of his rest cure would depend upon its incorporation with, rather than its rejection of, the psychological approach. In 1910, Edwin Branwell of Edinburgh neatly inverted Mitchell's perspective. In cases of hysteria, "a disease of psychic origin which is curable by psychical methods," he believed the rest cure was useful in providing the optimal conditions for the use of psychological suggestion and persuasion. "Isolation," Bramwell explained, "although now rightly regarded as no more than an adjuvant in the treatment of hysteria, in that it permits of the application of psycho-therapeutics under the most advantageous circumstances, is none the less essential." Bramwell interpreted virtually every aspect of the rest cure as salutary for its psychological, rather than physical, effect. The milk diet had a "moral and disciplinary effect," drugs were unnecessary except as placebos and should therefore be particularly bad-tasting, and isolation would give the physician "the satisfaction of knowing that [the patient] is, for the time being, under his complete control."[25]

Bramwell clearly illustrated the shift in paradigms which was taking place at the turn of the century. The somatic perspective upon which Mitchell based his treatment emphasized the physical benefits and nerve force regenerative power of the rest cure; those who adopted the later psychological perspective, against which he was opposed, countered that the rest cure was in fact a psychological treatment. It may be argued that the rest cure was both and neither;

the two most favoured elements, which ensured its longevity, were control and convenience. The control by the physician and the total submission of the patient produced the optimum conditions for whatever aspect of treatment the physician wished to stress, while the institutional convenience of having an immobile, isolated patient was self-evident. Though Mitchell originated his treatment as an individualized program, it was geared from the outset for the sanitarium. The seclusion of one or a few patients for weeks at various locations was awkward and unprofitable for the practitioner; the accumulation of many patients under one roof, however, all requiring little medical supervision, physical restraint, expensive diet, or occupation, could be extremely convenient and very profitable. These factors probably had much to do with the continuing use of Mitchell's rest cure at institutions such as Homewood well into the 1930s.

Hobbs practiced the rest cure on a variety of neurotic patients, not simply on neurasthenics. Jean K. (#268, 1913), for example, who suffered from melancholia, was given a "circular and rain bath each morning" and took about "twelve to fourteen glasses of milk a day." Elizabeth McK. (#320, 1913), the wife of a "niggardly" farmer, was "run down," "depressed," and "particularly averse to taking food." Her treatment was "entirely confined to tonics, with the view of building up her physical condition. She takes half an ounce of cod liver oil extract after each meal and on retiring. She gets a daily bath, full massage, and takes four glasses of milk at each meal."

Even morphia addicts were treated with the rest cure. Besides withdrawal therapy, Shirley V. (#514, 1918) was put on a course of "hydrotherapy and massage along with short walks in the afternoon to counteract [her] suffering." For hyperactive neurasthenics, Homewood offered a modified rest cure. Mary F. (#172, 1915) was "controlling her restlessness to [a] greater degree" a fortnight after admission "and showing better judgment regarding her exercise. Massage is also helping her," Barnes reported. "Her various treatments practically keep her at rest during morning, and it is usually twelve noon before she is up and dressed." As these cases indicated, Hobbs's variation of the rest cure included the use of hydrotherapy.

HYDROTHERAPY

By the time of its inauguration at Homewood in 1907, hydrotherapy already had a long history in Europe and North America. In 1747, John Wesley, founder of Methodism, wrote *Primitive Physic or an Easy and Natural Method of Curing Most Diseases* in which he claimed that

"almost every disease could be cured by water properly applied."
Philadelphia's Benjamin Rush espoused the cause of mineral water
and cold baths in 1786. The effect, he wrote, "was to wash off impurities from the skin, promote perspiration, drive the fluids from
the surface to the internal parts of the body ... [and] stimulate the
nervous system."[26] In the 1830s, hydrotherapy was popularized as
a therapeutic agent by an Austrian folk-healer, Vincenz Priessnitz.
Soon after Priessnitz's system arrived in North America a decade
later, "several large water-cure journals began to be published, two
medical schools of hydrotherapy opened, and in a few years a
hundred or more practitioners, male and female, were dispensing
therapy with much desired cleanliness." In its Victorian form, hydrotherapy or hydropathy involved exercise, massage, sweating, and
reducing as well as bathing and water drinking. The appeal of this
treatment, particularly for women, was great: "I never had to deal
with a Physician possessed of the same delicacy and consideration
for female modesty," one convert wrote while her sister added, "It
is a happy change indeed from poisonous drugs to pure cold water.
Would to heaven, I had come here when I was first taken sick; instead
of being butchered by Pill givers. How many hours of pain and
anguish I might have been spared."[27]

The hydropathic method generally adopted in North America was
devised by Joel Shew, leading New York hydropath and editor of
the *Water-Cure Journal*. Shew found that water "functioned best when
administered gradually through the skin" through the use of a wet
sheet pack, in which the patient would be wrapped, then secured
and topped by a feather bed. The patient "remained in his cocoon
from twenty-five minutes to several hours, depending upon the seriousness of his condition and his ability to work up a good perspiration." He was then unwrapped, immersed in cold water, and
briskly rubbed down.[28]

By the 1900s, the old water cures of the 1840s had been codified
into a system of therapeutics of great significance to somaticists. In
1902, Edward Angell, a New York neurologist, couched in medical
terms what had long been recognized by the general public as common sense. He stated that a better label would be "thermotherapy,"
since "practically it is the varying degree of heat or cold employed
which accomplishes the purpose." "In general," he explained, "the
influence of heat is sedative to the circulation, relaxing to the muscles,
and calmative to the nervous system ... Cold, however, is a more
important agent in hydrotherapy than heat ... The lower the temperature, the briefer should be the application."[29]

In Canada, that a market for hydropathic treatment existed was
made evident by the popularity of the mineral water spas located

throughout Ontario in the nineteenth century. People flocked to London, St. Catharines, and Ottawa, among other places, to use the waters that were supposed to contain properties conducive to good health if taken in moderate doses or if bathed in. Frederick Neal, a local historian, estimated that at the height of its business, twenty to twenty-five thousand people visited the Sandwich spa on a holiday. The waters were reported to be effective in curing "rheumatism, liver disease and nervous prostration" as well as "gout, dyspepsia [and] 'female disease.'"[30]

It is therefore not surprising that Hobbs realized the potential of hydrotherapy both as a therapeutic measure and as a drawing card. His interest would be further engaged by the fact that Kraepelin was an advocate of prolonged warm baths for the treatment of mental disease.[31] At Homewood, Hobbs used hydrotherapeutic equipment designed by New York's Simon Baruch and by 1915, there were "three complete suites for the administration of Hydrotherapy." Each suite contained "hot air cabinets, a central table from which are operated rain, needle, spray, shower, perineal, jet and Scotch douches, a sitz tub, shampoo table, and provision for the application of hot and cold packs."[32] In his address to the Canadian Medical Association in 1908, Hobbs compared the circulatory system to a "highway" for the "products of maintenance and growth" and by which "waste and repair" products were eliminated. Therefore, any agent having "the slightest influence" would have an effect upon disease. Cold water, which lowered blood pressure and benefited respiration, muscles and tissues, was specified for neurasthenia and melancholia. In neurasthenic cases, Hobbs advised practitioners not to "frighten" the patient and risk losing his "confidence"; therefore, cold baths should be worked up to slowly.[33]

George D. (#690, 1917), a neurasthenic also suffering from tuberculosis, was "very fearful about taking exercise, also fearful about taking his baths, thinks that they are too severe for him." However John G. (#771, 1916), another neurasthenic, had arrived "very discontented" and did not think he would remain, but "after the second hydro-bath he said that he felt they were going to be beneficial to him." Mary B. (#61, 1911) observed, "It was the baths I came for, to see if I could get to sleep ... Mrs C. said when she couldn't sleep she took the baths. I was going to the Hospital at home, but they haven't the baths there." Helena P. (#412, 1910), however, declared that she would not take her baths, "even if she has to stay here till doom's day."

In the melancholic, Hobbs continued, "the Scotch douche used freely all over the body markedly stimulates the circulation and imparts a sense of well-being substituting the depression." Baths were specified for alcoholism, "morphinism," "cocainism," and in cases of exhaustive psychoses or psychoses developing after serious illness, Hobbs recommended baths of as low as sixty degrees, citing Baruch's dictum, "Let not the fear of cold water deter anyone from resorting to cold affusions in these desperate cases. They are the hydriatic substitute for digitalis and alcohol."[34]

Hydrotherapy was also used in the asylum as a form of restraint. Harrington Tuke of the York Retreat recognized the delicate balance between treatment and punishment. In England, "the [cold] douche would not be recognized as part of moral treatment," since its use as shock value would not produce permanent good effects. Its only value, therefore, would be as a tonic. Warm baths, on the other hand, were "more valuable" than any other remedy in the treatment of mental diseases for both melancholia and mania. Restraint in a warm bath for acute mania, Tuke believed, for two hours would be effective, unlike the practice in certain French asylums which, he stated, kept patients in baths for the "absurd" period of twelve or fifteen hours.[35]

Hobbs was an advocate of the use of the continuous bath as a form of restraint for those patients suffering from "excitement," restlessness, and insomnia. The patient would be wrapped in sheets, suspended in a "comfortable hammock" in tepid water, and remain there for three or four hours until he or she "experienced marked relief, bec[ame] quiet, [took] liquid nourishment freely, [fell] into a peaceful sleep" and woke up "quiet and self-contained," thereby avoiding the need for a depressant. In two sample cases, however, both female, the patients had to be revived with stimulants following their sessions in the continuous baths. As was the case with other forms of treatment and restraint, hydrotherapy was a powerful if potentially dangerous component of the asylum's therapeutic arsenal.[36]

ELECTROTHERAPY

Electrotherapy was another popular treatment of the late nineteenth century that Hobbs used, albeit not very enthusiastically. Electrotherapy was the application of galvanic (direct) and faradic (alternating) currents as well as of static electricity to various parts of the body. As a mild form of therapy, at least when properly applied, it became extremely popular in the 1880s and 1890s among the growing numbers of middle-class women who visited physicians on a regular basis. As the electrotherapist Alphonso D. Rockwell noted in 1879, "It might be almost considered a panacea for this class of cases."[37]

Electrotherapy was a natural by-product of the somatic paradigm, in which nervous energy in the body, "the vital force," was perceived to be electrically generated by the brain; therefore, logically, it could be recharged by an outside electrical force. The public was fascinated with the mystery of electricity, with the way it was beginning to transform work and recreation; by association people proceeded to a faith in the therapeutic power of the new technology. As Caleb Brown raved "a force that can propel cars, run the heaviest machinery, light a city or enable us to talk across the miles of space, or break up molecules into their ultimate atoms, must have some effect, when properly used, upon the metabolism of the human organism."[38] Not all physicians, however, shared this view. The mystery associated with the modern "miracle" was criticized by those wishing to eliminate the spiritual element from medicine: "The vulgar are captivated with the marvelous" and "fascinated with the buzz of a battery; they are ever ready to worship unseen or mysterious forces," wrote a critic of electrotherapy.[39]

In his analysis of electrotherapy after he had used it in his practice for ten years, the American neurologist Morton Prince discussed the benefits and drawbacks. (It is worthwhile noting that soon after this discussion, Prince was converted to the new psychoanalytic theory). Electrotherapy, he wrote, was "one of the most valuable remedies" in the treatment of neuralgia, but it was only a temporary palliative. In neurasthenia, electricity was an "excellent tonic" and relieved nervousness and insomnia, but here too the effect was "largely moral ... It is in no sense a cure for true neurasthenia." While electrotherapy was valuable in dispelling insomnia, Prince argued that it was important to delve into and treat the cause of insomnia, which required psychological technique. Yet electrotherapy was an important substitute for medication. As for the "organic destructive diseases of the spinal cord and brain [locomotor ataxia, disseminated sclerosis, and progressive muscular atrophy]" for which "your textbook" will advise using electricity, Prince countered, "shirk it"; it would not be of the slightest value. He concluded that the most important value of electrotherapy was the "influence of suggestion – purely or wholly."[40]

Faced with such criticism, it is not surprising that thirteen years later, in 1903, electrotherapists were still endeavoring to achieve professional respectability. As Edmund Owen of London's St. Mary's Hospital commiserated with his peers, electrotherapy "has hitherto received but scant professional courtesy and recognition in England ... The orthodox practitioner has been apt to regard it askance, and, passing by, has drawn his gown around him lest by chance it should become soiled by contact with it."[41]

The dilemma for the electrotherapists was not the limited effec-

tiveness of the treatment, but the unlimited availability of 'unqualified' practitioners. "The public have taken to electrical treatment
with extraordinary enthusiasm ... with, or without, the knowledge
or approval of their medical attendants. But I imagine that they have
derived the greater satisfaction ... when they have resorted to it
surreptitiously." Physicians as a professional enclave had not been
able to corner the equipment, and they subsequently suffered not
only financially but also in reputation because of these "unsavoury"
competitors. As Owens recounted, "A lady of good position and
education [was] sent by a consulting physician to receive electrical
treatment at the hands of a Surgeon ... The lady said that she was
rather apprehensive as to the effect of electrical treatment ... as her
heart was 'weak' ... The Surgeon said that he would examine her
heart. To this [she] replied, 'Oh, I did not think *you* could do that,
being a quack!'"[42]

The installation of electrical equipment at Homewood was undertaken by Hobbs and the board of directors not so much because
of great faith in its benefits as its value "in the way of advertising."
During his European tour, Hobbs had discovered electrotherapy to
be a fashionable treatment in institutions abroad. Closer to home,
competition had developed from private wards affiliated with general hospitals. In Boston, for example, St. Margaret's Hospital,
opened in 1881 and catering to the middle classes, offered electrical
treatments.[43] The installation of Homewood's equipment, Hobbs
agreed, would "have the sanitarium in all respects up to the highest
standards of the most modern institutions of the time." The board
decided that "while there might be some difference of opinion
among medical men as to the effectiveness of electrical treatment,
it would no doubt be in the interests of the sanitarium to have such
equipment." In its advertisement of 1915, Homewood's electrotherapy was specified for the treatment of "pain, insomnia, paralysis, etc.," but significantly not for its most generally popular purpose,
gynaecology.[44]

Hobbs's relative neglect of electrotherapeutics was due in part to
professional considerations. Electrotherapeutics in gynaecology had
been for many women and some physicians a welcomed alternative
to surgery. George J. Engelmann noted, for example, that electrical
treatment avoided "that nervous excitement so frequently caused by
the thought of a surgical operation" and allowed the patient "to
continue her daily vocation."[45] H.H. Hahn added, "In electricity we
possess an energy which is capable of curing ... without putting (a
woman's) life in jeopardy, or mutilating her body, but leaving her
as nature made her, a woman and not a *thing*."[46] Such sentiments

would leave a physician like Hobbs, by avocation and vocation a gynaecological surgeon unimpressed. More importantly, they ran in direct opposition to a significant element of his asylum therapeutics.

REPRODUCTIVE AND SEXUAL SURGERY

Gynaecological surgery was philosophically rooted in the late Victorian revival of the classical concept that the reproductive organs were central to a woman's mental and emotional well-being. Two factors in Victorian society were essential elements of this revival, the campaign for increased female participation in political and economic life and the somatic paradigm in medicine. The movement of middle-class women beyond the domestic sphere encountered considerable conservative opposition. Politicians, clergymen, educators, and physicians argued that female emancipation was unnatural and threatened the stability of the home, and by extension, of society. These opponents emphasized the differences between the sexes that rendered the female constitutionally incapable of achieving full equality. The center of this constitution was the reproductive system. Indeed, it seemed, as Professor Hubbard of New Haven, Connecticut concluded in 1870, that "the Almighty, in creating the female sex, had taken the uterus and built up a woman around it."[47]

The contribution of medicine to this debate revolved around the reflex theory of the human organism – every part of the body, physical or mental, was affected by every other part. The uterus was considered a particularly unstable and influential part of the female organism. Another factor was the somatic perception of the necessity for the conservation of nervous energy. Too much brain work on the part of middle-class women, it was argued, would divert vital energy from the reproductive organs and produce inferior offspring, perhaps even cause sterility. Quoting the British *Lancet* in 1881, the editors of the *American Journal of Insanity* maintained that the higher education of women was an "economic mistake." "In the ordinance of nature," they concluded, "the female is endowed with a force tending to the reproduction from her arrested or suppressed organism of the perfect organism of the male." By raising a "warning voice against jeopardizing the feminine stock and the entire race by encouraging women to stray beyond their appointed sphere," the editors revealed the political motivations behind the physiological theory.[48]

Puerperal insanity received considerable attention from physicians at the end of the nineteenth century, since by its nature it seemed to prove the centrality of the uterus. Such disorders were blamed partly on the stresses of childbearing in an age of increased 'civilization' and the new experiences women enjoyed. H.A. Tomlinson, superintendent of St. Peter's Hospital in Minnesota, argued that "when women are warring against their natural position in relation to the reproduction of the species," the "competition of social and industrial life" could lead to "disturbances of the nervous system associated with the bearing of children."[49]

Richard Bucke was a leading Canadian exponent of the importance of the female reproductive system – the raison d'etre of female existence – to a woman's mental health. His theory involved the operation of the great sympathetic nervous system, in his opinion the most important machinery of the human organism. This system linked the major organs, glands, and particularly the testes, ovaries, and uterus to the brain. Dysfunctions in any of these organs would lead to emotional disturbances. Bucke believed that women were lower on the evolutionary scale, so that their nervous systems were more highly developed in comparison to their brains, and the emotional reactions to physical disabilities therefore were more intense. Since the reproductive organs were the most sensitive influence on the mental health of a woman, Bucke attempted to prove in the late 1890s that attacking, correcting, or removing the offending organ would restore sanity and well-being.[50]

There were a few voices raised against the direct connection between the reproductive organs and insanity in women. Significantly, they were primarily women's voices. Although Clara Barrus of the Middletown, New York State Hospital, one of the few female assistant physicians, acknowledged that after systematic physical examinations of women in her institution, it was "the exception rather than the rule to find an insane woman with normal pelvic organs" and therefore inevitable to question "how much these abnormalities have to do with the causation of insanity," she demurred at concluding a direct relationship existed, stating rather that the experiences of the insane were as "human being[s]" first, "with the addition of those of ... being of the female sex."[51] Another advocate of the importance of other predisposing factors was Isabel Davenport, former gynaecologist at the Illinois Hospital for the Insane at Kankakee. "The laity, and many general practitioners," Davenport noted, "attach too much importance to pelvic disorders as an etiological factor in insanity and expect altogether too much from the treatment and removal of these disorders ... Unless there are conditions existing in the brain which make insanity possible, the diseased condition of the pelvic organs would not produce insanity."[52]

There were also male voices less willing to stray beyond clinical evidence to overarching theory. In his discussion of puerperal insanity, W.F. Menzies of the Lancashire County Asylum in Liverpool, England, argued that "many persons have been, as their friends say, 'queer' for years, but it require the extra strain attendant upon the functions of reproduction to precipitate them into an attack of actual insanity." Victims of puerperal insanity were often neurotics on the borderline of insanity or were those who had undergone multiple, closely-spaced pregnancies and were debilitated by "want, domestic tyranny, or actual physical disease."[53]

Despite these objections, gynaecological surgery for nervous and mental disorders was a regular procedure from the 1870s to the end of the century. Thousands of young middle- and upper-class women, usually in their thirties, underwent bilateral ovariotomies on healthy organs for the treatment of amenorrhea, dysmenorrhea, and any other form of "pelvic pain, hysteria or convulsive disorder." By 1906, it was estimated that 150,000 women had undergone "Battey's operation," so named for its originator, Robert Battey. Even if this figure was inflated, the number of operations was still extremely large, particularly given a purported mortality rate of thirty to thirty-three percent. The vogue for Battey's operation, which had at least the one positive side effect of greatly advancing the study of the reproductive system, was popular among many surgeons for the "brilliance and facility of the operation."[54] Ovariotomies were also advanced as a eugenics measure. William Goodell, professor of clinical gynaecology at the University of Pennsylvania, in fact concluded that the removal of the ovaries of the insane would benefit society, if not always result in mental recovery for the patient. "It [may well] be deemed [in the progressive future] a measure of sound policy ... to stamp out insanity by castrating all the insane men and spaying all the insane women."[55]

There was enthusiasm in Canada as well for the potentialities of the ovariotomy. In 1876, Lapthorn Smith, gynaecologist to the Montreal Dispensary, believed that the acceptance of the operation "would alone suffice to stamp our age as one of great progress in the treatment of those affections which are peculiar to women." The centre of surgical work in the ovariotomy in Canada was Montreal at the Montreal General and Royal Victoria hospitals. At the Montreal General, five ovariotomies were performed in 1884 and twenty-two in 1900, while forty-five such operations were performed at the Royal Victoria in 1895 alone. Ovariotomies were also performed at the Victoria General Hospital in Halifax and the University of Toronto.[56]

Some Canadian physicians were more cautious. "The removal of the normal ovaries is always a question in morals as well as in medicine," the *Canadian Practitioner* asserted, "and cannot be evaded in either relation without evil results." Other members of the medical profession were critical of the surgery because they were concerned about the effects enforced menopause would have upon women. They thought it would induce "morbid brooding, low spirits, melancholy, suicidal impulses and even insanity." There was also concern that the operation would "desex" a woman, affecting the secondary sex characteristics, diminishing the female sex drive, and most importantly, eliminating the ability for procreation ("a crime against society").[57]

By the 1890s, the tide was turned against the operation by physicians who questioned the sacrifice of "many a sinless ovary" to the career-building goals of some practitioners. More importantly, American state charity boards, characterizing the surgery as "brutal and inhumane," disallowed its practice in mental institutions. Thomas Morton, surgeon to the Pennsylvania Hospital, argued in 1893 that superintendents "now regard with disfavour the castration of women as a cure for mental disorders," since symptoms tended to persist "long after the removal of the alleged offending organs." On ethical grounds, Morton averred that it would be a matter "of grave doubt whether a relative or guardian ... has the moral or legal right to give consent to the unsexing of the insane person."[58]

Despite the fact that gynaecological surgery among the insane was declining in popularity, Richard Bucke sanctioned 226 such operations on chronically insane patients between 1895 and 1900. As an assistant physician at the London Asylum, Hobbs was an enthusiastic partner in Bucke's surgical experimentation and in fact performed the actual surgery. He and Bucke published a series of articles in the 1890s announcing and defending their experiments.[59] In these articles, Hobbs acknowledged that such surgery had aroused "much controversy and no small amount of bitterness" in some sections of the United States and that the "special work" had been characterized as "brutal and inhuman," but he insisted that "the eradication of pelvic disease among our female insane is the most important advance that we have made in this institution." He claimed that fully one-quarter of all women in the asylum were there "because of the special infirmities of their sex and the disasters and penalties of their lives as wives and mothers."[60]

Although the government ordered the operations discontinued in 1901 in public hospitals, Hobbs remained unregenerate and in 1907, he requested a surgical unit for Homewood. Langmuir responded,

"I have expressed doubts in previous letters as to the propriety of placing what you call an 'Operating Room' in the Sanitarium, more particularly as there is a General Hospital within a few hundred yards of Homewood, and moreover, some members of the medical profession have stated to me that there is no necessity for such an adjunct." Hobbs argued that "a surgical suite is just as much a necessity as any other department. In the past we have worked under great difficulties having had to use a bedroom and have dangerous solutions such as Bichloride of Mercury and Carbolic around in the corridors." He added, "it is not absolutely necessary to advertise the fact that we have an operating room, nobody suggested this."[61] The facilities were approved, and Hobbs examined and operated on a number of women – neurasthenics, manic-depressives, melancholics, and epileptics – with the avowed goals of both curing their mental and correcting their physical disorders.

Some cases obviously lent themselves to surgical intervention. Ethel H. (#225, 1916), a twenty-eight year old neurasthenic with heart trouble, suffered "very, very severe pain at her menstrual period," leaving her "practically worn out [and] always tired." She attempted to carry on her domestic chores, and "as a result [became] quite hyperactive in between menstruations, only further wearing herself out." Ethel was very discontented at Homewood ("the patients get on my nerves"), and her family arrived a week after admission "fully decided to take the patient home and before they interviewed the physician they had all her things packed up. The physician discussed the condition with them fully, pointing out the line of treatment that should be followed ... After considerable deliberation they decided that ... she would get help here if she could get help any place." While a "full curretage" was performed on Ethel, she declined any further surgery. Louise W. (#526, 1905), diagnosed with neurasthenia and hysteria, was reported to be "anxious to have some surgical work done to relieve her of the pain and distress resulting from [an] old pelvic inflammation."

Other cases failed to show mental improvement, and the propriety of the superintendent in performing the surgery was questionable. Eliza M. (#347, 1916) who suffered from depression following a mild cerebral hemorrhage, was operated on by Hobbs to repair a prolapsed uterus. She made no mental recovery. Nellie B. (#44, 1920), who was uniformly depressed and debilitated from having five children, the oldest at the time of her treatment under the age of nine, was treated without success for three months. Hobbs then gave her a pelvic examination, found "the uterus forward, slightly longer than normal, and a very lax, lacerated perineum." Obtaining permission "from the husband to have this repaired," Hobbs performed the surgery. There was no mental change. A gynaecological examination was made on Sylvia G. (#194, 1915) "in view that this might lessen the excitement during the menstrual period." However "nothing abnormal" was found "except hemorrhoids. Dilation and curettement was done."

Violet C. (#91, 1918), an epileptic, was operated on for a chronic appendicitis. "Liver, gall bladder, spleen, stomach, bowel, all carefully examined – no defects." Barnes noted her as making "satisfactory progress" from the operation, although she experienced a seizure the following morning and suffered a dangerously high septic fever as a result of the surgery, for which she was purged intensively. When discharged two months later, it was noted that the patient "cannot be said to have made any progress."

Homewood's female patients, unlike London's inmates, were able to make their voices heard, particularly those aware of Hobbs's reputation. Lela S. (#512, 1910) enjoyed the "treatment and baths" but did not want to return to Homewood as an in-patient when she was back "in the excitement" stage of her "neurasthenia." She finally agreed to return upon the promise "that she should not be submitted to a vaginal examination." In the case history of Margaret McL. (#326, 1914), who suffered from manic-depression, it was noted in boldface that she was said to have *prolapsus uteri*. She was not, however, operated on for it, probably due to her intense fear before an earlier vaginal examination ("I walked the floor that night.").

In contrast to Hobbs, Lett was neither qualified to attempt nor sympathetic to the cause of gynaecological surgery. He made his views apparent in 1892 when he noted that Susan McK. (#139, 1892) had never been quite right since, under an anaesthetic, she had had "some uterine operation performed by Dr Emily Stowe" (a leading Canadian feminist). In 1894, Lett recorded (perhaps smugly, given his relations with Bucke) that a female patient had died, having never recovered from a "severe surgical operation at London, Ontario." The patient had been a "noisy raving maniac" who had died from exhaustion and the "cancerous condition of [the] brain and other internal organs."[62]

One of the very rare instances when Lett undertook surgery of a sexual nature was in the treatment of a male patient who engaged in masturbation. The idea that masturbation was a deviant act was first popularized in an anonymous English pamphlet, "Onania, or the Heinous Sin of Self-Pollution," published in 1710; the pamphlet was an advertisement for a patent medicine. That masturbation was a mental disease as well as a sin was advanced by Simon-André Tissot,

Swiss physician and hygienist, who theorized that because sexual intercourse increased peripheral circulation, all sexual activity that caused the blood to rush to the head dangerously starved the nerves and increased the possibility of insanity. Masturbation was particularly risky because it could be indulged in secretly and at a tender age. With the widespread confinement of the insane in the eighteenth century, physicians observed large numbers of patients masturbating and made the false connection between the habit and the cause of insanity.[63]

According to Edward Spitzka, a leading American neurologist, masturbatory insanity was indeed a serious condition for teenagers who usually were victims of a "bad heredity." The symptoms he described were common in the stereotypical diseased: he would be "cowardly, apprehensive, and disinclined to manly sports, but ... subject to violent and dangerous impulses ... Males are at first timid towards the other sex, and later lose all normal sexual desire; females, on the contrary, are apt to be aggressively erotic. The disease may progress to an irritable dementia, with filthy, destructive and quarrelsome propensities, or, if dementia is less complete ... may [produce] a selfish, deceitful, malicious and cruel disposition."[64]

In 1877, Daniel Clark, superintendent of the Toronto Asylum, described masturbation as the "enshrouded moral pestilence," practiced in "numberless homes in every part of our land." Like all "such vices," masturbation was "against the State ... [producing] the enfeebled body and weak intellect" which fell prey to any "depravity and self-abasement."[65] Shortly after his appointment as medical superintendent of the London Asylum, Richard Bucke demonstrated his belief, as a somaticist, in the direct relationship, through the nervous system, of masturbation and insanity by "wiring" fifteen male patients in an effort to stop their habit. Wiring was a process of infibulation; a silver wire ring was placed through the foreskin. Bucke placed great hopes upon the operation. When the first patients were wired, he wrote, "[I] intend to make this operation simple and perhaps modified a good deal in the course of the next six months. There is no doubt that if a plan could be hit upon of stopping this vice M ± a good many cases could be relieved and cured which are now hopeless."[66]

The operations were not successful, however. Lett, observing the process at London, was never convinced that masturbation could be the sole cause of insanity. He believed, rather, that with an "adequate" hereditary predisposition masturbation was an exciting cause of insanity and would also manifest itself as a symptom. "When present," he suggested, "it hampers treatment, retards recovery, and in many instances precludes the possibility of a cure."[67] The patient Lett wired was Percival W. (admitted 27 September 1884) who had been insane for three months due to a prolonged attack of typhoid fever. It was clear to Lett that he had been masturbating, so he wired him. Although the wire was kept in place for four months, when it was removed, the patient began masturbating again. Other instances of suspected or observed "self-abuse" at Homewood were noted by Lett, but he took no further action.

SALVARSAN THERAPY

An area of sexual dysfunction in which Homewood had more positive results was the treatment of venereal disease. Syphilitic cases which required institutionalization were those in the tertiary stage of the disease during which the heart, brain, spinal cord, and nervous system were under attack. Patients exhibited locomotor ataxia or tabes dorsalis, the loss of functional control of the legs due to the disintegration of the spinal cord, or more commonly were diagnosed as having general paresis of the insane (GPI). Psychiatrists were well aware that research in combatting venereal infections was an integral aspect of curing mental illness. As Prince Morrow, foremost American venereologist concluded, "the elimination of these diseases would render one-third, possibly one-half, of our institutions for defectives unnecessary."[68]

The Academy of Medicine in Toronto estimated in 1914 that between five and fifteen percent of the Canadian population was infected with syphilis.[69] In 1907, however, Paul Ehrlich of Germany had discovered the syphilis-attacking properties of his "magic bullet," 606, an arsenical. This vanguard of the new science of chemotherapy first arrived in North America in 1910 under the trade name of salvarsan.[70] The salvarsan course was a heroic one; reactions ranged from nausea, fever, and skin eruptions to liver failure. Some patients died as a result of the treatment. Many practitioners in 1910 were unskilled in intravenous application and injected salvarsan subcutaneously, with diminished benefits. Therefore the institutions whose surgical staff were most skilled were more likely to be credited with good clinical results.[71]

Prior to the discovery of salvarsan, Homewood treated syphilitic patients with mercury, cinchona tonic (quinine), or potassium iodide. Before 1903, five patients in the sample population were diagnosed paretics, although many other alcoholics and "neurasthenics" had had a history of syphilis or had died from symptoms strongly indicative of paresis. (See table 12.) In 1913, the Wasserman test was instituted, and by 1920 an additional nineteen male and four female patients were diagnosed as syphilitic. Although three of these patients were treated with strychnine and mercury, the remainder were systematically treated with salvarsan or one of its derivatives: neosalvarsan, diarsenol, or neophenarsenyl.

Homewood's physicians were probably introduced to salvarsan therapy by one of North America's experts, Simon Flexner of the Rockefeller Institute, who was Paul Ehrlich's American agent for the testing of salvarsan,[72] and who visited Homewood on behalf of a neurasthenic patient. Homewood's physicians and administrators were certainly aware of the importance of the work and the possibilities it afforded their institution. Hobbs reported that five cases had been so treated in 1917, "two of whom have recovered and returned to their homes and three are improving under treatment. It is too soon definitely to say that this special line of treatment will become permanent. If our success continues it will effect the saving of many lives in the future." The success of the treatment, President F.C. Jarvis added, "would no doubt give our institution an outstanding reputation on this continent."[73] Indeed, the arsenical treatment of syphilitic insanity ushered in a new era of interventionist psychiatry, which would further manifest itself in the twentieth century with insulin shock therapy, psychosurgery, electro-convulsive therapy, and an expanding psycho-pharmacopeia.

The diagnostic practices of both Lett and Hobbs were based on early and largely unshaken convictions, Lett's in the primacy of hereditary influence and Hobbs's in the belief that mental illness could be traced ultimately to physical disorder. In any event, however, a psychoanalytic approach was not practical in their asylum. The moral manager's tools were fresh air, labour, and entertainment, the somaticist's were the kitchen, the baths, and the beds. The psychoanalyst's resources were unlimited time, intensive training, and a high physician to patient ratio. Neither Lett's nor Hobbs's intuitions and training, nor the exigencies of an institution, of operating budgets, of patient, family, and community expectations made it likely that psychoanalytic diagnostic techniques would be adopted under their regimes.

In the same way, therapeutics that emphasized the value of physical well-being in psychological recovery were more easily instituted than the intense, private, psychoanalytic approach that would compete for professional attention after the turn of the century. Hobbs's approval of hydrotherapy and disdain of electrotherapy were personal preferences. That he failed to ban the latter – that he was in fact obliged to advertise it – demonstrated the financial realities of the business of asylum management. The longevity of the rest cure, on the other hand, was indicative of the success of a therapeutic device when professional favour, patron approval, and financial benefit coalesced.

The First Mrs Rochester: Family Motivations for Commitment and the Dynamics of Social Redundancy

The history of asylums traditionally has been based upon annual reports and intra-professional medical publications. Accordingly, there has been much emphasis upon types of treatment and their failure to cure, the latter demonstrated by the steady accumulation of a chronic patient population. Yet, as Gerald Grob has argued, the institutionalization of large numbers of incurables and the construction of more asylums to meet further demands were not anticipated nor desired by the founders and the physicians.[1] The increase in the custodial populations was not a manifestation of the failure of the institution, but of its functional success in meeting the needs of families. As Grob further observed in 1980, "historical studies about conditions within the family that led to [commitment] are still lacking. But it is quite clear that in many instances, families decided on institutionalization [to preserve] their internal integrity."[2]

The literary richness of many of Homewood's patient histories not only uncovers these needs and conditions but opens a window to the lives of late Victorian middle-class families as well. While the families of the mentally ill may not be 'typical,' their differences should not be overdrawn, particularly when there were few universally accepted definitions of insanity and especially of neuroses. Once a family recognized and accepted a member as mentally ill, the decision to commit was not inevitable, even in more severe or destructive cases. As Henry Harbin had noted in his study of contemporary family psychiatry, "the basic assumption underlying the hospital treatment approach ... has been an individually oriented (either biological or psychological) model of madness. Yet most people are placed in the hospital because their family or the community is unable to tolerate their disturbing behaviour, no matter what the etiology of the illness happens to be."[3]

Table 7
Person(s) Committing Patients

	Female	Male
Family	453	327
Physician	74	145
Patient (self-admitted)	7	34
Friend	3	22
Outside authority (e.g. sheriff)	4	7
Employer	0	3
Army official	1	1
Nurse or attendant	1	1
Unknown	24	27
Total	567	567

The family, in fact, had a number of options to exhaust: to ignore the behaviour, to care for the individual at home, or to admit him to a rest home, hospital, or asylum. The decision to commit, therefore, may be seen as a family strategy in a time of crisis. As table 7 illustrates, admissions to Homewood were primarily at the instigation of the family, particularly in the case of women. Every family has its own standard of tolerable behaviour. As the primary unit for social control, the family or its dominant members monitor the behaviour of each individual member and decide when that behaviour becomes too disruptive to be acceptable. Louise C. (#86, 1902), an alcoholic, clearly had over-taxed the tolerance of her husband. In a lengthy, impassioned letter to Dr Hobbs, he wrote, "She is the most selfish woman you ever met; everything is judged by how it affects herself — her children or family are nothing to her if they don't agree with her wishes she is the biggest hypocrite you ever saw." He instructed that "the sooner she is made to realize that she is in your Sanitarium for treatment and not there on any pleasure trip the better for herself."

The case histories discussed below will reflect what the families involved regarded as standards of acceptable middle-class conduct. Inappropriate behaviour in these instances included refusal to work, public display, and sexual promiscuity. Patients were also committed for behaviour disruptive to family harmony, ranging from violence to irritability. (See table 8.)

The willingness to work was a highly value-laden behaviour pattern in the family and in the community. Thus, depending upon his or her labouring role in the household, in the workshop, or on the farm, a non-producer could range from being an irritant to a major

Table 8
Behaviour Cited by Families as the Motivation for Committing Patients

	Female	Male	Total
BEHAVIOUR INCOMPATIBLE WITH MIDDLE-CLASS STANDARDS OF PROPRIETY			
Refusal to work	13	7	20
Masturbation	3	14	17
Public display	7	4	11
Sexual excesses or perversions	0	6	6
Financial irresponsibility	3	2	5
Promiscuity	2	0	2
BEHAVIOUR DISRUPTIVE TO FAMILY HARMONY			
Irritability towards family	43	27	70
Violence towards family	8	23	31
Jealousy and suspicion	14	9	23
Insubordination towards parents	1	11	12
Refusal to have sexual relations with spouse	2	0	2

crippler of the family economy. Among the late Victorian middle class, at a time when the gap between adolescence and self-support was growing and children could be emotionally and financially dependent upon their parents for longer periods than in the previous century or among the working classes, the refusal of children to contribute their labour to the family was particularly worrisome.[4] The asylum was the alternative taken by some parents to curb idleness in their offspring.

Fatherless boys were especially difficult to control. Arthur D. (#693, 1913), diagnosed with neurasthenia and "mental excitement," appeared to be an incorrigible rather than mentally ill seventeen-year-old. His mother, a "very highly strung, nervous" widow, was unable to control him. Arthur smoked pipes and cigarettes, "runs away frequently from his mother ... Spending money wildly, buying motorcycles, and hiring carriages. Running away frequently to neighboring Cities, and last week ran away to Toronto, spending all his money, and then forging cheques on his Mother." When Arthur entered the asylum, the symptoms he manifested included attempting to run away, inquiring "if there were any girls to play with around here," and asking "if he would be allowed to smoke, and to have his revolver, and knives with him ... He walked about the corridor with his hat on, with an air of considerable importance." Arthur was visited often by his mother until he escaped nine months after admission.

Susie K. (#266, 1905) was a twenty-two-year-old single woman who "helped at housework" at home. The referring physicians described her as "quiet, passive," and "moody". Her mother stated that she "does nothing unless forced [and] becomes somewhat cross when compelled to do anything." She showed "no interest in general work or welfare of the place." After two years of her listlessness and inactivity, her mother could no longer cope, and committed her as insane, although she was discharged two months later. John B. (#612, 1910), thirty-three years old and living on his parents' farm, had changed from being a "quiet industrious citizen to a lazy boisterous person." He "lies in bed a good part of the day and wanders round at night," and "indulges in all kinds of silly talk."

Henry P. (#978, 1914) displayed more distinctive symptoms of mental illness, yet it would be external factors which led to his commitment. Aged thirty, Henry had been a clerk for the CPR in a northern Ontario town; he had graduated from McGill Medical School and worked for a year in a hospital. Described as a "good mixer, fond of company," and "never extravagant," Henry was noticed to be acting "peculiar" – nothing more – until he threw a glass of ginger ale on the floor and cried that there was acid in it. In a few days, he was sent to the first of a series of asylums far from home. The decisiveness of the family's response was due to the fact that the ginger ale episode had created a public scene at his father's victory party after his election as mayor. Although, in hindsight, his family noted Henry had been behaving oddly, his behaviour had been tolerated until he had broken another tenet of Victorian society: respectability.

Other public officials found it too socially costly to keep mentally unsound family members at home. Hugh S. (#1050, 1885), the alcoholic son of a senator, was admitted when his father became "disgusted to think that one belonging to me will go round the streets of Toronto and through the slums spending the money that he never earned." Harriet X. (#528, 1913), a resident of western Canada, was a forty-three-year-old mother of six children ranging in age from nineteen to five. She had been a "strong, wiry girl" of an "athletic turn," and had had a good public school and college education. Married at twenty-one, Harriet's confinements were "all more or less difficult." At the last birth, she had suffered "considerable tearing and laceration," and required surgery. Although her husband stated that she was of a "cheerful disposition," she had lately been exhibiting "a great deal of anxiety regarding the welfare of the children." At the same time, her husband was elected mayor of their large city, and Harriet's duties grew "considerably." Along with the social functions and committees attendant upon the office, a visit from the Governor-General provided additional public duties for which she "faithfully gave her time and energy." Given the daunting prospect for a mother of six of performing these duties along with her domestic chores (in the context of 1912 technology), it is not surprising that Harriet suffered a physical breakdown, succeeded by mental symptoms. She was nursed at home until she demanded to be allowed to attend social functions, at which point she was sent to Homewood, many hundreds of miles away from the eyes of the local citizens.

Physicians who referred such individuals to asylums were sympathetic towards the middle-class drive for respectability. In fact, by "ascribing unconventional ideas and actions to insanity, (alienists) set themselves up as the guardians of the respectable code, and of the social system it buttressed."[5] When charges of wrongful confinement had been raised in the British press in the 1840s, one anonymous physician admitted that "thinking of two evils, it is better to risk the confinement of an eccentric person improperly, than to leave him at liberty to become a disgrace to himself and his family."[6]

By the second half of the last century, the admission of a household member exhibiting behaviour intolerable to the standards of the middle-class family was facilitated by the widespread medical acceptance of the diagnosis of neurasthenia or nervous exhaustion. Neurasthenia was a term coined by the American neurologist George Miller Beard in 1869 to describe a malaise considered to be affecting a growing segment of the Victorian middle class. Late nineteenth-century neurologists likened the human body to an electrically powered machine, possessed of a "limited amount of nervous energy." When the machine became over-stimulated, whether by the modern urban stresses of the "railroad, the steam engine, the telegraph, and the increased mental activity of women," the body would break down, and require an extended period of rest in a secluded environment, preferably a sanitarium.[7]

Alfred Hobbs believed that there was a strong hereditarian element in the "cultivation of these noxious neurotic weeds. An alcoholic parent, a syphilitic progenitor, a restless, nervous mother, an epileptic brother, or an insane sister will be found somewhere perched on the family tree if diligently sought for in at least sixty percent of all histories of neurasthenia." The neurasthenic was "supersensitive; a perfect barometer of restlessness ... He fears he is going insane [and is] restless and discontented with himself and everybody else ... The universe looks blue to him. His own mental picture throws deep shadows; there is no silver lining."[8] Yet for all that, the diagnosis of neurasthenia was a badge of success akin to the executive ulcer. In his address to the Ontario Medical Association in 1905, New York physician William B. Pritchard termed it "a disease of bright intellects; its victims are leaders and masters of men, each one a captain of industry ... The neurasthenic is the arche type [sic] of the poohbah."9

Beard listed over seventy symptoms of neurasthenia, including "insomnia, flushing, drowsiness, bad dreams, cerebral irritation, dilated pupils, pain, pressure and heaviness in the head ..."10 So popular was the diagnosis that by 1901, it was termed "the newest garbage can of medicine."11 Neurasthenia was a relatively innocuous diagnosis and facilitated the movement of middle-class patients into asylums. Since few individuals would never exhibit at least some neurasthenic symptoms, it was not difficult for a physician, faced with behaviour which families could no longer tolerate, to arrive at a diagnosis satisfactory to himself, family members, and, frequently, the patients themselves. As table 1 indicates, neurasthenia was the primary diagnosis among patients admitted to the Homewood Retreat between 1883 and 1920. Table 9 illustrates the range and frequency of symptoms cited in neurasthenic cases.

Perhaps nowhere was there more universal agreement among physicians and laymen, with respect to the need for control on behaviour, than on controlling sexual promiscuity in women. Physicians frequently "confused insanity with immorality, especially sexual, and with other forms of nonconformist behaviour."12 Alice H. (#218, 1910) led a life considered immoral by her family and aggravated the situation with her profanity and open promiscuity. She, on the other hand, perceived her trouble as "one of constant and unwarranted persecution by the members of her family." In letters to her at the institution, male family members clearly detailed the motivations behind her commitment. Her brother-in-law wrote, "the existing method of 'living,' if you can call an endless sarcasm of argument and wrangling, living at all, simply can't go on any longer." Her brother added, "People who are laws onto [sic] themselves end up in lunatic asylums and that's what a lunatic is, a person who is a law onto herself ... Unless you can become an entirely changed woman, you will have to stay in an asylum somewhere all your life ... If you acted sanely, people would in time forget that you were in an asylum. Your social life is spoiled here for several years and you would have to live very quietly. *It's better that people should think you insane than that they should think you a bad immoral woman, and that's what many people thought till they heard you were in an asylum, which of course explained things*" (italics added).

The most obvious form of disruptive behaviour to produce an institutional response was violence. Violent family members were less likely to bc taken home by kin if the violence were directed to

Table 9
Symptoms of Neurasthenia

| | Frequency Cited[a] | | |
Symptoms	Female	Male	Total
Melancholia	52	35	87
Insomnia	35	22	57
Restlessness or mania	23	26	49
Delusions or obsessions	26	21	47
Nerves or anxiety	26	20	46
Neuralgia or dizziness	22	15	37
Feelings of persecution	19	14	33
Lack of concentration	12	21	33
Suicidal tendencies	14	15	29
Hysteria or emotionalism	22	6	28
Choking, tremors, back or heart pain	15	13	28
Antagonistic attitude	12	15	27
Hypochondria	16	5	21
Physical depreciation	11	10	21
Fatigue or weakness	8	12	20
Lack of ambition	8	12	20
Reclusive behaviour	13	6	19
Gastrointestinal disorders	15	3	18
Violence	9	6	15
Eating disorders	9	5	14
Tendency to wander	6	7	13
Sexual irregularities	9	3	12
Financial irresponsibility	2	4	6
Filthy habits	1	4	5
Malingering	1	1	2

[a]In the majority of neurasthenic cases, more than one symptom was cited; each has been tabulated separately.

the family rather than to strangers. Family members sometimes asked outright that the offender be committed for an indefinite period – in fact be incarcerated in the asylum without parole. Thomas M. (admitted 28 August 1888), an alcoholic, possessed a temper so violent that his wife was "broken down in health and cannot live with him." His son "wanted to know how long [Dr Lett] could detain him and if we could make this a permanent home for him. I replied [that] as long as he remained insane I could help him." Charles S. (#1070, 1910) was feared by his "nearest," especially "his wife being with him alone most of the time. While he has never threatened either his own life or the life of others," his physician believed there was "always a danger." While Charles apparently made a fair mental recovery from a diagnosed involutional melancholia, he was never visited while in the asylum.

Arthur R. (#1016, 1892), a fifty-year-old "gentleman," had attempted suicide and exhibited delusions of grandeur. The immediate cause of his commitment was his "uncontrollable" sexual propensity. "Of late [he] attacked [his] wife who is ill in bed after confinement with ruptured organs and attempted to have connection doing her serious injury." Arthur was uncontrollable despite the fact that he had become totally blind and suffered from multiple sclerosis. His symptoms were strongly indicative, however, of general paresis of the insane, the tertiary stage of syphilis. As might be expected, Arthur was never visited in the two years he spent at Homewood prior to his death.

Arthur had exhibited another symptom which was disruptive to family harmony: unwarranted jealousy towards his wife. Pathological jealousy was one of the most dangerous mental symptoms since there was a likelihood that it could lead to the murder of a spouse or another individual "as retribution for an often imaginary infidelity."[13] Thomas B. (#591, 1884) was committed after he became suspicious of his wife, and she believed he would harm her. Thomas H. (#815, 1919) also had become "restless, suspicious and made [unjustified] charges of infidelity against his wife."

Yet even instances of overt violence against family members did not necessarily lead to permanent confinement. Joanna R. (#445, 1887) was described as mentally unsound for eleven years and "sometimes very violent." Paranoid, delusional, and manic, Joanna beat her children "severely," forcing her daughter to "leave home at night to avoid maltreatment." After six years of confinement, she was discharged at her family's request on condition that a nurse be provided, and that she "sleep with wire screens." Della B. (#36, 1888), a twenty-one-year-old single girl from Mobile, Alabama, was another intractable case. A victim of mania supposedly caused by a "love affair," Della had been force-fed for "several months," was "filthy" in habits, and went through the "full line of medication including hypnotics, opiates, sedatives, massage, emenagogues, swedish movement and electricity." She gained weight at Homewood and showed some improvement; she baked a "delicious cake" and played piano, although she also attacked her nurse "savagely." Despite these incidents, and Lett's reporting in confidence to her brother that she habitually masturbated, her mother visited her frequently, brought her jewellery, and after nine months of treatment, took her home accompanied by a private nurse hired from the Homewood staff.[14] In this case, strong and persistent representations by physicians, family, and friends could not persuade Mrs B. to accept her daughter's apparently hopeless condition or the need for institutionalization, despite Della's patent unsuitability for home care.

If institutionalization was a decision made primarily by family members, social forces beyond the control of individual households also influenced and limited the choices available, particularly for individuals whose behaviour was less dramatic than that exhibited by Della and Joanna. The commitment process was greatly influenced by the presence or absence of another individual, usually a family member, who took responsibility for home care. The demographics of the nineteenth century did not auger well for this. As Katz, Doucet, and Stern have demonstrated, Canadians were on the move.[15] Constantly searching for cheap land and economic advancement, this mobile population was tardy in establishing the roots necessary for the proper care of the old or the sick.

In absolute terms, the extended family also was shrinking. At the turn of the century, a high adult mortality rate persisted as the fertility rate continued to fall. In 1900, one-quarter of all American children under fifteen years would lose one parent while one in sixty-two would lose both. Consequently, in their adult years these orphans were less likely to have kin to care for them should they experience a period of mental illness.[16] The decline in fertility was apparent in the halving of the average size of completed families. In 1851, a Canadian woman would have borne an average of 7.02 children while by 1921 the average had dropped to 3.54 children.[17] This demographic shift had "potentially important implications for old people and for society. Those who did not marry and those who had no or few living children might need public welfare ... Some 56 percent of [American] women over 44 who were living in or admitted to almshouses in 1910 had borne no children."[18]

Along with the diminuition of the pool of potential caregivers was the lessening of the sense of moral responsibility for kin members which was an integral part of the effect of a capitalist economy upon human relations – the process of reification.[19] Reification permeated family life, producing, as Shorter termed it, "economic egoism."[20] Unlike its pre-industrial antecedents, the family under industrial conditions was no longer a multifaceted corporate entity, responsible not only for food, shelter, and clothing, but for education, medicine, and care for the aged and infirm. As Eli Zaretsky stated, "so long as the family was a productive unit based upon private property, its members understood their domestic life and 'personal' relations to be rooted in their mutual labour."[21] The result of the removal of labour from the home (apart from domestic maintenance and childcare) and the decline of real property ownership, was the separation of personal life and labour – a bifurcation which held ramifications for the traditional social welfare functions of the family. Harry Braverman concluded:

The ebbing of family facilities, and of neighborly feelings upon which the performance of many social functions formerly depended, leaves a void. As the family members, [working] away from home, become less able to care for each other in time of need, and as the ties of neighbourhood, community and friendship are reinterpreted on a narrower scale to exclude onerous responsibilities, the care of humans for each other becomes increasingly institutionalized ... In addition, the pressures of urban life grow more intense and it becomes harder to care for any who need care in the conditions of the jungle of the cities. Thus understood, the massive growth of institutions ... [represents] the clearing of the market place of all but the 'economically active' and 'functioning' members of society.[22]

The individualization of household members was accompanied by the privatization of the nuclear family and its glorification as the centre of personal fulfillment. The closed windows draped with heavy brocades which characterized the middle-class home represented families turning inward from a society perceived as something "alien, impersonal, remote and abstract – a world from which pity and tenderness had fled in horror ... Yet the very conditions that gave rise to the need to view privacy and the family as a refuge from the larger world made it more and more difficult for the family to serve in that capacity."[23] Kin members, as well as employees, were increasingly measured by economic worth in the capitalist psyche. Ross McCormack, in his study of English immigrants, noted that "family relationships could be ruthlessly instrumental. In 1905 a Portsmouth woman living with her son and daughter-in-law in Winnipeg lost her sight and thus her ability to contribute to the family economy; she was turned out of the house and deported."[24] In her discussion of life-history interviews conducted with individuals born before 1908 and living in Hamilton, Ontario, Jane Synge contrasted the experiences of farm families, where "unneighbourliness" or neglect of elderly parents would be subject to severe social censure, with the recollections of urban dwellers, whose parents feared "being deserted in old age."[25]

The separation of productive (that is, wage-earning) and nonproductive elements of society had particularly detrimental effects for women. The economic dependency of wives and daughters was "the hallmark of middle-class respectability."[26] Yet, as Peter Stearns has observed, "Is it too fanciful to suggest that the dependence preached on women generally, of every age, served as a logical preparation for the special dependence of old age? Dependence of course is a nasty word, and heightened institutionalization reflects its harshness when there was no alternative."[27] The dependency which accompanied old age was a socio-economic consequence of a natural life-course event. Other life-course events which affected women's independence were spinsterhood (a word which took on its present perjorative meaning in the 1750s) and widowhood. The common thread of these life stages is that such women were not perceived as housewives – the only respectable state for the Victorian and Edwardian lady. Indeed, these dependent women had become redundant women. When these disesteemed, though natural, life stages were coupled with mental illness, the double burden of dependence/redundancy left women especially vulnerable to institutionalization.

That this pattern was evident at Homewood is clear when its case histories are examined for patients who were committed not on the basis of extreme changes in behaviour or worsening of mental symptoms but due to factors external to their mental state: the death of an important family member, for example, or the marriage of another. These factors resulted in the patients' loss of familial role or of a caregiver. Given the lack of economic opportunity and the deficiency in education for women, and the persistence of the patriarchal family at the turn of the century, it should not be surprising that, among Homewood's patients, socially redundant females outnumbered males by a ratio of five to one. (See table 10.)

The permanently unmarried middle-class woman was the focus of much discussion and concern throughout the nineteenth century. In England, it was estimated that fifteen percent of women would reach their fifties without being married. Contemporary observers blamed the surplus of women upon war casualties, male emigration, and the tendency for Victorian middle-class men to postpone marriage until it was economically feasible. Modern demographers, however, have noted that the increase in spinsterhood had actually been a product of the eighteenth century, and that the rate had remained fairly constant throughout the nineteenth. Increased urbanization, however, rendered the spinster population more visible.[28] In Catholic countries, taking the veil was an option pursued by many middle-class women until alternatives in employment existed. British writers like Mary Astell and Lady Mary Wortley Montagu "lamented the lack of the kind of association and professional outlet for the middle-class women in Protestant England that the convent bestowed on the continent."[29]

Table 10
Categories of Social Redundancy Cited as Reasons
for Commitment

	Female	Male
Loss of role or caregiver for unmarried at home	37	4
Loss of spouse through death or desertion	18	10
Spinsterhood/Bachelorhood	10	0
Total	65	14

In Canada, a similar schism between French and English cultures existed. In Quebec, Marta Danylewicz noted, land scarcity, migration, and constricted economic opportunities had lowered the provincial marriage rate from nine per thousand in 1830 to 6.6 per thousand in 1880. Fully thirty-three percent of the women in Montreal were single at forty in 1881. The convent absorbed many of these women. In 1881, 4.4 percent of single females over twenty were nuns, while by 1921, 9.1 percent had entered convents.[30] In the nation at large, the percentage of women between the ages of 45 and 49 who were single rose from 8.2 percent in 1851 to 11.1 percent by 1921.[31] As figures can, these cloak a great deal of suffering.

The plight of the spinster was seen by many observers, particularly female, as the glaring failure of respectable society to provide for members who had been bred to uphold middle-class culture. No gentleborn woman, it was understood, was ever completely safe from the possibility of economic hardship. Mary Agnes FitzGibbon, for example, was the niece of John A. MacDonald and the wife of a gentleman of titled family. When her husband was committed to an insane asylum, she became the sole support for herself and her daughter and took up journalism. In 1896, FitzGibbon described the redundant female as "the non-professional woman, usually the daughter of a professional man, and she is generally in every sense a 'gentlewoman' ... She has been brought up by her parents in a sort of haphazard way. The possibility of matrimony is a sort of mirage on the horizon. She is really fitted only to fill a niche in some household."[32]

A "niche" does not evoke a position of power or permanency, but its lack could evoke contempt. London's Saturday Review graphically illustrated reified relations in its commentary: "Married life is a woman's profession, and to this life her training – that of dependence

– is modelled. Of course, by not getting a husband, or losing him, she may find she is without resources. All that can be said of her is, she has failed in business and no social reform can prevent such failures."[33]

This narrow indictment failed to account for the inequities, both societal and familial, that exacerbated the plight of the spinster and of all women alone. Limited job opportunities and gender-based wage differentials meant that single women faced many more economic hardships and were less likely to be able to protect themselves financially in periods of unemployment, sickness, or in old age.[34] The only respectable employment open for middle-class women was that of governess or companion. To be in service in another middle-class home was often degrading as well as difficult, lonely work. Jeanne Peterson concluded that the ambiguity of the governess's social status caused inconsistency and confusion in her relations with her employers and other servants, which led to the high proportion of governesses in insane asylums.[35] What other options were there for these socially isolated women in middle-class society? The aristocratic practice of continued financial support for retired servants was a casualty of capitalism. Lengthy service was "much less the rule" in middle-class households, and "paternalism was expensive."[36]

The exploitation of the governess was not limited to Britain, as illustrated by the case of Ella A. (#16, 1917), a twenty-seven-year-old single companion. Ella had experienced a "healthy infancy and childhood," was very fond of school and attended a private academy until she was eighteen, studying painting, drawing, and music – all designed to prepare her to fill a niche. Possessed of a "bright, cheerful temperament," Ella performed her household duties properly and "if anything was overconscientious." Seventeen months prior to commitment, she was employed as a companion to a rich lady whose husband was serving overseas and whose life was "social affairs." Ella was nominally the governess of a twelve-year-old, but her duties grew considerably: she "would rise at seven, get child ready for breakfast and breakfast at eight, devoted whole time to child or mother as she could manage servants, household, pack and unpack" for her mistress's many trips. Ella would be left in charge of the household for weeks at a time, and there were "employed servants of whom she was in fear. They indulged in [alcohol]. When the child was sick she was practically a professional nurse." Learning from an outsider that her health had exceedingly deteriorated, Ella's parents wrote her mistress asking she be released. Her employer minimized the reports, and it was with "great difficulty" that consent was finally granted. Her parents were "greatly shocked at her appearance" and placed Ella in a general hospital. She weighed sixty-nine pounds and suffered "the greatest possible degree of emaciation."

Among Homewood's patients, social isolation frequently resulted from family strategies. Maintenance of a respectable lifestyle in Victorian middle-class society was often a difficult endeavour. Patricia Branca estimated that model budgets allowed only twelve percent of the annual income to cover not only education costs, but also servant's wages, charities, and incidental expenses.[37] The placement of sons in businesses and professions was expensive and was likely to displace the daughter's claim to a proper education or a dowry. Even gainfully employed daughters who lived at home "committed a high proportion of their income to the family economy, underwriting not only their share of the family budget but also the education costs of their brothers."[38] It was also a common practice for families to keep home one daughter to care for a surviving parent in old age. This was accomplished by actively discouraging daughters from marriage and paid employment, through convincing youngest daughters from an early age that they were "too weak and/or infirm to consider marriage," or simply because only one child survived to care for a widowed parent.[39] In Daniel Scott Smith's study of older Americans, he found that eighty percent of such singly surviving children lived with their mothers in 1900.[40]

The girl at home began life "as the primary object of affection to many," and then "came by degrees to be first to none," as the ranks of significant others were depleted with the natural passage of time.[41] Many of these women found their way to Homewood. Mary A. (#3, 1916) was a thirty-seven-year-old whose mother had been an invalid most of her life. As "the oldest girl, [Mary] has been the head of the house, directing all the domestic details, and at the same time devoting herself most assiduously and self-sacrificiously to her mother's care. Her early assumption of domestic responsibilities rendered her a very serious minded and careful girl." Mary had "no close associations at all among men" except her mother's doctors, and later her own. She complained of being "very nervous, very much run down [and] feeling weak." She was sent to hospital to have a "slight nasal operation," but her physician felt that there was "very little the matter with her and so told her. This upset her considerably and she began to lose confidence in him." Her subsequent "persecutory delusions" were in relation to her doctor. Mary was, however, "amenable" and "anxious to recover her health." When she was institutionalized, she deteriorated rapidly. She had to be forced-fed and between periods of improvement, became "restless, emotional and depressed." She was visited by her family twice in three years and was subsequently transferred to the public asylum in Verdun, Quebec.

Mary W. (#525, 1916), aged forty-nine, had acted as housekeeper for her mother in Dartmouth, Nova Scotia. Upon her mother's death, she had lived with her brother and his wife. She admitted "for sometime past her relationships in her brother's home have not been very cordial. She has been easily irritated, without cause, and that this has given rise to much unpleasantness in the home. Her brother eventually found out that the relationships between his wife and the patient were not good and he insisted upon her leaving the home and taking rooms." Mary decided to take up voluntary war work in England, and her brother arranged the passage, but at the last moment she refused to go and since that time had become increasingly seclusive, depressed, and unable to sleep. She came to Homewood reluctantly, but signed a voluntary application, "as she knows that it is her brother's desire that she place herself under sanitarium care." Mary showed improvement at Homewood, but her depression and homesickness worsened with the "inability to get her brother to set any definite date for his coming to take her home." She remained three years, until her brother transferred her to the Quebec asylum.

Social isolation and economic dependency due to life-course transitions were the experiences of many widows as well. In 1911, 8.2 per cent of female Canadians over fifteen years of age were widowed.[42] With a declining birth rate, the likelihood of widows being childless rose, which may have worsened their situation. As Smith concluded, "A simplistic view of the conjugal family system might lead one to think that not marrying was the most obvious decision leading to an isolated old age. A conjugal family system is, after all, based on relationships established by marriage. Marriage did erode ties to kin of orientation, but in 1900 those who did not marry had not erased that linkage ... Childless widows, not spinsters, were the losers in the great gamble, marriage, of a conjugal family system."[43]

One big loser in this gamble was Margaret F. (#163, 1919), a seventy-seven-year-old childless widow. At the time of her husband's death, "considerable money was left to her and she and the stepson have looked after this jointly." Her stepson, who obviously believed the money should have been left to him, described Margaret as having "practically no education" and "no idea of the value of money." The two had a functional relationship, however, until a third party entered: Margaret's nephew. According to the nurse accompanying Margaret, the nephew had been trying to "confiscate" some of her funds, and the stepson ordered that he not be allowed to visit the patient. Margaret exhibited only very mild symptoms of senility, and given her financial resources, she easily could have been provided with home care. Her peremptory commitment to Homewood was probably related to the struggle for money in which she was caught. Safely ensconced in the institution, Margaret could be declared insane by the court on her stepson's initiative, and the family fortune would be protected. With no children or allies to look after her interests, Margaret was institutionalized, never visited, and died six months after commitment.

Social redundancy and the increase in female commitment to asylums was a pattern apparent throughout North America and Great Britain. In Victorian England and Wales, applications to admit women to institutions had consistently outnumbered male applications. In 1871, the census revealed that for every one thousand male lunatics, there were 1,182 females. By 1872, out of a total of 58,640 certified lunatics in England and Wales, 31,822 were women.[44] In her study of first admissions to the York Retreat, Anne Digby determined that between 1796 and 1910, "women usually outnumbered men [and] the difference ... showed a widening, if fluctuating, disparity." By 1910, 61.3 percent of first admissions were female. Digby concluded that "this trend reflected that in other mental institutions during our period ... The growing preponderance of female over male patients [after 1850] may well have been a response to contemporary psychiatry's stress on women's peculiar vulnerability to mental shipwreck." Another revealing York statistic was the marital status of first admissions; overall, single and widowed patients comprised 67.3 percent and of these, "women consistently outnumbered men among the single and the widowed."[45]

Similar findings were uncovered in Nancy Tome's study of the Pennsylvania Hospital for the Insane. "Whereas at the old eighteenth century hospital (c. 1780–1830) men had outnumbered women by 70 to 30 percent, at the new asylum (1841–1883), the sexes were divided more evenly, 55 to 45 percent." The greatest shift was among single female patients who rose in numbers from thirty-one percent prior to 1830 to forty to forty-three percent after 1840.[46]

In Canada, the public system was based upon equal distribution of male and female beds so that sex differentials cannot be accurately determined. At Homewood, however, after an initial period of stagnation prior to 1900, the percentage of female admissions consistently grew, and, in fact, was ultimately responsible for the retreat's success. (See figure 1.) With respect to marital status, of those patients for whom marital status was noted, fifty-three percent of women were single, divorced or widowed, while only forty-five percent of men were unmarried. (See table 11.)

Table 11
Marital Status

Status	Male			Female		
	N^o	%	% excluding unknown	N^o	%	% excluding unknown
Married	127			86		
Married with children[a]	90			141		
Married and pregnant	n/a			6		
Total	217	(38)	(55)	233	(41)	(47)
Single	157			204		
Divorced, separated, deserted	5			8		
Unmarried with child	0			2		
Widowed	14			45		
Total	176	(31)	(45)	259	(46)	(53)
Unknown	174	(31)		75	(13)	
Total	567	(100)	(100)	567	(100)	(100)

[a]Details of family life for many male patients, particularly for alcoholics, were sparse because they were not considered relevant to the patients' condition. Therefore, the number of married men with children was probably underrepresented.

If we dismiss the presumption, popularly believed by centuries of physicians, that women were more 'prone' to insanity, we are left to conclude that they were in fact less powerful and more dispensable in the family economy. Young and Willmott have pinpointed this phenomenon to the nineteenth century; the growth of industrial society removed economic functions from the home without altering the authority of the head of the household. The economic contributions of women no longer matched their dependent status; consequently the family became assymmetrical – with the power, authority and economic resources concentrated in the hands of the master of the house.[47] The exercise of power within the family should be understood "not only as the circumstances in which the will of one person triumphs over that of another, but the circumstances in which the views, interests or wishes of one category or group (men) are normally given precedence, in which case there is no struggle or conflict, but rather superiority is taken for granted."[48] Such superiority would manifest itself in decisions crucial to the household, including the decision to commit.

The future of redundant women in the household, therefore, was dependent upon the good nature of the male head or upon his sense of moral obligation. As discussed above, that moral obligation may have been easily exhausted in the private, individualistic haven of the Victorian and Edwardian home, in which case, the standards for tolerated behaviour correspondingly increased. As the diagnosis of neurasthenia demonstrated, mental symptoms requiring commitment were not only mania, suicidal depression, or violence. Consider the case of Fanny E. (#156, 1919) who lived with her sister's family for only ten days following surgery and was committed for being "hysterical, irritable, ugly" and lacking in "affection" for her relatives. Or Mary H. (#230, 1909), a widow who showed no appreciation for the "lovely home" with which her "kind and considerate" relatives had provided her. "On the contrary, she is always fretting and complaining and worrying about one thing or another, and making herself a constant source of annoyance and uneasiness on the part of her relatives."

In none of these cases is the behaviour of the family portrayed in anything but the best possible light. In the case of Charles and Ida P. (#406, 1890), although both parties displayed neurotic symptoms, only one partner was hospitalized, an outcome demonstrative of the family's power structure. Upon marriage, Charles uprooted Ida from her kin and settled her in a small Nebraska town, and their first year of marriage, Charles insisted, had been "perfectly happy." One month after their first anniversary, Ida gave birth to twins; raising two babies presented a difficult prospect in a pioneer setting. Charles recognized that "the work and care ... of nursing and tending two delicate babes seemed to wear my dear, young wife down much," but he "looked to the future and hoped the little ones would more than repay us." Twenty-two months later, Ida gave birth to another child and was therefore caring for three babies under two years old. During this pregnancy, Ida was "irritable and nervous and worried much over the coming child and the addition to her already numerous and heavy cares." While her husband "was very sorry for her," she "would not believe that and at times talked very spitefully and unjustly to me about the matter." For his part, Charles admitted that he was "of a hasty temper" and "often lost patience with her." Her major, lasting delusion was the fear that she was pregnant for a third time. During this period, Charles threatened suicide several times but was not committed. Ida's final breakdown occurred following an attack of influenza, an extremely debilitating illness at the turn of the century.[49] In the midst of a bitter quarrel, Charles put his revolver to his head and threatened "to put myself beyond the reach of her accusations." Later that day, Ida became hysterical and did not eat or sleep for two days until she was sent back to her family. She was committed to Homewood when her sisters could no longer take the strain of caring for her. The dynamics of this tragic family have fascinating implications. Had the roles been reversed, had

Charles, overburdened with work and physically debilitated, come home to a bad-tempered wife who repeatedly threatened suicide, Ida still would more likely have been the one committed.

It would appear, then, that the realities of the household in late Victorian and Edwardian middle-class society rendered certain elements – socially redundant women in particular – more susceptible to institutionalization than others. The reification of family relations increased the material and emotional costs of maintaining non-productive members who were disruptive to family harmony. Public display, idleness, and sexual promiscuity, behaviours incompatible with middle-class standards of propriety, became symptoms of middle-class illnesses. While violent and destructive actions had customarily been regarded as evidence of insanity, few of the socially redundant patients admitted to Homewood exhibited these symptoms. Rather, they were irritating, obnoxious, and exasperating, and the explosion of medical interest in neuroses, or neurasthenia, facilitated popular acceptance of institutional care for these patients. The evidence would suggest that irritability was a luxury of the powerful in an individualistic age.

Hearth to Homewood: Domestic Life, Mental Breakdown, and Responses to the Institution

As I have outlined in the previous chapter, families had many motivations, based on personal and social realities, prompting them to institutionalize their relatives. This should not, however, cloud the very real evidence of patients with mental illness whom the asylum attempted to cure. Many of these illnesses found their roots in or were exacerbated by conditions in the household. This was recognized by Victorian alienists, who used the term heredity to include the range of inherited, congenital, and environmental causes of insanity. The household continued to influence the asylum's patients, and the asylum itself, beyond the point of the identification of mental illness and the subsequent decision to commit. This chapter, then, investigates family-related causes of mental breakdown and family responses to the institution itself.

Any investigator of the intimate and intricate relations in the historical family is to some degree diving into murky waters, although such inquiry is perhaps less risky when dealing with data of the not-too-distant past. In this investigation of family-related causes of mental breakdown, the stress points of the life-cycle, a useful concept from the field of family psychiatry, are used as a basis for discussion. McCubbin, Cauble, and Patterson have adapted a table of stress points or periods from the work of Erik Erikson and other developmental psychologists. These periods range from the pre-natal stage to extreme old age, and include the 'careers' of the family: establishment of the marriage, birth of the first child, entry of children into school, families with adolescents, the 'launching stages,' the empty nest, and finally retirement.[1]

For inhabitants of the nineteenth century, as well as today, each stage of the life cycle was accompanied by its own stresses and pressures. In many households, however, there were excessive or extraordinary strains – unstable or oppressive familial relationships, broken homes, child abuse, unhappy marriages – which tested and sometimes overwhelmed the emotional and mental stability of individual members. Mental health was also affected by physical or external factors such as puerperal disorders and other illnesses, overwork, and the most significant cause of mental breakdown in this study, grief at the loss of a close family member and household disruption accompanying death. (See table 12.)

Every individual will encounter some of these stress situations in the course of life. Given the higher mortality rates at the turn of the century, our great grandparents would have experienced the most universal of them, death in the family, more frequently than we do. Most people, then as now, would not require psychiatric care as a result of the stress created by a death in the family or by some other strain of family living – yet some would. Because of emotional instability, because of a combination of stress situations, because of illness, some would require institutional care. The individual patient histories of those who came to Homewood for help in recapturing their mental health provide the data for the discussion and conclusions that follow.

That asylum physicians like Alfred Hobbs, although unimpressed by the theories of Sigmund Freud, were aware of the dysfunctional effects child abuse and incest might have upon the young is apparent in the history of fourteen-year-old Ruth H. (#227, 1919). From the age of eight, subsequent to her parents' divorce, Ruth began exhibiting behavioural problems including hysteria, depression, extreme fear, and "exalted ideas." Her family physician reported that, while living with her mother and grandmother, she was forced to sleep alone on the third floor while her mother "carried on down below, stayed out all night with men, etc." The physician added, "also her mother was crazy enough to possibly have taught her to masturbate or something like that by fooling with her. I never could satisfy myself as to that point. It certainly is a very sad case with a bad prognosis I fear."

Incest, the extent of which is only now being estimated with the lifting of the shroud of secrecy around it, in the nineteenth century was associated with overcrowded slum conditions and the 'bestial' nature of working-class inhabitants. Such conditions, which led in Britain to the establishment in 1889 of the National Society for the Prevention of Cruelty to Children, and in Ontario to the passage in 1893 of an Act for the Prevention of Cruelty to, and better Protection of Children, did not lead reformers to pursue the issue of incest in

Table 12
Precipitating Causes or Explanations for Mental Illness Entered in the Files

Causes/Explanation	Female	Male	Causes/Explanation	Female	Male
RELATED TO FAMILY RELATIONSHIPS			**RELATED TO PHYSICAL HEALTH**		
Bereavement	36	12	(excl. venereal diseases)		
Family relations	21	20	Debility following illness		
Deterioration of marriage			(e.g. influenza)	49	24
or divorce	19	15	Senility	14	23
Childbirth	22	n/a	Epilepsy	10	7
Sterility	4	1	Masturbation	1	13
Broken home	3	0	Gynecological disorders	11	n/a
Retirement	0	4	Stroke	5	4
Pregnancy	2	n/a	Cerebral inflammation	0	7
Immorality of patient	1	1	Menstruation	5	n/a
Idleness	1	1	Menopause	5	n/a
Child abuse	1	1	Insomnia	3	0
Excessive sexual demands			Headaches	2	1
by spouse	1	0	Rheumatism	0	2
Sexual dysfunction	1	0	Congenital defect	1	1
Incest	1	0	Goitre	1	0
Syphilis from spouse	1	0	Tumor	1	0
Prenatal trauma	0	1	Sunstroke	0	1
Marriage of child	1	0	Chorea	0	1
Marriage of friend	1	0	Sclerosis	0	1
Total	116	56	Facial rash	0	1
			Total	108	86
RELATED TO EMOTIONAL HEALTH					
Exhaustion from			**RELATED TO VENEREAL DISEASES**		
overwork	42	16	Syphilis	0	32
Stress	26	9	Gonorrhea	0	2
Financial worries	4	18	Alcoholism and Syphilis	0	2
Nervous temperament	12	8	Total	0	36
Loneliness	10	5			
Worry over Great War	11	3	**RELATED TO ADDICTIONS**		
Disappointment over love			Addiction to drugs	21	35
affair	6	2	Iatrogenic addiction	29	23
Trauma	2	3	Recreational addiction	0	3
Shellshock	1	3	Alcoholism	21	159
Religious revival			Total	71	220
excitement	1	2			
Rape	2	0	**SUDDEN ONSET WITH**		
Shock	2	0	**UNKNOWN CAUSE**	6	18
Immigrant dislocation	2	0			
Hypochondriasis	1	0			
Seance excitement	0	1			
Cannot handle prosperity	1	0			
Total	123	70			

Note: The precipitating cause was the event or condition noted by the referring physician, a family member, or the patient him/herself to be most directly responsible for commitment. Other conditions, however, may have been present.

the middle-class home.² Two further examples from the Homewood files, however, demonstrated its presence and the ensuing emotional devastation.

The father of Mary X. (#113, 1914) had been a successful politician for fifteen years. "High strung. Possessed of strong sensual ideas and was a normal [heterosexual] pervert, and when the patient was seventeen years of age he attempted to commit sexual crimes with her." Her mother developed epilepsy at the menopause and "died in convulsions." The mother's marriage had been "forced upon her, and it is expected that the patient was conceived before the marriage. This is only a suspicion." Mary's five brothers were all alcoholics and her sister had been hospitalized for melancholia with "distinctly suicidal tendencies." "The attempt of her father upon [Mary] ... seemed to upset all the family relationship[s] to a marked degree, and [had] always had a marked effect upon the patient."

The story of Agnes P. (#411, 1913), also a victim of incest, provides an example of male physicians not being able to accept or comprehend incestuous or deceitful behaviour among their own kind. Agnes, a physically beautiful woman of thirty-seven, had suffered from neurasthenia, had been treated at Homewood, and then had been sent to recover at her uncle's home in California. She was readmitted within a year and recounted,

The first month out there ... my uncle [a physician, gave me a gynaecological] examination after which I felt so relieved, as it removed the erroneous idea that I had some internal trouble, then he told me to come each month for a while for treatment, a few days before my period ... I hoped never to have to tell anyone else the dreadful truth so locked it in my heart ... My uncle had always made much of me from a child and he now pursued the same way of touching me. Sometimes my ankle or further until I stopped him ... One morning he thrust his hand down the back of my middy waist, in such a horrible way that I felt sick for two days, insulted and depressed. The next time ... I drew back ... He said, "Don't you love me?" ... I then broke down and cried a little. [After being told by another doctor to] unwind to my uncle [Agnes began receiving "treatments" from him, which consisted of stretching] the uterus with three different sized instruments, the last one was large and hurt dreadfully. [After further depression] then went on a treatment of which I will not give details, it was horrible and suitable for one depraved and unrepentant. [Her uncle sent her home after she fixated on the idea that she was to bear an illegitimate child]. After coming home, I told my parents everything. I could see they were very troubled [and told them to write the uncle and confirm this was done "in treatment". The uncle wrote back] repudiating what I had said in every particular. [Agnes, however, insisted that] what I told you about

California was the absolute truth. Dr Barnes said he believed every word my uncle wrote.

In May 1914, she drowned herself. While the therapeutic tools which Barnes and his associates possessed to help Agnes were limited, sadly, so was their professional and male-centred perspective.

The records of other patients, the products of unstable family life, also serve to demonstrate the family's role in mental breakdown, a role uniformly called heredity. The records of 196 patients, or twenty-two percent of the sample, refer to other family members who have exhibited mental disorders or deviant behaviour. For instance, the family of Florence T. (#503, 1913), a neurasthenic, was described as "of a very highly strung, nervous make up." Oliver M. (#914, 1884) had mentally unstable "uncles, aunts and cousins." Lett recollected that a cousin of Oliver at the London Asylum had been "one of the worst patients" there. Helen S. (#477, 1891), a nurse engaged in "literary work, "had been injecting as much as ten grains of morphine daily because of "trouble and unpleasant domestic relations." A "peculiarly nervous and hysterical person," Helen's addiction was evidently inherited. Lett wrote, "two of [her] grandfather's brothers ... died of D.Ts. Her grandfather drank as a young man but gave it up and took to smoking heavily consuming 30-40 cigars a day. One of her paternal uncles drinks heavily and has done so all his life. Her father a drinker all his life, her brothers both drink heavily. Her sister ... is the only one of the family not addicted to some such habit. My patient says she never cared for alcohol, and though wine was in constant use in the house, she never had any desire for it. But morphine from the first took strong hold upon her."

Another common family-related cause of mental breakdown was an unhappy marriage. Marriage in late Victorian and Edwardian society has been described by Eli Zaretsky as in a state of crisis. The removal of many of the economic bases for the family as well as the concomitant rise in expectations for marriage based upon "love ... mutual affection and respect, trust, fidelity [and] pre-marital chastity" meant that at least one partner in many marriages was doomed to disappointment, particularly in a society with such separate spheres and expectations for men and women.[3] Given the limited opportunities women had for self-expression outside the household, they were likely to suffer from this disappointment.

At the same time that young women were beginning to believe in romance as the basis for marriage, a belief stoked by the domestic novels they read so assiduously, the emphasis upon the individual, an essential feature of a maturing industrial economy, made them less tolerant of parental direction in mate selection. Women were "demanding more from marriage ... resisting forced sexual relations and seeking closer personal bonds with husbands."[4] An unhappy marriage was no longer popularly considered a "spiritual opportunity," but a cage.[5] However, there were few options, short of desertion, for escaping such marriages. Furthermore, the continuing decline in adult mortality rates meant that the expected length of marriage had increased by century's end. Changes in attitudes and in the divorce laws after the turn of the century finally made it possible to end an unhappy marriage; it has been estimated that by 1924 one in seven marriages ended in divorce.[6]

High marital expectations and disappointing realities were recounted by many Homewood patients. Lucy T. (#507, 1917), for example, stated that her "husband is a fiend incarnate – that he is a Dr Jekyll and Mr Hyde and has always abused her sexually, and every other way from the time of her honeymoon." Martha S. (#458, 1902) was diagnosed as a neurasthenic, a condition brought about from "grieving over domestic infelicity." She "does not want to live with [her] husband" and had tried to commit suicide. Amitta M. (#353, 1917) "became melancholic and low spirited" following the discovery of her daughter's secret marriage and pregnancy. Amitta's own marriage "had not been happy. Evidently incompatibility of temperament – Had the children and had to take care of them. Husband a good worker, not alcoholic, but patient found she did not like him as well as she thought she did."

To many Victorian and Edwardian women, as the English feminist Henrietta Muller observed, "sexual intercourse [was] an unpleasant and fatiguing obligation."[7] Ending excessive childbearing was the goal for many feminists and birth control advocates who sought to improve the quality of life for women like Elizabeth M. (#320, 1913), a sixty-two-year-old farmer's wife. Elizabeth had undergone thirteen pregnancies and raised eleven children to adulthood with great affection, despite the fact that her husband was a "niggardly" man and "hard" on the family. This was a "cause of discouragement" to the patient. Though "fond of company," Elizabeth never travelled nor visited much, and, after forty years of this life, she became "weak," "pale," "run down," and severely depressed.

At thirty-one years old, Nellie B. (#44, 1920) had four living children under nine years and had lost a three-year-old child. While her domestic relations were described as "fairly happy," she had been "under considerable stress in the raising of a large family, the husband's sexual demands being considered as extreme." "She has been gradually depreciating for some little time, keeping very late hours working for the children, and their care in the day time has lately made her irritable. This has made the children fretful and a vicious circle has been established." Her physician added, "In my opinion her family life has been the main cause of her breakdown. Her husband thinks he is kind to her, but his kindness is the wrong type." When her husband came for her after five months of treatment, she "absolutely refused" to board the train with him, and subsequently was transferred to a public asylum.

The physical costs of child-rearing were exacerbated at the turn of the century by the increased demands upon the middle-class mother to play a primary, if not a sole role, in the socialization and education of the child.[8] Childcare manuals warned of the dangers of leaving such crucial tasks in the hands of servants or to chance. Toronto psychologist William Blatz asserted that while "it formerly was believed that mother instinct or mother love was the simple and the safe basis from the problems of training, it is now known that a much more reliable guide is the kitchen timepiece."[9] That timepiece might be one of the housewife's few helpers, as the shrinking of the household and increased geographical mobility reduced the access to a larger support network of kin and friends who could share the work. As for domestic tasks, it may be argued that such inventions as gas and electricity, refrigeration, washing machines, and indoor plumbing, which lessened the load of domestic housework, were as welcome to women as were the improvements in health care associated with reproduction. While, clearly, developments in technology may have made household tasks easier, it is also arguable, as Ruth Schwartz Cowan has demonstrated, that these devices raised expectations for cleanliness, food preparation, and menu variety.[10] Indeed, the precipitating factor in the mental breakdown of some of the women who came to Homewood was the arrival of visitors, whose presence increased the amount of domestic toil to an unendurable level.

The cases below detail a pattern of stress building up under the burden of childbearing and rearing. Jessie W. (#532, 1917) had three children under ten years. Her husband stated "that she never seemed to have any satisfaction in intercourse, but she did not object. For a year they have avoided relations because it seemed to affect her nervous condition." Rosalie R. (#413, 1916) had her adenoids removed in the same week her three children also had that operation, and she tended them while she recovered. She broke down from the combined stress of being an "active" and "ambitious" professional nurse and housewife. Lucy N. (#380, 1918) had three children under seven years. She "nursed the baby until about a month ago, when she gave up, finding that it was overtaxing her strength to a very great degree." She became nervous, ill, and tired, finding "the care of the children a considerable burden, and [herself] inadequate to the task of caring for them." Her family visited often and arranged for Harvey Clare, in his capacity as government inspector, to investigate her case, but Lucy's hyperactivity and restlessness heightened to the point where she could be controlled only if kept in a dry pack in the continuous bath for six hours a day.

Men also, of course, experienced the stresses of overwork, particularly those related to providing an adequate living for the family. For the middle class at the turn of the century, the growth of the consumer society raised aspirations for affluence. The economy offered the housewife "little in the way of jobs, yet it provided seemingly unlimited possibilities for consumerism." Such material desires could create great strain in a marriage. Elaine Tyler May's study showed that there were a growing number of women in the United States who filed for divorce on the grounds of lack of material comforts. In more than one instance, the divorce proceedings also indicated that a man's ability to provide for his wife's desires was equated by his spouse with his manhood.[11] Given the anxiety created by low job satisfaction and increased competition, divorce may not have been the only outcome for such casualties of the consumer economy.

Robert D. (#694, 1913), a fifty-six-year-old farmer, was "honest, sober-minded," and supported a family of six children. He took on extra construction work, and was responsible for a work crew about whom "he worried a great deal, lest an accident should result from their carelessness. Patient had to do his own work at home, before going to this work at seven o'clock in the morning. After going home at night, he had to do his own chores. The work was very hard on him, and he soon became nervous. He complained of weakness and loss of appetite, and began to sleep poorly." Albert D. (#697, 1920) "had always farmed and done considerable buying and selling of stock and was always inclined to worry, especially if he thought he was losing. He always worked very hard, and was always in a bustle and very busy." James F. (#749, 1914), an ex-clergyman, "left Church duties five years ago and went into the Real Estate business in Winnipeg. Things went well up to two years ago, when hard times came in and he found it hard to realize on his various properties. He had taken a very active part in the Provincial and Municipal Elections in Manitoba during the past year and it has been too much for him. Since the breaking out of the war his business has come to a standstill, and he is afraid that he will lose everything that he has. Began at this time to lose sleep, and his worries were added to by the insistence of his son, eighteen years old, who wants to enlist and go to the front."

The single most statistically significant factor in family life responsible for mental breakdown, however, was not financial worry but the extended illness or the death of a close family member. When this loss was not anticipated and could not be prepared for, the grief and dislocation attendant upon it might be emotionally devastating.[12] John D. (#704, 1919), born in Elora, Ontario, practised medicine in Montana. He was an alcoholic, and took various drugs to sober himself up until he became a bromide addict as well. He had begun drinking to excess when "his little girl aged four years died of acute intestinal toxemia. This greatly upset him, and caused him considerable worry." Mae B. (#33, 1913), aged forty-two, had been "apparently in good health until her husband died a year ago last July. Married at the age of 21 – never had any children. The husband and wife were very much attached to one another. She always received the utmost care and every want was supplied ... The shock of the husband's death was severe," and she experienced choking sensations and a "sense of depression and weight" in her stomach. Similarly, Margaret B. (#59, 1919) had been "quite healthy all her life" until her eldest son was killed in France in 1916; she subsequently experienced dizziness and severe headaches. Emily C. (#94, 1915) was unable to cope with her husband's lengthy final illness. With each attack of "hemorrhage" he suffered, she became "very nervous and suffered from diarrhoea." (See appendix 2.)

As in Emily's case, nursing a family member through the final illness was doubly draining emotionally. Dying at home was usually the only option at the turn of the century, and it was not without physical and emotional costs to family members. Nursing was primarily the realm of the woman, and many women (and some men) broke down under the strain of constant nursing and lack of sleep. James M. (#926, 1892) began using laudanum to help him sleep following the "double calamity" of nursing his wife and his sister through their final illnesses. Francis P. (#407, 1915) nursed her father during his last illness; "lost a good deal of sleep [and] was exceedingly anxious in regard to him. She was hyperactive – hurrying through all [the] work she had to do and not doing it with the same care as was her habit. Sleep was practically nil." Agnes K. (#257, 1916) developed severe depression following her son's maniacal episode, which lasted five days, and during which she did not sleep.

A declining adult mortality rate increased the prospect that at least one spouse would reach the empty nest stage, a stage difficult for women who lost their household functions and nurturing roles as well as companionship. For instance, Matilda R. (#440, 1916) was a widow with two sons. Her younger son had married,

and the patient immediately became filled with the idea that the young couple were inexperienced, that they would not be able to get along on his bank salary, and she took them into her home, rather than permit them to live in an apartment which had been planned. [She subsequently grew] quite depressed, sleepless [and fearful something was] going to happen to her boy. [She was committed by her children and remained convinced] that her boy at home is not well ... and this in spite of the fact that she has a letter from him telling her that he is very happy with his wife and that she need have no cause for anxiety.

After seven months of treatment, which consisted primarily of inducing her to eat, she was moved to a public asylum.

The family, as discussed above, had a great deal of control over the hospital system. It identified and labelled mental illness; accepted, with the advice of a physician, the institutional alternative; and maintained both direct and indirect influence over treatment, accommodation, and length of commitment.[13] In a private asylum such as Homewood, financial considerations rendered the family's input crucial. If the family wanted short or lengthy periods of care, if they wanted a particular treatment, their wishes usually prevailed.

Hospitalization for milder forms of mental disorder, and of more affluent members of society, only became a viable alternative with the popular acceptance of the disease model of insanity from the 1840s onward.[14] In a discussion of contemporary treatment of schizophrenia, Anderson and Reiss concluded that labelling the patient as someone with a serious illness can be advantageous, since such a perspective will enable the family "to continue to support the patient during those times when he is unable to function at full capacity. Furthermore, labelling the patient as having an illness decreases the tendency to assign negative and emotional meanings to symptoms. If the family can believe that the patient is neither malingering nor attempting to communicate a malicious message, there is decreased anger at the patient and the treatment team."[15]

The negative aspect of this process is that once the identification of serious illness is made, treatment may be forcibly administered as it would in the case of life-threatening physical illnesses. In 1891, Richard Dewey, an American psychiatrist, cogently concluded that the "only persons generally known to have gone voluntarily to any insane asylum are perhaps the reporters ... [who sham] insanity, for the sake of informing the public what was going on 'behind the bars.'"[16] This statement was made in spite of the boom in private asylums, obstensibly geared towards the voluntary patient, which took place in the last two decades of the nineteenth century. It therefore was apparent that even the 'voluntary' patient probably was hospitalized without his or her complete consent.

Committing family members regularly used deception. Dr Charles Buchanon, superintendent of the Potomac Asylum, Washington, considered the problem "Should the insane be deceived?" in 1892. He recounted the tale of another superintendent who "bluntly resented" the use of deceit, stating that he would not have the "love and confidence" of patients admitted in this way. But, Buchanon responded, what lunatic voluntarily would go to a place which would signify for him "a living death?" Buchanon actually stated that the only alternatives available were "force or deceit," deceit being the "lesser of two evils."[17] Homewood patients were deceived with predictably negative results. For example, John C. (admitted 11 January 1889) "was very much excited when he found out that his friends had deceived him and brought him here under false pretenses. [He] demanded his liberty and it was found necessary to put him in the back ward [for refractory patients]." Cora F. (#168, 1916) "was brought away from home under misapprehension, being told that she was going on a trip with her husband, but on arriving in Guelph he told her that he was taking her to a YMCA. She came noisily into the institution, entered the office asking everyone if this was the YMCA. When told it was not she began to be emotional, told her husband that he was deceiving her," and refused to trust the admitting physician.

Once the individual had become an inpatient, the family's role altered. In many instances, the family relinquished all further responsibility for the patient's care. As the psychiatrist Henry Harbin has noted, the decision to commit "galvanizes the family or support system into action because no one can deny the seriousness of the issue any longer." But once "the family brings the patient to the hospital, they often feel a reduction of anxiety; sometimes this decreases their motivation to change" or even their desire to have any contact with the patient in the future.[18] Thomas Krajewski and Harbin have outlined three standard types of family reactions to institutionalization, all of which are represented in case histories at Homewood: the uninvolved, over-involved, and pseudo-involved families.[19]

The uninvolved family preferred to distance itself as much as possible from the patient. The family, having made the decision that they wanted the patient out of their lives, "are usually comfortable with a custodial approach" to treatment. When the patient improved to the point that discharge was being considered, "this type of family becomes quite fearful that the patient will again be forced upon them," and they will attempt "to manipulate the various hospital hierarchical levels in order to have the patient remain at the hospital."[20] Elizabeth O'H. (#393, 1892), a member of an uninvolved family, had the dubious distinction of having been evicted from Brigham Hall Asylum, New York, after thirty years. Her family physician wrote, "[Superintendent] Burrill's course ... has been so extraordinary and he appears to be actuated by so much feeling that I am almost prepared to hear of his doing anything." After "suddenly" demanding Elizabeth's removal, Burrill was offered more money by the family. He never replied. A date was set for her departure, but when the physician who was to take her away was delayed, Burrill threatened that if "she were not removed by that date he would send her to Toronto under the custody of an officer and leave her at [the physician's] house. It was at this point that I saw Mr Langmuir." It was apparently Elizabeth's "excessive devotion" to Burrill that precipitated her removal. The consternation with which her family faced the prospect of her homecoming after thirty years and under such circumstances is probably hard to overestimate.

The overinvolved family, on the other hand, is usually "too close to the patient and [has] a difficult time disengaging" from their control over the patient's life. The family may try to "control the staff" and demand special privileges for the patient.[21] The wife and daughter of Alex C. (#639, 1915) visited "nearly every day." Winnifred A. (#12, 1913) was visited often by her family. Although her behaviour was becoming more uncontrolled, she was discharged on probation at the request of her mother, who wished to "try her at home for a time." An extreme example of overinvolvement was the family of Mabel H. (#229, 1917), who took "advantage of the near situation and are with her almost all the time. They also, especially the sisters, are extremely [difficult], criticizing and [refusing to be satisfied]. In fact, they are altogether unreasonable. Patient says she was in the hospital at Hamilton two years ago for one week. It is probable that the one week duration was due to this same condition." Homewood discharged her two weeks later.

Family involvement also might represent judicious concern as in the case of Edwin H. (#807, 1915). He was a very "tidy, neat and orderly" patient, who led a very "easy and methodical life" at the asylum. When his wife visited, she stayed "all week [taking him for] daily walks [and being] very well satisfied with his improvement." Involvement might have allayed the family's guilt and anxiety over the decision to commit, as in the case of Sarah B. (#45, 1886). Following her admission for "hysterical mania" and "nervous irritability lasting several days," her mother wrote,

I cannot leave without a line to say that my dear child's characteristics [are] of a loving domestic character. [Sarah is] fond of all her family surroundings and housekeeping and of her relatives. These occupy her mind and when not herself is led but requires leading. She will ... submit to all that is kindly offered. Naturally of a very nice delicate ladylike disposition ... she will feel deeply any kindness you can bestow when ill as well as when better. If you will [act] motherly [and] friendly [to her], her mother will be very grateful. It is very trying to me to part with her but trusting her characteristics will be studied ... I go home with confidence in your kindly care ... Please think of her specially tonight ... She is soothed by singing when dejected.

As Krajewski and Harbin asserted, overinvolvement may also entail demanding certain treatment or even diagnosis. The sister of Bella C. (admitted 28 January 1891) was "anxious that [Lett] should make a positive diagnosis as to ovarian trouble which she believes is the cause of insanity." This diagnosis would, for the sister, have fewer negative connotations than admitting the possibility of a hereditary form of insanity.

The most difficult family type for the asylum to deal with was the pseudo-involved. This type "maintains the myth of a close, caring and supportive family but this is primarily a group defense mechanism that masks their ambivalence about themselves and having the patient home again." They are "at first described as very concerned family members. What ultimately happens is that when the family realizes that they must reintegrate the patient, they become resistant ... The basic theme behind this family is that they want to look like they are strong and competent but are actually unable to provide a supportive setting and do not want demands placed on them."[22] Henry A. (admitted 31 July 1888) had a daughter who visited frequently and showed great concern for his condition. When his wife, however, intended to visit and "possibly to remove him," their daughter told Lett in advance that as signee for his reception, she did not want Henry discharged. A month later, the daughter again asserted that Mrs A. was not to take the patient home without her consent: "she having her father's welfare at heart." Henry was visited frequently by his family, but there was no record of his discharge.

As in Henry's case, family wishes were extremely important in the decision to discharge. James Greenley, in his study of a New England state psychiatric hospital, found that family desires were the crucial factor in determining when and if a patient left the hospital, more important than either the danger the patient might pose for others or professional judgment.[23] He posited several possible explanations for the family's influence on the psychiatrist's decision. First, the patient could more successfully be placed in the home if the family approved and thus would be "supportive" rather than undermining. Second, many psychiatrists, dealing with heavy workloads and hoping to lessen the "nuisance factor" might follow the wishes of the family and discharge the patient "Against Medical Advice." Conversely they might hold the patient for "non-family placement." The family factor was clear: "of those families who wanted the patient out, for instance, eighty-seven percent have visited their relatives six or more times by this time." Those families the staff needed to contact themselves were not likely to favour release.[24] This pattern prevailed at Homewood. The wishes of the family – not the diagnoses, nor the success or failure of drugs, baths, or rest cure – were primarily responsible for discharge. (See tables 13 and 14.)

Mabel W. (#534, 1919), for example, was "taken home today by her mother and her aunt, and this against the advice of the physicians. She is a potential suicide and they were so warned. It is thought that this patient is taken home as a result of a mis-statement of facts made possibly by a former patient ... It is very much regretted that her friends would not listen to the advice of the physicians." (See tables 15 and 16.) A family might decide to request a patient be prematurely discharged for a variety of reasons, including a change in family situation, finances, or the need for the patient's labour. Henry P. (#979, 1888), who escaped twice and was returned by his family, was finally sent home "due to the death of his father-in-law." Margaret A. (#20, 1883), a violent and destructive girl, was transferred to Hamilton as her family "cannot continue the expense." Alfred M. (#949, 1890) was also taken home to "try" in order to reduce costs.

A patient might also succeed in initiating his or her discharge. Emeline A. (#14, 1897), a housewife, was "doing nicely." A month after admission, her "husband visited her today and completely upset her. [He] couldn't get away from her without a scene so he took her home." Edith C. (#87, 1918), forty-five years, was described as a "very temperamental" social "butterfly," who had been raised in a

Table 13
Relation between Behaviour Precipitating Admission and Length of Stay

Behaviour Precipitating Admission	Months of Stay								
	Less than 1 mo.	1–2 mos	3–5 mos	6–8 mos	9–11 mos	12–17 mos	18–24 mos	24+ mos	Unknown
FEMALE									
Violence	4	10	6	5	4		1	4	2
Delusions	7	24	32	10	4	4	1	5	4
Depression	13	29	39	13	5	7	1	2	2
Addiction	11	21	26	1	3	1			9
Dementia	5	4	6	1	2		1	2	
Agitation	13	26	23	10	6	3	2	1	
Unmanageable	4	11	15	1	4	4		2	1
Destructiveness	2		1		1				
Hysteria	2	6	4	3				2	
Epilepsy			1		2				1
Stopped work	1	1	2					1	
Physical illness		4	6	4					2
Manic-depression	1		3			1			
Not given	14	16	14	4	1	4	1	4	1
MALE									
Violence	2	6	8	5		1	1		
Delusions	15	18	20	2	4	1	1	9	6
Depression	16	24	20	5	1	1		2	2
Addiction	52	67	58	19	11	6		2	2
Dementia	4	10	9	3	4	2	1	5	
Agitation	10	16	8	2	1	1		1	1
Unmanageable	2	2	6	3				2	2
Destructiveness	1								
Hysteria	2	6						1	
Epilepsy	3	1	2						
Stopped work	3	1	2						
Physical illness	3	7	1	2		2		1	1
Manic-depression	1	2							
Not given	8	17	8	3	2	2			3

"very luxurious" style until her father lost a great deal of money. She had been married, unhappily, to an alcoholic until they separated five years prior to commitment, and she had recently renewed an attachment with a childhood friend who was married to an invalid. Depressed over this situation and over business worries, Edith swallowed poison and was placed under nursing care. At Homewood, her suicidal tendencies necessitated her residence in a closed ward. She consequently wrote "very long and worrying letters to various members of her family, complaining of her surroundings, her treat-

Table 14
Relation between Number of Visits to Patients and Length of Stay

| | Months of stay | | | | | | | |
| | Less than 1 month | 1–2 mos | 3–5 mos | 6–8 mos | 9–11 mos | 12–17 mos | 18–24 mos | 24+ mos |
Visits								
FEMALE								
0	35	50	54	14	9	3	1	2
1	13	26	16	7	6	2		2
2		8	11	5	1			3
3		6	10			2		1
4		4	3	5	3	3		5
5+	2	5	5	1		5	2	5
MALE								
0	43	72	46	10	7	2	2	7
1	12	16	15	7	2	2		2
2	3	6	7	3		2		1
3	4	4	6	2	3	2		1
4	2	3	5	1	2	1	1	4
5+	1	5	3	1		3		4

ment, her lack of exercise, the character of the patients with whom she associates, etc. By every possible means in her power she endeavors to convince her relatives that she is perfectly well ... and that they must come for her immediately." Dr Barnes took pains to add to her file that "many of the statements in her letters are not strictly in accord with facts." The complaints succeeded, however, in securing her release.

A contributing factor in premature discharge, and what could be considered the reverse of social redundancy, was the importance of the patient to the household. As Barrett, Juriansky, and Gurland have documented in their study of emergency discharge from a state psychiatric hospital, "a patient was more likely to remain out of the hospital if he was actively involved with the family to whom he was discharged." "If the patient 'always' contributed to the family he remained out of the hospital, whereas if he 'never' did he was more likely to return. If a patient helped with household chores, helped with child care, or helped support the family financially, he was more likely to remain out of the hospital."[25] This description naturally fits the housewife, and, at Homewood, a housewife, particularly with young children, was an excellent candidate for premature discharge, regardless of its effect on the patient's health. Nellie L. (#282, 1918) had five children ranging in ages from nine months to nine years. She was a manic, delusional patient who had to be force-fed, but

Table 15
Types of Discharge

	Female	Male
Improved	104	130
Recovered	99	109
"Discharged"	91	115
At kin's initiative	113	71
Transferred	63	38
Died	35	38
Unimproved[a]	34	20
Escaped	3	28
Not given	25	18
Total	567	567

[a]Unimproved may also represent some patients who left at kin's initiative.

her husband would not let her remain longer than one week: "It is absolutely impossible to advise him as to the care that his wife should receive."

The family's input to institutional care did not end with discharge. Mental illness, in one respect, is a terminal disease; once the diagnosis of insanity is made, notwithstanding later pronouncement of full recovery, the individual will always be in a "post-patient phase" to his family and the community.[26] This is apparent in the ease and rapidity with which a family would decide to re-commit a former patient, and in the frequency with which prior commitment was seen as justification for future commitment and even, in itself, as part of the diagnosis of insanity.[27] Prior commitment was a powerful weapon in the hands of the family. When used to "coax the patient" into acting normal, the threat to re-commit enabled the family to relinquish its responsibility for any relapse and subsequent rehospitalization.[28]

William B. (#598, 1884) was taken home on his uncle's recognizance with the assurance that "if ever again unsteady, he shall agree to return." Simeon X. (#829, 1907), a member of a leading Toronto family, signed a detailed contract as a precondition to his probation:

1. To entirely abstain from taking any alcoholic beverage.
2. To refrain from visiting church or any club, hotel, saloon, restaurant, tea-room or theatre.
3. To dismiss no servants.
4. To undertake no business transactions, and to sign no cheques or documents.

Table 16
Stated Explanations for Removal of Patients by
Kin prior to Recovery

	Male	Female	Total
"Try at home" or with private nurse	14	13	27
Housewife duties		24	24
Financial exigencies	4	17	21
Worried about patient's welfare	7	10	17
Taken home with threat to readmit	10	5	15
"Against Doctor's Advice"	9	6	15
Family saw improvement	3	11	14
Patient's pleading	2	7	9
Husband's duties or loss of income	7		7
Family occasion	1	2	3
"Try at home" prior to public asylum	1	2	3
Parental or kin initiative: no explanation noted	11	18	29
Total	69	115	184

5. To remain at the residence every morning until 9 am and after 5 pm every evening.
6. To co-operate cheerfully in all matters with the direction of my daughter, who will assume the whole responsibility of my probational residence at home.
7. In the event of the necessary absence of my daughter from home, then I will cordially comply with the guidance and directions of her aunt in all the foregoing particulars.

Simeon's large estate holdings and lofty social position were over-shadowed by his identity as former psychiatric patient; he was reduced to accepting the complete authority of his daughter and sister-in-law in rather farcical circumstances. One can imagine, for example, Simeon skulking past the parlor towards the front door, only to be met by a lady waving a contract under his nose in righteous indignation.

Nineteenth-century alienists recognized the influence family life had upon mental and physical health and termed it heredity. Removal of patients from their homes had been, after all, the rationale for institutionally based moral treatment. As a somaticist, Hobbs was particularly responsive to the physical stresses of family life, such as excessive childbearing and overwork, which could produce mental breakdown. Both he and Lett were sensitive to the psychological ramifications of unhappy marriages, incest, and child abuse, although these factors would have far more importance in the Freudian era. Although it was not especially cited by either physician, grief, and its attendant dislocation, were statistically the most significant family-related causes of mental breakdown. In many instances, the tragedy of personal loss must have been compounded by the tragedy of institutionalization. Yet commitment was not necessarily a one-way trip. Patients were removed from the asylum because of financial exigencies, housekeeping duties, family emergencies, or simply the loneliness of family members. In this respect, the walls of the asylum were far more fluid than the image of a total institution would allow.[29]

CHAPTER SEVEN

Daily Life at Homewood: The Sub-Culture of Work

Whatever the therapeutics favoured by Lett and Hobbs, sanctioned by the board, or approved of by patients and their families, it was the poorly paid, overworked nurses and attendants who carried out the physicians' directives with, often enough, it is likely, scant regard for the rationale behind the treatments or the motivations of the families. While the patients of the Homewood Retreat were drawn primarily from the same class as the directors and physicians, the nurses and attendants were "drawn almost exclusively from a social class – and often from ethnic and religious groups – widely different from those of trustees and medical staff." However, it was these nurses and attendants who "helped to shape a hospital sub-culture in many ways sufficient unto itself and not easily amenable to control by formally constituted authority."[1] The daily realities of asylum life had more to do with social identification than social class.

This is not to say that great transformations in asylum staffing did not take place at the turn of the century. The evolution of the nursing profession as a whole was reflected in the asylum in the upgrading of educational requirements, the feminization of attending staff, and the improvement in standards of personal conduct and professional demeanour. Poor working conditions and the isolation of asylum life, however, rendered psychiatric nursing a stepchild of the profession during this period. The association in the public mind of male attendants with brutality and anachronistic therapeutics prevented these asylum workers from a thoroughgoing participation in professional reform; indeed, reform was perceived in part to be a reduction in male staff. Given the asylum's casually selected, ill-paid, and stress-ridden workforce, the therapeutic successes which occurred at Homewood were truly remarkable.

The supreme figure of the asylum family was the medical superintendent. How did he feel about his pre-eminent role? Charles
Nichols of the Government Hospital of Washington, D.C., compared
managing an asylum to "living over a volcano all the time ... [I] cannot
command the security necessary either to happiness or the highest
usefulness."[2] The work was dangerous, as the superintendents were
frequently reminded in their publication, the *American Journal of
Insanity*, which diligently reported "the martyrology of psychiatry":
those too frequent injuries or deaths at the hands of patients. It also
recorded calamities of a different nature that befell superintendents
– apoplexy, burns, and suicide. The most tragic incident in Victorian
Canada was the fatal knifing in 1885 of William George Metcalfe,
superintendent of Rockwood Asylum, by a patient whom the doctor
had always treated "with all possible kindness."[3]

The superintendents rarely found satisfaction in their relationships with their colleagues in other areas of the medical profession.
In the Canadian *Medical Record* of 1897, J.V. Anglin directed his
comments to those physicians ignorant of the realities of asylum care.
"It will be a pleasure," he wrote, "to disabuse your minds of mis-
conceptions, to raise the cloud of calumny from the sick in mind,
for certainly those can have no idea of how interesting and satisfactory the work is, who have told me with a suggestive gesture, that
they would not take charge of the insane for anything, as if it were
similar to caring for some wild beast instead of our own flesh and
blood."[4]

Reflecting upon his tenure at Homewood, Harvey Clare wryly
admitted, "I came to Homewood five years ago, quite convinced that
five years, if it did not kill me, it would pretty near satisfy me. Now
I have signed a contract to remain longer ... Sometimes I may con-
fess, the load is a little more than I would like to carry. Superintendents of Homewood before now have broken down in a nervous
or mental way, and I have no thought of staying until I break ...
Last week I spoke to a man who had been superintendent of a public
hospital for fifty years, and he said, 'It must be nice to have a small
compact private hospital.' He did not realize any more than I did,
that the friends of every patient demand full value for every dollar
they pay."[5]

Clare, like Drs Farrar, Hobbs and Lett before him, was buttressed
by a staff that alternatively could put the institution on the map or
its superintendent into an early grave. In 1913, Homewood's staff
consisted of the superintendent, assistant superintendent, two physicians, and a third-year intern. There were on staff twenty-six
nurses, six of whom were on night duty, and twenty-four attendants

"of whom six take night duty." Also employed were a matron, four office staff, a gardener, arts teacher, two stablemen, a painter, three engineers, and a fireman, twenty-five kitchen employees, three groundsmen, and a chauffeur – a total of ninety-seven persons in all.[6]

Given the formidable size of this support staff over and above 123 patients, it is interesting to note that when J.W. Langmuir, chairman of the board of directors, suggested the delegation of some of the superintendent's functions, Hobbs strenuously objected. "My position as Superintendent of The Homewood," he argued, "is a peculiar and unusual one, and cannot be compared with any other position in any institution in Canada. Of necessity I am as follows: Medical Superintendent; Chief Physician; Bursar; Treasurer; Steward. The admission of a patient comes through my hand. The medical care and supervision finally rests with myself and my judgment ... I am responsible for the financing of the institution, as this cannot very well be dissociated from my position, and I have also to keep an eye on all inside and outside work ... There is practically no way of dissociating any of these departments from my position, otherwise the institution will suffer material loss."[7] Hobbs jealously guarded the powers of his office, even at the cost of "overwork, ill-health and political harassment."[8] The full extent of his authority, however, and that of Stephen Lett, was often more apparent than real, dependent as it was upon the quality and co-operation of the staff they directed.

Nowhere was the transformation from Victorian to modern asylum more evident than in the qualities and experiences of the women hired for the position of matron. The first matron, Amy Murray, was engaged in 1885. She proved herself "efficient, untiring and zealous in the performance of her work," but she did not remain long in the job, for which she was paid $250 yearly in 1886.[9] Mrs Murray was replaced by Alice Finch, a most colourful matron. A physician's widow, Mrs Finch was an intelligent and capable matron. She also liked men, particularly men among the patient population. That Mrs Finch's extramural activities appeared to have escaped Lett's attention for quite some time places doubt upon his real abilities to administer as well as treat. When he finally woke up to his matron's duplicity, his reaction was anything but decisive. Indeed, Mrs Finch's long tenure at Homewood revealed much about Lett's inadequacy as superintendent. He surely should have seen the handwriting on the wall, or at least in his own journal, which read:

29 JUNE 1888 Mrs Finch took A. and W. in buggy to races.

2 JULY 1888 Mrs Finch gone to Berlin for day with A.
13 JULY 1888 W., A. and F. gone to concert with matron.
20 JULY 1888 Mrs Finch with W. to band concert.
1 AUGUST 1888 Mrs Finch with W. to theatre.

Apparently Mrs Finch enjoyed a fuller social life than the superintendent. That Lett had lost control of his matron was clear in the extraordinary entries in his journal between November 1888 and February 1889, which were written in a variation of the morse code.[10] Both in the content and the format of the entries, Lett made apparent his inability to properly supervise his matron and possibly an element of paranoia in his own personality. The entries read:

28 NOVEMBER 1888 – Re Mrs Finch: I learned today that when she was downtown yesterday with three of the gentlemen, she sent one of them into William's store for a bottle of whisky ... The whisky was refused on the ground that they were not allowed to sell it. I was also informed that twice last summer she had obtained it in [?]. I had sent her for it for use in the house.

Mrs Finch apparently did not stop at supplying alcohol to the patients.

1 DECEMBER 1888 – Re Morphia: Upon going to my stock of morphia today I was surprised to find the tin half empty. I purchased it full only a short time ago ... It is therefore certain that someone has taken it and as I have always been careful to keep the surgery locked and permit no one to have my keys, someone must have a key to [it].

3 DECEMBER 1888 – Re Surgery: Someone was in the surgery during the time Mrs L. and myself were in town this morning. The mark I had made was disturbed. This settles the fact of someone having a key during the time Mrs Lett and I were out at Mr Powells. This evening someone went to the stamp drawer in my desk and disturbed a key there which unlocks the surgery [which apparently had not been secure].

12 DECEMBER 1888 – Re Mrs Finch: [Director] Hedley informs me that when she was in Toronto she wrote to Edgar asking him to lend her [?] dollars. He took the letter to Langmuir who was much annoyed and asked Hedley to get an [affadavit?] of it. I gave him my theory why she did such a foolish thing. [Unfortunately Lett does not elaborate upon his theory].

15 DECEMBER 1888 – Re Mrs Finch: [Nurse] Ross asked me if I had sent her a white powder on Wednesday week last which was to be taken in milk and made her feel very sleepy. That Mrs Finch had given it to her saying I had ordered it. From what Ross says there is no doubt it was

morphia ... Ross says that F. wants to get rid of [Nurse] Lydia because the latter knows too much about her [In November, Mrs Finch had complained that Lydia was "overbearing and inclined to insolence" and she and Lett came to the conclusion that Lydia should be replaced].

Mrs Finch is wearing a fob chain which she says [Attendant] Max gave her. I know she is aware that he is taking cocaine. Can it be possible that she is treating Max? If so it would account for the loss of morphia in my surgery.

16 DECEMBER 1888 – Re Mrs Finch: Lydia tells me that Mrs F. seldom goes into the wards except when she goes round with me in the morning and when going round with the night nurse and that she does not know when she went into the patients' rooms last to inspect.

Mrs Butt [?] here today. She would make a good housekeeper having had good experience in England and would probably do for Matron.

Yet Lett did not discharge Mrs Finch. On 28 January 1889 he gave her a "positive order that I would not permit her to have men in her room that if she continued to do so she might take it as a notice to leave." Even this proscription was lifted less than a month later to give her "special leave ... to have three of the Gents in her room for a game of cards."[11] Matters came to a head when Marion Freeman, a nurse whom Lett had fired, showed him the "testimonial she had received from Mrs Finch." It showed satisfaction with her work and said she was "honest and truthful." It was "quite at variance" with the one Lett had given the matron and allowed her to read, and "also at variance with the matron's own report. Effect of the matron's testimonial will be to override mine which need not be produced. Asked matron for an explanation." This discussion "led to other matters and I spoke of the entries [in the journal]. She denies in toto the allegations which are there set forth, she admits having [?] whisky from Watsons on one or two of three occasions and explains ... [end of entry]."[12]

In June 1889 Mrs Finch announced her plans to resign. The discussion of the board of directors following this terse statement by the vice president can only be imagined: "Dr Lett informed me that he was looking out for a successor to Mrs Finch, the Matron, who intends leaving next August to be married to an ex-patient, Mr S. He adds that she has been engaged to three other patients since coming to the Retreat."[13]

There is a footnote to the adventures of Matron Finch. She died suddenly the following year. According to her obituary, which Lett saved, Alice Finch never married Mr S. or anyone else following her departure from Homewood. She died alone in a Chatham board-

inghouse: just retribution, Lett may have thought, for this trans-
gressor of Victorian morality.[14] From a modern perspective, Mrs
Finch's activities may be looked upon in a more charitable light.
Given the constricted economic opportunities for women in the
1880s, and the limited society she would encounter as a live-in employee of the retreat, it was logical, if unethical, for her to look at
marriage to a patient as a way out of the asylum and as a means to
better her status. The patients with whom she associated, although
alcoholic, were middle or upper class and a marriage to one of them
could have been highly advantageous. Regardless of her motivations,
however, Mrs Finch was representative of staffing problems in the
disorderly nineteenth-century hospital, where "swearing, cardplay-
ing, drinking and 'impertinence' were typical grounds for discharge," not only of attendants, but of patients as well.[15] Mrs Finch's
departure signalled the end of an era, at least in the asylum in
Guelph.

Mrs Finch was succeeded by Miss Rogers in August 1889. She
appeared to be a more level-headed and trustworthy matron, although one year later, Lett was again writing in his private code:
"The matron went out driving with Mr W. yesterday ... and did not
return until [?] p.m. I spoke to her this morning and said it was not
right to do so, that she would get herself talked about all over town,
that that was the way the trouble commenced with the former matron
and that I did not like it."[16] She did not have to be warned again.

Rogers was replaced by Mrs Webber, whose salary was increased
in 1902 to $300 placing her on par with the chief attendant (whose
duties were fewer). When Webber resigned in 1906, the superintendent took a major step towards the professionalization of his staff
by appointing a head nurse and a matron, both trained in their
fields. From this time on the nursing and housekeeping at Homewood were separate functions.[17] However, until 1927 and the appointment of Esther Northmore, who stayed at Homewood for
twelve years, there was a rapid turnover of the heads or superintendents of nursing. The contrast between Miss Northmore and Mrs
Finch could not have been more striking, nor more demonstrative
of the transformations in hospital care wrought in the four pivotal
decades around the turn of the century.[18] A fitting portrait of the
qualities of her supervision was the affectionate reminiscence of her
former student, Elva Young: "Miss Northmore was determined to
finish the job our parents had started. To make young ladies of us
... discipline would be taken into it ... On duty or in classes, we
dressed in our complete uniform – starched bib and apron, cap –
the whole bit ... Even off duty, this was the dress for classes or for

summons to Miss Northmore's office. Remember the pattern on that red carpet?"[19]

Even more than upon the matrons and supervisors, the success of moral treatment depended upon the capabilities and sympathies of the nurses and attendants who dealt with the patients on a daily basis. John Conolly, one of the first to adopt the treatment by "moral principles" in the public asylum in Hanwell, England, recognized the crucial function of a competent staff:

The character of particular patients, and of all the patients of a ward, takes its colour from the character of the attendants placed in it. On their being proper or improper instruments – well or ill-trained – well or ill-disciplined ... depends whether many of his patients shall be cured or not cured; whether some shall live or die; whether frightful accidents, an increased mortality, incalculable uneasiness and suffering, and occasional suicides, shall take place or not."[20]

The standards for staff behaviour were systematized by the British Medico-Psychological Association in 1885 in its *Handbook for Attendants on the Insane*. The ideal attendant, it was recommended, "knows his own mind," has "attained self control," and "possesses those moral qualities summed up in character."[21] In Canada, Daniel Clark had printed a *Handbook for Attendants* for use at the Toronto Asylum in 1880 while Homewood printed its own set of rules entitled *What Experience Has Taught*.[22] Attendants and nurses in all Victorian asylums were responsible for the patients' cleanliness and dress, meals, exercise, occupation, amusement, "general quietness and good conduct" and "calls of Nature," all in an appropriately firm yet sympathetic manner at "wages comparable to agricultural workers" for attendants and to domestics for nurses.[23]

In 1889, the wages for a starting male attendant who was to be "single, strictly temperate and [have] good references" were fifteen dollars per month. Wages for an experienced night nurse were eight dollars per month.[24] In comparison, labourers for the Toronto Street Railway, who were at the bottom of the utility's pay scale, were paid eight dollars per six-day week during the same year. Female piece-workers at the Crompton Corset Company, which moved to Berlin (Kitchener) from Toronto for the express purpose of lowering wages, were paid $2.50 to four dollars per week.[25]

By 1891, Homewood's female nurses were being offered ten dollars per month. The high staff turnover was indicated by a graded pay scale that in 1902 offered male attendants sixteen dollars for each of the first three months of service, seventeen dollars for the next three, and eighteen dollars thereafter. A veteran attendant therefore would have completed six months of service. While Homewood, of course, supplied room and board, lodgings were not separate from the patients until 1912, and, as one attendant complained in resigning, the "sugar [was] all sand [and] the butter and meat not fit for use at the attendant's table."[26]

Given the long hours, low pay, social and geographical isolation, and the unpleasant aspects of asylum work, it is not surprising that "asylum service has been looked down upon in the past as worse and more degrading than the lowest menial service," as the *Medical Press and Circular* commented in 1900.[27] Asylum work was an "occupation of last resort"; in 1837, Dr Browne had described attendants as "the unemployed of other professions ... If they possess physical strength and a tolerable reputation for sobriety, it is enough; and the latter quality is frequently dispensed with."[28]

In 1912, Britain's National Asylum Workers Union agitated for a legal reduction in their working hours that commonly ranged from seventy to ninety hours per week exclusive of meals. The union was unsuccessful; the superintendents argued that the duties were "light" in terms of time spent playing games and dressing the patients. Dr Cassidy of the Lancaster Asylum, in fact, believed that more than one day's holiday per month was "distinctly demoralizing."[29] The position of Britain's attendants, not very different one expects from that of Homewood's, was creatively expressed by an anonymous attendant-poet in 1912:

Repulsive work we have to do, and bear obscene abuse,
And undergo a mental strain from which there is no truce;
Our tempers through the live long day are tried full a time;
But if we make the slightest slip 'tis counted as a crime.

They say, 'the sorrows of these creatures almost make us weep,
And we must ease their sufferings, but we must do it cheap;
So down we'll keep the wages bill by all means in our power,
There's plenty glad to get a job at nothing much an hour.'[30]

The situation was no better in American asylums. In its report of 1896, the Tennessee Board of State Charities bluntly stated, "It is impossible to secure a cultured or refined person as an attendant upon the insane for the compensation provided." The historian Gerald Grob argued that the retention of mechanical restraints was made necessary by the under-staffing and poor quality of attendants and concluded, "Long hours, arduous duty in wards filled with difficult patients, and ... low pay made it difficult to attract ... high quality personnel ... Indeed, even the possible attraction of regular employment was not a sufficient inducement at a time when periodic economic depressions created either irregular employment or unemployment."[31]

Because of the questionable quality of attendants, asylum workforces became "punishment-centred bureaucracies" backed by the power of the law. In Ontario, the owner, superintendent, and staff of private lunatic asylums were liable for prosecution for willful abuse, mistreatment or neglect of patients as first outlined in the Private Lunatic Asylums Act of 1853.[32] Attendants' behaviour off-duty was circumscribed as well; tardiness, drunkenness, and even marriage could lead to dismissal. An illicit card game could bring an abrupt end to employment after years of service. Attendants, of course, had to be caught to be disciplined, and given the high patient-physician ratio in public asylums and the preoccupation of medical superintendents with administrative tasks, the attendants and nurses remained to a large extent an independently functioning unit.

In Canada, the problems and responsibilities unique to asylum work were discussed by Dr Richard Bucke of the London Asylum in 1877, in his keynote address to the annual attendants ball. He asked,

Why is it that we require more patience [and] more intelligence ... in dealing with lunatics than in dealing with sane people? It is because insanity is not confined ... to a derangement of the intelligence ... What we have to contend against ... is not so much false ideas and defective reasoning processes, but the far more formidable departures from mental health, of evil desires, vicious habits, malignant passions: it is the manifestations of these which make necessary on the part of the attendants superior qualities of head and heart, which often drive the physicians well nigh to despair.[33]

Significantly, such "superior qualities" were not possessed in sufficient numbers by London's staff, as indicated by the high staff turnover (including the transfer of Stephen Lett to Toronto) and ill-feelings engendered during the first year of Bucke's tenure. "Such changes have caused and will cause me more pain than anybody else," he informed his staff, "though perhaps you do not believe that. You probably think it is a pleasure or a matter of indifference to me to report or discharge any officer or employee." In only a year, Bucke's tone of optimism, intimacy, and shared purpose had been replaced by one of isolation, distance, and bitterness.[34]

At the Homewood Retreat, the want of qualified workers willing to take or maintain asylum employment meant that, even when staff members were known to be incompetent, there was often little alternative to their retention. Lett's experience with attendant Henry Gosling is an example. Five days after his arrival, Gosling was "much discontented about his work." Lett gave him "a long talking to and told him to consider the matter for a few days. If he thought he could content himself all right, if not he had better leave." Gosling resigned the following day. Three weeks later, he returned to be special attendant to one patient. That evening, Gosling came in drunk, and having no money, Lett gave him two dollars to "get out of town." Eleven days later Gosling was back doing night duty and in a fortnight was back as special attendant.[35]

The growth in opportunities for working class women in other sectors of the economy, particularly in industry, added to staffing difficulties. In 1888, only four applicants answered the advertisement for a female attendant, "none of which had asylum experience." Finding staff for the more menial tasks was even harder. The "lack of freedom, the isolation or loneliness, and the low status" of domestic service rendered it well behind "shop, office and factory work as occupations preferred by native Canadian women." Hobbs reported in 1900 that "the question of obtaining the proper kind of help both for the wards, kitchen, laundry and other domestic work is becoming serious. I have experienced much difficulty and expense in this direction during the past year and finally was obliged to close the laundry and put the washing out and I think without increasing the cost. I fear there will have to be a general increase of wages all round in order to secure and retain what is necessary under this heading."[36]

By 1918, "the question of employees [had become] a very serious one. The unrest pertaining to all departments of industry has more or less affected the Homewood. During the month of May the matron had to meet an ultimatum from her maids in the kitchen."[37] The administration attempted to redress the labour problem by recruiting immigrants from among the domestic servants that were "actively recruited" in Britain by the federal and provincial governments. Between 1870 and 1930, "over 250,000 women immigrated to Canada stating their intended occupation as domestic service." Once in Canada, however, many domestics failed to keep their bargains and left employment early.[38] Homewood's experience was no different from other employers: "For many months in the early part of the year we were shorthanded in the kitchen as well as in the nursing staff," Hobbs reported, "and your president and myself with the active co-operation of the CPR and the Immigration Department imported a number of girls for the kitchen as well as a number of graduate nurses. The experiment has not been entirely satisfactory, as a spirit of unrest seems to prevail among the newcomers. Two of the nurses have paid up their passages and left, and two of the maids bolted with attendants that they had picked up here while in the institution. The immigration department are endeavouring to locate the two maids to deport them."[39] Hobbs was probably naive to believe that two domestics, of whom there was such a great shortage in Canada, were likely to be deported, regardless of the assurance of the immigration department.

The Great War made Homewood's labour shortage even more acute. In 1915, Hobbs reported that "there have been a large number of resignations during the last year, particularly among the male employees, the majority of whom have enlisted in the Canadian Force[s]. In connection with this, The Homewood can point with pride to the fact that seven of our former medical assistants are now overseas or on their way to the front, also chief attendants, chef, painters, fireman and a large number of attendants and ex-patients." By 1916, eight assistant physicians were in the forces, among whom one, Captain Ireland, was reported killed. Major Reason, another former assistant physician became commanding officer of the large military hospital at Shorncliffe, England.[40]

Like that of the nation at large, Hobbs's patriotic enthusiasm had dimmed somewhat by 1916. "It has been a very trying year for everybody concerned," he wrote, "and the difficulties encountered have been unusual." Attendants were "constantly required to be replaced, many enlisting." Hobbs averted the potentially crippling loss of Assistant Medical Superintendent Barnes, who "withstood one or two requests to go overseas" but who "felt his duty lay here." Hobbs was forced, however, to increase Barnes's salary when he agreed to remain, and later renovated apartments in the Colonial for Barnes and his bride. At the same time, the number of patients was decreasing due to the "financial stringency caused by [the] War." Potential patients were either kept at home or sent to the public asylums.[41]

As the war was coming to an end in 1918, the scarcity of help had placed an "increasing burden upon the staff." Hobbs found it "impossible to carry out effective work with a limited staff and an inferior class of attendants. Our good men have all volunteered or been drafted, and gone overseas, and have not yet returned ... A good many men that we have had have been inferior in every possible way, making the occurrence of tragic accidents possible [three suicides had in fact occurred]. There has been a limited supply of female nurses, owing to the many attractions offered by other professions."[42] As will be discussed below, conditions had indeed deteriorated by 1920, although this may be a reflection of a general trend that began about a decade earlier.

As in other institutions, the duties required of Homewood's attendants and nurses militated against the retention of a qualified workforce. In 1888, Lett entered the reponsibilities of the night nurse, whose duties were considerably lighter than those expected of the day staff, into her report book:

She shall commence her duties punctually at 10:00 at which time she will accompany the matron ... to every patient ... During the night she must be vigilant, and note everything going on in the ward. Visit each patient once, or oftener if necessary ... Attend carefully to any that are sick, administer medicine or nourishment as prescribed. Get up such patients as are wet or dirty in their habits at regular times. Except Maggie A. ... She is to spend as short a time as possible at her midnight meal, and not leave the ward during her time of duty.[43]

For the superintendent, the problem was to find staff who could stay awake. In 1888, Lett instructed the matron to give Ellen McGowan two-weeks notice because she was not reliable; "though I have not detected her in the act there appears to be no doubt but that she goes to sleep on duty and makes incorrect reports as to the condition of the patients." The matron reported two days later that Ellen was again asleep on duty. Lett "gave her a good talking to and told her if she did not keep awake all night I would dock her wages at the end of the month."[44]

It would be unfair to blame these derelictions simply on laziness or irresponsibility; shift work, difficult in the best of situations, must have been particularly hard on attendants who had to reside inside a crowded asylum with little soundproofing. Night attendant Max Rosenthal was an experienced and competent employee. When he had to be awakened in his chair by Lett during the superintendent's rounds, he complained that "he had gotten no sleep the day before as Maggie A. had been so noisy and kept him awake." As dangerous as asylum work was for physicians, the dangers were immediate for the attendants. Lett cautioned Mrs Finch about letting the nurse dress Maggie alone with the doors locked, "as should Maggie become excited and violent she would kill Mary before assistance could reach her."[45]

The daily drudgery and stress, however, did more damage to the health of employees than patient violence could. The more experienced and conscientious the attendants, the more likely their health would be to break down. Between July 1888 and December 1889, for example, the head nurse, chief attendant, and nurse Ross, an employee with two years' experience, were among the many who resigned or took extended leaves to recuperate. In Ross's case, Lett "promised to take [her] back in [a] month if well enough for duty."[46] Drunkenness, another reaction to the stress and drudgery, was a chronic problem as certain employees were continually suspected of imbibing on their nights out. Attendant Thomas Hill "stayed out all night, said [it] was raining so hard." Lett told him "not to do so again that staying out at night was one of my serious objections to having a married man as attendant." Hill drowned his sorrows in another fashion when Lett "found the smell of liquor on him." When Hill said "he had taken some for a cold," Lett directed, "I would not have him take it for a cold or anything else and he must not take it again."[47] That Hill did not receive instant dismissal for the drinking offense was more indicative of the shortage of good attendants than exceptional benevolence on Lett's part.

As I noted at the beginning of this chapter, the daily realities of life in a hospital, general or mental, produce a bond of shared experience or a sub-culture shared between the attendants and patients. In hospitals like Homewood where attendants resided in the institution and had few holidays, they could be expected to identify to an even greater degree with patients. That this happened is evident in the following three instances: the reactions of attendants to censure or stress was to imitate the behaviour of the patients.

When Ellen McGowan was discharged and her last month's wages were docked because she persistently slept through night duty, to Lett's consternation, she began "acting very queer." "She is either simulating or is under the influence of some drug. I think the former perhaps mixed up with some hysteria," he concluded. When nurse Ross broke down from overwork, she became "quite hysterical ... nervous, unable to lay still." Although Lett gave her chloral, potassium bromide, and an opiate, she remained delirious for two days. In her 'delirium,' "she spoke of the excuses Nurse Lydia would make to the Matron in order not to take the patients out walking so that she might get at her own sewing."[48]

When the night attendant Darling came in drunk one night, Lett discharged him, paid him off, took his keys and "told him to leave at once." Darling refused to go and when Lett gave him "the option of being locked up in his room or going down to the Police cells he chose the former. [Whereupon] I locked him in and ordered Attendant Hill to bring him some supper in about an hour afterwards. Attendant Swaffield came to me and said, 'Darling was smashing the windows.' I went up and found he had smashed all the windows in his room, battered the door, smashed the plaster on his wall and smashed a chair. [I] removed him to a shuttered room and gave him a sleeping draft [of] chloral."[49]

For Darling, Hill, and other attendants, an essential, if not the most essential, requirement for their employment was physical strength. During the late nineteenth century, male hospital attendants cared for the alcoholics, the violent, the mentally ill, and male patients suffering from genito-urinary disorders. Education directed at male attendants was virtually nonexistent and trained female nurses replaced them. In 1886, the McLean Asylum Training School, established in 1882, enrolled male attendants in its program, but the experiment was not successful. Homewood followed the general pattern; its nursing school did not offer any formal education to its male attendants. There was little motivation for advancement for the long-term or for overly qualified male attendants.[50]

For female attendants, the situation was different but by no means ideal. At the turn of the century, Dr Greene, medical superintendent of Northampton's Berry Wood Asylum, complained that "the asylum nurse is rather looked down upon in some places, as if she belonged to an inferior order of the nursing profession."[51] Even within the nursing profession, asylum work was not of particularly high status, perhaps because psychiatric nursing was a specialty "that was not especially successful in creating a specific self-identity. This was so partly because of the generalized nature of the work, the inability to define a body of data whose mastery would become a precondition for a specialty."[52]

Improvement in status for psychiatric nurses did indeed lag behind the professionalization of general hospital nursing. One of the few attractions of asylum work for trained nurses from the general hospital was the possibility of a rapid promotion to a supervisory position, especially to matron, although such opportunities were, of course, limited. The first Canadian psychiatric nurses were the French religious sisters who established a hospital ward in Quebec City in 1714. The first training for psychiatric nurses has been credited to the commencement of regular programs in 1921 at the Brandon, Manitoba asylum. This was followed by training programs in the other three western provinces. However, if 1921 is indeed the earliest credible date heretofore, then the distinction of operating the first psychiatric nursing school in Canada must instead be claimed by either the Homewood school of nursing, established in 1906, or by the Rockwood asylum training school for nurses, which opened in Kingston even earlier – in 1888[53] In actual practice, the beginnings of psychiatric nursing as a profession rather than as glorified menial labour was signalled in a speech by Dr Tuttle of the McLean Asylum in 1886 to the Association of Medical Superintendents of American Institutions for the Insane. He reported, "We relieved nurses of a great deal of drudgery by employing on each side of the house men and women to scrub the floors, make the beds, wash the dishes and windows, and other labor that our nurses formerly did and still do."[54]

The first sign at Homewood of the professionalization of its nurses was the adoption of uniforms in 1902. When the formal training program began four years later, as was common practice, it provided a cheap labour force for the institution as well as nursing training. Provincial accreditation was crucial for attracting students, and the institution was forced to continually upgrade its program in order to get it.[55]

In correspondence with Inspector Bruce Smith in 1913, Hobbs could not see how his nurses were inferior. "My graduate nurses ... undergo a training of two years and three months, undergo a strict course of lectures, and pass a very strict severe standard for their examinations." Smith, however, recommended that there be at least one nurse "with regular hospital training to supervise each ward and carry out the physicians' orders." By 1918, the program had been upgraded to a two and one-half year training course with a post-graduate training of six months in "some General Hospital." Obstetrical training was provided with local physicians. In 1919, however, the Ontario legislature failed to pass a bill "for recognition of our nurses, as was promised ... Without this we cannot hope to improve and maintain sufficient staff of nurses, which are so necessary to the welfare of the institution."[56]

The professionalizing initiatives by the general nursing establishment left Homewood's nurses in the cold. "A tenth of the nurses in the Province have banded themselves as the Ontario Nursing Association," Hobbs complained, "and have made themselves so exclusive that the nurses in smaller hospitals and mental institutions cannot become members ... A very strong deputation waited upon the Provincial Secretary and made representations to him ... and pointed out the menace to the country at large that such official regulations would produce. We hope the next session will see our nurses registered with other nurses from all hospitals, even if they have to take a postgraduate course of three or four months on subjects that they are deficient in." The directors subsequently lobbied for the establishment of an accredited training school; provision for one finally passed the legislature in 1922.[57]

Homewood's physicians recommended that the new training school involve a three-year program, with a minimum requirement for entrance of one year in high school. At Homewood, Hobbs claimed, "We are trying to lay more stress on study, trying to develop along more serious educational lines so that our nurses will be better adapted to meet our private patients." Homewood was forced to continually upgrade its program and facilities because of the "unwillingness on the part of young ladies to come to Homewood to train, and [the] scarcity of nurses. Reason – standards of nurses are very low and type of work expect[ed]. Toronto graduate nurses and staff absolutely refused to do maid's work." Along with an improved curriculum, Homewood also realized that they would have to provide "better standards of amusements and entertainments" to compete for nursing students of good quality. The erection of a new separate nurses' home in 1924 helped to make Homewood more appealing to prospective nurses.[58]

The professionalization of asylum nursing had immediate benefits for the institution, although how much the nursing staff benefitted is less certain. On the one hand, the two- or three-year training program provided a steady supply of cheap labour, but then the graduates not retained by the institution would be sent out to find their own way in an uncertain market. The feminization of nursing had the advantage to the asylum of reducing the payroll; wage differentials based upon gender were constant in spite of training differentials. The association of the male attendant with brutality and the female nurse with a natural and benevolent 'calling' provided a philosophical justification for the shift in staffing. However, the increase in females was not necessarily perceived by the administration as constituting an inherently better labour force. "We have a good staff of nurses in training and we have had no trouble," Clare reported in 1935. "This to you may seem an ordinary statement but in my life I have seen a great deal of difficulty and trouble aroused from the misconduct of silly young girls who are away from home for the first time."[59]

Homewood's nursing school did not have a lengthy existence. Its closure in 1939 was part of an international trend resulting from the economic depression of the 1930s. Small nursing schools throughout North America were closed due to an oversupply of nurses, and even a scheme to increase the number of jobs by reducing the working hours of those already employed failed to save the schools. Elva Young recalled the closing of the school: "Our Derniere

Class – the graduates of 1939 – were a determined lot, almost defiant
... Thirteen would-be graduates were to be in that class ... and these
thirteen young nurses wanted their Graduation Day to be Friday,
June 13th, 1939" as a form of protest against the closing of the
school. Miss Northmore, bowing to the popular suspicion about the
unlucky date, said "that would never do." "Finally, however, with
much determination on the girls' part, Friday, June 13th, 1939,
became their Graduation Day."[60]

Of the paramedical specialties introduced into asylum care in the
early twentieth century, occupational therapy was one of the most
popular. At Homewood, the issue of patient employment had always
been a sensitive one given the asylum's middle-class orientation and
its attempt to distance itself from the public asylum. In 1908, however, citing the frequent requests of friends that "some work [be]
given to patients," Hobbs suggested starting an arts and crafts department. The benefit of "diversional occupation," he argued, "was
directed at the mentally and physically 'overactive.'" It would break
up "wrong associations of ideas" and direct activities into "normal
and healthy channels." In cases of depression, "congenial work stimulates and interests the morbid mind." In the transfer papers for
Henry M. (#924, 1903), Dr D.R. Burrill of the Brigham Hall Sanitarium in Canandaiga, New York revealed the benefits and also the
form occupational therapy traditionally took. Henry's periods of
excitement, Burrill wrote, "are not of long duration. Work at that
time helps to calm him. When excited we have had him push the
floor polisher though attended by some swearing." John S. (#1043,
1890) was happiest when engaged in some temporary carpentry
work for the Retreat. "He must be employed he says or he will die,"
Lett wrote. "No man can stand to be idle who has been used to hard
work like he has all his life."[61]

Occupational therapy as a specialty, an early twentieth-century
development, was important in dispelling notions that patient work
was an institutional cost-saving scheme and an inexpensive way to
keep patients amused. Susan E. Tracy used the term "invalid therapy" in her 1910 publication *Studies in Invalid Therapy*, and taught a
course at the Massachusetts General Hospital on the subject in the
following year. The professionalization of occupational therapy was
stimulated by the support and leadership it obtained from male
psychiatrists. George Edward Barton of the Sheppard and Pratt
Hospital in Maryland began agitating for a national organization
after 1914. He endeavoured "to exclude individuals concerned
merely with 'arts and crafts' and 'largely without any knowledge of
medicine whatever,' and urged that such terms as 'occupational

workers' be dropped in favor of a designation that included 'ther-apeutics.'"[62]

The occupational therapy department at Homewood was begun in 1912 with the engagement (at sixty dollars per month plus board) of Miss Scott, a Canadian graduate of the Pratt Institute of Brooklyn, New York. She organized activities in "certain branches of industrial work, such as the making of leather articles in various forms, brass work, knitting, etc.," and the department proved to be a "great suc-cess." "It fills in the spare time of the patients," Hobbs reported, "keeps them busy, at the same time turning their energies into useful work. This is all free, and a gift of the institution to the patients. The only expense involved is the cost of the raw material on which they work."[63]

From its inception at Homewood, the staff working in occupational therapy had to have some form of professional training. It is inter-esting, and perhaps also inevitable, that by 1925, occupational ther-apy had evolved into a department with goals similar to that of the nineteenth-century public asylum: a therapeutic goal – to direct the energies of the patients, but also a utilitarian goal – to reduce the operating budget. The president of Homewood's board reported that the department had been made "increasingly useful" to the patients, with "practically no expense" to the institution. A special "repair service" for patients' clothing was installed, with the bulk of the work handled in the patients' classes: "This service has added distinctly to the comfort and appearance of patients unable satis-factorily to take care of their own needs."[64]

The transformations in asylum personnel from the 1880s to the 1920s were dramatic and cosmetic at the same time. In training and professional demeanour, there was a wide gulf between the cor-rupting influence of Mrs Finch and the starched efficiency of Miss Northmore. Working conditions, responsibilities, and wages for gen-eral personnel did not change substantially during this period, how-ever, despite attempts to integrate the nursing staff into the professional mainstream. The nature of the work also hampered the efforts of the institution to upgrade the quality of its personnel. As evident in the evolution of occupational therapy, changes in no-menclature and the advent of specialists did not necessarily produce substantive changes in either the activities or the rationale behind them.

Regardless of the degree of innovation, the efforts of the orderly, scientifically oriented asylum were constantly compromised by the subversive activities of the patient population. Homewood's patients fought, screamed, stole, sued, and showered their physicians with unwonted affection. The existence of a large neurotic, alcoholic, and addicted population in residence aggravated the propensity for disorder, as sane patients found novel methods to assuage their boredom by annoying the staff. This tendency towards rebellion, it will be argued in subsequent chapters, was an inevitable consequence of moral treatment; the patriarchal superintendent produced on the one hand, dependent, child-like patients, and on the other, rebellious, raucous "adolescents." Perhaps the true paradigm of the asylum is that of the extended family. And if the family is the basis for other societal groups, then the asylum, with its varying levels of authority figures and the combination of positive and destructive relationships existing under one roof, certainly resembled its mother institution.

CHAPTER EIGHT

Resistant Patients and the Reactive Institution

The patient's life at a psychiatric hospital like Homewood included every aspect of social interaction: authority figures, friendship, language, uniforms, regulations, and routine, all of which could have overwhelmed past identities and experiences. Up to a point, the Homewood Retreat resembled a total institution.[1] Yet for the majority of patients, a number of circumstances worked against their alienation from the external world. Frequent contact with family and friends provided a window on the outside. A high rate of staff turnover, particularly at the supervisory level, detracted from the establishment of 'big nurse' territories. Administration was sometimes so inefficient that a virtual state of anarchy existed. This made staff brutality a possibility but also meant that patients might be left alone. In 1890, for example, a record three patients escaped from the institution, separately, on the same day.[2]

The key factor militating against Homewood becoming a total institution was the lack of money. Finances were a chronic problem for public asylums, but for a proprietary asylum, they were a critical one. As long as the patient at the proprietary asylum had the support of at least one influential family member, he or she could demand to be taken home or to another place of treatment. In addition, the middle-class composition of Homewood's patient population meant that the sane or voluntary patients there could react to asylum policies and treatments; unlike the poorer patients in public asylums, they had resources. They could pay to go elsewhere, and they had the wherewithal to bring themselves to the attention of outsiders. They could complain to family members, lawyers, newspapers, and even board members about treatments they were getting or failing to get. They would also be likely to have heard about new therapeutic techniques, about patient rights, and about what other institutions had to offer.

Had the Homewood Retreat possessed an ideal staff, its effectiveness and efficiency would still have been compromised by the
actions of its patient population. As Nancy Tomes has observed,
"troublesome inmates played a significant role in the demise of moral
treatment."[3] In theory, activities, baths, and moral persuasion should
have sufficed in the care of the insane; in practice they did not.
Mechanical restraints, chemical restraint (that is, sedatives and hypnotics), ward therapy, and isolated acts of violence became a cus-
tomary part of institutional existence, as the control of resistive
patients became an end in itself. The payment of fees and even the
active concern of the family members could not, ultimately, prevent
many patients from gradually sinking into a malaise caused by occasional repression, habitual neglect, and relentless boredom.

For the patients, the retreat was often a far different environment
than their families had envisaged and their physicians had intended.
By their reactions, and the institution's subsequent responses, the
patients helped to shape an asylum that may not have been better
or worse than perceived by outsiders, but that was unique all the
same.

CHEMICAL RESTRAINT

An essential though sometimes lamentable feature of asylum treatment was the use of drugs. Medication could have two functions at
the institution, therapeutic and restraining. New discoveries and
vogues in medication were reflected in the various hypnotics, stimulants, sedatives, and antibiotics employed by the institution. The
choice appeared to be based upon the personal preferences of the
attending physicians.

When Lett began treating patients in 1883, he relied at first upon
tonics, a favoured choice of moral managers. Tonics or stimulants
became very popular in the second half of the nineteenth century
because, it was believed, they helped restore nervous energy. The
basis for this belief lay in the fact that these medicines produced
changes in "pulse, respiration, appetite, digestion or skin color."[4]
Widely used stimulants included arsenic (which had the added benefit of lightening the female complexion to the fashionably tuber-
cular shade of pale), quinine, and strychnine. The most popular
stimulant was beverage alcohol, usually in the forms of whisky and
brandy, while iron tonics were commonly prescribed. Helen M.
(#357, 1884), a manic-depressive, apparently was treated solely with
tonics. On admission, extremely depressed and run down, she was
put on an iron tonic. After "some improvement," she had a "bad
turn of depression," and Lett changed the tonic to citrate of iron

and quinine. After Helen H. (#222, 1892), in an "erotic passion," grabbed him when he made his rounds, she was taken off her iron tonic, Lett noted tersely.

Over the years, Lett employed an increasing number and variety of medications. In this he was not alone. "Taking advantage of numerous developments in pharmacology throughout the second half of the century," William Rothstein noted, "physicians continued to use therapies to 'make an impression on the patient' – to use the words of their forebears. New antipyretics continued to reduce fevers at any cost. Analgesics and anodynes continued to relieve pain and hypnotics to induce sleep despite their addictive properties and other undesirable side effects."[5]

Antipyretics replaced bloodletting and had the same purpose, to lower temperature. The favoured antipyretics of the nineteenth century were aconite, a vegetable poison, quinine, the alkaloid isolated from the cinchona bark in 1820, whose benefits in malaria rendered it the panacea for all fevers in the 1870s and 1880s, and the synthetics developed in the 1880s including antipyrine, derived from coal tar. Among analgesics, the most important for the better part of the century were opium and its alkaloid derivative, morphine. Cocaine was specified for sinus problems and as a stimulant and anaesthetic. Awareness of the possibility of addiction, unfortunately, lagged decades behind use of the drugs.

The favoured hypnotics of the century were chloral hydrate and sulphonal. Carlos MacDonald of the Auburn, New York asylum for the criminally insane preferred the action of chloral hydrate, which he believed was "probably unequalled" as a hypnotic. He considered it to be most beneficial in the early stages of insanity, when insomnia was a persistent problem.[6] As assistant physician at the London Asylum, Lett had been particularly enthusiastic about the value of chloral hydrate. He found the drug useful "in all cases of acute mania where the patient has not so deteriorated as to require free use of stimulants." Where chloral hydrate produced "sleep and quietness," it had none of the "evil effects" of opium; it did not "derange" the digestive system, check secretions, constipate the bowels, nor produce drowsiness.[7]

In his study of "The Modern Hypnotics" in 1889, Henry Wetherill found much success in treating the "insomnia of inebriety and the morphia habit" with hyoscine, from the vegetable group. He also found paraldehyde, an ether derivative, useful in melancholia, hysteria, and the "delusions of fear [and] doubt," although it had a major drawback in its "burning, acrid, choking" taste. Sulphonal, also from the ether series, not a narcotic and therefore not beneficial to insomniacs, was a pure hypnotic, "increasing [and] prolonging the natural tendency to sleep."[8] Sulphonal had relatively few side effects, unlike opium, which in 1905 was still specified for mental illness. By this time, the use of opium was indicated primarily in cases of melancholia to ward off severe attacks where suicide was a possibility. In other forms of insanity, however, "beware of the medical man who is too handy with his hypodermic."[9] W.A. McClain blamed the routine overmedication of asylum patients in Europe and North America on the "pernicious" practice of "political preferment" that led to the hiring of incompetents. Young and inexperienced physicians medicated rather than conduct "real" examinations, particularly on female patients, and failed to correct problems which McClain considered to be widespread with respect to the reproductive organs. Like Hobbs, McClain opposed "the habit of thinking that all insane persons are suffering from some mysterious affections [sic] of that still more mysterious and intangible something called mind."[10]

Despite the various physical and psychological ailments for which medication was specified, the administration of drugs at the asylum was, in a majority of cases, for the purposes of restraint and control. Contemporaries understood that the misuse of drugs was the consequence of the institution's need to keep order by pacifying disruptive patients. In 1881, H.B. Wilbur of the United States acknowledged that "chemical restraint" was directly related to mechanical restraint; both tended to be abused by some institutions.[11] In 1899, Dr Hitchcock reported to the British Medico-Psychological Association that "at almost every asylum with which I was connected before I went to York, I have seen two 16-ounce bottles [of sedatives] made up for the males and females, given night after night to be used at discretion for patients who were noisy. I have seen this most detrimental treatment pushed until many patients have been at death's door."[12] Even the York Retreat succumbed to the necessities for chemical restraint. With the introduction of the bromides and chloral hydrate in the 1860s, these drugs were used to control restless patients. A patient at York in 1878 charged that chloral "was being used to 'quench the poor sufferers into quietness.'"[13]

In theory, the application of proper techniques of moral treatment should not have involved the systematic use of chemical restraints. In practice, however, overmedication underwrote, at the same time as it competed with, moral treatment. Patients in asylums of ever-increasing size, whose management was left more and more in the hands of attendants, often could not be coaxed or cajoled into their occupations, baths, or rest. The subsequent struggles became ends

Table 17
Use of Hypnotics and Sedatives at Homewood, 1883–1920

	Instances of Use		
Hypnotic or Sedative	Lett Regime (1883–1900)	Early Hobbs Regime (1901–10)	Later Hobbs Regime (1911–20)
Bromides	13	2	9
Opium	6	1	15
"Sedatives"	1	1	19
Chloral	19		1
Barbituates		2	17
Hyoscine	1	1	12
Cannabis	6		
Paraldehyde	3		3
Sulphonal	4		
Trional			4
Total of instances used	53	7	80	(140)
Percent of total instances hypnotics and sedatives were used	38%	5%	57%	(100%)

in themselves. As proponents of mechanical restraint understood, the form restraint took might be less relevant in the minds of the patients than the act of restraint, that is, the denial of the patients' desired activities. When Kate T. (#508, 1917), a "noisy" and "antagonistic" patient required morphia and hyoscine by hypodermic because she would not "co-operate," her reaction, "I'll make noise enough to raise the roof to spite physicians," would have been the same had mechanical restraints been used. When medication was overused, there was no longer any rationalization for moral treatment; increasing rates of medication indicated the system of therapeutics was breaking down.

In table 17, medications used to sedate and control at Homewood have been grouped to demonstrate the extent of such drug use and the changes in popularity of the various forms of medication. These figures can be compared in table 18 with the number of admissions during three periods of Homewood care, roughly corresponding to the Lett administration, the early years of Hobbs's tenure, and the later years of his administration. During the Lett administration, there was an excessive reliance on medication to sedate the patient population. Drug usage dipped substantially during the early years of Hobbs's tenure, only to rise again after 1910. The suggestive

Table 18
Admissions during Lett and Hobbs Administrations, 1883–1920

	Lett Regime	Early Hobbs Regime	Later Hobbs Regime	
Admissions	179	318	629	(1126)[a]
Percent of admissions	16%	28%	56%	(100%)

[a]Eight patients in the sample population were admitted after 1920.

v-curve in frequency of medication is graphed on figure 2. Apparently the first half of Hobbs's administration was a 'high water mark' in the practice of moral treatment at Homewood. Despite a steady increase in the number of patients, drug use was kept to a minimum. This probably was the result of Hobbs's personally active role in treatment. By the last decade, due to his failing health, Hobbs retreated to administrative duties and the occasional surgical intervention. The staffing difficulties attendant on the Great War probably also exacerbated the medication problem. With Hobbs's semi-retirement, patient care was delegated to assistant physicians, including medical students, but primarily to attendants. Consequently, more and more hypnotics and sedatives were used to maintain a smooth-running institution.

MECHANICAL RESTRAINT

An extremely controversial issue among medical superintendents throughout the late nineteenth century was the use of mechanical restraints. The physicians were aware that, to the public mind, nothing so typified the repressive nature of the asylum as the use of straps, muffs, camisoles, and crib-beds. For themselves, the alienists knew that use of mechanical restraints signalled the failure of moral treatment. Yet violent, destructive, and excited patients had to be controlled, and public pronouncements and personal preferences did not make the problem disappear.

In 1877, Eugene Grissom defended the use of restraints which he denied were "used as punishment, in any sense" in American asylums. Restraint was essential to an individual who "would otherwise dash out his brains, as the crutch is to the shrunken limb." Advocates of mechanical restraint claimed that it prevented personal antagonism between the patient and attendant by providing an alternative to "the threatening glances, or the hard grasp of four or five attendants." They argued that its removal, much heralded in some institutions, really required the substitution of another form of restraint since violent patients would have to be controlled in some way. "We have to choose," Grissom argued, "between the hypnotic power of drugs, affording the 'chemical restraint of the brain cell,' or the manual restraint of the strong arms of attendants, or that of solitary imprisonment in seclusion [or] mechanical restraint." During his administration of the London Asylum, Henry Landor preferred minor forms of restraint to seclusion: "The use of the hand-muffs," he wrote, "might be resorted to without doing any violence to the feelings of the most advanced advocate of non-restraint, and in my opinion, would be preferable to long confinement in a small badly ventilated room."[14]

In 1891, Clark Bell, an American attorney and president of the New York Medico-Legal Society, solicited the views of medical superintendents concerning the issue of restraint. Bell, who was a critic of the practice, noted that even John Conolly, the 'father' of non-restraint, permitted its use in surgical cases and at night for the "highly suicidal," and when necessary, used "chemical restraint" to control his patients. Dr Theodore Diller was representative of the view that the use of restraints was a decision to be made within the asylum. Diller perceived the public concern regarding restraints to be threatening to the professional independence of the physicians; medical decisions should not be made by outsiders. As Diller noted, asylum superintendents had many forms of restraint including forced feedings, drugs, and baths. The argument that mechanical restraint alone was too dangerous was "absurd," he argued. It "is a measure of treatment, a remedy of peculiar value – one which in certain cases, cannot be supplanted by any other from which an equally good result can be obtained." C.K. Bartlett, of the Minnesota Hospital for the Insane, averred that non-restraint was an ideal only possible in "rich asylums" where "experienced help" was abundant, room was "unlimited," and all shared the "same nationality."[15]

Alice Bennett, medical superintendent of the Norristown, Pennsylvania State Hospital, however, propounded the view which the public and some superintendents were beginning to share: total abolition of mechanical restraint. Bennett believed that "nothing is more certain than that mechanical restraint is incompatible with 'moral treatment,' and that resort to it destroys at once any personal influence that may be brought to bear." Far from restraining, Bennett argued, mechanical restraints would direct the aggressive impulse, heightened by feelings of "resentment and revenge" into other outlets "for evil." W.T. O'Reilly, inspector of Ontario asylums, shared Bennett's viewpoint. "Restraint," he boasted, "is done away with forever in our asylums. No handcuffs, straight jackets, padded rooms or anything of that kind is used. What has taken their place? Nothing; there is no need for anything. The necessity for restraint arose only because restraint was used. It is true there are people subject to paroxysms ... By giving [them] work and exercise these paroxysms are made less frequent and less dangerous. But if a lunatic will occasionally break glass and tear his clothes, it is a great deal better to let him do it than to make his outbreaks more frequent and more dangerous by tying his hands or otherwise forcibly restraining him."[16]

In 1894, C.K. Clarke stated that non-restraint "has been the principle in nearly all Canadian institutions for ten years."[17] In the 1870s and 1880s, Daniel Clark of Toronto and Richard Bucke of London both became vocal advocates of non-restraint. This had not always been the case. In 1878, Bucke believed Landor, his predecessor, to have used "as much restraint as in any restraint asylum." "For my own part," Bucke added, "I am persuaded that the use of mechanical restraint variously applied ... is the most useful ... and least injurious of any form of restraint that can be used." By 1885, however, Bucke considered "restraints and seclusion" to be "unnecessary and injurious."[18] Opponents of mechanical restraint cited its brutalizing effects upon its users: "When we tie a man up like an animal, it is harder to regard him as a patient. Our finer feelings are benumbed by such practices."[19]

Yet Bennett herself had offered one cautionary proviso which was at the heart of the dilemma. "Much depends upon the attendants," she admitted, "they must be without preconceived notions, and should be intelligently interested in the principles they are carrying out." While an advocate of non-restraint, Daniel Clark agreed that it was "easy to adopt" where the nurse to patient ratio was one to six. Where it was one to sixteen, as in his own Toronto Asylum, non-restraint was more difficult.[20] Given the attendants' situation — understaffing, poor pay, long hours and disagreeable conditions — Bennett's comment indicated that non-restraint was an ideal for which an asylum should strive, rather than a reality easy to achieve.

Other Canadian alienists were more critical of the popular sentiments for non-restraint. Joseph Workman indirectly blamed its advocates for the tragic death of Kingston's William Metcalfe. As he wrote to C.K. Clarke, "If a mad dog should be seen by you running towards one of your children, ... would you deliberate long on the subject of restraint? ... We may not shoot madmen, but honestly tell me, had you possessed prophetic power, and could it have been revealed to you that Maloney would some day ... slay Dr Metcalfe, would you have shed tears over the anticipative half hour's [restraint] of him[?]"[21]

In 1889, Lett expounded his personal views on restraint in a rare commentary in his journal. He recounted,

> Libbie B.'s sister came up today especially to see me. She thought of writing to me to know if I had any objections to putting a jacket on Libbie. She felt that it would be for her own good to do so ... it would prevent her wearing herself out with so much motion of the limbs and yet permitted a certain amount of movement ... In all I quite agreed with Miss B. and told her that my chief reason [for not] was the popular prejudice ... with regard to mechanical restraints and the popular and erroneous fad amongst some asylum officials regarding non-restraint ... My rule for adopting mechanical restraint was if the patient is dangerous to herself or others I adopted it, or in cases where the friends of the patients wished it provided such wishes coincided with my views. [Miss B. replied that] she would rather see her sister with it on than without it and plenty of warm clothing could [then] be kept on her. To this view I quite concur.[22]

In both the Lett and Hobbs administrations, patients were placed in jackets, camisoles, "mild restraint," "restraining sheets," and shuttered rooms because of violence, masturbation, self-mutilation, filthiness, excitement, and destructiveness. The shuttered room was the reward for James D. (#695, 1909), for instance, after he had a "fistic encounter with another patient during the week, in which he was the victor."

Hobbs's contribution to restraint methods was the introduction of the continuous bath. (See appendix 7.) The restraint characteristic of the baths was evident to the board of visitors. During their inspection of 1913, they noted that no patient was under restraint, "though two were at the time of inspection under treatment in the baths." In fact the continuous bath, in which a patient would be wrapped in sheets and suspended in water for hours, could be a debilitating form of punishment.[23] Jane McC. (#291, 1918) was placed in the continuous tub daily, "some lessening of her excitement while in the tub, but this is again markedly in evidence as soon as she is removed." While Jane became "considerably reduced," it had not "yet had any appreciable effect in diminishing her physical strength." She fainted as a result of treatment and had to be revived with stimulants; however her destructive and filthy habits necessitated her return: "in this way it has been possible to keep her more cleanly." The continuous bath had a similar debilitating effect on

Annie B. (#63, 1919), who was destructive, excited, and incoherent on the morning after her admission. She was put in the continuous bath "for the day, where she quieted down considerably." The following day she was "more or less exhausted" and "stimulants were required on account of her weak condition."

FORCED FEEDING

Artificial feeding was also a common form of aggressive treatment. Asylum physicians accepted forced feedings as a fact of life. Dr Cobbold, medical superintendent of Britain's Earlswood Asylum, claimed that there would "always ... be a certain number of patients who ... will not swallow" by any other means. Writing in 1882, Cobbold was aware, however, that artificial feeding was bad for public relations, and he was opposed to it except as a last resort: "When the public mind is, causelessly, as I believe, somewhat uneasy upon the subject of the care and treatment of the insane, it is most undesirable that the idea should become general that insane persons are needlessly subjected to the discomfort of having tubes passed into their stomachs, even though the object be to supply them with the food necessary to their sustenance and recovery."[24]

Artificial feeding was particularly used on female patients or conversely, it was a response to a particularly female behaviour. In 1820, George Jepson of the York Retreat described an effective technique: "fasten the patient in a chair a little leaning backward with a person to hold the head and another the hands. If the patient refuses to open her mouth it becomes necessary to force it open."[25] At the Pennsylvania Hospital for the Insane, it was noted that "the sight of the stomach pump" caused a woman "to make an effort and eat the soup herself."[26] The incidence of artificial feeding at Homewood reflected events in other asylums; thirty-seven women and ten men in the sample population were forcefed at some point.

Elaine Showalter has characterized the cases of "fasting girls" and anorexia nervosa, first identified in 1873, as forms of "female cultural protest." Florence Nightingale argued, "To have no food for our heads, no food for our hearts, no food for our activity, is that nothing? If we have no food for our body, how all the world hears of it ... One would think we had no head or hearts, by the indifference of the public towards them. Our bodies are the only things of any consequence." "When only the body was regarded as important," Showalter concluded, "anorexic girls paraded physical starvation as a way of drawing attention to the starvation of their mental and moral faculties."[27] At the asylum, women had few other avenues for protest. With little physical access to the outside world, even to the perimeters of the grounds, female patients had fewer opportunities than men for either escape or receiving contraband, while physical weakness kept most of them under control. The cultural conditioning that inculcated passivity and submission may have caused women to direct their resistance inward – they stopped eating or tried to commit suicide. Even within the confines of the asylum, it would appear that women found their confinement more exacting, and their choices for rebellion more limited, than men.

WARD THERAPY

Another form of punishment which often was accompanied by mechanical restraint, chemical restaint, or forcible feeding was transfer to another division or building – or what has been termed ward therapy. In his account of the state hospital at Northampton, Massachusetts, David Rothman described the mechanics of ward therapy:

  The patient received a ward assignment, determined almost exclusively by his behaviour in the institution. The quiet and orderly patient went to one ward, the noisy to another, the violent to still another ... In this way, classifications in a state mental institution were much closer to those of a prison than those of a hospital: both of them placed inmates according to custodial, not treatment, criteria. In fact, the resemblance between cell block assignment and ward assignment was even closer, for the state hospital would often reward or punish a patient by placing him on a better or worse ward.[28]

With the expansion of Homewood into separate buildings, Hobbs and his staff practiced a form of ward therapy. Patients were transferred for "screaming," uncleanly habits, "disrupting interviews with other patients," "constant annoyance," excitement, attempted suicide, noisiness, violence, and "yelling fire." Others would be transferred for "improvement" and "better conduct."[29] The patients indeed considered ward therapy to be a "most potent weapon." Hazel C. (#97, 1912), "exalted, egotistical and vain," became so excited she was transferred to B4 until, "very much improved," she was sent to B1. The perception of her improvement was based partly on her acknowledgment that in her "recent excitement ... she said and did many things that were abnormal. 'I am afraid I am very difficult to manage, and gave you all a lot of trouble.'" When her "disturbing" behaviour again produced a transfer, she went "willingly on suggestion of physician" to B4 and controlled herself "very well"; subsequently she only remained twelve days there.

When Margaret D. (#127, 1920) became disturbed due to "neu-ralgic attacks," her second transfer to B3 brought the following state-ment, "Well it is my own fault that I am here – you warned me that I would have to control myself if I were to be permitted to remain on B1. I know that you cannot have disturbance such as I created over there." She was re-transferred after a week. That the patients were indeed 'playing the game' was indicated by the letter of apology written to the superintendent by Ruth H. (#227, 1919), following her transfer to B4. There was a "strong suspicion on the part of the physicians that this letter was written at the instigation and probably partially dictated, by Mrs B. [another patient]." Grace C. (#102, 1914), while considered "not so secretive," was still suspected of hid-ing her views: "she did not voice her delusional ideas as formerly, although it is presumed that direct questioning ... would bring them out."

Ward therapy was not invariably successful. For their part, the physicians did not always scruple at using the threat of ward shift as a repressive measure. When Alice M. (#345, 1918) swallowed poison, she was removed to B4 "for closer observation." When asked her reason for attempting suicide, she replied that "she became so depressed and felt that she would never get away from here." In the next few days, she "continually ask[ed] that she may be taken to the open division again" and was "fearful" that it would never hap-pen. After a month in the closed division, Alice was successful in committing suicide.

Finally, whenever Senator X (#880, 1920) became "irritable and hyperactive," he was removed to the Bungalow "where he very rap-idly calmed down." The senator "possesses a horror for the bungalow and we find this is the best place to keep him quiet." How much was this fear real or imagined? The difficulty in examining asylum rec-ords is that so much of it is aimed at public relations, either in the form of annual reports, board minutes, newspaper articles, or ad-vertisements. Much of Homewood's records are of this type. In 1923, however, with the resignation of Hobbs, Fred Jarvis, president of the sanitarium, commissioned Dr C.K. Clarke, a leading Toronto psychiatrist, to undertake a critical assessment of the institution. Clarke's remarks were candid and devastating. He alluded to the high standard of service Homewood had maintained, but observed that "of late, owing to the failing health of Dr Hobbs, it has fallen back to a certain extent." The "most glaring and outstanding defect," Clarke found, was the Bungalow:

I have sent a very large number of patients to Homewood, but it is equally true that I have had several removed because my conscience would not permit me to allow these people to be retained in the Bungalow Department, as almost any psychiatrist will agree that its influence for harm is great. The building is not only an anachronism, but has done incalculable harm to the reputation of Homewood ... After having visited all of the ... institutions in Canada, and a very large number both in the United States and Europe, I can truthfully say that nowhere have I seen anything more open to criticism. [In appearance, it was] suggestive of a second rate country gaol ... Its interior is calculated to depress the inmates and perpetuate their mental worry rather than cheer them up and help to their recovery. They are shut out from the world ... and [the] attendants ... are not anxious to give their best in the way of treatment.[30]

The Bungalow's shuttered rooms were "glorified prison cells of the most disagreeable character." In Clarke's opinion, the Bungalow could not be renovated; "it should be pulled down and ... [a] psychopathic hospital substituted for it." That Homewood's facilities for the acutely insane should have been so inferior is especially striking when compared to the progress and promise during the early days of Hobbs's regime. Clarke's further remarks also help explain the breakdown and deterioration that could be inferred from the dramatic increase in the use of chemical and mechanical restraint after 1910. The operative factor in this decline, as he observed, was lack of supervision. With Hobbs's failing health and increasing delegation of authority to assistants, the possibilities for abuse and neglect also increased. Clarke noted that a major drawback to the Bungalow was its complete isolation from the main institution. "Even yesterday as we went through we found a patient secluded in an absolutely dark dungeon, and that the seclusion had been done by the attendant, and without reference to any of the officials."

Other equally archaic practices lent themselves to patient abuse. Clarke had been sent by a "prominent Ontario family" to look at a member "so violent" that a male attendant was detailed to look after her. "When I visited the institution," Clarke related, "she had been in an altercation with this male attendant, during which she had received a fractured jaw. It was a very embarassing condition of affairs [but] I smoothed things out with the relatives and suggested ... that the wisest thing ... would be the transfer of the patient to a public institution. This was done and the result was that the patient gave no trouble after the transfer, but was easily managed and amenable to routine treatment." This scene could easily have taken place in 1793 rather than 1923.

Patients defended themselves against the asylum's restraining methods in various ways. Two particular resistive behaviours are the subject of the remainder of this chapter.

COMPLAINTS

The asylum administrators were often tried by the stream of complaints, both serious and trivial, that they received from the patient population. These complaints took the form of visits to the superintendent's office, letters home, and occasionally the initiation of lawsuits against the institution. Legal action against an asylum, especially a private one, could be very damaging to its reputation. In the public mind, at the turn of the century, the asylum was still synonymous with abuse and unlawful subjection. Sensational novels such as Charles Reade's *Hard Cash*, Ebenezer Haskell's *The Trial of Ebenezer Haskell*, and Georgina Weldon's *How I Escaped the Mad-Doctors*, as well as the publicity generated by the patients' rights crusade organized by Elizabeth Packard of the United States in the 1860s and 1870s, promoted the idea that many inhabitants of asylums were victims of wrongful confinement. "Some minds positively revel in conjuring gruesome pictures that have for their background the harrowing experiences related in Reade's *Hard Cash*," complained Edward Runge, superintendent of the St. Louis, Missouri insane asylum. "Collusion between the victim's kindred and the authorities is either charged openly or more often mysteriously whispered about."[31]

In 1883, John Chapin, medical superintendent of the Welland Asylum in New York, published a passionate diatribe against the purveyors of public complaints about institutions like his own. The guilty parties in particular were the newspapers, electioneering politicians, discharged attendants, and ex-patients. "So frequently, causeless, undeserved and unexpected, have been the attacks upon the asylums for the insane," Chapin exclaimed, "that it has, probably, been the personal experience of some here present to enjoy a momentary sensation of relief after gleaning the morning papers to find they have not been publicly charged with the commission of some grave offense."[32]

Homewood was particularly vulnerable to public distrust. As C.K. Clarke observed in 1923, "much of the criticism levelled at Homewood is based on the assumption that it is merely a mercantile venture, developed for the gratification of a group of business men ready to exploit the misfortunes of their fellow citizens for the purpose of profiting by them."[33] This perception was heightened each time a patient, whom Runge characterized as "court-cranks," began legal proceedings against the institution.[34] Because of the possibility of being charged with collusion with family members for monetary gain, the superintendents had to be extremely careful when relations requested to be given powers of attorney. In 1891, when Mr M. was approached by his family to sign such a document, Lett first ensured that he understood what it would mean: "I then put several questions to him to test his mental capacity on business matters." Lett appeared convinced when M. disapproved of his young daughter being sent away to school, and gave instructions "not to let his daughters go out to meetings at night."[35]

Complaints were also handled by the board of visitors who made unannounced visits to the asylum, and who took special interest in patients at the request of their families or in those patients who had written them letters. Mr G., for example, was "specially conversed with and he states that he is kindly treated by Dr Lett." Miss L., on the other hand, had complained of her "being confined on the charge of insanity." In 1922, Maud H. (#210, 1919) a delusional patient, had escaped from the institution and had to be returned from Toronto. During her absence, she initiated proceedings to be presented to court on a writ of habeas corpus, but the judge refused to grant it. Although all authorities concerned were of the opinion "that she is a mental case," steps were being taken "through the patient's husband and the provincial Inspector to have this patient removed from this institution." Dickinson H. (#787, 1912), an alcoholic, talked of writing a "disparaging description of the institution, after he left it." While he admitted "he might not be able to make any very unfavourable criticism of the place, yet the mere fact that it had been criticized, could not fail to be hurtful to the reputation of the institution."[36]

When M.C. (#632, 1905) was discharged, he wrote a bitter letter of complaint to Hobbs:

Since my return home my mother has shown me some of the letters you wrote her. Others she burned. [M's complaints, which if, as Hobbs wrote, were "exaggerated", nevertheless revealed a patient's perception of his treatment. Among his charges was that Hobbs had seen M.] twice or at most thrice, professionally (if your coming into my room twice and looking at me in the smoking room once may be dignified by the name of professional visits). [Another common complaint was that as a sane, alcoholic patient, M. could not find] rest and quiet among a lot of lunatics, idiots and a syphilitic. [When M. was refused his razor because other patients on the floor] might get into other patients' rooms, the doors having no locks, and cut their throats and perhaps the throats of other patients as well [was it not] a nice place to get peace and quietness in?

M.C. also raised the popular perception of Homewood as a money-gouging enterprise: "Your place is run largely upon a financial basis – to create large dividends and to make the stocks valuable is not blameworthy and you are, I believe, adept at the business but the law as it stands makes you too much of a boss and autocrat."[37]

Stephen Lett encountered two serious and embarassing lawsuits in the 1880s brought by patients Agnes H. and John S. According to her attorney's legal memorandum, Agnes (#206, 1888) had voluntarily entered the asylum for the treatment of a chloral habit. She charged, however, that "far from any attempt being made to fulfill the obligations undertaken by the authorities, there was an entire disregard of them and the surroundings of the patient were such as would drive a person in good health as to body and mind into a state of nervous disorder." The food was "revolting to any persons other than lunatics," there was little "supervision, sympathy or care expressed," her mail was intercepted, and only one "filthy" bath was available for all the female patients. On three occasions, Agnes charged, she was seized "roughly" by the nurses and was "injured." Homewood's solicitors, whose defence was based primarily on the psychological effects of the chloral habit, were anxious about one aspect of her charges in particular – the lack of separation from insane patients: "the patient was placed amongst those suffering from the most debasing form of insanity where all is not of propriety and common decency where grown women [engaged in] noises, mutterings, gestures, facial language and filthy and repulsive actions."

The provincial government was concerned about the political fallout from the case. Inspector O'Reilley, during Lett's absence, visited Homewood and attempted to convince the matron, Mrs Finch, to take a position in another asylum. Lett considered this "a most contemptible piece of business ... and quite beneath the dignity of the office he holds as government inspector."[38] While Lett might have been ethically correct in this judgment, such public remarks were not politically astute. Had Homewood failed, it is doubtful whether he would have found another position in the Ontario asylum system.

Another serious lawsuit was that initiated by John S. (#1063, 1889), a paretic who sued for his release. This case was especially sensitive since John's brother was a leading member of the Montreal establishment, and John insisted that he had been committed at the "instrumentalities" of his family. John would not listen "to any reason" and brought suit for his release. Although the suit was unsuccessful, it is worth noting that John was accorded special privileges at Homewood including a private attendant, special foods, and freedom to post letters unread. The efforts of the physicians were met with vilification quite often. John's actions had been instigated by another patient, William T. When William's family urged Lett, and then Langmuir, to take William back, Lett refused, stating, "had it not been for T.'s action in this matter we would not now be involved in this lawsuit." William had written another patient, Lett noted, displaying "the animus [he] bears towards me and confirms me in the wisdom of refusing to have such a miserable man in the house. Why T. should bear this feeling towards me I know not as I have always treated him like a gentleman and I can only look upon it as the action of a weak intellect ... I pity more than blame a man in his condition."39

Hobbs was also faced with serious lawsuits, such as that Maurice D. instituted in 1910. According to Hobbs, Maurice was legally admitted and "changed his mind and demanded to be released." His solicitor and his wife however "strongly protested ... and requested that he be retained at all hazards." At issue was the fact that Maurice was an American and the point was raised as to the right of the sanitarium to detain an alien. Hobbs was anxious that the matter be determined "once for all," as many present and future admissions would be affected by the court's decision. In 1920, an ex-patient, George A., sued Homewood for "illegal detention and abuse." While the sanitarium was successful in defeating the suit, the superintendent was angered by the actions of the court: "After wasting the time of the court with the most trivial evidence possible [that is, damaging the reputation of the sanitarium], Mr Justice Orde took it out of the hands of the jury [by stating] that the statute of limitations [had run out] and that there was not one tittle of evidence produced to show that this man did not receive but the kindest possible treatment while here as a patient."40

In 1888, when the (mostly alcoholic) gentlemen began complaining about the food, swearing at the attendants, and demanding more privileges, Lett saw this (probably with no pun intended) as "simply the outcome of a spirit of insubordination which is brewing." This spirit of insubordination, that is, the development of a patient subculture, often shared with attendants, led to lawsuits (as in the John S. case), the smuggling of contraband (alcohol or drugs), and escapes. After Thomas P. (#989, 1915) lost his parole when he informed his physician that he would return from town at his "convenience," he tried to send letters by "the underground method which is wrapping the letters in a newspaper and dropping it from the verandah. These were picked up by an attendant who handed them to the doctors."41 It is not clear in this instance whether the physician was being facetious, or whether an informal system of mail delivery had in fact been devised. Patients with parole privileges certainly did carry mail for others. Jacob C. (#659, 1919), for example, posted letters for other patients "which he knows is strictly against the rules." Jacob had his parole cancelled for this reason and because he had been "interviewing two or three lawyers in the city" to get his release.

Don McL. (#898, 1919), who was "improving," became "more or less under the influence of one of the patients ... who does all he can to urge him against the staff." From the physician's viewpoint, Jacob and Don had both been influenced by David L. (#878, 1919), a morphia addict "very contrary" to the physicians. In fact, David was transferred to another ward to separate him from Jacob because they "were indirectly from their talk having a bad influence on the rest of the patients."

Patients also complained about violent attendants. As Gerald Grob has observed, staff violence towards patients tended to be spontaneous responses of anger rather than systematic patterns of oppression.[42] The employment of a workforce that was not always ideal, coupled with the actions of a difficult, potentially violent patient population, provided many situations which could upset the delicate balance between management and oppression. Moral treatment failed when confrontational episodes and tragedies caused by negligence occurred with greater frequency, usually during periods when a strong, central authority was absent. In table 19, these incidents have been grouped into the three periods of administration. In figure 2, the rates of confrontational incidents and accidents, use of hypnotics and sedatives, and admissions, have been correlated to illustrate the apparent success of moral treatment during Hobbs's early administration, and its apparent failure during the Lett years and especially during the later years of the Hobbs administration.

For the asylum administrators and physicians, charges of abuse made by the insane were agonizingly difficult to deal with. As the editors of the *American Journal of Insanity* noted in 1882, "no ... duty was more unpleasant than having to listen to complaints of ill-treatment." The superintendent required "tact, experience and sagacity" to sort through the testimony of patients and attendants.[43] The charges might be trivial or serious. When patient S. complained that Ira Carpenter, an attendant, had insulted him, Carpenter explained that no offence had been intended: "He had been brought up a Quaker amongst whom it is the custom to call people by their surnames and not say Mr." Lett decided, however, to discharge him. When Reverend Edwin H. (#807, 1915), a feeble, elderly gentleman, wandered off the premises, the attendant "unnecessarily used a certain amount of force with him, with the result that his wrists became

Table 19
Failures of Moral Treatment: Incidence of
Confrontation and Negligence

Years	Male	Female	Total	%
1883–1900	16	14	30	17
1901–10	9	3	12	7
1911–20	47	89	136	76
Total	72	106	178	100

Notes: This table includes every case in which one or more of
the following were noted in the sample population: disruptive behaviour, violent behaviour, mechanical restraint,
confinement in bath packs, artificial feeding, solitary confinement, escape, accidental death, suicide.

Instances in tables 17, 18, and 19 are most likely underrepresented. Approximately one-third of the sample files have extremely sparse data subsequent to admission. As C.K. Clarke
noted, (see p. 131), violent, destructive, and other intractable
insane cases were housed, after Homewood's expansion, in
back wards and separate buildings, such as the Bungalow,
and received the least amount of direct attention from the
house physicians. Instances of neglect, abuse, or overmedication in these wards would therefore tend to be underrepresented.

somewhat swollen and his dignity injured." The attendant was also
discharged. For those unable to speak, the physicians had to note
physical signs such as mysterious bruising. When Mr A. (admitted
31 July 1888) was discovered to be bruised, Lett could not find out
the cause, but assumed it was due to his restlessness and the "very
loose" condition of his tissues.

Violent patients threatened both inmates and employees; Helen
H. (#222, 1892) gave Fannie G. "a mauling," while Carrie W. (#529,
1920) made two assaults upon an elderly patient "scratching her in
the face."[44] Lucy N. (#380, 1918) "made a very violent assault upon
the nurse, breaking the nurse's glasses, tearing her clothes and physically abusing her." Ethel McK. (#318, 1917) struggled with the night
supervisor to try to secure from her a nailfile, "making the remark
that if she had it she would plunge it through her heart." Rosalie P.
(#413, 1916) threw a shoe at a physician, "inflicting a gash in the
scalp about an inch long. Questioned as to why she does this, she
says that she is subject to impulses of this kind and should not be
blamed for giving way to them, and that it is the business of the
institution to protect her."

Figure 2
Incidents of Confrontation, Negligence, and Sedation by Decade

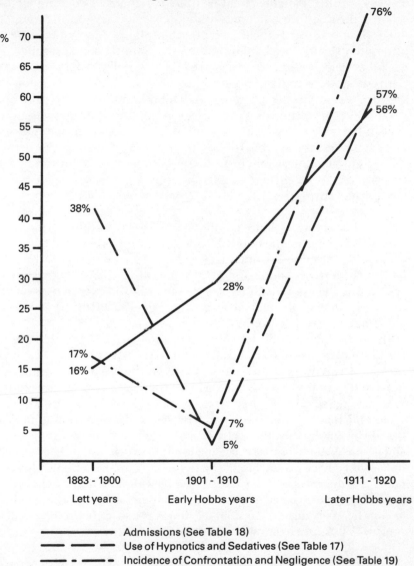

Admissions (See Table 18)
Use of Hypnotics and Sedatives (See Table 17)
Incidence of Confrontation and Negligence (See Table 19)

(Percentages represent percent of total incidents, sedations, and admission for sample population, 1883–1920)

More common than physical abuse was negligence resulting in injury or death. Patients could be quite ingenious in devising methods for their self-destruction, although carelessness on the attendant's part was occasionally responsible. Janie M. (#333, 1884) attempted suicide by drinking ammonia a nurse had given her to wash her hair. Amitta M. (#353, 1917), in the midst of a protracted depression, tried to hang herself with a stocking. The prevention of suicides was a chronic dilemma. As Hobbs admitted, "the problem of absolute protection is as yet unsolved in any institution for the care of the insane, especially so when the cream of would-be suicides are committed to asylums for treatment ... We have tried to better the existing conditions by introduction of glass panels in the doors of certain rooms, all night lights, a larger night staff, and careful [systematic] inspection of each suspected patient and his room on retiring."[45]

Yet other acts of violence could not be so easily justified. Nineteen-twenty was a particularly bleak time for 'moral treatment'; in that year, Rebecca L. was scalded to death in the continuous bath after her nurse left her alone for fifteen minutes. This tragedy, which resulted in a lawsuit instituted by the patient's widower, was as much the consequence of understaffing as negligence; the nurse had been alone in charge of "eleven violently insane patients."[46]

By 1920, the male refractory ward was degenerating into an arena for violent confrontation. Foster S. (#1044, 1920), a sixty-year-old farmer, was paranoid and manic. Once on the wards, he became so noisy and excitable, he was locked in his room. His case history reads:

On Thursday night he was quite noisy, barricading his room, throwing the bed around against the wall and pushed the bed up against the door and propped himself against that, and the wall, so that the attendants could not get in ... They got the fire hose and tried to scare him. He mistook the hose for a gun and said, 'Shoot away,' that he wished he were dead anyway ... However, they succeeded in forcing an entrance whereby patient kicked one of the attendants in the stomach. It was necessary to use him a little roughly and he received a slight mark over his left eye.

Albert D. (#697, 1920), a 36-year-old farmer, also experienced a questionable variety of moral treatment when admitted during a manic episode.

MARCH 6 On admission patient was placed on A2, he was in a very excitable condition. He kicked one of the attendants very severely and tore another one's trouser leg. Placed in observation room, he would not stay in bed and was very religious. Kept repeating in a loud voice portions of Scripture ... Three drahms of Bromide were administered, which he refused to take, but by holding his nose we succeeded in making him swallow it. This quieted him to some extent, although he did not rest well that night ... This morning condition much the same. Bowels have not moved, so was given large dose of Cascara in his milk, which it was necessary to administer artificially. I might say, also, that he had to be fed on Friday with the tube.

MARCH 8 This morning patient is very much better ... He asked to be given water to wash, also to have his teeth and mouth cleansed ... Then said he would eat and take any medicine which we thought necessary ...

MARCH 16 On Saturday afternoon, a slight redness was noticed over the bridge of the patient's nose. By Sunday morning this had increased in size until the whole nose was involved, being of a deep red color and slightly swollen. This looked suspicious of erysipelas. ... Treatment [vaccine] was instituted. Temperature 102°.

MARCH 20 Very much better but refuses to eat sufficient amount ... Anticipating tube feeding him but at present are fearful of starting up an infection on top of the erysipelas.

MARCH 27 Patient ... catatonic, resistive, and found it necessary on Monday to start artificial feeding three times a day ... On Thursday he took his food voluntarily ... The face now is normal, except for a few sores on his upper lip ...

APRIL 17 Patient's condition shows considerable variation mentally ... For some reason or other, he has taken a dislike to the physicians ...

APRIL 24 On Friday [the ward physician] had a long talk with the patient. He said he was feeling a great deal better ... He rather took exception to the treatment he received when he first came in ... I argued the point with him and he said he was handled rather roughly ... He could not see how it took four men to bring him over to the ward.

ESCAPE (ELOPEMENT)

Some patients demonstrated their displeasure with asylum life by escape, or what was then termed elopement. Attempting escape was a male option; few women were given day paroles or were left unsupervised so that opportunities to escape did not arise often. Among the sample population, twenty-eight men and three women succeeded in escaping. Escape was a possibility particularly for alcoholic patients, many of whom made it clear that they did not differentiate between their asylum residence and prison. Charles D. (admitted 8 October 1888) escaped several times, and on other occasions was placed under lock and key because an attempt was expected. He was finally successful in 1889 when he escaped to the United States.[47] About the same time, William C. (#638, 1884), also an alcoholic, escaped twice using wires and a small key which "by careful manipulation will slip the bolt back. Without actually trying myself," Lett admitted, "I could not have believed it possible." During William's first admission to Homewood in 1884, he had to be sought and returned by peace officers three times; Lett wanted to discharge the "confounded nuisance" on the grounds of "vicious conduct" as per the Asylum Act. Langmuir's response was that escape was not considered vicious under the act; it was in fact a "natural impulse." William was discharged as an incurable.[48]

Asylum commitment, by its nature, will not be viewed as a positive experience by most patients. For a few, however, the retreat lived up to its name, becoming a sanctuary from a stressful world. George B. (#586, 1884) returned voluntarily to stay "a short while as his house is full of visitors and he cannot stand the excitement." Charles T. (#1089, 1906), an alcoholic, never left. Charles carried the mail, operated the "moving picture shows," and exchanged greetings over his wireless until his death in 1925. On Stephen and Annie Lett's fifteenth wedding anniversary, the matron and a number of the patients "got up a little supper and presented us with a very flattering, humorous and pleasing address, accompanied by a handsome 'berry dish.'" As Lett reminisced in the aftermath of a pleasant evening, the patients' "expressions of esteem and satisfaction ... are more than my most sanguine expectations could have looked forward to, and is a most satisfactory expression of the value of this institution to our suffering fellow creatures."[49] Despite the sincerest efforts of the physicians, however, the sentiments of Moses C. (#654, 1906), an evangelical minister committed for manic behaviour and extravagant spending, must have been shared by many patients:

Dear Dr Hobbs,
    Your remarks astonished me. 'It is not a question of sympathy, but of health.' Does not a healthy and sound mind crave sympathy? On the other hand, is there not something lacking when a man's heart and conscience seem as hard as rock? ... This is not the first occasion on which I have been called a fool and a crazy man ... Of course I did not then have the slightest expectation that man would go as far as this as to lock me up in an asylum ... I believe and cannot do otherwise than believe it to have been a mistake on the part of my friends, and therefore I can forgive them. My prayer is: Father, forgive them for they know not what they do. But the feeling of

loneliness and homesickness that comes over me from time to time is almost more than I can bear.

Moses C.

The asylum could be a place of loneliness and overcrowding, of brutality and neglect, but also of emotional sustenance and physical rejuvenation. The common threads that ran through the experiences of Homewood's patients reflected the advantages of proper administrative supervision and the baneful consequences of its absence. Despite the fact that a certain percentage of patients, by virtue of their personalities and behaviour, inevitably would encounter and resist asylum control, the high incidence of the use of chemical restraints, mechanical restraints, forcible feedings and violence indicated that at times the system broke down. When Lett and Hobbs were forced to delegate authority during their periods of illness, the increased incidents of violence and resistance were evidence of the weakness inherent in a pyramidal administrative system. Homewood's experiences in the control of its patients made it clear that if rehabilitation was to be more than an ideal, proper and consistent supervision through all the ranks was imperative.

CHAPTER NINE

Because There is Pain: Medical Treatment of Alcoholism

The use and abuse of alcohol were matters of continuing debate for the medical profession in Victorian Canada, as they were for the country at large. Practitioners had been active in the early temperance movements of the 1830s and 1840s but their roles had become eclipsed by laymen, and many physicians became disaffected as moderate temperance gave way to radical prohibition. This disaffection was also the consequence of the concurrent vogue for alcohol as a therapeutic agent, which divided the profession, exposed it to public censure, and undermined the promotion of the exclusive medical management of alcoholism.

The failure to win popular support for the treatment of alcoholism, or inebriety, as a medical problem – as opposed to a moral issue – affected Homewood's approach to alcoholic patients. During the first years of its existence, the asylum's survival depended on income from a male alcoholic patient population. However, this dependence at a time when the public was generally antagonistic toward alcohol use and vehemently condemnatory of abuse, gave the asylum a reputation that probably prevented other, more 'respectable' patients being recommended for admission.

A large alcoholic population also held ramifications for the internal administration of the asylum. Alcoholics were notoriously unstable patients, prone to short-term stays, relapses, and generally disruptive behaviour. The subsequent actions of the superintendent towards these patients developed into a pattern of paternalism not unlike that in the households they had left behind. So disreputable did the inebriate become by the turn of the century that Alfred Hobbs considered the decline of alcoholic admissions to be not an indication of a general decline in alcoholism, but of the increased status Homewood had achieved in the community.

Alcohol was an essential household item for much of the nineteenth century. As a beverage, it was considered safer than milk or water, and until the 1830s and 1840s, cheaper than tea or coffee.[1] Alcohol was also popularly believed to have medicinal qualities; it stimulated and supported the system, prevented fevers and infectious diseases, and furnished the stamina necessary for hard physical labour.[2] Given the widespread popularity of alcohol as well as its use as a therapeutic agent, the rise in consumption, which peaked in the 1830s, was inevitable.[3] In response, the Canadian temperance movement was organized in both English and French Canada in the 1830s and 1840s and achieved general, if temporary, popular support. In the 1840s, it was estimated that one-third of the total population of Canada East and Canada West had pledged to abstain from alcohol.[4]

By mid-century, the early temperance fervour had cooled and pledges were quietly broken. Those in the core of the movement, predominantly Protestant and middle class, were convinced that prohibition could eliminate indigency and disease.[5] Dissatisfied with the failure of earlier campaigns, temperance advocates began to lobby the federal government for legislated prohibition.[6] As a consequence of these endeavours, the Canada Temperance Act, or Scott Act, proclaimed in 1878, provided for a system of local option; this legislation, however, was rejected by the voters in every Canadian district by 1889.[7] In 1892, a royal commission on the liquor traffic was established. Its recommendations, which would form the basis for national prohibition in 1918, included a call for the removal of alcoholics from common jails and their placement in "proper places where they can be restrained indeterminately."[8]

This recommendation was a small victory for experts on alcohol abuse in the medical profession who had lobbied for special asylums for half a century.[9] The experts considered inebriety to be a hereditary neurotic disorder for which alcohol abuse was only a catalyst – a far more moderate view than that implied in the epithets used by the prohibitionists to describe victims of the 'demon rum.' In further contrast to prohibitionist sentiment, many practitioners considered the effects of alcohol to be not only benign, in small doses, but even therapeutically beneficial in stimulating the "vital power" essential to the natural healing processes.[10] Many medical practitioners and all prohibitionists were clearly on a collision course. This was no less true in Ontario's asylums where physicians using alcohol found themselves forced to defend their choice of therapeutics.

In 1877, the "use of spirits" in the medical treatment of the insane became an issue in the Ontario legislature. This produced no

Table 20
Chloral Hydrate and Opium Used as Hypnotics and
Sedatives in Toronto, London, and Kingston
Asylums, 1875–1878

Drugs	Quantity	Total Patients	Total used per patient
TORONTO			
Chloral Hydrate	25½ oz.	3,469	3.21 grs.
Opium	6½ oz.	3,469	.90
Morphia	2 dr.	3,469	.03
LONDON			
Chloral Hydrate	62 oz.	2,975	10.0 grs.
Opium	28⅔ oz.	2,975	4.62
Morphia	1 oz 1 dr.	2,975	.11
KINGSTON			
Chloral Hydrate	258⅔ oz.	1,720	72.12 grs.
Opium	22⅓ oz.	1,720	6.23
Morphia	2½ oz.	1,720	.69

Source: ARIP (1879), no. 8.
Note: The following preparations of opium "have been ex-
cluded from the quantities used by the different asylums, viz:
Tinc. Camph. Co. and Pulv. Co., as these drugs were not
used to quiet patient."

difficulties for John Dickson of Kingston's Rockwood Asylum, who
considered alcohol to be "a most destructive agent to every organ
or tissue of the body either in a state of health or disease."[11] At this
time, however, he was in the minority. Toronto's Joseph Workman
declared that "total abstainers should leave the domain of medicine."
London's Henry Landor added that alcohol tended to "restore the
vital powers."[12] The staunchest defender of alcohol therapy, however, was Daniel Clark, Workman's successor at Toronto. He con-
ceded that "alcohol as a beverage has done incalculable injury to
society. In health no one needs it, and in disease it has to be given
with discretion and judgment." Clark pointed out, however, that its
removal from the asylum's pharmacopeia often led to an increased
reliance on other drugs "more pernicious" than alcohol. In comparing drug use at three Ontario asylums between 1875 and 1878
(see table 20), he noted that Dickson's 'dry' Kingston Asylum prescribed ten times as much chloral hydrate and nearly four times as
much opium as the 'wet,' and far larger, Toronto and London asylums.[13]

By the end of the century, the tide was turning in favour of the
prohibitionists. Dickson was replaced as temperance advocate in the
asylum community by the more formidable Richard Bucke, who

removed alcohol from the shelves of the London Asylum and credited this action for a "remarkable" one percent drop in the patient death rate.[14] Although practitioners chose other alternatives to alcohol in therapeutics, they did not entirely leave the field; coincident with the rise of alcohol therapy was the formulation of the disease concept of alcoholism.

Many in the medical profession believed treating alcoholism was their prerogative. William Westcott, a British physician, no doubt voiced the sentiments of many practitioners when he wrote in 1900, "The relief of the sufferer from alcoholic excess is a purely medical question of medicinal treatment on ordinary therapeutic lines, and ... the tendency to inebriety can only be overcome by a period of hygienic restraint in an institution regulated by law and managed by medical men who have had experience in the treatment of mental degeneracy and physical incapacity."[15]

Because the personality changes and behaviour patterns resulting from inebriety so resembled insanity, the experts, most of whom had had experience practicing in asylums, described it in the same terms as insanity, and eventually concluded that alcoholism was in fact a manifestation of a previous mental imbalance. T.D. Crothers, the premier American authority, stated that inebriety "is insanity, obscure and masked, starting from the same range of physical causes, following the same lines of progress, and curable in substantially the same way."[16] By casting alcohol abuse in a form palatable to the middle-class patient, that is, as a physical condition worthy of sympathy rather than as vicious conduct, the experts in treating inebriety were creating a profitable market for their therapies and their institutions. In Canada, such treatment could be found at the Homewood Retreat under Stephen Lett.

Both the institution and Lett's professional career were shaped by the asylum's inebriate patients. Lett had outlined his conception of inebriety in an 1889 newspaper article, in which he differentiated between the vice of drunkenness, the product of a weak moral fibre, and the disease of inebriety, the consequence of chronic drunkenness. Where "vice and sin are the factors," he concluded, "we may safely leave the treatment to the care of the clergy and other well meaning people." When disease was present, however, "it rests with medical men and the state to take action." Lett argued that men drink because "there is pain," a "feeling of disturbance" produced by a hereditary predisposition which "makes the victims an easy prey to the ravages of such stimulants."[17]

His hereditarian views concerning alcoholism apparently found favour with prospective patients. For much of the late 1880s and 1890s, the proportion of alcoholic patients at Homewood was substantial, in fact essential for the survival of the institution. (See figure 3.) Yet alcoholic patients were notorious for short stays. As Toronto's Daniel Clark noted, "Many of the wealthy go voluntarily to pleasant asylums when remorse is on them after a long debauch," but would then leave when the urge returned.[18]

As early as 1886, Homewood's president was complaining of failure in keeping the "unfortunate inebriate" under treatment. "The short stay of so many of the patients," wrote J.W. Langmuir, "may in many cases be accepted as a satisfactory evidence of the good work done by the Retreat. Unfortunately, however, a short stay in the Retreat cannot in all cases be regarded as proof that the patient has derived permanent benefit from his sojourn in the Institution ... Everything must be done to induce the unfortunate ... to remain ... for a sufficiently long period to effect a perfect cure of his malady."[19] The directors approved a policy of refusal to admit inebriates for periods of less than six months. With low admission figures and a faltering balance sheet, however, this policy was impossible to enforce. Lett devised a rate scale based upon the length of time the alcoholic remained and still was forced to demand four-weeks payment in advance from inebriates. (See appendix 6.) Alcoholic patients were able to use the fact that they were housed with the insane to convince their relatives to take them home; yet while revenues were so low, there could be no possibility of providing inebriates with a separate ward.

The problem of Homewood's dependency on its alcoholic patients was compounded by the craze for the gold cure. The cure, created by Dr Leslie Keeley of Dwight, Illinois, was a treatment for alcoholism based on the detoxification effects of a gold-coloured serum composed of atropine and strychnine. Treatment required a three-week session at a franchised Keeley Institute. The phenomenal success rate Keeley claimed, the short period of treatment, and the optimistic sociable character of the various Keeley clubs and centres ensured the immediate success of the cure. So popular was it, and so dependent was the institution on alcoholic patients, that Lett, while condemning the cure as quackery, was forced to adapt it for use at Homewood: "Inebriates will have gold cure," he reported. "Therefore your superintendent has found it necessary to practice it here, and although the remedies under this plan of treatment have been kept a profound secret by the Keeley Company, yet, through Experiment and otherwise I soon developed a formula for 'Gold Cure' which, if not identical, is closely allied to the Keeley formula and under similar circumstances will give the same results."[20] When the craze for the gold cure subsided, difficulties remained for Home-

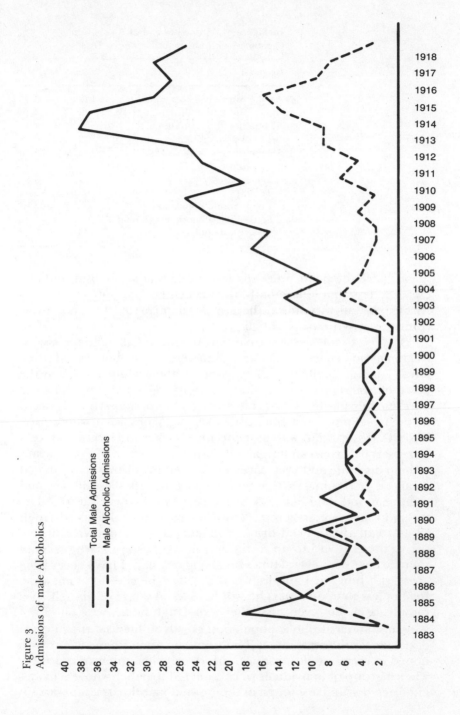

Figure 3
Admissions of male Alcoholics

——— Total Male Admissions
– – – Male Alcoholic Admissions

Table 21
Incidence of Alcoholism and of Alcoholism
Combined with Other Addictions or Diseases

Diagnosis	Male	Female
Alcoholism	149	19
Alcoholism and addiction	19	12
Alcoholism and neurasthenia	9	4
"Alcohol psychosis"	9	0
Alcoholism and syphilis	2	0
Alcoholism and addiction to cigarettes	1	0
Total	189	35
Total sample population	567	567
Percentage of alcoholics in total sample population.	33%	6%

wood, since the public were still convinced that alcoholism could be cured in less than one month. Consequently, Lett's attempts to institute gradual withdrawal therapy was interpreted by many to be thinly disguised money-gouging.

As table 21 indicates, a substantial one-third of all male admissions to Homewood between 1883 and 1920 were for alcohol-related problems. For the families of these patients, the asylum was often the place of last resort. Homewood's patrons were both hopeful for a cure and pessimistic about achieving it and were similarly ambivalent in their feelings about their afflicted kin. A physician whose wife, Mary C. (#92, 1899) was an inebriate, sent her to Homewood "as a last resort before seeking legal separation ... I have tried every means to help dissuade and even threaten her but my efforts have proved a failure ... Hoping Dr that you will give her the best of care and treatment and send her back to me cured in the near future." The father of an inebriate wrote, "It is four years since I learned Hugh [S. (#1050, 1885)] liked drink. Thinking to cure him we sent him off to travel [then] to an institution in the Eastern states ... Since then he has been several times on a long drunk ... I have never been cross with him but I am disgusted ... After [he goes to Homewood for not less than one year] he will have to take care of himself." Six months later, however, his father took Hugh home.

A substantial alcoholic population greatly influenced the internal dynamics of the institution. The domestic atmosphere the asylum hoped to create could produce unforeseen consequences especially when a group of individuals were gathered together whose activities had been disruptive enough in their own domestic circles to warrant their institutionalization. Nancy Tomes described the occasional spree at the Pennsylvania Hospital for the Insane, during which a male patient would venture out, only to return a short time later, usually "gloriously drunk." "For some patients, elopement served only as a short-term release during which they eluded supervision and tasted forbidden pleasures (chiefly liquor) with every intention of returning to the asylum's security."[21] The frequency of such prodigalities, however, would indicate that these brief lapses of discipline were more than isolated incidents but were an inevitable, though unforeseen, consequence of moral treatment – that is, the adoption of the family model of institutionalization. Indeed, the treatment and maintenance of the alcoholic patient at Homewood was a fascinating portrait of the paternalistic institution and of patterns of authority relations developed in the home and replicated in the asylum.

Charles McD (#881, 1912) was admitted twelve times between 1912 and 1918. A typical month went as follows:

2 SEPTEMBER 1915 This week patient was given parole of two hours each afternoon on condition that he return no later than five p.m. and that he refrain from entering some of the objectionable stores downtown.

9 SEPTEMBER 1915 Patient continues to show very good control. On Thursday visited the Toronto Exhibition with a nurse.

15 SEPTEMBER 1915 On Sunday last patient was out motoring and came home feeling rather overjoyed. Suspected of taking stimulant but this was not proven, so that his parole was not cancelled. Has been going downtown the last couple of days regularly.

19 SEPTEMBER 1915 Yesterday patient was out in the morning ... It was suspected that he had been taking stimulant, acting very strangely at tea time ... Came home partly under the influence of liquor at night and this morning his parole was cancelled indefinitely.

23 SEPTEMBER 1915 On Monday patient went downtown and came home at tea time, very talkative and slightly irritable. [He later returned] under the influence of liquor. His parole was cancelled, after which time he showed very fair control. Yesterday he demanded that he be given his parole, said that he was going to leave and had to go downtown to make arrangements. This morning was discharged, with the orders that he never return.

Yet Charles would return on four more occasions. While this is an extreme example, it would appear that for patients of this type, the asylum was used as a surrogate and a companion to the home. Charles was not so much treated as overseen and tolerated, granted

favours and privileges until such time as he blatantly broke the house
rules and was 'grounded.' When he exhausted the patience of the
physicians, he was thrown out, that is, he returned to his own home
until such time as he was no longer tolerated there. In this type of
situation, which was fairly common among alcoholic patients, treatment seemed doomed to failure from the start, since unmotivated
patients replicated domestic behaviour patterns of rebellion, secre-
tiveness, and irresponsibility in the asylum, and the asylum inevitably
responded like the home.

Particularly during the 1880s, when the asylum had a dispropor-
tionately large number of alcoholic patients, Lett had considerable
difficulty controlling some patients who were insubordinate and deceitful. Stephen W. (admitted 29 June 1888) was disgruntled that
he would have to remain six months rather than three and said he
would write his wife to demand his liberty. Lett "reasoned with him
[and] told him [he] was aware [it was] only [a] few weeks since Stephen had [a] strong hankering for stimulants and although he re-
sisted impulse he couldn't do so when thrown in temptation's way."
When Lett added what course he would adopt should Stephen attempt to escape, he went upstairs "in a rage saying 'well I suppose
I must consider myself locked in.'" After Stephen tore up letters of
complaint he had written his family, Lett removed the restrictions.
"He is so full of whims that there is no satisfying him," the superintendent complained, "what he will want today probably the next
time it is laid before him he will object to it."[22]

The exchange of paternalistic authority was demonstrated in the
case of Patrick R. (admitted 31 December 1888). When his father
took him home on probation, Lett told him that he had "no faith in
[Patrick] doing well as [he] showed no disposition to reform." Lett
"fully explained" to Patrick that he was only on a leave of absence
and if he drank "whilst out [he] would have to come back." Lett
received a letter from his father two days later stating that Patrick
had "got drunk the next morning" and requesting that Lett come
to get him. This happened twice. On a third occasion, Patrick went
out drinking with another patient. Lett "said [he] would write fathers
to take them home. Did so."[23] The revolving doors of home and
asylum illustrated that such treatment did no more than grant the
family a respite from the patient's disruptive behaviour. It is interesting to note that the tolerance level of the asylum was also not
inexhaustible.

The difficulties in controlling alcoholics were not limited to male
patients. Ina B. (#53, 1912) was an especially obnoxious patient.
Aged forty-four, Ina had used stimulants "more or less constantly"

since she was twenty. She had also used paregoric and chlorodyne
(see chapter 10) on occasion to reduce the amount of alcohol she
drank. The stimulants and narcotics had first been used to relieve
"very painful menstruation." Ina worked in an office, and found it
necessary to take as much as two quarts of Canadian whisky in
twenty-four hours to get her through her working day. While her
physical condition had improved at Homewood, she had "broken
every possible rule of the institution, and particularly in regard to
mingling with the opposite sex.

Wherever men were, there she was to be found. The most flagrant abuses
of any leniency shown, were committed by the patient. From early morning
until late at night, she was on the verandah, speaking to all that passed, or
mingling indiscriminately among patients on the lawn. Further than that,
she would hold conversations with friends of patients, and give wrong
impressions of the institution, offer her opinion as to what should be done
with the patient, going so far as to advise the friends to remove them, in
fact her whole attitude has been one of antagonism towards the institution.

Ina was also not above attempting to bribe a mentally defective
patient to bring her whisky, banging pots in the diet kitchen at two
o'clock in the morning when she did get intoxicated, waking up the
entire female wing, and demanding she be served meals on a tray,
like other patients. A night on the Vista ward settled her down
somewhat, although her attitude remained "unchanged."

The anarchic tendencies of an alcoholic patient population rendered
it undesirable once the problems of numbers had been resolved. In
1904, Alfred Hobbs found "gratifying" the fact that nervous and
mental cases comprised eighty percent of admissions. Hobbs shared
none of Lett's sympathy for the inebriate, believing that "the less the
Sanitarium is known as an inebriate institution, the better will be its
moral atmosphere in the eyes of the profession, and more attractive
will it be to the general public." Lett's "diseased unfortunates" had
become "alcoholic degenerates" who would "heap abuse upon the
institution at every opportunity" for failing "to pander to their depraved appetites."[24] Hobbs clearly was reflecting popular sentiment
concerning alcohol which, less than two years later (in 1906) would
generate the reintroduction of temperance legislation in Ontario.
By that time, the medical profession was no longer as greatly divided
over the alcohol issue as it had been during the late nineteenth
century, when the vogue in alcohol therapeutics had coincided with
the rise of temperance legislation.

The views of specialists like Stephen Lett in the treatment of inebriates met with considerable opposition from temperance advocates. Emphasis on hereditary and psychological factors in the etiology of alcoholism was opposed by pious temperance reformers, who believed that individual sin and moral degeneracy were responsible for drunkenness. Alcohol therapeutics was sufficiently controversial within the medical profession to prevent the presentation of a united front for controlling alcoholism as a medical preserve. Without this unity, the medical profession discovered that not only did it fail to influence public policy, but it was also forced to defend its own choice of therapeutics. As the superintendents of the Homewood Retreat had discovered, the treatment of alcoholics also forced them to defend their choice of patients.

The Aristocratic Vice: Medical Treatment of Drug Addiction in the Nineteenth Century

The Homewood Retreat's experiences with drug addicts were somewhat different from its dealings with alcoholics, at least in terms of professional recognition. The relatively recent discovery of the process of addiction and its treatment enabled Stephen Lett to enter the field early on. He subsequently was able to create a sound reputation for himself and the Retreat in addiction therapy. The nascent disease of addiction, not yet as value laden as alcoholism, allowed practitioners more professional freedom and less therapeutic interference in treating their patients, most of whom were the socially respectable.

Although by 1928, the "dope fiend" was portrayed as a "miserable, emaciated, furtive individual with pinpoint pupils, trembling hands [and] a sallow complexion,"[1] in 1881, "opium eating" was "an aristocratic vice [prevailing] more extensively among the wealthy and educated classes than among those of inferior social position ... The merchant, lawyer, and physician are to be found among the host who sacrifice the choicest treasures of life at the shrine of Opium."[2] Indeed, for most of the nineteenth century, drug addicts did not constitute a deviant social group, but were simply individuals guilty of a specific moral transgression. By the 1920s, addicts were clearly social deviants, so defined by both illness and by vice, and they required institutional isolation.

What caused this transformation in attitudes? Improved technology and pharmaceutical advancement produced more severe cases of addiction while shrinking the pool of potential opium addicts. Government regulation, which should be viewed as the culmination of the shift in attitudes, was produced at least as much by bigotry as by a threat to public health, but it was responsible for curtailing legal supplies of narcotics. The most important factor in the creation of the modern public perception of drug abuse, however, was the definition of addiction as a disease by the medical profession. In Europe, the United States, and in Canada, from the 1870s to the end of the century, the medical profession was in the process of creating and defining a new disease and a new group of diseased.

In the first half of the nineteenth century, opium was an essential element in the physician's pharmacopeia. In raw gum form, as morphine, laudanum, or paregoric, opiates were as widely used as aspirin is today.[3] They were prescribed by physicians, dispensed by pharmacists, and sold in general stores and by mail-order houses. Most patent medicines contained opiates. Because of its exceptional qualities as an anodyne – Benjamin Rush deemed opium "God's Own Medicine" – physicians prescribed opium for gastrointestinal disorders, fevers, rheumatic and arthritic pain, hysteria, syphilis, smallpox, diabetes, cholera, and cancer. Opium also had a long and useful history as a drug for self-medication, for earaches, toothaches, insomnia, dysentery, and for soothing fretful infants. It was especially popular in swampy regions, such as the English fens and the southern American states, with a high prevalence of malarial diseases. Opium was considered invaluable in rural areas without access to physicians or in regions with strong traditions of folk medicine.[4]

The recreational use of opiates was popularized by the Romantic authors. Coleridge, Keats, and Poe were among those who were opium "habitués." They were popularly believed to have written many of their works while "under the influence."[5] The most important writer of this group was Thomas De Quincy, whose *Confessions of an English Opium-Eater* was said to have inspired many to experiment with opiates. As one American lawyer and addict lamented, the *Confessions* "kindled within me a desire to experience for myself the grand dreams to which the drug gave birth in him."[6] Despite the publicity given to famous literary addicts, it has been demonstrated that by the mid-nineteenth century, with easy access to opium, British addiction levels were stable and even falling, as the general population successfully regulated its consumption of opiates.[7]

With the introduction of the hypodermic syringe in the 1850s, and its general use in private practice by the 1870s, however, the nature of opiate abuse was changed.[8] Subcutaneous injection of morphine was at first heralded by the medical profession as lacking opium's side effects, including addiction.[9] The benign administration, and swift dramatic effect, of the hypodermic syringe also had great psychological appeal to the medical profession. Demoralized into "therapeutic nihilism" by the public (and professional) rejection of "heroic" treatment (that is, bleeding, cupping, and purging) in the period prior to the advent of modern synthetic drugs, medical practitioners hailed the morphine injection as evidence that they could cure or at least kill pain.[10] In cases of severe and chronic pain, even a physician aware of the danger of addiction found it difficult, or impossible, to cut off a patient crying out for the needle. The realities of a rural or widely-scattered practice also forced many physicians to teach patients and their families to administer morphine themselves, and the use of the hypodermic soon escaped the control of the medical profession.[11] However, physicians were concerned that so powerful a drug should be so easily available to the public and believed that opiate use and abuse was somehow a medical problem, despite the fact that no addiction "germ" could be found (since all diseases were believed to be organically based) and that addiction appeared to be a condition brought on voluntarily. The general population, on the other hand, accustomed to self-medication, and often hostile to physicians' encroachment on hitherto non-professional spheres, did not share this concern.

The breakthrough for the medical profession came in 1877 with the publication of Edward Levinstein's *The Morbid Craving for Morphia*. Levinstein was the first to describe "morphinism" as a pathological state rather than a habit but also as a "human passion" like gambling, drinking, or smoking. The treatment he recommended, however, dealt more with the moral failings than with the physical disease. It was, in fact, brutal – "harsh, immediate withdrawal" with the patient isolated in a locked room for a week guarded by two male nurses[12]. If the patient lived through the ordeal, and Levinstein described the symptoms of minor and complete collapse, he left the sanitarium cured. Relapse was viewed as the failure of the individual, not of the treatment.

Levinstein's treatment was modified in Britain and North America, but its underlying assumptions, of addiction as a disease and of the moral failing of the individual addict, were not. Norman Kerr, founder of the British Society for the Study and Cure of Inebriety, linked opiate abuse to alcoholism and incorporated it into the temperance movement. Kerr argued that intemperance in the use of alcohol or drugs was a disease of a "depraved, debilitated or defective nervous organization," despite the fact that the majority of cases of addiction were caused by the misuse of hypodermic syringes by physicians, that habits were formed because of chronic conditions and not in pursuit of recreation, and that moderate cases of addiction did not of necessity preclude normal, day to day functioning so long as supplies were maintained.[13]

Kerr's views were controversial at the time, in part because the opium users physicians usually encountered were professionals and others of "high social standing" who did not display "inferior moral intellect." The disease theory, therefore, had to be altered to suit the typical addict. Thomas D. Crothers, an American authority on addiction, modified George Beard's concept of neurasthenia. Neurasthenics were individuals whose nervous systems were rendered too delicate by civilization to deal with an excess of mental exertion, and Crothers considered them to be highly susceptible to opiate addiction.[14]

J.B. Mattison, the foremost American specialist, disagreed with Crothers, arguing that addicts were generally normal people who had become addicted through medical treatment. He also maintained, however, that addiction, once it occurred, was a disease requiring treatment in a controlled environment. Mattison advocated rapid reduction therapy, whereby the patient was weaned from the drug over a period of eight days to two weeks, and also stressed the need to strengthen the patient's nervous system with tonics, hot baths, and bromides.[15]

In Canada, Stephen Lett, an early advocate of the disease concept of drug abuse among Canadian practitioners, was the first well-known addiction specialist. As noted earlier, his position as head of a private asylum enabled him to obtain valuable clinical experience in the treatment of opium and other "neuroses," and through the publication of a number of articles, he established himself as Canada's authority on drug abuse. In an address before the American Medical Association in 1891, Lett argued that addiction should not be regarded as "only a vice, which the patient can at once abandon if he only wishes to do" so, an opinion, he stated, which was held by "at least ninety percent of the medical men of [Ontario] who are not themselves victims of drugs." His speech was sponsored by the board of directors of Homewood on the grounds that the institution would thereby gain wider renown and an increased clientele.[16] As was the case in Britain and the United States, the treatment of addiction at Homewood was motivated by the imperatives of the patient, the physician, the institution, and the medical profession.

Lett considered Levinstein's method, "abrupt and total withdrawal," to be a "barbarous, inhuman and dangerous procedure, involving, as it does, the most exquisite torture." Lett's treatment consisted of the gradual withdrawal of the opiate, effected by "decreasing the amount in fractions of a grain at each dose." When the point was reached where only one grain was consumed in twenty-four hours, Lett "usually [employed] from three to four weeks" until the final dose would be 1/6000 of a grain." Following Mattison, Lett sustained his patients with tonics, bromides, and cannabis indica. Gradual reduction therapy was ideal for the private asylum for a number of reasons: it provided the least discomfort to the patients and would therefore be a more attractive treatment; it reduced the risk of collapse; it required the active participation of a qualified practitioner; and it was only feasible in the controlled environment of an institution. It also required a lengthy and expensive stay.[17]

Lett saw addiction as a disease in strictly physiological terms since, like Levinstein, he believed that when a patient's body was free of morphine, he was recovered. He did not propose that there was a psychological component, even though he did note that "with very much broken down and highly nervous patients, I permit them to retain their syringe and morphia ... it is a source of much comfort to them."[18] High rates of relapse and the inability to discover actual physical manifestations of the disease did not deter practitioners like Levinstein, Kerr, Mattison, and Lett from continuing to accept the disease model of addiction. Not recognizing that their own therapeutics were partly responsible for the problem, their failure to cure was viewed as the moral failure of the addict.

To illustrate the experiences of an addict at Homewood, a composite case will be presented: By the time of his admission in 1893, Dr M., a Toronto physician, thirty-five years old and married, had been addicted to morphia for six years. He had first experimented with it in medical school but refrained from drugs for several years until he resorted to morphine to get relief from various problems such as rheumatism, gastralgia, and the stress of overwork. Because he had access to hypodermic syringes, his addiction was swift and severe. After four years of physical and mental degeneration and a series of unsuccessful cures, he tried another drug touted as an antidote for opiate addiction – cocaine – with, as Lett wrote, "the usual result": double addiction.[19] After an especially bad bout, Dr M. submitted to the urgings of his wife and colleague and signed an application of voluntary admission. His wife added a note to "please keep the matter secret" and to allow him a "lamp to read at night." Dr M. arrived at Homewood by train, accompanied only by his friend, since his wife did not want to bear the blame of having him committed. Dr Lett tested his urine for drug levels, discovering them to be much higher than the patient knew or admitted. Dr M. spent his first days in isolation, with Lett in constant attendance, administering morphine in minute doses to determine how much was needed to "sustain" the patient. Lett did not administer cocaine, believing that withdrawal therapy could only be attempted with one drug, but M.'s withdrawal symptoms were so severe the first night that Lett was forced to send out for a supply of cocaine. M. was permitted to keep his hypodermic syringe for a week, until he was

comfortable with his surroundings, then the morphia was administered orally in gradually reduced doses. During the first few weeks,
M. was given chloral hydrate or cannabis to produce sleep. M. did
"splendidly" until New Year's day, when he went on a drunken binge,
although he soon recovered, and the reduction treatment was continued. Dr M. amused himself by reading, playing chess, strolling
the grounds, and going to the races. He was released "in excellent
health" one week after his last, minute dose. He had been in Homewood seven months. Despite Lett's hopeful prognosis, Dr M. returned eighteen months later.

The nineteenth century has been called the "dope fiend's paradise," and Homewood's patients suffered from a variety of addictions
apart from opium.[20] Chloral hydrate, for example, was discovered
to have therapeutic value in 1869, and within a year became a favourite sleeping potion in North America.[21] Chloral, as it was called,
was considered "unequalled" as a hypnotic, and was widely used in
insane asylums in cases of mania or chronic insomnia.[22] As assistant
physician at the London Asylum, Stephen Lett was enthusiastic about
the value of chloral, although his superior, Henry Landor, believed
that a bottle of "the very best Scotch ale, or the best Dublin stout"
was "more pleasant to take" and not "less effective in its operation."[23]
Six chloral addicts were admitted to Homewood between 1883 and
1900, three men and three women, with one case complicated by
alcoholism and another by morphia taken to break the chloral
habit.[24]

Cocaine, isolated from the coca leaf in 1855, found widespread
popularity in the 1880s when Sigmund Freud and others attested
to its value as a local anaesthetic and stimulant and as a specific
treatment against opiate addiction. Arthur Conan Doyle's experiences as a physician are reflected in Sherlock Holmes's struggle with
addiction to cocaine.[25] All eight of the cocaine addicts admitted to
Homewood before 1900 were male; seven of these were also addicted
to alcohol or opium.[26] Stephen Lett referred to these cases in the
Canada Lancet in 1898. Most of those addicted to cocaine, he concluded, were "neurotics, and like many such are always on the outlook for some medicine or stimulant to quiet their unstable nervous
organization." Cocaine was easily accessible in patent medicines and
by prescription from "the dentist, rhinologist and general practitioner." Lett graphically evoked the cocaine "habitué:"

Nutrition soon becomes impaired, accompanied by emaciation and ane-
mia; sunken eyeballs with dark areola round the eyes, prominent cheek
bones and general pallor makes the subject a most ghastly spectacle. As the

Table 22
Addictions of All Patients Admitted for Substance
Abuse prior to 1900

	Male		Female		Total	
	No.	%	No.	%	No.	%
Alcohol	139	55.5	10	22	149	50.5
Opium[a]	52	21	23	51	75	25
Alcohol plus non-opiate	37	15	5	11	42	14
Cocaine[b]	8	3	0	0	8	3
Other[c]	4	1.5	4	9	8	3
Unknown	10	4	3	7	13	4.5
Total	250	100	45	100	295	100

[a]Opium represents addiction to one or more of the following: morphia, laudanum, "morphia and other narcotics and stimulants," "laudanum and liquor," "inebriate and opium," narcotics, chlorodyne.
[b]Includes cocaine and opium.
[c]Chloral, chloroform, paraldehyde, bromides, sulphonal, tobacco, drugs.

malady becomes more chronic, mental symptoms in the form of hallucinations and delusions supervene. Persons seen or heard at a distance are construed into bands of enemies plotting to rob, physically disable, or murder, and as a result the patient makes complaints and lays charges against innocent persons.[27]

Chloroform,[28] bromides, chlorodyne,[29] sulphonal, and tobacco were other addictions treated at the asylum. Thomas B. (#608, 1891), a paraldehyde addict readmitted four times over a four-year period, was considered by Lett to be unique enough to be reported in *The Medical Times and Register*. Previous to this case, a paraldehyde habit was considered extremely unlikely "owing to the disagreeable odor and taste of the drug."[30] Opium, however, remained the drug of choice for addicts. Of non-alcoholic addicts admitted to Homewood in the nineteenth century, over one-half were opium addicts. Homewood's patients took their opium in morphine injections, laudanum tonics, with whisky, cocaine, or "other narcotics and stimulants." (See tables 22 and 23.)

The stated causes of addiction varied but they can be grouped under several broad categories as physiological, social, emotional or hereditary causes, and prior addiction. As a matter of fact, drugs other than alcohol were mainly taken to cure pain. In an age in

Table 23
Drug Addictions among Sample Population

Diagnosis	Male	Female
Opium	32	29
Chloroform	0	2
Atropine	0	1
Chloral	0	1
Chlorodyne	0	1
Paraldehyde	1	0
Alcoholism and addiction	19	12
Multiple addiction	9	3
Addiction and neurosis	4	7
Addiction (unspecified)	5	6
Addiction and delusions	0	1
Total	70	63
Total sample population	567	567
Percentage of total sample addicted	12%	11%

which physicians treated symptoms, not diseases, efficacious anaes-
thetics, analgesics, sedatives, and hypnotics were widely used. Patients
cited epilepsy, rheumatism, asthma, bad teeth, peritonitis, and Civil
War wounds as the initial reasons for taking opium. Emotional problems such as those caused by business failure or family trouble, stress
or overwork, drove other people to drugs. Whisky was used to break
off opium habits, cocaine was used to break off morphine, and paraldehyde was taken to break the habit of chloral; this process invariably led to multiple addictions. That heredity was not seen as
important in cases of drug addiction can best be explained by the
association of drug addiction with the "better classes" in the nineteenth century. Addicts came from families whose accomplishments
and social standing rendered them anything but "degenerate," and
who themselves were the first to chastise the intemperate "other
half."

Among the addicts admitted to the Homewood Retreat, two sub-
groups were noteworthy. William Osler wrote, "The [opium] habit
is particularly prevalent among women and physicians," and Homewood's statistics bore this out.[31] One-half (49%) of the women admitted to the inebriate branch before 1900 were addicted to opiates,
while only one-fifth (20%) of the men admitted were so addicted.
Women were susceptible to drug abuse because opiates were specified for the whole range of "female disorders." Patients used laudanum or morphine injections to relieve the pains of a "fibro-cystic

growth," of menstruation, and of menopause.[32] There were also less tangible female ailments, depression, insomnia, neurasthenia, "restlessness and hysteria,"[33] psychological, and psychosomatic disorders which drove many women to use narcotics and stimulants. Mood-altering drugs, first introduced by physicians and druggists for physical complaints, became habits for women in need of emotional release, especially in a culture where saloons and alcohol were male preserves. Women who "never knowingly would touch liquor would drink it and opiates as 'medicine.'"[34] The popular rest cure for women might also have exposed many women to drugs. As the American physician George Butler cautioned, "there is very little doubt that bromide, chloral and other drug habits are created during the rest cure."[35] Elizabeth M. (#356, 1892), a middle-aged opium addict, was introduced to opiates by her doctor. She insisted she had not taken any drugs for some time, and her physician concurred. Lett found, however, significant levels of morphine in her urine. Upon further questioning, Lett discovered that Elizabeth had been "taking a tonic prescribed by her physician which she found having a wonderfully soothing effect and which she took with great regularity."

Sarah M. (#379, 1887) was a chloral addict who had been continuously over-dosing herself with the drug for two days. Her husband's letter graphically illustrated the pain sustained by the addict and the suffering endured by the family, as far as it could be tolerated:

[Sarah] goes up today to Guelph to see the Retreat and talk with you ... She does not intend to stay unless she likes it (she won't like it) and will want to come back. I dare not go up with her as she will suspect I was taking her away to an asylum ... She thinks she is going on a visit to see our boy Frank at the [agricultural college] ... Dr Ross said this morning ... the only chance of saving her life is to send her there ... She is in poor health and has a good deal of infirmities – the change of life on her every three or four weeks causes her great pain ... I know she thinks she is awful bad in order to get either stimulant or chloral. She will get awful bad or think she is when she finds she can't get away – and will storm or rave about what she will do – then she will declare she is dying – and implore you to send for me. She always sends for me when she is dying and she has been going to die such hundreds of times this last five years.

The other significant group of addicts were associated with the health care field: physicians, druggists (see table 24), nurses, and female relatives of physicians. This group made up over one-third (36%) of all of Homewood's non-alcoholic addicts before 1900. Almost one-

Table 24
Occupations of Male Morphia and Cocaine Addicts
Admitted prior to 1900

	No.	%
Physician	20	35
Clergy	3	5
Commerce	3	5
Druggists	2	3
Other	3	5
Unknown	27	47
Total	58	100

fifth (18%) of female morphia addicts were nurses. As in the case of physicians, ready access to hypodermic syringes was considered responsible for the severity of the addiction, the drug first being taken for problems such as "rheumatism," and then perhaps continued because of "trouble and unpleasant domestic relations."[36] As could be expected, druggists had the most exotic addictions. William P. (#976, 1893), for example, "went through the whole pharmacopeia" in search of relief from migraine headaches. He took a combination of "Soda Bromide, caffeine citrate and antipyrine," six glasses of brandy daily, and "at times a little chloral and morphia every other night." Lett's paraldehyde case, Thomas B., was also a druggist, a young man who first became addicted to chloral "through insomnia [from] the disturbed sleep attendant to this business." He suffered four relapses, one of which was caused by "the dominion elections. He gave both his clerks leave to go out and ... the strain [of his business] was too much for him."

Physicians were highly susceptible to drug addiction.[37] Peer pressure, especially in medical school, was deemed responsible for introducing medical practitioners to the use of alcohol and opiates. While there are no precise statistics on the number of physician-addicts in Ontario in the nineteenth century, in each year between 1883 and 1890, a few physicians entered Ontario's asylums as patients. The one designated case of addiction at the London Asylum in the 1870s was that of a physician who had become "manic from morphia abuse and the strain of a 'hard country practice.'"[38] At the Homewood Retreat, one-third (33%) of male addicts admitted in the nineteenth century were physicians who used opium. Three-quarters of Homewood's cocaine addicts were physicians who had easiest access to the new miracle drug and apparently had most need of its qualities as stimulant and supposed cure of opiate addiction.[39]

In the nineteenth century, alcoholism and "morphinism in medical men" was a serious concern of and embarassment to the medical profession. When T.D. Crothers published a statement that ten to twenty percent of physicians were "intemperate in the use of alcohol and drugs," the *American Journal of Insanity* was quick to denounce the "extremist."[40] However, J.B. Mattison stated that out of three hundred addicts whom he had treated, 118 cases were physicians. Mattison did not believe the high rate was due to "frequent handling of morphia" but to "non-fatal disorders," "neuralgia," and the "anxious hours, the weary days and wakeful nights." Mattison also blamed the "careless curiosity" of junior physicians who dabbled in self-experimentation, and the "too frequent use of morphia" in general practice. Physicians were also guilty of "ignorance or unbelief as to the ... snareful power of morphia."[41]

Because of overwork, their access to pure drugs, and their unwillingness to seek professional help, physicians had the most serious addictions and were the worst patients.[42] They tended to leave treatment early and suffer relapses often. The average patient took between two and four grains of opium at admission to Homewood; physicians had much higher levels in their systems. Drs Thatcher G. (#768, 1891) and Charles S. (#1036, 1898) required fifteen grains of morphia per day to sustain them. Thatcher had been "out of it once or twice but always went back to work almost the day he took his last dose, consequently [he] was soon into it again." Dr Edward W. (#1103, 1891), twenty-six years old, who first took morphia for "bad teeth" at the age of fifteen, used seventy grains of morphia "and as much cocaine every twenty-four hours." He arrived with ulcers from injections on his arms and legs "about 5–6 inches long by about 3 inches broad." One year after admission, Lett wrote, "after a long and patient struggle both for himself and his physician, he is at last fairly righted and is sustained by 1 ⅛ grain every four hours taken by the mouth, the syringe having been abandoned about ten days ago." Edward left in "excellent" health but was readmitted twice in the next five years. Dr James McM. (admitted 21 October 1889) arrived addicted to forty-five grains of morphia and seventy-five grains of cocaine per day. Reduction treatment was physiologically successful, but as Lett wrote, "the case has been an unsatisfactory one all through ... the man has no mind above the gratification of his own personal comfort ... I was obliged during the latter stages especially to keep him under lock and key ... He is sure to return to it again. No good results could be expected from a person with so low an order of intellect."

Many patients, but addicts in particular, submitted to a variety of cures both before and after treatment at Homewood. As table 25 indicates, twenty-six percent of male and thirty-three percent of

Table 25
Previous Institutionalization of Homewood Patients

	Male		Female	
	No.	%	No.	%
Previous institutionalization	110	19[a] 26[b]	150	26[a] 33[b]
No previous institutionalization	306		310	
Unknown	151		107	

[a]Percentage of total sample population
[b]Percentage excluding unknown cases

female patients had tried other treatments.[43] Many, believing in the benefits of fresh air and change in environment, went to "the seaside" or on European tours. Patients made the rounds of the asylum circuit in New York, Michigan, and Massachusetts and were treated with chloroform, bromides, tonics, and other substances, none of which had satisfactory results. The most heroic course was abrupt withdrawal either at an institution or at home. Helen S. (#477, 1891), for instance, suffered from hysterical paralysis after such a course, while Marguerette O. (#396, 1892) went "almost blind [probably from atropine]." Cures for drug addiction were rarely lasting. As table 26 demonstrates, twenty-two percent of Homewood's patients entered more than once, forty percent of patients who relapsed entered more than twice. Given that Homewood was often not the first nor the last asylum entered, the true relapse rate may have been much higher. As table 27 illustrates, readmissions were common among alcoholics and addicts. In some cases, there were no serious attempts made to stay off the drugs, as in the case of James McM., cited above, or Augustus P. (#990, 1884), a barrister who got drunk "immediately on his leaving his Guelph quarters." In other instances, however readdiction occurred innocently. James N. (#958, 1891), "nicely cured," had bowel trouble. The physician treating him "gave him laudanum per rectum." Elizabeth M., also cited above, was given opium in a cough mixture – by a physician aware of her history.

Following his discharge, Frederick D. (#703, 1884) wrote to Lett, recounting the hard road to recovery and re-integration into the community experienced by former drug users. "About one year ago," the patient wrote,

I was at your place and in no very comfortable condition ... I can say with perfect truth that knowingly I have not taken the least particle of morphine

Table 26
Re-admissions to Homewood

No. of times Patients Re-admitted	Male		Female		Total	
	No.	%	No.	%	No.	%
0	413	73	475	84	888	78
1	80	14	67	12	147	13
2	42	7.5	14	2.5	56	5
3	9	1.5	4	.5	13	1.2
4	11	2	4	.5	15	1.3
5	6	1	2	.3	8	1
6	3	.5	1	.2	4	.3
8	1	.2			1	0
9	2	.3			2	.2
Total (2–9 times)	74	13	25	4	99	9
Total	567	100	567	100	1134	100

in any form ... I carry my hypodermic syringe in my case ... use it when I think I ought ... but have never used it on myself ... For a long time I would not carry morphia in any form ... after a while I sent for a syringe and left it at a Drug Store ... As I grew stronger in mind and body, I began to carry it with me ... Do you think it dangerous? ... If I do break down, you will see me very soon after.

The attitudes of others towards the ex-addict could also increase the likelihood of relapse; the abstainer might be unable to resume his "pre-addiction" social identity, because his experiences as an addict had "set up communication blocks" with those from whom he hoped to receive support.[44] As Frederick wrote, friends "sometimes annoy me by asking unnecessary questions about my health which is only a polite way of asking me if I have freed myself from the [vile] habit, but I have learned to answer in a way that cuts off all discussion without giving offense."

Family responses to addiction followed patterns similar to those evidenced when patients with other diagnoses were committed to the asylum. Intolerable behaviour or changes in circumstances also preceded the admission of addicts to Homewood. Mary S. (#450, 1885), a physician's widow, used laudanum and liquor for "fifteen or twenty years." She was admitted only when she began taking overdoses, and when her nephew realized "she must have it and cannot do without it." That it had taken her nephew twenty years to recognize Mary's addiction should indicate the relatively recent understanding of the nature of addiction, as well as the probable absence of home care. Sidney G. (#752, 1884), an artist, drank lau-

Table 27
Relation between Re-admissions and Diagnosis

Diagnosis	Number and Percentage of Re-admissions								Total
	0	%	1	%	2	%	3 +	%	
Neurasthenia	271	81	45	13.5	11	3.5	7	2	334
Alcoholism	116	63	37	20	16	8.5	16	8.5	185
Depression	114	88	13	10	3	2			130
Addiction	67	64.5	14	13.5	13	12.5	10	9.5	104
Agitation	55	78	9	13	4	6	2	3	70
Alcoholism and addiction	23	70	2	6	3	9	5	15	33
Other	238	87	27	10	6	2	3	1	274
Not given	4	100							4
Total	888	78	147	13	56	5	43	4	1134

danum for ten years. His wife committed him after he increased his dosage "from four to five ounces" of opium and when he ceased to work. Johnston A. (#574, 1884), a physician addicted to "drink and opium," was admitted after attempting to take the life of his wife. He also had "prescribed and administered" drugs to patients while under the influence.

As demonstrated above in the case of Dr M., who was only "cured" when kept under lock and key, the notion of voluntary admission was problematic. Sarah M., the chloral addict cited earlier, was inveigled into the asylum through the misapprehension that she was visiting a friend. Coercion and compulsory commitment were advocated by adherents of the vice-disease model in Britain, but these issues were not broached by Lett in his essays on treatment.[45] Provincial Inspector O'Reilly, however, stated that "to make an Inebriate Asylum anything more than a sobering-up establishment, the conductors of it should be clothed with authority to detain and control an inebriate for an indefinite length of time, months or years, if necessary. The same policy in respect to his personal liberty should prevail [as for] a lunatic."[46] The acceptance of the concept of addiction as disease demanding medical management rather than as merely a vice, was a prerequisite to the acceptance of involuntary asylum confinement of the addict.

The frustration O'Reilly experienced at the failure to cure addiction was shared by other specialists and asylum superintendents who reached the same conclusion: if the disease of addiction could not be cured, it was not the fault of the diagnosis but of the patient.[47] Physicians recognized addiction as a social problem without being able to label it as such. Within the essentially paternalistic paradigm, the only solution to the disease of addiction appeared to be legislating the temptation out of the reach of the morally weak. The first moves to limit the availability of opiates in Ontario was The Pharmacy Act of 1875, although it still permitted over the counter sale of opium by registered druggists.[48] It was not until 1908 that opium and cocaine were banned from patent medicines by the Proprietary or Patent Medicine Act.[49] Criminalization of opiate use also occured in that year, and was produced at least as much by racism as by a public health problem. In 1908, following his investigation of the Vancouver riot of 1907, Mackenzie King undertook a private study of the opium trade in Canada.[50] His report depicted "the ruin of white women" and other "moral calamities" 'caused' by the Chinese opium trade.[51] The federal government subsequently passed The Opium Act of 1908 which banned the "import, manufacture and sale of opiates for non-medical purposes."[52] The Opium and Drug Act of 1911 made it a criminal offense to smoke, possess, or deal in opium and cocaine, or to be found in "opium resorts."[53] Both acts were specifically aimed at the Chinese Canadian community.

That opiate use was associated with the alien indicated that by 1908 opium was no longer an integral part of the popular culture. Most of its uses had been rendered obsolete by chloral, the bromides, and eventually the new synthetic drugs, such as aspirin. Improvements in sanitation, and the pure food and milk legislation, substantially decreased the cases of gastrointestinal disorders for which opium was a specific.[54] The older generation of respectable middle-aged addicts had largely died out, leaving only a residue of younger users "hooked" (through recreational rather than iatrogenic use) on the expensive and outlawed opiate derivatives: morphine and heroin.[55] By the 1920s, the furtive dope fiend was entrenched in the public imagination.

Homewood's addicted patients in the nineteenth century were physicians and barristers, housewives and politicians – individuals of high social standing who were able to maintain their status after institutionalization, and who alternately tried asylums, travel, and tonics to break their habits. As long as the use of narcotics and stimulants was so common, drug addiction was seen as an unfortunate consequence of accessibility, similar to the current view of alcoholism. The disease model of drug abuse opened up a new area of expertise for the medical profession, but produced a no-win situation for the addict. Physicians could not cure a social problem which they had helped to create; yet failure to cure the "disease" was viewed as the moral failure of the individual addict, the consequence of which was often voluntary or compulsory institutionalization.

CHAPTER ELEVEN

Conclusion

When the Homewood Retreat opened its doors in 1883, its founders believed that they had embarked upon a profitable enterprise. Because there was a demonstrated need in the nation for mental health care for the middle class, the founders predicted their venture would find quick success. But the business of asylum keeping, as they were soon to learn, was a speculative one at best. The weighty bureaucratic structure under which the institution laboured rendered the retreat as tied to governmental direction as the public asylums, but without the cushion of taxpayers' funds. An unforeseen consequence of managing a proprietary asylum was its dependence upon the vagaries of public whim; far from being the sinister madhouse evoked in the popular mind, the proprietary asylum was forced by necessity to grant a greater voice than the provincial institutions to its paying patients and their kin.

This interference was part of the challenge faced by the Homewood Retreat's first two medical superintendents, Stephen Lett and Alfred Hobbs. They were also affected by the uncertain state of psychiatry at the turn of the century. Homewood's superintendents could not rely upon solidly established medical theory to support their claims for professional autonomy, particularly before 1900. The one psychiatric concept for which there was consensus in medical thought, hereditarianism, was not likely to win popular favour among the respectable patrons of the institution.

The careers of Stephen Lett and Alfred Hobbs reflected transformations in the medical profession generally. In the 1880s and 1890s, Lett largely limited diagnostics to superficial observation, and offered his patients a system of therapeutics primarily based upon traditional moral management: routine, occupation, healthful diet, and mild exercise. This reliance upon custom reflected Lett's apprenticeship in Ontario's public asylum system; his brand of psychiatry, apart from his work with addicts, differed little from the practices common at mid-century. Alfred Hobbs, on the other hand, can be viewed as a more transitional figure in Canadian psychiatry. Although also a product of the provincial system, he was more interested in those contemporary advances in neurology which produced increasingly localized etiological conceptions of insanity. As a somatic interventionist, Hobbs was more thorough, instituting physical examinations, blood testing, and the compilation of detailed patient histories. Consequently, Hobbs was a clear forerunner of the scientific, research-oriented psychiatrist of the twentieth century. By remaining in tune with advances in the wider medical world, he was able to attract the attention of the all-important family physicians who in turn brought Homewood to the attention of the relatives of the mentally disordered.

Despite Hobbs's innovations and the adoption of a modern system of patient classification, ward designation and consequently treatment itself continued to be based on manageability rather than type of disease. Placement on this basis degenerated into a system of ward therapy with occasionally unfortunate results for the patients. The professional requisite of the proprietary asylum was interventionist therapy; paying patients and their families demanded active treatment for their fees. Asylum therapeutics after 1900 was based upon the rest cure, which demonstrated the advantages of convenient, economical, and benign therapeutic measures.

In contrast, Lett's gradual withdrawal course in the treatment of addictions, while benign in operation, was a lengthy, drawn-out procedure to which many patients objected and which the superintendent found difficult to impose. Lett's experiences with habit cases brought into sharp relief the extent to which the institution was dependent upon the patients. As Hobbs also discovered, in the use of electrotherapy and surgery, the power of the patient to shape the proprietary asylum was manifest. While hydrotherapy, like the rest cure, was a therapeutic measure approved of by the physicians and most of the patients, electrotherapy was a treatment for which Hobbs had little favourable regard. He was forced, however, to employ it at Homewood because of its popular appeal. On the other hand, Hobbs's specialty, gynaecological surgery, through which he had established his reputation, did not meet the approval of all of his patients. Significantly, and in sharp contrast with the public asylums, the will of the paying patient prevailed; where she raised opposition to such surgery, it was abandoned.

Another influential element in the dynamics of the asylum was the family. The family's influence upon diagnosis and commitment was pre-eminent, as it was in the determination of the course and length of treatment; relatives suggested or demanded types of treatment and decided if and when the patient would return to the family. But if the family was central to the institution, so was the institution essential to the family. Certain features of late Victorian and Edwardian households – the economic dependency of women, the inequities inherent in a patriarchal system, and the inexorable realities of the life cycle – often enough produced a socially redundant residuum, overwhelmingly female, that required an institutional setting in which to end its days. This setting, in the guise of the Homewood Retreat, was not a total institution, subject as it was to family interference and patient input, rather it was modelled, in many ways, on the patriarchal family itself. The varying levels of equivocal authority, reward and punishment, rebellion and secrecy, negligence and caring intervention, mirrored the dynamics of a household. Especially in the treatment of alcoholics, the actions and responses of the physicians and patients directly imitated reactions in the patients' homes. Consequently, the division between home and asylum was often blurred.

If the asylum may be seen, to some degree, as a family strategy in times of crisis, then the accumulation of custodial populations may have been not so much an unfortunate, as a primary function of the institution. What is the result when functional custodialism is devalued, as demonstrated in the recent trend toward de-institutionalization of mental patients? As Philip Hepworth warned in 1979, "In our wish to rid ourselves of institutions, we have not stopped to think of some of the functions served by large institutions in the past. For the mentally ill they provided refuge, and for their relatives and friends respite. If we simply use the advances in modern medicine to keep the mentally ill out of hospitals, what are the consequences going to be for families and home communities? Almost certainly anxiety, fatigue, and disruption, unless adequate support services are provided."[1] Unless government, and the taxpaying public, are totally committed to the provision of universal, diverse, and properly maintained community services for the mentally ill, the asylum will have to retain its primary custodial role.

In its internal social structure, the asylum functioned as a patriarchal institution, albeit not always a disciplined one. The family's input, the patients' reactions, and the uncertain quality of the staff undermined the power of the authorities at the Homewood Retreat.

The population of the asylum lent itself to disorder, and direct, consistent, and active supervision on the part of its administrators was crucial to control that population benevolently and therapeutically. Untrained, disorderly staff were gradually replaced by trained, specialized health care workers, which was a reflection of general transformations in hospital care at the turn of the century. Yet the unpleasant aspects of asylum work ensured that understaffing and unqualified personnel would remain problems throughout the period. The shortage of desirable workers, so essential to avoiding a repressive environment, made abuse, neglect, and over-medication inevitable. This was particularly evident in periods of inadequate supervision, such as the final years of both the Lett and Hobbs administrations. When proper supervision was present, however, it was possible for the proprietary asylum to achieve its creative, therapeutic potential.

The asylum, then, should be viewed as process: a series of dynamic interactions between directors, administrators, families, employees, and patients. In the end, if the Homewood Retreat fell short of the therapeutic and financial goals envisaged by its founders, it nonetheless fulfilled an important medical and social function in the lives of its middle-class, emotionally disturbed patients in late nineteenth- and twentieth-century Ontario.

Appendices

Prospectus of 1883

This Association has been organized under the provisions of the "Act Respecting Private Asylums for Insane Persons and Inebriates," (Statutes of Ontario, 42 Victoria, Cap. 28), for the purpose of founding a Hospital and Retreat for the care and treatment of the better classes who are insane, or who, as inebriates, require temporary seclusion and care.

The necessity for such an establishment has long been known to all who have taken any interest in such matters; but it has been brought home with peculiar force to the minds of at least three of the promoters of the present Association from the fact of their having been officially connected, in different capacities, for many years with the Public Asylums of the Province. Within the past fifteen years Ontario has provided most liberally for her insane poor, and has done something towards supplying accommodation in her Public Asylums for the mentally afflicted, whose friends were able to pay in part for their treatment and support. No separate provision, however, has been made, either by the Province or by private individuals, for the insane drawn from the higher and more affluent classes of the community. The friends of these unfortunates have, in consequence, been reluctantly compelled either to search in a foreign country for the special comforts and care which their cases required, or to commit them to one of the large Public Asylums of the Province. The former course has been attended with great expense, inconvenience and delay, and what is perhaps more objectionable, the practical separation of the patient from family and friends. In the latter case there are all the drawbacks which are incident to the indiscriminate association of persons of all ranks and conditions in the generally overcrowded wards of a Public Asylum, with the greatly divided attention of an overtaxed medical staff, and the hard and monotonous surroundings of such establishments.

The HOMEWOOD RETREAT has its origin and raison d'être in the foregoing considerations, and it is the aim and object of its founders to supply and adequately meet the long felt want referred to.

The Association has been fortunate in securing as a site for the RETREAT a piece of land in the outskirts of the City of Guelph, about 20 acres in extent, richly wooded and well cultivated, and possessing peculiar advantages for such a purpose, being elevated, healthy and picturesque. The Buildings will occupy the higher portions of the land, which command an extensive view of the surrounding country. The pleasure grounds and gardens of the establishment slope gently down from the Building to the River Speed, which forms the natural boundary of the property on the south. The wing intended for the patients is being built upon a plan carefully considered by experts in Asylum architecture, and is provided with all the appliances and conveniences which modern science considers requisite for the care or comfort of the inmates.

It will be seen from the accompanying map that the Asylum occupies a central and convenient position in Ontario, and that it possesses facilities of access by rail from almost every part of Ontario, and also from many of the great railway centres of the neighbouring States.

The Association particularly desire, both in their own interest and in the public interest, that the RETREAT should be at all times open to the most searching oversight and inspection by competent persons entirely unconnected with the proprietors. It has accordingly been provided, at the special instance of the promoters of the Association, by an Act passed by the Ontario Legislature in its last session, that the HOMEWOOD RETREAT shall not only be inspected by Government officials in the same way as the Public Asylums of the country, but shall also be subject to further, and probably more rigid, inspection by a local Board comprised of gentlemen of the highest standing and intelligence in the county, namely, the County Judge, the Clerk of the Peace, the Warden of the County, and a local physician to be nominated by the Government of Ontario.

The RETREAT will for the present afford accommodation for only fifty patients – twenty-five of each sex – a number not too large to permit the Medical Superintendent to make a careful study of each individual case in its special phases, symptoms and history – a most important factor in the successful treatment of the patient.

The Institution will be under the medical superintendence of Dr Stephen Lett, who for the past thirteen years has been Assistant Medical Superintendent in the largest Public Asylums in this Province. Dr Lett will reside in the building, and give his undivided attention to the treatment and welfare of all entrusted to his care, in which he will have the assistance of a competent staff.

A few special cases of inebriates and of persons addicted to the morbid use of opium, or other narcotic drug, will be admitted to the institution for treatment.

Application for admission must be made to the Medical Superintendent, either personally or by letter, giving a short outline of the circumstances, history and symptoms of the proposed patient, whereupon the requisite blank forms will be furnished with full instructions as to their execution.

The rates charged will, of course, vary with the condition and requirements of the patient. It will be the aim of the proprietors to furnish at as reasonable a charge as possible, whatever special comforts or accomodation the friends of the patient may desire, such as the use of carriage, extra rooms, special attendants, etc. It will be readily understood that all such detail must necessarily be subject to arrangement with the Medical Superintendent.

Payments are required to be made strictly three months in advance, and the bond of two responsible parties must be given for future payments. In cases where the bondsmen are not known, evidence of their financial responsibility must be furnished.

It is expected that the RETREAT will be ready for occupation about the 1st November next.

Dr Lett will be happy to furnish further information to any who may apply to him for that purpose, either verbally or by letter, at the Toronto Asylum.

STEPHEN LETT
TORONTO, Sept. 15th, 1883.

Prospectus of 1915

Board of Management
President
Fred. C. Jarvis, Esq. – Toronto, Ontario
Vice-President
A.D. Langmuir, Esq. – Toronto, Ontario
General Manager, the Toronto General Trusts Corporation
Directors
Hon. Featherston Osler, K.C., D.C.L.
Toronto
James A. Hedley, Esq. – Toronto
Edward Galley, Esq. – Toronto
Henry Howitt, M.D. – Guelph
T.S. Hobbs, Esq. – London
W.A. Cameron, Esq. – Toronto
Resident Staff
Medical Superintendent – A.T. Hobbs, M.D.
Asst. Medical Supt. – E.C. Barnes, M.D.
Physicians
J.R. Boyd, M.D.   E.W. McBain, M.D.
Matron
Miss Ada Hobbs
Graduate of the Macdonald Institute, Guelph
Instructor of Handicrafts
Miss Marion Bathgate
Board of Visitors
His Honor
The Judge of the County of Wellington
Chairman
The Sheriff of the County of Wellington

The Clerk of the Peace of the County of Wellington
Dr. T.J. McNally, District Health Officer
Dr. Harvey Clare, Asst. Superintendent of
The Hospital for Mental Diseases for Toronto
Inspector
Provincial Inspector of Hospitals and Public
Charities for the Province of Ontario

The Homewood Sanitarium is pleasantly situated amongst picturesque surroundings on the outskirts of the City of Guelph, which is the county town
of Wellington, and the centre of one of the most prosperous farming communities in Ontario. Its situation is fully 800 feet higher than Lake Ontario,
which is twenty-five miles to the south. It is one of the healthiest cities in
North America. Guelph streets are wide, and the houses are, for the greater
part, built of the clean gray stone that is quarried in the neighborhood. At
the extreme west end of the city lies the group of buildings that comprise
the Homewood Sanitarium, which nestle among its own trees, and is separated from the city by the calm, placid waters of the River Speed. Its
situation is an ideal one. It is the essence of peace and restfulness, without
any suggestion of loneliness. It is the very spot for successful treatment of
patients suffering from nervous and mental disquietude.

The Manor Building is in the Colonial style, with what might very easily
be termed an architectural blending with the French pensionnat. The Manor
flanks the Administration Building on three sides. The east wing is the ladies'
section; the west side is occupied by the men. There is a maximum of sunlight
in each room. Each apartment is bright, homelike and furnished in excellent
taste. In the Manor, the nervous and convalescing patients find a home life
that rapidly leads to a speedy and permanent convalescence. The Manor
suites are models of quiet taste and luxury. Each bed-room has hot and cold
running water, and its spacious and beautifully furnished sitting rooms,
drawing rooms, writing and receptions rooms offer the elegance and comfort of refined [living].

[The] Sun Verandah, in the eastern wing of the Manor. One does not
need to dwell upon the glory, the splendor, or the health-giving properties
of sunshine. On such a verandah as this the germs born of dust and darkness
have little chance to develop.

[The] charming Manor bedroom is exactly what a sleeping room should
be – airy, cheerful, where sleep comes easily, and when the night is done
the aroused sleeper feels that it is good to be alive and look out once more
on a beautiful world.

[In] the men's sitting rooms ... one can read, chat and pass a quiet hour
in a pleasant way. This is a particularly cheerful room, and one that is
appreciated by every male guest at the Homewood.

[The] ladies' sitting room in the Manor [faces] the morning sun, and looking at it, you easily realize the restful influence it has on the patient who is convalescing from an attack of nervous breakdown.

The Colonial Building is an imposing structure of white limestone, quarried in the immediate neighborhood, with a frontage of three hundred feet. Its spacious verandahs and balconies especially appeal to the visitor whose impression is heightened on entering the fine rotunda and handsome reception rooms. The special features in evidence here for the treatment, care and protection of the patients are in close harmony with the most advanced ideas in psychiatry. The Colonial Building, which has a south aspect, is devoted to the care of those quiet patients whose cases are under a special observation to determine the exact course of treatment their individual cases require. It will be readily understood that an efficient staff of nurses is maintained here, nurses who have quiet voices and sympathetic hearts, and who are capable of making an intelligent reading of the conflicting indices offered by the newly arrived patient ...

No modern Sanitarium for Mental and Nervous ailments is complete in its equipment unless it is provided with a surgical suite. The Homewood is well equipped in this respect. The operating room is constructed on modern lines, and its appointments and equipment are the best that can be obtained. The most improved methods in surgery are in evidence at the Homewood, and it has brought back many a patient to the sunshine of life and the enjoyment of good health. There is no doubt whatever of the splendid utility of modern surgery as a curative aid to many patients who seek the Homewood for restoration to health.

Electrical machines are in evidence at the Homewood for the treatment of pain, insomnia, paralysis, etc., that may afflict any of its patients. The appliances are the best that can be devised ...

Billiards, Bowling and the Gymnastics ... have each their admirers. Billiards mildly stimulates the brain, mildly exercises the muscles and has a soothing effect on the nerves. Alley bowling is a much more active game, and is a popular pastime during the fall and winter. A well equipped gymnasium is provided where carefully regulated gymnastic exercises are carried out under the direction of a competent instructor.

In addition, life at the Homewood is made more pleasant by concerts, dances, and motion pictures, given weekly during the spring, autumn, and winter months. Divine services are held every Sunday morning during the winter months, and are conducted by the clergymen of different denominations of the city of Guelph.

Outdoor sports that are not too strenuous are encouraged at the Homewood. The exercise of all the muscles of the body increases the circulation, improves the respiration, and in this way acts as a natural tonic in the upbuilding of the patient whose nerves have been shattered by worries and overwork.

Within a few minutes' walk of the Sanitarium is the Golf Club House, which has a lovely view that dominates the landscape for miles around in each direction. On the hottest day in summer you can always find a cool corner on the southern verandah. The golf course is one of nine holes, and is being improved each year. Patients whose condition permits of playing should bring their clubs. The Homewood patients have the privilege of the Golf Club course on the payment of a small weekly fee.

One of the most popular sports at the Homewood is Lawn Tennis. It appeals to those desiring vigorous exercise and interests the onlooker as well. Permanent cinder courts are in evidence, as well as the smooth, well-kept grass lawns. The fine old trees surrounding the lawns afford a number of shady nooks from which to observe the game, and also afford rest to the tired performers when the play is done. It is a game that requires a good eye and quick action, and appeals especially to the younger patients of the Sanitarium.

"Ye Old English Game of Bowling-on-the-Green" is a popular diversion with all the Homewood residents. The turf of the bowling lawns resembles a first-class Wilton carpet, and they are as level as a billiard table. The game appeals to patients of all ages, and although not strenuous, requires a steady hand and some skill to make a good bowler. Many games are played with the City and Visiting Clubs during the summer, and much interest is excited by the frequent contests held between teams of patients and nurses of the different buildings. These matches always arouse the greatest interest and keenest enthusiasm.

Hydrotherapy has long been recognized as a most efficient aid in the treatment of nervous and mental disease. For over ten years this therapeutic measure has been in daily use at the Homewood, and the results obtained have been so uniformly satisfactory that no expense has been spared to completely equip and organize this department in the Sanitarium.

With all advances in technique and equipment the Homewood has kept pace so that at the present time there are three complete suites for the administration of Hydrotherapy in all its branches. Each suite contains hot air cabinets, a central table from which are operated rain, needle, spray, shower, perineal, jet and Scotch douches, a sitz tub, shampoo table, and provision for the application of hot and cold packs. In fact, everything requisite for the carrying out of the most rational and approved methods of Hydrotherapy in the treatment of nervous, depressed and physically depreciated patients is to be found in each department.

For patients whose mental sickness is accompanied by excitement, restlessness and insomnia, the continuous baths have proved very efficacious. Wrapped in sheets, suspended in a comfortable hammock, in water whose temperature ranges between 92° and 95°, which is the body surface heat, the patient soon experiences marked relief, becomes quiet, takes liquid nourishment freely, falls into a peaceful sleep, and wakes up in three or four hours quiet and self-contained for the rest of the day. All this done through the agency of a carefully regulated bath without the aid of any depressing drug.

As a therapeutic measure, diversional occupation has been found to be a valuable remedial agent in the treatment of nervous and mental ailments. Systematically applied and judiciously carried out in patients who are mentally over active and possessing an abundant physical energy it breaks up wrong associations of ideas and directs their activities along normal and healthy channels.

If inaction is depressing in those who are well, how much more so is it in those whose sickness is of a depressed nature? Congenial work stimulates and interests the morbid mind and attractive employment is the foe of morbid introspection. It enlarges the patient's mental horizon, and, as a re-educative factor in re-arranging disassociated ideas, it is unexcelled.

Occupation has a decided tranquillizing influence on the restlessness of neurasthenia, but it should not be pushed to the point of fatigue.

The occupation should be new, that is something to which the patient is not accustomed in order to arrest and hold his attention.

Monotony is avoided by the variety of the work and it may be varied to suit almost any taste or fancy.

Recognizing all these factors as being of value, the Homewood management has provided a series of large bright rooms and furnished them with the necessary appliances, benches, tools, tables, looms, etc., and, above all, a capable, willing and attractive instructor.

The handicrafts cover a wide field and consist of basketry, wood carving, china painting, weaving, stencilling, leather, wool, wood and copper work. These offer a sufficient and attractive range to suit any individual taste.

All this is done without cost to the patients, except the few cents that they pay the teacher for the raw material with which they work. The finished articles are the property of the patients, and, taken home by them, act as kindly reminders of the good work done for them by this important department of the Homewood.

A view of Guelph from the Homewood lawns makes two things at once apparent – the apparent nearness and the real distance of the city, owing to the course of the River Speed, which holds the grounds of the Homewood inviolate from the steps of the would-be intruder. It would be impossible to secure a more complete privacy, or a more pleasant seclusion than is enjoyed amongst the grassy slopes, shaded walks and the lovely lawns of the Homewood Sanitarium. Here you feel the perfect charm of refined seclusion; here you feel that while the world is near, you are sheltered from its grosser side. It is perfect peace, perfect rest. It is the Homewood ...

Address Dr. A.T. Hobbs, Superintendent
Guelph, Ontario

The Life Chart of Emily C. (#94, 1915)

Age	Event or Symptom
11+	Neuralgia
15	Lung congestion
16	Left private school to help with children at home
27	Marriage
28	Nervousness and neuralgia begins
	Lost child at birth
30	Lost child at birth
31	Lost child at birth and developed milk leg
46	Pelvic operation
	Onset of mental symptoms (nerves)
50	Emily and husband end travelling lifestyle
51	General hospital for 1½ months for nerves
	Sanitarium for 5 months for neuralgia
	Gallstone attack
53	Death of husband after lengthy illness
	Insomnia, fear, functional paralysis
	Entered asylum

Note: This chart was derived from the facts given in the patient's history.

Sample Patient History and Admitting Interview, Clara B. (#27, 1916)

Clara Bertha B.
Admitted on Voluntary Application October 10th, 1916
Female 42 Single.
Occupation: Patient was in business until 33 years of age, when she left off business and remained at home because she found it too trying.

FAMILY HISTORY
Father: Dead, aged 62. Diabetes.
Mother: Living, age 69. Fair health.
Brothers: 1, age 51, good health.
Sisters: 3, 2 older and one younger than patient. Good health. 1 sister died, age 15. Peritonitis. No mental history in family.

PAST HISTORY
Patient has always been very supersensitive, religious and introspective.

On May 18th, 1916, patient went to hospital in London and was operated on for Uterine-myoma. Operation – hysterectomy. Made good physical recovery, but was noticed however reading her bible a good deal when convalescing.

About a month ago patient visited Detroit, when she became excited. She visited a physician there and had a secondary operation, which was said to be circumcision. She did not improve however, and her brother the Minister was sent for from New Brunswick. Coming to Ingersoll he found his sister, as he termed it, "excited." He says that she repeats to herself, "I am afraid, I am afraid that God is going to leave me, and that I am going to be lost." She has left the house two or three times with the desire to go away and pray in the woods.

After her return home from the hospital she wrote letters to the surgeon who operated on her, stating her love for him. When she first visited the

Doctor she said that he was the one she saw in a vision, and he was to remove the tumor, and therefore he was called upon to do it.

She is capricious in her diet, poor sleeper, and very restless at times.

A.T.H. [Alfred Thomas Hobbes]

OCT. 11 EXAMINATION BY E.C.B.

What is your full name?   Clara Bertha B.

What is your age?   Well, I always – I just about forget, doctor, but I thought it was 39 – I have not really kept track of it.

Date of your birth?   I cannot tell you that – the 9th of June – but I cannot tell you the year.

You think you are 39? I know it is somewheres around there.

Where were you born?   At Ingersoll.

Have you lived there all your life?   Yes, all my life.

Were you a pretty healthy girl?   Just about – at first, you know, doctor – seemed to be healthy as a baby mamma said, and then took whooping cough, used to bleed at the lungs a lot, and from then never seemed to be what you would call robust.

Any serious illness?   No. Of course, when I ever had my sickness on or anything, used to have lots of fainting spells – used to faint away about every time I had them on. And then you see when I had my operations that was all cut away.

How long did you attend school?   Until 14. I was going farther but could not at the time.

Did you take up any studies outside of school?   Well, I was starting music, which I was very sorry I did not keep up, but father passed away suddenly, you see. Very fond of music and have no doubt I would have taken it up if father had lived. But he died suddenly and I had to go into the store and help my sister, and then we put our younger sister through.

How long since your father died?   About 19 years ago.

How long did you continue to work in the store?   Eleven years, and then my nerves seemed to be completely done and I stayed home then and helped mother with the work and that, and then thought that I would try to take up my music, but our house was large and it was too much for mother, and father signing notes for men and losing so much money we had to curtail our expenses, you see, and could not do as some people would do. He would let people get into his debt so and never make them pay – books and books of debts. Not only that but he got in very friendly with a man, in fact two men, and they just robbed him of $8,000 in one case, which crippled him in his younger days. It has been wonderful since father passed away, every person has been so kind and it seemed as though they came right to our store. My older sister has much different character than I, seems to be a character that would draw any person and the business just seemed to prosper in her hands, and then she is clever, too, you know – a very clever business woman.

Who came with you? My brother and mother came with me.

What time did you get here? I don't know, doctor, I suppose about noon hour. My brother wanted to go away – he has a large church in ... New Brunswick, and the people only gave him two Sundays off. At that time, I was just as though I was crazy almost, the way I acted, but I will tell you all that, but I would rather tell you that alone.

Any reasons for your coming here? Well, I didn't want to come here, doctor. I thought if I would go with brother and probably go around visiting amongst his church people, you know – he is a beautiful singer and prayer with his sick people – and I thought if I could go around with him like that that perhaps I would get blessed in my soul and be healed, but in the night time I feel as though I would like to put an end to myself.

Did you ever attempt to do yourself any harm? Oh, no doctor, I never thought of such a thing – at least, I feel as though I want to do it, yet I know what will be the end of things if I do.

You know it is not the proper thing to do? Oh, yes.

How long have you been feeling this way? Since July.

That was the beginning of it? Yes, I never had anything like that before. God always seemed so close to me.

Date of operation? That was in May (1916) – Oh, I wish I had never been operated on, doctor.

You apparently did very well afer the operation until July? Oh, yes. Yes, so many people seemed to be praying for me that I seemed to get over it with no trouble, doctor, and my own doctor said I was too religious. He said that if I should go out of my mind at all it would be on religion. I would rather tell you alone. I thought yesterday that I could not tell you.

When the patient was left alone with the physician she immediately began to give a description of her difficulties. Summed up, it is as follows:

That at various times during her earlier life, she became the subject of sexual uneasiness, and this was followed by some self-abuse. Later on this was discontinued and did not appear again until recently, that is, the masturbation. At various times in her life she has been attracted to members of the opposite sex, and on one or two occasions has been proposed to, which proposals came from men for whom she felt no regard. Those that were fond of her and she fond of them, always excited [her] sexual desires. She thinks that this was entirely an offence to God and that for being the victim of these sensations God was displeased with her, that He had forsaken her. Since about July 1st of this year these sexual instincts have been aroused much more frequently and to a much greater degree than ever before, and masturbation has been present on a few occasions. She is fully convinced, however, that God has departed from her, that she is going to perdition, and that if she is to still continue to be the prey of what she thinks an unnatural sexual sensation she would be much better dead, and she expressed rather emphatically the fact that suicide, although wrong, is something that she would very seriously consider if she cannot recover.

E.C.B. [Edward C. Barnes]

OCT. 17   Since the original notes were made in regard to this patient's condition, she has continued depressed, crying whenever interviewed by the physician, introducing many religious topics into her conversation, this being self-accusatory, and also accusing herself of having fallen in love with her former physician, something, she says, she should not have done, and that this has given rise to sexual manifestations which have been abhorrent to her but which she could not overcome. She pleads with the physician that he will not think wrong of her because she has told him of these things.

Physically, she is inclined to neglect her body welfare, taking only very small quantities of food, and this in spite of urging of nurses and physicians that she should do better in this regard.   E.C.B.

OCT. 28   Patient has been introduced to the Arts and Crafts department almost since her admission, and is doing fairly good work – her depression is lessened while thus engaged, but whenever interviewed by the physician she reverts to her delusional ideas of self-accusation and self-depreciation. When spoken to in regard to taking a greater quantity of food, she becomes more depressed and more emotional, says that she does not need food, that God will provide for her. In spite of this assertion, she takes a certain quantity but this under compulsion.   E.C.B.

NOV. 1   The general condition of the patient has not changed since the last note, except that she is taking her food a little better and not showing quite so much mental distress.

It should be noted that she has spent a great deal of time reading her Bible and other religious books, and also spends considerable time in prayer at different periods of the day.   E.C.B.

NOV. 7   The letter addressed to Dr Barnes is enclosed [the letter is absent from the case history]. It gives a very fair idea of her train of thought.   E.C.B.

NOV. 8   Patient discharged today in the care of her sister. This against the advisability of the physicians. Patient is by no means well enough to be away from hospital supervision, but the wishes of the family are acceded to as there is no way of convincing them that the patient is too sick for home care. If anything, she was a little improved just prior to her discharge, but by no means stable, and her delusional ideas were more or less freely expressed.   E.C.B.

APPENDIX FIVE

Prospectus of 1934

THE TREATMENT OF NERVOUS AND MENTAL DISEASES
The means adopted for treating cases of mental and nervous disease have changed greatly during the past one hundred years. Where formerly lack of knowledge, ignorance and fear brought into being appliances and methods that have long since been discarded, experience and observation now have shown that these illnesses may be cured permanently if only they are taken in hand early enough to ensure recovery.

Today at Homewood Sanitarium the patient is surrounded with an atmosphere of kindness, sympathy, patience and cheerfulness, with all irritating agencies removed, and after careful investigation into the cause of his illness, the appropriate treatment is accorded him. Only by this means can the desired results be obtained.

The cause of mental diseases has always aroused a great deal of interest, as well as much speculation and argument. Many and varied have been the opinions expressed. Such illness has been attributed to witchcraft, religious excitement, over-work or worry due to domestic unhappiness or financial loss; but when these cases are properly analysed, the cause may usually be placed under one of four headings, hereditary taint, unhealthy environment, toxic conditions and traumatism.

The treatment recommended even yet differs widely, ranging from rigid dietetic rules, physical exercises, rest in bed or the Weir Mitchell treatment, to the use of electricity, baths, salt rubs, irrigations or massage. While each of these may have its own value, no one remedy can rightly be applied in all cases. Everything that is wrong in the patient's physical condition must be corrected as far as possible, whether it be tonsils, teeth, eyes, heart, gall bladder or liver. His mental condition must be improved by means of normal sleep, freedom from worry, cheerful surroundings, quiet and intelligent nursing attention and some occupation that will interest but not irritate. This can only be accomplished by a skilled observer, for no two patients are alike in their conditions and needs, and what will benefit one may be actually harmful to another.

Each patient must have careful physical examination, including all necessary laboratory work. These examinations may have to be repeated three or four times and while this is being done the patient himself must be studied, his family history and all phases of his life from his earliest years, together with the history of his illness from the time it first manifested itself. Then, and not till then, can the proper treatment be considered and determined ...

Treatment – The medical treatment of patients at Homewood consists of thorough and frequent mental and physical examinations, with appropriate treatment for any physical ailments which may exist. In addition to this, there are several other aids to treatment, such as:

1. Hydrotherapy, consisting of hot and cold wet packs, cabinet baths, spray baths, shower baths and continuous hot baths.

2. Electrotherapy which includes quartz lamps, carbon lamps, sunlight lamps, vibrators, etc.

3. Occupational Therapy, which is carried on every day and in which patients are encouraged to interest themselves. It may be weaving, leatherwork, brasswork, or woodwork ... The making of bird houses has been a favourite pastime ... Occupational therapy also includes such games as tennis, indoor and outdoor bowling, baseball, football, golf, billiards, bridge, chess, etc.

4. Massage is used with many patients every day and is useful to soothe and satisfy, and it often aids in securing sleep for them ...

Any further information that may be desired will be gladly furnished by Harvey Clare, M.D., Medical Superintendent.

Schedule of Prices for Inebriates

1894

Inebriates: 4 weeks treatment $30.00 per week
Inebriates: 8 weeks treatment $25.00 per week
Inebriates: 12 weeks treatment $15.00 per week
Inebriates: After 12 weeks treatment $12.00 per week
Opium cases: $15.00 per week
Cocaine cases: Price of cocaine + $15.00 per week
Insane [and nervous]: $12.00–$15.00 per week according to case.

The above prices to include board, washing and lodging, the services of the ordinary staff, medical and otherwise, and medicines. Special attendant $10.00 per week extra and the larger rooms $3.00 per week extra.

Source: Annual report of the medical superintendent, 15 December 1894.

1895

Owing to the short terms which inebriates will remain ... I have been obliged to grade on scale of prices to meet the new order of affairs as follows:

Inebriates: 4 weeks treatment $120.00 spot cash
Inebriates: 8 weeks treatment $20.00 per week
Inebriates:12 weeks treatment $15.00 per week
Inebriates: After 12 weeks treatment $12.00 per week
Opium cases: $15.00–$25.00 per week according to rooms occupied or any
              special features the case may present.
Insane [and nervous]: $12.00. $15.00. $20.00 and $25.00 per week ac-
              cording to the nature of case, special requirements
              and rooms.

Source: Annual report of the medical superintendent, 15 December 1895.

Instructions for the Use of the Continuous Baths at the Homewood Sanitarium

1 Patients must be placed in a sheet or pack before being brought to the bath.
2 Patients must never be put into the bath until the bath is filled and tested by the hand, by the elbow, by the thermometer on the wall, and by the thermometer in the bath.
3 Anoint patient with olive oil or vaseline before placing in bath.
4 Head nurse must not allow nurses to remain on duty in continuous bath-rooms for a period exceeding two hours.
5 Nurses must never leave the patient for a moment. Always remember the patients may drown themselves if left alone, or turn on the tap and scald themselves.
6 The temperature of the water must never be above 98 degrees, the correct temperature for the average patient is 96 degrees. Alcoholic patients require a temperature of 98 degrees.
7 An ice-bag or cold compresses to the head must be used if the temperature of the water is 98. Frequent drinks of cold water must be given to patient.
8 If patient shows pallor, weakness or blueness of the lips, remove at once from the bath, rub vigorously, and give hot drinks.
9 The temperature of the water, the pulse and the respirations must be charted every 15 minutes, and any important utterances.
10 Contra indications for bath are menstruation and extreme weakness.

Source: Homewood Archives (photograph of original instructions)

Abbreviations

AN	*Alienist and Neurologist*
AHR	*American Historical Review*
AJI	*American Journal of Insanity*
ARIP	Ontario. Legislative Assembly. *Sessional Papers.* "Annual Report of the Inspector of Prisons, Asylums and Public Charities."
ARIP (London)	"Appendix: Report of the Medical Superintendent, London, Ontario Asylum for the Insane."
ARIP (Rockwood)	"Appendix: Report of the Medical Superintendent, Rockwood Asylum for the Criminally Insane."
ARIP (Toronto)	"Appendix: Report of the Medical Superintendent, Ontario Asylum for the Insane at Toronto."
ARMS	Guelph, Ontario, Homewood Sanitarium Collection. *Board of Directors Minutes*, "Annual Report of the Medical Superintendent."
BD	Homewood Sanitarium Collection. *Board of Directors Minutes.*
BHM	*Bulletin of the History of Medicine*
BMJ	*British Medical Journal*
BMSJ	*Boston Medical and Surgical Journal*
CHA	*Canadian Historical Association*
CHR	*Canadian Historical Review*
CIPA	Archives of Ontario. Ministry of Health. RG 10. "Correspondence of the Inspector of Prisons and Asylums."
CJMS	*Canadian Journal of Medicine and Surgery*

CMAJ	*Canadian Medical Association Journal*
CMR	[Canada] *Medical Record*
CMS	Homewood Sanitarium Collection. "Correspondence of the Medical Superintendent."
CMSJ	*Canadian Medical and Surgical Journal*
CP	*Canadian Practitioner [and Medical Review* 1899 to 1921]
HS/SH	*Histoire Sociale/Social History*
JAMA	*Journal of the American Medical Association*
JHMAS	*Journal of the History of Medicine and Allied Sciences*
JNMD	*Journal of Nervous and Mental Diseases*
JSA	*Journal of Studies on Alcohol*
LJ	Homewood Sanitarium Collection. *Journal of the Medical Superintendent* [Dr Lett]
LPH	University of Western Ontario. D.B. Weldon Library. Regional Collection. *Bucke Papers.* London, Ontario Asylum for the Insane.
MH	*Medical History*
MN	*Medical News*
MR	*Medical Record*
MSR	*Medical and Surgical Reporter*
QJI	*Quarterly Journal of Inebriety*
RSO	*Revised Statutes of Ontario*
VB	Homewood Sanitarium Collection. *Visitors Minute Book.*

Notes

CHAPTER ONE

1 Parry-Jones, *The Trade in Lunacy*. For more recent studies on the treatment of and attitudes towards the insane in Great Britain, see the excellent MacDonald, *Mystical Bedlam*, Porter, *Mind-Forg'd Manacles*, and Scull, *Museums of Madness*.

2 Walton, "Treatment of Pauper Lunatics," 191. Moral treatment was based upon the premise that the insane could be controlled and treated through the use of what we would call behaviour modification techniques. Through actively engaging the patient in a regular schedule of moderate labour and recreation, and providing him or her with a proper diet and plenty of rest, the asylum superintendent strove to lessen the disturbing manifestations of mental illness without resorting to physical restraints. Moral treatment, the foundation of institutional care throughout the nineteenth century, is termed milieu therapy in contemporary psychiatry.

3 Digby, *Madness, Morality and Medicine*, xiv. For treatment in Ireland, see Finnane, *Insanity and the Insane*.

4 Tomes, *A Generous Confidence*, xi.

5 Grob, *The State and the Mentally Ill*; Dwyer, *Homes for the Mad*. For attitudes towards the insane in the US, see Jimenez, *Changing Faces of Madness*.

6 Brown, "Living with God's Afflicted." Baehre's "Ill-Regulated Mind" investigates attitudes towards the insane in nineteenth-century Ontario. See Dissertations and theses section of bibliography for these works. (Dissertations and theses are identified by "diss." hereafter.)

7 Sims, "Asylum for the Insane at Kingston," diss.

8 Shortt, *Victorian Lunacy*.

CHAPTER TWO

1 Belcher, *Address to Humanity*, quoted in Parry-Jones, *Trade in Lunacy*, 226.
2 Halliday, *Letter to Lord Robert Seymour*, quoted in Parry-Jones, *Trade in Lunacy*, 84.
3 Homewood Sanitarium, *Prospectus of 1915*, 29.
4 Katz, "Directory of Super Hospitals."
5 Parry-Jones, *Trade in Lunacy*, 1. See also 7–11.
6 Great Britain. *Statutes*, 14 Geo. 3, c. 49.
7 Great Britain. *Statutes*, 9 Geo. 4, c. 41; 5 and 6 Vict., c. 87; 8 and 9 Vict., c.100. See Parry-Jones, *Trade in Lunacy*, 17–20.
8 Upper Canada. *Statutes*, 3 Wm 4, c. 45. See Baehre, "Lunacy Legislation" for a useful discussion of early legislation affecting madhouses.
9 See Heagerty, *Four Centuries*, 270–80.
10 See Baehre, "Lunacy Legislation," 17–20.
11 Upper Canada. *Statutes*, 14 and 15 Vict., c. 81.
12 Morgan, *Canadian Men and Women* (1912), 636.
13 Brown, "Living with God's Afflicted," 220–1.
14 ARIP, 1885, no. 11.
15 See Vogel, *Modern Hospital*, 1–3.
16 See Shortt, "Canadian Hospital," 4–7.
17 See Tomes, *A Generous Confidence*, 108–13.
18 BD, 30 December 1885. Information on the first years of the Homewood Retreat are sparse, since a fire which gutted the original building, the Guthrie homestead, on 6 January 1911 destroyed most of the early records.
19 BD, 20 June 1887; "Prominent Lawyer Called by Death," *Toronto Globe*, 7 October 1926; Morgan, *Canadian Men and Women* (1912), 573.
20 Morgan, *Canadian Men and Women* (1898), 622. For an entertaining account of E.A. Meredith's life, see Gwyn, *The Private Capital*.
21 For example, Ernest Frederick Jarvis, married to the daughter of E.A. Meredith, later served on Homewood's board of directors. *Might's Directory*, n.p.: *Who's Who and Why*, 456.
22 Johnson, *History of Guelph*, 250; Stewart, *Guelph*, 106.
23 "Private Asylums Act," *RSO* (1887) c. 246, ss. 8, 31, 72–3; ARIP, 1885, no. 11.
24 "Private Asylums Act," *Ontario Statutes* (1885) 48 Vict., c. 53 s. 5. See Sicherman, "Paradox of Prudence," 220.
25 "Inebriate Asylums Act," *Ontario Statutes* (1873) 36 Vict., c. 33, s. 13. Drug addicts were admitted by the provisions of "The Private Asylums Act" *Ontario Statutes* (1883) 46 Vict., c. 28 s. 11.
26 Tuke, *Insane in U.S. and Canada*, 209; ARIP, 1885, no. 11.

27 ARIP, 1884, no. 8; BD, 17 October, 31 December 1885, 6 January 1887.
28 BD, 14 September 1907, 4 June 1910; ARMS, 15 December 1890, 15 December 1891.
29 Brown, "Living with God's Afflicted," 222; ARMS, 31 December 1888. See appendix 6 for Homewood's rates in the early years.
30 Shortt, *Victorian Lunacy*, 53.
31 BD, 9 January 1890. *Ontario Statutes* (1873) 36 Vict., c. 33.
32 BD, 10 January 1889, 9 January 1890.
33 BD, 31 December 1891; ARMS, 24 November 1897.
34 Lett to Langmuir, 19 February 1900, recorded in BD, 10 March 1900.
35 BD, 19 January 1901; VB, 19 December 1901. More information about Annie Lett's role at Homewood is unfortunately absent from the records.
36 Hobbs to Langmuir, 20 December 1901, as recorded in BD.
37 BD, 13 January, 18 July, 1903; ARMS, 8 January 1904.
38 ARMS, 23 December 1904, "New Homewood," *Globe*, 14 September 1907.
39 Langmuir to Hobbs, 5 June 1907 as recorded in BD, 7 July 1907.
40 ARMS, 13 January 1916, 11 September 1918.

CHAPTER THREE

1 Morgan, *Canadian Men and Women* (1898), 579.
2 Vogel, *Modern Hospital*, 59–60.
3 ARIP (London), 1871, no. 6. For more information on the Landor years at the London Asylum, see Krasnick, "In Charge of the Loons."
4 Shortt, *Victorian Lunacy*, 96.
5 Rosenberg, "Bitter Fruit," 191.
6 See ibid., 217–20 and Ackerknecht, *History of Psychiatry*, 54–5 for detailed discussions of hereditarian thought in psychiatry.
7 See Haller, *Eugenics* and Dain, *Clifford W. Beers*, for the social ramifications of hereditarianism and the origins of the mental hygiene movement.
8 ARIP (London), 1872, 155. See Krasnick, "Because There is Pain," for more on the medical treatment of alcoholism in Victorian Canada.
9 Landor to Langmuir, 19 March 1876, 24 July 1876, CIPA, box 230, file 6598.
10 Langmuir to Lett, 9 January 1877, ibid.
11 Shortt, *Victorian Lunacy*, 7, 24.
12 Bucke to Langmuir, 29 March 1877, Langmuir to Lett, 25 April 1877, CIPA, box 230, file 6598. Their feud lived on. At a cricket match between the two asylums, Bucke complained that Lett and his wife had

snubbed him, allegedly indicating, in Lett's case, "a mental or moral aberration scarcely short of insanity." Bucke to Langmuir, 30 August 1877, CIPA.

13 Langmuir to Metcalfe, 25 April 1877, Metcalfe to Langmuir, 26 April 1877, Clark to Langmuir, 26 April 1877, Metcalfe to Langmuir, 8 May 1877, CIPA, box 250, file 6905.

14 See McCaughey, "Professional Militancy," for more on professional overcrowding in Ontario, especially 96–8.

15 Pitts, "AMSAII," 6. For a recent study of the founders of the AMSAII, see McGovern, *Masters of Madness*.

16 Morgan, *Canadian Men and Women* (1898), 579, 190.

17 Clark, "Reflexes," 86–93.

18 See Blustein, "Hollow Square," for the growth of American neurology.

19 Griesinger is quoted in Brown, "Shell Shock," 309.

20 Ackerknecht, *History of Psychiatry*, 75.

21 See Clark, "An Animated Molecule," for his views on the causation of insanity.

22 Clark's neglect of asylum affairs was noted by Joseph Workman, his predecessor at the Toronto Asylum and Homewood's consulting physician emeritus. When Workman referred a Toronto patient, James S. (#1045, 1888) to the private asylum, he crustily observed that, according to the patient's wife, Clark had seen "very little of him – once a week, and he had to enquire from the keeper about his condition – that was so like the truth that I could not refrain from believing the statement, but I deemed it prudent to be silent. Mrs. S. regretted [her husband's] commitment to the [Toronto Asylum]. I said it was a pity he had not been sent to Guelph." Workman was in fact successful in spiriting the case to Homewood, and chortled, "It will do you no hurt that they have tried Daniel and found out some of his virtues."

23 Langmuir to Clark, 22 March, Lett to Langmuir, 13 April 1881, CIPA, box 250, file 6905.

24 Griffin and Greenland, "Psychiatry in Ontario," 273. The scarcity of early records makes a temporal discrepancy difficult to resolve. Although Lett was transferred to Hamilton in the summer of 1883, Homewood's first prospectus directs inquiries to him at the Toronto Asylum in September. (See appendix 1.) Presumably the prospectus was printed before his transfer, and Toronto was a more prestigious institution to which to refer.

25 Pitts, "AMSAII," 194–5. In fact, "over one-third of the [American] proprietary institutions opened after 1865 were operated by former assistant physicians." By 1883, assistant physicians revealed their own professional consciousness, forming the American Association of As-

sistant Physicians of American Institutions for the Insane, which was absorbed when the AMSAII opened membership to assistant physicians in 1885. Ibid., 200.

26 LJ, 25 December 1890.

27 ARMS, 15 December 1890, 15 December 1896.

28 ARMS, 1 March 1895.

29 See Lett, "Why Do Men Drink?" 264–9.

30 "Alfred T. Hobbs," *Guelph Mercury*, 26 May 1931.

31 Morgan, *Canadian Men and Women* (1912), 537.

32 Bucke to Robert Christie, 1 April 1895, CIPA, box 220, file 6460.

33 For a thoughtful discussion of these gynaecological experiments, see Shortt, *Victorian Lunacy*, 141–59.

34 Bucke to James Stratton, 30 November 1900, Alexander McPhedran to Christie, 11 January 1900, CIPA, box 220, file 6460.

35 Hammond, "Maudsley's Physiology," 86; ibid., *Treatise on Diseases*, 376. See Blustein, "New York Neurologists," for a thorough discussion of Hammond, Beard, and other pioneers of the specialty of neurology.

36 Stratton to Hobbs, 12 April 1901, CIPA, box 220, file 6460.

37 Haller and Haller, *Physician and Sexuality*, ix–x. See Mackintosh, "The Profession and the Public," for a Canadian view of the role of the physician.

38 Andrews, "Alienist and General Practitioner," 2; Meyers, "Neurology," 240.

39 See p. 45 and Mitchell, "Treatment by Rest," for a discussion of his successes with the rest cure.

40 BD, 23 December 1905, 13 January 1916.

41 Patients Henry W. (#1128, 1909), Griffin R. (#1009, 1895).

42 See Showalter, *The Female Malady*, 3–4.

43 Bucke, "To Medical Practitioners," 16 November 1897. After Hobbs's retirement, Bucke attempted to keep the surgery going, citing the "great mass of instruments and trained nurses" that would be lost if the unit shut down. Hobbs had continued to operate, after he left the public service, on female patients who had been slated for surgery some time earlier, and whose "fathers were very anxious" to have the operation performed. Once Inspector Christie got wind of this, however, he ordered Hobbs to "stop at once." Bucke to Stratton, 30 November 1900, Christie to Bucke, 13 May, Bucke to Christie, 14 May 1901, CIPA, box 220, file 6460.

44 BD, 14 January 1905, 1 April 1920; Ontario. College of Physicians and Surgeons, registration files, "Barnes, Edward C."

45 "Guelph Doctor was outstanding as Psychiatrist," *Globe and Mail*, 6 August 1949.

46 "Obituary-Farrar," BD, 18 January 1923.

47 For an appraisal of the effects upon therapeutics and admissions of contemporary private mental health care facilities, see Schlesinger and Dorwart, "Ownership and Mental Health Services."

CHAPTER FOUR

1 Hobbs, "Wound Infection," 89.
2 See Ackerknecht, *History of Psychiatry*, especially 77–8, for a useful account of Kraepelin's work.
3 See Burnham, *Psychoanalysis*, especially 66–8, for the diagnostic and therapeutic consequences of Kraepelin's classifications.
4 Hobbs to Langmuir, 8 January 1909, CMS.
5 Sicherman, "New Psychiatry," 24.
6 Meyer, "Objective Psychology," 860.
7 Sicherman, "New Psychiatry," 24.
8 ARMS, 14 January 1908.
9 VB, 3 April 1916. See pp. 130–3, for the use of ward therapy as a disciplinary measure at Homewood.
10 Brown, "Shell Shock," 312, 321.
11 Ibid., 321.
12 See Burnham, *Psychoanalysis*, 18 and Grob, *Mental Illness and American Society*, 120, for the reception of Freudian ideas in American institutions.
13 See Brown, "Ernest Jones," for an excellent account of the Canadian reception of Freudian psychology.
14 See Hale, *Freud and the Americans*, for psychotherapeutic ideas in the United States before Freud, especially 221–2.
15 Hobbs, "Some Aspects of Neurasthenia,"13.
16 Anglin, "Nursing the Insane," 181–3.
17 See Grob, *Mental Illness and American Society*, 13–14.
18 Donald Gregg of the Boston Psychopathic Hospital made this remark in "Drugs," 476–7.
19 Homewood Sanitarium Collection, *Prospectus of 1934*, 7.
20 See Morantz, "Feminist History," especially 651–3 for the reception and functions of the rest cure in the United States.
21 Meyers, "Neurasthenia in some of its relations to insanity," 394.
22 Hobbs, "Present Methods," 515.
23 Mitchell, "Treatment by Rest," 2033–5.
24 Ibid., 2036–7.
25 Bramwell, "Hysteria," 296–7, 301–3.
26 Weiss and Kemble, *Water-Cure Craze*, 2–3. See also Cayleff, *Wash and Be Healed*, a recent analysis of women and the American hydropathy movement, and Turner, *Taking the Cure*, an anecdotal account of the European spas.

27 Legan, "Hydropathy," 268, 272–4.

28 Ibid., 274.

29 Angell, "Hydrotherapy," 600, 603.

30 Neal, *Township of Sandwich*, 58–61. Connor points out the differences between spas and hydropathy in his "Preservatives of Health," 136–8.

31 Santos and Stainbrook, "Psychiatric Nursing," 67.

32 Homewood Sanitarium Collection, *Prospectus of 1915*, 24. The "douche" was a localized stream of water aimed at exciting the nervous system. A scotch douche alternated hot and cold water. A perineal douche would be a stream of water aimed at the perineum, or pelvic floor and was specified for perinatal injuries, while a sitz tub was a regular wash tub, one-third full of water, in which the patient sat with the feet remaining outside. It stimulated the nerves of the bowels and the pelvis viscera. See Cayleff, *Wash and Be Healed*, 97.

33 Hobbs, "Hydrotherapy," 761–3.

34 Ibid., 764–5. Baruch, the father of the famous American financier Bernard Baruch, published the standard medical text, *Principles and Practices of Hydropathy* in 1898.

35 Tuke, "On Warm and Cold Baths," 111.

36 Homewood Sanitarium Collection, *Prospectus of 1915*, 24. The cases, Annie B. (#63, 1919) and Jane McC. (#291, 1918) are discussed on pp. 128–9.

37 Rockwell, *Lectures in Electricity*, 63. See Longo, "Electrotherapy in Gynecology," for an informative examination of the procedure and its use in the nineteenth-century United States.

38 Brown, "Use of Electricity," 968–9.

39 Scudder, "Electro-therapeutics," 97–9.

40 Prince, "Electricity," 315–16, 318. See Corbet, "Electro-therapy," for a Canadian view.

41 Owen, "Electrotherapeutics," 2.

42 Ibid., 3.

43 Vogel, *Modern Hospital*, 102.

44 BD, 11 July 1914; Homewood, *Prospectus of 1915*, 22.

45 Engelmann, "Electro-therapy and Surgery," 330–1.

46 Hahn, "Electricity in Gynecology," 328.

47 Hubbard was quoted in Wood, "Fashionable Diseases," 3.

48 "Special Brain Work," 450–1.

49 Tomlinson, "Puerperal Insanities," 70.

50 ARMS (London), 1896. See Krasnick, In Charge of the Loons," 178.

51 Barrus, "Gynaecological Disorders," 476–7.

52 Davenport, "Five Cases," 513,520.

53 Menzies, "Puerperal Insanity," 147–8.

54 Longo, "Battey's Operation," 250, 256, 261. Robert Battey, a gynaecological surgeon in the American south in the second half of the

nineteenth century, developed the procedure of bilateral ovariotomies as a cure for amenorrhea, dysmenorrhea, and a variety of other non-pathological symptoms.

55 Goodell, "Extirpation of the Ovaries," 295.
56 Smith, *Canada Medical Record*, 4 (February 1876) 130 is quoted in Mitchinson, "Ovariotomies," 135.
57 CP, 19 (July 1894) 493, and 9 (September 1884), 272.
58 Longo, "Battey's Operation," 26–8. Morton, "Removal of Ovaries," 398–9.
59 See, for instance, Bucke, "Surgery among the Insane," and "200 Operative Cases."
60 Hobbs, "Gynaecology," 412 and "Surgical Treatment," 171.
61 Langmuir to Hobbs, 7 June, Hobbs to Langmuir, 25 June 1907, recorded in BD.
62 BD, 15 December 1894.
63 See Comfort, *Anxiety Makers*, 53–77, Bullough and Bullough, *Sin, Sickness and Sanity*, 59 and Neuman, "Masturbation," 3–11, for eighteenth- and nineteenth-century concepts of masturbatory insanity.
64 Spitzka, "Cases of Masturbation," 415.
65 "Dr Clark's Remarks," 1 October 1877, LPH, *Scrapbook*.
66 LPH, Journal of the Medical Superintendent, 6 March 1877.
67 Lett, "Insanity to Masturbation," 363.
68 Morrow, "Social Diseases," 629. See Brandt, *No Magic Bullet*, and Cassel, *Secret Plague*, for attitudes towards and treatment of syphilis in the United States and Canada respectively. Compare Cassel with Buckley and McGinnis, "Venereal Disease."
69 "Academy meeting," CP, 39 (1914) 168–73.
70 See Ward, "Salvarsan," for the American reception of the drug.
71 See ibid., especially 48–53 and Vogel, *Modern Hospital*, 70, for problems regarding administration of the medication.
72 Vogel, *Modern Hospital*, 71 n. 62.
73 ARMS, 11 January 1917; BD, 11 January 1917.

CHAPTER FIVE

1 See Grob, *Mental Institutions in America* and *Mental Illness and American Society*.
2 Grob, "Abuse in American Mental Hospitals," 304. Tomes and Fox have reached similar conclusions. After examining correspondence at the Pennsylvania Hospital, Tomes found that commitment was a response to a "level of deviant behaviour which the family could no longer tolerate." *A Generous Confidence*, 109. Even where admissions were by warrants from the courts, they were most likely initiated by

families. In his study of commitments for insanity in California between 1870 and 1930, Richard Fox discovered that "the most common petitioners, in order of frequency, were relatives [who] comprised 57 percent, doctors 21 percent, and police 8 percent … Through the insane commitment procedure, the government in effect 'socialized' such troubling behaviour, relieving relatives of the real burden and … the cost of caring for a family member whom they considered disturbed." *So Far Disordered*, 84, 97. See also Dwyer, *Homes for the Mad*, chap. 4 and Mackenzie, "Social Factors," 147–74.

3 Harbin, "Family Treatment," 4.

4 Bliss, *A Living Profit*, 29–30. According to Carroll Smith-Rosenberg, this transformation commenced with the decline of rural crafts and the rise of urbanization and geographical mobility. The middle-class family was robbed of its "instrumental centrality" and "generational relations – principally between fathers and sons – altered dramatically. No longer was the father's power to determine the economic choices, and thus control the future of his maturing sons, unquestioned …" Smith-Rosenberg, "Sex as Symbol," S218–19.

5 McCandless, "Liberty and Lunacy," 377.

6 [London] *Times*, letter to editor from "Vigil," 5 October 1844, as quoted in McCandless, "Liberty and Lunacy," 373.

7 Sicherman, "Paradox of Prudence," 220. Early Canadian writings on neurasthenia include Clark, "Neurasthenia," Collins and Phillips, "Etiology and Treatment," Shirres, "Plea for the Neurasthenic," Meyers, "Neurasthenia," "Neurology and Prevention," and "Neurasthenia and relations to Insanity," and Pritchard, "American Disease." American sources include Beard, *American Nervousness*, Mitchell, *Fat and Blood*, Foster, "Common Features," Jewell, "Varieties and Causes," and "Nervous Exhaustion," and King, "Treatment of Nervous Diseases." Rankin, "Neurasthenia," was a representative British contribution. See also Nye, "Degeneration," for an account of French views of neurasthenia, and Fye, "H. Newell Martin," for a biography of a noted American scientist who suffered from neurasthenia and alcoholism and, at one point, was a Homewood patient.

8 Hobbs, "Some Aspects of Neurasthenia," 13–14.

9 Pritchard, "American Disease," 985–7.

10 Beard, *American Nervousness*, 7.

11 Brill, "Diagnostic Errors," 123.

12 McCandless, "Liberty and Lunacy," 367.

13 Brandon, "Physical Violence," 1.

14 LJ, 12 August 1888.

15 See Katz, Doucet and Stern, *Social Organization*, ch. 3.

16 Uhlenberg, "Death and the Family," 172.

17 Beaujot and McQuillan, "Demographic Change," 59.

18 Smith, "Life Course," 292.

19 In an industrial society, people compare each other's material possessions, and indirectly, their own market and social value. The significance of material objects is raised from "simply representing a usevalue to also representing a social value. It is in this context that social relations develop between things. The material objects almost take on a life-like quality of their own. This process, whereby material relations develop between people, and social relations develop between things, is referred to as reification." Michael Warsh, "Domestic Concatenations," 4.

20 Shorter, *Modern Family*, 259.

21 Zaretsky, *Capitalism*, 29–30.

22 Braverman, *Labor and Monopoly Capital*, 279–80.

23 Lasch, "Social Pathologists," 183.

24 McCormack, "Networks among British Immigrants," 365.

25 Synge, "Work and Family Support," 139–40, 144.

26 Gorham, *Victorian Girl*, 11–12.

27 Stearns, "Old Women," 53.

28 Hartman, *Victorian Murderesses*, 112.

29 Hufton, "Women Without Men," 371.

30 Danylewicz, *Taking the Veil*, 52, 17.

31 Gee, "Marriage," 315.

32 Barber, "Queen Mary's Coronation," 147.

33 Strachey, *The Cause*, 92.

34 Hufton, "Women without Men," 358.

35 Peterson, "Victorian Governess," 13.

36 Ibid., 9. See also Showalter, "Victorian Women and Insanity," 317.

37 Branca, *Silent Sisterhood*, 58 n. 22.

38 Danylewicz, *Taking the Veil*, 67.

39 Gittins, "Marital Status," 262. See also Chudacoff and Hareven, "From the Empty Nest," especially 73–82.

40 Smith, "Older Americans," 294.

41 Catharine Maria Sedgwick, unmarried American novelist, to Frances Watson, 25 March 1816 in Mary E. Dewey, *Life and Letters of Catharine Sedgwick* (New York: 1974), 102–3 as quoted in Mintz, *Prison of Expectations*, 165.

42 Prentice et al, *Canadian Women*, 412.

43 Smith, "Older Americans," 292.

44 Showalter, "Victorian Women and Insanity," 315–16.

45 Digby, *Madness, Morality and Medicine*, 174–6.

46 Tomes, *A Generous Confidence*, 322.

47 Young and Willmott, *The Symmetrical Family*, 31. See also Edgell, *Middle Class Couples*, 69.

48 Lewis, "Restructuring Women's Experience," 16.
49 See Collier, *Plague of the Spanish Lady*, for a discussion of the influenza pandemic of 1919.

CHAPTER SIX

1   McCubbin, Cauble and Patterson, *Family Stress*, xii.
2   Wohl, "Sex and the Single Room," 197–216. For more on the establishment of Ontario's children's aid societies, see Jones and Rutman, *In the Children's Aid.*
3   Zaretsky, *Capitalism*, 43.
4   Hartman, *Victorian Murderesses*, 66, 231.
5   Showalter, "Family Secrets," 101.
6   Lasch, "Social Pathologists," 83.
7   Bland, "Marriage Laid Bare," 128.
8   Lasch, "Social Pathologists," 82.
9   Blatz and Bott, *Parents and the Pre-school Child*, viii. While this manual was published in 1928, it reflected attitudes which were becoming predominant at the beginning of the century. See Strong-Boag, "Intruders in the Nursery," 160–73.
10 Cowan, "Technological and Social Change," 247–8.
11 May, "Pressure to Provide," 158–9.
12 See Uhlenberg, "Death and the Family," 169–72.
13 Spitzer, Weinstein and Nelson, "Family Reactions," 187.
14 Tomes, *A Generous Confidence*, 219.
15 Compare this with the comments of Alice H.'s family; "It's better that people should think you insane than that they should think you a bad, immoral women [see p. 68]." Anderson and Reiss, "Family Treatment," 87.
16 Dewey, "Voluntary or Self-Commitment," 71.
17 Buchanon, "Should the Insane be Deceived?" 669–71.
18 Harbin, "Family Treatment," 15–16.
19 Krajewski and Harbin, "Family Changes the Hospital?" 145.
20 Ibid., 149.
21 Ibid., 146.
22 Ibid., 151.
23 Greenley, "Patient's Family," 219–22.
24 Ibid., 223–4, 231.
25 Barret, Juriansky and Gurland, "Community Tenure," 958–64. See Withersty and Kidwell, "Measuring the Effects," 180.
26 Spitzer, Weinstein and Nelson, "Family Reactions," 187.
27 Ibid., 194–6.
28 Anderson and Reiss, "Family Treatment," 85.
29 See chap. 7 for a discussion of the total institution.

CHAPTER SEVEN

1 Rosenberg, "Inward Vision," provides an analysis of the shaping of a sub-culture within the nineteenth-century general hospital, 347.
2 Nichols to Dix, 4 July 1869, Dorothea Dix Papers, Houghton Library, Harvard University, Cambridge, Mass. as quoted in Tomes, *A Generous Confidence*, 277.
3 See, for instance, "The Martyrology of Psychiatry," *AJI* (1890) 290–3, 421 and (1885) 259–64.
4 Anglin, "Nursing," 177.
5 BD, 16 January 1930.
6 VB, 25 June 1913.
7 BD, 27 June 1910.
8 Tomes, *A Generous Confidence*, 280.
9 ARMS, 10 January 1885; BD, 9 January 1886.
10 After considerable experimentation, I was able to decode these entries. Since the code was not standard morse, and the spacing often unclear, there remain a few blanks. I have been unable to decipher numbers, but this detracts little from the substance of the text.
11 LJ, 23 February 1889.
12 LJ, 1 February 1889.
13 BD, 1 June 1889.
14 "Obituary: Alice Waller Finch," *Chatham Planet*, 8 November 1890.
15 Rosenberg, *Care of Strangers*, 35.
16 LJ, 30 September 1890.
17 The first head of housekeeping, Erie Shand, was a graduate of the Ontario Agricultural College. Shand resigned after three years, citing "better money in Long Island," and was replaced by Dr Hobbs's sister Ada, a graduate of Guelph's MacDonald Institute. BD, 30 July 1902, 4 August 1906, 21 August 1909.
18 Between 1922 and 1927, six head nurses were appointed. See BD, 15 July 1922, ARIP, 19 December 1923, VB, 1 April 1925, ARMS, 19 January 1928. Esther Northmore resigned in 1939 to serve as a nursing sister in the Canadian armed forces.
19 Young, "Life in Residence," 5.
20 Conolly, *Lunatic Asylums*, 83.
21 British Medico-Psychological Association, *Handbook for Attendants*, 373, as quoted in Carpenter, "Asylum Nursing," 130.
22 Brown, "Living with God's Afflicted", diss., 263; LJ, 9 January 1908. Homewood's set of rules for personnel, *What Experience Has Taught*, was cited in Dr. Lett's Journal, but unfortunately a copy has not survived.
23 *Regulations and Orders for the Government of the Wiltshire County Asylum,*

Devizes (1882) as quoted in Carpenter, "Asylum Nursing," 130–2. Carpenter presents a detailed account of the asylum attendants' tasks and failed attempts at organization in Britain. See also Smith, "Behind Closed Doors."

24 LJ, 18 September 1889, *Toronto Mail*, 24 November 1890.

25 The factory closed after the Berlin women struck for higher wages. Kealey, *Canada Investigates Industrialism*, 103, 86–7.

26 *Toronto Mail*, 15 January 1891; ARMS, 31 December 1902; LJ, 13 August 1888.

27 "The Future of the Asylum Service," 21 March 1900.

28 Browne is quoted in Carpenter, "Asylum Nursing," 134.

29 *Select Committee on Asylum Officers (Employment, Pensions and Superannuation) Bill*, 1911, minutes of evidence, as quoted in Carpenter, "Asylum Nursing," 133.

30 *National Asylum Workers' Union Magazine*, February 1912 as quoted in Carpenter, "Asylum Nursing," 141–2.

31 Tennessee Board of State Charities, *Report* (1896), 19 as quoted in Grob, *Mental Illness and American Society*, 19–20.

32 Province of Canada, *Statutes*, 14 and 15 Vict., c. 81. Compare with the British Lunacy Act of 1890, especially ss. 322–4.

33 LPH, *Scrapbook*, 19 March 1877.

34 "Speech to Employees," ibid., 1878.

35 LJ, 20–1 November, 12–13, 24 December 1889, 6 January 1890.

36 LJ, 18 December 1888; ARMS, 15 December 1900.

37 ARMS, 11 September 1918.

38 See Barber, "Women Ontario Welcomed," especially 148–58.

39 ARMS, 16 January 1920. The Canadian Pacific Railway was profitably involved in recruiting immigrants. It provided steamship services for their journey across the ocean, rail services for transport to western Canada, cheap land (huge tracts were granted to the railroad by the government during construction), and was the primary carrier for crops, farm implements, and supplies once immigrant settlers established homesteads.

40 ARMS, 11 January 1917.

41 ARMS, 22 June 1916, VB, 3 April 1916, BD, 13 January 1916.

42 ARMS, 9 January 1919.

43 LJ, 1 September 1888.

44 LJ, 16–18 August 1888.

45 LJ, 6, 29 July 1888.

46 LJ, 6 April, 2–3 July, 28 September, 15 December 1888.

47 LJ, 8, 19 October 1888, 23 February 1889.

48 LJ, 19 August, 3–5 December 1888.

49 LJ, 11 July 1890.

50 Mericle, "Psychiatric Nurse," 30.
51 *Asylum News* (1900) 42–3 as quoted in Carpenter, "Asylum Nursing," 136.
52 Grob, *Mental Illness and American Society*, 258.
53 See Gibbon and Mathewson, *Canadian Nursing*, especially chap. 6. *The Canadian Encyclopedia* credits the Brandon Asylum with the first nursing school; Brown, "Living with God's Afflicted", diss., 264, cites the opening of the Rockwood Asylum school in 1888.
54 Tuttle was quoted by J.A. Campbell, "Remarks on the use and abuse of Seclusion," *Journal of Mental Science* 32 (1886), 351.
55 BD, 30 July 1902.
56 BD, 15 September 1913, VB, 25 June 1913, 18 July 1918, ARMS, 16 January 1920.
57 ARMS, 21 January 1921, BD, 15 July 1922.
58 A consequence of the professionalization of Homewood's nurses was the diminuition of the role of male attendants. By 1925, Clare had introduced seven nurses on the men's side which he claimed was a "great improvement." By 1935, male attendants clearly were being phased out. ARMS, 18 January 1923, 15 January 1925, 16 January 1936, VB, 18 September 1925.
59 ARMS, 16 January 1936.
60 Shryock, "Nursing," 208; Young, "Life in Residence," 7.
61 ARMS, 9 January 1908; Homewood Sanitarium Collection, *Prospectus of 1915*, 26.
62 Grob, *Mental Illness and American Society*, 258–9.
63 BD, 6 July 1912.
64 ARMS, 14 January 1915, 16 January 1924, 15 January 1925.

CHAPTER EIGHT

1 In his influential study, *Asylums*, Erving Goffman described the characteristics of total institutions (including homes for the aged, mental hospitals, jails, and army barracks) as follows: "First, all aspects of life are conducted in the same place and under the same single authority. Second, each phase of the member's daily activity is carried on in the immediate company of a large batch of others, all of whom are treated alike and required to do the same thing together. Third, all phases of the day's activities are tightly scheduled, with one activity leading at a prearranged time into the next, the whole sequence of activities being imposed from above by a system of explicit formal rulings and a body of officials," 6.
2 LJ, 17 October 1890.
3 Tomes, *A Generous Confidence*, 15.

4 See Rothstein, *American Physicians*, especially 182–94, for the more popular items of the nineteenth-century pharmacopeia, and see Warner, *The Therapeutic Perspective*, for a thorough account of Victorian medical practice in the United States.

5 Ibid., 186.

6 MacDonald, "Hydrate of Chloral," 363.

7 ARIP (London), 1872, 155.

8 Wetherill, "Modern Hypnotics," 33, 38, 43.

9 Rogers, "Use of Opium," 554.

10 McClain, "Routine Medication," 516–17.

11 See Wilbur, "Chemical Restraint," 271–92.

12 S. Hitchcock, "Autumn Meeting of the Northern and Middle Division of the Medico-Psychological Association, 1899," *Journal of Mental Science* 46 (1900) 83, as quoted in Santos and Stainbrook, "Psychiatric Nursing," 70.

13 E.B.C., "Letter written to a Friend in 1878," typescript in York Retreat Library, as quoted in Digby, *Madness, Morality and Medicine*, 129.

14 Grissom, "Mechanical Protection," 30, 32; ARIP (London) 1872, 22.

15 Bell, "Mechanical Restraint," 3, 10–11, 23.

16 Ibid., 15–16; O'Reilly, *Toronto Mail*, 1890, as recorded in LJ.

17 Clarke, "Care of the Insane," 381.

18 ARIP (London), 1878, 274. See Brown, "Living with God's Afflicted," 288, for Daniel Clark's opposition to mechanical restraint.

19 Anglin, "Nursing the Insane," 177.

20 Bell, "Mechanical Restraint," 19, 28.

21 C.K. Clarke Papers, "Workman to Clarke," 7 May 1888, Clarke Institute, as quoted in Brown, "Living with God's Afflicted," 288 n. 119.

22 LJ, 3 November 1889.

23 VB, 1 December 1913.

24 Cobbold, "Forcible Feeding," 349–50.

25 York Retreat, G. Jepson to W. Alexander, 1 September 1820, Borthwick Institute of Historical Research, as quoted in Digby, *Madness, Morality and Medicine*, 132.

26 Pennsylvania Hospital for the Insane, "William Moon to Kirkbride, 12 June 1870, as quoted in Tomes, *A Generous Confidence*, 198.

27 Nightingale, *Cassandra*, 41–2; See Elaine Showalter's discussion of anorexia nervosa in *The Female Malady*, 127–31, Edward Shorter's "Anorexia Nervosa," 69–96, and Joan Brumberg's definitive account, *Fasting Girls*.

28 Rothman, *Conscience and Convenience*, 340–1.

29 Cases 16, 17, 96, 143, 214, 299, 353, 404, 433 were the cited instances of bad conduct. Cases 97 and 300 were obedient patients.

30 See Clarke to Jarvis, 17 March 1923, especially 1–3.

31 For the story of Ebenezer Haskell, see Tomes, *A Generous Confidence*, 253–7; Runge, "How to Deal with the Insane," 636.
32 Chapin, "Public Complaints," 33.
33 Clarke to Jarvis, 17 March 1923, 1.
34 Runge, "How to Deal with the Insane," 633.
35 LJ, 1 January 1891.
36 VB, 4 October 1894, 2 September 1896, 10 May 1922.
37 M.C. to Hobbs, 13 September 1905, in patient file, 1, 3.
38 Legal memorandum, 23 May 1888 as recorded in O'Reilly to Lett, 14 June 1888, in patient file; LJ, 6 July 1888.
39 LJ, 20–1, 26 October, 12 December 1889.
40 There is unfortunately no more personal information on these two patients. See BD, 1 September 1910, 21 January 1921.
41 LJ, 6 August 1888.
42 Grob, "Abuse in Hospitals," 298.
43 "Complaints," 74.
44 LJ, 28 October, 15 November 1888.
45 LJ, 9 September 1890, BD, 21 January 1921.
46 See "Nurse Not Guilty," *Guelph Mercury*, 8 December 1920.
47 LJ, 8 October 1888, 10 May 1889.
48 LJ, 11 October 1884, 11 April 1889; CMS, Lett to Langmuir, 13 December 1884, O'Reilley to Lett, 20 December 1884, Langmuir to Lett, 26 December 1884. The statutory reference was *Ontario Statutes*, 36 Vict., c. 33, s. 15 and 46 Vict., c. 38, s. 10.
49 LJ, 12 June 1889, 8 August 1891.

CHAPTER NINE

1 The literature on drink is vast. See, for instance, Lender and Martin, *Drinking in America*, especially 46–56, and Brian Harrison, *Drink and the Victorians*, especially 38–42. For recent research on drinking habits, temperance, and the treatment of inebriety in Canada, see my *Drink in Canada: Historical Essays* (forthcoming).
2 See Williams, "Alcohol as Medicine," especially 546–57, for a thorough account of the medicinal uses for alcohol.
3 Garland and Talman note the high density of taverns and saloons in Upper Canada in the 1830s. See "Pioneer Drinking Habits," especially 172–3.
4 See Noel, "Temperance, Evangelism," especially 1–5, 49–54, for the early temperance movement in the province of Canada. See also Barron, "Genesis of Temperance," Davis, "Prohibition in New Brunswick," and Decarie, "Something Old, Something New," for more on the Canadian temperance movement.

5 See Blocker, *Alcohol, Reform and Society*, Burnham, "New Perspectives," Clark, *Deliver Us From Evil*, Gusfield, *Symbolic Crusade*, and Kobler, *Ardent Spirits*, for American prohibition.

6 See Chapman, "New Brunswick and Maine," and Spence, *Prohibition in Canada*.

7 Local option was reintroduced in Ontario in 1906. Prohibition was legislated for the province in 1916 and for Canada in 1918, a move facilitated by the wave of patriotism and the extraordinary powers enjoyed by the federal government during the Great War.

8 Canada. Royal Commission on the Liquor Traffic, *Report*, 503.

9 For more on the evolution of the disease model of inebriety in the nineteenth century, see Wilkerson, "Concept of Alcoholism," Levine, "Discovery of Addiction," McLeod, "The Edge of Hope," and Quen, "Isaac Ray on Drunkenness."

10 For more on the theoretical bases for the use of alcohol in therapeutics, see Warner, "Physiological Theory," especially 243–8, Blackader, "On the Action of Alcohol," and "The Pathologic Impulse."

11 ARIP (Rockwood), 1878, 301.

12 Workman is cited in LPH, *Scrapbook*, 19 May 1876. Landor commented in ARIP (London), 1873, 155.

13 ARIP (Toronto), 1880, 281–2.

14 ARIP (London), 1885, 69. For a more detailed account of the Canadian medical debate over temperance and the use of alcohol in therapeutics, see Krasnick, "Because There is Pain."

15 Westcott, "Inebriety," 664. See also Beard, "Causes of Recent Increase," Kerr, *Inebriety*, Palmer, *Inebriety*, Skae, "On Dipsomania."

16 Crothers, "New Clinical Studies," 783. See also his *The Disease of Inebriety*.

17 Lett, "Why Do Men Drink?" 264–5. See also his "Report on Inebriety," and "Life Assurance and Inebriety."

18 Clark, "Dipsomaniac," 112.

19 BD, 31 December 1885.

20 BD, 21 April 1892; ARMS, 15 December 1892. For more on the gold cure in Canada, see Warsh, "Adventures in Maritime Quackery."

21 Tomes, *A Generous Confidence*, 239.

22 LJ, 13 July, 1 August, 22 September 1888.

23 LJ, 22, 26 December 1890, 10 January, 5 April 1891.

24 ARMS, 23 December 1904.

CHAPTER TEN

1 Terry and Pellens, *The Opium Problem*, 2.

2 *Catholic World* (1881), as quoted in Brecher, *Licit and Illicit Drugs*, 18.

3 Morphine is the chief active ingredient in opium. Laudanum is one grain opium to 25 drops alcohol. Paregoric is one grain opium to 480 drops alcohol and was a popular medicine for infants. See Brecher, *Licit and Illicit Drugs*, 18.

4 For the medicinal use of opium in nineteenth-century Britain, see Peters, "British Medical Response," especially 457–61; Berridge and Edwards, *Opium and the People*, Parssinen, *Secret Passions*, and Scott, *The White Poppy*. For opium use in the United States, see Courtwright, *Dark Paradise*, Musto, *The American Disease*. For Canadian events, see Solomon and Green, "The First Century" and Rublowsky, *The Stoned Age*.

5 Alethea Hayter has challenged this myth in *Opium and Romantic Imagination*. See Seigel, "Wilkie Collins," Macht and Gessford, "Dante Gabriel Rossetti," and Pearsall, "Victorian Oblivion."

6 de Quincey, *Confessions*. See Schiller, "Thomas de Quincey." The addict was quoted by Calkins, *Opium-Appetite*, 159. See also Morgan, *Yesterday's Addicts*, 115.

7 Berridge and Edwards, *Opium and the People*, 47.

8 The American civil war accelerated widespread use of the hypodermic syringe on this continent. See Courtwright, "Opiate Addiction," 101–11.

9 Berridge, "Victorian Opium-Eating," 454. For an early recognition of the problem, see Allbutt, "Abuse of Hypodermic Injection."

10 Berridge and Edwards, *Opium and the People*, 140–5.

11 Parssinen and Kerner, "Disease Model," 279.

12 Levinstein, *Morbid Craving*, 40. See also Anders, "Morphine Habit," Ball, *Morphine Habit*, and Richardson, "On the Morphia Habit."

13 See Parssinen and Kerner, "Disease Model," 279–80, and Berridge and Edwards, *Opium and the People*, 151–61. See also Harding, *Opiate Addiction*.

14 See Courtwright, *Dark Paradise*, 127–34, and Jaffe, "Addiction Reform" for the American view of inebriety and its application to drugs. Nineteenth-century literature includes Crothers, "Treatment of Morphinism," and Mann, "Morphia Habit."

15 See Peters, "British Medical Response," 483–5.

16 Lett, "Opium Neurosis," 828–33; ARIP (Homewood), 1891, 164; BD, 31 December 1891. See also Lett, "Opium Habit," "Diagnosis of Morphia Addiction," and "Prognosis of Drug Habits."

17 Lett, "Opium Neurosis," 829–31. On cannabis use, see Burr, "Two Cases," Hindmarch, "Cannabis Sativa," and Sloman, *Reefer Madness*.

18 Lett, "Opium Neurosis," 832–3.

19 Erlenmeyer, "Cocaine in the Treatment of Morphinomania," and "Cocaine in Morphine Habit."

20 Brecher, *Licit and Illicit Drugs*, 3; Parssinen and Kerner, "Disease Model," 276.

21 Morgan, *Drugs in America*, 13. See also Inciardi, "Changing Life of Mickey Finn."

22 MacDonald, "Hydrate of Chloral," 363–4. See also Balfour, "Hydrate of Chloral."

23 ARIP (London), 1872, 155.

24 Hugh MacD. (#875, 1887), Michael D. (admitted 15 June 1888), Thomas B. (#608, 1890), Sarah M. (#379, 1887), Caroline B. (#55, 1893), Jane A. (#4, 1898).

25 See Morgan, *Drugs in America*, 16–18, Chapman, "Drug Use," 21, and Berridge and Edwards, *Opium and the People*, 223–4. For more on cocaine, see Hammond, "Remarks on Cocaine," Grinspoon and Bakalar, "Coca and Cocaine," and "Cocaine and its Abuse." Thornton discusses Freud's experimentation in *Freud and Cocaine*.

26 Frank W. (#1113, 1890), AES (admitted 19 August 1890), Edward W. (#1103, 1891), Thatcher G. (#768, 1891), Clarkson C. (#646, 1891), Frederic R. (#1007, 1897), Harry McC. (#866, 1896), MTR (admitted 15 May 1895).

27 Lett, "Cocaine Addiction," 829–30.

28 Incidence of anaesthetic addiction succeeded the realization of the euphoric qualities of ether, nitrous oxide, and chloroform. "Ether frolics," similar to the pot parties of the late twentieth century, were popular diversions in the early nineteenth century. Diethyl ether was shipped "by the tons" to areas of Ireland during the temperance years of the mid-nineteenth century. Sir Benjamin Ward Richardson, a leading British physician, noted in 1878 that "the main street of Draperstown smelled like his surgery." See Nagle, "Anaesthetic Addiction," 25–30 and Browning, "Chloroform Habit."

29 In England in 1848, John Collis Browne patented chlorodyne, a mixture of chloroform and morphia. It became popular as a cure for cholera, bronchial and gastrointestinal disorders, and neuralgia. Chlorodyne was a target of anti-patent medicine reformers in the medical profession. See Berridge and Edwards, *Opium and the People*, 126–31.

30 *Medical Times and Register*, 9 September 1893. See also Stucky, "Paraldehyde Habit." Paraldehyde, used as a hypnotic, was a colorless liquid with a strong odor and burning taste. It was prepared by treating aldehyde with hydrochloric acid.

31 Osler, *Principles and Practice*, 1005.

32 Helen S. (#477, 1891) and Lucy S. (#448, 1892).

33 Haller and Haller, *Physician and Sexuality*, 274.

34 Stage, *Female Complaints*, 167.

35 Butler, "Limitations of the Rest Cure," 210. For more on bromide

addiction, see Baker, "Use of the Bromides," Cross, "Bromide Intoxication," and Seguin, "Abuse and Use of Bromides."

36 Kate R. (#434, 1889), Helen S. (#477, 1891).

37 They remain so today. In a study conducted at Homewood of physi-
cian-patients admitted between 1960 and 1967 (n = 93), one-quarter
(26.9%) were diagnosed with drug addiction and a further thirty percent with alcoholism. The author concluded that addiction "was almost an occupational hazard for the medical profession." The
narcotics addiction rate among physicians is currently thirty to one
hundred times that of the general population. Vincent, "Doctors as
Patients," 405. See Tokarz et al, *Beyond Survival*, 8. See also Henderson, "Addicted Doctors," and Garb, "Narcotic Addiction." Compare
with "Drug Addiction in the Medical Profession," written in 1900.

38 Joseph M., casebook no. 926, admitted to the London Asylum in
1875.

39 Addiction was not always an obstacle to an illustrious career. William
S. Halstead, a founder of Johns Hopkins Medical School and one of
the greatest of American surgeons, was successively a cocaine and
morphine addict during his adult life, including the period when he
developed aseptic techniques in surgery. See Brecher, *Licit and Illicit
Drugs*, 33–4 and Bett, "W.S. Halstead."

40 "Alcoholism and Morphinism," 559.

41 Mattison, "Morphinism," 186–8.

42 For a study of present-day physicians in addiction treatment, see
Waring, "Medical Professionals," 257–64.

43 The figures for tables 25 to 27 are related to the sample population,
1883 to 1920, for whom such information was noted.

44 Lindesmith, *Addiction and Opiates*, 148.

45 See Parssinen and Kerner, "Disease Model," 280, and Peters, "British
Medical Response," for the problems of coercion.

46 ARIP, 1889, 53.

47 See Berridge and Edwards, *Opium and the People*, 165.

48 Other sales outlets, such as mail order houses and grocery stores,
were prohibited from selling opiates. Licensed physicians were still
permitted to dispense medication. *RSO*, 1877, c. 145.

49 *Canada Statutes*, 1908 7–8 Edward 7, c. 56.

50 For an account of the Vancouver riot and its aftermath, see W. Peter
Ward, *White Canada Forever*.

51 King, "Report in Losses," *Sessional Papers*, 1908, no. 74f, 9–18, and
"Need to Suppress Trade," ibid., 1908, no. 36b, 7. For racist and sen-
sational accounts of the opium den, see Burke, *Limehouse Nights* and
Murphy, *Black Candle*.

52 *Canada Statutes* 1908 7–8 Edward 7, c. 50.

53 *Canada Statutes* 1911 1–2 George 5, c. 17.

54 Berridge and Edwards, *Opium and the People*, 70.

55 Heroin was isolated in 1898. See Terry and Pellens, *The Opium Problem*, 76, and Courtwright, *Dark Paradise*, 147. See also "Caution regarding Heroin," and Guggenheim, "Heroin."

CHAPTER ELEVEN

1 Hepworth, "Personal Social Services," 103.

Bibliography

The following bibliography is comprehensive. In addition to those items I refer to specifically in the notes, I have included articles, books, and dissertations and theses, primarily Canadian and American, but also British, that would be useful for researchers in the field. The bibliography has been divided into primary and secondary sources as follows:

I Primary Sources
  1 Archives of Ontario
  2 College of Physicians and Surgeons of Ontario
  3 University of Western Ontario Regional Collection
  4 Government Documents – Canada, Ontario, Great Britain
  5 Publications of Stephen Lett
  6 Publications of Alfred Hobbs
  7 Books (1790 to 1932)
  8 Articles (1790 to 1932)
II Secondary Sources
  1 Books
  2 Articles and chapters in books
  3 Dissertations and theses

PRIMARY SOURCES

Archives of Ontario

HOMEWOOD SANITARIUM COLLECTION
  Acts on Sanitaria
  Annual Reports 1883–1925
  Applications for Voluntary Admission 1883–1923
  Casebooks, male and female 1883–94

Cash Journal 1919–23
Cash Receipts and Disbursements 1902–12
Centennial Clinical Report 1983
Correspondence of the Medical Superintendent 1909
Daily Diary 1888–91
Day Books 1889–1922
Drug Books 1880s–1890s
Expense Ledgers 1914–22
General Ledgers 1883–1923
Insane Patients Commitment Forms 1883–1925
Journals 1905–22 ·
Journal of the Medical Superintendent 1885–91
List of Shareholders 1917–23
Medical Casebook 1883–91
Minute Books 1888–1900
Minutes of the Board of Directors 1883–1933
Patient Records (on microfilm) 1883–1925
Patient Registers, male and female 1883–1936
Petty Cash Books 1898–1923
Prospectus and Statement of Purpose of Homewood Retreat Association 1883
Prospectus/Advertising Circulars 1883, 1915, 1935
Stock Certificates
Visitors Minute Books 1884–1942

College of Physicians and Surgeons of Ontario

Registration Files 1866–1912

University of Western Ontario Regional Collection

Richard M. Bucke Papers
London, Ontario Asylum for the Insane
  Scrapbook 1877–8
  Medical Superintendent's Journal 1877–84

Government Documents

CANADA
  Census 1880–81
  House of Commons *Debates* 19 May 1922
  Parliament. Commission to Enquire into the Working of the Prohibitory Liquor Law in the United States. *Report* 1874
  Parliament. Royal Commission on the Effects of the Liquor Traffic.

Minutes of Evidence 1895
  Report 1895
Parliament. Commission of Inquiry into the Non-medical Use of Drugs.
Interim Report, 1970
  Report 1972
Statutes of Canada 1908, 7 and 8 Edward 7, c. 56, "An Act Respecting Proprietary or Patent Medicines."
Statutes of Canada 1911, 1 and 2 George 5, c. 17, "An Act to Prohibit the Improper Use of Opium and Other Drugs."

ONTARIO
Legislative Assembly.
  Debates 1874–8
  Sessional Papers, "Annual Report of the Inspector of Prisons, Asylums and Public Charities," 1878–1923.
Ministry of Health, "Correspondence of the Inspector of Prisons and Asylums," 1875–7.
Statutes of Upper Canada 1839, 2 Vict., c. 11, "An Act to Erect a Provincial Asylum at Toronto."
Statutes of the Province of Canada 1853, 14 and 15 Vict., c. 81, "An Act for the Regulation of Private Lunatic Asylums."
Statutes of the Province of Ontario 1873, 36 Vict., c. 33, "An Act to Provide for the Establishment of an Hospital for the Reclamation and Cure of Habitual Drunkards."
Revised Statutes of Ontario 1877, c. 221, "An Act Respecting Private Lunatic Asylums."
Revised Statutes of Ontario 1877, c. 145, "The Pharmacy Act."
Statutes of the Province of Ontario 1882–3, 45 Vict., c. 28, "An Act Respecting Private Asylums for Insane Persons and Inebriates."
Revised Statutes of Ontario 1887, c. 246, "An Act Respecting Private Lunatic Asylums."

GREAT BRITAIN
Statutes of Great Britain 1774, 14 Geo. 3, c. 49, "An Act for Regulating Madhouses."
Statutes of Great Britain 1828, 9 Geo. 4, c. 41, "The English Madhouse Act."
Statutes of Great Britain 1842, 5 and 6 Vict., c. 87, "The Lunatic Asylums Act."
Statutes of Great Britain 1845, 8 and 9 Vict., c. 100, "The Lunatics Act."

Publications of Stephen Lett

"Acute Mania," *Canada Lancet* 7, no. 10 (1875): 287–9.

"Cocaine Addiction and its Diagnosis," *Canada Lancet* 31, no. 4 (1898): 829–32.

"The Great Social Problem," *Ottawa Evening Journal*, 4 September 1889.

"Homewood Retreat," *Guelph Herald*, 21 March 1891.

"Life Assurance and Inebriety," *Monetary Times*, 3 April 1891.

"The Opium Habit and its Treatment," *CP* 4, no. 10 (1884): 301–7

"The Prognosis of Drug Habits with some reference to Treatment," *Canada Lancet* 34, no. 1 (1900): 1–4.

"The Relationship of Insanity to Masturbation," *Canada Lancet* 19, no. 12 (1887): 360–3.

"Some Points in the Diagnosis of Morphia Addiction," *QJI* 20, no. 4 (1898): 427–30.

"The Treatment of Drunkards," *Monetary Times*, 9 May 1890.

"Treatment of the Opium Neurosis," *JAMA* 17, no. 22 (1891): 828–33.

"Why Do Men Drink?" *QJI* 19, no. 3 (1897): 264–9.

Publications of Alfred Hobbs

"Gynecology among the Insane," *American Medico-Surgical Bulletin* 9, no. 13 (1896): 412–14.

"Hydrotherapy on Mental and Nervous Diseases," *CP* 33, no. 12 (1908): 761–6.

"A Plea for the Radical Operation for Hernia among the Insane," *CP* 22, no. 8 (1897): 567–72.

"The Role of Wound Infection as a Factor in the Causation of Insanity," *AJI* 56, no. 1 (1899): 89–94.

"Some Aspects of Neurasthenia and their Treatment," *CP* 34, no. 1 (1909): 13–20.

"Some Present Methods of Treatment of Patients at the Asylum for Insane, London, Ontario," *CP* 23, no. 9 (1898): 513–25.

"Surgical Treatment of Patients at the Asylum for Insane, London, Ontario," *American Journal of Obstetrics* 38, no. 2 (1898): 170–80.

Books (1790–1932)

Ball, B. *The Morphine Habit*. Paris: n.p., 1885.

Baruch, Simon. *The Principles and Practices of Hydrotherapy: A Guide to the Application of Water in Disease*. New York: n.p., 1898.

Beard, George Miller. *American Nervousness: Its Causes and Consequences*. New York: G.P. Putnam's Sons, 1881.

Belcher, W. *Address to Humanity, containing a Letter to Dr Thomas Monro; a Receipt to Make a Lunatic and Sieze his Estate and a Sketch of a True Smiling Hyena*. London: for the author, 1796.

Blatz, William and Helen Bott. *Parents and the Pre-school Child*. Toronto:
Dent, 1928.

British Medico-Psychological Association. *Handbook for Attendants on the Insane*. 5th edition. London: Balliere, Tindall and Cox, 1908.

Browne, W.A.F. *What Asylums Were, Are, and Ought to Be*. Edinburgh:
1837. Reprint. New York: Arno Press, 1976.

Buchan, William. *Every Man His Own Doctor*. New Haven, Conn.: Nathan
Whiting, 1816.

Bucke, Richard Maurice. *Alcohol in Health and Disease*. London, Ont.: William Bryce, 1880.

– *Man's Moral Nature*. New York: G.P. Putnam's Sons, 1879.

Bucknill, John C. *Notes on Asylums for the Insane in America*. London: J & A
Churchill, 1876.

Bucknill, John C. and Daniel Hack Tuke. *A Manual of Psychological Medicine*. London: Hafner, 1858. Reprint. New York: Arno Press, 1968.

Burgess, T.J.W. *A Historical Sketch of our Canadian Institutions for the Insane*.
Toronto: Copp-Clark, 1898.

Burke, Thomas. *Limehouse Nights*. New York: Grosset and Dunlap, 1917.

Calkins, Alonzo. *Opium and the Opium-Appetite*. Philadelphia: J.B. Lippincott, 1871.

Caniff, William. *The Medical Profession in Upper Canada 1783–1850*. Toronto: Briggs, 1894.

Chadwick, Mary. *The Psychological Effects of Menstruation*. New York: Nervous & Mental Diseases Pub., 1932.

Clark, C.S. *Of Toronto the Good*. Montreal: Toronto Pub., 1898. Reprint.
Toronto: Coles Pub.: 1970.

Clarke, Edward H. *Sex in Education*. Boston: Osgoode, 1874.

Clarke, John. *Practical Essays on the Management of Pregnancy and Labour*.
London: J. Johnson, 1793.

Conolly, John. *The Construction and Government of Lunatic Asylums and Hospitals for the Insane*. 1847. Reprint. London: Dawson's of Pall Mall, 1968.

– *Treatment of the Insane without Mechanical Restraints*. Reprint, with introduction by R. Hunter and I. Macalpine. London: Dawson's of Pall Mall,
1973.

Coyne, J.H. *Richard Maurice Bucke*. Toronto: Henry Saunders, 1923.

Crothers, Thomas D. *The Disease of Inebriety*. New York: n.p., 1893.

Curwen, John. *History of the Association of Medical Superintendents of American Institutions for the Insane*. Harrisburg, Penn.: n.p., 1875.

Cutten, George B. *The Psychology of Alcoholism*. 1907. Reprint. New York:
Arno Press, 1981.

Darwin, Charles. *On the Origins of Species by Means of Natural Selection*.
London: John Murray, 1859.

de Quincey, Thomas. *Confessions of an English Opium Eater*. Edinburgh:
Adam & Charles Black, 1862.

Dewees, William P. *A Treatise of the Diseases of Females.* 4th ed. Philadelphia: Carey & Lea, 1833.

Dix, Dorothea. *Remarks on Prisons and Prison Discipline in the United States.* Boston: Munroe & Francis, 1845.

General Council of Medical Education and Registration of the United Kingdom. *British Pharmacopoeia, 1877.* London: Spottiswoode, 1877.

Halliday, W. *A Letter to Lord Robert Seymour: with a Report of the number of Lunatics and Idiots in England and Wales.* London: Underwood, 1829.

Hammond, William A. *A Treatise on the Diseases of the Nervous System.* 6th ed. New York: Appleton, 1876.

Howe, Joseph W. *Excessive Venery, Masturbation and Continence.* New York: Bermingham, 1883.

Kane, Harvey H. *Opium-Smoking in America and China.* New York: G.P. Putnam's Sons, 1882.

Keeley, Leslie E. *The Non-Heredity of Inebriety.* Chicago: S.C. Griggs, 1896.

Kerr, Norman. *Inebriety: Its Etiology, Pathology, Treatment and Jurisprudence.* London: H.K. Lewis, 1888.

Kirkbride, Thomas S. *On the Construction, Organization and General Arrangement of Hospitals for the Insane.* 1880. Reprint. New York: Arno Press, 1973.

von Krafft-Ebing, Richard. *Psychopathia Sexualis.* 1886. rev. ed. New York: Rebman, 1922.

Landor, Henry. *Hysteria in Children as Contrasted with Mania.* London, Ont.: Daily Free Press, 1873.

– *Insanity in Relation to Law.* London, Ont.: Daily Free Press, 1871.

Leake, John. *Medical Instructions Towards the Prevention and Cure of Chronic Diseases Peculiar To Women.* London: n.p., 1781.

Levinstein, Edward. *Morbid Craving for Morphia.* 1878. Reprint. New York: Arno Press, 1981.

Might Directory of Toronto. Toronto: n.p., 1883.

Mitchell, Silas Weir. *Clinical Lessons on Nervous Diseases.* Philadelphia: Lea Bros, 1897.

– *Dr North and His Friends.* New York: Century, 1901.

– *Fat and Blood.* 7th ed. Philadelphia: J.B. Lippincott, 1898.

Morgan, Henry J. ed. *Canadian Men and Women of the Time.* Toronto: William Briggs, 1898 and 1912.

Murphy, Emily J. *The Black Candle.* Toronto: Thomas Allen, 1922.

Nightingale, Florence. *Cassandra,* ed. Myra Stark. Old Westbury, N.Y.: Feminist Press, 1979.

The Opium Habit. New York: Harper & Bros., 1868.

Palmer, Charles F. *Inebriety: Its Sources, Prevention and Cure.* New York: Fleming H. Revell, 1896.

Pereira, Jonathan. *The Elements of Materia Medica and Therapeutics.* Philadelphia: Blanchard & Lea, 1854.

Rockwell, Alphonso David. *Lectures in Electricity in its Relations to Medicine and Surgery.* New York: W. Wood, 1879.

Ross, Alexander M. *Memoirs of a Reformer.* Toronto: Hunter, Rose, 1893.

Rush, Benjamin. *Medical Inquiries and Observations upon the Diseases of the Mind.* 5th ed. Philadelphia: Grigg & Elliot, 1812, 1835.

Shew, Joel. *Midwifery and the Diseases of Women.* New York: Fowler & Wells, 1853.

Tuke, Daniel Hack. *The Insane in the United States and Canada.* London: H.K. Lewis, 1885.

Who's Who and Why. Toronto: International Press, 1883.

Williard, Francis E. *Woman and Temperance or, The Work and Workers of the WCTU.* Hartford, Conn.: Park Pub., 1883. Reprint. New York: Arno Press, 1972.

Workman, Joseph. *On Crime and Insanity.* Montreal: Lovell, 1877.

Articles (1790–1932)

"Action of Paraldehyde." *AJI* 41, no. 4 (April 1885): 480–1.

"Alcoholism and Morphinism among Physicians." *AJI* 56, no. 3 (January 1900): 559–60.

Allbutt, T.C. "On the Abuse of Hypodermic Injection of Morphia." *Practitioner* 5 (1870): 327–31.

Allen, Nathan. "Effects of Alcohol on the Offspring." *Journal of Psychological Medicine,* n.s. 3 (1877–8): 209–14.

Anders, J.M. "The Morphine Habit." *Medical Bulletin* 21 (1899): 6–8.

Andrews, Judson B. "The Alienist and the General Practitioner." *MR* 43, no. 1 (7 January 1893): 2–5.

Angell, Edward B. "The Physiological Basis of Hydrotherapy." *American Journal of Nursing* 3 (1902–3): 600–6.

Anglin, James V. "Nursing the Insane." *CMR* 25, no. 4 (January 1897): 177–94.

"Annual report of Walnut Lodge Hospital, Hartford, Conn." *QJI* 18, no. 1 (January 1896): 44–50.

Anstie, [Francis]. "On Indiscriminate Stimulation in Chronic Disease." *Practitioner* 3, no. 1 (July 1869): 34–42.

Baker, L.W. "The Continuous Use of the Bromides." *Medical Register* 4 (1888): 533–5.

Balfour, G.W. "Hydrate of Chloral." *Edinburgh Medical Journal* 15 (1870): 1011–15.

Barrus, Clara. "Gynecological Disorders and their Relation to Insanity." *AJI* 51, no. 4 (April 1895): 475–91.

Beard, George Miller. "Causes of the Recent Increase of Inebriety in America." *QJI* 1, no. 1 (December 1876): 25–44.

Bell, Clark. "Mechanical Restraint in the Care and Treatment of the Insane." *Medico-Legal Journal* 9 (1891–2): 384–99; 10 (1892–3): 1–32.

Bennett, Alice. "Mechanical Restraint in the Treatment of the Insane." *Medico-Legal Journal* 1 (1883–4): 285–96.

Bigelow, Horatio R. "Gynecological Electro-therapeutics." *MN* 56, no. 19 (10 May 1890): 499–503.

Blackader, A.D. "On the Action and Therapeutic Employment of Alcohol, being an Epitome of Recent Contributions to the Subject." *Montreal Medical Journal* 31 (1902): 951–65.

– "Recent Views on the Therapeutic Value of Alcohol." *Montreal Medical Journal* 34 (1905): 811–16.

Blodgett, Albert N. "The Management of Chronic Inebriates and Insane Drunkards." *AN* 4, no. 1 (January 1883): 36–57.

Bramwell, Edwin. "Remarks upon the Treatment of Hysteria with Special Reference to the Rest Cure." *CP* 35, no. 5 (May 1910): 296–305.

Brill, A.A. "Diagnostic Errors in Neurasthenia." *Medical Review of Reviews* 36 (1930): 123.

Broom, John. "The Wet-Sheet Pack and Chloride of Ammonium as Valuable Therapeutics in the Treatment of Some Forms of Delirium Tremens." *BMJ* 2 (16 November 1878): 720.

Brown, Caleb. "The Use of Electricity by the General Practitioner." *JAMA* (1898): 31.

Browning, A.G. "The Chloroform Habit." *Louisville Monthly Journal of Medicine and Surgery* 18 (1911–12): 232–7.

Buchanon, Charles M. "Should the Insane be Deceived?" *AJI* 49, no. 4 (April 1892): 669–71.

Bucke, Richard Maurice. "The Growth of the Intellect." *AJI* 29, no. 1 (July 1882): 36–54.

– "Mental Evolution in Man." *JAMA* 29, no. 17 (23 October 1897): 821–4.

– "The Moral Nature and the Great Sympathetic." *AJI* 35, no. 2 (October 1878): 229–53.

– "The Origin of Insanity." *CP* 17, no. 12 (16 May 1892): 219–24.

– "Sanity." *AJI* 47, no. 1 (July 1890): 17–26.

– "Surgery among the Insane in Canada." *Proceedings of the American Medico-Psychological Association* 5, NO. 1 (1898): 1–19.

– "Two Hundred Operative Cases – Insane Women." *Proceedings of the American Medico-Psychological Association*, 7, no. 1 (1900): 99–105.

Bucknill, John C. "On some Relations between Intemperance and Insanity." *BMJ* 1 (3 March 1877): 254–5.

Burr, Charles W. "Two Cases of Cannabis Indica Intoxication." *Therapeutic Gazette* 40 (1916): 554–6.

Butler, George F. "The Advantages and Limitations of the Rest Cure." *Journal of the Michigan State Medical Society* 2, no. 5 (May 1903): 206–10.

Carman, J.H. "The Danger of Opium Smoking as a Therapeutic Measure." *MR* 26, no. 18 (November 1884): 501.

"Caution regarding Heroin." *Maritime Medical News* 12, no. 4 (April 1900): 144.

Chambers, Francis T., Jr. "A Psychological Approach in Certain Cases of Alcoholism." *Mental Hygiene* 21, no. 1 (January 1937): 67–78.

Chapin, John B. "Public Complaints against Asylums for the Insane and the Commitment of the Insane." *AJI* 40, no. 1 (July 1883): 33–49.

Chenery, E. "The Effects of Alcohol on Offspring." *QJI* 4, no. 2 (April 1881): 91–101.

Clark, Daniel. "An Animated Molecule and its Nearest Relatives." *AJI* 35, no. 2 (October 1878): 189–228.

– "Crime and Responsibility." *AJI* 47, no. 4 (April 1891): 496–506.

– "Neurasthenia." *CP* 13, no. 7 (July 1888): 209–13.

– "The Public and the Doctor in Relation to the Dipsomaniac." *CP* 13, no. 4 (April 1888): 109–15.

– "Reflexes in Psychiatry." *CJMS* 5 (1899): 86–93.

– "The Relationship of Mind and Body." *AJI* 49, no. 1 (July 1892): 1–25.

Clark, L. Pierce. "A Psychological Study of some Alcoholics." *Psychoanalytic Review* 6, no. 3 (July 1919): 268–95.

Clarke, C.K. "The Care of the Insane in Canada." *AJI* 50, no. 3 (January 1894): 381–5.

– "The Fourth Maudesley Lecture," *Public Health Journal* 10, no. 12 (December 1923): 531–41; 11, no. 1 (January 1924): 9–15.

Clarke, C.K. and C.B. Farrar. "One Thousand Psychiatric Cases from the Canadian Army." *Canadian Journal of Mental Hygiene* 1, no. 4 (January 1920): 313–17.

Clarke, J. St. Thomas. "Treatment of the Habit of Injecting Morphine by Suddenly Discontinuing the Drug." *Lancet* 2 (20 September 1884): 491.

Cleaves, M. Abbie. "The Medical and Moral Care of Female Patients in Hospitals for the Insane." In *Proceedings of the Sixth Annual Conference of Charities*, edited by F.B. Sanborn, 73–83. Boston: A. Williams, 1879.

"Cocaine in the Morphine Habit." *AJI* 42, no. 3 (January 1886): 357.

"Cocaine and its Abuse." *Maritime Medical News* 11, no. 10 (October 1899): 368.

Collins, Joseph and Carlin Phillips. "The Etiology and Treatment of Neurasthenia, An Analysis of 333 Cases." *CJMS* 7, no. 2 (February 1900): 131–8.

"Complaints by Insane Patients." *AJI* 39, no. 1. (July 1882): 74.

Cook, George. "The Relations of Inebriety to Insanity." *AJI* 18, no. 4 (April 1862): 321–49.

Corbet, G.G. "Electro-Therapy." *Maritime Medical News* 17, no. 1 (January 1905): 1–7.

Cross, W.D.S. "Bromide Intoxication." *CMAJ* 35, no. 3 (September 1936): 283–9.

Crothers, Thomas D. "Is Alcoholism Increasing among American Women?" *North American Review* 155 (1892): 731–6.

– "Clinical Studies of Inebriety." *MSR* 35, no. 7 (12 August 1876): 125–8.

– "Clinical Studies of Inebriety – Hints of the Pathology." *MSR* 49 (27 September 1879): 268–71.

– "Clinical Studies of Inebriety – Some Obscure Symptoms." *MSR* 41 (19 July 1879): 51–4.

– "Dangers from the Injudicious Use of Alcohol in the Sick Room." *MSR* 39 (20 July 1878): 48–51.

– Inebriety and Heredity." *QJI* 8, no. 2 (April 1886): 72–80.

– "Neuratrophia – The Cause of Inebriety: A Clinical Study." *AN* 4, no. 1 (January 1883): 104–12.

– "Sketch of the Late Dr. J. Edward Turner, the Founder of Inebriate Asylums." *QJI* 12, no. 1 (January 1890): 1–14.

– "Some Clinical Indications for the Use of the Electric Light Bath." *Journal of Advanced Therapeutics* 21 (1903): 20–6.

– "Some New Clinical Studies on Inebriety." *BMJ* 2 (25 September 1897): 782–3.

– "Treatment of Morphinism." *CJMS* 9, no. 5 (May 1901): 307–17.

Davenport, Isabel M. "Five Cases of Hysterectomy in the Insane." *AJI* 53, no. 4 (April 1897): 513–20.

Davis, N.S. "Inebriate Asylums." *QJI* 2, no. 3 (June 1878): 80–8.

Dennis, F.W. "The Therapeutic Value of Alcohol," *MR* 60, no. 17 (26 October 1901): 676.

Dewey, Richard. "The Jury Law for Commitment of the Insane in Illinois." *Chicago Medical Recorder* 35 (2 February 1913): 72–84.

– "Voluntary or Self-Commitment to Insane Hospitals." *Proceedings of the National Conference on Charities and Corrections*, edited by Isabel Barrows, 71–8. Boston: George H. Ellis, 1891.

Douglas, Charles J. "Historical Notes on the Sanatorium Treatment of Alcoholism." *MR* 57, no. 10 (10 March 1900): 410–11.

"Drug Addiction, especially in the Medical Profession." *JNMD* 27, no. 5 (May 1900): 294–5.

Engelmann, George J. "Electro-therapy and Surgery in Gynaecology," *Transactions of the American Gynaecological Society* (1888): 13.

Erlenmeyer, A. "Cocaine in the Treatment of Morphinomania." *Journal of Mental Science* 31 (1885–6): 427.

– "The Morphia Habit and its Treatment" *Journal of Mental Science* 34 (1888–9): 116.

Farrar, Clarence B. "Rehabilitation in Nervous and Mental Cases among Ex-soldiers." *AJI* 76, no. 2 (October 1919): 145–57.

– "The Revival of Spiritism: Psychologic Factors." *Archives of Neurology and Psychiatry* 5, no. 6 (June 1921): 670–86.

– "War and Neurosis with some Observations of the CEF." *AJI* 73, no. 4 (April 1917): 693–719.

"The Future of the Asylum Service." *Medical Press and Circular* (21 March 1900).

Fischer, Louis. "The Opium Habit in Children." *MR* 45, no. 7 (17 February 1894): 197–9.

"Forcible Feeding of the Insane." *AJI* 39, no. 3 (January 1883): 349–50.

Foster, G.W. "Common Features in Neurasthenia and Insanity." *AJI* 56, no. 3 (January 1900): 395–417.

Fox, Fortescue. "Stimulants and Narcotics: Their Use and Abuse." *Nineteenth Century* 18 (December 1885): 923–39.

Goodell, William. "Clinical Notes on the Extirpation of the Ovaries for Insanity." *AJI* 38, no. 3 (January 1882): 294–302.

Gray, John P. "Hints on the Prevention of Insanity." *AJI* 41, no. 3 (January 1885): 295–304.

Gregg, Donald. "A Comparison of the Drugs Used in General and Mental Hospitals." *BMSJ* 171 (1917): 476–7.

Grissom, Eugene. "Mechanical Protection for the Violent Insane." *AJI* 34, no. 1 (July 1877): 27–58.

Gross, Samuel D. "Brunonianism, Toddism and Other Isms." *North American Medico-Chirurgical Review* 5, no. 1 (January 1861): 66–83.

Grosvenor, J.W. "What Shall We Do With Our Alcoholic Inebriates?" *Canada Lancet* 28, no. 9 (May 1896): 299–303.

Hahn, H.H. "Electricity in Gynaecology: based on an Experience of over 1000 Applications." *JAMA* (1893): 20.

Hammond, William A. "Henry Maudesley's Physiology and Pathology of the Mind." *Nation* (1867): 86.

– "Remarks on Cocaine and the so-called Cocaine Habit." *JNMD* 13 (1886): 754–9.

Haskell, William G. "The Keeley Cure for Inebriety." *Arena* 16 (1896): 222–7.

Hattie, W.H. "The Prevention of Insanity." *CMAJ* 1, no. 11 (November 1911): 1019–26.

Howard, Henry. "The Increase of Insanity – What is the Cause?" *CMSJ* 5 (1876): 1–8.

Hughes, Charles H. "Experience of an Opium Eater during the Withdrawal of the Drug." *AN* 4, no. 1 (January 1883): 26–35.

– "The Successful Management of Inebriety without Secrecy in Therapeutics." *AN* 15, no. 1 (January 1894): 1–11.

"Hydrotherapy in Mental Diseases" *AJI* 44, no. 3 (January 1888): 414–5.

"Hydrotherapy in States of Mental Excitement." *AJI* 50, no. 2 (October 1893): 295–7.

"Inebriety among Women." *MR* 42, no. 20 (5 November 1892): 544.

"Influence of Menstruation on Chronic Psychoses." *AJI* 51, no. 3 (January 1895): 393.

Ives, A.W. "Neurasthenia." *Detroit Medical Journal* 3, no. 4 (July 1903): 191–3.

Jewell, J.S. "Nervous Exhaustion or Neurasthenia in its Bodily and Mental Relations." *JNMD* 6, no. 1 (January 1879): 45–55; no. 3 (July 1879): 449–60.

– "The Varieties and Causes of Neurasthenia." *JNMD* 7, no. 1 (January 1880): 1–16.

"The Keeley Cure Exposed." *MR* 43, no. 19 (13 May 1893): 593.

Keeley, Leslie E. "Does Bi-Chloride of Gold Cure Inebriety?" *Arena* 7 (1893): 450–60.

– "My Gold Cure." *North American Review* 153 (1891): 759–61.

Kerr, Norman. "International Congress of Inebriety: Opening Address." *QJI* 9, no. 3 (July 1887): 129–42.

King, James K. "Treatment of Nervous Diseases in Sanitariums." *AN* 15 (1894): 12–26.

Landor, Henry. "Probationary Leave of Absence." *AJI* 32, no. 4 (April 1876): 475–87.

Langmuir, John Woodburn. "The Asylums, Prisons and Public Charities of Ontario, and their System of Management." *Canadian Monthly and National Review* 18 (1880): 239–47.

"The Late Robert Bentley Todd, M.D. F.R.S." *BMJ* 1, no. 1 (11 February 1860): 111–12.

Lord, Henry W. "Hospitals and Asylums for the Insane." In *Proceedings of the Sixth Annual Conference on Charities and Corrections*, edited by F.B. Sanborn, 83–94. Boston: A. Williams, 1879.

"Lunatics as Witnesses." *AJI* 40, no. 2 (October 1883): 224–5.

Mann, Edward C. "Intemperance and Dipsomania as related to Insanity." *MR* 10 (6 November 1875): 756–8.

– "The Nature and Treatment of the Morphia Habit." *Montreal Medical Journal* 23, no. 1 (July 1894): 1–6.

Mason, Theodore L. "Anniversary Address." *QJI* 1, no. 1 (December 1876): 1–17.

Mattison, J.B. "Cocainism." *MR* 42, no. 17 (22 October 1892): 474–7; 43, no. 2 (14 January 1893): 34–6.

– "The Modern and Humane Treatment of the Morphine Disease." *MR* 44, no. 26 (23 December 1893): 804–6.

– "Morphinism in Medical Men." *JAMA* 23 (4 August 1894): 186–8.

– "Morphinism in the Young." *Archives of Pediatrics* 12, no. 11 (November 1895): 812–16.

"Medical Society Meeting." *Toronto Mail*, 13 December 1889.

Menzies, W.R. "Puerperal Insanity," *AJI* 50, no. 2 (October 1893): 147–85.

Meyer, Adolf. "Objective Psychology and Psychobiology with Subordination of the Medically Useless Contrast of Mental and Physical." *JAMA* 65, no. 10 (4 September 1915): 860–3.

Meyers, D. Campbell. "Neurasthenia." *Canada Lancet* 33 (1899–1900): 503–6.

– "Neurasthenia in some of its Relations to Insanity." *CP* 29, no. 8 (August 1904): 393–4.

– "Neurology and The Prevention of Insanity in the Poor." *CP* 30, no. 5 (May 1905): 235–43.

– "With Déjérine at the Salpétrière." *Canada Lancet* 28, no. 3 (November 1895): 81–2.

Mitchell, Silas Weir. "The Treatment by Rest, Seclusion, etc. in Relation to Psychotherapy." *JAMA* 50, no. 25 (20 June 1908): 2033–7.

Morrow, Prince A. "The Relations of Social Diseases to the Family." *American Journal of Sociology* 14 (March 1909): 629.

Morton, Thomas G. "Removal of the Ovaries as a Cure for Insanity." *AJI* 49 (1893): 397–401.

Munson, J.D. "Asylum Dietaries." *AJI* 52, no. 1 (July 1895): 58–66.

McClain, W.A. "Routine Medication in Asylum Practice." *MR* 48, no. 15 (12 October 1895): 516–18.

MacCoy, Cecil. "Some Observations on the Treatment of Neurasthenia at the Dispensary Clinic." *Brooklyn Medical Journal* 17, no. 9 (September 1903): 399–401.

MacDonald, Carlos F. "Hydrate of Chloral." *AJI* 34, no. 3 (January 1878): 360–7.

Mackintosh, D. "The Mutual Relation of the Profession and the Public." *Maritime Medical News* 12, no. 7 (July 1900): 217–30.

Niles, H. Roland. "Hydrotherapy in the Treatment of Mental Diseases." *AJI* 55, no. 3 (January 1899): 443–7.

"Obituary – A.T. Hobbs." *Guelph Mercury*, 26 May 1931.

"Obituary – Farrar." *Globe and Mail*, [n.d.], Homewood Archives.

Ogston, Francis. "An Address on the Use and Abuse of Alcohol." *BMJ* 2 (2 November 1878): 655.

Ordronaux, John. "Is Habitual Drunkenness a Disease?" *AJI* 30, no. 3 (April 1874): 430–43.

Owen, Edmund. "An Address on the Future of Electrotherapeutics." *BMJ* 1 (3 January 1903): 1–5.

"The Pathologic Impulse to Drink." *Maritime Medical News* 11, no. 4 (April 1899): 139–40.

"The Pecuniary Value of the Keeley Cure." *MR* 43, no. 16 (22 April 1893): 499.

"Personal Purity." *Guelph Herald*, 22 February 1890.

"The Prevention of Masturbation." *CJMS* 1, no. 11 (November 1876): 394.

Prince, Morton. "The True Position of Electricity as a Therapeutic Agent in Medicine." *BMSJ* 123, no. 14 (25 September 1890): 313–18.

Pritchard, William B. "The American Disease: An Interpretation." *Canada Lancet* 38, no. 11 (June 1905): 982–95.

"Proposed Legislation for the Treatment of Inebriates in Canada." *QJI* 23, no. 2 (April 1901): 234–5.

Pursell, John. "The Alcoholic Treatment in Exhausting Diseases." *BMJ* 2 (15 September 1860): 722–3.

Putnam, James Jackson. "Remarks on the Psychical Treatment of Neurasthenia." *BMSJ* 132 (23 May 1895): 505–11.

Rainear, A.R. "The Proper Recognition of Electrotherapeutics." *MN* 82, no. 25 (20 June 1903): 1161–3.

Rankin, Guthrie. "Neurasthenia: The Wear and Tear of Life." *BMJ* 1 (2 May 1903): 1017–20.

"The Relation of Drink and Insanity." *British Journal of Mental Science* 22 (July 1876): 265–87.

Richardson, Benjamin Ward. "Notes on the Administration of Alcohol in the Treatment of Disease." *Lancet* 1 (1 January 1876): 6–8.

– "On the Morphia Habit and its Treatment." *BMJ* 2 (1883): 1194.

"The Rights of the Insane." *AJI* 39, no. 4 (April 1883): 411–32.

Rogers, Arthur W. "Some Remarks on the use of Opium in Mental Diseases." *Wisconsin Medical Journal* 3, no. 10 (March 1905): 554–9.

Rosebrugh, Abner M. "The Treatment of Inebriates." *CJMS* 4 (1898)229–33.

– "The Treatment of Inebriety." *CJMS* 3 (1898): 237–44.

Rosebrugh, A.M. and R.H. Coleman. "Hospitals for Inebriates: A Cottage Hospital for Toronto." *CP* 36, no. 6 (June 1911): 351–4.

Runge, Edward C. "How to Deal with the Insane: A Medico-Legal View." *AJI* 56, no. 4 (April 1900): 631–44.

Russel, Colin K. "A Study of Certain Psychogenetic Conditions among Soldiers." *CMAJ* 7, no. 8 (August 1917): 704–20.

– "War Neuroses: Some Views on Diagnosis and Treatment." *Archives of Neurology and Psychiatry* 1, no. 1 (January 1919): 25–38.

Russell, James. "Insanity: Its Causes and Remedies." *CP* 27, no. 11 (November 1902): 627–32.

Scudder, John M. "Electrotherapeutics." *Eclectic Medical Journal* (1895): 45.

Seguin, Edward C. "The Abuse and Use of Bromides." *JNMD* 4 (1877): 445–62.

Sharkey, Seymour J. "Morphinomania." *Nineteenth Century* 22 (September 1887): 335–42.

– "The Treatment of Morphia Habitués by Suddenly Discontinuing the Drug." *Lancet* 1 (29 December 1883): 1120–1.

Shew, A.M. "Progress in the Treatment of the Insane." *AJI* 42, no. 4 (April 1886): 429–51.

Shirres, David A. "A Plea for the Neurasthenic." *Montreal Medical Journal* 35, no. 3 (March 1906): 161–79.

Skae, David. "On Dipsomania." *Journal of Psychological Medicine* 11, no. 2 (1 April 1858): 349–64.

Smith, P.C. "The Meaning of the Term 'Neurasthenia' and the Etiology of the Disease." *BMJ* 1 (4 April 1903): 781–2.

Spitzka, Edward C. "Cases of Masturbation." *AJI* 45, no. 3 (January 1889): 415–16.

Stucky, T.H. "Case of Paraldehyde Habit." *MSR* 70 (1894): 91.

Sweeney, M.J. "Sixty Grains of Morphine at a Dose." *MR* 46, no. 18 (3 November 1894): 565.

Tomlinson, H.A. "The Puerperal Insanities." *AJI* 56, no. 1 (July 1899): 69–88.

"Treatment of Morphinism and Chloralism." *AJI* 47, no. 2 (October 1890): 252–3.

TPW, "The Redundancy of Spinster Gentlewomen." *The Living Age* 227, no. 2943 (1 December 1900): 529–44.

Tuke, Harrington. "On Warm and Cold Baths in the Treatment of Insanity." *Journal of Mental Science* 4, no. 26 (July 1858): 532–52; 5, no. 27 (October 1858): 102–14.

Walker, Henry F. "Some Remarks on the Morphine Habit." *MR* 48, no. 20 (16 November 1895): 692–4.

Waugh, William F. "The Morphine Habit – Home Treatment." *Medical Brief* 23, no. 10 (October 1895): 1185–7.

Weijl, S. "On the Psychology of Alcoholism." *Psychoanalytic Review* 15, no. 1 (January 1928): 103–4.

Westcott, William W. "Inebriety: Its Causes and Cure." *Journal of Mental Science* 46, no. 195 (October 1900): 653–73.

Wetherill, Henry M. "The Modern Hypnotics." *AJI* 46, no. 1 (July 1889): 28–47.

"W.G. Jaffray." *Globe and Mail*, 29 December 1949.

Wilbur, H.B. "Chemical Restraint in the Management of the Insane." *Archives of Medicine* 6, no. 3 (December 1881): 271–92.

"Women versus Special Brain Work." *AJI* 37, no. 4 (April 1881): 450–1.

Wood, Henry. "Does Bichloride of Gold Cure Inebriety?" *Arena* 7 (1893): 145–52.

Woolley, B.M. "Opium and Its Excessive Use." *MR* 45, no. 14 (7 April 1894): 444–5.

Workman, Benjamin. "Asylums for the Chronic Insane in Upper Canada." *AJI* 24, no. 1 (July 1867): 49–51.

Workman, Joseph. "Asylum Management." *AJI* 38, no. 1 (July 1881): 1–15.
– "Moral Insanity: What is it?" *AJI* 39, no. 43 (January 1883): 334–48.

SECONDARY SOURCES

Books

Ackerknecht, Erwin H. *A Short History of Psychiatry*. 2d ed. Translated by S. Wolff. New York: Macmillan, 1954.
Agnew, G. Harvey. *Canadian Hospitals 1920 to 1970: A Dramatic Half-Century*. Toronto: University of Toronto Press, 1974.
Al-Issa, Ihsan. *The Psychopathology of Women*. Englewood Cliffs, N.J.: Prentice-Hall, 1980.
Anderson, Michael. *Approaches to the History of the Western Family*. London: Macmillan, 1980.
– *Family Structure in Nineteenth Century Lancashire*. Cambridge University Press, 1971.
Ariés, Philippe. *Centuries of Childhood: A Social History of Family Life*. Translated by Robert Baldick. New York: Vintage Books, 1962.
Bacchi, Carol Lee. *Liberation Deferred? The Ideas of the English-Canadian Suffragists 1877–1918*. Toronto: University of Toronto Press, 1983.
Ball, John C. and Carl D. Chambers, eds. *The Epidemiology of Opiate Addiction in the United States*. Springfield, Ill.: Charles C. Thomas, 1970.
Banks, Joseph A. *Prosperity and Parenthood: A Study of Family Planning among the Victorian Middle Classes*. London: Routledge & Kegan Paul, 1954.
Banks, Joseph A. and Olive. *Feminism and Family Planning in Victorian England*. Liverpool: University of Liverpool Press, 1964.
Barker-Benfield, G.J. *The Horrors of the Half-Known Life: Male Attitudes towards Women and Sexuality in Nineteenth-Century America*. New York: Harper Colophon, 1976.
Berger, Carl. *Science, God and Nature in Victorian Canada*. Toronto: University of Toronto Press, 1983.
Berridge, Virginia and Griffith Edwards. *Opium and the People: Opiate Use in Nineteenth-Century England*. London: Allen Lane, 1981.
Bilson, Geoffrey. *A Darkened House: Cholera in Nineteenth-Century Canada*. Toronto: University of Toronto Press, 1980.
Bjork, Daniel W. *The Compromised Scientist: William James and the Development of American Psychology*. New York: Columbia University Press, 1983.
Bledstein, Burton J. *The Culture of Professionalism: The Middle Class and the Development of Higher Education in America*. New York: W.W. Norton, 1976.

Bliss, Michael. *A Living Profit: Studies in the Social History of Canadian Business 1883–1911*. Toronto: McClelland & Stewart, 1974.

Blocker, Jack S. *Retreat from Reform: The Prohibition Movement in the United States*. Westport, Conn.: Greenwood Press, 1976.

– ed. *Alcohol, Reform and Society: The Liquor Issue in Social Context*. Westport, Conn.: Greenwood Press, 1979.

Borland, Marie, ed. *Violence in the Family*. Atlantic Highlands, N.J.: Humanities Press, 1976.

Boyer, Paul. *Urban Masses and the Moral Order in America 1820–1920*. Cambridge: Harvard University Press, 1978.

Braceland, Francis J. *The Institute of Living: The Hartford Retreat; 1822–1972*. Hartford, Conn.: priv. pub., 1972.

Branca, Patricia. *Silent Sisterhood: Middle Class Women in the Victorian Home*. London: Croom-Helm, 1975.

Brandt, Allan M. *No Magic Bullet: A Social History of Venereal Disease in the United States since 1880*. New York: Oxford University Press, 1985.

Braverman, Harry. *Labor and Monopoly Capital: The Degradation of Work in the Twentieth Century*. New York: Monthly Review Press, 1974.

Brecher, Edward M. et al. *Licit and Illicit Drugs*. Boston: Little, Brown, 1972.

Brown, Richard D. *Modernization: The Transformation of American Life 1600–1865*. New York: Hill & Wang, 1976.

Brumberg, Joan Jacobs. *Fasting Girls: The Emergence of Anorexia Nervosa as a Modern Disease*. Cambridge: Harvard University Press, 1988.

Bullough, Vern L. *Sex, Society and History*. New York: Science History Pub., 1976.

Bullough, Vern L. and Bonnie. *Sin, Sickness and Sanity: A History of Sexual Attitudes*. New York: New American Library, 1977.

– *The Subordinate Sex: A History of Attitudes towards Women*. Urbana: University of Illinois Press, 1973.

Burnham, John C. *Psychoanalysis and American Medicine 1894–1918*. New York: International University Press, 1967.

Bynum, William F., Roy Porter, and Michael Shepherd, eds. *The Anatomy of Madness: Essays in the History of Psychiatry*. London: Tavistock, 1985.

Calder, Jenni. *The Victorian Home*. London: B.T. Botsford, 1977.

Caplan, Ruth B. *Psychiatry and the Community in Nineteenth-Century America*. New York: Basic Books, 1969.

Cassel, Jay. *The Secret Plague: Venereal Disease in Canada 1838–1939*. Toronto: University of Toronto Press, 1987.

Cayleff, Susan E. *Wash and Be Healed: The Water-cure Movement and Women's Health*. Philadelphia: Temple University Press, 1987.

Chambers, Clarke E. *Seedtime of Reform: American Social Service and Social Action 1918–1933*. Ann Arbor: University of Michigan Press, 1963.

Chertok, Leon and Raymond de Saussure. *The Therapeutic Revolution from Mesmer to Freud.* Translated by R.H. Ahrenfeldt. New York: Brunner/Mazel, 1973, 1979.

Chesler, Phyllis. *Women and Madness.* New York: Doubleday, 1972.

Clark, Norman H. *Deliver Us From Evil: An Interpretation of American Prohibition.* New York: W.W. Norton, 1976.

Clark, Robert A. *Mental Illness in Perspective: History and Schools of Thought.* Pacific Grove, Calif.: Boxwood Press, 1973.

Clarke, Edwin, ed. *Modern Methods in the History of Medicine.* London, Athlone Press, 1971.

Coleman, William R. *Biology in the Nineteenth Century: Problems of Form, Function and Transformation.* New York: Wiley, 1971.

Collier, Richard. *The Plague of the Spanish Lady: The Influenza Pandemic of 1918–1919.* New York: Atheneum, 1974.

Comfort, Alex. *The Anxiety Makers: Some Curious Preoccupations of the Medical Profession.* London: Panther, 1967.

Cook, Ramsay. *The Regenerators: Social Criticism in Late Victorian English Canada.* Toronto: University of Toronto Press, 1985.

Cook, Ramsay and Wendy Mitchinson, eds. *The Proper Sphere: Woman's Place in Canadian Society.* Toronto: Oxford University Press, 1976.

Cooper, David. *Psychiatry and Anti-psychiatry.* London: Paladin, 1967, 1974.

Cosbie, Waring G. *The Toronto General Hospital 1819–1965: A Chronicle.* Toronto: Macmillan, 1975.

Courtwright, David T. *Dark Paradise: Opiate Addiction in America before 1940.* Cambridge: Harvard University Press, 1982.

Cowan, Ruth Schwartz. *More Work for Mother: The Ironies of Household Technology from the Open Hearth to the Microwave.* New York: Basic Books, 1983.

Cravens, Hamilton. *The Triumph of Evolution: American Scientists and the Heredity-Environment Controversy 1900–1941.* Philadelphia: University of Pennsylvania Press, 1978.

Dain, Norman. *Clifford W. Beers: Advocate for the Insane.* Pittsburgh: University of Pittsburgh Press, 1980.

– *Concepts of Insanity in the United States 1789–1865.* New Brunswick, N.J.: Rutgers University Press, 1964.

Danylewicz, Marta. *Taking the Veil: An Alternative to Marriage, Motherhood, and Spinsterhood in Quebec, 1840–1920.* Toronto: McClelland & Stewart, 1987.

Davis, Allen F. *Spearheads for Reform: The Social Settlements and the Progressive Movement 1890–1914.* New York: Oxford University Press, 1967.

Defries, R.D. ed. *The Development of Public Health in Canada.* Toronto: Canadian Public Health Association, 1940.

Degler, Carl N. *At Odds: Women and the Family in America from the Revolution to the Present.* New York: Oxford University Press, 1980.

Delamont, Sara and Lorna Duffin, ed. *The Nineteenth-Century Woman: Her Cultural and Physical World*. London: Croom-Helm, 1975.

Demos, John. *A Little Commonwealth: Family Life in Plymouth Colony*. New York: Oxford University Press, 1970.

Deutsch, Albert. *The Mentally Ill in America*. Garden City, N.Y.: Doubleday, Doran, 1937.

Digby, Anne. *Madness, Morality and Medicine: A Study of the York Retreat 1796–1914*. Cambridge: Cambridge University Press, 1985.

Ditzion, Sidney. *Marriage, Morals and Sex in America: A History of Ideas*. New York: Bookman, 1953.

Donegan, Jane B. *Women and Men Midwives: Medicine, Morality and Misogyny in Early America*. Westport, Conn.: Greenwood Press, 1978.

Donnelly, Michael. *Managing the Mind: A Study of Medical Psychology in Early Nineteenth-Century Britain*. London: Tavistock, 1983.

Dorland's Illustrated Medical Dictionary. 25th ed. Philadelphia: W.B. Saunders, 1974.

Drachman, Virginia G. *Hospital with a Heart: Women Doctors and the Paradox of Separatism at the New England Hospital 1862–1969*. Ithaca, N.Y.: Cornell University Press, 1984.

Drinka, George F. *The Birth of Neurosis: Myth, Malady and the Victorians*. New York: Simon & Shuster, 1984.

Dublin, Thomas. *Women at Work: The Transformation of Work and Community in Lowell, Massachusetts 1826–1860*. New York: Columbia University Press, 1979.

Dubos, Jean and Rene Jules. *The White Plague: Tuberculosis, Man and Society*. Boston: Little, 1952.

Duffy, John. *Epidemics in Colonial America*. Baton Rouge: Louisiana State University Press, 1953.

– *The Healers: A History of American Medicine*. Urbana: University of Illinois Press, 1979.

Duffy, John and Edward M. Litin. *The Emotional Health of Physicians*. Springfield, Ill: Charles C. Thomas, 1967.

Duncan, Robert C., Rebecca G. Knapp and M. Clinton Miller III. *Introductory Biostatistics for the Health Sciences*. New York: John Wiley & Sons, 1977.

Dwyer, Ellen. *Homes for the Mad: Life Inside Two Nineteenth-Century Asylums*. New Brunswick, N.J.: Rutgers University Press, 1987.

Edgell, Stephen. *Middle Class Couples: A Study of Segregation, Domination and Inequality in Marriage*. London: George Allen & Unwin, 1980.

Ehrenreich, Barbara and Dierdre English. *Complaints and Disorders: The Sexual Politics of Sickness*. Brooklyn, N.Y.: Feminist Press, 1973.

– *For Her Own Good: 150 Years of the Experts' Advice to Women*. Garden City, N.Y.: Anchor Press, 1979.

Ellenberger, Henri. *The Discovery of the Unconscious.* New York: Basic Books, 1970.

Erikson, Erik H. *Childhood and Society.* 2d ed. New York: W.W. Norton, 1963.

Feder, Lillian. *Madness in Literature.* Princeton: Princeton University Press, 1980.

Finnane, Mark. *Insanity and the Insane in Post-Famine Ireland.* London: Croom-Helm, 1981.

Flugel, J.C. *The Psychoanalytic Study of the Family.* London: Hogarth Press, 1960.

Foucault, Michel. *Discipline and Punish: The Birth of the Prison.* Translated by Alan Sheridan. New York: Vintage Books, 1979.

– *Madness and Civilization: A History of Insanity in the Age of Reason.* Translated by Richard Howard. New York: Vintage Books, 1965.

Fox, Richard W. *So Far Disordered in Mind: Insanity in California 1870–1930.* Berkeley: University of California Press, 1978.

Friedson, Eliot. *Professional Dominance.* New York: Atherton, 1970.

Fromm, Erich. *Escape from Freedom.* New York: Rinehart, 1941.

Gibbon, John M. and Mary S. Mathewson. *Three Centuries of Canadian Nursing.* Toronto: Macmillan, 1947.

Gillis, John R. *Youth and History: Tradition and Change in European Age Relations 1770–Present.* New York: Academic Press, 1974.

Gilman, Alfred G., Louis S. Goodman and Alfred Gilman. *Goodman and Gilman's The Pharmacological Basis of Therapeutics.* 6th ed. New York: Macmillan, 1980.

Gilman, Charlotte Perkins. *The Yellow Wallpaper.* Old Westbury, N.Y.: Feminist Press, 1973.

Godfrey, Charles M. *Medicine for Ontario.* Belleville, Ont.: Mika, 1979.

Goffman, Erving. *Asylums: Essays on the Social Situation of Mental Patients and Other Inmates.* Chicago: Aldine, 1962.

Goldstein, Jan. *Console and Classify: The French Psychiatric Profession in the Nineteenth Century.* Cambridge: Cambridge University Press, 1987.

Gould, Stephen Jay. *The Mismeasure of Man.* New York: W.W. Norton, 1981.

Grob, Gerald N. *Edward Jarvis and the Medical World of Nineteenth-Century America.* Knoxville: University of Tennessee Press, 1978.

– *Mental Illness and American Society 1875–1940.* Princeton: Princeton University Press, 1983.

– *Mental Institutions in America: Social Policy to 1875.* New York: Free Press, 1973.

Grob, Gerald N. *The Origins of the State Mental Hospital in America.* New York: Arno Press, 1973.

– *The State and the Mentally Ill: A History of the Worcester State Hospital In*

Massachusetts 1830–1920. Chapel Hill: University of North Carolina Press, 1966.

Gusfield, Joseph R. *Symbolic Crusade: Status Politics and the American Temperance Movement*. University of Illinois Press, 1963.

Gwyn, Sandra. *A Private Capital: Ambition and Love in the Age of MacDonald and Laurier*. Toronto: McClelland & Stewart, 1984.

Hale, Nathan G., Jr. *Freud and the Americans: The Beginnings of Psychoanalysis in the United States 1876–1917*. New York: Oxford University Press, 1971.

– *James Jackson Putnam and Psychoanalysis*. Cambridge: Harvard University Press, 1971.

Haller, John S., Jr and Robin M. *The Physician and Sexuality in Victorian America*. New York: W.W Norton, 1974, 1977.

Haller, Mark H. *Eugenics: Hereditarian Attitudes in American Thought*. New Brunswick, N.J.: Rutgers University Press, 1963.

Hallowell, Gerald A. *Prohibition in Ontario 1919–1923*. Ottawa: Ontario Historical Society, 1972.

Handel, Gerald. *The Psychosocial Interior of the Family*. Chicago: Aldine, 1967.

Harbin, Henry T. ed. *The Psychiatric Hospital and the Family*. Jamaica, N.Y.: Spectrum, 1982.

Harding, Geoffrey. *Opiate Addiction, Morality and Medicine: From Moral Weakness to Pathological Disease*. London: Macmillan, 1988.

Hareven, Tamara K., ed. *Anonymous Americans: Explorations in Nineteenth-Century Social History*. Englewood Cliffs, N.J.: Prentice-Hall, 1971.

– *Family and Kin in Urban Communities 1700–1930*. New York: New Viewpoints, 1977.

– *Transitions: The Family and the Life Course in Historical Perspective*. New York: Academic Press, 1978.

Harris, C.C. *The Family and Industrial Society*. London: George Allen & Unwin, 1983.

Harris, Chris, ed. *The Sociology of the Family: New Directions for Britain*. Keele: University of Keele Press, 1979.

Harrison, Brian. *Drink and the Victorians: The Temperance Question in England 1815–1872*. London: Faber & Faber, 1971.

Hartman, Mary S. *Victorian Murderesses*. New York: Pocket Books, 1978.

Hartman, Mary S. and Lois W. Banner, eds. *Clio's Consciousness Raised: New Perspectives on the History of Women*. New York: Harper Torchbooks, 1974.

Hayter, Alethea. *Opium and the Romantic Imagination*. London: Faber & Faber, 1968.

Heagerty, John S. *Four Centuries of Medical History in Canada*. Toronto: Macmillan, 1928.

— *The Romance of Medicine in Canada*. Toronto: Ryerson, 1940.

Hinsie, Leland E. and Robert J. Campbell. *Psychiatric Dictionary*. 3d ed. New York: Oxford University Press, 1960.

Hollingshead, August B. and Fredrick C. Redlich. *Social Class and Mental Illness*. New York: John Wiley & Sons, 1958.

Houghton, Walter E. *The Victorian Frame of Mind 1830–1870*. New Haven, Conn.: Yale University Press, 1957.

Hunter, Richard A. and Ida Macalpine. *Psychiatry for the Poor: 1851 Colney Hatch Asylum – Friern Hospital 1973*. London: Dawson of Pall Mall, 1974.

Hurd, Henry M. *The Institutional Care of the Insane in the United States and Canada*. Baltimore: Johns Hopkins University Press, 1916.

Ignatieff, Michael. *A Just Measure of Pain: The Penitentiary in the Industrial Revolution 1750–1850*. London: Pantheon Books, 1978.

James, William. *The Principles of Psychology*. Cambridge: Harvard University Press, 1950, 1981.

Jameson, Eric. *The Natural History of Quackery*. London: Michael Joseph, 1961.

Jarvis, Edward. *Insanity and Idiocy in Massachusetts: Report of the Commission on Lunacy 1885*. Introduction by Gerald N. Grob. Cambridge: Harvard University Press, 1971.

Jimenez, Mary Ann. *Changing Faces of Madness: Early American Attitudes and Treatment of the Insane*. Waltham, MA: Brandeis University Press, 1987.

Johnson, Leo. *A History of Guelph 1827–1927*. Guelph Historical Society, 1977.

Jones, Andrew and Leonard Rutman. *In the Children's Aid: J.J. Kelso and Child Welfare in Ontario*. Toronto: University of Toronto Press, 1981.

Jones, James H. *Bad Blood: The Tuskegee Syphilis Experiment*. New York: Free Press, 1981.

Jones, Kathleen. *Mental Health and Social Policy 1845–1959*. London: Routledge & Kegan Paul, 1960.

Katz, Michael B. *The People of Hamilton, Canada West: Family and Class in a Mid-nineteenth-Century City*. Cambridge: Harvard University Press, 1975.

Katz, Michael B., Michael J. Doucet and Mark J. Stern. *The Social Organization of Early Industrial Capitalism*. Cambridge: Harvard University Press, 1982.

Kaufman, Martin. *Homeopathy in America: The Rise and Fall of a Medical Heresy*. Baltimore: Johns Hopkins University Press, 1971.

Kealey, Greg, ed. *Canada Investigates Industrialism: The Royal Commission on the Relations of Labor and Capital*. Toronto: University of Toronto Press, 1973.

Kett, Joseph F. *The Formation of the American Medical Profession: The Role of Institutions 1780–1860*. New Haven, Conn.: Yale University Press, 1968.

– *Rites of Passage: Adolescence in America 1790 to the Present*. New York: Basic Books, 1977.

Kobler, John. *Ardent Spirits: The Rise and Fall of Prohibition*. New York: G.P. Putnam's Sons, 1973.

Laing, R.D. *The Politics of Experience and the Bird of Paradise*. Middlesex: Penguin, 1967.

– *The Politics of the Family*. Toronto: CBC, 1969.

Laing, R.D. and A. Esterson. *Sanity, Madness and the Family*. 2d ed. New York: Basic Books, 1971.

Lasch, Christopher. *Haven in a Heartless World: The Family Besieged*. New York: Harper, 1977.

Laslett, Peter. *Family Life and Illicit Love in Earlier Generations*. Cambridge: Cambridge University Press, 1977.

Leacy, F.H., ed. *Historical Statistics of Canada*. 2d ed. Ottawa: Statistics Canada, 1983.

Leavitt, Judith W. *Brought to Bed: Childbearing in America 1750 to 1950*. New York: Oxford University Press, 1986.

Leavitt, Judith W. and Ronald L. Numbers, eds. *Sickness and Health in America*. 2d ed. Madison: University of Wisconsin Press, 1985.

Leigh, Denis. *The Historical Development of British Psychiatry*. New York: Pergamon, 1961.

Lender, Mark E. and James K. Martin. *Drinking in America: A History*. New York: Free Press, 1982.

Lerner, Gerda. *The Creation of Patriarchy*. New York: Oxford University Press, 1986.

Lewis, Jane, ed. *Labour and Love: Women's Experience of Home and Family 1850–1940*. Oxford: Basil Blackwell, 1986.

Lief, Alfred, ed. *The Commonsense Psychiatry of Dr Adolf Meyer*, New York: McGraw-Hill, 1948.

Lindesmith, Alfred R. *Addiction and Opiates*. Chicago: Aldine, 1947, 1968.

Lubove, Roy. *The Professional Altruist: The Emergence of Social Work as a Career 1880–1930*. Cambridge: Harvard University Press, 1965.

Marcus, Stephen. *The Other Victorians*. New York: Basic Books, 1964.

Martindale, Don and Edith. *The Social Dimensions of Mental Illness, Alcoholism and Drug Dependence*. Westport, Conn.: Greenwood, 1971.

Melosh, Barbara. *The Physician's Hand: Work Culture and Conflict in American Nursing*. Philadelphia: Temple University Press, 1982.

Mintz, Stephen. *A Prison of Expectations: The Family in Victorian Culture*. New York: New York University Press, 1983.

Moore, Judith. *A Zeal for Responsibility: The Struggle for Professional Nursing in Victorian England 1868–1883*. Athens: University of Georgia Press, 1988.

Moran, Richard. *Knowing Right from Wrong: The Insanity Defence of Daniel McNaughtan*. London: Collier-Macmillan, 1981.

Morgan, H. Wayne. *Drugs in America*. Syracuse, N.Y.: New York University Press, 1981.

– *Yesterday's Addicts: American Society and Drug Abuse 1865–1920*. Norman: University of Oklahoma Press, 1974.

Musto, David F. *The American Disease*. New Haven, Conn.: Yale University Press, 1973.

Macalpine, Ida and Richard Hunter. *George III and the Mad Business*. London: Allen Lane, 1969.

McCubbin, Hamilton, Elizabeth Cauble, and Joan M Patterson, eds. *Family Stress, Coping and Social Support*. Springfield, Ill.: Charles C. Thomas, 1982.

MacDermot, H.E. *One Hundred Years of Medicine in Canada*. Toronto: McClelland & Stewart, 1967.

McDermott, John J., ed. *The Basic Writings of Josiah Royce*. Chicago: University of Chicago Press, 1969.

MacDonald, Michael. *Mystical Bedlam: Madness, Anxiety and Healing in Seventeenth-Century England*. New York: Cambridge University Press, 1981.

Macfarlane, Alan. *Marriage and Love in England 1300–1840*. Oxford: Basil Blackwell, 1986.

McGovern, Constance M. *Masters of Madness: Social Origins of the American Psychiatric Profession*. Hanover, N.H.: University Press of New England, 1985.

McKeown, Thomas. *The Modern Rise of Population*. London: Edward Arnold, 1976.

– *The Role of Medicine: Dream, Mirage or Nemesis?* London: Nuffield Prov. Hospitals Trust, 1976.

McLaren, Angus and Arlene Tigar. *The Bedroom and the State: The Changing Practices and Politics of Contraception and Abortion in Canada 1880–1980*. Toronto: McClelland & Stewart, 1986.

MacNab, Elizabeth. *A Legal History of the Health Professions In Ontario*. Toronto: Queen's Printer, 1970.

Naylor, C. David. *Private Practice, Public Payment: Canadian Medicine and the Politics of Health Insurance, 1911–1966*. Kingston: McGill-Queen's University Press, 1986.

Neal, Frederick. *The Township of Sandwich (Past and Present)*. Windsor, Ont.: privately pub., 1909.

Neaman, Judith S. *Suggestion of the Devil*. Garden City, N.J.: Anchor Books, 1975.

Nett, Emily M. *Canadian Families: Past and Present*. Toronto: Butterworths, 1988.

Nicholson, G.W.L. *Canada's Nursing Sisters*. Toronto: Samuel Stevens, Hakkert, 1975.

Nissenbaum, Stephen. *Sex, Diet and Debility in Jacksonian America: Sylvester Graham and Health Reform.* Westport, Conn.: Greenwood Press, 1980.

Parker, Gail, ed. *The Oven Birds: American Women on Womanhood 1820–1920.* Garden City, N.Y.: Doubleday, 1972.

Parr, Joy, ed. *Childhood and Family in Canadian History.* Toronto: McClelland & Stewart, 1982.

Parry-Jones, William L. *The Trade in Lunacy: A Study of Private Madhouses in England in the Eighteenth and Nineteenth Centuries.* London: Routledge & Kegan Paul, 1972.

Parssinen, Terry M. *Secret Passions, Secret Remedies: Narcotic Drugs in British Society 1820–1930.* Philadelphia: Institute for Study of Human Issues, 1983.

Peck, Martin W. *The Meaning of Psychoanalysis.* New York: Permabooks, 1950.

Perrucci, Robert *Circle of Madness.* Englewood Cliffs, N.J.: Prentice-Hall, 1974.

Peterson, M. Jeanne. *The Medical Profession in Mid-Victorian London.* Berkeley: University of California Press, 1978.

Pivar, David J. *The Purity Crusade: Sexual Morality and Social Control 1868–1900.* Westport, Conn.: Greenwood Press, 1973.

Platt, Anthony. *The Child Savers: The Invention of Delinquency.* Univ. of Chicago Press, 1969.

Polanyi, Karl. *The Great Transformation.* New York: Rinehart, 1944.

Porter, Roy. *Mind Forg'd Manacles: A History of Madness in England from the Restoration to the Regency.* Cambridge: Harvard University Press, 1988.

– *A Social History of Madness: Stories of the Insane.* London: Weidenfeld & Nicolson, 1987.

Prentice, Alison et al. *Canadian Women: A History.* Toronto: Harcourt, Brace, Jovanovich, 1988.

Pressman, Jack D. *Uncertain Promise: Psychosurgery and the Development of Scientific Psychiatry in America 1935 to 1955.* Philadelphia: University of Pennsylvania Press, 1986.

Rapoport, Robert N., Michael P. Fogarty and Rhona Rapoport, eds. *Families in Britain.* London: Routledge & Kegan Paul, 1982.

Reed, James. *From Private Vice to Public Virtue: The Birth Control Movement and American Society since 1830.* New York: Basic Books, 1978.

Reese, William L. *Dictionary of Philosophy and Religion.* Atlantic Highlands, N.J.: Humanities Press, 1980.

Reverby, Susan M. *Ordered to Care: The Dilemma of American Nursing, 1850–1945.* New York: Cambridge University Press, 1987.

Reverby, Susan M. and David Rosner, eds. *Health Care in America: Essays in Social History.* Philadelphia: Temple University Press, 1979.

Riese, Walther. *The Legacy of Philippe Pinel: An Inquiry into Thought on Mental Alienation.* New York: Springer, 1969.

Risse, Guenter B., Ronald L. Numbers, and Judith W. Leavitt, eds. *Medicine without Doctors: Home Health Care in American History*. New York: Science History, 1977.

Roberts, Wayne. *Honest Womanhood: Feminism, Femininity and Class Consciousness among Toronto Working Women 1893 to 1914*. Toronto: New Hogtown Press, 1976.

Roland, Charles G., ed. *Health, Disease and Medicine: Essays in Canadian History*. Toronto: Hannah Institute, 1984.

Roland, Charles G. and Paul Potter. *An Annotated Bibliography of Canadian Medical Periodicals 1826–1975*. Toronto: Hannah Institute, 1979.

Rooke, Patricia T. and R.L. Schnell. *Studies in Childhood History: A Canadian Perspective*. Calgary: Detselig, 1982.

Rose, Phyllis. *Parallel Lives: Five Victorian Marriages*. New York: Alfred A. Knopf, 1984.

Rosen, George. *Madness in Society*. London: Routledge & Kegan Paul, 1968.

Rosenberg, Charles E. *The Care of Strangers: The Rise of America's Hospital System*. New York: Basic Books, 1987.

– *The Cholera Years: The United States in 1832, 1849, and 1866*. Chicago: University of Chicago Press, 1962.

– ed. *The Family in History*. Philadelphia: University of Pennsylvania Press, 1975.

– *No Other Gods: On Science and American Social Thought*. Baltimore: Johns Hopkins University Press, 1961, 1976.

– *The Trial of the Assassin Guiteau: Psychiatry and Law in the Gilded Age*. Chicago: University of Chicago Press, 1968.

Rosenkrantz, Barbara G. *Public Health and the State: Changing Views in Massachusetts 1842–1936*. Cambridge: Harvard University Press, 1972.

Ross, Dorothy. *G. Stanley Hall: The Psychologist and Prophet*. Chicago: University of Chicago Press, 1972.

Rothman, David J. *Conscience and Convenience: The Asylum and its Alternatives in Progressive America*. Boston: Little, Brown, 1980.

– *The Discovery of the Asylum: Social Order and Disorder in the New Republic*. Boston: Little, Brown, 1971.

Rothstein, William G. *American Physicians in the Nineteenth Century: From Sects to Science*. Baltimore: Johns Hopkins University Press, 1972.

Rowntree, Benjamin S. *Poverty: A Study of Town Life*. New York: Macmillan, 1901.

Rublowsky, John. *The Stoned Age: A History of Drugs in Canada*. New York: Putnam, 1974.

Ryan, Mary P. *Cradle of the Middle Class: The Family in Oneida County, N.Y. 1790–1865*. Cambridge: Cambridge University Press, 1981.

– *The Empire of the Mother: American Writing about Domesticity 1830–1860*. New York: Haworth, 1982.

– *Womanhood in America*. New York: New Viewpoints, 1975.

Schreber, Daniel Paul. *Memoirs of my Nervous Illness*. Translated by Ida Macalpine and Richard A. Hunter. Cambridge: Harvard University Press, 1988.

Scott, James Maurice. *The White Poppy: A History of Opium*. London: Heinemann, 1969.

Scull, Andrew T. *Museums of Madness: The Social Organization of Madness in Nineteenth Century England*. New York: Penguin, 1979.

– ed. *Madhouses, Mad-doctors and Madmen: The Social History of Psychiatry in the Victorian Era*. Philadelphia: University of Pennsylvania Press, 1981.

Seaborn, Edwin. *The March of Medicine in Western Ontario*. Toronto: Ryerson, 1944.

Sennett, Richard. *Families against the City: Middle Class Homes of Industrial Chicago 1872–1890*. New York: Vintage Books, 1974.

Shorter, Edward. *The Making of the Modern Family*. New York: Basic Books, 1975, 1977.

Shortt, S.E.D. *Victorian Lunacy: Richard M. Bucke and the Practice of Late Nineteenth Century Psychiatry*. Cambridge: Cambridge University Press, 1986.

– ed. *Medicine in Canadian Society: Historical Perspectives*. Montreal: McGill-Queen's University Press, 1981.

– *Psychiatric Illness in Physicians*. Springfield, Ill.: Charles C. Thomas, 1982.

Showalter, Elaine. *The Female Malady: Women, Madness and English Culture 1830–1980*. New York: Pantheon, 1985.

Simmons, Harvey G. *From Asylum to Welfare*. Downsview, Ont.: National Institute on Mental Retardation, 1982.

Skultans, Vieda. *English Madness: Ideas on Insanity 1580–1890*. London: Routledge & Kegan Paul, 1979.

– *Madness and Morals: Ideas on Insanity in the Nineteenth Century*. London: Routledge & Kegan Paul, 1975.

Slater, Michael. *Dickens and Women*. London: J.M. Dent, 1983.

Sloman, Larry. *Reefer Madness: The History of Marijuana in America*. Indianapolis: Bobbs-Merrill, 1979.

Smith, Roger. *Trial by Medicine: Insanity and Responsibility in Victorian Trials*. Edinburgh: Edinburgh University Press, 1981.

Smith-Rosenberg, Carroll. *Disorderly Conduct: Visions of Gender in Victorian America*. New York: Oxford University Press, 1985.

Spence, Ben H. *Liquor Control in Canada*. Toronto: Canadian Prohibition Bureau, 1928.

Spence, Ruth E. *Prohibition in Canada*. Toronto: Ontario Branch of Dominion Alliance, 1919.

Splane, Richard B. *Social Welfare in Ontario 1791–1893*. Toronto: University of Toronto Press, 1965.

Stacey, Margaret and Marion Price. *Women, Power and Politics*. London: Tavistock, 1981.

Stage, Sarah. *Female Complaints: Lydia Pinkham and the Business of Women's Medicine*. New York: W.W. Norton, 1979.

Starr, Paul. *The Social Transformation of American Medicine*. New York: Basic Books, 1982.

Stewart, Robert A. *A Picture History of Guelph 1827–1978*. Guelph: Ampersand, 1978.

Stone, Lawrence. *The Family, Sex and Marriage in England 1500–1800*. New York: Harper & Row, 1979.

Strong-Boag, Veronica, ed. *A Woman with a Purpose: The Diaries of Elizabeth Smith 1872–1884*. Toronto: University of Toronto Press, 1980.

Strug, David L., S. Priyadarsini, and Merton M. Hyman, eds. *Alcohol Interventions: Historical and Sociocultural Approaches*. New York: Haworth Press, 1986.

Sykes, Gresham M. *The Society of Captives: A Study of a Maximum Security Prison*. Princeton: Princeton University Press, 1958.

Szasz, Thomas S. *The Manufacture of Madness*. New York: Harper & Row, 1970.

– *The Myth of Mental Illness*. rev. ed. New York: Harper & Row, 1974.

Tannahill, Reay. *Sex in History*. New York: Stein & Day, 1980.

Tatham, M. Ruth. *A Social History of Riverslea*. Guelph: Homewood Sanitarium, 1983.

Terry, Charles E. and Mildred Pellens. *The Opium Problem*. New York: Hadden Craftsmen, 1928.

Thornton, E.M. *Freud and Cocaine: The Freudian Fallacy*. London: Blond & Briggs, 1982.

Tilly, Louise A. and Joan W. Scott. *Women, Work and Family*. New York: Holt, Rinehart & Winston, 1978.

Tokarz, J. Pat et al. *Beyond Survival*. Chicago: AMA, 1979.

Tomes, Nancy J. *A Generous Confidence: Thomas Storey Kirkbride and the Art of Asylum-Keeping 1840–1883*. Cambridge: Cambridge University Press, 1984.

Turner, E.S. *Taking the Cure*. London: Michael Joseph, 1967.

Tyler, Alice Felt. *Freedom's Ferment: Phases of American Social History from the Revolution to the Outbreak of the Civil War*. New York: Harper, 1967.

Vicinus, Martha ed. *Suffer and Be Still: Women in the Victorian Age*. Bloomington, Ind.: Indiana University Press, 1972.

– *A Widening Sphere: Changing Roles of Victorian Women*. Bloomington, Ind.: Indiana University Press, 1977.

Vogel, Morris J. *The Invention of the Modern Hospital, Boston 1870–1930*. Chicago: University of Chicago Press, 1980.

Vogel, Morris J. and Charles E. Rosenberg. *The Therapeutic Revolution: Es-

says in the Social History of American Medicine. Philadelphia: University of Pennsylvania Press, 1979.

Walker, Nigel. *Crime and Insanity in England.* Edinburgh: Edinburgh University Press, 1968.

Walkowitz, Judith R. *Prostitution and Victorian Society: Women, Class and the State.* London: Cambridge University Press, 1980.

Walsh, Mary R. *Doctors Wanted: No Women Need Apply, Sexual Barriers in the Medical Profession 1835–1975.* New Haven: Yale University Press, 1977.

Walter, Ronald G., ed. *Primers for Prudery: Sexual Advice to Victorian America.* Englewood Cliffs, N.J.: Prentice-Hall, 1974.

Ward, Peter. *White Canada Forever.* Montreal: McGill-Queen's University Press, 1978.

Warner, John Harley. *The Therapeutic Perspective: Medical Practice, Knowledge, and Identity in America 1820–1885.* Cambridge: Harvard University Press, 1986.

Warsh, Cheryl Krasnick. *Drink in Canada: Historical Essays.* Toronto: McClelland and Stewart, forthcoming.

Wiebe, Robert H. *The Search for Order 1877–1920.* New York: Hill & Wang, 1967.

Weiss, Harry and Howard Kemble. *The Great American Water-Cure Craze: A History of Hydropathy in the U.S.* Trenton, N.J.: Past Times Press, 1967.

Wohl, Anthony S. ed. *The Victorian Family: Structure and Stresses.* New York: St. Martin's Press, 1978.

Young, James Harvey. *The Toadstool Millionaires: A Social History of Patent Medicines in America before Federal Regulation.* Princeton: Princeton University Press, 1961.

– *The Medical Messiahs: A Social History of Health Quackery in Twentieth-Century America.* Princeton: Princeton University Press, 1967.

Young, Michael and Peter Willmott. *The Symmetrical Family.* New York: Pantheon, 1973.

Youngson, A.J. *The Scientific Revolution in Victorian Medicine.* New York: Holmes & Meier, 1979.

Zaretsky, Eli. *Capitalism, The Family and Personal Life.* New York: Harper Colophon, 1976.

Articles and Chapters in Books

Ackerknecht, Erwin H. "Diathesis: The Word and the Concept in Medical History." *BHM* 56, no. 3 (Fall 1982): 317–25.

– "A Plea for a Behaviorist Approach in Writing the History of Medicine." *JHMAS* 22, no. 3 (1967): 211–14.

Adams, Maurianne. "Family Disintegration and Creative Reintegration: The Case of Charlotte Brontë and Jane Eyre." In *The Victorian Family:*

Structure and Stresses, edited by Anthony S. Wohl, 148–79. New York: St. Martin's Press, 1978.

Allderidge, Patricia. "Hospitals, Madhouses and Asylums: Cycles in the Care of the Insane." *British Journal of Psychiatry* 134, no. 4 (April 1979): 321–34.

Allodi, F. and H.B. Kedward. "The Evolution of the Mental Hospital in Canada." *Canadian Journal of Public Health* 68, no. 3 (May/June 1977): 219–25.

Anderson, Carol M. and Douglas J. Reiss. "Family Treatment of Chronic Schizophrenia: The Inpatient Phase." In *The Psychiatric Hospital and the Family,* edited by Henry T. Harbin, 79–101. Jamaica, N.Y.: Spectrum, 1982.

Anderson, Michael. "The Social Position of Spinsters in Mid-Victorian Britain." *Journal of Family History* 9, no. 4 (Winter 1984): 378–93.

Ayers, Pat and Jan Lambertz. "Marriage Relations, Money and Domestic Violence in Working Class Liverpool, 1919–39." In *Labour and Love: Women's Experience of Home and Family 1850–1940,* edited by Jane Lewis, 195–222. Oxford: Basil Blackwell, 1986.

Baehre, Rainer. "Lunacy Legislation in Upper Canada 1792–1867." Department of History, York University, Toronto. Photocopy.

Barber, Marilyn. "The Gentlewomen of Queen Mary's Coronation Hostel." In *Not Just Pin Money: Selected Essays on the History of Women's Work in British Colombia,* edited by Barbara K. Latham and Roberta J. Pazdro, 141–58. Victoria: Camosun College, 1984.

– "The Women Ontario Welcomed: Immigrant Domestics for Ontario Homes, 1870–1930." *Ontario History* 72, no. 3 (September 1980): 148–72.

Barker-Benfield, G.J. "The Spermatic Economy: A Nineteenth-Century View of Sexuality." In *The American Family in Social-Historical Perspective,* edited by Michael Gordon, 2d ed, 374–402. New York: St. Martin's Press, 1978.

Barrett, J.E., J. Juriansky, and B. Gurland. "Community Tenure following Emergency Discharge." *American Journal of Psychiatry* 128 (1972): 958–64.

Bator, Paul A. "The Struggle to Raise the Lower Classes: Public Health Reform and the Problem of Poverty in Toronto, 1910–1921." *Journal of Canadian Studies* 14, no. 1 (Spring 1979): 43–9.

Beaujot, Roderic P. and Kevin McQuillan, "The Social Effects of Demographic Change: Canada 1851–1981." *Journal of Canadian Studies* 21, no. 1 (Spring 1986): 57–69.

Bellomo, J. Jerald. "Upper Canadian Attitudes towards Crime and Punishment." *Ontario History* 64, no. 1 (March 1972): 11–26.

Berman, Alex. "The Thomsonian Movement and its Relation to American Pharmacy and Medicine." *BHM* 25, no. 5 (September/October 1951): 405–28; no. 6: 519–38.

Berridge, Virginia. "Victorian Opium Eating: Responses to Opiate Use in Nineteenth-Century England." *Victorian Studies* 21, no. 4 (1978): 437–61.

Bett, W.R. "W.S. Halsted (1852–1922): Cocaine Pioneer and Addict." *British Journal of Addiction* 49 (1954): 53–9.

Biggs, C. Lesley. "The Case of the Missing Midwives: A History of Midwifery in Ontario from 1795–1900." *Ontario History* 75, no. 1 (March 1983): 4–20.

Bland, Lucy. "Marriage Laid Bare: Middle Class Women and Marital Sex c. 1880–1914." In *Labour and Love: Women's Experience of Home and Family 1850–1940*, edited by Jane Lewis, 123–48. Oxford: Basil Blackwell, 1986.

Bliss, Michael. "Pure Books on Avoided Subjects: Pre-Freudian Sexual Ideas in Canada." In *Studies in Canadian Social History*, edited by Michiel Horn and Ronald Sabourin, 326–46. Toronto: McClelland & Stewart, 1974.

Blustein, Bonnie E. "A Hollow Square of Psychological Science: American Neurologists and Psychiatrists in Conflict." In *Madhouses, Mad-Doctors and Madmen: The Social History of Psychiatry in the Victorian Era*, edited by Andrew T. Scull, 241–70. Philadelphia: University of Pennsylvania Press, 1981.

– "New York Neurologists and the Specialization of American Medicine." *BHM* 53, no. 2 (Summer 1979): 170–83.

Bradbury, Bettina. "The Fragmented Family: Family Strategies in the Face of Death, Illness and Poverty, Montreal, 1860–1885." In *Childhood and Family in Canadian History*, edited by Joy Parr, 109–28. Toronto: McClelland & Stewart, 1982.

Brandon, Sidney. "Physical Violence in the Family: An Overview." In *Violence in the Family*, edited by Marie Borland, 1–25. Atlantic Highlands, N.J.: Humanities Press, 1976.

Brewster, Joan M. "Prevalence of Alcohol and other Drug Problems among Physicians." *JAMA* 255, no. 14 (11 April 1986): 1913–20.

Brookes, Barbara. "Women and Reproduction c. 1860–1919." In *Labour and Love: Women's Experience of Home and Family 1850–1940*, edited by Jane Lewis, 149–74. Oxford: Basil Blackwell, 1986.

Brown, Edward M. "What Shall We Do with the Inebriate?: Asylum Treatment and the Disease Concept of Alcoholism in the late Nineteenth Century." Department of Psychiatry, Brown University, Photocopy.

Brown, Thomas E. "Architecture as Therapy." *Archivaria* 10 (Summer 1980): 99–124.

– "Dr. Ernest Jones, Psychoanalysis and the Canadian Medical Profession, 1908–13." In *Medicine in Canadian Society: Historical Perspectives*, edited by S.E.D. Shortt, 315–60. Montreal: McGill-Queen's University Press, 1981.

Brown, Thomas E. "Shell Shock in the Canadian Expeditionary Force, 1914–1918: Canadian Psychiatry in the Great War." In *Health, Disease and Medicine: Essays in Canadian History*, edited by Charles G. Roland, 308–32. Toronto: Hannah Institute, 1984.

Buckley, Suzann and Janice Dickin McGinnis. "Venereal Disease and Public Health Reform in Canada." *CHR* 63, no. 3 (1982): 337–53.

Buerki, Robert A. "Medical Views on Narcotics and their Effects in the mid-1890s." *Pharmacy in History* 17, no. 1 (1975): 3–12.

Bullough, Vern L. and Martha Voght. "Homosexuality and its Confusion with the 'Secret Sin' in Pre-Freudian America." *JHMAS* 28, no. 2 (April 1973): 143–55.

Burgess, T.J.W. "A Historical Sketch of our Canadian Institutions for the Insane." *Transactions of the Royal Society of Canada* 4 (1898): 3–122.

Burley, Kevin. "Occupational Structure and Ethnicity in London, Ontario 1871." *HS/SH* 11, no. 22 (November 1978): 390–410.

Burnham, John C. "American Historians and the Subject of Sex." *Societas* 2, no. 4 (Autumn 1972): 307–16.

– "The Mind-Body Problem in the Early Twentieth Century." *Perspectives in Biology and Medicine* 20, no. 2 (Winter 1977): 271–84.

– "New Perspectives on the Prohibition 'Experiment' of the 1920s." *Journal of Social History* 2 (1968): 51–68.

– "Psychiatry, Psychology and the Progressive Movement." *American Quarterly* 12, no. 4 (Winter 1960): 457–65.

– "The Struggle between Physicians and Paramedical Personnel in American Psychiatry 1917–41." *JHMAS* 29, no. 1 (January 1974): 93–106.

Bynum, William F. "Chronic Alcoholism in the First Half of the Nineteenth Century." *BHM* 42, no. 2 (March/April 1968): 160–85.

– "Rationales for Therapy in British Psychiatry 1780–1835." *MH* 18, no. 4 (October 1974): 317–34.

– "Themes in British Psychiatry, J.C. Pritchard (1786–1848) to Henry Maudesley (1835–1918)." In *Nature Animated*, edited by Michael Ruse, 225–42. Dordrecht, Holland: D. Reidel, 1983.

Carlson, Eric T. and Norman Dain. "The Psychotherapy that was Moral Treatment." *American Journal of Psychiatry* 117, no. 3 (December 1960): 519–24.

Carpenter, Mick. "Asylum Nursing before 1914: A Chapter in the History of Labour." In *Rewriting Nursing History*, edited by Celia Davies, 126–41. London: Croom-Helm, 1980.

Cassedy, James. "An Early American Hangover: The Medical Profession and Intemperance 1800–1860." *BHM* 50, no. 3 (Fall 1976): 405–13.

Chapman, James K. "The Mid-nineteenth Century Temperance Movements in New Brunswick and Maine." In *Canadian History before Confederation: Essays and Interpretations*, edited by J.M. Bumsted, 444–61. Georgetown, Ont.: Irwin-Dorsey, 1972.

Chapman, Terry L. "Drug Use in Western Canada." *Alberta History* 24, no. 4 (Autumn 1976): 18–27.

Chodorow, Nancy and Susan Contratto. "The Fantasy of the Perfect Mother." In *Rethinking the Family: Some Feminist Questions*, edited by Barrie Thorne and Marilyn Yalom. London: Longman, 1982.

Chudacoff, Howard P. and Tamara K. Hareven. "Family Transitions into Old Age." In *Transitions: The Family and the Life Course in Historical Perspective*, edited by Tamara K. Hareven, 217–43. New York: Academic Press, 1978.

– "From the Empty Nest to Family Dissolution: Life Course Transitions into Old Age." *Journal of Family History*, 4, no. 1 (Spring 1979): 79–83.

Clark, Michael J. "The Rejection of Psychological Approaches to Mental Disorder in late Nineteenth Century British Psychiatry." In *Madhouses, Mad-doctors and Madmen: The Social History of Psychiatry in the Victorian Era*, edited by Andrew T. Scull, 271–312. Philadelphia: University of Pennsylvania Press, 1981.

Clemens, James M. "Taste Not, Touch Not, Handle Not: A Study of the Social Assumptions of the Temperance Literature and Temperance Supporters in Canada West Between 1839 and 1859." *Ontario History* 64, no. 3 (September 1972): 142–60.

Coburn, Judi. "I See and am Silent: A Short History of Nursing in Ontario." In *Women at Work: 1850–1930*, edited by Janice Acton et al, 127–64. Toronto: Can. Women's Educational Press, 1974.

Connor, J.T.H. "Preservatives of Health: Mineral Water Spas of Nineteenth Century Ontario." *Ontario History* 75, no. 2 (June 1983): 135–52.

Cook, Shirley J. "Social Background of Narcotics Legislation." *Addictions* 17, no. 2 (Summer 1970): 14–29.

Cott, Nancy F. "Passionlessness: An Interpretation of Victorian Sexual Ideology 1790–1850." *Signs* 4, no. 2 (1978): 219–36.

Courtwright, David T. "Opiate Addiction as a Consequence of the Civil War." *Civil War History* 24, no. 2 (1978): 101–11.

Cowan, Ruth Schwartz. "A Case Study of Technological and Social Change: The Washing Machine and the Working Wife." In *Clio's Consciousness Raised: New Perspectives on the History of Women*, edited by Mary Hartman and Lois Banner, 245–53. New York: Harper Torchbooks, 1974.

Coyne, James H. "Richard Maurice Bucke: A Sketch." *Proceedings and Transactions of the Royal Society of Canada*. 2d ser. 12 (1906): 159–96.

Craig, Barbara Lazenby. "The Canadian Hospital in History and Archives." *Archivaria* 21 (Winter 1985–6): 52–67.

Dain, Norman and Eric T. Carlson. "Social Class and Psychological Medicine in the United States 1789–1824." *BHM* 33, no. 5 (September 1959): 454–65.

Darroch, A. Gordon. "Occupational Structure, Assessed Wealth and Homeowning during Toronto's Early Industrialization 1861–1899." *HS/SH* 16, no. 32 (November 1983): 381–410.

Davidoff, Leonore, Jean L'Esperance and Howard Newby. "Landscape with Figures: Home and Community in English Society." In *The Rights and Wrongs of Women*, edited by Juliet Mitchell and Ann Oakley, 139–75. Harmondsworth: Penguin, 1976.

Davies, Celia. "Professionalizing Strategies as Time and Culture Bound: American and British Nursing, circa 1893." In *Nursing History: New Perspectives, New Possibilities*, edited by Ellen C. Lagemann, 47–63. New York: Teacher's College Press, 1983.

"Dean of Medical Corps, Gen. Fotheringham Dies." *Globe and Mail*, 20 May 1940.

Decarie, M. Graeme. "Paved with Good Intentions: The Prohibitionists' Road to Racism in Ontario." *Ontario History* 66, no. 1 (March 1974): 15–22.

– "Something Old, Something New... Aspects of Prohibitionism in Ontario in the 1890s." In *Oliver Mowat's Ontario*, edited by Donald Swainson, 154–71. Toronto: Macmillan, 1972.

Degler, Carl N. "What Ought to be and What Was: Women's Sexuality in the Nineteenth Century." *AHR* 79, no. 5 (December 1974): 1467–90.

Demos, John. "Old Age in Early New England." In *Turning Points: Historical and Sociological Essays on the Family*, edited by John Demos and Sarane Spence Boocock, 248–87. Chicago: University of Chicago Press, 1978.

"Dr Goldwin W. Howland was noted neurologist." *Globe and Mail*, 13 July 1950.

"Dr Joseph Workman." *AJI* 45, no. 4 (April 1889): 573–6.

"Dr William P. Caven: Family won medical fame." *Globe and Mail*, 24 September 1943.

"Dr W.T. Parry stricken at 80." *Globe and Mail*, 2 February 1940.

"Doctors and Addiction." *Fifth Estate*, 4 October 1983. CBC Toronto. Transcript.

Dodd, Dianne. "The Hamilton Birth Control Clinic in the 1930s." *Ontario History* 75, no. 1 (March 1983): 71–86.

Duquenin, Anthea. "Who Doesn't Marry and Why." *Oral History* 12, no. 1 (Spring 1984): 40–7.

Dyhouse, Carol. "Mothers and Daughters in the Middle Class Home: c. 1870–1914." In *Labour and Love: Women's Experience of Home and Family 1850–1940*, edited by Jane Lewis, 27–48. Oxford: Basil Blackwell, 1986.

Elder, Glen H. Jr. "The Life Course Perspective." In *The American Family in Social-Historical Perspective*. 3d ed, edited by Michael Gordon, 54–60. New York: St. Martin's Press, 1983.

Evans, A. Margaret. "The Mowat Era 1872–1896: Stability and Progress." In *Profiles of a Province*, edited by E.G. Firth, 97–106. Toronto: Ontario Historical Society, 1967.

Flegel, Kenneth M. "Changing Concepts of the Nosology of Gonorrhea and Syphilis." *BHM* 48, no. 4 (Winter 1974): 571–88.

Francis, Daniel. "The Development of the Lunatic Asylum in the Maritime Provinces." In *Medicine in Canadian Society: Historical Perspectives*, edited by S.E.D. Shortt, 93–114. Montreal: McGill-Queen's University Press, 1981.

Freedman, Estelle B. "Their Sister's Keepers: An Historical Perspective on Female Correctional Institutions in the United States 1870–1900." *Feminist Studies* 2 (1974): 77–95.

Freeman, Ruth and Patricia Klaus. "Blessed or Not? The New Spinster in England and the United States in the late Nineteenth and early Twentieth Centuries." *Journal of Family History* 9, no. 4 (Winter 1984): 394–414.

Fye, W. Bruce. "H. Newell Martin: A Remarkable Career Destroyed by Neurasthenia and Alcoholism." *JHMAS* 40, no. 2 (April 1985): 133–66.

Garb, Solomon. "Narcotic Addiction in Nurses and Doctors." *Nursing Outlook* (November 1965): 30–4.

Garland, M.A. and J.J. Talman, "Pioneer drinking habits and the rise of the temperance agitation in Upper Canada prior to 1840," In *Aspects of Nineteenth Century Ontario*, edited by F.W. Armstrong et al, 171–93. Toronto: University of Toronto Press, 1974.

Gee, Ellen M. "Marriage in Nineteenth-Century Canada." *Canadian Review of Sociology and Anthropology* 19, no. 3 (1982): 311–25.

Gidney, R.D. and W.P.J. Millar. "The Origins of Organized Medicine in Ontario 1850–1869." In *Health, Disease and Medicine: Essays in Canadian History*, edited by Charles Roland, 65–95. Toronto: Hannah Institute, 1984.

Gittins, Diana. "Marital Status, Work and Kinship, 1850–1930." In *Labour and Love: Women's Experience of Home and Family 1850–1940*, edited by Jane Lewis, 223–48. Oxford: Basil Blackwell, 1986.

Gorham, Deborah. "Flora MacDonald Denison: Canadian Feminist. In *A Not Unreasonable Claim: Women and Reform in Canada 1880s–1920s*, edited by Linda Kealey, 47–70. Toronto Women's Educational Press, 1979.

Gossage, Peter. "Absorbing Junior: The Use of Patent Medicines as Abortifacients in Nineteenth Century Montreal." *McGill Register* 3, no. 1 (March 1982): 1–13.

6

Greenland, Cyril. "The Compleat Psychiatrist: Dr R.M. Bucke's Twenty-Five Years as Medical Superintendent, Asylum for the Insane, London, Ontario 1877–1902." *Canadian Psychiatric Association Journal* 17, no. 1 (February 1972): 71–7.

– "Richard Maurice Bucke, M.D. 1837–1902: A Pioneer of Scientific Psychiatry." *CMAJ* 91, no. 8 (22 August 1964): 385–91.

– "Services for the Mentally Retarded in Ontario, 1870–1930." *Ontario History* 54, no. 4 (1962): 267–74.

Greenley, James R. "The Patient's Family and Length of Psychiatric Hospitalization." In *The Psychiatric Hospital and the Family*, edited by Henry T. Harbin, 213–37. Jamaica, N.Y.: Spectrum, 1982.

Griffen, Clyde. "Occupational Mobility in Nineteenth-Century America: Problems and Possibilities." *Journal of Social History* 5, no. 3 (Spring 1972): 311–30.

Griffin, John D. and Cyril Greenland. "Psychiatry in Ontario in 1880: Some Personalities and Problems." *Ontario Medical Review* 47, no. 6 (June 1980): 271–4.

Grinspoon, Lester and James B. Bakalar. "Coca and Cocaine as Medicines: an Historical Review." *Journal of Ethnopharmacology* 3 (1981): 149–59.

Grob, Gerald N. "Abuse in American Mental Hospitals in Historical Perspective: Myth and Reality." *International Journal of Law and Psychiatry* 3 (1980): 295–310.

– "Class, Ethnicity and Race in American Mental Hospitals, 1830–75." *JHMAS* 28, no. 3 (July 1973): 207–29.

– "Mental Illness, Indigency and Welfare: The Mental Hospital in Nineteenth-Century America." In *Anonymous Americans: Explorations in Nineteenth Century Social History*, 250–79. Englewood Cliffs, N.J.: Prentice-Hall, 1971.

– "Rediscovering Asylums: The Unhistorical History of the Mental Hospital." *Hastings Center Report* 7, no. 4 (August 1977): 33–41.

– "Reflections on the History of Social Policy in America." *Reviews in American History* 7, no. 3 (September 1979): 293–306.

– "The Social History of Medicine and Disease in America: Problems and Possibilities," *Journal of Social History* 10, no. 4 (June 1977): 391–409.

"Guelph Dr was outstanding as Psychiatrist [Harvey Clare]." *Globe and Mail*, 6 August 1949.

Guggenheim, W. "Heroin: History and Pharmacology." *International Journal of the Addictions.*" 2, no. 2 (1967): 328–35.

Gutman, Herbert G. "Work, Culture and Society in Industrializing America 1815–1919." In *Work Culture and Society in Industrializing America*, 3–78. New York: Vintage, 1966, 1977.

Haller, John S. Jr. "Concepts of Race Inferiority in Nineteenth-Century Anthropology." *JHMAS* 25, no. 1 (1970): 40–51.

Harbin, Henry T. "Family Treatment of the Psychiatric Inpatient." In *The Psychiatric Hospital and the Family*, 3–25. Jamaica, N.Y.: Spectrum, 1982.

Hammerton, A. James. "Feminism and Female Emigration, 1861–1886." In *A Widening Sphere: Changing Roles of Victorian Women*, edited by Martha Vicinus, 52–71. Bloomington, Ind.: Indiana University Press, 1977.

Hare, E.H. "Masturbatory Insanity: The History of an Idea." *Journal of Mental Science* 108, no. 1 (January 1962): 1–25.

Henderson, H.W. "Addicted Doctors: Responding to their Needs." *Canadian Family Physician* 29 (September 1983): 1691–9.

Hepworth, H. Philip. "Personal Social Services in the United States and Canada." In *The Social Welfare Forum*, edited by James E. Huddleston, 96–111. New York: Columbia University Press, 1979.

Hershberg, Theodore, Michael Katz, Stuart Blumin, Laurence Glasco and Clyde Griffen. "Occupation and Ethnicity in Five Nineteenth-Century Cities: A Collaborative Inquiry." *Historical Methods Newsletter* 7, no. 3 (June 1974): 174–216.

Hershon, Howard. "Alcoholism and the Concept of Disease." *British Journal of Addiction* 69, no. 2 (1974): 123–31.

Hess, Noel. "King Lear and Some Anxieties of Old Age." *British Journal of Medical Psychology* 60 (1987)209–15.

Hindmarch, Ian. "A Social History of the Use of Cannabis Sativa." *Contemporary Review* 200, no. 1276 (May 1972): 252–7.

Horne, James. "R.M. Bucke: Pioneer Psychiatrist, Practical Mystic." *Ontario History* 59, no. 3 (September 1967): 197–208.

Houston, Susan E. "Victorian Origins of Juvenile Delinquency: A Canadian Experience." *History of Education Quarterly* 12 (Fall 1972): 254–80.

Howell, Colin D. "Reform and the Monopolistic Impulse: The Professionalization of Medicine in the Maritimes." *Acadiensis* 11, no. 1 (Autumn 1981): 3–22.

Hufton, Olwen. "Women without Men: Widows and Spinsters in Britain and France in the Eighteenth Century." *Journal of Family History* 9, no. 4 (Winter 1984): 353–76.

Inciardi, James A. "The Changing Life of Mickey Finn: Some Notes on Chloral Hydrate Down Through the Ages." *Journal of Popular Culture* 11, no. 3 (1977): 591–6.

"In Memoriam: Clarence B. Farrar 1874–1970." *American Journal of Psychiatry* 127, no. 2 (2 August 1970): 223.

Jacyna, L.S. "Somatic Themes of Mind and the Interests of Medicine in Britain 1850–1879." *MH* 26, no. 3 (July 1982): 233–58.

James, Janet W. "Isabel Hampton and the Professionalization of Nursing in the 1890s." In *The Therapeutic Revolution: Essays in the Social History of American Medicine*, edited by Morris Vogel and Charles Rosenberg, 201–44. Philadelphia: University of Pennsylvania Press, 1979.

Jamieson, Lynn. "Limited Resources and Limiting Conventions: Working

Class Mothers and Daughters in Urban Scotland c. 1890–1925." In *Labour and Love: Women's Experience of Home and Family 1850–1940*, edited by Jane Lewis, 49–72. Oxford: Basil Blackwell, 1986.

Jimenez, Mary Ann. "Madness in Early American History: Insanity in Massachusetts from 1700 to 1820." *JSH* 20, no. 1 (Fall 1986): 25–44.

Johansson, Sheila R. "Sex and Death in Victorian England: An Examination of Age and Sex-Specific Death Rates 1840–1910." In *A Widening Sphere: Changing Roles of Victorian Women*, edited by Martha Vicinus, 163–81. Bloomington: Indiana University Press, 1977.

Jones, Bartlett. "Prohibition and Eugenics 1920–1933." *JHMAS* 18, no. 2 (April 1963): 158–72.

Jones, Kathleen W. "Sentiment and Science: The Late Nineteenth Century Pediatrician as Mother's Advisor." *Journal of Social History* 17 no. 1 (Fall 1983): 76–96.

Katz, Sidney. "Directory of Super Hospitals." *Chatelaine* 56 (May 1983).

Klein, Dorie. "The Etiology of Female Crime: A Review of the Literature." *Issues in Criminology* 8, no. 2 (Fall 1973): 2–30.

Kottman, Richard N. "Volstead Violated: Prohibition as a Factor in Canadian-American Relations." *CHR* 43, no. 2 (June 1962): 106–26.

Krajewski, Thomas and Henry T. Harbin. "The Family Changes the Hospital?" In *The Psychiatric Hospital and the Family*, edited by Henry Harbin, 143–54. Jamaica, N.Y.: Spectrum, 1982.

Krasnick (Warsh), Cheryl L. "Because There is Pain: Alcoholism, Temperance and the Victorian Physician." *Canadian Bulletin of Medical History* 3 (Spring 1985): 1–22.

– In Charge of the Loons: A Portrait of the London, Ontario Asylum for the Insane in the Nineteenth Century." *Ontario History* 74, no. 3 (September 1982): 138–84.

– "The Aristocratic Vice: The Medical Treatment of Drug Addiction at the Homewood Retreat, 1883–1900." *Ontario History* 75, no. 4 (December 1983): 403–27.

Kutcher, S.P. "Toronto's Metaphysicians: The Social Gospel and Medical Professionalization in Victorian Toronto." *HSTC Bulletin* 5, no. 1 (January 1981): 41–7.

Lasch, Christopher. "Origins of the Asylum." In *The World of Nations: Reflections on American History, Politics and Culture*, 3–17. New York: Knopf, 1974.

– Social Pathologists and the Socialization of Reproduction." In *The American Family in Social-Historical Perspective*, 3d ed., edited by Michael Gordon, 80–94. New York: St. Martin's Press, 1983.

Lavell, Alfred E. "The Beginnings of Ontario Mental Hospitals." *Queen's Quarterly* 49, no. 9 (1942): 59–67.

Lay, Jackie. "To Columbia on the Tynemouth: The Emigration of Single

Women and Girls in 1862." In *In Her Own Right*, edited by Barbara Latham and Cathy Kess, 19–42. Victoria: Camosun College, 1980.

Legan, Marshall. "Hydropathy in America: A Nineteenth Century Panacea." *BHM* 45, no. 3 (May/June 1971): 267–80.

Lender, Mark E. "Jellinek's Typology of Alcoholism: Some Historical Antecedents." *JSA* 40, no. 5 (1979): 361–75.

Leslie, Genevieve. "Domestic Service in Canada 1880–1920." In *Women at Work: 1850–1930*, edited by Janice Acton et al, 71–126. Toronto: Canadian Women's Educational Press, 1974.

Levine, Harry G. "The Discovery of Addiction: Changing Conceptions of Habitual Drunkenness in America." *JSA* 39, no. 1 (1978): 143–73.

Lewis, Jane. "Reconstructing Women's Experience of Home and Family." In *Labour and Love: Women's Experience of Home and Family 1850–1940*, 1–26. Oxford: Basil Blackwell, 1986.

– "The Working Class Wife and Mother and State Intervention, 1870–1918." In *Labour and Love*, 99–122.

Lidz, Theodore. "Adolf Meyer and the Development of American Psychiatry." *American Journal of Psychiatry* 123, no. 3 (September 1966): 320–333.

Macht, David J. and Nellie L. Gessford. "The Unfortunate Drug Experiences of Dante Gabriel Rossetti." *BHM* 6 (1938): 34–61.

May, Elaine Tyler. "The Pressure to Provide: Class, Consumerism and Divorce in Urban America 1880–1920." In *The American Family in Social-Historical Perspective*, 3d ed., edited by Michael Gordon, 154–68. New York: St. Martin's Press, 1983.

Mayer, Arno. "The Lower Middle Class as Historical Problem." *Journal of Modern History* 47, no. 3 (September 1975): 409–36.

Medjuck, Sheva. "Family and Household Composition, Moncton, N.B." *Canadian Journal of Sociology* 4, no. 3 (Summer 1979): 275–86.

Mericle, Bruce P. "The Male as Psychiatric Nurse." *Journal of Psychosocial Nursing* 21, no. 11 (1983): 28–34.

Mitchinson, Wendy. "A Medical Debate in Nineteenth-Century English Canada: Ovariotomies." *HS/SH* 17, no. 33 (May 1984): 133–47.

Modell, John and Tamara K. Hareven. "Urbanization and the Malleable Household: An Examination of Boarding and Lodging in the American Family." In *Family and Kin in Urban Communities, 1700–1930*, edited by Tamara Hareven, 164–86. New York: New Viewpoints, 1977.

Mora, George, "Vincenzo Chiarugi (1759–1820) and his Psychiatric Reform in Florence in the late Eighteenth Century." *JHMAS* 14, no. 4 (October 1959): 424–33.

Morantz, Regina M. "Making Women Modern: Middle Class Women and Health Reform in Nineteenth Century America." *Journal of Social History* 10, no. 4 (June 1977): 490–507.

– "The Perils of Feminist History." *Journal of Interdisciplinary History* 4, no. 4 (Spring 1974): 649–60.

Morgan, Edmund S. "The Puritans and Sex." *New England Quarterly* 15, no. 4 (1942): 591–607.

Morrison, Terrence. "Their Proper Sphere: Feminism, the Family and Child-Centred Social Reform in Ontario 1875–1900." *Ontario History* 68, no. 1 (March 1976): 45–64.

Mulgrew, Ian. "Fulton's Fight: Ex-minister, Judge Tells of Comeback from Drinking, Jail." *Globe and Mail*, 9 March 1984.

McBride, Theresa. "As the Twig is Bent: The Victorian Nanny." In *The Victorian Family: Structure and Stresses*, edited by Anthony Wohl, 44–58. New York: St. Martin's Press, 1978.

McCandless, Peter. "Build! Build! The Controversy over the care of the Chronically Insane in England 1855–1870." *BHM* 53, no. 4 (Winter 1979): 553–74.

– "Liberty and Lunacy: The Victorians and Wrongful Confinement." *Journal of Social History* 11, no. 3 (Spring 1978): 366–86.

McCaughey, Dan. "Professional Militancy: The Medical Defence Association vs the College of Physicians and Surgeons of Ontario 1891–1902." In *Health, Disease and Medicine: Essays in Canadian History*, 96–104. Toronto: Hannah Institute, 1984.

McConnell, Harvey. "Misguided Fears of Narcotic Abuse fail Good Pain Care: AMA Pres." *The Journal* [Addiction Research Foundation] 12, no. 3 (1 March 1983): 1–2.

Mackenzie, Charlotte. "Social Factors in the Admission, Discharge and Continuing Stay of Patients at Ticehurst Asylum, 1845–1917." In *The Anatomy of Madness: Essays in the History of Psychiatry*, edited by William Bynum, Roy Porter, and Michael Shepherd, 147–74. London: Tavistock, 1985.

McLaren, Angus. "Birth Control and Abortion in Canada 1870–1920." In *Medicine in Canadian Society: Historical Perspectives*, edited by S.E.D. Shortt, 285–314. Montreal: McGill-Queen's University Press, 1981.

MacLeod, Roy M. "The Edge of Hope: Social Policy and Chronic Alcoholism 1870–1900." *JHMAS* 22, no. 3 (1967): 215–45.

McNaughton, F.L. "Colin Russel: A Pioneer of Canadian Neurology." *CMAJ* 77 (1 October 1957): 719–23.

Nagle, David R. "Anaesthetic Addiction and Drunkenness: A Contemporary and Historical Survey." *International Journal of the Addictions* 3, no. 1 (Spring 1968): 25–39.

Naylor, C.D. "The CMA's First Code of Ethics." *Journal of Canadian Studies* 17, no. 4 (Winter 1982–3): 20–32.

Nett, Emily M. "Canadian Families in Social-Historical Perspective." *Canadian Journal of Sociology* 6, no. 3 (1981): 239–60.

Neuman, R.P. "Masturbation, Madness and the Modern Concepts of Childhood and Adolescence." *Journal of Social History* 8, no. 3 (Spring 1975): 1–27.

Nicholi, Armand M. "The Nontherapeutic Use of Psychoactive Drugs." *New England Journal of Medicine* 308, no. 16 (21 April 1983): 925–33.

"Noted City Physician Dr H.O. Howitt Dies." *Guelph Daily Mercury*, 4 May 1953.

Nye, Robert A. "Degeneration, Neurasthenia and the Culture of Sport in Belle Epoque France." *Journal of Contemporary History* 17, no. 1 (1982): 51–68.

Oppenheimer, Jo. "Childbirth in Ontario: The Transition from Home to Hospital in the early Twentieth-Century." *Ontario History* 75, no. 1 (March 1983): 36–60.

Parsons, Gail P. "Equal Treatment for All: American Medical Remedies for Male Sexual Problems 1850–1900." *JHMAS* 32, no. 1 (January 1977): 55–71.

Parssinen, Terry M. and Karen Kerner. "Development of the Disease Model of Drug Addiction in Britain 1870–1926." *MH* 24, no. 3 (July 1980): 275–96.

Pearsall, Ronald. "Victorian Oblivion." *Addictions* 12, no. 3 (Winter 1965): 20–3.

Peters, Dolores. "The British Medical Response to Opiate Addiction in the Nineteenth Century." *JHMAS* 36, no. 4 (October 1981): 455–88.

Peterson, M. Jeanne. "The Victorian Governess: Status Incongruence in Family and Society." In *Suffer and Be Still: Women in the Victorian Age*, edited by Martha Vicinus, 3–19. Bloomington: Indiana University Press, 1972.

"Prominent Lawyer [Frederick Jarvis] Called by Death." *Toronto Globe*, 7 October 1926.

Quen, Jacques M. "Isaac Ray on Drunkenness." *BHM* 41 (1967): 342–8.

Ramkhalawansingh, Ceta. "Women during the Great War." In *Women at Work: 1850–1930*, edited by Janice Acton et al, 261–308. Toronto: Canadian Women's Educational Press, 1974.

Roberts, Barbara. "A Work of Empire: Canadian Reformers and British Female Immigration." In *A Not Unreasonable Claim: Women and Reform in Canada 1880s–1920s*, edited by Linda Kealey, 185–201. Toronto: Women's Educational Press, 1979.

Roberts, David. "The Paterfamilias of the Victorian Governing Classes." In *The Victorian Family: Structure and Stresses*, edited by Anthony Wohl, 59–81. New York: St. Martin's Press, 1978.

Roberts, Wayne. "Rocking the Cradle for the World: The New Woman and Maternal Feminism, Toronto, 1877–1914." In *A Not Unreasonable Claim: Women and Reform in Canada 1880s–1920s*, edited by Linda Kealey, 15–46. Toronto: Women's Educational Press, 1979.

Rosenberg, Charles E. "And Heal the Sick: The Hospital and the Patient in Nineteench-Century America." *Journal of Social History* 10, no. 4 (June 1977): 428–47.
– "The Bitter Fruit: Heredity, Disease and Social Thought in Nineteenth-Century America." *Perspectives in American History* 8 (1974): 189–235.
– "The Crisis in Psychiatric Legitimacy: Reflections on Psychiatry, Medicine and Public Policy." In *American Psychiatry: Past, Present and Future*, edited by George Kriegman, Robert Gardner, and D. Wilfred Abse, 135–48. Charlottesville: University Press of Virginia, 1975.
– "Factors in the Development of Genetics in the United States: Some Suggestions." *JHMAS* 22, no. 1 (January 1967): 27–46.
– "Inward Vision and Outward Glance: The Shaping of the American Hospital 1880–1914." *BHM* 53, no. 3 (Fall 1979): 346–91.
– "The Place of George M. Beard in Nineteenth-Century Psychiatry." *BHM* 36, no. 3 (Fall 1962): 245–9.
– "Sexuality, Class and Role in Nineteenth-Century America." *American Quarterly* 25 (1973): 131–53.
– Social Class and Medical Care in Nineteenth-Century America: The Rise and Fall of the Dispensary." *JHMAS* 29, no. 1 (January 1974): 32–54.
Ross, Ellen. "Labour and Love: Rediscovering London's Working Class Mothers 1870–1918." In *Labour and Love: Women's Experience of Home and Family 1850–1940*, edited by Jane Lewis, 73–98. Oxford: Basil Blackwell, 1986.
Santos, Elvin H. and Edward Stainbrook. "A History of Psychiatric Nursing in the Nineteenth Century." *JHMAS* 4, no. 1 (January 1949): 48–74.
Scheff, Thomas J. "Control over Policy by Attendants in a Mental Hospital." *Journal of Health and Human Behaviour* 2 (1961): 93–105.
Schiller, Francis. "Thomas de Quincey's Lifelong Addiction." *Perspectives in Biology and Medicine* (Autumn 1976): 131–41.
Schlesinger, Mark and Robert Dorwart. "Ownership and Mental Health Services: A Reappraisal of the Shift towards Privately Owned Facilities." *New England Journal of Medicine* 311, no. 15 (11 October 1984): 959–65.
Scull, Andrew T. "From Madness to Mental Illness: Medical Men as Moral Entrepreneurs." *Archives Europeenes de Sociologie* 17 (1976): 279–305.
– "Mad-Doctors and Magistrates: English Psychiatry's Struggle for Professional Autonomy in the Nineteenth Century." *Archives Europeenes de Sociologie* 16 (1975): 218–51.
– Moral Treatment Reconsidered: Some Sociological Comments on an Episode in the History of British Psychiatry." *Psychological Medicine* 9, no. 3 (August 1979): 421–8.

Seigel, Shepard. "Wilkie Collins : Victorian Novelist as Psychopharmaco-
logist." *JHMAS* 38, no. 2 (April 1983): 161–75.

Shorter, Edward. "The First Great Increase in Anorexia Nervosa." *Journal
of Social History* 21, no. 1 (Fall 1987): 69–96.

Shortt, S.E.D. "Before the Age of Miracles: The Rise, Fall and Rebirth of
General Practice in Canada 1890–1940." In *Health, Disease and Medicine:
Essays in Canadian History*, edited by Charles Roland, 123–52. Toronto:
Hannah Institute, 1984.

– "The Canadian Hospital in the Nineteenth Century: An Historio-
graphic Lament." *Journal of Canadian Studies* 18, no. 4 (Winter 1983/4):
3–14.

– "The Influence of French Biomedical Theory on Nineteenth Century
Canadian Neuropsychiatry: Bichat and Comte in the Work of R.M.
Bucke." Paper presented to the Twenty-eighth International Congress
for the History of Medicine, Paris, 1982.

– "The New Social History of Medicine: Some Implications for Research."
Archivaria 10 (Summer 1980): 5–22.

– "Physicians and Psychics: The Anglo-American Medical Response to
Spiritualism 1870–1890." *JHMAS* 39, no. 3 (July 1984): 339–55.

Showalter, Elaine. "Family Secrets and Domestic Subversion: Rebellion in
the Novels of the 1860s." In *The Victorian Family: Structure and Stresses*,
edited by Anthony Wohl, 101–16. New York: St. Martin's Press, 1978.

– "Victorian Women and Insanity." *Victorian Studies* 23, no. 2 (Winter
1980): 157–81.

Shryock, Richard. "Nursing Emerges as a Profession: The American Experience." In *Sickness and Health in America*, 2d ed., edited by Judith
Leavitt and Ronald Numbers, 203–15. Madison: University of Wisconsin Press, 1985.

Sicherman, Barbara. "The New Psychiatry: Medical and Behavioural Science 1895–1921." In *American Psychoanalysis: Origins and Development*,
edited by Jacques M. Quen and Eric T. Carlson, 20–37. New York:
Brunner/Mazel, 1978.

– "The Paradox of Prudence: Mental Health in the Gilded Age." *Journal
of American History* 62, no. 4 (March 1976): 890–912.

– "The Uses of a Diagnosis: Doctors, Patients and Neurasthenia." *JHMAS*
32, no. 1 (January 1977): 33–54.

"Single Women on Relief." *Canadian Forum* 16 (March 1937): 5.

Smelser, Neil. "The Victorian Family." In *Families in Britain*, edited by
R.N. Rapoport, M.P. Fogarty and R. Rapoport, 59–74. London: Routledge & Kegan Paul, 1982.

Smith, Daniel Scott. "Life Course, Norms and the Family System of Older
Americans in 1900." *Journal of Family History* 4, no. 3 (Fall 1979): 285–98.

Smith, F. Barry. "Sexuality in Britain 1800–1900: Some Suggested Revi-
sions." In *A Widening Sphere: Changing Roles of Victorian Women*, edited

by Martha Vicinus, 182–98. Bloomington: Indiana University Press, 1977.

Smith, L.D. "Behind Closed Doors: Lunatic Asylum Keepers, 1800–1860." *Social History of Medicine* 1, no. 3 (December 1988): 301–328.

Smith-Rosenberg, Carroll. "Beauty, the Beast and the Militant Woman: A Case Study in Sex Roles and Social Stress in Jacksonian America." *American Quarterly* 23, no. 4 (October 1971): 562–84.

– "The Female World of Love and Ritual: Relations between Women in Nineteenth Century America." *Signs* 1, no. 1 (Autumn 1975): 1–29.

– "The Hysterical Woman: Sex Roles and Sex Conflict in Nineteenth Century America." *Social Research* 39 (Winter 1972): 652–78.

– "Sex as Symbol in Victorian Purity: An Ethnohistorical Analysis of Jacksonian America." In *Turning Points: Historical and Sociological Essays on the Family*, edited by John Demos and Sarane Spence Boocock, 212–47. Chicago: University of Chicago Press, 1978.

Smith-Rosenberg, Carroll and Charles Rosenberg. "The Female Animal: Medical and Biological Views of Woman and her Roles in Nineteenth Century America." *Journal of American History* 60, no. 2 (September 1973): 332–56.

Snell, James G. "The White Life for Two: The Defence of Marriage and Sexual Morality in Canada 1890–1914." *HS/SH* 16 (May 1983): 111–28.

Solomon, R. and M. Green. "The First Century: The History of Non-medical Opiate Use and Control Policies in Canada 1870–1970." *UWO Law Review* 20, no. 2 (1982): 307–36.

Speisman, Stephen A. "Munificent Parsons and Municipal Parsimony: Voluntary vs Public Poor Relief in Nineteenth Century Toronto." *Ontario History* 65, no. 1 (March 1973): 33–49.

Spiegel, David. "Mothering, Fathering and Mental Illness." In *Rethinking the Family: Some Feminist Questions*, edited by Barrie Thorne and Marilyn Yalom, 95–110. London: Longman, 1982.

Spitzer, Stephen P., Raymond M. Weinstein and Herbert L. Nelson. "Family Reactions and the Career of the Psychiatric Patient: A Long Term Follow-Up Study." In *The Psychiatric Hospital and the Family*, edited by Henry T. Harbin, 187–212. Jamaica, New York: Spectrum, 1982.

Spragge, George W. "The Trinity Medical College." *Ontario History* 58, no. 2 (June 1966): 63–98.

Starr, Paul. "Medicine, Economy and Society in Nineteenth-Century America." *Journal of Social History* 10, no. 4 (June 1977): 588–607.

Stearns, Peter N. "Old Women: Some Historical Observations." *Journal of Family History* 5, no. 1 (Spring 1980): 44–57.

Stevenson, George H. "Bucke and Osler: A Personality Study." *CMAJ* 44, no. 2 (February 1941): 183–8.

Young, Elva M. "Life in Residence." Paper presented to the Homewood
Sanitarium Nurses Reunion, 6 October 1976. Photocopy.

Dissertations and Theses

Baehre, Rainer K. "The Ill-Regulated Mind: A Study in the Making of
Psychiatry in Ontario 1830–1921." Ph.D. diss., York University, 1985.

Barron, F. Laurie. "The Genesis of Temperance in Ontario 1828–1850."
Ph.D. diss., University of Guelph, 1976.

Brown, Thomas E. "Living with God's Afflicted: A History of the Provincial Lunatic Asylum at Toronto 1830–1911." Ph.D. diss., Queen's University, 1980.

Casselman, Ian. "The Secret Plague: Venereal Diseases in Early Twentieth Century Canada." Master's thesis, Queen's University, 1981.

Clarke, Ian H. "Public Provision for the Mentally Ill in Alberta, 1907–
36." Master's thesis, University of Calgary, 1973.

Connors, Stephen. "J.W. Langmuir and the Development of Prisons and
Reformatories in Ontario, 1868–1882." Master's thesis, Queen's University, 1982.

Davis, Claude Mark. "Prohibition in New Brunswick 1917–27." Master's
thesis, University of New Brunswick, 1979.

Edington, Barry. "Formation of the Asylum in Upper Canada." Ph.D.
diss., University of Toronto, 1981.

Gosling, Francis G. III "American Nervousness: A Study in Medicine and
Social Values in the Gilded Age 1870–1900." Ph.D. diss., University of
Oklahoma, 1976.

Jaffe, Arnold. "Addiction Reform in the Progressive Age: Scientific and
Social Responses to Drug Dependence in the United States 1870–
1930." Ph.D. diss., University of Kentucky, 1976.

Lunbeck, Elizabeth. "Psychiatry in the Age of Reform: Doctors, Social
Workers and Patients at the Boston Psychopathic Hospital 1900–1925."
Ph.D. diss., Harvard University, 1984.

McCandless, Peter. "Insanity and Society: A Study of the English Lunacy
Reform Movement 1815–1870." Ph.D. diss., University of Wisconsin,
1974.

McGovern, Constance. "Mad-Doctors: American Psychiatrists 1800–
1860." Ph.D. diss., University of Massachusetts, 1976.

Noel, Janet. "Temperance, Evangelism, Drink, Religion and Reform in
the Province of Canada 1840–1854." Master's thesis. University of
Ottawa, 1978.

Pitts, John A. "The Association of Medical Superintendents of American
Institutions for the Insane 1844–1892: A Case Study of Specialism in
American Medicine." Ph.D. diss., University of Pennsylvania, 1979.

– "The Life and Work of Richard Maurice Bucke: An Appraisal." *American Journal of Psychiatry* 93, no. 2 (March 1937): 1127–50.

Stone, Alan A. "The New Paradox of Psychiatric Malpractice." *New England Journal of Medicine* 311, no. 21 (22 November 1984): 1384–7.

Stone, Robert. "A White Hand Haunts Americans." *Globe and Mail*,
13 January 1987.

Strong, Bryan. "Towards a History of the Experiental Family: Sex and
Incest in the Nineteenth-Century Family." *Journal of Marriage and the
Family* 35, no. 3 (August 1973): 457–91.

Strong-Boag, Veronica. "Canada's Women Doctors: Feminism Con-
strained?" In *A Not Unreasonable Claim: Women and Reform in Canada
1880s–1920s*, edited by Linda Kealey, 109–30. Toronto: Women's Educational Press, 1979.

– "Intruders in the Nursery: Childcare Professionals Reshape the Years
One to Five, 1920–1940." In *Childhood and Family in Canadian History*,
edited by Joy Parr, 160–78. Toronto: McClelland and Stewart, 1982.

– "Setting the Stage: National Organization and the Women's Movement
in the Late Nineteenth Century." In *The Neglected Majority*, edited by
Susan Trofimenkoff and Alison Prentice, 87–103. Toronto: McClelland
& Stewart, 1977.

Synge, Jane. "Work and Family Support Patterns of the Aged in the
Early Twentieth Century." In *Aging in Canada: Social Perspectives*, edited
by Victor W. Marshall, 135–44. Toronto: Fitzhenry & Whiteside, 1980.

Tomes, Nancy J. "A Generous Confidence: Thomas Storey Kirkbride's
Philosophy of Asylum Construction and Management." In *Madhouses,
Mad-doctors and Madmen: The Social History of Psychiatry in the Victorian
Era*, edited by Andrew T. Scull, 121–43. Philadelphia: University of
Pennsylvania Press, 1981.

– "A Torrent of Abuse: Crimes of Violence between Working Class Men
and Women in London, 1849–1875." *Journal of Social History* 11, no. 3
(Spring 1978): 328–45.

Trecker, Janice L. "Sex, Science and Education." *American Quarterly* 26,
no. 4 (October 1974): 352–66.

Turner, Frank M. "The Victorian Conflict between Science and Religion:
A Professional Dimension." *Isis* 69, no. 248 (September 1978): 356–76.

Tyor, Peter L. "Denied the Power to Choose the Good: Sexuality and
Mental Defect in American Medical Practice 1850–1920." *Journal of Social History* 10, no. 4 (June 1977): 472–89.

Tyor, Peter L. and Jamil S. Zainaldin. "Asylum and Society: An Approach to Institutional Change." *Journal of Social History* 13, no. 1 (Fall
1979): 22–47.

Uhlenberg, Peter. "Changing Configurations of the Life Course." In
Transitions: The Family and the Life Course in Historical Perspective, 65–98.
New York: Academic Press, 1978.

– "Death and the Family." In *The American Family in Social-Historical Perspective*, 3d ed., edited by Michael Gordon, 169–77. New York: St. Martin's Press, 1983.

Verbrugge, Martha H. "Women in Medicine in Nineteenth Century America." *Signs* 1, no. 4 (Summer 1976): 959–72.

Vincent, M.O. "Alcohol: Use or Misuse?" *Modern Medicine of Canada* 29, no. 10 (October 1974).

– "The Alcoholic: Who is He? How Did He Get There?" *Report on Alcohol* (Summer 1972): 3–30.

– "Are You Hooked Dr? Addiction among Physicians." *Canadian Family Physician* 22 (April 1976): 401–4.

– "Female Physicians as Psychiatric Patients." *Canadian Psychiatric Association Journal* 21 (7 November 1976): 461–6.

– "Physicians and Alcoholism." *Report on Alcohol* (Summer 1969): 5–27.

Vincent, M.O., E.A. Robinson and L. Latt. "Physicians as Patients: Private Psychiatric Hospital Experience." *CMAJ* 100, no. 9 (1 March 1969): 403–12.

Vincent, M.O. and C.F. Story. "The Disappearing Manic-depressive." *Canadian Psychiatric Association Journal* 15, no. 5 (October 1970): 475–83.

Walker, R.B. "Medical Aspects of Tobacco Smoking and the Anti-tobacco Movement in Britain in the Nineteenth Century." *MH* 24, no. 4 (October 1980): 391–402.

Walter, Richard D. "What Became of the Degenerate?" *JHMAS* 11, no. 4 (October 1956): 422–9.

Walton, John K. "Lunacy in the Industrial Revolution: A Study of Asylum Admissions in Lancashire 1848–50." *Journal of Social History* 13, no. 1 (Fall 1979): 1–22.

– "The Treatment of Pauper Lunatics in Victorian England: The Case of Lancaster Asylum 1816–1870." In *Madhouses, Mad-doctors and Madmen: The Social History of Psychiatry in the Victorian Era*, edited by Andrew T. Scull, 166–200. Philadelphia: University of Pennsylvania Press, 1981.

Ward, Patricia S. "The American Reception of Salvarsan." *JHMAS* 36, no. 1 (January 1981): 44–62.

Ward, W. Peter. "Family Papers and the New Social History." *Archivaria* 14 (Summer 1982): 63–73.

Warfe, Chris. "The Search for Pure Water in Ottawa 1910–1915." *Urban History Review* 8, no. 1 (June 1979): 90–112.

Waring, E.M. "Medical Professionals with Emotional Illness: A Controlled Study of the Hazards of Being a 'Special Patient.'" In *Psychiatric Illness in Physicians*, edited by S.E.D. Shortt, 257–64. Springfield, Ill.: Charles C. Thomas, 1982.

Warner, John H. "The Nature Trusting Heresy: American Physicians and the Concept of the Healing Power of Nature." *Perspectives in American History* 11 (1977–8): 291–324.

– "Physiological Theory and Therapeutic Explanation in the 18 British Debate on the Medical Use of Alcohol." *BHM* 54, no. mer 1980): 235–57.

Warsh, Cheryl Krasnick. "Adventures in Maritime Quackery: The E. Keeley Gold Cure Institute of Fredericton, N.B." *Acadiensis* 1 (Spring 1988): 109–30.

– "The First Mrs Rochester: Wrongful Confinement, Social Redund and Commitment to the Private Asylum, 1883–1923." CHA *Histor Papers*, Windsor, 1988.

Warsh, Michael L. "Domestic Concatenations: The Reification of Soci Relations in Family Law." Faculty of Law, University of New Brunswick. Photocopy, 1988.

Watkins, Susan Cott. "Spinsters." *Journal of Family History* 9, no. 4 (Wint 1984): 310–25.

Weiner, Dora B. "Health and Mental Health in the Thought of Philippe Pinel: The Emergence of Psychiatry during the French Revolution." In *Healing and History: Essays for George Rosen*, edited by Charles E. Rosenberg, 59–85. New York: Science History, 1979.

Welter, Barbara. "The Cult of True Womanhood 1820–1860." *American Quarterly* 18, no. 2 (Summer 1966): 151–74.

Williams, Sarah E. "The Use of Beverage Alcohol as Medicine 1790–1860." *JSA* 41, no. 5 (1980): 543–565.

Withersty, David J. and E. Raymond Kidwell. "Measuring the effects of Family Involvement on a Psychiatric Inpatient Unit." In *The Psychiatric Hospital and the Family*, edited by Henry Harbin, 173–86. Jamaica, New York: Spectrum, 1982.

Wohl, Anthony S. "Sex and the Single Room: Incest Among the Victorian Working Classes." In *The Victorian Family: Structure and Stresses*, 197–216. New York: St. Martin's Press, 1978.

Wood, Ann Douglas. "The Fashionable Diseases: Women's Complaints and their Treatment in Nineteenth Century America." In *Clio's Consciousness Raised: New Perspectives on the History of Women*, edited by Mary Hartman and Lois Banner, 1–22. New York: Harper Torchbooks, 1974.

– "The War Within a War.": Women Nurses in the Union Army." *Civil War History* 18 (September 1972): 197–212.

Woodward, John and David Richards. "Towards a Social History of Medicine." In *Health Care and Popular Medicine in Nineteenth-Century England*, 15–55. London: Croom-Helm, 1977.

Wortis, J. "Adolf Meyer: Some Recollections and Impressions." *British Journal of Psychiatry* 149 (1986): 677–81.

Wrigley, E. Anthony. "Reflections on the History of the Family." In *The Family*, ed. Alice S. Rossi, Jerome Kagan, and Tamara K. Hareven, 71–85. New York: W.W. Norton, 1978.

Sims, Catharine. "An Institutional History of the Asylum for the Insane at Kingston, 1856–1885." Master's thesis, Queen's University, 1981.

Tomes, Nancy J. "The Persuasive Institution: Thomas Storey Kirkbride and the Art of Asylum-keeping 1841–1883." Ph.D. diss., University of Pennsylvania, 1978.

Wilkerson, A.E. "A History of the Concept of Alcoholism as a Disease." Ph.D. diss., University of Pennsylvania, 1966.

Index